PRAISE FOR THE WORKS

The Royal Art of Poison

"Morbidly witty."

—Marilyn Stasio, *New York Times*

"You'll be as appalled at times as you are entertained."
—*Bustle*, one of The 17 Best Nonfiction Books
Coming Out In June 2018

"A heady mix of erudite history and delicious gossip."
—Aja Raden, author of *Stoned*

Mistress of the Vatican

". . . immensely readable and compelling . . . An expert on—and descendant of—European royal families, she skillfully uses letters, diaries, newssheets of the time, and biographies to tell this personal tale, set during unforgiving times. Highly recommended for public and academic libraries."
—*Kirkus Reviews*

Sex with the Queen

"Herman bares all the hot and heavy details about the lewd lives of royal lovers. . . . The addictively good dish is worth, if not a king's ransom, then at least the cover's price tag."
—*Entertainment Weekly*

". . . the salacious details about the sometimes-outlandish characters . . . make this book sparkle brighter than a crown jewel."
—Emily McCombs, *Bust*

Sex with Kings

"Open *Sex with Kings* at almost any page and you'll find yourself immersed in a bawdy, deliciously appealing illicit scene occurring in the highest places."
—*New York Times Book Review*

"An irreproachably researched and amusingly written history of European monarchs' jezebels."
—*Kirkus Reviews* (starred review)

"*Sex with Kings* is . . . a lot more fun than Danielle Steel or Dan Brown."
—*Washington Post Book World*

SEX

with

PRESIDENTS

ALSO BY ELEANOR HERMAN

Nonfiction

The Royal Art of Poison

King Peggy *(with Peggielene Bartels)*

Mistress of the Vatican

Sex with the Queen

Sex with Kings

Murder in the Garden of God

Blood of Gods and Royals Series

Dawn of Legends

Reign of Serpents

Empire of Dust

Legacy of Kings

Voice of Gods

Queen of Ashes

SEX

with

PRESIDENTS

The Ins and Outs of
Love and Lust

in the White House

ELEANOR HERMAN

wm

WILLIAM MORROW
An Imprint of HarperCollins*Publishers*

P.S.™ is a trademark of HarperCollins Publishers.

HarperCollins books may be purchased for educational, business, or sales promotional use. For information, please email the Special Markets Department at SPsales@harpercollins.com.

A hardcover edition of this book was published in 2020 by William Morrow, an imprint of HarperCollins Publishers.

FIRST WILLIAM MORROW PAPERBACK EDITION PUBLISHED 2021.

Designed by Nancy Singer

Interior images @ Amili/Shutterstock (historical costume); @ Varlamova Lydmila/Shutterstock (wedding rings); @ Morphart Creation/Shutterstock (White House); @ Vkilikov/Shutterstock (Thomas Jefferson); @ Christophe BOISSON/Shutterstock (American postcard); @ ullstein bild Dtl./Getty Images (White House photo)

Library of Congress Cataloging-in-Publication Data has been applied for.

ISBN 978-0-06-302191-4

21 22 23 24 25 LSC 10 9 8 7 6 5 4 3 2 1

To Mary Frances Manning, who eased for me the loss of my mother. You are family.

CONTENTS

There is no one whose sexual life, if it were broadcast, would not fill the world at large with surprise and horror.

—W. SOMERSET MAUGHAM

INTRODUCTION

*I*t is a truth universally acknowledged that the Achilles' heel is located nowhere near a person's foot but rather higher up. It has always been this way with humankind. In the beginning, Eve gave Adam an apple and, let's face it, he probably gave her a banana in return. They suddenly realized what those strange body parts were for and as a result got kicked out of Paradise. Fast-forward to the 1490s, when a new plague swept Europe, rotting private parts, bones, and noses with excruciating pain, followed by madness and death. Spread by sexual contact, syphilis, as one sixteenth-century apothecary put it, "Comes from choosing beds unknown and plugging holes best left alone." Few, alas, could bring themselves to stop plugging those unknown holes.

Who among us hasn't had at least one sexual encounter that was unwise, unsafe, or unethical? We risk losing marriages, friends, and even our lives for a sweet coupling that lasts minutes and the soaring exultation of an orgasm measured in seconds. The sex drive mocks logic and is resistant to common sense. This primeval instinct overpowers us, causing us to lose all self-control. Such loss of control never has more explosive consequences than when played out in the bedrooms of world leaders. Those dalliances affect not just an individual, a marriage, or a family. They affect entire nations.

Of course, some political leaders lose their self-control more often than others. "You know, I get a migraine headache if I don't get a strange piece of ass every day," President John F. Kennedy told British prime minister Harold Macmillan in 1962. Kennedy used sex with strangers not just as aspirin, but also to project a presidential image. On September 26, 1960, an hour and a half before the first-ever televised live presidential debate, Democratic nominee Kennedy cavorted with a prostitute in his Chicago hotel room for fifteen minutes. During the debate, he appeared relaxed, radiant, and confident. The Republican nominee, Richard M. Nixon—tense, sweating, and gray-skinned—looked as if he hadn't been laid in years. Chicago mayor Richard J. Daley said, "My God, they've embalmed him before he even died." Kennedy won the debate by a large margin among the seventy million television viewers. He was so pleased with his performance that he arranged to bed prostitutes right before every debate after that.

Donald Trump follows in a historic tradition of scandalous presidential sex. Weeks before the 2016 presidential election, his lawyer and fixer Michael Cohen paid porn star Stormy Daniels $130,000 for her silence about a one-night stand she had allegedly had with Trump ten years earlier. The resulting lies, cover-ups, shifting narratives, denials, and eventual admissions have resulted in Cohen sitting in the slammer for three years for campaign finance violations and the possibility that the president himself might be indicted after leaving office. And all because of— according to Stormy Daniels—two minutes of really bad sex.

Despite the American reputation for prudery, many of our leaders have had a colorful sexual past. One beloved president suffered a fatal stroke in his mistress's presence. Another was gay.

At least two first ladies were so fed up with their husband's philandering that they almost certainly had affairs of their own, one with a woman. Three presidents have been accused of rape. Another had a thirty-year affair and seven children with his enslaved woman, and a leading presidential hopeful had a love child with his mistress while his wife was dying.

Why have so many national leaders been adulterers? Henry Kissinger, the secretary of state and national security advisor under presidents Nixon and Ford, had an explanation: "Power is the ultimate aphrodisiac." And he should know. With his Coke-bottle glasses, unprepossessing features, and a German accent thick as blutwurst, Kissinger was known as "Dr. Strangelove" in Washington circles. Still, as one of the nation's most influential men, Kissinger bedded Hollywood's sexiest sirens.

Edgar Faure, prime minister of France twice in the 1950s, said, "When I was minister, some women resisted me." This is not surprising, as he was balding and bespectacled with thick lips and ears like Dumbo. "Once I became prime minister," he added, "not even one."

In the course of exploring the sex scandals of U.S. presidents and European leaders, we will discover the answers to several burning questions. For instance, what is sex like with the president of a nation? Does the man's charisma, his passion and zest for power make it better than with an average Joe—Donald Trump aside? Fortunately, letters and biographies illuminate both the delights and disappointments of presidential passion. More importantly, we will explore the issue of whether a strong sex drive has any relevance to political success or failure. Does rampant adultery show a lack of character, the stamina needed to run the country, or a bit of both?

And why have first ladies stayed married to such disgraceful philanderers—with the exception of one Italian who notified her husband of her intention to divorce by publishing her grievances in a major daily newspaper? Do these women make a Faustian bargain? They accept a life of luxury and fame as the price for humiliation and betrayal that everyone in the world knows about? Why did Hillary stick to Bill like glue—rambling on about a vast right-wing conspiracy—instead of throwing his gasoline-soaked clothes out the White House bedroom window, running downstairs, and setting them on fire? Why does Melania stay with Donald, giving vent to her fury in passive-aggressive fits of wearing inappropriate jackets and slapping his hand away on the red carpet? What kind of woman would make such a deal? Is any amount of money worth it?

What about presidential girlfriends? What's in it for them? Centuries ago, royal mistresses bedding smelly old kings received premium pay packages: titles, lands, castles, and jewels. But presidential mistresses would be more likely to receive rewards along the lines of an official White House paperweight. Is it the excitement that attracts these women? Being, for a few minutes, at the epicenter of the universe? Do some of them set out to bag a powerful man, like JFK's countless girlfriends who gleefully disported themselves on the first lady's sheets? Is getting the president in bed a kind of trophy?

We will examine the differences between the American reaction to such love affairs and people of other nations. When Americans have caught their leaders with their pants down around their ankles, they have often reacted with shock and outrage. Astonishingly, the founding strain of puritanism brought to Plymouth, Massachusetts, by a few dozen bleak souls in 1620 existed until quite recently in the American character—even four centuries and 330 million citizens of all nationalities later, a kind of virus from hell, resistant to time, genetic dilution, and common sense.

Lyndon Johnson once raged to his mistress, "If a man can't do a little of what he's not supposed to, he ain't much of a man. Hell, our country is so outdated. Why can't we do like the Chinese and fuck all the women we want and populate the world like the good Lord wanted us to? What is so goddamned wrong with that? In this fucking Victorian society, we've become stalemated by fucking only one woman."

Many Europeans would agree. From time immemorial, their reaction to such behavior has been a slow smile followed by a wink. Perhaps it should come as no surprise that France has the unique distinction of being the only nation where a president is known to have died while receiving oral sex from a mistress in the presidential palace, a fact that swells some Gallic breasts with pride.

We will also investigate the changing role of the press in such scandals. Since the 1790s, the American press has, at times, formed a barricade of complicit silence, maintaining the fiction of presidential dignity in the face of adultery, orgies, abortions, and sweaty grappling in White House closets. At other times, reporters scenting a sex story have resembled sharks in a feeding frenzy.

Lastly, we will examine the recent death of American puritanism. Because the truth is no one even pretends to care about political sex scandals anymore, not even evangelical Christians, who hold their nose when they vote for Donald Trump.

SOURCES

*N*ational leaders are, by their very nature, the subjects of copious written material. Most such material focuses on policy issues, with love affairs, if they are mentioned at all, a mere footnote. In some cases, the absence of juicy sex stories is not due to the unsullied conduct of the president, but because of a dearth of detailed information in the form of love letters, autobiographies, and newspaper reports.

For instance, James Garfield, who was president for only six months in 1881 before being felled by an assassin's bullet, had an affair in 1862 with an eighteen-year-old *New York Times* correspondent named Lucia Calhoun. His passionless wife, Lucretia, found the girl's love letters and convinced him to give up the relationship. What wouldn't we give to read those letters from a sex-obsessed teenager to the thirty-one-year-old future president. But, alas, thin-lipped Lucretia most probably poured whale oil on them and burned them.

James Buchanan (served 1857–1861)—often ranked as the worst U.S. president ever for his bungling of events leading up to the Civil War—had a thirteen-year affair with a man, William Rufus King, who was vice president for six weeks in 1853 as he fought a losing battle against consumption. Buchanan was the only U.S. president who never married, but he and King often lived together. In political circles, they were known as Mr. and Mrs. Buchanan, or Miss Nancy and Aunt Fancy, terms at the time used to denote gay men. When King served as ambassador to France in 1844, Buchanan wrote to a friend, "I am so solitary and alone having no companion with me. I have gone wooing to several gentlemen but have not succeeded with any of them."

Many in political circles understood the nature of their relationship, but the press never reported a word about it, even in a time of fevered yellow journalism. Historians believe this was because the press couldn't begin to grapple with the concept of homosexuality. Considered unnatural and unspeakable, it was also unwritable. Ironically, this morbid prejudice against homosexuality served at times to protect gay individuals. Though there were no newspaper articles on the relationship, we might have hoped to have some of the hundreds of letters Buchanan and King wrote each other as their political duties often separated them. These letters were evidently consigned to the flames by prim relatives who had cleaned out the desks of the deceased and, as they read hot and steamy gay love letters, felt their heads explode. And so almost nothing is known of the love affair of President Buchanan and Vice President King.

We have, alas, only the broadest outlines of another unusual affair. Richard Mentor Johnson of Kentucky, who served as Martin Van Buren's vice president from 1837 to 1841, called his enslaved woman Julia Chinn his wife, even though mixed-race marriages were illegal. He installed her as the mistress of his plantation, where they raised their two daughters as ladies, both of whom married rich white gentlemen. Newspapers excoriated him. One wrote, "He has endeavored often to force his daughters into society, that the mother in her lifetime, and they now, rode in carriages, and claimed equality. The idea of voting for him is loathed beyond anything that has occurred with us."

After Julia Chinn died, he took a second enslaved woman as his mistress but sold her at auction when he discovered she had been unfaithful. He brought his third African American mistress to Washington, D.C., and took her to social gatherings as his wife. It was not Johnson's choice of sex partners that caused the furor. He was, after all, only following in the footsteps of Thomas Jefferson. His insistence that his mistresses be recognized as social equals, though enslaved African Americans, created the resentment.

Nor is much known about Richard Nixon's affair with Hong Kong cocktail hostess Marianna Liu, whom the FBI believed was a spy for the Communist Chinese. They had met in 1966 at the bar where she worked in the Hilton Hotel, enjoyed a fling, and saw each other periodically. When Nixon announced his candidacy for the presidency in 1968, the FBI grew concerned. The Chinese government often placed gorgeous spies in Hong Kong cocktail lounges to seduce Western businessmen and politicians. Liu mysteriously owned extensive real estate in Hong Kong, far beyond the means of her modest salary, and the father of one of her closest friends was a general in the Red Army. Agents feared Liu could blackmail a future U.S. president. Undeterred, Nixon invited her to the White House and arranged for her to become a permanent U.S. resident.

Fortunately for us, most high-level U.S. political sex scandals are well documented. Some of the leaders themselves have written about their romances. Founding Father Alexander Hamilton published a hundred-page booklet about his illicit love affair. The rapturously pornographic love letters of Warren G. Harding speak for themselves, as do Woodrow Wilson's more discreet missives. Newspapers covered in graphic detail Thomas Jefferson's relationship with his enslaved woman Sally Hemings, Grover Cleveland's illegitimate child with a seamstress, Gary Hart's weekend with a blonde, and Bill Clinton's affairs with a lounge singer and an intern.

Warren Harding's young lover Nan Britton, mother of his child, was the first presidential mistress to write a kiss-and-tell book, in 1927. *The President's Daughter* was so graphic for the time that no publisher would touch it; she self-published and made herself a fortune. Dwight Eisenhower's lover, Kay Summersby, wrote of their wartime romance as she lay dying in 1975.

Several of John F. Kennedy's mistresses have written memoirs: "Mafia Moll" Judith Campbell, Swedish aristocrat Gunilla von Post, and White House intern Mimi Beardsley. Retired White House servants also published recollections of presidential misbehavior. In her memoirs, seamstress Lillian Parks saw Franklin Roosevelt's secretary Missy LeHand wandering in and out of his bedroom in her nightgown and Eleanor Roosevelt's girlfriend Lorena Hickock sleeping on the daybed in the first lady's bedroom. Dog keeper Traphes Bryant wrote of Kennedy's nude swimming parties in the White House pool. President Trump's one-night stand, porn star Stormy Daniels, not only wrote a book but also tweets about her liaison.

We even know the names some U.S. presidents called their penises. Warren Harding dubbed his appendage "Jerry." Lyndon Johnson named his "Jumbo" and sometimes waved it around when he was mad about Vietnam, showing off its impressive eight-and-a-half-inch length to envious male staff and admiring journalists. Bill Clinton dubbed his "Willard." It is tempting to believe that Richard Nixon called his "Tricky Dick," but we can't be sure.

THE CHANGING WHITE HOUSE

*T*he presidential residence at 1600 Pennsylvania Avenue in Washington, D.C., has had various names since John Adams moved into a smoky, partially finished shell in 1800: the President's House, the Executive Mansion, and the White House. According to a popular myth, the building wasn't called the White House until after it was whitewashed in 1814 to cover the scorch marks left by British arsonists. The fact is that the building has been white since its first paint job in 1798, and it was referred to as the White House in several newspapers before the Brits burned it. In 1901, President Theodore Roosevelt officially dubbed it the White House.

In 1902, Roosevelt built the West Wing after his wife complained about the presidential offices just down the hall from her bedroom—most presidents used the Lincoln Bedroom as their office until that time. She wanted a completely domestic space for the family, a cocoon of privacy, where she could walk out of her bedroom in curlers and a bathrobe without running into visiting dignitaries. Roosevelt razed a collection of ghastly mid-Victorian greenhouses to the west of the residence to build office space for himself and his staff, though his office was rectangular. His successor, William Taft, expanded the West Wing and created the first Oval Office to mirror the oval rooms on the south side of the White House. In 1933, Franklin Roosevelt, unhappy with the West Wing, redesigned it, creating the current Oval Office on the old laundry drying yard, in part because a room without corners made it easier for a wheelchair-bound individual to navigate. It was a bit larger than the first Oval Office and had more private access to the residence, useful for a handicapped president who pretended to the American people that he was not disabled. The same year, FDR built the White House swimming pool between the main building and the West Wing, as he found swimming an enjoyable form of physical therapy.

By the time of the Truman presidency, the White House was falling apart, its great age exacerbated by other factors. In the late nineteenth century, the building had been updated with modern amenities: running water, radiator heating, and electricity, with heavy pipes and wires run throughout the walls and floors. Further updates included an elevator, along with several bathrooms with marble fixtures, yet no braces were inserted to support the additional weight. Worse, in 1927 an entire third floor was added, providing fourteen much-needed new guest rooms, bathrooms, and storage areas, but causing tremendous structural strain. The building periodically shook, as if in a minor earthquake, and enormous cracks appeared in the walls. In the summer of 1948, the leg of first daughter Margaret Truman's baby grand piano sank through the decayed floor of her upstairs sitting room, causing plaster to crash down in the Family Dining Room below. She wrote, "For most of 1948, we lived in a forest of steel pipes in our bedrooms and sitting rooms. They were supposed to hold up the ceilings, but they could do nothing about the rot that was destroying the old timber."

Experts agreed that the White House was standing "purely from habit" and was in danger of imminent collapse, sending the president, his family, his staff, and all those historic antiques into a mushroom cloud of splinters and pilasters. Architects came up with three proposals: tear down the White House and build a new one on the site; build a new presidential residence elsewhere in the District of Columbia; or restore the existing structure. Fortunately, the third option was chosen. Truman and his family moved across the street to Blair House, which had been used as guest quarters for visiting dignitaries, while the White House was gutted down to the original bare stone walls. These were shored up from below by a new concrete foundation, and from within they were braced by a steel skeleton, which would support the weight of the rebuilt interior.

FDR's swimming pool, outside the main White House structure, survived the renovation. John F. Kennedy used it to treat his appallingly bad back, heating it up to 100 degrees. Richard Nixon, on the other hand, didn't like to swim. In 1970, he covered over the pool—it's still down there somewhere—beneath a new press briefing room. Before that, presidents gave press conferences in various rooms of the White House itself, which allowed journalists to traipse through and nose about. Nixon, secretive and paranoid with good reason, as it turned out, exiled reporters to the West Wing and out of his dark, Brylcreem-slicked hair. Or so he thought.

1

THE MEN WHO BECOME PRESIDENT: RISK-TAKING NARCISSISM

*I*t is a logical assumption that most sane people would not want to become president of a nation. Who in their right mind would want the unceasing stress, the death threats, the vicious criticism, and the constant chaos? The majority of those in possession of good mental health would choose peaceful, middle-class anonymity hands down over bone-grinding torture in an impressive palace.

When George Washington's vice president, John Adams, considered running for president in 1796, his wife, Abigail, warned, "You know what is before you—the whips, the scorpions, the thorns without roses, the dangers, anxieties, the weight of empire." Yes, yes he did. And he wanted it anyway.

And, indeed, there is a dark side to the dazzling confidence, the charm, and the talent to persuade and inspire possessed in such stunning quantities by many world leaders. In 2009, a team of psychologists identified a disorder they called "hubris syndrome." This illness is not genetic or inherent; it does not appear by early adulthood as most personality disorders do, including its evil twin, narcissistic personality disorder. Hubris syndrome *is acquired by wielding power over a period of time.* In other words, power *triggers* the illness. And when the power is gone, the illness subsides.

Characteristics include impulsivity, restlessness, recklessness, contempt for the advice of others, and overweening pride. Those who have it see the world as an arena in which to wield power and seek glory. They focus obsessively on their personal image, lose contact with reality, and see themselves as omnipotent messiahs. Unable to admit they have made a mistake, they find themselves increasingly isolated. No matter what horrors occur on their watch, they believe that history will vindicate them.

Long before the 2009 study, nineteenth-century American suffragist Elizabeth Cady Stanton noticed the correlation between imprudence and power. She wrote, "I have known statesmen, soldiers, scientists, men trusted with interests and empires devoted to the public good, whose patriotism no one doubted, yet reckless of their business and family affairs."

Lillian Parks, a White House seamstress who observed presidents from 1909 to 1960, said, "Maybe you're a lot better off married to an average American. As far as I can see, no average man ever became President . . . The White House uses people up like soap."

Some of the characteristics of world leaders are also the manic symptoms of bipolar disorder: increased energy and restlessness, euphoria, irritability, wild mood swings, unrealistic beliefs in one's abilities, poor judgment, increased sex drive, the need for little sleep, and a denial that anything is wrong.

Lyndon Johnson exhibited clear symptoms of both bipolar

and narcissistic personality disorders. As president, he had an obsessive need for secrecy and labeled anyone who disagreed with him a Communist, a traitor, or a spy in the pay of the Kennedy family. Refusing to take any personal responsibility for poor choices—such as sinking the country ever deeper into the Vietnam conflict—he blamed all his failures on a conspiracy of his enemies. For days on end, he would lie in bed with the covers pulled over his head, then jump up and make a hundred phone calls in a row. Johnson's press secretary George Reedy said that he walked "on air" one minute and then was ready to "slash his wrists" the next. Worried about Johnson's behavior, his special assistant Richard Goodwin consulted psychiatrists, who provided him some comfort. Johnson's personality type, they said, in its inspirational, indefatigable expression, could achieve great things like leading "a Senate or even an entire country." Which was true. On the domestic front—with Medicare, Head Start, and the Voting Rights Act—Johnson accomplished as much as Franklin D. Roosevelt. In other words, some leaders are successful *because* they are crazy.

While not all politically ambitious men have hubris syndrome or bipolar disorder in their full-blown expression, many are narcissistic risk-takers with feelings of invincibility. Seekers of high sensation, risk-takers feed upon the thrill of knowing they could get caught doing something they shouldn't. Afterward, they triumph in knowing they didn't get caught. They outsmarted everyone. And they are, primarily, in love with themselves.

Easily sexually aroused, they are always searching for the next burst of excitement. On his trips abroad, French president François Mitterrand, in his sixties, often disappeared with young women for a couple of hours after his speeches. A friend of his once remarked that he already had a wife and a mistress of many years, and a revolving harem of other lovers. "You are no longer twenty," she chided. "What's the point?"

Mitterrand replied solemnly, "You cannot understand. When I descend the tribunal, after the effervescence of the speech, I need to end in the arms of a woman."

There appears to be little difference between the thrills of seeking public power, with crowds of adoring fans, to seeking pubic power, with an adoring audience of one. The same compulsions that send a man hurtling toward the White House can also send him into a foolhardy tryst with a woman. High political office and dangerous sex are, in fact, all about hubris and power.

Research has shown that the severity of hubris syndrome, bipolar disorder, and narcissistic personality disorder spikes with increased power, resulting in ever riskier behavior. Warren G. Harding routinely had sex in a closet in the Oval Office, in one case when his wife was pounding angrily on the office door. As governor of New York, Franklin Roosevelt assigned his secretary and mistress, Missy LeHand, the bedroom next to his so that she could take dictation at any hour of the night, he said. In the White House, she lived a floor above Roosevelt but still wandered into his bedroom in her nightgown with no steno pad in hand, shocking the servants.

John F. Kennedy had sex with secretaries and prostitutes in the White House swimming pool and in his wife, Jackie's, bed. Lyndon Johnson's wife, Lady Bird, once walked into the Oval Office to find him in flagrante delicto with one of his secretaries on a sofa. A furious Johnson ordered the Secret Service to install a buzzer system. "If we saw Lady Bird heading for the elevator or stairs," an agent recalled, "we were to ring the buzzer."

As governor of Arkansas in the 1980s, Bill Clinton suggested he and his mistress, nightclub singer Gennifer Flowers, have sex during a party at the governor's mansion in the first-floor bathroom—with Hillary in the next room. According to Flowers, she turned him down. He also wanted to have sex with her in the state capitol building. "He liked the idea of having sex on his desk or on the floor with all his staffers right outside," she recalled in her 1995 memoir, *Passion and Betrayal*. "Bill felt an enormous sense of power from leading me into sexual adventures. He thought he was bulletproof in his relationship with me . . . He seemed to think nothing could ever touch him in an adverse way."

Donald Trump's risk-taking surprised former *Playboy* Playmate Karen McDougal, with whom he reputedly had an affair from 2006 to 2007. She told CNN's Anderson Cooper that Trump didn't care whether people saw them together and didn't seem to feel at all guilty about cheating on his wife. She said they made love in his home in New Jersey and once in his gilded Trump Tower apartment in New York City, where he lived with his wife and their young son, Barron. According to Karen, she asked, "Aren't you afraid to bring me here?"

Trump replied, "They won't say anything."

Porn star Stormy Daniels has a similar Donald Trump story. In an interview with *In Touch* magazine, she said, "He didn't seem worried about [anyone finding out about their tryst]. He was kind of arrogant. It did occur to me, 'That's a really stupid move on your part.'"

In 1912, the charismatic British politician David Lloyd George, who became prime minister in 1916, began a lifelong relationship with his secretary, Frances Stevenson, eventually fathering her child. It was an affair that could have ruined him politically had it come to public attention.

Italian prime minister Silvio Berlusconi went a tad further in his narcissism than his political colleagues, hanging up placards in all his palaces that read "Long Live Silvio!" He had private orgies, one of which featured twenty young women in naughty nun costumes dancing around an eight-foot-tall phallus, singing, "Thank God for Silvio!" In 2009, a psychiatrist said he suffered from "a personality with unlimited egocentricity."

"I am, far and away, the best prime minister that Italy has ever had in its one-hundred-and-fifty-year history," he said as he prepared to step down from office after a scandal involving sex with an underaged prostitute. He seemed to have forgotten that under him the Italian economy had tanked, unemployment had skyrocketed, and government services had ground to a halt.

According to their lovers, the risky behavior of Harding, Johnson, Kennedy, Clinton, Trump, Lloyd George, Mitterrand, and Berlusconi involved unprotected sex. In at least three cases (Lloyd George, Kennedy, and Clinton) this resulted in unwanted pregnancies and abortions. Not only did Lloyd George father a child with his mistress, but Harding, Mitterrand, and possibly Johnson did, too. Kennedy suffered from chronic chlamydia, a venereal disease, which may have caused Jackie's difficulty in having healthy children; out of a total of five pregnancies, she had one miscarriage, one stillbirth, and one infant who lived thirty-nine hours. There is a clear pattern among these men of recklessness, feelings of invincibility, and little concern for the collateral damage they caused to their wives and lovers.

Perhaps Michigan representative Candice Miller summed it up best in 2011, when she responded to a question about New York congressman Anthony Weiner tweeting photos of his wiener. "What is it with these guys?" she asked. "Don't they think they're going to get caught?"

Sadly, the answer is no. Or worse: they don't even care.

2

ALEXANDER HAMILTON AND THE IMPULSE OF PASSION

*A*merica's first political sex scandal began just fifteen years after the signing of the Declaration of Independence. A Founding Father, Alexander Hamilton never became president, yet his influence on the nation's history was far greater than that of many who did. His handling of the scandal has offered lessons to philandering politicians right up to President Trump, lessons most have unwisely chosen to ignore.

* * *

On a sizzling summer day in 1791, twenty-three-year-old Maria Reynolds called on the handsome, thirty-six-year-old Alexander Hamilton, then serving as the first U.S. treasury secretary, at his redbrick house in Philadelphia, ostensibly to ask for help. They had never met, but it was common for men of wealth and importance to accept visits from strangers seeking assistance. Hamilton must have been delighted that this particular stranger was so attractive.

Though we have no description of Maria's appearance, men seemed to go weak in the knees in her presence. Given the written records about her, and her own impassioned letters, we can paint a picture of this Drama Queen Sex Siren. She has huge breasts that she flaunts in her low-cut gowns, and a tiny waist. Her thick hair, which she leaves unpowdered, is the cascading wild tumble so fashionable at the time. Her big eyes are framed by long, dark lashes that she bats, but only at men. She is always ready to smile—let us give her dimples. Her voice is low and throaty, redolent of jazz and cigarettes, even though they haven't been invented yet. She positively radiates sex.

She told Hamilton that her husband, James Reynolds, had abandoned her for another woman, and she needed funds to return to her family in New York. She had turned to Hamilton as he was from New York and might be sympathetic to a fellow citizen in trouble. Perhaps Maria was also aware that the chivalrous Hamilton often assisted damsels in distress and had heard of his reputation as a ladies' man.

As Hamilton listened to her pathetic tale of abuse by James Reynolds—probably accompanied by a torrent of tears—he must have sized her up. The delectable young woman was offering herself to him in return for travel expenses. The temptation was irresistible. But Hamilton's wife, Eliza, and their four young children were just yards away from him. He told Maria that he wanted to help her, but she had come at an "inopportune time," as he later wrote. He got her address—a local boardinghouse—and promised to bring her thirty dollars, a substantial sum, about $800 in today's money. Clearly, he was intending to pay for more than stagecoach fare to New York.

"In the evening I put a bank-bill in my pocket and went to the house," he later confessed. "I inquired for Mrs. Reynolds and was shewn upstairs, at the head of which she met me and conducted me into a bedroom. I took the bill out of my pocket and gave it to her. Some conversation ensued from which it was quickly apparent that other than pecuniary consolation would be acceptable."

And so began the lurid affair that would trumpet Hamilton's sins in the tabloid press, tarnish his reputation, and humiliate his wife. Because Maria Reynolds didn't get dressed and take the next stagecoach home. She stayed in Philadelphia, enjoying an impassioned relationship with the treasury secretary. When, soon after the affair began, Eliza Hamilton took the children on a long visit to her father in Albany, Hamilton entertained Maria in the marital home and had sex with her on the marital bed. And when James Reynolds returned and reconciled with his wife, Hamilton continued seeing her. Soon, Alexander Hamilton, the second most important man in the country, and the brightest mind in that time of exceptionally bright minds, found himself the dim-witted victim of a tawdry extortion scheme that had targeted him in advance.

It was a strange, dark, and stupid detour in Hamilton's extraordinary life that, until this point, had arced ever upward. His was a rags-to-riches story, the stuff of an adventure novel. He had been born out of wedlock, a stain, in his time and place, that branded him as less-than, as if God himself had marked the boy as a moral misfit. His illegitimacy made him combative, ambitious, insecure, and swaggering, eager to prove he was the smartest guy in the room, and usually succeeding.

In 1772, community leaders in St. Croix, in the British West Indies, wanted to provide Hamilton—who was either sixteen or eighteen, records are unclear—with a brighter future. His mother was dead, his father had abandoned him years earlier, and he subsisted as a lowly clerk, reading every book he could get his hands on. Talented, personable, and brilliant, Hamilton's potential could never be realized on the sleepy little island. Benefactors raised funds to send him to New York to receive a sterling education.

In 1773, he entered King's College, now Columbia University, in New York City, where he impressed his professors and bolted through his studies, devouring legal and philosophical books in the library. He became an avid supporter of the Revolutionary cause, writing pamphlets and giving fiery speeches. When the university closed during the British occupation of New York, Hamilton put down his books, picked up his musket, and joined a militia, now reading every book he could on military strategy and history. Commissioned in February 1776 as a captain of artillery, he impressed his commanding officers with his precision drills of men in immaculate military dress, his profound military knowledge, and his valor in the Battle of Princeton on January 3, 1777.

Two weeks after the battle, George Washington, commander in chief of the Continental Army, invited Hamilton to join his staff as aide-de-camp, and soon relied on his administrative abilities and wide-ranging knowledge from all that reading. Though immensely popular with most, Hamilton's frankness insulted some, for his razor-sharp words could cut and slice just as efficiently as his razor-sharp bayonet. His friend William Sullivan said, "He was capable of inspiring the most affectionate attachment, but he could make those whom he opposed fear and hate him cordially." In fact, Hamilton loved being hated, dueling with words, and never-ending controversy.

Hamilton also loved women, with whom he flirted outrageously, and women loved him back. A slight figure at five foot seven, Hamilton had something delicate about him, almost feminine. With wavy chestnut hair and alert blue eyes, he had a face of elegant and surprising angles: a broad forehead, high cheekbones, beautifully molded thin lips, and a perfectly curved jaw. Hamilton's most distinguishing feature was his nose: high-bridged, bony, and irregular, thrust out impudently into the world, a metaphor in cartilage for its owner.

In 1780, he married Elizabeth Schuyler, daughter of General Philip Schuyler, one of New York's richest men, a true love match. Elizabeth—called Eliza and sometimes Betsey or Bess—was a pretty woman with dark brown hair, usually powdered white, with a little snub nose, full chin, and petite and shapely figure. But it was her charm that won the most admiration. Tench Tilghman, another one of George Washington's aides, described her as "a brunette with the most good-natured, lively, dark eyes that I ever saw, which threw a beam of good temper and benevolence over her whole countenance." In 1788, a French visitor, Brissot de Warville, said Eliza was "a delightful woman who combines both the charms and attractions and the candor and simplicity typical of American womanhood."

The first rumors of Hamilton's adultery came not long after his marriage and were disturbing indeed, as they concerned Eliza's sister, the vivacious, flirtatious Angelica. Only eighteen months older than Eliza, in 1777 Angelica had married the fabulously wealthy John Church. If she had been single three years later, it is quite possible that Hamilton would have married Angelica instead. Angelica was as different from Eliza in personality as she was in looks. She was taller and blond, with a long nose, and looked rather like an attractive collie in heat. A sophisticated fashion diva who would, in coming years, charm the elite of London and Paris, Angelica was, in short, more like Hamilton himself.

Those who saw Hamilton and Angelica—and sensed the crackling sexual energy between them—assumed they were lovers. Angelica never concealed her admiration for Hamilton, not even from Eliza. One missive in particular raises eyebrows. "I love him very much," she wrote her sister, "and if you were as generous as the old Romans, you would lend him to me for a little while . . . Ah! Bess! You were a lucky girl to get so clever and so good a companion." Hamilton wrote to Angelica in an equally flirtatious tone. Eliza never showed any sign of jealousy but seemed flattered that her older, more worldly sister thought so highly of Hamilton. She must have believed there was no physical relationship between the two. Maybe she was right. Or maybe not.

Prudish John Adams believed Hamilton and Angelica were having an affair, and it wasn't his only one. "His fornications, adulteries and his incests [an apparent insinuation that he had slept with his sister-in-law] were propagated far and wide," Adams wrote.

Most of Hamilton's substantial energy, however, would be directed not at fornications, adulteries, and incests, but at forming a new, sustainable U.S. government. The unity of the thirteen states fractured after the Redcoats sailed home. Each state—with its distinct personality, economy, boisterous hopes, and thundering fears—had its own ideas about governance. The Articles of Confederation, enacted in 1777, loosely regulated thirteen mini-kingdoms, granting states great power and severely limiting the central government. There was no provision for a chief executive and no federal taxing power. Indeed, no one wanted to mention the "t" word. Weren't taxes the reason they had rebelled against Great Britain to begin with? Many Americans felt that, with the Brits gone, now was the time to truly enjoy themselves in some kind of giant national frat party with limitless kegs.

Freedom is a wonderful concept, bankruptcy less so. The combined total loans from European banks to the thirteen states and the Continental Congress was some $79 million (more than

$2 billion in today's money), and the U.S. had no way to repay it. Welching on loans meant the young nation wouldn't be able to borrow more. Due to the lack of funds, soldiers had gone unpaid for years. Some had lost farms; others feared they would be thrown into debtors' prison upon leaving the army. Many soldiers marched on Congress demanding their pay.

Clearly, Hamilton believed, what was needed was a federal government collecting taxes, paying back old loans, negotiating new ones, and regulating trade, and an army run by the federal government rather than a hodgepodge of state militias with different uniforms, training, equipment, and regulations. But to do so, the Articles of Confederation had to be replaced with a Constitution. In 1787, Hamilton, who had been practicing as a lawyer, was named a delegate to what we know as the Constitutional Convention in Philadelphia. Many other delegates, particularly from the South, feared strong federal power, as it reminded them of the heavy-handed overreach of Great Britain they had so recently shaken off.

After four months of blistering debate and quite a few compromises on both sides, the Constitution was completed in September and ratified the following June. Hamilton's push for a strong central government had become law, and the basic elements of our present system of government—three equal branches of government and two legislative houses—came into effect. George Washington was chosen as the nation's first president to great acclaim. Given the fractious politics of the time, only a man of his superhuman dignity could preside over the squabbling sure to ensue.

Washington knew he would need a Cabinet, even though the Constitution didn't mention one. He appointed Hamilton as secretary of the treasury, Thomas Jefferson as secretary of state, and a Revolutionary War hero, Henry Knox, as secretary of war. Hamilton's department started off with thirty-nine employees. State had only five. War—which had no war to run—had two, Knox and a clerk.

Hamilton had to create a customs service on the spot, which would account for 90 percent of government revenue, and pushed Congress to form what would become the U.S. Coast Guard to prevent smuggling. By late 1790, he had already amassed a sizable government surplus. Loans were being paid back, government securities had tripled in value, and the country was enjoying high economic growth. In 1792, Hamilton created a national mint: most coins in circulation at the time were Spanish doubloons, British pounds, and French guineas.

The Constitution does not mention political parties and George Washington did not belong to one. But almost immediately, politicians fell into one of two categories. Those like Hamilton who wanted a strong central government became known as Federalists. Those like Jefferson who wanted states to have the dominant power called themselves anti-Federalists, though they soon became known as Democratic-Republicans, naming themselves after the ancient Roman republic which had thrown off the tyranny of kings. Confusingly, they soon became known as Republicans, and by the 1820s, Democrats.

The feud of the early 1790s is still with us today. Today's Republicans generally support a smaller government, greater states' rights, less federal control, and reduced taxation and regulation. Today's Democrats support greater regulation and federal control, greater government debt, and higher taxation.

The American press, which had gleefully lampooned King George III, his taxes, and his soldiers, now turned to partisan politics, an eighteenth-century version of Fox News and MSNBC.

Each paper was either Republican or Federalist and spent much of its ink skewering the other side with little regard to facts, gleefully spreading fear and hate. Americans devoured the vitriol. Then, as now, citizens loved good stories that gripped the heart and stirred up righteous anger. They enjoyed booing the villains, cheering the heroes, and shedding tears for victims. It was easier to see the world in clear, comforting black and white, rather than in fifty shades of confusing, morally ambiguous gray. Moreover, the news they chose confirmed the beliefs they held already, helping them avoid the discomfort of realizing they may, in fact, be wrong.

In his countless newspaper columns eviscerating Republicans, Hamilton presented himself as a paragon of virtue—a tactic that would later come back to haunt him. Writing of himself in the third person, he issued this challenge to his opponents: "Mr. Hamilton can, however, defy all their malevolent ingenuity to produce a single instance of his conduct, public or private, inconsistent with the strict rules of integrity and honor." In September 1791, when his affair with Maria raged at a fever pitch, he boasted to a Federalist politician that he was a man whose character was above reproach. "I pledge myself to you and to every friend of mine," he wrote, "that the strictest scrutiny into every part of my conduct, whether as a private citizen or as a public officer, can only serve to establish the perfect purity of it."

It is almost inconceivable that a genius like Hamilton, knowing he had powerful enemies, would allow himself to have a yearlong affair with a trollop like Maria Reynolds and subject himself to the threat of blackmail. When Maria's now-reconciled husband asked Hamilton for a cushy government job, that should have been the first clue something was wrong. Sensing Reynolds was a sleaze, Hamilton politely demurred—he would never compromise the public trust by placing this man in government—but he didn't cease contact. Maria, he later explained, wouldn't let him. "She employed every effort to keep up my attention and visits," he recalled. "Her pen was freely employed, and her letters were filled with those tender and pathetic effusions which would have been natural to a woman truly fond and neglected."

"I have kept my Bed those tow days," Maria wrote in one such illiterate effusion, "and now rise from My pillow wich your Neglect has filled with the sharpest thorns I no longer doubt what I hae Dreaded to no but stop I do not wish to se you to say any thing about my Late disappointments No I only do it to Ease a heart wich is ready Burst with Greef I can neither Eate or sleep I have been on the point of doing the moast horrid acts at I shudder to think where I might been what will Become of me."

As if her letters weren't disturbing enough, Maria's past was darker than Hamilton knew. She had married the much older Reynolds when she was fifteen, and he soon began pimping her. The son of her first landlady in Philadelphia, Richard Folwell, later wrote, "She told me, so infamous was the perfidy of Reynolds, that he had frequently enjoined and insisted that she should insinuate herself on certain high and influential characters—endeavor to make assignations with them and actually prostitute herself to gull money from them." For a time, Maria dabbled in outright prostitution. Gentlemen hoping for an assignation left letters in her entryway and "at night she would fly off as was supposed to answer their contents."

Unaware of her sordid past, Hamilton believed Maria was truly in love with him, and it must have flattered his vanity. This exotic, oversexed woman—we can picture her leaving scorch marks on the sheets—was quite different from his honest, reliable wife of eleven years. His obsession for Maria led him to persuade

Eliza to stay in Albany for as long as possible. Worried that his wife might return home to find Maria in her bed, he wrote, "Let me know beforehand your determination that I may meet you at New York." When, in late August, she seemed on the point of returning home, he wrote, "Much as I long for this happy moment, my extreme anxiety for the restoration of your health will reconcile me to your staying longer where you are . . . Think of me—dream of me—and love me my Betsey as I do you." In September, when Eliza started for home, he advised her, "Don't alarm yourself nor hurry so as to injure either yourself or the children."

Was Maria Reynolds his only love affair? We don't know of any others for certain, but probably not. The fact that hours after he first met her, he hotfooted it to her rooms with money in his pocket indicates he did not suffer the hesitation and pangs of conscience of a first adultery. John Adams traced Hamilton's libertine ways back to his time as aide to George Washington during the Revolution, after which Hamilton committed "debaucheries in New York and Philadelphia," where he had made "his audacious and unblushing attempts upon ladies of the highest rank and purest virtue." Adams's wife, Abigail, concurred. "Oh, I have read his heart in his wicked eyes," she wrote. "The very devil is in them. They are lasciviousness itself."

Even with both spouses back home, Maria and Hamilton continued the affair, Hamilton under a pretense of friendship with the oily James Reynolds. Then, on December 15, 1791, Reynolds informed Hamilton that his wife had confessed her affair to him. "I am very sorry to find out that I have been cruelly trated by a person that I took to be my best friend instead of that my greatest Enimy. You have deprived me of every thing that's near and dear to me," he wrote.

"Instead of being a Friend, you have acted the part of the

most Cruelist man in existence, you have made a whole family miserable. She ses there is no other man that she Care for in this world. Now Sir you have bin the Cause of Cooling her affections for me. She was a woman. I should as soon suspect an angiel from heven and one where all my happiness was depending. And I would Sacrefise almost my life to make her Happy. but now I am determed to have satisfaction."

Maria, too, sent a letter, stating that if Hamilton didn't reply to James, he would write Mrs. Hamilton of the affair. "O my God," Maria wrote, "I feel more for you than myself and wish I had never been born to giv you so mutch unhappisness do not rite to him no not a Line but come here soon do not send or leave any thing in his power Maria."

And so, Hamilton found himself charged with ruining a marriage by alienating the wife's affections, a serious legal predicament at the time. The threat of informing Eliza must have been much more frightening, especially since she was then pregnant with their fifth child. He explained, "No man tender of the happiness of an excellent wife could, without extreme pain, look forward to the affliction which she might endure from the disclosure, especially a public disclosure, of the fact. Those best acquainted with the interior of my domestic life will best appreciate the force of such a consideration upon me. The truth was that . . . I dreaded extremely a disclosure—and was willing to make large sacrifices to avoid it."

Large sacrifices indeed. Reynolds began squeezing Hamilton for blackmail money—some $1,100 (about $30,000 in today's money)—over the course of several months. Even then, Hamilton continued to bed Maria, often with James's acquiescence. He must have been sexually obsessed by the woman, needing her as an addict does a drug that sweeps him to heights of euphoria and then, as it wears off, dashes him into hell. At those moments when he found the strength to try to break up with her, she wept, implored, and sent impassioned misspelled letters laced with vague threats.

It was an unfortunate stroke of fate when James Reynolds's friend, Jacob Clingman, ran into Hamilton at the Reynolds home in April 1792. Clingman had impressive political connections; he had served as a clerk of the first speaker of the House of Representatives, Republican Frederick Muhlenberg of Pennsylvania. Why, Clingman wondered, would the second most important man in the country be on such intimate terms with his lowlife friend? Reynolds—unwilling to admit he had been pimping his wife—explained that Hamilton, far from being the epitome of virtue he bragged about, was giving him money to speculate in government securities on his behalf. Hamilton, who had enacted laws preventing government officials from dealing in government securities, had been breaking his own ethical regulations and had secretly made $30,000 ($830,000 today) from this criminal activity, Reynolds said. When Clingman doubted this story, Reynolds had him wait outside Hamilton's office while he went in. Minutes later, he came out with $100 (the equivalent of $2,800 in 2020).

Hamilton, horrified to have run into Jacob Clingman at Reynolds's home, finally understood the threat to his career and refused to see Maria again. He ignored her wailing pleas and gave her husband a final payment of $50 ($1,400 today). He must have felt intense relief when the annoying pair stopped contacting him, and his life returned to normal. It was over, he thought. But he was wrong.

The Reynolds affair might never have come to light if James Reynolds and Jacob Clingman had not been charged in November 1792 with defrauding old Revolutionary War soldiers, just six months after Hamilton's affair with Maria ended. Stewing in a cell, Reynolds asked Hamilton to spring him, and Hamilton refused. Whatever threat Reynolds posed, Hamilton was certainly not going to use his political position to free a vile criminal.

Unlike Reynolds, Clingman was no hard-core scoundrel and soon found himself out on bail. He told his former boss, Congressman Muhlenberg, that Reynolds possessed evidence of Hamilton's illegally amassing a fortune from speculation. Clingman gave the congressman several letters from Hamilton to Reynolds that seemed to back up his claim. Horrified, Muhlenberg invited two other Republicans, Senator James Monroe and Representative Abraham B. Venable, both of Virginia, to join in the investigation. They were delighted to be in a position to crucify the obnoxious, swashbuckling leader of the Federalist Party.

The delegation first visited Reynolds in jail, where he dropped threatening hints but refused to say another word until he was freed. But as soon as he got out, he briefly visited Hamilton and disappeared. When the trio called on Maria, she said Hamilton had instructed Reynolds to "leave the parts, not to be seen here again," because her husband "could tell them something that would make some of the heads of departments tremble."

Hamilton's guilt seemed clear. But before sending a report to President Washington, the investigators felt it gentlemanly to at least give Hamilton a chance to explain himself. On December 15, they met with the treasury secretary and showed him his own handwritten letters to James Reynolds. Hamilton immediately acknowledged he had written them and told the entire Maria Reynolds saga in such exquisitely painful detail that one of his visitors—we can picture him wildly waving his hands—begged him to stop. But Hamilton couldn't put the brakes on his cathartic confession. He showed them Maria's poorly spelled love letters and her husband's sulky demands for money. Blushing furiously, the trio promised the matter would remain confidential. Hamilton asked for copies of the correspondence they had shown him for his records.

His request proved a mistake. James Monroe tasked John Beckley, a clerk of the House of Representatives who hated Hamilton, to copy them. Beckley made another set of copies for himself and, it seems, gave them to Hamilton's political nemesis, Thomas Jefferson.

For years, Hamilton had torn Jefferson and the Republicans to shreds in his newspaper columns. Now, on January 5, 1793, in Monroe's column on the "Vindication of Mr. Jefferson," he sent a thinly veiled warning to Hamilton. "I shall conclude this paper by observing how much it is to be wished that this writer [Hamilton] would exhibit himself to the public view, that we might behold in him a living monument of that immaculate purity to which he pretends and which ought to distinguish so bold and arrogant a censor of others."

Hamilton got the message. His enemies had the power to humiliate him. Perhaps that is why he never made a bid to become president. Even though he had been born on the Caribbean island of Nevis, the Constitution, realizing that no contenders for the presidency for decades to come would have been born as American citizens, stipulated that anyone holding U.S. citizenship on or before the 1787 adoption of the Constitution could run for office, no matter what their citizenship at birth. Surely, he must have wanted to be president.

Though Hamilton's enemies knew of the affair, Eliza did not. She lived in ignorant bliss, thinking she had the best husband in the world. Maria Reynolds's marriage, however, was not so resilient. In 1793 she divorced James—oddly enough, for adultery—and married Jacob Clingman the day her divorce was finalized.

In January 1795, Hamilton resigned his treasury post. Ironically for someone accused of venality, Hamilton left his government office much poorer than he had entered it, with only $500 (some $10,200 today) to his name. He went back to his profitable law practice, which netted him several times his government salary, to repair the damage.

In the fall of 1796, during the presidential election to replace George Washington, Hamilton wrote twenty-five articles over five weeks in the *Gazette of the United States* disparaging Thomas Jefferson. Perhaps, because it had been four years since Jefferson and his other enemies had learned about Maria Reynolds, Hamilton thought they would never use the information. Perhaps he just couldn't help inserting himself in a provocative way into the election. The result was predictable, especially once the calming force of George Washington had vanished from the presidency, replaced by the irascible John Adams. The Republicans were ready to take down Hamilton.

In June 1797, they hired a tabloid journalist named James Callender to write a series of pamphlets innocuously titled *The History of the United States for 1796*, reporting on Hamilton's tenure as treasury secretary. Callender, a hack writer who dipped his pen in venom, had fled to the U.S. from his native Edinburgh, Scotland, to evade a sedition charge by the British government. In his pamphlets, Callender promised to cut Hamilton down to size and reveal his rank hypocrisy. "We shall presently see this great master of morality, although himself the father of a family, confessing that he had an illicit correspondence with another man's wife," he wrote. But that wasn't all. Callender accused Hamilton of having made a fortune by speculating in government securities and stated the money he had paid Reynolds wasn't for blackmail related to adultery, but for speculation. He published all the letters Clingman had given to the trio of investigators.

"So much correspondence could not refer exclusively to wenching," Callender pointed out. "No man of common sense will believe that it did . . . Reynolds and his wife affirm that it respected certain speculations." Callender accused Hamilton of writing Maria's misspelled love letters himself to make his illegal activity look like an ordinary love affair.

Hamilton realized a dignified silence would only encourage speculation about his speculation, a smear that would tarnish his reputation as a government official forever. He would be remembered for rumors of corruption rather than all his numerous public acts and the institutions he'd built from nothing. He decided to accept public humiliation for the affair while proving the allegations of corruption false.

Hamilton rage-wrote a detailed hundred-page booklet he titled *Observations on Certain Documents Contained in No. V and No. VI of "The History of the United States for the Year 1796," in Which the Charge of Speculation Against Alexander Hamilton, Late Secretary of the Treasury, Is Full Refuted. Written by Himself.* In it, Himself explained his relationship with Maria and James Reynolds in squirm-inducing detail. The first thirty-seven pages were purgative confession mingled with self-examination; the remaining fifty-eight pages comprised the misspelled letters of the Reynoldses. In no way, he insisted, did this tawdry affair have anything to do with compromising the public trust. He maintained his honor as an incorrupt and incorruptible public official by sacrificing his honor as a husband.

"The charge against me," he wrote, "is a connection with one

James Reynolds for purposes of improper pecuniary speculation. My real crime is an amorous connection with his wife, for a considerable time with his privity and connivance, if not originally brought on by a combination between the husband and wife with the design to extort money from me." If he had been a corrupt official, he pointed out, he certainly would have chosen a worthier accomplice than the sleazebag James Reynolds. "It is very extraordinary, if the head of the money department of a country, being unprincipled enough to sacrifice his trust and his integrity, could not have contrived profit sufficiently large to have engaged the cooperation of men of far greater importance than Reynolds," he wrote. And the paltry sums he gave Reynolds—usually thirty or fifty dollars at a time—would hardly have amassed the fortune he had supposedly stashed somewhere.

Hamilton's main concern in publishing the pamphlet was how it would affect his wife.

> With such men, nothing is sacred. Even the peace of an unoffending and amiable wife is a welcome repast to their insatiate fury against the husband . . . This confession is not made without a blush . . . I can never cease to condemn myself for the pang which it may inflict on a bosom eminently entitled to all my gratitude, fidelity, and love. But that bosom will approve that even at so great an expense, I should effectually wipe away a more serious stain from a name which it cherishes with no less elevation than tenderness.

He concluded, "Thus has my desire to destroy this slander, completely, led me to a more copious and particular examination of it, than I am sure was necessary. The bare perusal of the letters from Reynolds and his wife is sufficient to convince my greatest enemy that there is nothing worse in the affair than an irregular and indelicate amour. For this, I bow to the just censure which it merits. I have paid pretty severely for the folly and can never recollect it without disgust and self condemnation."

Initially, it seemed as if his self-vindication had been a mistake. His supporters were aghast, his enemies delighted. "Humiliating in the extreme," said Henry Knox. Hamilton's old friend Robert Troup observed that Hamilton's "ill-judged pamphlet has done him inconceivable injury."

The Republican press had a field day with the pamphlet. Callender summed up Hamilton's defense: "I am a rake and for that reason I cannot be a swindler." Similarly, the Republican newspaper the *Aurora* mocked Hamilton's defense as "I have been grossly . . . charged with . . . being a speculator, whereas I am only an adulterer. I have not broken the eighth commandment . . . It is only the seventh which I have violated."

While Hamilton's affair remained the butt of Republican jokes, his reputation for public integrity remained undiminished. His embarrassing pamphlet dispelled any notions of impropriety in office. Perhaps David Cobb, a Federalist judge from Massachusetts, summed it up best in a letter to Henry Knox: "Hamilton is fallen for the present, but even if he fornicates with every female in the cities of New York and Philadelphia, he will rise again, for purity of character after a period of political existence is not necessary for public patronage."

Eliza never publicly commented on the Reynolds affair, though it surely must have mortified her to learn not only of her husband's adultery, but that the partner of his choice was an uneducated prostitute, rolling around with him in Eliza's own bed. She must have recalled Hamilton's letters to her that summer of 1791, urging her to stay in Albany for as long as possible. Later events proved that she wholeheartedly forgave him. As for Hamilton, he became more attentive than ever to his wife and children. He wrote her, "In proportion as I discover the worthlessness of other pursuits, the value of my Eliza and of domestic happiness rises in my estimation."

Though in private practice as a lawyer, Hamilton remained an influential mover and shaker, frequently advising members of President John Adams's Cabinet and serving as inspector general for the army. Once his bitter enemy Thomas Jefferson became president in 1800, however, Hamilton's influence in government decreased. His handsome nineteen-year-old son, Philip, died in a duel in 1801, so devastating his sister that she sank into mental illness. Hamilton found solace in religion and sat mostly on the sidelines, philosophizing. In an 1802 letter to a friend, he wrote, "Men are rather reasoning than reasonable animals, for the most part governed by the impulse of passion." Though he was discussing the heated political controversies of the day, he was probably also speaking about himself.

For his part, Thomas Jefferson was finally in a position to examine Hamilton's old treasury files for proof of theft. Licking his chops, he asked his new treasury secretary, Albert Gallatin, to find him "the blunders and frauds of Hamilton." Gallatin, who also disliked Hamilton, dived in "with a very good appetite," as he later recalled. "Well, Gallatin, what have you found?" Jefferson asked hopefully. Gallatin replied despondently, "I have found the most perfect system ever formed. Any change that should be made in it would injure it. Hamilton made no blunders, committed no frauds. He did nothing wrong." He added, "I think Mr. Jefferson was disappointed."

Jefferson's vice president, Aaron Burr, an unpopular individual, knew Jefferson did not want him as his running mate in the 1804 election and made a heated bid to become governor of New York. Burr lost, but he could not accept that his defeat was due to his terrible reputation in both public and private life: deflowering virgins, seducing wives, raping slaves, taking bribes, and stealing from the estates of his legal clients. He turned his beady eyes on Alexander Hamilton, who had spoken and written against him, and challenged him to a duel. Prickly Hamilton, still the impoverished, orphaned bastard boy at heart despite all his accomplishments, felt he needed to defend his honor.

None of Hamilton's family members had any idea of his dueling plans. He told his friends he would waste his shot, sending it into a tree or the air. Burr, however, spent his days in target practice. At seven o'clock in the morning of July 11, 1804, the two men, their seconds, and a doctor met at the infamous Weehawken Dueling Grounds across the Hudson River from New York City. Though details are unclear, it seems Hamilton did indeed waste his shot, while Burr shot to kill. The bullet sliced through Hamilton's spine, paralyzing him, and damaging his liver and diaphragm. Though Hamilton did not die instantly, it was clearly a mortal wound.

He was rowed back across the river to the home of a friend and put to bed. When Eliza arrived, she was frantic with grief and horror. Though suffering intense pain and heavy blood loss, Hamilton wanted to see his children one last time. Eliza lined all seven of them up at the foot of his bed, from twenty-year-old Angelica to two-year-old Philip, named after his deceased brother. Thirty-one hours after the duel, Alexander Hamilton died at the age of forty-nine.

Hamilton's untimely death devastated his wife. God, Eliza said, had given her all her life's joy in her first decades, and now the remainder would be filled with sorrow. "I have remarked to you that I have had a double share of blessing and I must now look forward to grief," she told a friend. "For such a husband, his spirit is in heaven and his form in the earth and I am nowhere any part of him is." She read his letters so often they eventually crumbled in her hands. She wore decayed bits of a love sonnet he had written her in a little bag around her neck.

Eliza devoted her remaining years—there were to be fifty of them—to burnishing Hamilton's rather tarnished reputation. His death had not stopped Jefferson and Adams from heaping slander on him, and Hamilton, for once, was in no position to defend himself with a flood of accusing newspaper columns. She employed thirty assistants to organize his voluminous papers into a biography.

In 1802, Hamilton had built a beautiful family home in Harlem, the Grange, in what was then a rural area of Manhattan, and planned to pay off his debts of more than $50,000 (some $1.2 million in today's money) over the next few years with his lucrative legal fees. To keep the family from destitution, Hamilton's good friends solicited donations from more than a hundred people, raising more than $80,000. Still, with seven children to raise and educate, Eliza was often reduced to begging friends for small loans to stay afloat. Two years after Hamilton's death, she and two other women founded the New York Orphan Asylum Society, the first private orphanage in New York. Eliza poured herself into helping children who, as her husband had been as a child on St. Croix, were alone, destitute, frightened, and dreaming of a life that didn't seem possible.

Eliza's rival for Hamilton's love, Maria Reynolds, also had some tough times. With the publication of Hamilton's 1797 pamphlet, she was known throughout the United States as a whore, happy to be pimped by her own husband, and even worse, a woman with very bad grammar and spelling. She and her second husband, Jacob Clingman, soon hightailed it out of the U.S. and moved to Great Britain. In 1806, she returned to Philadelphia using the name Maria Clement, with no Clingman in sight. No record exists of a divorce, so perhaps Clingman died, or maybe she just dumped him.

She found employment as the housekeeper of a Dr. Mathew, who became enamored of her—naturally—and married her in 1808. For the first time in her turbulent life, Maria, now in her forties, became respectable and respected. No longer a sexpot proudly sporting a ripped bodice, she found God and became active in the Methodist Church, proving Benjamin Franklin's observation that "when women cease to be handsome, they study to be good." A friend of Maria's in her later years said, "She enjoyed . . . the love and good will of all who knew her." Well into middle age Maria was described as "highly amiable and handsome." She died at the age of sixty in 1828.

Eliza's undiminished, rude good health shocked those who saw her climbing over fences in her eighties. In 1848, at the age of ninety-one, she moved to Washington, D.C., to live in her daughter's home near the White House, where she was often entertained. In the years leading up to the Civil War—which Hamilton's extraordinary vision had foreseen—everyone wanted to meet the woman who, seventy years earlier, had danced the minuet with George Washington.

Despite her unabated vigor and constant activity, Eliza suffered the loss of her husband every day during those long years. A visitor to her house recalled her playing a game of backgammon by the fire. "When the game was done," he said, "she leaned back in her chair a long time with closed eyes, as if lost to all around her. There was a long silence, broken by the murmured words, 'I am so tired. It is so long. I want to see Hamilton.'"

She died at ninety-seven on November 8, 1854.

3

THOMAS JEFFERSON'S
PURSUIT OF HAPPINESS

*E*veryone with an ounce of sense knows that karma is a bitch. Certainly, that is what President Thomas Jefferson discovered in 1802. Five years earlier, he had employed the scandal-rag journalist James Callender to trumpet Alexander Hamilton's adulterous affair with Maria Reynolds. Now Jefferson found himself hoist with his own petard when his hired gun, feeling under-rewarded for his efforts, turned on Jefferson, exposing in his trademark shrill, nasty prose a scandalous amour of the president's own.

* * *

On June 26, 1787, Abigail Adams, wife of John Adams, the first American ambassador to Great Britain, greeted a special visitor in London: Thomas Jefferson's younger daughter, just arrived on the *Robert*, commanded by Captain Ramsey. Nine-year-old Polly hadn't seen her father since 1784 when he went to France to conduct commercial negotiations, leaving Polly in the care of her aunt. Now she would recuperate with the Adamses from the five-week trip across the Atlantic, and then journey on to her father in Paris. Little Polly did not arrive in England unaccompanied, of course. She had a traveling companion to look after her.

Jefferson had hoped to find a "careful English woman" traveling on the *Robert* who would agree to look after Polly. Unable to do so, he wanted one of his mature enslaved women to undertake the task, but that woman was recuperating from childbirth. Polly's companion ended up being another of Jefferson's slaves: fourteen-year-old Sally Hemings, the half-sister of his deceased wife, Martha. (Sally's enslaved mother, Elizabeth Hemings, daughter of an African woman and a white man, had had six children with John Wayles, Martha's father.) The result of what developed in Paris—and what would continue for many decades afterward—would shake the 1804 presidential election, cause Jefferson's family to craft a carefully purged history, and tear apart families until the present day.

Immediately after retrieving Polly, Abigail wrote Jefferson, "The old Nurse whom you expected to have attended her was sick and unable to come. She has a Girl about 15 or 16 with her . . ." But within twenty-four hours of observing Sally, Abigail seemed to have had a frisson of foreboding. Perhaps it would be better to send Sally back to Virginia immediately. "The Girl who is with her is quite a child," she wrote, "and Captain Ramsey is of the opinion will be of so little service that he had better carry her back with him. But of this you will be a judge." On July 6, Abigail wrote even more disparagingly, "The Girl she has with her wants more care than the child, and is wholly incapable of looking properly after her, without some superior to direct her." The Girl, evidently, didn't even warrant the use of her name.

It is hard to imagine why Abigail ridiculed Sally for irresponsibility. At the time, a fourteen-year-old enslaved individual stood at the cusp of adulthood and would have been accustomed to working long hours quite efficiently. The Hemingses' light skin—Sally was three-quarters white—and their family relationship with Jefferson gave them privileged status among his slaves. Instead of breaking their backs in the fields, the boys were taught trades, and the girls worked in the house. It is likely that Sally had looked after other enslaved children at Monticello, sewed, and worked in the kitchen and laundry. How then could she have been "wholly incapable" of looking after Polly?

Could it be that the prudish Abigail disliked Sally because she showed too much spunk and not enough deference? Perhaps Sally had a confidence the prim northerner did not like in a servant. Was Sally too familiar with little Polly who was, in fact, her niece? Was she just bubbling over with excitement to leave the plantation for the first time in her life, cross the Atlantic Ocean, and arrive in sprawling, bustling London?

Or had Abigail Adams heard rumors that Jefferson had an eye for young mulatto girls, as mixed-raced people were called at the time? Puritanical in outlook and scrupulously faithful to each other, Abigail and John Adams enjoyed sneering at the immoral sexual behavior of others. It may be significant that Abigail thought that Sally was older than she was—fifteen or sixteen—indicating she was well developed for her age. Additionally, Sally was reported to be "very handsome," according to her son with Jefferson, Madison. Jefferson's white grandson, Thomas Jefferson Randolph, described Sally as "light colored and decidedly good looking." According to Isaac Jefferson, an enslaved man who became overseer of Monticello in 1797, Sally was "mighty near white" with "straight hair down her back." In his 1781 book, *Notes on the State of Virginia*, Jefferson wrote that white skin was more aesthetically pleasing than black because it enabled whites to blush, displaying their emotions and "the expression of every passion," which he found quite charming. He added that "flowing hair" was a particularly important attribute of Caucasian beauty, and that mulattoes had "superior intellect" to those of fully African descent.

The Adamses had spent a great deal of time with Jefferson while he and John negotiated the commercial treaties in Paris two years earlier. They must have seen that Jefferson, in his forties, still radiated virility, turning the ladies' heads. His astonishing height alone—he was almost six foot three in an age when the average man was five foot seven—would have made him stand out in a crowd. In addition, he was trim and handsome, with hazel eyes, reddish hair, a sensuous mouth, and a strong jaw. Perhaps, too, Abigail noticed that Sally resembled Jefferson's beloved late wife, Martha, since they had the same father. If that were the case, Sally might prove an irresistible temptation to the lusty bachelor who owned her.

Lusty though he was, Thomas Jefferson would never truly get over his wife's untimely death. Indeed, the life path he had carefully designed in his youth had taken surprising turns both tragic and fortuitous. Born in rural Virginia in 1743, the son of a well-to-do planter, he had received a sterling education, entering the College of William & Mary in Williamsburg at sixteen and two years later commencing his studies in law. Blessed with an omnivorous appetite for learning, he studied Latin, Greek, French, philosophy, mathematics, history, ethics, politics, and agriculture. He was fascinated by the world around him and, over the years, collected mastodon bones, studied the stars, cultivated 330 types of vegetables and 170 kinds of fruit, designed buildings, tinkered with inventions, and analyzed the Bible and wrote his own version, which he thought made a lot more sense than the original. His ravenous curiosity compelled him to collect thousands of books.

Admitted to the Virginia bar in 1767, Jefferson practiced law and served as a delegate to the Virginia House of Burgesses from 1769 to 1775. In 1772, the twenty-nine-year-old married Martha Wayles Skelton, a twenty-three-year-old widow, with whom he was deeply in love. Like Jefferson, Martha was an avid reader. She played the piano beautifully, often accompanied by Jefferson on the violin. She kept his house and entertained his friends and birthed his babies. In addition to his law practice and political responsibilities, Jefferson ran his five-thousand-acre plantation and built his new house on a hill, which he called Monticello, "little mountain" in Italian. It was, for a short time, the life he had dreamed of. Farming. Raising a family with a beloved wife. Dabbling in local politics while working as a country lawyer.

And then, in 1775, the course of this calm, predictable life was swept up into the whirlwind of the Revolution. That year, aged thirty-two, he was one of the youngest delegates to the Continental Congress. There he became friends with John Adams, a delegate from Massachusetts. As Adams soon learned, while Jefferson could be witty and warm with friends, revealing the treasures of his encyclopedic knowledge, he shrank from strangers, often avoiding eye contact. Sitting amid the nation's most powerful, argumentative men in the Continental Congress, he was positively tongue-tied. Adams said, "I never heard him utter three sentences together" and compared him to "the great rivers, whose bottoms we cannot see and make no noise."

Perhaps because of his height, Jefferson slouched when standing up and when seated rolled onto one hip. Seeing himself as a farmer-spokesman for the common folk, he usually dressed casually, sometimes even sloppily. It was easy for the older, more experienced men at the Continental Congress to ignore him as a rather stupid country bumpkin. But Adams, aware of Jefferson's vast knowledge and abilities, especially his powerful writing style, pushed to have him write the initial draft of the Declaration of Independence. Though Congress made changes to his document, it is Jefferson's words that ring throughout history: *We hold these truths to be self-evident, that all men are created equal, that they are endowed by their Creator with certain unalienable Rights, that among these are Life, Liberty, and the pursuit of Happiness.*

After an unsuccessful stint as governor of Virginia from 1779 to 1781, Jefferson felt he was poorly suited to public service and just wanted to return home, continue building his house, and spend time with his family. His wife, Martha, was sickly. She had given birth to six children during their decade-long marriage—though only two would live more than a few years—and she seemed to become sicker with each pregnancy. She never recovered from the birth of her last child in 1782. A few months later, on her deathbed, Martha made Jefferson swear he would never remarry. Jefferson's overseer, Edmund Bacon, later recalled, "Holding her hand, Mr. Jefferson promised her solemnly that he would never marry again."

When Martha died, Jefferson fainted. For weeks, he was inconsolable, his grief frightening those around him. He stayed in his room, walking "incessantly night and day only lying down occasionally when nature was completely exhausted," according to an early biographer who interviewed members of Jefferson's immediate family. He must have been suffering from clinical depression, yet he managed to rouse himself enough to serve in Congress in 1783 to 1784.

Still, his friends believed he needed a change of scene. In the summer of 1784, he was sent to Paris to join John Adams and Benjamin Franklin to negotiate commercial treaties with several countries. He brought with him his twelve-year-old daughter, Martha, called Patsy as a child; and James Hemings, Sally's nineteen-year-old brother, with the object of training him as a French cook.

Upon landing, Jefferson cast his comfortable sloppiness immediately aside. Here in France he would be representing his country and meeting King Louis XVI, Queen Marie Antoinette, and other power brokers. He powdered his hair and dressed in pastel brocades with diamond buttons, embroidered waistcoats, silk stockings, and frothy lace cravats and cuffs. For formal events he buckled on a jeweled sword. He sent Patsy to board during the week at the Abbaye Royale de Panthemont, the most exclusive convent school in Paris, though she returned home on weekends.

In 1785, the commercial treaties ratified, Franklin returned to Philadelphia, Jefferson replaced him in Paris, and Adams took up the position as U.S. ambassador in London. Jefferson rented the opulent Hôtel de Langeac—a sprawling, gated estate abutting the Champs-Élysées with a courtyard, gardens, and outbuildings. Here he entertained in the grand style, often inviting thirty people to dinner at a time, and far outspending his government allowance. But one of Jefferson's weaknesses—and one which would have horrific consequences for his enslaved people at Monticello—was his need to play the role of Lord Bountiful, the world's most generous and elegant host, regardless of whether he could afford it or whom it might hurt.

Perhaps because of the constant round of entertaining, Jefferson didn't follow Abigail's advice and send Sally back to Virginia. Another pair of young, well-trained hands would come in handy. Moreover, Jefferson had known Sally from the time she was a small child, arriving with her family at Monticello as part of his wife's inheritance from her father. When Jefferson had left Virginia in 1784, Sally was eleven. Perhaps he remembered her as an industrious worker, helping around the house. He sent a servant to London to escort his daughter and Sally to the Hôtel de Langeac. And on July 15, Sally Hemings arrived in Paris, no longer a flat-chested child, but a nubile girl budding into womanhood.

Though it is not known exactly what work Sally did for Jefferson, we can assume that during the week she ran errands, sewed, and helped her brother prepare meals. Perhaps she took care of Jefferson's linen and clothing and bustled around his bedroom dusting and tidying. She must have looked after his daughters when they returned home on the weekends. She would have helped them dress, curl their hair, and keep their clothing clean and pressed. At fifteen, Patsy attended various social events. Sally would have stood back against the wall watching her mistress dance and play cards, brought her a cup of punch or plate of food, or assisted her on the chamber pot.

As the personal maid of the American ambassador's daughter, Sally, too, was expected to look fashionable, attired in silk and satin, though with less decoration than her niece. Jefferson's records show that he spent a good amount on her clothing, taking her around personally to milliners, apparently without Patsy in tow. It is curious that a man in his august position would have accompanied his slave to dress fittings, when his housekeeper would have been a more appropriate choice.

Sally might have loved not only the gorgeous French fashions, but the entire Paris experience. She had been used to the slow plantation rhythm of a few hundred people methodically feeding animals, pulling plows, and weeding tobacco. Now she was in a metropolis of seven hundred thousand people, the largest city in Europe. Right outside her door, princely carriages rattled past. Prostitutes and street vendors flaunted their wares. Actors set up impromptu street theaters. Beggars displayed maimed limbs and suppurating sores. For the first time in her life, Sally had her own money. Jefferson paid her sporadic wages, as he did her brother James and had done for her relatives back at Monticello. She could march into an upscale store and buy herself something lovely. Perhaps she and her brother visited museums or the theater, or sipped coffee at a café.

But for Sally and James Hemings, the most exciting thing about Paris could have been the Freedom Principle, which stated that enslaved individuals could claim their freedom at the Admiralty Court. It seems that James Hemings was intending to stay in Paris after Jefferson departed. He paid for French lessons with a tutor to perfect his knowledge of the French language. As a master chef in a noble household—an enviable and highly respected position—he could have commanded a high salary.

Meanwhile, in France the popular disgust with government mismanagement and overspending rose to a boil. Hail, floods, and drought destroyed crops, resulting in starvation across France even as the government raised taxes. On July 14, 1789, thousands of citizens unleashed their rage in Paris, storming the Bastille prison, that symbol of royal suppression. Jefferson was thrilled that France was following in America's footsteps. "My fortune has been singular to see in the course of fourteen years two such revolutions as were never seen before," he wrote.

Excited as he was by political events in France, Jefferson was itching to take his daughters back home and return a few months later without them. Enjoying her stay in the convent, Patsy told her Protestant father she wanted to become a nun. Jefferson, who had great difficulty telling anyone flat-out no, took her into society more, sometimes to as many as three balls a week, where she was such a success that he feared she would fall in love with a Frenchman and beg to marry him. In that case, Jefferson might never see her again. He was terribly afraid of losing those he loved—his father had died when Jefferson was thirteen, and he had lost not only his wife but four of their six children. "I am born to lose everything I love," he lamented to a friend in 1787.

Moreover, Jefferson was not entirely comfortable with the education his daughters were receiving. As America's ambassador, he had done what was expected by sending them to their prestigious convent school where they learned music, dancing, art, and languages. That was fine, in its way. Back in Virginia they would attend a dance now and then and amuse themselves at home playing the piano, painting, or reading a book in French. But, as he complained to his sister-in-law, nothing the girls learned there would make them particularly "useful in [their] own country." Better, Jefferson believed, that they know how to make a pudding and mend a shirt.

Jefferson found French women—with their sharp wit, fierce self-confidence, and devastating attractions—a bit frightening, perhaps even emasculating. These Gallic Amazons wore powdered hair a foot high, with ostrich feathers waving another two feet above that. They had white lead–painted faces with black beauty spots and bright red cheeks, and rustled in poofed satin gowns, trailing clouds of heady perfume in their wake.

It's not that he wasn't attracted to these bold women. In August 1786, Jefferson had had an intense affair with twenty-seven-year-old Maria Cosway, a talented portrait painter resident in London, who was visiting Paris with her husband, Richard, also an artist. She had a full face, wide blue eyes under dark brows, a straight little nose, and pouting lips. Her golden hair was piled high and tumbling down to her shoulders in the popular 1780s coiffeur of a whirlwind destroying a wig store. For a month, while Richard Cosway painted portraits, Jefferson and Maria visited châteaux, strolled in gardens, and took carriage rides in the countryside. They had fallen deeply in love. Jefferson wrote of being smitten with "a generous spasm of the heart," and we can imagine he experienced other generous spasms as well. He was overcome with grief when her husband took her away a month later, though he soon got over it.

In the winter of late 1787 and early 1788, the dazzling Angelica Church, who had been living in London with her husband, visited Paris. The sister-in-law of Alexander Hamilton—with whom he was presumed to have had an affair—captivated Jefferson as much as she had his political enemy. Theirs was, most likely, a gallant flirtation; effusive demonstrations of affection were fashionable at the time. But as far as a long-term relationship was concerned, Jefferson yearned for a more comfortable type of woman like his late wife, one who loved nothing so much as sitting in a rocking chair by the fire, knitting.

Someone, in fact, like Sally Hemings. By the time Jefferson prepared to return to Virginia, the lovely girl was sixteen. Here was a young woman who could never have emasculated him, never could have threatened him. Never could have *left* him. She could not demand marriage and try to make him break his promise to his late wife. A man could not marry his slave. Legally, she was required to do his bidding as long as she lived. Sally, for Jefferson, was the perfect solution.

And what about Sally? How did she feel about him? We know frustratingly little about her as a person, her thoughts and feelings, hopes and dreams and disappointments, and barely anything about her relationship with Jefferson. As an enslaved woman, she leaves us no portraits, no letters or diaries. We do not know if she was literate, though her brother James was. And we have no idea when the affair began. Did he set out immediately to seduce the pretty fourteen-year-old? Or did the daily contact over two years gradually result in feelings on both sides?

Our only source of information was her son with Jefferson, Madison Hemings, who, in 1873 at the age of sixty-eight, spoke with a journalist from an Ohio newspaper. Regarding Sally's tenure in Paris, Madison said, "During that time, my mother became Mr. Jefferson's concubine . . . When he was called back home she was enceinte [pregnant] by him. He desired to bring my mother back to Virginia with him, but she demurred. She was just beginning to understand the French language well, and in France she was free, while if she returned to Virginia she would be re-enslaved. So she refused to return with him." It was, for a time at least, Sally Hemings's own declaration of independence.

Again, Jefferson was in danger of losing someone he cared for, as well as his unborn child. In France, he could not force Sally to return with him. "To induce her to do so," Madison continued, "he promised her extraordinary privileges and made a solemn pledge that her children should be freed at the age of twenty-one years. In consequence of his promises, on which she implicitly relied, she returned with him to Virginia. She trusted Jefferson over French law, with her life and the lives of her children." Madison described their pact as a "treaty," a bargain on both their parts.

Did Sally Hemings love Thomas Jefferson more than freedom? Or did she merely tolerate him but longed to see her mother, brothers, and sisters in Virginia again? Did she believe that her relationship with the plantation master would raise her family's status even higher, obtaining greater comforts and privileges for them all? Was she afraid of remaining in Paris, pregnant and alone?

And why didn't her brother James, a master chef, fluent in French, stay and claim his freedom? It is likely that he planned to return to France with Jefferson in early 1790 and wanted to spend some time visiting his family at Monticello whom he hadn't seen in five years. Whatever the reason behind their extraordinary decisions to return to slavery, on October 22, 1789, Sally and James Hemings set sail for Virginia, looking back at France, as the freedom they could have had dwindled on the horizon and disappeared.

Just four months later, James's plan to return to France and freedom were ruined when President George Washington appointed Jefferson the first U.S. secretary of state. Jefferson—and James—would not be returning to Paris. They would be going to the interim U.S. capital, New York. James was stuck in slavery, though Jefferson would free him in 1796 once James had trained his brother Robert as a master chef to replace him.

After Jefferson's daughter Patsy married in February 1790, he gave her several slaves, but not Sally, who had been her lady's maid for two years in France and would have, under other circumstances, been the logical choice. Yet Jefferson ended up sending Sally's fourteen-year-old niece.

It is intriguing how every household slave at Monticello is mentioned in family correspondence *except* Sally Hemings, and her absence from the letters is a clue in itself. After Jefferson's death, Patsy sifted through his documents to prepare them for publication. Numerous letters that did not reflect well on Jefferson were not published. Let us imagine that Patsy found the following note she had written her father decades earlier: "Dear Father, I am in sore need of a lady's maid. It's a pity Sally can't be the new maid, but I understand she is big with child. Please send me someone else." Surely, she would have consigned such a missive to the flames, along with anything else mentioning Sally.

Jefferson's daughters must have understood the nature of his relationship with Sally Hemings, especially when she gave birth to several light-skinned children, at least some of whom resembled him. As awkward as the relationship must have been for his daughters, they likely appreciated the fact that Jefferson did not remarry and sire legitimate children who could draw off their expected inheritance. This kind of family upheaval happened quite frequently in an era when so many young women died in childbirth. Sally's children could never inherit for two reasons: they were illegitimate, and they were slaves. But Sally's baby, born most likely in the spring of 1790, seems to have died in infancy; Madison's mention of this pregnancy more than eighty years later is the only extant reference to it.

As secretary of state, Jefferson found himself increasingly at odds with Alexander Hamilton, the secretary of the treasury. The vastly differing views that had first become apparent while negotiating the Constitution continued to inflame their hatred for each other as the nation fell into two political parties. Jefferson found himself, along with James Madison, the leader of the Republican Party, Hamilton in charge of the Federalists. Jefferson rejected national debt, banks, and vibrant commerce. He believed the most virtuous life was farming, pulling your plow—or better yet, watching your slaves pull your plow—over the rich earth to bring forth food.

While Hamilton enjoyed fierce vocal debate, Jefferson could not bear to argue with anyone and disliked those who did. He saw disagreement as bad manners. In a letter to John Adams he wrote, "I do not love difficulties. I am fond of quiet, willing to do my duty, but made irritable by slander and apt to be forced by it to abandon my post." If Hamilton poked holes in his proposals, Jefferson, clearly passive-aggressive, would not jump up and respond angrily. He would sit quietly, plotting revenge in the form of nasty newspaper columns, using aliases.

At the end of 1793, Jefferson resigned from his position as secretary of state, feeling snubbed by President Washington, who mostly sided with Hamilton, and returned to Monticello. He ran for president in 1796 and came in second after John Adams, which, according to the electoral system of the time, meant the nation had a Federalist president, John Adams, and a Republican vice president, Jefferson, who labored to undermine everything the president did. He secretly worked with the French to thwart Adams's policies and wrote nasty anonymous newspaper articles about the irascible chief executive tearing off his wig and kicking it across the room in rage. Picture Hillary Clinton as Donald Trump's vice president, or vice versa, and you will understand the strange and horrible politics of the late 1790s.

When Jefferson won the presidential election of 1800, he sought to portray himself as a man of the people. For two weeks after his inauguration, he stayed at his boardinghouse near the Capitol and dined at the common table. Once ensconced in the White House, Jefferson often answered the door himself wearing an old robe and bedroom slippers. When William Plumer, a Federalist from New Hampshire, arrived at the White House and saw the slouching, slovenly Jefferson open the door, he naturally assumed he was a servant, and a poorly dressed one at that.

In one case, Jefferson's dress resulted in a diplomatic furor. On November 29, 1803, Anthony Merry, the new British ambassador to the U.S., arrived at the White House to present his credentials in a blue dress coat with gold braid, white breeches, white silk stockings, a feathered hat, and a dress sword. Jefferson ambled into the room wearing slippers "down at the heels," as a furious Merry wrote his superiors in London, woolen stockings, and old clothing of "utter slovenliness." Not only did Merry feel that he had been personally insulted, but he viewed Jefferson's appearance as an insult to King George III, whom he represented. And it probably was, when we consider how Jefferson had powdered and curled his hair and sported brocade suits with diamond buttons while serving in France. To make matters worse, while Jefferson and Merry were speaking, the president of the United States of America repeatedly kicked his rotten old slipper up in the air and caught it on his toe. Soon after, when Merry and his wife arrived for a White House dinner, they found that the traditional system of ranked seating had gone out the window, replaced by a kind of unseemly musical chairs as guests fought over the most honorable seats. The ambassador boycotted official functions.

And now, as president, Jefferson's bad karma came back to haunt him. James Callender, the hack journalist he had hired to publicize Alexander Hamilton's tawdry love affair with Maria Reynolds, became furious that Jefferson, as president, wasn't doing enough to reward him. He demanded that Jefferson appoint him postmaster of Richmond as payment for services rendered, a demand Jefferson refused. Callender decided to poke around Charlottesville and Richmond to see what dirt he could dig up on his former employer. And it wasn't very hard to learn of Sally Hemings. It seemed that her thirteen-year relationship with the president was the best-known secret in the commonwealth of Virginia.

A vicious racist, Callender was disgusted by the news. Jefferson, a man Callender had worked with and looked up to for several years, was a traitor to the white race. Callender would humiliate him publicly, as well as Sally Hemings and their children. "It is well known that the man, whom it delighteth the people to honor, keeps, and for many years has kept, as his concubine, one of his slaves," Callender wrote in the September 1, 1802, issue of the *Richmond Recorder*. "Her name is SALLY." It was just the first salvo in a cruel attack. The September 14, 1802, issue of another Richmond newspaper, the *Virginia Federalist*, reported that, according to multiple sources, "Mr. J," a man in a position of great power, had "a number of yellow children and that he is addicted to golden affections."

Though Callender was correct that Sally had given birth to five children by then, three of them had died. Either he didn't know that, or he didn't want to portray Sally as a figure worthy of sympathy. It served Callender's purpose to present Jefferson as populating the world with countless mixed-race bastards. He reported that Sally's oldest child, the one born soon after she returned from France, was still living and called "President Tom," bore "a striking resemblance to the President," and was "putting on airs."

Callender called Sally "the African Venus," "Dusky Sally," "Yellow Sally," and "Black Sal," and indicated she lived in the pigsty at Monticello. "A slut as common as the pavement," she had sex with thirty men of all colors. Learning that three teenaged enslaved girls worked in the White House kitchen, Callender crowed that Jefferson kept a "stable of mulatto girls" there for his sexual pleasure. Sally was caricatured in newspaper cartoons and ridiculed in ribald ballads. Newspapers in Europe commented on her.

Jefferson maintained a dignified silence about the accusations, which was easier to do in a time when there was no threat of a microphone being stuck in your face. Moreover, unlike Hamilton, he had not been falsely accused of financial crimes that he would have felt obligated to deny. There is no record in his family papers—of course not—about the reactions of Jefferson, his family, and Sally herself to Callender's vitriol. The one thing Sally had possessed was her privacy, her dignity. Now the entire world knew her name, her shame, her love—if love it was—and her bargain. Now millions of people saw her as the Black Whore of Babylon. We can assume her large, supportive family buoyed her up, as did Jefferson himself. Perhaps he sent her encouraging letters from Washington, which the family later burned.

Callender's last months were difficult ones. Though readers loved his florid, nasty prose, some of those who knew him personally were heartily sick of him. In December 1802, one of his former defense attorneys beat him on the head with his walking stick. In March 1803, a group of Republicans attacked his newspaper office. Another former friend in an open letter in the Richmond *Examiner* suggested that Callender, once he stopped drinking whiskey, should swallow a dose of James River water. A few months later, Callender did just that. He was found drowned in the James River in three feet of water, reportedly too drunk to stumble to shore. Either that, or one of his literary victims had murdered him.

While Callender had hoped his disreputable revelations would prevent Jefferson from enjoying a second term, his plan did not work. In November 1804, Jefferson won 162 out of 176 electoral votes, winning on a strong economy, low taxes, and the triumph of the Louisiana Purchase. In 1803, he had bought some 828,000 square miles of territory from France for $15 million (some $340 million in today's money), doubling the size of the United States with a pen stroke. Perhaps his best-known accomplishment in his second term was the return in 1806 of the two-year expedition led by Meriwether Lewis and William Clark to explore the new territory and beyond, all the way to the Pacific, mapping the land, initiating diplomatic relations with native peoples, and bringing back plants, seeds, and minerals.

In 1809, Jefferson left office and returned to Monticello to play the role of virtuous resplendent farmer. Soon after, his daughter Patsy—now going by her legal name of Martha—separated from her abusive, alcoholic husband and moved back to Monticello with her eight children. It must have been awkward having her father's enslaved mistress at the house, along with all those nearly white enslaved children who looked just like the author of the Declaration of Independence. Martha demanded that Jefferson send them all away to one of his other plantations, but he refused.

Jefferson, who always loved to entertain, providing countless guests with the finest food and wines, now reveled in hospitality so extreme it was almost pathological. Any stranger could knock on his front door and stay as an honored guest in Hotel Monticello, where no one ever paid a cent. Entire ravenous families arrived with their hungry servants and famished horses, sometimes staying weeks at a time. Jefferson, whose finances had always been precarious, had left the White House poorer than he had arrived because of his lavish entertaining. Now he was racking up more debts, and completely unconcerned by the work he was giving his enslaved people—changing bed linens, doing laundry, cooking, cleaning hearths, and emptying chamber pots. But there would be far worse consequences.

Sally Hemings kept out of the way of Monticello visitors, quietly going about her business. "It was her duty, all her life which I can remember, up to the time of father's death, to take care of his chamber and wardrobe, look after us children and do such light work as sewing," her son Madison recalled. Jefferson made sure that his private quarters were strictly off limits to the countless visitors wandering through the house. During his presidency, he had had "porticles" built, structures attached to the exterior of his private living area, with louvered blinds, which prevented people from peering into his bedchamber.

It was a good idea, because many of the visitors to Monticello had read about the African Venus and were keeping an eye out for her. In 1811, one visitor, Elijah Fletcher of Vermont, reported after his visit, "The story of black Sal is no farce. That he cohabits with her and has a number of children by her is a sacred truth and the worst of it is, he keeps the same children as slaves, an unnatural crime which is very common in these parts."

Of the seven children Sally had with Jefferson, only four survived to adulthood. The boys—Beverly, born in 1798, Madison in 1805, and Eston in 1808, when Jefferson was an impressive sixty-five—learned the craft of fine furniture making in the Monticello carpentry shop. His daughter Harriet, born in 1801, learned to weave and spin. Back in Paris in 1789, Jefferson had promised Sally that he would free their children when they turned twenty-one, a promise he did not fulfill. It is likely that he was afraid they would leave him if freed and, as we know, he had a deep-seated fear of losing those he loved.

In 1822, when Beverly was twenty-four, he was fed up enough to simply walk away from Monticello, and Jefferson did not pursue him. Soon after, twenty-one-year-old Harriet decided to leave, too. The Monticello overseer, Edmund Bacon, reported that he gave her $50 (more than $1,000 today) and put her on a stagecoach north, probably to join Beverly. Bacon described Harriet as "nearly as white as anybody, and very beautiful." Both Beverly and Harriet lived as white people in Washington, D.C., and married well-to-do whites. After several years, they changed their names so no one could trace them back to their black family and stopped writing home.

In a spectacular coincidence, eighty-three-year-old Thomas Jefferson died on July 4, 1826, the fiftieth anniversary of the founding of the United States, as did the only other signer to become president, John Adams. The two had started off as friends, became rabid enemies, and finally reconciled in their final years. Indeed, Adams's last words were, "Jefferson lives," but Jefferson had died a few hours before.

Jefferson's death had horrific consequences for his slaves. Six months after his death, his surviving daughter, who inherited his staggering debts, advertised "130 Valuable Negroes" to be auctioned off. How tragically ironic that Thomas Jefferson—who penned the most powerful words of liberty and equality in human history—ended up sending these people to the auction block, to have their lives uprooted, their families separated, to work for new and perhaps cruel masters. The laws for freeing slaves were complex and designed to make it difficult. Many whites feared that freed slaves would wreak revenge for their heinous treatment. They wanted them either to remain enslaved or go back to Africa. Yet Jefferson could have freed a good portion during his lifetime, and freed them all in his will, as George Washington had done in his. But doing so would have deprived his white family of valuable property at a time when they would be dealing with his massive debts.

Jefferson officially freed only two slaves during his lifetime, Sally Hemings's two brothers, James and Robert, in the 1790s, though they had to work for it. He had allowed two of his children with Sally to head north. In his will, he freed two more sons with Sally, twenty-one-year-old Madison and eighteen-year-old Eston, whom he called his "apprentices." His will did not free Sally; wills were recorded in the county courthouse where any nosy person could read them. Jefferson's daughter Martha informally gave Sally—who was her aunt—"her time," allowing her to live as a free person.

Sally moved into a rented house on Main Street in Charlottesville and later moved into her son Madison's house. Before she died in 1835 at the age of sixty-two, Sally gave her sons precious, carefully harbored mementos of Jefferson: a pair of eyeglasses, shoe buckles, and an inkwell, apparently all that she had left of him. Perhaps she had truly loved him after all.

In 2017, archeologists tore out a tourists' bathroom in Monticello's basement under the South Terrace and, based on the description of Sally's room by Jefferson's grandson, declared it to be Sally's. It is being restored and furnished, a tribute to the nation's most famous unknown African American woman.

Over the years, Thomas Jefferson's white descendants have not only bent over backward to deny his relationship with Sally Hemings but twisted themselves into pretzels. Not only were any references to Sally destroyed soon after his death, but in the 1850s, Thomas Jefferson Randolph, Martha's son, bruited it about that the late Peter Carr, one of Jefferson's nephews by his sister Martha, had fathered Sally's children. The story was published and generally accepted. The oral history of the Hemings family was ridiculed as a pack of lies, uppity black people desperately trying to latch on to the saintly Thomas Jefferson.

A 1998 DNA test on Jefferson's white descendants and a descendant of Eston Hemings, however, upset the applecart. It showed that Peter Carr could not have been the father. There were seven other male Jeffersons who could have been, including his younger brother Randolph. Although Randolph had never been mentioned as a possibility before the test, his name was put forward by people desperately grasping at DNA straws. Moreover, Randolph, though he lived only twenty miles from Monticello, had visited only four times as documented in Jefferson's obsessive-compulsive recordkeeping—in September 1802, September 1805, May 1808, and sometime in 1814—none of which coincided with the conception of Sally Hemings's children. Nor was he in Paris when Sally conceived her first child. However, since Madison Hemings's recollections of his mother's tales are the only indication of this child, some historians believe there is insufficient proof of its brief existence.

The fact is that during a period of nineteen years from her arrival home from Paris in 1789 until the birth of her seventh child in 1808, Sally Hemings never conceived when Jefferson was away from Monticello. This indicates she may never have had another sexual partner. One compelling detail is that on July 11, 1797, Jefferson arrived at Monticello after a long stay in Philadelphia, and thirty-eight weeks later Sally had a baby. Another is that Jefferson noted the fathers of all his female slaves' children in his farm book except for the children of Sally Hemings. He never listed their father. Nor were there any rumors in that gossipmongering era of Jefferson having any other lover. It seems the two of them stayed faithful to each other until death.

4

GROVER CLEVELAND'S
HIGH CHARACTER

*P*erhaps Grover Cleveland learned a valuable lesson from Alexander Hamilton on how to deal with a political sex scandal: tell the truth. For his refusal to lie, spin, and shred the truth, he has been applauded in the history books. But there is a darker side to his story. Three U.S. presidents have been accused of rape. Grover Cleveland was the first. Unlike the two who followed him, he never denied it. And, despite the expected squawks of puritanical outrage, most voters didn't care.

* * *

On the evening of December 15, 1873, thirty-three-year-old Maria Halpin walked briskly down the freezing streets of Buffalo, New York, on her way to a friend's birthday party at a nearby hotel restaurant. She had no idea, as she saw a man coming toward her, his black broadcloth coat and top hat visible in the yellow gaslight, that her life was about to veer horribly off course in a scandal that would rock the nation.

As he approached, Maria recognized Grover Cleveland, a lawyer finishing up his term as county sheriff, and she greeted him in pleasant surprise. Cleveland, thirty-six, lived a block and a half from Maria's rooms in Mrs. Randall's boardinghouse and had been courting the stunning widow for several months now. We do not know how they first became acquainted. Perhaps it was at the nearby Episcopal church they both attended. Or maybe he had first seen her at the Flint & Kent department store, where she waited on him behind the counter in the lace and cloak section.

Cleveland had been immediately attracted to the elegant beauty with an hourglass figure. At five foot eight, Maria was nearly a head taller than most women and moved with a regal poise. She had jet-black hair, sky-blue eyes, full lips, and white skin set off by the mourning she still wore three years after the death of her husband from tuberculosis. With two young children to support, Maria left her daughter in the care of her father in New Jersey and took her son to Buffalo, where she accepted a job in a new department store. Graceful, charming, and beautiful, she soon become a top salesperson.

"He sought my acquaintance," Maria later recalled of Cleveland, "and obtained an introduction to me from a person in whom I had every confidence, and he paid me marked attention." Cleveland was "persistent," she said. Maria asked some of the other congregants in her church about Cleveland's character, which, "so far as I then knew, was good, and his intensions I believed were pure and honorable." It seemed the prosperous, popular Mr. Cleveland was finally looking to marry.

Cleveland wasn't a handsome man, but he had a jovial personality and a keen intelligence. Six feet tall, he was built like a bull, with brown hair, bright blue eyes, and a small hooked nose over a walrus mustache. An imposing individual, he radiated virility and power. He lived in a hotel, reveling in the bachelor life, eating in fine restaurants, smoking cigars, playing cards, and drinking with his friends.

The son of a Congregational minister, Cleveland had grown up in Central New York, studied law, and was admitted to the New York bar in 1859. His income was sizable, and he sent most of his earnings back to his widowed mother and younger sisters. He would, by any standards, be an excellent catch.

On that dark December street, Cleveland invited Maria to dinner. She declined, telling him about the birthday party. Her friend and other guests would be waiting for her, she said. But Cleveland kept urging her to accept his invitation until she finally agreed, and the two of them headed to the popular Ocean Dining Hall & Oyster House. After an enjoyable dinner, he walked her to her lodgings. He had done so before, Maria said, and knew that her ten-year-old son was living with her. Perhaps that is why, with her son in the next room, she always felt safe.

We only have Maria's account of what happened in her rooms that night. As soon as they were alone, she said, he got on top of her and "by use of force and violence and without my consent" had intercourse with her. "Up to that hour my life was as pure and spotless as that of any lady in the city of Buffalo. There was not the slightest shadow of suspicion over me." Now she knew she was a "ruined" woman.

We can picture her, bruised, torn, humiliated, miserably pulling down her skirt and wiping tears from her face. She told him she would report the rape to the authorities. "He told me that he was determined to ruin me if it cost him $10,000," she recalled, "if he was hanged by the neck for it. I then and there told him that I never wanted to see him again and would never see him and commanded him to leave my rooms, which he did."

Cleveland knew that Maria would have a hard time making any charges stick, and if by any chance she did, as the local sheriff, he would be in an excellent position to make them disappear. It was generally believed a woman could not be raped unless she was overpowered by more than one man. Every man knew that women could keep their legs closed if they really wanted to and, failing that, the self-welding mechanism on their vaginas would kick into action. Resistance was viewed as spirited foreplay. A "real" rape victim's injuries had to be substantial: broken bones and enormous bruises. Anything else was seen as consensual, after which the woman had second thoughts and made a false report of a crime. And pregnancy was a sure sign she had enjoyed the sex.

It didn't help Maria's case that she had led what was then considered a dubious lifestyle to begin with. For one thing, she was a woman living without a male relative or a female chaperone. For another, she walked the streets alone at night to attend events like birthday parties in hotel restaurants. She had accepted a man's invitation to dinner issued on the street. Even worse, she had invited a man up to her rooms. A virtuous woman would never have done any of those things. And, as far as we know, she suffered no broken bones or horrifying bruises from her struggle. The law would have assumed that, even if she had struggled briefly at the beginning of the attack, she consented to the sex by the end.

As bad as things stood, they got much worse. Six weeks after the assault, Maria realized she was pregnant. She had few options. She could try to induce an abortion by swallowing poison, or she could go to a backstreet abortionist, risking her life. If her pregnancy became known, she would lose her job and her reputation. She did not feel she could tell her father what had happened; he would have blamed her. The best path open, she decided, would be to marry her rapist. And so, she chose "to inform him of the consequences of his actions . . . he being the proper person to whom I could tell my trouble."

Maria wrote Cleveland a note demanding that he come see her at Mrs. Randall's. When he arrived at her rooms, in "despair" she told him of her pregnancy and insisted that he marry her. He was furious.

"What the devil are you blubbering about?" he cried. "You act like a baby without teeth." After a while, according to Maria, he calmed down, said he "would do everything which was honorable and righteous" and "promised that he would marry me."

Over the next several weeks, Cleveland gave Maria some money, raising her hopes that this nightmare might end up working out. But he never agreed to set a wedding date. When her pregnancy began to show, she left her job at the department store. She confided to her pastor what had happened, who reached out to Cleveland about his duty to marry her. Cleveland, though he "acknowledged his fault," said he was not certain that he was the father. He would, however, be willing to help support the child. Maria, realizing Cleveland would not marry her, fell into a deep depression.

Cleveland arranged for the top obstetrician in Buffalo, Dr. James E. King, to deliver the baby at the only hospital in town that served unwed mothers. There, on September 14, 1874, Maria gave birth to a boy, whom Cleveland named Oscar Folsom Cleveland for his best friend. Two days later, Dr. King took the baby from Maria and put him in the care of his sister, who was due to give birth any day. For the next year, Minnie Kendall raised her son and Maria's as twins. It is not known why Cleveland took the baby from his mother. Perhaps he was afraid of her showing up at his prestigious law office with a wailing baby, clamoring for money and marriage.

He allowed Maria to see her son briefly on two occasions. Both times she cried and begged to keep him. Perhaps Cleveland began to have some sympathy for her. Maybe, too, he finally realized she would not try to shame him publicly. Whatever the reason, after a year, he instructed Minnie Kendall to give Maria her son back. Overjoyed, Maria once again begged Cleveland to marry her. They could live as a family. It wasn't too late. "Marriage was the only step possible to even partially repair the wrong he had done," she explained. It would wipe clean the "stain on her honor." He again refused. And Maria, severely depressed, began to drink heavily.

Her supportive neighbor Mrs. Baker said, "She took to drink to drown the grief that was consuming her." Learning about her alcohol abuse, Cleveland grew concerned that his child might be in danger. He asked a friend of his, a judge, to visit Maria to persuade her that her drinking endangered her toddler. If she placed her son in the Buffalo Orphan Asylum, Cleveland would give her money to start her own dressmaking shop in Niagara Falls. It was all for the good of her son and herself. Exhausted, sick with grief and depression and liquor, Maria agreed to everything. She signed legal papers surrendering all claims to her son and giving him to the orphanage. On March 9, 1876, under the name of Oscar Halpin, the eighteen-month-old was officially placed in the Buffalo Orphan Asylum. Maria set off for Niagara Falls to begin a new life.

But within days she realized she had made a tremendous mistake. She returned to Buffalo and, on April 28, grabbed her son from the orphanage and fled. The police found her in an apartment on July 10, 1876, and tore a shrieking Oscar from her arms. Then they dragged her kicking and screaming into another waiting carriage.

When the carriage stopped less than an hour later, Maria looked out the window and saw she had arrived at the Providence Lunatic Asylum where she was committed against her will. The following morning, she was evaluated by Dr. William Ring, who could tell she had been drinking. Otherwise, he found her well-spoken and ladylike. He sat spellbound and horrified by her tale of rape, the loss of her child, and now her unjust imprisonment in an insane asylum. He told her she was free to leave whenever she wanted, but he advised her to rest there a few days. On July 21, somewhat recovered from her ordeal, she checked herself out.

Maria consulted a top Buffalo lawyer about getting her son back, who told her she also had grounds to sue for "assault and abduction." As he moved forward with the case, her brother-in-law Simeon Talbott said the family would not put up with a "public scandal." Her family—her old father, her two older children—would be "bowed down in an exposure of Maria's shame." Talbott handed her an agreement signed by Grover Cleveland stating he would pay her $500 (more than $12,000 today) if she agreed to give up Oscar and never make any claim against his father for anything. Totally defeated, Maria signed. On January 1, 1877, Dr. James E. King, who had delivered Oscar, and who had placed him with his sister for a year, removed the two-year-old from the orphanage and began formal adoption proceedings. His only child had died a couple years earlier at the age of ten, and his wife longed for another. Oscar Folsom Cleveland became James E. King Jr. No longer living in a rented room with an alcoholic mother, no longer one of dozens of unwanted children in the orphanage, now Maria's baby lived with prosperous parents in a large house with a wide front porch and fenced lawn.

When Grover Cleveland ran for mayor of Buffalo in 1881, he must have been delighted that Maria Halpin had left town years earlier for parts unknown, especially as he was running on a platform of honesty, responsibility, and clean government. A gang of crooks had been running city hall for years, the mayor and city council giving themselves commissions on all public works contracts. This meant that contracts were awarded to the highest bidder at taxpayer expense. Vowing to stop such corrupt practices, Cleveland, a Democrat, was swept into office in a Republican city on a wave of public disgust at the status quo. He took office January 1, 1882.

When the city council awarded an unscrupulous businessman a contract more than $100,000 ($2.5 million today) higher than the lowest bid to clean the city streets—and gave themselves generous kickbacks—Mayor Cleveland vetoed it, stating, "I regard it as the culmination of a most bare-faced, impudent, and shameless scheme to betray the interests of the people." The story made the newspapers across the state, and the people of Buffalo—Republican and Democrat alike—stood squarely behind their mayor. The contract was voided. Cleveland's new sewer system ended up costing $764,000, half the price of the $1.5 million estimate the previous council had received.

By August, only seven months into his job as mayor, Democratic Party leaders asked Cleveland to run for governor. He agreed and quickly won the nomination and then the governorship in a landslide. Now he started cleaning up the massive corruption in New York State. Newspaper articles praising Cleveland appeared across the U.S., and in early 1884 party power brokers asked him if he would consider running for president. Initially, Cleveland was hesitant. He had had "a woman scrape" a decade earlier, he explained. He could only pray that it would not come out. The party officials didn't mind, probably because most politicians had had "woman scrapes." Besides, Cleveland's battles with corrupt politicians were the talk of the nation. At the 1884 Democratic National Convention, General Edward S. Bragg of Wisconsin nominated Cleveland with the words "We love him for the enemies he has made."

Dr. George Lewis of Buffalo had watched Cleveland's meteoric political rise with increasing dismay. Back in 1876, a patient of his had brought her friend, Maria Halpin, to ask him for advice. She had related the whole sordid tale of her rape by Grover Cleveland, and while Lewis sympathized greatly, he told her he didn't see how he could help. He hadn't said a word to anyone about Maria's visit when Cleveland was elected mayor in 1881 and then governor a year later. But now, in July 1884, as the presidential conventions were quickly approaching, he told Maria's story to the Reverend George H. Ball, pastor of the Free Baptist Church.

Appalled, Ball started investigating. He went to the Buffalo department store where Maria had worked, and her supervisors confirmed she had left after becoming pregnant with Cleveland's child. Ball next interviewed Dr. William Ring at the lunatic asylum, who also corroborated Maria's story, as did her former landlady. But Ball could not find Maria herself. She had disappeared from Buffalo eight years earlier. Undeterred, Reverend Ball began writing to newspaper editors, accusing Cleveland of the "grossest licentiousness," though it was too late to stop his nomination as the Democratic presidential candidate on July 11. No paper printed his letter, but many journalists were certainly interested in learning more. They interviewed Ball, the landlady, the lunatic asylum doctor, and Maria's former colleagues at the department store.

On July 21, the *Evening Telegraph* broke the story of Cleveland's bad behavior, titled "A Terrible Tale." Part of the tale was a letter from Ball, who remained anonymous, accusing Cleveland of "habitual immoralities with women," "debauchery," and drunken, bloody bar fights, along with Maria's "seduction" and her involuntary commitment to an insane asylum. Meanwhile, Ball wrote, Cleveland pretends "before the great American public that he is a model of virtue, pre-eminently worthy of being honored by their votes and being exalted as an example of ambitious youth to imitate . . . It would be criminal to allow the virtuous to vote for so vile a man as this under a false impression that he is pure and honorable. It is painful to think of his offenses and shameful, infinitely shameful, to have such a man commended to the suffrages of a Christian nation. It is enough to alarm all decent people . . ." The *Evening Telegraph* described Maria as a woman of "culture, proud spirit and hitherto unblemished life," who had been "shamed," "disgraced," and "dishonored."

Though no word of rape had been uttered, even a seduction might have been enough to derail Cleveland's campaign, and his advisers were apoplectic. Desperate, they split up and ran around the city trying to buy up every copy of the offending newspaper from the newsstands. The paper gleefully printed more. Charles Goodyear, Cleveland's friend, telegraphed him in Albany asking for instructions on how to proceed with the scandal. Cleveland was celebrating the twentieth birthday of Frances Folsom, daughter of his deceased best friend, Oscar, along with her mother, Emma. For ten years, he had been nervously anticipating the other shoe to drop. Or, as the *Evening Telegraph* put it, "The mine that has long slumbered under the feet of Grover Cleveland has at last been exploded."

Without missing a heartbeat, Cleveland telegraphed back: "Whatever you do, tell the truth." Yes, he was the father of Maria's son. But his supporters, concerned that voters would reject him for not having been a virgin at the age of thirty-six, spun an exculpatory tale. The real father was Oscar Folsom who, being dead, was in a poor position to deny the charge. When Cleveland learned that newspapers were getting ready to carry the Folsom story, he was livid. He wrote to Daniel Lockwood, a Democratic congressman from Buffalo:

> I learned last night that McCune [Charles McCune, editor of the *Buffalo Courier*] had started the story and told it to newspapermen that I had nothing to do really with the subject of the Telegraph story—that is, that I am innocent—and that my silence was to shield my friend Oscar Folsom. Now is this man crazy or does he want to ruin anybody? Is he foolish enough to suppose for a moment that if such was the truth (which it is not, so far as the motive for silence is concerned) that I would permit my dead friend's memory to suffer for my sake? And Mrs. Folsom and her daughter at my house at this very time! I am afraid that I shall have occasion to pray to be delivered from my friends . . . This story of McCune's of course must be stopped. I have prevented its publication in one paper at least.

But Democratic Party leaders felt they had to fight back as the Maria Halpin story ran in more than one hundred newspapers across the country. Many editors noted that the governor hadn't denied the accusation. Horatio King, publisher of the *Christian Union* magazine, ignored Cleveland's instructions and wrote a particularly damning story about Maria Halpin for the *New York World*. A decade earlier, when Governor Cleveland was "sowing his wild oats" as every young man does, the story went, he began a relationship with Maria Halpin, who was "not a good woman by any means." Maria had been having affairs with three other men at the same time, all of them married. King described the real father in terms that make it clear he was referring to Oscar Folsom: "The man who in reality was the father of the infant had an interesting daughter whom he idolized. He was in constant dread lest his offense should reach his wife and child, and Cleveland, being the only unmarried man, relieved him of the embarrassment by shouldering all of the responsibility. That man is dead, and the child is his perfect image in manner and looks. Cleveland acted a heroic part, suffering the obloquy that his friends might not bring unpleasantness to their hearthsides." Cleveland was, in fact, not a vile seducer of innocent womanhood, but a self-sacrificing hero.

Maria, meanwhile, was living with her late aunt's husband, James Seacord, in the village of New Rochelle, New York, eighteen miles outside of New York City. She had lived quietly, keeping house for her uncle after her aunt's death, and making dresses to earn a little extra money. We can only imagine Maria's shame as she read the Terrible Tale. When a neighbor asked her whether the allegations against Cleveland were true, she replied, "They are, and God knows they are true, too."

Frantic Democratic political operatives tracked her down and attempted to persuade her to issue a statement "pronouncing the story of her alleged relations with the governor a base fabrication." She did not respond. Then her twenty-one-year-old son, Frederick, received a telegram from Cleveland's political adviser William Hudson, asking for a meeting in Manhattan. When Frederick arrived, Hudson told him it was in his mother's best interests to publicly deny a relationship with Cleveland. He then showed him a statement he wanted her to sign calling the Terrible Tale "false and malicious." It went on, "I received from Mr. Cleveland uniform kindness and courtesy. I have now and have always had a high esteem for Mr. Cleveland. I have not seen him in seven or eight years."

If Maria signed the statement, she would be paid $10,000 ($260,000 in today's money), and Frederick would receive a job with the commissioner of the New York State Board of Public Works. Maria didn't sign it, but she agreed to Hudson's suggestion to disappear from the media feeding frenzy for a time and went into hiding on the west side of Manhattan. Her Democratic handlers told her she could leave her refuge at any time, but if she did so, someone would probably try to kill her as many Cleveland supporters had been making death threats. While she was in hiding without access to newspapers, the pro-Cleveland press dragged her name through the mud.

One aspiring fiction writer from the *Boston Globe* pretended he had sat down with Maria in James Seacord's house for an interview. "Mrs. Halpin is evidently an epileptic," he wrote, "and she has every symptom of insanity. Her eyes are glassy; she cannot look her questioner in the face; she has the trembling twitching of the muscles and the sudden starts at every unexpected noise peculiar to insane persons."

"I have been very sick and am very sick now," she supposedly said. "I will not live six months I know. I hope that Mr. Cleveland will be elected, and I would not want to put anything in the way of his success. I do not wish Mr. Cleveland any harm. I have no quarrel with Mr. Cleveland. He is a good, plain, honest-hearted, nice man who has always been friendly to me and used me kindly. It is a shame that the newspapers should have issued such lies. I would not harm a hair on the head of Mr. Cleveland."

Maria's brother-in-law Simeon Talbott, who had negotiated

the $500 settlement years earlier, received a letter from Cleveland urging him to make a public statement declaring that Cleveland had always treated Maria with respect. If he did so, the governor promised him "anything I could wish for in case he was elected." Cleveland added that he had never authorized Horatio King to publish such lies about Maria. When Talbott discussed Cleveland's request with Maria, she said she would rather die than issue any public statement that would support Cleveland's candidacy.

The Democratic political machine was not just defending its candidate, it was seeking to take down his opponent with similar salacious tales. Operatives dug up dirt on Republican nominee James Blaine indicating that back in 1851 he had had a literal shotgun wedding, at which the bride's brother held a gun to his head during the entire ceremony, and the bride had a baby eleven weeks later. Presenting Cleveland with corroborating documents, his aides boasted that this would "more than" offset the Maria Halpin story. Cleveland took the papers, tore them to pieces over a trashcan, and then tossed them into the fire. "The other side can have a monopoly of all the dirt in this campaign," he said.

When the shotgun marriage story made its way into the *Indianapolis Sentinel*, Cleveland said he was "very sorry it was printed. I hope it will die out at once." It turned out the true story was not damning at all. Blaine and his wife had married a year before their son was born, but nine months after the ceremony they discovered the preacher had not possessed a proper license, so they married again.

But the scandalized Reverend George Ball wasn't finished yet with his own dirt. In a letter to the Buffalo *Evening Telegraph*, George Ball described Cleveland as a "champion libertine, an artful seducer, a foe to virtue, an enemy of the family, snare to youth, and hostile to true womanhood . . ." Ball thundered, "The issue is evidently not between the two great parties, but between the brothel and the family, between indecency and decency, between lust and law . . . between the degradation of women and due honor, protection and love to our mothers, sisters, and daughters."

For their part, Cleveland's allies did all they could to undo the damage of the Terrible Tale. If Ball could use the press to vilify their candidate, they could use it to defend him. On August 11, the *Buffalo Courier* defended Cleveland's forcible committal of Maria in an insane asylum. "There was no abduction. The authorities had acted in the best interests of the child. There was no cruelty. The mother was in a state of intoxication, and she was removed lawfully and with no more force than was necessary."

Cleveland found a defender in none other than Mark Twain, who scoffed, "To see grown men, apparently in their right mind, seriously arguing against a bachelor's fitness for President because he had private intercourse with a consenting widow! Isn't human nature the most consummate sham and lie that was ever invented?" Twain was assuming the relationship had been consensual.

It was fortunate for Cleveland that his opponent, James Blaine, though a faithful husband and family man, had a ghastly reputation for corruption. As speaker of the House in 1869, he had been accused of accepting $130,000 ($2.5 million today) in bribes to secure land grants for portions of the Transcontinental Railroad. Though he was never criminally charged, during the 1884 election some of his correspondence regarding the odiferous deal surfaced, ending with the instruction, "Burn this letter."

At a meeting where Cleveland supporters discussed the two scandals—Cleveland's illegitimate son and Blaine's corruption—a journalist summed it up. "Well," he said thoughtfully, "from what I hear, I gather that Mr. Cleveland has shown high character and great capacity in public life, but that in private life his conduct has been open to question, while, on the other hand, Mr. Blaine in public life has been weak and dishonest, while he seems to have been an admirable husband and father." Those gathered nodded in agreement. "The conclusion I draw from these facts," the journalist continued, "is that we should elect Mr. Cleveland to the public office which he is so admirably qualified to fill and remand Mr. Blaine to the private life which he is so eminently fitted to adorn."

In early September, having hidden for a solid month, Maria showed up at her uncle's house "crushed in spirit and broken in health." She had finally realized the Democratic Party wanted her out of sight until the November election. Now, with access to newspapers, she learned what they had been writing about her. She was a whore. A lunatic. A drunkard. Fury gave her strength. She decided to give an in-depth interview to a sympathetic newspaper, Manhattan's *Morning Journal.*

"Grover Cleveland is the father, and to say otherwise is infamous," she declared. "The attempt to connect the dead Oscar Folsom with me or my boy, of which I hear, is cruel and cowardly. I had but a very slight acquaintance with Oscar Folsom. It does not seem possible after all I suffered for Grover Cleveland and my boy's sake that an attempt will be made to further blacken me in the eyes of the world . . ."

She continued, "My sufferings, subsequently my fruitless efforts to have him fulfill his promise of marriage, his neglect of myself and my child, my abduction and violent treatment by his hired tools were truthfully but only partially told in the *Buffalo Telegraph* of July 21. It would be impossible to cover the events that made up those years of shame, suffering, and degradation forced upon me by Grover Cleveland."

The reporter asked Maria about a rumor going around that she was considering issuing a statement vindicating Cleveland. "Maria Halpin drew herself up," the reporter wrote, "as preparing for a supreme effort, and replied in a most impressive and earnest manner, 'Me, make a statement exonerating Grover Cleveland? Never! I would rather put a bullet through my heart.'"

The September 27 issue of *Judge* magazine blazoned on its cover a color cartoon called "Another Voice for Cleveland." It showed Maria, her face planted in a handkerchief, holding a squalling infant with "Where's my Pa?" coming out of his mouth, even though by this time their son was ten years old. A fat-bellied Cleveland—bearing a tag on the bottom of his coat that read "Grover the Good"—is so upset his top hat is falling off. Republicans roared with laughter at the cartoon, and "Where's my Pa?" became their rallying cry. When Cleveland spoke at campaign events across the country, hecklers in the audience jeered, "Where's my Pa?"

On October 22, Henry Ward Beecher—a popular clergyman and social reformer—spoke at a Cleveland rally in Brooklyn, New York, calling Maria Halpin a "harlot and a drunkard." Maria, reading the papers the following day, was so furious she decided to fight back in the press once more and invited Charles Banks, the owner of the *New Rochelle Pioneer*, to meet with her. Banks helped her write an affidavit, which he published. She began:

> I would gladly avoid further publicity of this terrible misfortune, if I could do so without appearing to admit the foul and false statements concerning my character and habits . . . I deny that there was anything in my actions or against my character at any time or place up to the hour I formed the acquaintance of Grover Cleveland

on account of which he or any other person can cast the slightest suspicion over me. My life was as pure and spotless as that of any lady in the City of Buffalo—a fact which Grover Cleveland should be man enough and just enough to admit, and I defy him or any of his friends to state a single fact or give a single incident or action of mine to which any one could take exception. I always felt that I had the confidence and esteem of my employers . . . and this I could not maintain if I had been the vile wretch his friends would have the world believe. He sought my acquaintance and obtained an introduction to me from a person in whom I have every confidence, and he paid me a very marked attention. His character, so far as I knew, was good, and his intentions I believed were pure and honorable.

The details of the night of her ruin were too "revolting" to be made public, Maria wrote. But "there is not and never was a doubt as to the paternity of our child, and the attempt of Grover Cleveland or his friends to couple the name of Oscar Folsom or anyone else with that of the boy, for that purpose, is simply infamous and false."

Republican papers picked up her story; Democratic ones ignored it or dismissed it as false. But the statement must have been cathartic for Maria who, unburdening herself of a decade of mute victimhood, wasn't done yet. She submitted to Banks another statement detailing the rape. She began with meeting Cleveland on the street, of his pressing her to accept his dinner invitation, and his accompanying her to her rooms afterward. "While in my rooms," she wrote, "he accomplished my ruin by the use of force and violence and without my consent." Finally, she had spoken of the rape. If Cleveland's supporters waited with bated breath for him to angrily dismiss the accusation of rape, they were sorely disappointed. He never addressed it, which many voters saw as an admission of guilt. The burning question was: Would they care?

When election day, November 4, came around, Cleveland lost his home county, Erie, because of Maria Halpin's story. He won big in Manhattan, which cared mostly about his reputation for low taxes and cutting bureaucratic red tape. In the national popular vote, however, he won by only 25,000 votes out of ten million cast. A difference of just 600 votes in strategic states would have lost Cleveland the election. His supporters didn't care that he won by a hair. They just cared that he won. Many of them ran out into the streets crying:

> *Hooray for Maria! Hooray for the kid!*
> *We voted for Grover and damned glad we did!*
> *Ma, Ma, where's your pa?*
> *Gone to the White House, hahaha!*

It is important to remember that only men could vote in the 1884 election. It is likely, given Cleveland's slim majority, that if women had voted he would not have been elected. While many readers criticized the *Telegraph* for breaking the sensational and highly indelicate story, a Mrs. O. K. Smith of West Eager Street in Buffalo wrote the editor shortly before the election, "All honor to the bravest paper in Buffalo! Women, if you have any influence, use it." Whatever influence they used, it wasn't quite enough.

The biggest takeaway from the 1884 election is that the majority of voters, forced to choose between a corrupt candidate and a rapist, chose the rapist. Whatever Grover Cleveland had done to Maria Halpin, it hadn't cost them a dime. He had never stolen from his constituents—indeed, quite the opposite; he had prevented others from doing so—and had kept taxes low. Then there was the matter of his honesty. Given that he never bothered to deny the rape, he certainly wouldn't lie to them about politics.

As president, Cleveland refused to fire government employees for the sin of being Republican and said anyone who was doing a good job could stay. He reduced the number of federal employees, feeling that government had become bloated. He was a president in the mold of the old Republicans—government should keep its stinking hands off as much as possible. Thomas Jefferson would have loved him.

Since the birth of Frances Folsom, Cleveland had served as a kind of godparent to her. After Oscar died in a carriage accident when Frances was eleven, Cleveland became the court-appointed administrator of his estate. He remained in close contact with Frances as she grew up, frequently visiting her and her mother, Emma, so much so that newspapers hinted he would propose to Emma, which she herself believed. "I don't see why the papers keep marrying me to old ladies," he groused to an assistant as Frances morphed into an elegant young woman. "I wonder why they don't say I am engaged to marry her daughter." They probably didn't say he was engaged to marry Frances because she was twenty-seven years younger, radiantly beautiful, and seemed more like the daughter of the old, gray, obese president. Tall for her time at five foot seven, with a slender but shapely figure, she had thick chestnut hair, violet eyes, and a pert, intelligent face.

Cleveland visited Frances at Wells College in Aurora, New York, a place where her mother, Emma, could not intrude on their rendezvous, and frequently sent flowers. Emma Folsom, realizing which way the wind was blowing, was not pleased to learn that all this time her daughter had been the object of his affections. On June 2, 1886, Cleveland became the first—and until now, the only—president to marry in the White House. Twenty-one-year-old Frances was the youngest first lady in history and soon became immensely popular. The Clevelands would have five children.

Cleveland lost the 1888 election to Republican nominee Benjamin Harrison. As Frances Cleveland left the White House, she told a servant, "Now, Jerry, I want you to take good care of all the furniture and ornaments in the house, for I want to find everything just as it is now, when we come back again." When asked when she would return, she responded, "We are coming back four years from today." The Clevelands moved to New York City, where Grover returned to the practice of law.

Frances Cleveland had been correct. Her husband bounced back into office in the next presidential election. Grover Cleveland is the only U.S. president to serve two nonconsecutive terms—1885–1889 and 1893–1897. His second term was marred by strikes and a depression. Even so, his reputation for probity and good character survived the troubles of his second term. Maria Halpin's accusations of rape were soon forgotten.

Her son with Cleveland, James E. King Jr., became a physician and a pioneer in the field of gynecology. He was married briefly, had no children, and died in 1947 at the age of seventy-two. He never reached out to his birth mother, nor did she try to contact him.

As for Maria, after the scandal died down, she married James Seacord, her uncle by marriage. Nearly seventy, he was sickly and fragile. Most likely, the marriage offered her a safe haven and a bit of financial security. In 1899, a widow for the second time, she married again, a man named Wallace Hunt. In 1902, Maria Halpin died of bronchial pneumonia at the age of sixty-two. "Do not let the funeral be too public," she told her husband in her final illness. "I do not want strangers to come and gaze on my face. Let everything be very quiet. Let me rest."

5

WOODROW WILSON'S
THROBBING PULSES

*W*oodrow Wilson might have resembled a prim Sunday school teacher or, by his own description, "a rare bookworm . . . incapable of sentiment, smileless and given over to dead love." But underneath his bow tie and button-down shirt surged a raging libido.

* * *

In October 1915, Mary Allen Hulbert had every reason to hope that her life was going to change. At fifty-three, she was a faded beauty, though still slender. She had lost much of her substantial divorce settlement to bad investments and a wastrel son and now lived in a shabby apartment in Los Angeles.

But she had had two amazing strokes of luck in recent years. The first was that her lover of several years, Woodrow Wilson, had been elected president of the United States in 1912. The second was that his wife of thirty years, Ellen, had died of kidney disease in August 1914. Bereft, Wilson had written Mary soul-wrenching letters describing his loneliness. Now that the year-long mourning period was over, he was bound to remarry. More than any other man on the planet, Wilson needed the companionship of a lively, fun-loving woman. And though he had loved Ellen dearly, her bouts of depression had caused him to take the vivacious Mary as a lover in the first place. Because of her devotion to her husband, Ellen permitted it.

Surely, the time had come when Wilson would invite Mary to visit him in Washington again. Surely, he would propose to her, and they could be together the way she had always dreamed. No more financial difficulties. No more dreary little apartments. No more pulling her hair out over her alcoholic son starting one doomed business venture after another. Mary would be first lady of the United States, an international celebrity, living in wealth and style, married to the man she passionately loved.

But when Mary sat down to read the newspaper on that golden October day, she must have shrieked out loud. For there, on the front page, was the news that President Woodrow Wilson had announced his engagement to Mrs. Edith Galt, the wealthy widow of a Washington, D.C., jeweler. The bride-to-be, the paper announced, was thirty-eight—the writer had gallantly shaved off five years—and "a woman of unusual beauty" who was always "modishly gowned." The headline also trumpeted—in a sop to American women who might have resented the president for remarrying so soon after his mourning ended—that the president had finally come out for "woman suffrage." The happy couple would be married in December. "Gay Capital Season Sure," crowed the headline.

We can picture Mary staring at the words that shattered her hopes, destroyed her dreams, and broke her heart, words that swam on the page as her eyes filled with tears. And then, she let the pages flutter to the floor.

Mary Allen Hulbert Peck had met Wilson back in February 1907, when he was vacationing in Bermuda without his wife in the hopes of reducing his blood pressure. A few months earlier, he had gone temporarily blind in one eye due to a burst blood vessel and may have had a small stroke. While doctors of the time could diagnose high blood pressure, they had no way to treat it other than prescribing rest and relaxation. And Wilson sorely needed both. As president of Princeton University, he had been mired in constant bitter arguments with faculty and alumni over the school's future. If he did not reduce his stress, doctors warned, he could have a catastrophic—perhaps fatal—stroke. Ellen could not join him as she was caring for their sick daughter.

Wilson was immediately enchanted by the island, so "warm and soft and languid," where the daily tumult of Princeton seemed "remote and theoretical." He was eager to be "irresponsible"— and he was—"and so renew my youth"—and he did.

Since 1892, Mary had been spending her winters in Bermuda to get away from her overbearing husband. Mary Hulbert had been a widow with a young son when she married a wealthy widower, Thomas Peck, in 1890. The marriage was an almost immediate failure. Stressed and depressed at home in Pittsfield, Massachusetts, with her husband's annoying children and feuding parents, in Bermuda she was "joyous, with an almost pagan delight in basking in its beauty," as she later described it. She soon elbowed her way into the center of the island's social scene, entertaining the most famous visitors, including Mark Twain. Known for her "frank courting of susceptible males," Mary Peck was "a bewitching woman, and a snare for men folk," according to one Bermuda matron. Another mentioned "a little restless look of unfulfillment about her eyes and mouth that gave grounds for romantic speculation," a polite Edwardian description of a well-heeled tart.

With thick, dark hair piled high, large, pale blue-gray eyes, and pretty features, Mary Peck glided from luncheons to beach picnics to balls in large feathered hats and large feather boas. It was her confidence and engaging conversation that attracted most, her "absorbing way of listening to the words of wisdom uttered by a *man*," as Wilson's cousin later described her.

In February 1907, a friend of Mary's invited her to dinner to meet Woodrow Wilson, whom she had read about in the papers. There Mary was introduced to a prim-looking, silver-haired gentleman with a long face, a lantern jaw, calm gray eyes, and a pince-nez perched on the bridge of his aristocratic nose. At five foot eleven and 170 pounds, he was dapper in his high, starched collars and top hat. Despite his resemblance to a hanging judge, Wilson had an impish sense of humor and a love of playfulness.

Sparks flew between them that first night as they conversed animatedly about the nature of freedom. Wilson was enthralled. Here was a free spirit, a woman of wit and vivacity, all the things his wife, poor devoted Ellen, was not. He saw Mary again the next night and the following day wrote to her from the port just before he boarded his homeward-bound ship. "It is not often that I can have the privilege of meeting anyone whom I can so entirely admire and enjoy," he gushed. Back in Princeton, he sent her two books of essays, one of them authored by himself, so "that you may know me a little better."

Mary wrote back that she had hesitated to tell him "what knowing you has meant to me." A flurry of enthusiastic letters bounced from Bermuda to Princeton and back. Wilson told her that her letters served "to keep me in heart amidst much unrewarding toil."

Most men who embark on a love affair after more than twenty years of marriage have fallen out of love with their wives. Not so Woodrow Wilson. He was still deliriously in love with Ellen, whom he had met in 1883. The twenty-six-year-old Atlanta lawyer had gone to Rome, Georgia, on business and seen a pretty, twenty-three-year-old woman in church. She had apple cheeks, golden-brown hair, and large, velvety brown eyes that impressed him as "splendid, mischievous, laughing." Wilson thought to himself, "I'll lay a wager that this demure little lady has lots of life and fun in her!" She did not, in fact. Her father would soon die in an insane asylum, possibly from suicide, and her brother was repeatedly institutionalized throughout his life. Compared to them, Ellen had won the genetic lotto of the family with only moderate depression. Though she would never be the life of the party, she would prove herself highly intelligent and loyal.

A talented artist, Ellen had considered remaining single and devoting herself to her landscape painting, but Wilson pressed his suit so ardently she found resistance was futile. He peppered her with letters. "Never was a man more dependent than I am upon love and sympathy," he wrote, and it was true. Woodrow Wilson would love the three women in his life with an obsessive intensity. He and Ellen were engaged five months after their first meeting and married after he had finished his doctoral program at Johns Hopkins in 1885.

The Wilsons had three daughters in quick succession. Ellen not only raised his children and ran his home, she devoted herself to helping his career, organizing his papers, translating scholarly articles from German, and entertaining his business contacts, giving up her own dreams of being a professional artist. In 1890, he accepted the chair of political economy and jurisprudence at his alma mater, Princeton. He was immediately popular with his students and soon become a leader among the faculty.

The Wilsons seemed to have had a fulfilling sex life. Wilson wrote Ellen that she was not only "an intellectual man's close confidante, companion, counsellor, but also *Love's Playmate*, led on to all the sweet abandonments and utter intimacies of love."

But Ellen knew she disappointed in one regard. Her husband loved whimsy and laughter. After dinner, he romped with their daughters and danced wildly around the house. He rejoiced in spirited conversation, droll quips, and witty repartee, especially in the company of women. Without them, he seemed to wilt. Ellen, however, "considered herself a grave and sober person," according to her daughter Nell. She could not provide lightheartedness to a man who needed it nearly as much as he needed air. But she had a solution. "Since you have married someone who is not gay," she often told him, "I must provide for you friends who are." She found lively female friends whom she invited frequently to dinner and, when he traveled, encouraged him to "go to see some of those bright women."

In 1902, Wilson became Princeton's new president. A powerful speaker, he traveled the country lecturing on government issues. Ellen, raising children and nursing a conga line of sick relatives, rarely went with him. Their love letters after nearly two decades of marriage were intensely romantic. She wrote, "Surely there was never such a lover before, and even after all these years it seems almost too good to be true that you *are* my lover."

Ellen must have been leery of her husband's new best friend as letters from the ebullient Mrs. Peck arrived with irritating frequency, and when they did an overjoyed Wilson sat down immediately to pen his reply. In January 1908, Wilson returned to Bermuda once again to lower his blood pressure, though the trip surely raised Ellen's own because she couldn't go with him this time either; she was caring for her brother who had had a nervous breakdown. She must have worried about Wilson rejoining this middle-aged Circe of Bermuda, with a knack for turning men into drooling dogs. But she sent him off anyway, after issuing an "injunction," a warning of some sort.

It must have been challenging for Wilson to remember his wife's injunction once he had returned to the Land of the Lotus-Eaters. He and Mary saw each other every day, walking along the beach, picnicking, reading to each other, discussing life and people and politics. "I found him longing to make up as best he might for play long denied," Mary later wrote, in a cutting allusion to poor morose Ellen. They also discussed Wilson's political ambitions. Should he run for governor of New Jersey? Important men in the Democratic Party suggested he do so, and he had always wanted to enter politics. Mary encouraged him to follow his dream.

Wilson wrote long letters to Ellen describing the fun he was having with Mary, adding, "While she delights me, you enslave me." Surely this made his wife feel much better. He showed Mary a picture of Ellen, who must have examined the sad, dark eyes staring out of a plump face with a twinge of triumph. She told him she wanted to keep it.

He wrote Ellen, "I brought two pictures of you with me . . . and Mrs. Peck is so charmed with them that she insisted upon keeping one of them on the mantel-piece of her drawing room, so that it sometimes seems as if my darling were there." He wanted the three of them in that drawing room, all happy together. It seems he needed both women to complete himself and desperately hoped that Ellen and Mary, out of their love for him, would understand.

When Wilson returned to Ellen after his winter fling, the poor woman must have been more depressed than ever. She accused him of "emotional love" for Mary. Wilson denied it, though his protestations of innocence were belied by his letters to "his precious one, his beloved Mary," recalling their "delectable walks to the South Shore when you were like a gay child of nature, released into its native element, and I felt every quickened impulse of the blood communicated to me."

In the spring of 1909, Mary separated from her husband and moved to New York City. Wilson was overjoyed—not only was she single, she was living close by—and Ellen must have been less so. He visited Mary frequently, called her on the telephone, and thought of her with "admiration and longing," as he waited for her next letter. "I must keep in constant touch with you, if my spirits are to be steady and my tasks well done," he wrote.

In the winter of 1910, Wilson went to Bermuda again for his blood pressure. Ellen must have been thrilled that Mary was in New York taking care of her dying mother. On the island, Wilson dreamed of his two loves and wrote them frequently. He told Ellen that she was "so exactly what I want and need" and "I am very, very lonely without my love to sustain me." He informed Mary that she was "perfectly satisfying and delightful, so *delectable*" and "I am lonely wherever I go because you are not there!" Wilson informed her he could not go anywhere on the island without thinking of her. All his "pulses throbbed" as he entered the cottage that she had loaned him. "It seemed to me a mere romance to be in it, after all the thoughts I had had of it, and the peculiar associations. If you could have been there it would have been perfect . . ."

Mary replied saucily, "Does the bougainvillea fling itself over the cottages as of old? Why, why can I not be there—to fling myself where I would!"

Ellen, always more sedate, wrote her husband, "It is quite impossible to express my love. It is greater than ever, and I had thought that too was impossible!" Ten days later, she vowed, "I would give my life, ah! how freely to make life happier for you. I love you with all my heart and soul and strength and mind." Perhaps she was telling him she was permitting his affair so that he could be happy.

Ellen even called on Mary in New York when she took her daughter Nell to see a play there. She cheerfully wrote Wilson that she'd had "a delightful little visit" with his friend. We can only wonder how delightful the visit truly was. Clearly, Ellen was working hard to prevent Mary from becoming a scandal. Because if a man's wife called on his reputed mistress, she couldn't really be his mistress, could she? And if Wilson were going to have the political future he had long dreamed of, the scandal of Mary could not be permitted to derail it.

As the university squabbles resolved themselves to the satisfaction of Wilson's opponents, he decided that after twenty years at Princeton, it might be time for him to finally dive into politics. On September 25, 1910, he was nominated for New Jersey governor. He campaigned on a strong progressive platform and became known for his rousing speeches, easily beating his Republican opponent 54 to 43 percent.

Wilson was such a popular governor—enacting laws for workers' compensation and restricting child labor and public corruption—that many Democratic power brokers wanted him to run for president in 1912. Both Ellen and Mary encouraged him, yet both felt, too, that something would be irretrievably lost. As first lady of New Jersey, Ellen had already given up much of the stress-free home life she had so enjoyed and would lose it altogether if Wilson became president. Mary worried he might cease contact with her completely to avoid scandal. But it was too late for that. When Wilson campaigned in Chicago in early April 1912, burglars broke into his hotel room and stole a suitcase full of letters but no valuables. Clearly, it was a political hit job. Wilson must have waited with dread for the other proverbial shoe to fall.

The Democratic National Convention, which started on June 25 in Baltimore, was of particular interest as the Republican convention held a week earlier had resulted in two candidates who would, most likely, split the vote. Incumbent president William Howard Taft was nominated after a brutal contest with former president Theodore Roosevelt, who stormed off announcing he would form a third party. The Democrats had an excellent chance of capturing the White House, which had been Republican ever since Grover Cleveland left office in 1897.

On July 2, on the forty-sixth ballot, Woodrow Wilson was nominated as the Democratic candidate for president of the United States. He wrote Mary—who was now divorced and took the name of her first husband, Hulbert—that his feelings would never change, and she was always in his thoughts, "a noble, sweet, free, unspoiled inspiriting" woman, for whom "nature found a fit form." He complained that sixteen newspaper reporters had been assigned to follow him, "to know where I am, who is with me, and what I am doing at all times. They must move as I move, go where I go . . . All eyes are watchful of my slightest action." He would not be sneaking to New York to visit her anytime soon.

The October surprise was the surfacing of Woodrow's letters from Mary. Theodore Roosevelt's campaign heard that someone was "hawking" the letters, which were reported to be "salacious and incriminating." When Roosevelt's campaign managers suggested they obtain and publish them to tank Wilson's candidacy, Roosevelt replied they would be "entirely unconvincing" because "no evidence would ever make the American people believe that a man like Woodrow Wilson, cast so perfectly as the apothecary's clerk, could ever play Romeo!"

Wilson won the presidential election with 435 electoral votes, compared to 88 for Roosevelt and 8 for Taft. A few days after his inauguration, Wilson wrote to Mary in Bermuda that he had finally found the time "for which I have waited with such impatience, to write to my dear, dear friend." Her letters, he insisted, were a help to him in the midst of his troubles. When he did not hear back from her, he protested, "Do you really want to know what the present President of the United States lacks and *must* have, if he is to serve his country . . . He needs *pleasure* and the unaffected human touch!" He urged her to contribute to the "success of a national administration" by writing him.

When Wilson moved into the White House, the staff was a bit afraid of him "because the President looked so stern with his long, lean face," according to one. But they soon learned of Wilson's joy in playfulness. "The strangest thing about the President was that he was really a frustrated actor," wrote Lillian Parks, whose mother, Maggie Rogers, worked as a White House maid. "Mama would find him making faces, clowning and doing a jig with his daughters, or taking a very serious part in a play, and speaking with one arm raised dramatically."

As first lady, Ellen stepped outside the traditional role of hosting social events and took a particular interest in improving the slum housing—often with no running water—in Washington's numerous alleyways. A serious, joyless individual, she disliked wearing beautiful gowns, even complaining that she had to put on a clean blouse every day or her White House maid would quit. When Eleanor Roosevelt came to Washington in 1913 as the wife of the new assistant secretary of the navy, she described the first lady as "a nice, intelligent woman but not overburdened with charm."

The White House staff, however, loved her. According to Lillian Parks, her mother "always came home shaking her head in amazement because a woman of such importance and such high rank could be so gentle. It was as if Mrs. Wilson wanted to make the world around her a little better place to live in."

Ellen's despondency must have been increased by Mary Hulbert's visit to the White House beginning on May 9, 1913. The first lady absented herself, pleading other commitments. Wilson took Mary on drives in the Virginia countryside with his cousin Helen Bones, who served as Ellen's personal secretary, as chaperone. Helen remarked that the first lady had proved herself "a pretty good politician" by inviting Mary Hulbert to stay in the White House, giving the "friendship" the gloss of respectability.

And so things continued with President Wilson and his two women, until the summer of 1914 when everything changed. On June 28, Wilson received a telegram that Austro-Hungarian Archduke Franz Ferdinand and his wife had been assassinated in Sarajevo. As Europe prepared for war, Wilson kept the U.S. firmly on the sidelines, hoping to mediate. It was a hot summer, and Ellen became unwell and feverish, despite the newfangled White House "cold-air machine": swiftly revolving fans blowing over seven tons of ice in the White House basement. The first lady had a hard time keeping her food down and grew weaker by the day. Doctors diagnosed Bright's disease, an obsolete term that included various diseases of the kidneys. She had experienced her first kidney trouble twenty-five years earlier after her third pregnancy.

Now she was suffering the symptoms of kidney failure: swelling of the face, nausea, and backache. Her nights were "full of pain."

As the European powers lurched into a world war, Wilson spent every moment he could with Ellen, holding her hand with his left hand as he wrote urgent memos with his right. Now and then, he was forced to leave the room to deal with the looming bloodbath in Europe. When he was away, she called for him continually. In a moment of clarity, she took the hand of her physician, Dr. Cary Grayson, and said, "Doctor, if I go away, promise me that you will take good care of my husband." She also told Grayson that the "Peck affair," as she called it, was the "only unhappiness her husband had ever given her."

"Even in the last moment of her life, her thoughts were with others," wrote Lillian Parks. "The President was with her when she died on August 6, 1914, and he came out of the room saying that her last words had been for the slum-dwellers of Washington, asking that something be done for them." When Wilson realized she was gone, he wrenched himself away, staggered to the window, and wept bitterly. Dr. Grayson later said, "A sadder picture no one could imagine. A great man with his heart torn out."

Lillian Parks wrote, "Mama heard the President talking to his dead wife as he stood beside the body. She happened to be in the room at twilight when the President came in and stood looking at his wife's face. He picked at the lace on her dress, and Mama could hardly keep from crying at this wistful, hopeless scene. The President spoke aloud, brokenly, 'Never, never, never.' Then he walked out."

Americans—especially American women—mourned Ellen Wilson greatly. Lacking in charm though she might have been, she had in many ways transformed the role of first lady. As the first to undertake social welfare causes, Ellen was a tremendous inspiration to Eleanor Roosevelt when she became first lady nineteen years later. Ellen was also the first to campaign with her husband and watch him address Congress. And she left the American people a lasting legacy by creating the White House Rose Garden.

Within hours of Ellen's death, Wilson wrote Mary, "Of course you know what has happened to me; but I wanted you to know direct from me. God has stricken me beyond what I can bear . . . I never dreamed such loneliness and desolation of heart possible."

Mary had already fired off a letter as soon as she heard the news. "It seems incredible," she wrote, "that this terrible thing has come to you now, when you need that sweet love to help you in this terrible time."

Wilson told his chief adviser and longtime friend, "Colonel" Edward House, that he could "not think straight" and "had no heart in the things he was doing." He wanted and needed a woman. Washington socialites made bets on whether he would remarry before his first term expired. Mary, knowing him as well as she did, understood better than most that he could not live long without a female companion. She hoped, when the time came, it would be her, after all the love they had shared. Yes, she was older and not as attractive as she had been eight years earlier when the affair began. The stress of her divorce, a drunken adult son, and her financial difficulties had affected both her health and her appearance.

There was, of course, the added disadvantage that marrying a divorcée—and one whose name had been whispered with his while his lamented wife had been alive—might jeopardize his winning a second term. But why not marry after his reelection, more than a year after the mourning period was over? Ellen herself wouldn't have minded. She had told her friends, "I hope Woodrow would marry again. He cannot live alone."

Wilson found his new love quite unexpectedly, in March 1915, as he rounded a corner on the second floor of the White House and almost smacked into a striking woman with muddy shoes. She was forty-three-year-old Edith Bolling Galt, five foot nine, with Rubenesque curves, who had accompanied her friend Helen Bones—Wilson's cousin—to her White House apartment to have tea. The president was gobsmacked by the sight of her, muddy shoes notwithstanding. Edith had a wide, handsome face, thick, black hair, deep blue eyes, and strong, dark eyebrows. As they chatted, he found she was charming, confident, and amusing. He invited her for dinner and, after her departure, pumped Helen for information about her.

Edith had been born to a family of modest means in rural Virginia. In 1896, she had married Norman Galt, owner of Galt's Jewelers, known as "the Tiffany's of Washington," and helped her husband run the revered establishment where Thomas Jefferson had bought a silver service for the White House in 1802. Edith was not terribly attracted to Norman, but she was attracted to his lifestyle and the Washington social scene, and they lived happily enough. In 1908, Norman Galt died of a liver infection at the age of forty-five, leaving his childless thirty-five-year-old widow with some $6 million in today's money. In early 1915, she became acquainted with Helen Bones, and the two frequently walked in Rock Creek Park for fresh air and exercise. When Helen invited Edith to tea in her White House apartment that day, Edith demurred. She wouldn't want to run into the president of the United States wearing muddy shoes. Helen assured her there was no chance of that; the president was out playing golf.

Edith dined at the White House for the first time on March 23 and soon became a regular guest. "She's a looker," said Pat McKenna, the White House doorkeeper. "He's a goner," said Arthur

Brooks, Wilson's valet. "He couldn't," said some. "Wait and see," others predicted. "Suddenly the President was effervescent and full of jokes," wrote Lillian Parks.

Two months after their first meeting, Wilson proposed to Edith. But she said it was too soon. His wife had only been dead nine months. Wilson protested that it had already been "a lifetime of loneliness and heartache" since Ellen's death. "I would be less than a gentleman if I continued to make opportunities to see you without telling you that I want you to be my wife," he said.

Wilson wrote her, "Here stands your friend, a longing man, in the midst of a world's affairs which he cannot face with his full strength unless you come into this heart and take possession. Will you come to him some time, without reserve and make his strength complete?"

Edith told him her first marriage had not been a passionate one and indicated she had never much liked sex. "If you can quicken that which has laid dead so long within me," she wrote, "I promise not to shut it out of my heart." He would gladly undertake the task, he rejoined. "There is a heart to be rescued from itself—a heart that never made complete surrender . . . that final divine act of self-surrender which is a woman's way to love. She must be taken by storm—and she shall be!"

Wilson was evidently successful in awakening Edith's interest in sex. They would drive out into the countryside, park, and close the curtains on the car windows. And there was certainly something going on between them in Wilson's private White House quarters (etiquette forbade the president from calling on a private citizen). "Seeing you as I saw you last night," he wrote, "my radiant, wonderful Darling, is like being present while life is created." Wilson was overwhelmed at being "the instrument of it." He wrote that she "turns to her lover and throws the gates wide—no, not quite wide yet, but wide enough to show him the sweet and holy places where her true spirit lives."

Having had a look at Edith's sweet and holy places between the gates, he would lie awake at night pretending she was in his arms. He complained that his lips "can speak nothing worthwhile all day long for lack of your kisses." He started signing his letters "Tiger."

She was his "*perfect playmate*," one who could "match and satisfy every part of me, grave or gay, of the mind or of the heart—the man of letters, the man of affairs, the boy, the poet, the lover." Indeed, Edith, with her vivacity, her unabashed self-confidence, and her hearty laugh, was far more suited to Wilson than Ellen had been.

What interested Edith even more than sex, however, was power: sharing *power* with the president of the United States. She enjoyed his romantic letters, she wrote, but "I enjoy even more the ones in which you tell me of what you are working on for then I feel I am sharing your work and being taken in partnership as it were . . . I feel so close to you when I know what you are doing."

Wilson, who was still writing to Mary, hadn't mentioned a word about Edith, nor had he told Edith about Mary. This caused him some awkwardness when, in May 1915, Mary, who had been staying in Hot Springs, Virginia, wanted to visit her lover at the White House on the way home to New York. Wilson tried to discourage her from coming, citing his busy schedule. She did not take the hint, however, and arrived at seven thirty on the morning of May 31. That afternoon, Mary accompanied Wilson, his daughter Margaret, and Helen Bones to Arlington Cemetery, where the president made a speech observing Memorial Day. They all made sure Mary was on the four o'clock train to New York. It was a stroke of great good fortune that Edith had been unable to attend the Arlington events as she had houseguests. Wilson must have mopped his face with his handkerchief in relief as Mary's train whisked her north.

In June, Wilson proposed again, and this time Edith accepted him, though they couldn't release the news until after the year of mourning was over. Now the president was in a real pickle. What should he do about Mary? He decided to send her some money. She had written him that her son wanted funds to start yet another business, this one in California, where she would be joining him. Wilson bought two mortgages she held for $7,500 ($190,000 today). Though Mary had never given him the slightest hint that she considered blackmailing him with his letters, he must have been worried what a scorned woman might do when she heard about his engagement to Edith.

Despite the world war raging in Europe, Wilson was "simply obsessed" with Edith. Some of his staff were concerned that the president of the United States was acting like a lovesick teenager while Europe was consumed by war and his wife's body was still cooling in her grave. In a bizarre, cruel manipulation, Wilson's son-in-law Treasury Secretary William Gibbs McAdoo lied to the president about having received an anonymous letter claiming that Mary Hulbert Peck was showing around the president's love letters. McAdoo hoped Wilson's fear of scandal might cool his relationship with Edith.

But the maneuver backfired spectacularly. Wilson reckoned that if he did not tell Edith about Mary before the papers broke the story, she might very well dump him. The same day, September 18, 1915, he sent Edith a scrawled note, asking to meet in her home—etiquette be damned—to discuss "something personal." Edith agreed at once, and that evening, Wilson confessed to his affair with Mary Hulbert Peck. Though we don't know exactly what was said, we do have the letters Wilson wrote Edith in the following days rehashing his story, which he called "a passage of folly and impertinence, long ago loathed and repented of."

He insisted his embarrassment was not because "the lady to whom [the letters] are addressed was not worthy of the most sincere admiration and affection, but because I did not have the moral right to offer her the ardent affection which they express." The revelation of his affair would, Wilson said, "make the contemptible error and madness of a few months seem a stain upon my whole life." He added, "I am deeply ashamed and repentant . . . But none of this lessens the blame or the deep humiliating grief and shame I suffer, that I should have so erred and forgotten the standards of honorable behavior by which I should have been bound."

As Edith listened, she must have felt that she was watching Wilson fall off his pedestal in horrifying slow motion. She could not bring herself to forgive him immediately and told him she would think about their relationship. But by the next morning, she was "ready to follow where love leads" and promised that "whether the wine be bitter or sweet, we will share it together." The wedding was still on. Wilson was further delighted to hear from Edward House that Mary had not, in fact, tried to sell his letters.

And so on that October day, Mary read of her lover's upcoming marriage in the newspaper. She must have been equally devastated that Wilson had not had the courtesy to write to her before the public announcement, that he had been so uncaring as to let her learn the news in this hurtful way. When she did receive his letter, she saw that it had been postmarked only two days before the announcement, not long enough for it to travel all the way to California. He had "not been at liberty to speak of it sooner," he wrote. It seems likely that Edith, who had been micromanaging the announcement, did not want to give Mary any special preference.

It took Mary a few days to pull herself together enough to respond on October 11:

Dearest Friend,

I have kissed the cross. We are very glad you have found happiness and that you had time to think of us in the midst of it. I need not tell you again that you have been the greatest, most ennobling influence in my life. You helped me to keep my soul alive and I am grateful. I hope you will have the happiness that I have missed. I cannot wish you greater. We are well, and both working at the business that your friendly purchase of the mortgages made it possible for us to embark upon . . . She [Edith] is very beautiful and sometime perhaps I may meet her. I wish you had told me before, for your letter was only mailed the 4th, and the newspapers had already published the fact. The cold peace of utter renunciation is about me, and the shell that is M.A.H. [Mary Allen Hulbert] still functions. It is rather lonely, not even an acquaintanceship to make the air vibrate with the coming warmth, perhaps of friendship. God alone knows—and you—partly, the real woman Mary Hulbert, all her hopes and joys, and fears, and mistakes. I shall not write you again this intimately but must this once . . . Write me sometime, the brotherly letters that will make my pathway a bit brighter. And believe me ever

Your friend,
Mary Allen Hulbert.

P.S. This is rather a whine but it is the best I can do—now. God bless you!

It was a stunningly gracious letter from a woman suffering such utter heartbreak. Wilson's engagement to Edith was a slap in the face of not only Mary, but also of Ellen. On the back of Wilson's letter to her, Mary scrawled, "How could he so soon?" She then swallowed hard and wrote Edith a letter wishing her happiness. Wilson, feeling more miserably guilty than ever, sent Mary another $7,500.

Woodrow Wilson and Edith Galt were married on Saturday, December 18, 1915, at her house, with only forty guests in attendance. A Secret Service agent reported that the day after the wedding, he saw Wilson dancing down a White House corridor singing a popular song, "Oh, you beautiful doll, you great, big, beautiful doll!" and clicking his heels.

Wilson's money didn't last Mary very long, probably because her son wasted it. By 1916, she was reduced to "tramping the streets of California towns," she later wrote, "selling books which nobody seemed to want; buying furniture at auctions and trying to sell it to affluent people, sitting in the casting offices of moving picture studios in Hollywood hoping to do 'atmosphere' parts for five or ten dollars a day, cooking for ranch hands." She sold her own furniture to make ends meet and was evicted from one apartment for not paying rent. She had fallen far from the unrivaled queen of the winter social season in Bermuda.

And so, when a Republican operative knocked on her door asking to buy her letters from President Wilson, he assumed she would eagerly accept the huge sum he offered. The 1916 presidential election was coming up, and the Republican Party wanted to prevent Woodrow Wilson's reelection at all costs. According to Mary's recounting of the event, her visitor looked around her modest room and remarked that a woman of her breeding should have a larger apartment. Surely an extra $250,000 ($6 million in today's money) would come in handy? She stared at him. Or $300,000 ($7.3 million)? Or more? The men he represented could raise just about any sum she wanted. She would, however, have to travel abroad for a time. The United States would no longer be a suitable place for her to reside.

Having heard him out, Mary told him that the letters were honorable ones that would only reflect well on President Wilson's character, adding "I am not that sort of a woman." Then she told him to get lost. Offers continued to roll in up to half a million dollars (nearly $12 million today). The answer was still a firm no. Woodrow Wilson had been—would always be—the love of her life. She would rather suffer all the indignities poverty could offer than betray him. Concerned that someone might break in and steal the letters, she put them in a safe-deposit box. It was a good thing, too. Because Wilson only narrowly defeated the Republican candidate, Supreme Court Justice Charles Evans Hughes, with 277 electoral votes to 254. If Mary's collection of the president's love letters to her while he was married to Ellen had been published, he likely would have lost the election.

It is uncertain, though, that they would have been published at all in a major newspaper. Back in the 1912 election, journalists were well aware of Wilson's relationship with Mary Peck—among themselves they called Wilson "Peck's bad boy"—but didn't print a word about it. At the Democratic National Convention that year, journalist David Lawrence heard rumors involving Wilson and Peck "whispered about the corridors." And in 1915, reporters knew the supposedly inconsolable widower was having an affair with the voluptuous Edith Galt. Considering the shrieking newspaper articles about Alexander Hamilton and Maria Reynolds, Thomas Jefferson and Sally Hemings, and Grover Cleveland and

Maria Halpin, why were journalists so painfully discreet about Woodrow Wilson and Mary Peck?

Wilson benefited from a sudden radical shift in American journalism. From the dawning of the American colonies until the early twentieth century, members of the press were considered socially inferior tradesmen like carpenters, wielding not saws but pens to produce sleazy articles. Then journalists organized themselves into an elite profession, founding the National Press Club in 1908 and adhering to a code of ethics. Journalism schools were established at universities. The 1914 Journalist's Creed stated, "I believe that no one should write as a journalist what he would not say as a gentleman." And gentlemen did not gossip about other gentlemen's love lives.

Moreover, early twentieth-century legislators passed laws to prevent muckraking journalists publishing articles on political sex scandals. In 1900, the California legislature prohibited the publication of any article "which tends to expose the individual so caricatured to public hatred, ridicule or contempt." Other states quickly followed suit. The sponsor of Pennsylvania's law stated that "the Commonwealth is interested that those who render her service should be treated with deference and respect, so that when they go forth in performance of her functions those to whom they are sent may feel that they are vested with authority." Political opponents could, however, have printed up their own pamphlets and distributed them, causing outrage and protests, which may have been covered by major news outlets.

As America's leaders confronted the great struggles of World War I, the press became even more determined to insulate presidents from sex scandals. Still, one journalist must have had the good old days of salacious news stories somewhere in his subconscious when, on October 9, 1915, the *Washington Post* printed the most embarrassing typo in its long history. In describing President Wilson's activities of the day before, a front-page exclusive stated that the president took his fiancée to the theater, and "rather than paying attention to the play the President spent the evening entering Mrs. Galt" instead of "entertaining Mrs. Galt."

On April 6, 1917, the U.S. finally declared war on Germany. Though the conflict lasted only nineteen months for America, the losses were staggering: 53,000 killed, 204,000 wounded, and another 63,000 dead of the influenza epidemic that swept the world beginning in 1918. Yet the other Allies had lost far more. They wanted revenge. And Wilson warned that harshly punishing Germany would create a backlash of anger that would only result in another world war. He worked tirelessly to create a League of Nations, a body where disputes would be peacefully resolved. The Covenant of the League of Nations required members to respect freedom of religion and treat racial minorities fairly. It was incorporated into the Treaty of Versailles, which officially ended the war.

The Wilsons spent six months in Europe cleaning up the post-cataclysm mess at the Paris Peace Conference, where Woodrow started behaving oddly. He irritated the other statesmen by insisting they reopen issues that had already been settled. On occasion, the entire conference had to be adjourned because he hadn't read his papers. He accused his French servants of spying on him, and when his hosts removed some furniture in his official residence, he saw it as part of a diabolical plot. He ate less than ever and suffered excruciating headaches. On the morning of April 28, 1919, while Wilson was signing letters, his handwriting suddenly deteriorated. He could barely write his name when he signed the peace treaty. Back home, when several senators wanted amendments to the treaty before the U.S. agreed to it, Wilson stubbornly refused.

He decided to take his case for an unamended treaty to the American people and, against the wishes of Dr. Grayson and Edith, undertook an arduous twenty-seven-day trip to the West Coast, with speaking engagements all along the way. He spoke of his fear that American children would have to fight another world war if the League were not in place to prevent it. But Wilson was like Cassandra, the Trojan prophetess cursed with seeing a horrifying future that no one believed.

In Los Angeles on September 21, the Wilsons met with Mary, whom Wilson had not seen in four years. Edith, just like Ellen before her, went reluctantly along with the visit to show her "disdain" for the "slander" about his relationship with Mary. Edith damned Mary with faint praise, describing her as "a faded, sweet-looking woman," while the ever-slender Mary later commented how shocked she was at Edith's weight; she was much fatter than she had appeared in newspaper photos. When Wilson expressed his regret about the gossip Mary had endured because of their friendship, Edith snapped, "Where there's so much smoke, there must be some fire." Mary, who had heard rumors that Edith had been sleeping with the German ambassador before the war, retorted, "Then maybe you were von Bernstorff's mistress!"

Perhaps the strain of the meeting, on top of his exhaustion and unceasing, years-long stress, tipped Wilson over the edge into a full-on stroke. Just three days later, his face suddenly changed. He said, "I am not in a condition to go on. I have never been in a condition like this, and I just feel as if I am going to pieces." Then he started to cry.

Canceling the remaining five stops on the trip, the presidential train raced to Washington, seventeen hundred miles away.

The president could barely walk from the train to his limo. He began drooling from the left side of his mouth. Back in the White House, at 8:00 a.m. on October 2, Edith found him awake but unable to move. A specialist arrived and discovered that Wilson's left leg and arm were completely paralyzed. He had no feeling on the left side of his body, the left half of his face was drooping, and he was completely blind in his left eye.

The Constitution had no provision for a president suffering a serious physical disability. Edith, unwilling to inform the American people of her husband's condition, decided she would run the country for him until he improved. She forced Dr. Grayson to lie about Wilson's health, claiming he was merely suffering from exhaustion. The vice president, Thomas R. Marshall of Indiana, was not allowed to see him. He kept up with the president's health by reading the newspapers every morning, filled with lies Edith had given them.

Edith took important papers into Wilson's bedroom and came out with his "instructions." It was unlikely the president was able to issue any instructions. Ike Hoover, who served as White House chief usher, recalled, "He appeared just as helpless as one could possibly be and live." In the middle of the night, Wilson would pick up a little flashlight and turn it toward a picture of his first wife, stare at it, turn off the flashlight, and do it again. And again. Grayson said that the president "could articulate but indistinctly and think but feebly."

Members of Congress were refused permission to see Wilson and guessed what was happening. They knew the country needed strong leadership to deal with unemployment, inflation, and striking workers. Instead, the acting president was a former jeweler's wife who had never completed high school. Senator Albert Fall, a Republican from New Mexico, spoke for many when he pounded his fist on the table of the Senate Foreign Relations Committee and shouted, "We have a petticoat government! Mrs. Wilson is President!"

Even though Wilson slowly improved, with the irascibility of a stroke victim, he refused to make the changes to the treaty that Congress wanted. It would be all or nothing. On March 19, 1920, the treaty was voted down. If Edith had allowed her husband to resign and the vice president to take over, the U.S. would likely have ratified the Treaty of Versailles and joined the League of Nations. Though more than forty countries from around the world joined the League, without the force of the U.S. behind it, it was a creature without a spine, powerless to alter the events leading up to World War II.

Perhaps Wilson's most bizarre plan of all was to run for a third term as president. There were no rules to limit a president to two terms until 1951, and Wilson hoped the delegates to the 1920 Democratic National Convention would nominate him. Fortunately, they did not. They chose James Cox, whose running mate was a handsome, up-and-coming young man named Franklin Delano Roosevelt.

Deeply depressed after Warren Harding's inauguration in 1921, Wilson moved to an elegant home not far from the White House where Edith took care of him, reading to him, tucking his napkin under his chin at meals, and holding his hand when he burst into tears. On February 3, 1924, as he lay dying, he told Dr. Grayson, "I am a broken piece of machinery. I am ready." He called out to Edith when she stepped away from his bedside. Her name was the last thing he ever uttered.

For the next thirty-seven years, Edith Wilson devoted herself to creating a fitting legacy for her husband. Her first step was to get those blasted letters back from Mary Hulbert. Edith had authorized Ray Baker, Wilson's press secretary at the Paris Peace Conference, to write Wilson's definitive biography; now she instructed him to visit Mary and persuade her to turn them over. Mary told him she needed the money the letters could bring, and she would be happy to sell them to a buyer friendly to Wilson's memory. A donor, Wilson's friend and adviser Bernard Baruch, stepped up and bought them for $31,500 (some $473,000 today).

Several months after she had sold them, Mary wrote Baker, "You understand that the loss of those documents leaves me bereaved. I hated selling them. I wanted to give them. I am satisfied however that they have found their safe and right honors . . . I am grateful for your beautiful and delicate handling of the friendship." Mary died in New York City in 1939 at the age of seventy-seven. We can imagine she cherished those eternally sunlit Bermuda days with Woodrow Wilson until her last breath.

Edith Wilson was successful in burnishing her husband's reputation. By the time she died, Wilson was considered one of the best U.S. presidents ever with an astonishing vision that foresaw World War II and the formation of the United Nations. Active socially and philanthropically on the Washington scene, she was on the inaugural platform on that bitter cold day in January 1961 when John F. Kennedy took the oath of office, discreetly sipping bourbon from a silver flask to keep herself warm. She died that year on December 28, Woodrow Wilson's birthday, at the age of eighty-nine, in the same bed, in the same room where he had died. Perhaps her greatest legacy to the American people is the Twenty-Fifth Amendment, enacted in 1967, which provides measures to ensure that the vice president becomes "acting president" if the president is "unable to discharge the powers of duties of his office."

6

WARREN G. HARDING'S
EXCRUCIATING JOY

*W*arren Gamaliel Harding exuded a raw animal magnetism irresistible to many women. His security guards had to keep his female fans from following him around and making embarrassing scenes. Pundits of the day believed he won the 1920 election only because featherbrained women—newly given the vote—were smitten by his sex appeal rather than his policy goals.

Harding's sex life involved a rotating buffet of delectable young women. But the American public had no idea of the president's philandering until his former mistress, the mother of his illegitimate child, wrote a scandalous tell-all book, the first of its kind, that shook the nation.

* * *

On a hot summer's day in 1922, First Lady Florence Harding marched grimly to the Oval Office. This time she was determined to catch her husband, Warren, red-handed with a girl. Her trusted Secret Service agent Harry Barker had just informed her that Harding's trusted Secret Service agent Walter Ferguson had smuggled a blonde into the office five minutes earlier.

But as Florence approached the door opening onto the hallway, Ferguson blocked it, explaining that Secret Service regulations permitted no entry from that door, not even to the first lady. She would have to go through the office of Harding's secretary, George Christian. As Florence turned around and raced to Christian's office, Ferguson entered through the hallway door he had been guarding and told the president—who had taken the girl into a closet to muffle the noise—that his wife was on the way. As Harding pulled up his trousers, Ferguson grabbed the girl, took her out the hallway door, and told her to meet him at his car. Meanwhile, the first lady was delayed a few moments by George Christian, who knew what was up. When she barged into the Oval Office, she found her husband sitting innocently at his desk, quietly perusing papers. She flew back through Christian's office and into the hallway to find Ferguson idly guarding the door. Perhaps he was studying his fingernails. "She stood and glared at me like she couldn't believe it," he reported.

President Theodore Roosevelt's acid-tongued daughter, Alice Roosevelt Longworth, heard all about the episode from White House chief usher Ike Hoover. "It was really rather a close call," she said. "Stumbling in closets among galoshes, she pounding on the door, the girlie with panties over her head. That sort of thing. My God, we've got a President who doesn't know beds were invented, and he was elected on a slogan of Back to Normalcy!"

Florence was long used to her husband's infidelities. A good-natured fellow who didn't want to hurt anybody, Harding just couldn't help himself when it came to sex. Tall and well-built, with a face of bold, carved features like those of a Roman god, he exuded pheromones of such wild sexuality they turned women into howling cats in heat, even as he grew portly and gray. Debutantes, actresses, wives, widows, prostitutes, teenagers, and socialites stalked him, sent him love letters, and boldly offered their bodies. His staff had a name for women they needed to extricate him from: "lollapaloozas."

Ironically, thirty years earlier Florence had been a lollapalooza herself. The daughter of Amos Kling—the richest and meanest man in Marion, Ohio—at nineteen she became pregnant by a neighbor, twenty-year-old Henry DeWolfe. Amos threw her out of the house. Scholars debate whether Florence and Henry ever married, but all agree that DeWolfe, a hopeless alcoholic, abandoned Florence and their son in less than two years, and after an estrangement of four years she divorced him (which she could also have done for a common-law marriage). Her father agreed to raise her son, but Florence, defiantly independent, did not go home in shame. She supported herself by teaching piano to local children. When she was thirty, she went to the home of Dr. George Harding to teach his daughter. There she met the girl's older brother, Warren. Five years her junior, Harding owned a struggling newspaper, the *Marion Star.*

Smitten to the core, Florence avidly pursued him. She rudely interrupted his conversations with other women at social events. One day, hearing that he would be returning from visiting a girlfriend, Florence waited for him at the train station. Spotting her, he tried to escape out of the other side of the train. "You needn't try to run away, Warren Harding," Florence cried. "I can see your big feet!" He allowed her to drive him home in her buggy.

Harding liked beautiful, feminine young women, and bossy bespectacled Florence wasn't pretty, even in her youth. But she had an intelligent face, alert blue-gray eyes, and thick, dark hair.

She also had a keen sense for business and saw enormous opportunity in Harding's newspaper. He listened with interest as she described ways to make the paper profitable. Harding knew himself to be a bit too lackadaisical to achieve great success; his favorite pastimes were sex, drinking, and playing poker. In Florence, he saw a woman who could organize his life and perhaps help him realize his dream of becoming a politician. And it wouldn't hurt if she one day managed to inherit some of old man Kling's money. At their 1891 wedding, Florence announced that she was now going to work to make her husband president of the United States.

A *Star* writer said, "She had faith in his future. She believed he had the making in him of a great man. She urged him on and on." Florence immediately took the newspaper in hand. She negotiated lower interest rates for loans, greatly increased circulation by drafting an army of schoolboys on bicycles to provide home delivery, and raised advertising rates. A strong advocate of women's rights, she hired Ohio's first female reporter, and she even learned how to wield a wrench to fix the printing presses herself. As Warren put his feet up on the editor's desk and smoked a cigar, Florence made the paper a tremendous financial success. "Florence Harding?" said one Marion lady. "Runs her house, runs the paper, runs Warren; runs everything but the car, and could run that if she wanted to."

But Warren didn't much like being run by the "Duchess," as he called her, and escaped as frequently as he could. He traveled to Republican meetings across the state where he drank, played poker, and had sex with women. After eighteen months of marriage, he fell into a deep depression and eventually checked into the renowned Battle Creek Sanitarium run by Dr. J. H. Kellogg, who believed that the cereal he invented—cornflakes—would cure depression and reduce the insatiable libidos of his male patients.

The cornflakes didn't work for Harding's libido, alas. Soon after returning from the sanitarium in 1894, Harding got Florence's best childhood friend, Susan Pearl McWilliams Hodder, pregnant. Susan left for Nebraska, where Harding sent child support for their daughter. Her pregnancy so upset Harding that he bounced back to Battle Creek.

But no matter how many cornflakes Warren Harding ate, he never did manage to give up women. The men in town understood. One of them said, "Anyone who lives with Florence Harding *deserves* extra-curricular activities." Another recounted the story of plumbers going into the home of a local widow to fix a sink. "And who comes out of the master bedroom but Harding in shirt sleeves. He had obviously just bedded down the woman of the house. He guffawed and then asked the plumbers to give him a ride downtown."

Florence knew, of course, about her husband's illegitimate daughter and the constant stream of women. She vacillated between blazing fury and resigned acceptance. As far as emotional pain was concerned, she wrote in her diary, she learned to "shut it away in my mind's secret cupboard and lock the door upon it." She also chose to enjoy her life no matter how badly the men in it were behaving. "No man, father, brother, lover or husband, can ruin my life," she wrote. "I claim the right to live the life the good Lord gave me, myself."

In 1899, Harding ran for state senate and, though a Republican, won in a heavily Democratic district. A charismatic speaker, he was extremely popular with other legislators for his ability to find a compromise. His constituents, too, loved him, particularly the women. Florence never let him out of her sight, even sitting in the statehouse gallery to watch the legislators at work. Harding became Ohio's lieutenant governor in 1904 and started to get national headlines as one of the most popular speakers on the Midwest summer lecture circuit. Gripping his arm tightly, Florence went along on the tour. "The way to keep a husband," she often said, "is never to let him travel alone."

But the biggest threat to Florence's marriage would not be a one-night stand with a stranger. It would be Florence's best friend. Carrie Phillips—tall, voluptuous, with wide blue eyes and strawberry-blond hair—was married to Jim Phillips, owner of a prosperous Marion hardware store. In 1905, when Florence was in the hospital with kidney disease and Jim Phillips in the Battle Creek Sanitarium eating cornflakes for depression, Warren and Carrie began a torrid affair. Even though Carrie lived nearby, Harding wrote her passionate letters—thirty, forty, fifty pages long. Hopelessly romantic, deliriously ardent, he blended the physicality of sex with rapturous poetry and apocalyptic religion. Indeed, reading the missives alone might suffice to tip some women into an earth-shattering orgasm.

My Darling:

There are no words, at my command, sufficient to say the full extent of my love for you—a mad, tender, devoted, ardent, eager, passion-wild, jealous, reverent, wistful, hungry, happy love— unspeakably encompassing, immeasurably absorbing, unendingly worshipping, unconsciously exalting, unwillingly exacting, involuntarily expounding, everlastingly compensating . . . It is the prayer and benediction of my heart; the surpassing passion of my body, the conviction and consecration of my mind, and the hope and heaven of my soul. I love you thus, and more. I love you more than all the world and have no hope of reward on earth or hereafter, so precious as that in your dear arms, in your thrilling lips, in your matchless breasts, in your incomparable embrace. To have and to hold you, in happiness to you, exclusively in satisfying and satisfied love, would be the triumph of living and loving.

In another, he told her, "I'd pet and coddle and kiss and fondle and admire and adore, utterly impatient until I made you the sweetest and purest and darlingest wanton . . . There is one engulfing, enthralling rule of love, the song of your whole being which is a bit sweeter—the 'Oh Warren! Oh Warren!' When your body quivers with divine paroxysm and your soul hovers for flight with mine . . ."

When Florence returned from the hospital, she was not healthy enough to travel with him on the next summer's speaking circuit. Harding and Carrie met in hotel rooms across the Midwest. Back in Marion, they met in each other's homes when their spouses were out. One morning, the Harding cook spotted Carrie wearing bright-colored shoes at the market. A few hours later, when the cook started to enter the Harding kitchen through the rear, she was stopped in her tracks by the sight of Warren, his trousers about his ankles, standing with his back to the door, and Mrs. Phillips spread out "on the kitchen table—still in those shoes!"

Oddly, Florence's sharp, suspicious eye never fell on her best friend. When the two couples cruised to Europe in 1909, Warren and Carrie made love on the ship's deck after their spouses had gone to bed. "I want to weld bodies, to unite souls," he wrote soon after. "I want the divine embrace, the transcending union, the blissful affinity, and with them all the excruciating joy and unspeakable sweetness that I never did know and can only know when fastened by you."

In 1911, encouraged by all those letters, Carrie suggested they both obtain divorces and marry. But Warren hemmed and hawed. True, Florence had aged greatly since their wedding twenty years earlier. Her hair was gray, her face rather puckered and sunken. Though she was still trim, her ankles had swollen. Harding no longer found her sexually attractive—if he ever had—and, it seems, they had stopped having sex some time ago. But Florence stalwartly supported him, his newspaper, and his political career with her wily acumen and forceful determination. Even if they were no longer lovers, they were partners and friends. His wife was bossy, to be sure, but she buoyed him up while nasty Carrie tore him down, deriding his dreams of high political office. There was more than self-interest in his reluctance, however. He knew of Florence's painful past—the father who beat her bloody with a switch, the pregnancy, the abandonment, the years of shame and grinding poverty. He could not hurt and betray her.

Furious, Carrie sent a love letter to his home hoping Florence would open it. She did. And realized that she had been doubly betrayed. Florence wrote in her diary, "Most of the pain in this world is located in the hearts of women . . . Passion is a very transient thing. To me, love seems to have been a thing of tragedy." Raging, Florence dragged her husband to a divorce lawyer.

But Warren didn't want a divorce. He wanted wild raucous sex with Carrie and a marriage partnership with Florence. Somehow Florence and Warren came to an agreement. They would stay married. After this crisis, she became bossier than ever, and he became more deferential to the Duchess.

"Love, to a man," she wrote bitterly in her diary, "is a sensation only. Never a complete giving of himself to one forever." She wrote that her relationship with him was "platonic affection, good fellowship."

In September 1911, Carrie Phillips took her fourteen-year-old daughter, Isabelle, to Germany, leaving behind her rather stupid husband—who remained blissfully unaware of his wife's infidelity with his best friend—to run the hardware store. But she secretly met Warren in Montreal for a New Year's Eve rendezvous. As both of them reached their climax, the bells of midnight pealed out their joy at the New Year in a kind of orgasm all their own. "The bells rang the chorus," Warren recalled in a letter, "while our hearts sang in rapture without words, and we greeted the New Year from the hallowed heights of heaven." He continued, "Fate timed that marvelous coincidence. It was impossible for us to have planned, and I count it to be one of the best remembered moments of my existence."

After another quick tryst in New York, on September 15, 1913, he wrote, "At New York, I had given you all—the very last passions, I thought, in a perfectly ecstatic loving, and I was prostrate from the excessive joy of it, dead from rapture . . . You set me aflame with the fullness of your beauty and the fire of your desire, and you loved me, gave me your unfailing kisses, and intoxicated me with your breasts, and then imprisoned me in your embrace and gave me transport—God! my breath quickens to recall it."

When an ocean came between them, Harding liked to put on his bathrobe—which she wore when they were together— and, wrapped in her scent, masturbate in front of a roaring fire in his study. One evening, he wrote Carrie, he dreamed of her "to alarming release. I called your name aloud thrice, begging you to come, and a voice upstairs responded, wanting to know what I wanted."

It was Florence, wondering what he was yelling about.

After war broke out in Europe in 1914, Carrie—who had become a rabid supporter of the kaiser and all things German—moved back to Marion with her daughter, much to Florence's chagrin. Warren was now running for the U.S. Senate, and he met Carrie in hotel rooms as he campaigned across the state. He won the Senate seat by more than 102,000 votes.

After the election, Carrie demanded Warren buy her a car. At first, he refused, but then, remembering all those letters, he caved and got her a Cadillac. Florence had no idea that the impressive new set of wheels her former friend and current enemy drove around town had been paid for by Warren. And poor, dim Jim Phillips didn't think there was anything odd about his best friend buying Carrie a Cadillac.

In 1915, the Hardings moved to Washington, D.C., and Warren took up his seat in the U.S. Senate. While he was popular with just about everyone, Florence hated her new city and felt the other politicians' wives were harshly judging her. She was right. One Washington society matron wrote of the Hardings, "That evening, I decided that the junior senator from Ohio was a stunning man with a powerfully masculine quality to charm a woman. That night his white-haired, kidney-troubled wife, whose chin was lifted haughtily each time she scented challenge, served all our drinks and did not play. Woman-like, I noticed her neck was withering and her ankles thickly swollen almost before I realized that she was rich in spirits, a determined and a jealous wife. By the calendar year she was five years older than her husband, but by all that matters in a marital partnership, she was far, far older than her easy-going, play-loving partner. Ill-health and a tendency to worry over what might happen, plus her nagging temperament had helped to wear her body . . . Hers was the ambition, what he had was charm, an ability to get along with assorted persons, friendliness and a love of jovial companions."

Millionaire Evalyn Walsh McLean, owner of the Hope Diamond, was much kinder. "She had been lovely in her youth," Evalyn wrote. "Anyone could tell that. Her eyes were blue, her profile finely chiseled, but her mouth was a revelation of her discontent. She was ambitious for herself and Warren."

When Florence fell ill with the old kidney complaint, Evalyn visited her. "You know, this town, Washington, is an awful place," Florence muttered, lying flat in bed, "the most awful town I have ever lived in."

"Why, Mrs. Harding, I love Washington. Why don't you like it?" Evalyn inquired.

"I'll tell you," she said, pushing herself up to a seated position. "Every woman in this town is after Warren . . . It's so. I'll keep him close to home, until I am up again."

Evalyn wrote, "At parties she was bound to grow alert each time he vanished from her sight. 'Where's Warren?' she would ask and then more shrilly pipe, 'Warren!'"

Though there was a twenty-six-year gap in their ages—when Florence moved to the capital she was fifty-five and Evalyn twenty-nine—they soon became best friends, and Florence settled into Washington life. Always an advocate for helpless, abused things as she herself had been, Florence joined the Animal Rescue League, the Humane Society, and the SPCA. When she saw a drunken man whipping his horse after it had fallen in front of the wagon, she ran into the street, tended to the horse, pulled the whip out of the man's hand, and gave it to his wife. "If you have to, use the whip, but not on the horse," she advised.

As pressure mounted on the U.S. to join the Allies in the European war, Carrie Phillips so defiantly defended the German cause back in Marion that the Secret Service investigated her as a possible German spy. Harding, made aware of the investigation, begged her to tone down her shrill defense of the kaiser. In response, Carrie wrote Warren that if he voted for war with Germany, she would reveal his love letters to her husband and the public. But when Congress—including Senator Harding—voted to declare war in April 1917, she kept his letters to herself. Revenge, of course, is sweet. But money is sweeter. She would hold on to them awhile.

Even after her threat to reveal his letters, Harding couldn't stop writing new ones. He concluded one such missive by asking her to destroy it. "Such a letter is a peril," he wrote. "I know and ought not send it. I endanger you, and no sane man ever pens such a missive. But no sane man ever loves as I do . . ."

In the midst of war, hot sex, and Carrie's threats of blackmail, Warren must have been intrigued to receive a letter from a twenty-year-old girl he had known in Marion. Nan Britton was the daughter of Sam Britton, a friend of Harding's. When Sam died in 1913, his widow, Mary, asked Harding for help, and he arranged a teaching position for her. "Maybe I can do something for Nan," he told Mary.

It had been a joke in Marion that Nan, at twelve years old, had developed a burning crush on Harding, who was thirty-one years her senior. She hid outside the *Star* office until he emerged and followed him home. She scribbled in her schoolbooks "Warren Harding—he's a darling" and wrote "I love Warren Harding" on her classroom blackboard. She covered her room with his campaign posters.

"Nan was a pretty girl, blonde and slender," recalled her best friend, Ellen Metzger. "In those days, we girls were movie crazy and we couldn't wait until school was out to go to a movie or to read movie magazines. But Nan wasn't interested in the movie stars; all she could talk about was Harding . . . I don't believe Mr. Harding encouraged her in any way. He didn't have to. Nan ran after him. He was so good looking, women chased him."

Nan recalled, "His pictures hung directly in front of my bed so that when I awoke in the morning, I looked into the handsome face of him whom I loved and saw his likeness the last thing before turning off my light." Everyone in Marion laughed at Nan's schoolgirl crush, everyone except Florence.

Now, in May 1917, Nan was finishing up secretarial school in New York. She wrote Harding in Washington and asked if he could use his influence to find her a good secretarial position. Eager to leave the hornet's nest of Washington to flirt with a sweet young thing, he raced up to New York and met her in the lobby of the Manhattan Hotel, where he had often rendezvoused with Carrie. "We became immediately reminiscent of my childhood," Nan later wrote, "and my adoration of him, and he seemed immensely pleased that I still retained such feelings. I could not help being perfectly frank."

When Harding suggested they go to his room, the bridal suite, "so that we might continue our conversation without interruptions or annoyances," she eagerly agreed. There they kissed passionately. "Oh, dearie, tell me it isn't hateful to you to have me kiss you!" he exclaimed. But Nan did not find it hateful at all. He tucked thirty dollars (some $600 in today's money) into her silk stockings and said, "I love you more than all the world, and I want you to belong to me. Could you believe me, dearie? I want you and I need you so."

Harding arranged for Nan to be hired as the secretary of the chairman of the U.S. Steel Corporation headquartered in New York. He continued to see her, dabbling in foreplay, even as he rendezvoused with Carrie. Finally, in July 1917, Harding and Nan met at New York's Imperial Hotel—a shady place used for such assignations where important men wouldn't run into anyone they knew except one another—where he registered as Mr. Harwick. They finally made love that afternoon. "I became Mr. Harding's bride—as he called me—on that day," Nan recalled.

As Nan and Warren were getting dressed, two house detectives broke into the room and caught the pair. They demanded to know Nan's name and age; she was, in fact, under twenty-one, the legal age of consent. Warren feared his entire career was ruined. He sat "disconsolately on the edge of the bed, pleading for them to allow me to go," Nan wrote. "'I'll answer for both, won't I? Let this poor little girl go!'" A detective told him they had already called the police and "You'll have to tell it to the judge!"

Then, one of the detectives picked up Harding's hat, saw his name on the band, and recognized him as a U.S. senator. They immediately apologized and even helped them sneak out of a side entrance before the paddy wagon arrived. Harding thankfully gave them a twenty-dollar bill. "I thought I wouldn't get out of that for under $1,000!" he said to Nan as they raced off in a taxi.

Harding and Nan frequently met in New York and Washington. Their rendezvous often lasted long, luxurious hours. "So potent was this spell which we had for each other," Nan wrote, "that for whole evenings we were its willing prisoners, living as in a dream, neither of us coming out from the intoxication of each other's presence until long after separation." Harding must have been a hot handful of man in the sack.

He sent her a photo of himself standing on the steps of the U.S. Capitol which she kissed so much it cracked and fell apart. "He confessed that it had been many years since his home situation had been satisfying," Nan wrote. "He spoke very freely to me about what he would do if Mrs. Harding were to pass on, he wanted to buy a place for us and live in the country. 'Wouldn't that be grand, Nan? You'd make such a darling wife!'"

In January 1919, Nan visited Harding in his Senate office and made love without a condom as, she wrote, "The Senate Offices do not provide preventive facilities for use in such emergencies." A month later, Nan knew she was pregnant.

In April, she returned to Washington and met Harding at the Willard Hotel, where she informed him of her condition. Calmly, Harding offered to procure her an abortion. Her sister Elizabeth, too, thought that was the only sensible route to go. But Nan, in awe that she was carrying the child of the man she idolized, refused. "I could not bring myself to destroy the precious treasure within me," she explained. Allowing Nan to make her own choice, Warren gave her a sapphire-and-diamond ring and the two performed a pretend marriage ceremony. "The ring was indeed a great comfort to me, helping to sustain me . . . It was a material evidence of a relationship which no wedding ceremony could have made more solemn or more sacred than that very own ceremony between ourselves, with God as our witness."

But Harding was still involved with Carrie, regularly adding more love letters to her mountain of blackmail material. And after he hired a tall, blond, beautiful new secretary, Grace Miller Cross, he started an affair with her, too, a sadomasochistic one, as sometimes she cut him and made him crawl in front of her naked, begging for forgiveness. Then there was a Washington woman named Augusta Cole, whom he also impregnated. He must have been relieved that Augusta, at least, agreed to have an abortion. A New York matron whose name has been lost to history committed suicide when Harding didn't divorce Florence and marry her. And amid all these histrionics and threats, there was little

Nan, sweet, undemanding, and grateful for whatever crumbs of attention he gave her. She was delighted when he gave her a winter coat.

Carrie Phillips, on the other hand, would not be silenced with a coat. In August 1919, she wanted him to buy her another new car and give her $10,000 ($150,000 today). By then her husband Jim was deeply in debt, and she saw her luxurious lifestyle slipping away. She once again threatened to release Harding's letters if he didn't cough up the money and the car. They came to an agreement.

When Nan's pregnancy began to show, she left her job at U.S. Steel and, with funds provided by Harding, rented rooms in a boardinghouse in the seaside resort of Asbury Park, New Jersey. She used an alias and pretended to be the wife of a soldier serving abroad. There, on October 22, 1919, she gave birth to a daughter whom she named Elizabeth Ann. Nan seems to have suffered from postpartum depression, exacerbated by being the single mother of a U.S. senator's child. She ate poorly, cried a lot, and said her nerves were "shattered." Finally, her sister took her to Chicago, leaving Elizabeth Ann in Asbury Park with a nurse. Harding had suggested they give the baby to his sister Charity to raise in California. But Nan could not give her up. Warren then promised that when Florence finally died of her kidney ailment, he would take the baby himself "and make her a real Harding!"

Florence, meanwhile, had no idea her husband had fathered a child with the obnoxious little girl from Marion who used to follow him around. Her mind was focused on politics. She watched hopefully as support in the Republican Party grew for choosing Warren as the 1920 presidential candidate. Jovial, glad-handing Harding had been an across-the-aisle bridge-builder in the Senate, finding the middle ground between progressivism and conservativism. He had been chosen to give the keynote address at the 1916 Republican National Convention, a nod to a man with a possibly presidential future.

In January 1920, Harding outlined his America First theme, which seems strangely familiar to us a century later, though in Harding's case, it was a reaction to the massacre of American men in the Great War. "Call it the selfishness of nationality if you will," he said, "I think it an inspiration to patriotic devotion. To safeguard America first. To stabilize America first. To prosper America first. To think of America first. To exalt America first. To live for and revere America first." Most Americans were disgusted at the cost America paid to extricate foreign nations from a bloodbath of their own making and heartily agreed with him. Additionally, Harding wanted to severely restrict the number of immigrants from southern and eastern Europe.

Florence, always interested in astrology and the occult, went with her friend Evalyn McLean to visit Washington's top fortune-teller, Madame Marcia. Wearing a dark veil so the seer wouldn't recognize her as the senator's wife, Florence gave her Warren's date of birth and asked what the future held for him.

Madame Marcia replied, "If this man runs for the presidency, no power on earth can defeat him. But you must know he will die a sudden death, perhaps of poison . . . This person will be the next president of the United States, but he will not live out his term. He will die in a sudden if not violent death. The end, when it comes, will be sudden, after an illness of short duration." Florence didn't know if she should be delighted that Warren would become president or horrified that he would die in office.

Carrie Phillips, too, was thinking about Warren's becoming president. Now that the stakes were higher, the orgasmic love letters were more valuable than ever. Carrie threatened to publish them if he didn't divorce Florence immediately and drop out of the presidential race. Warren politely offered to withdraw from the race, if that was her choice, to avoid disgrace. Or, if she waited until he became president, he would be in an excellent position to pay her substantial sums. He also assured her (despite the recent pregnancies, abortions, and suicides of his lovers) that he had never cheated on her. No fool, Carrie opted for the money.

Warren told Florence about Carrie's blackmail attempt and wondered if he should drop out of the race before the Republican National Convention, held in Chicago in June. Before the advent of the primary system in 1968, the Republican and Democratic national conventions were not the coronations they later became. They were cliff-hangers, where wheeling and dealing took place among a party's power brokers in smoke-filled rooms. And so, Florence traipsed back to Madame Marcia, having revealed her true identity. "He must stick," the psychic announced. "He will not be nominated until after noon on Saturday of the convention. But he will be nominated."

She was correct. At 6:00 p.m. on Saturday, June 12, Warren Harding was nominated as the Republican candidate for president. Three weeks after his nomination, Jim Phillips—informed by Carrie about the affair and not terribly upset about it—showed up at Harding's Senate office to ask about blackmail payments. Warren—prosperous but never rich—finally had to tell the Republican Party bosses about Carrie's extortion. They were horrified. The election of 1920 was the first time that American women would vote for president. Twenty million new female voters would not ignore a sex scandal the way most male voters had back in 1884 when Maria Halpin had accused Grover Cleveland of rape.

It is unlikely that any newspaper would have printed Carrie's steamy love letters. Harding benefited from the hands-off approach the press had with political sex scandals, just as Wood-row Wilson had. During the 1920 campaign, three newspaper reporters were invited to dine at the home of one of Harding's neighbors, an attractive widow. After dinner, the woman's eight-year-old child took them upstairs and proudly showed them Harding's toothbrush in the bathroom, explaining, "He always stays here when Mrs. Harding goes away." None of them investi-gated the matter further.

Harding even had the audacity to announce to journalists at the National Press Club, "It is a good thing I am not a woman. I would always be pregnant. I just can't say no"—perhaps the greatest headline never printed. Journalists also knew that during Prohibition, the Harding White House offered a full bar. Alice Roosevelt Longworth recalled, "No rumor could have exceeded the truth . . . trays with bottles containing every imaginable brand of whiskey stood about."

Perhaps Carrie was planning on publishing Harding's letters in pamphlet form and distributing them herself. Pamphlets could do great damage by causing protests and uproar that the press was obliged to cover. To solve the problem of Carrie Phillips, the Republican National Committee (RNC) solicited donations from Harding's richest friends and supporters to create an ample slush fund. An RNC representative called on Carrie in Marion. He would give her a lump sum of $25,000 ($321,000 today) and the promise of $2,000 ($26,000 today) a month, he said, as long as Harding remained in public office. In return, she would never discuss her relationship with Harding, never show the letters to anyone, and would betake herself and her husband on a very long cruise to Japan before the election. Carrie agreed.

With Carrie hushed up, the campaign moved forward at full speed. Florence came up with the idea of the front-porch campaign. Their Marion house—which she had helped design—had an enormous front porch with a circular area bulging out at one end and a white railing. The Hardings would not travel to meet voters but would invite the voters to come to them. In a rocking chair, Florence knitted and darned socks as Warren chatted amiably with supporters. It was a kind of before-the-war Disney World of traditional family values, a stage set where all that bloodshed on foreign soil had never happened, a dreamlike place of baseball games, apple pie, and church socials with fried chicken and watermelon, of good old American values like hard work and decency. It was a "Return to Normalcy," as his campaign slogan stated. Every storefront had red, white, and blue bunting except the hardware store owned by Jim Phillips.

Harding recognized Florence's campaigning savvy, which included novelties such as the extensive use of press photographers and newsreels, and the support of major Hollywood stars such as Charlie Chaplin. Warren "placed implicit confidence in his wife's judgment," said Florence's Marion neighbor Jane Dixon. He told his political advisers, "I'll consult Mrs. Harding about that and let you know." "Better ask the Duchess." "Talk with my wife. She will understand."

H. L. Mencken thought Harding's campaign pledges were tripe of the blandest, most bloviating kind, and we can only wonder what he would have thought of his love letters. "He writes the worst English that I have ever encountered," the writer remarked. "It reminds me of a string of wet sponges; it reminds me of tattered washing on the line; it reminds me of stale bean soup, of college yells, of dogs barking idiotically through endless nights. It is so bad that a sort of grandeur creeps into it. It drags itself out of the dark abysm of pish, and crawls insanely up the topmost pinnacle of posh. It is rumble and bumble. It is flap and doodle. It is balder and dash."

Still reeling from the horrors of bloody war, most Americans longed for the comforts of wet sponges and barking dogs. On November 2, 1920, Harding's birthday, he won in a landslide: 404 electoral votes compared to the Democratic candidate's 127 and thirty-seven out of forty-eight states in the most overwhelming presidential victory since 1820.

Nan Britton had been living with her sister Elizabeth and her husband in Chicago and working at the Harding campaign headquarters there. Upon hearing of her lover's victory, she took the midnight train for Marion. The next morning, Harding's Secret Service agent Tim Slade took her to a small house used by campaign clerical workers. There she sat on Warren's lap and cooed, "Isn't it wonderful that you are president?"

"This is the best thing that's happened to me lately, dearie," he replied. He asked about Elizabeth Ann, and Nan delightedly showed him pictures of the thirteen-month-old. Then he gave Nan $1,500 in the form of three $500 bills (about $20,000 today).

In January 1921, as Harding worked with his transition team, he arranged for Nan's sister Elizabeth to visit him in Washington. Hustled into his office, Elizabeth listened as the president-elect begged her and her husband to adopt Elizabeth Ann, who was still in New Jersey in the care of a nurse. Nan, he explained, with her bouts of severe depression and physical weakness, was in no position to take care of her. Moreover, he wanted the child to have a name and a traditional family. He volunteered to send Elizabeth $400 a month ($5,700) for the baby. Elizabeth saw the wisdom of his suggestion and pressed Nan to agree. The adoption took place in February, and the baby was brought to Chicago. Though Nan was delighted to be living with her child, the girl now had three parents, all arguing about how to raise her.

In the wee hours of the night before the inauguration, Warren snuck out of the presidential suite at the Willard Hotel to meet his former secretary, Grace Miller Cross, who had also taken a room there. But men from the Republican National Committee had heard about the planned rendezvous and, eager to avoid a new scandal, waited in the hall outside Harding's suite. When he emerged after midnight, they pushed Harding firmly back inside his room, then chased Grace out of the hotel with violent threats. Soon, however, they sent her, too, on a luxurious monthslong cruise abroad. Other young women kept popping up with Warren's love letters demanding money. There was a *Washington Post* employee named Miss Allicott, an Evalyn Ruby, and chorus girls Maize Haywood and Blossom Jones. The RNC slush fund would need constant replenishment throughout Harding's time in office.

Harding's 1921 inauguration was one of firsts: the first time the principals were driven in motorcars, the first time the wife of the new president had voted for her husband, and the first time the president took the oath of office with a loudspeaker so people could actually hear him.

As the band played "Hail to the Chief," Florence's joy was tempered by the memory of Madame Marcia's doom-filled prediction. She had been right about the nomination and the election, after all. Would her prediction of Warren dying in office also prove to be correct? She told Indiana senator Jim Watson, "I am filled with fear . . . It is the proudest day of my life, but we will not live through the four years."

Yet her ambition overcame her fear. As she stood on the North Portico waiting to enter the White House for the first time as first lady, she asked a senator, "Who was the most successful First Lady of the Land?"

"Mrs. Cleveland or Dolley Madison, I suppose," he replied.

"Watch me," Florence rejoined.

Then she turned to her husband and said, "Well, Warren Harding, I have got you the Presidency. What are you going to do with it?"

Feeling already the weighty responsibility of his position, he said, "May God help me, for I need it."

A week later, the debilitated President Woodrow Wilson and his wife, Edith, who had moved to a house nearby, drove past the White House. The place had been transformed. The Wilsons had shut off all public access for security reasons during the war and then due to the president's ill health. The White House, grim and darkened, where people talked in whispers, had been something like a funeral home. But Florence insisted that all the gates to the grounds be flung open, and hundreds of people were milling about the lawn. "The crowds of visitors were so interested in what was going on in the new administration," reported the *Los Angeles Times*, "that almost no one noticed the former President passing by."

Florence loved interacting with the public. At one reception she shook 6,756 hands. According to Lillian Parks, whose mother worked as a maid, "She would go running down the steps and greet the tourists, who came in to look around, with a big hello. They would be really startled!" The first lady was immensely popular with American women who saw her as a self-deprecating, folksy suffragette, a beloved auntie always ready with a witty quote.

Many commented that Florence enjoyed being first lady much more than Warren enjoyed being president. He hated having his every movement monitored and told Nan, "The White House is a veritable prison . . . I'm in jail, Nan! And I can't get out. I've got to stay." Wherever he went, he was trailed by Secret Service agents. And when he brought a girl into the White House, Florence's Secret Service agent Harry Barker would tell her. Which is what happened the day Florence almost found him in the closet having sex.

Perhaps because of that day, Florence finally learned that Nan Britton—the blonde in the closet with Warren—had become his mistress and had had his child. Gaston Means, an agent of the Bureau of Investigation who undertook special missions for the Hardings, reported in a 1930 book that Florence Harding asked him to follow Nan. Though Means was a crook and a swindler and later repudiated many of the shocking accusations in his book, his sex stories seem to have been accurate. Gaston wrote that Florence instructed him to get on Nan's train in Chicago bound for Washington. He noticed Nan immediately. "She was a most attractive young woman," he wrote, "blonde, fresh, vital. I took a seat in that car and watched her, and I also noticed that the other men in the car were watching her. She was decidedly the type to attract men.

"This attractive young woman," he continued, "with her bobbed blonde hair peeping from a closely fitting cloche, was really after all no more alluring than many other girls and women in whose presence I myself have seen President Harding all aflutter. But she was young, eager, panting, calling for sex-fulfillment, dazzled by his masculine beauty and his position, determined, flattered, seductive. And he loved girls . . . I had already seen enough of the President to know that he could no more resist a pretty girl or woman than he could resist food when hungry."

According to Means, Florence assigned him to investigate Nan's behavior with men from the age of twelve, when she had first started stalking Warren. Promiscuity with other men, she hoped, might indicate that her child was not Warren's. Means, interviewing schoolfriends and landladies, found that Nan had never shown any interest in the male sex—except for Warren Harding. Florence must have been deeply disappointed. She was even more so when Harding started sneaking out again, taking a few loyal Secret Service agents with him on his trysts.

The White House staff sensed Florence's nervousness. "The President was spending a lot of time away from the White House," wrote Lillian Parks. "Mama knew Mrs. Harding kept worrying about whom he was with . . . The more he stayed away, the more tense Mrs. Harding would get . . . She would try to keep him home, and once Mama was very shocked when Mrs. Harding shouted at him over the banister, 'You are not leaving this house tonight!'"

One night, when Warren was partying at the Love Nest, a rowdy bordello near the White House on K Street, a prostitute was hit on the head with a champagne bottle. As her friends tried to revive her, Harding, who was leaning against a mantel, drunk, was hustled out of the building by his Secret Service agents. The woman died.

If Nan had heard of Harding's extracurricular activities, she would have been devastated. Even believing as she did in his fidelity, she remained deeply depressed. "It is breaking my heart!" she wrote. "Our baby lost to me, and the world has my sweetheart!" When Harding gave her large amounts of cash—thousands of dollars in today's money—she would spend it immediately to induce a kind of quick high. "A new trinket might help to make me forget, at least while its newness lasted," she recalled. "Whenever I found myself eaten to distraction with too much thinking, I would go out to purchase a gaily colored gown or a hat or a pretty pin, eventually giving it away perhaps, but easing myself at least during the moment of buying. I used to drag my darling baby around with me on these mad hunts for happiness which, alas, never sparkled for the desolate even in caskets of diamonds and rubies . . . I surfeited Elizabeth Ann with toys. There was nothing she wanted that I did not immediately buy for her, often to my sister's disgust."

Harding's women troubles sowed the seeds of the corruption that would destroy his reputation. So many men had donated generously to his slush fund that he felt obliged to pay them back with high-level government positions. Harding trusted implicitly these good old boys who had gotten him elected, held the women at bay, and played poker with him.

He made his campaign manager, Harry Daugherty, the U.S. attorney general, a position Daugherty used to take hundreds of thousands of dollars in bribes to quash federal investigations. He also secretly sold liquor confiscated by agents enforcing Prohibition. Daugherty's assistant Jess Smith—who also accepted bribes for derailing investigations—committed suicide or was, quite possibly, murdered because he knew too much.

Harding's friend Charles Forbes became head of the new Veterans' Bureau, where, instead of looking after wounded veterans, he sold hospital medications to drug dealers, took kickbacks from purchasing agents, and gave himself commissions from selling army surplus material. His assistant, Charles Cramer, shot himself, leaving a suicide note addressed to Harding, which disappeared.

Another good friend, New Mexico senator Albert Fall, became secretary of the interior—where he caused the worst scandal of all, Teapot Dome, the name of a Wyoming oil field. Fall obtained control of the field from the navy, then leased oil production rights—with no competitive bidding—to Mammoth Oil. Suddenly, Fall was a wealthy man, with cattle ranches, several businesses, and a lavish lifestyle. It seemed clear that Mammoth Oil had rewarded him with huge bribes. Though the full scope of the scandal wouldn't come out for a couple of years, Fall had received $404,000 from the oil company (almost $6 million today).

"My God this is a hell of a job," Harding cried after hearing about the scandal. "I have no trouble with my enemies but my damned friends! My goddamned friends, they're the ones that keep me walking the floor at night." One night, White House chief usher Ike Hoover found the president sitting on the front lawn, sobbing that he hated his life. To friends he moaned, "And they called this the greatest position in the land—this nerve-wrecking, energy-sapping job—the Presidency of the United States!"

As Harding's popularity tanked, Florence pushed him to undertake an exhausting, fifteen-thousand-mile tour of the western states and become the first president to visit the American territory of Alaska. Harding wondered if it was a good idea. The stress of the office—exacerbated by the percolating corruption scandals—had taken its toll on his health. He had chest pains and, since he couldn't breathe lying down, he had to sleep propped up on pillows. Sometimes he had such shortness of breath he could hardly finish a sentence without gasping. His lips became puffy and blue, and his hands stiff and immobile. But Florence was determined to go. The trip would be good for him, she said, and would improve his popularity.

Harding's secretary George Christian begged him with tears in his eyes not to undertake the journey. "I can see nothing but a coffin in a funeral train coming back across the country," he said. But Warren—who had always wanted to see the beauties of

America's West and Alaska—decided to go. He made a new will shortly before his departure and sent Nan off on a cruise to Europe with some friends, hoping it would ease her depression.

As for the grueling "voyage of understanding," as the trip was called, Florence placed blind faith in her physician of many years, Dr. Charles Sawyer, called "Doc." Back in Marion, Doc had treated Florence for her numerous near-fatal, kidney-related illnesses. She credited him with keeping her alive, though that is debatable as Doc believed in the pseudoscience of homeopathy: giving patients minute doses of drugs that would produce symptoms in a healthy person similar to those of the disease. Doc was such an incompetent quack he couldn't tell that Warren was suffering from severe heart disease, even though other doctors who merely shook the president's hand could see it. And Doc wouldn't let his assistant physicians go near Harding if he wasn't around.

During the trip, Harding got sicker and sicker. Florence had to put ice on his swollen, blue lips. His eyes were so puffy he could hardly see, all signs that his heart could no longer pump sufficient oxygen through his body. At times, Florence had to give her husband's speeches for him. Coming back from Alaska on July 23, Harding and several others on the ship got food poisoning from shellfish. In Seattle on July 27, in the middle of a speech, he started gasping, dropped his remarks, and grasped the podium, probably suffering a mild heart attack. The rest of the trip was canceled.

Harding made it down to the Palace Hotel in San Francisco where he intended to recuperate. The incompetent Doc decided his attack had been caused by lingering food poisoning and Harding needed violent purgatives to get it out of his system. Quite possibly, Doc's medieval use of purgatives—which remove the body's potassium, a mineral required for healthy heart function— kicked Harding's already weakened heart into full-scale cardiac arrest. Sometime around 7:30 p.m. on August 2, Warren Harding died in his hotel bed. At the same time, 4:30 p.m. in Washington, D.C., the seer Madame Marcia told a gathering of her clients. "The President is dead."

Doc, in a panic, and Florence, protective of the man she believed had saved her life so many times, gave contradictory information about the president's exact time of death and who was in the room when it occurred. Florence refused to permit an autopsy, which would have revealed a heart attack as the cause of death and possibly resulted in a charge of negligent homicide against Doc. Doc wrote out a death certificate stating Harding had died of a cerebral hemorrhage. Given the conflicting stories about Harding's death, and the lack of an autopsy, many people believed Florence had killed her husband, either as punishment for his amours or to protect his legacy from all the corruption scandals about to break.

On August 3, 1923, Nan Britton was in Dijon, France, when she heard that President Harding had died the night before. "My heart pounded, and my cheeks felt strangely hot," she wrote in her autobiography. "Aloud I was saying to myself as I ran along, 'Oh, that could not be, that could not be! Of course, it is a mistake; oh, God, that just *could* not be!'" When she realized it was true, she wrote, "The world seemed without bottom. Things suddenly lost their meaning. I could not cry." And he had never once seen their daughter. She left on the next ship home.

Harding was placed in a coffin with a glass lid—his pallor covered by thick makeup, rouge, and lipstick, which only made him look ghastlier. The funeral train wended its way to Washington, exactly as his secretary had foreseen. People were disturbed to see that Florence never shed a tear. Indeed, she enjoyed looking at his dead body through the glass in his coffin. "Look at him," she told reporters as they gazed at the corpse, "more magnificent still in death!" For once in their marriage, Florence Harding knew exactly where her husband was and knew, too, he would never commit adultery again. Lillian Parks recalled, "Mama was shocked at how calm the First Lady was. 'She has turned to ice,' Mama said." Florence's odd behavior, too, added fuel to the murder rumors.

As soon as Harding was buried in Marion, Florence turned her attention to salvaging his reputation by dealing with his papers. Warren's secretary George Christian had a secret file marked "Heart-Throb Letters" which she proceeded to burn. There must have been many heartthrob letters because for five hot summer nights smoke billowed out of the Oval Office chimney. Realizing she didn't have enough time to read, sort, and burn all the compromising material before President Calvin Coolidge and his wife moved in, Florence instructed George Christian to stuff all the remaining presidential papers into ten-foot crates and cart them over to Evalyn McLean's suburban estate, Friendship. In the garden, she created a giant pyre of presidential papers, not all of them love letters. Many of Harding's official documents went up in that hecatomb. "We must be loyal to Warren," she said, "and preserve his memory."

During those days, Florence's face, hands, and arms were covered in soot as she fed papers to the flames: half of all Harding's presidential papers as well as many from his Ohio political career. She also destroyed much of her own correspondence and records of her early life. "Now that is all over," she told Evalyn as she shoveled the last embers, "I think it was all for the best." Curiously, her private diary escaped the conflagration, ending up in an Ohio barn auction, where it was discovered in 1997. Florence did not long outlive her husband. She finally died of her kidney ailment sixteen months after Warren on November 21, 1924.

Florence's bonfire of the vanities didn't help much to protect her husband's legacy. He was considered one of the least successful U.S. presidents, mostly because of the shocking corruption scandals associated with his administration that tumbled out in full public view soon after his death. Much anti-corruption legislation the Trump administration is coming up against was passed because of the Harding scandals: for instance, the 1924 change to the Internal Revenue Code allows the House Ways and Means Committee and the Senate Finance Committee to request the president's—or anyone else's—tax returns to conduct an investigation.

Carrie Phillips went to Germany in the 1930s, became the mistress of a prince, and lived in a castle on the Rhine. She returned to Marion, dumped Jim, who died in abject poverty in 1939, and raised German shepherds as a kind of paean to the dead kaiser. As senility settled in, she didn't bother to housebreak her dogs and lived in a house filled with their excrement. Sometimes she walked through downtown Marion—the scene of her former triumph as the town's wealthiest, most beautiful matron—naked except for a fur coat. She entered a nursing home, where she died in 1960. Soon after, her lawyer entered her house to see what valuables he might discover for her heirs. At the bottom of a closet, he found a shoebox crammed with poems and 250 love letters—some of them sixty pages long—from Warren Harding.

Desperate for money after Harding's death, Nan went to Warren's sister and told her about Elizabeth Ann. But unlike the shrewd Carrie Phillips, trusting little Nan had burned all of Harding's letters as he requested and had no proof that he had fathered her child. The family, already dealing with the corruption scandals ruining Warren's legacy, refused to give Nan anything. It would prove to be a massive mistake.

Nan wrote the first presidential kiss-and-tell book, *The President's Daughter*, published in 1927. As no publisher would take it, she decided to self-publish. When the government seized the printing plates from the printer, Britton successfully sued for their return. The book sold like hotcakes, making Nan a mint of money. On November 13, 1927, she held a press conference to introduce eight-year-old Elizabeth Ann to the world.

While the public reveled in Nan Britton's book about their affair, the press either ignored or disparaged it. One of the book reviewers explained the reluctance of journalists to cover any of Harding's indiscretions: "The majority feel . . . that it is not only beneath their dignity but a breach of their patriotic integrity to notice such terrible statements about a dead ex-President of the United States." Congressman John Tillman denounced Nan Britton's book on the floor of the House of Representatives, insisting that suppressing news of presidential adultery was "a matter of nation-wide interest and importance. It is a non-partisan question."

While many doubted over the years that Harding was Elizabeth Ann's father, proof came in 2015 when Elizabeth Ann's son, Jim Blaesing, was contacted by Peter Harding, Warren's grandnephew, suggesting a DNA test. It was a match.

"She loved him until the day she died," Jim Blaesing said. "When she used to talk about him, she would get the biggest smile. She just couldn't get enough of him. They were truly in love." Nan herself, who died in 1991 at the age of ninety-four, wrote that she looked back on the relationship "with absolutely no regrets. In the history of lovers, there was, I am sure, none to compare with Warren Gamaliel Harding. And to him I was, or so he has often said, the 'sweetheart incomparable.'"

7

FRANKLIN DELANO ROOSEVELT
AND THE GOOD-LOOKING LADIES

*F*DR was one of the most beloved and successful U.S. presidents. His dynamic leadership hoisted the nation out of the Depression. He deftly guided U.S. diplomacy and the armed forces through World War II to victory. His wife, Eleanor, was a world figure on her own merits, endorsing the rights of workers and minorities. There was never a breath of scandal about the president and first lady during FDR's administration. And yet both had steaming-hot love affairs that came out decades later.

* * *

When Eleanor Roosevelt decided to unpack her husband's leather valise in September 1918, she had no idea it would irrevocably alter her marriage and the rest of her life. Franklin was in no condition to unpack it himself as he had just been carried off his ship on a stretcher, suffering from double pneumonia caused by the Spanish flu, a pandemic that would cull some fifty million people around the world. As assistant secretary of the U.S. Navy, he had spent ten weeks in Europe visiting battlefields and top military brass. But he had collapsed almost as soon as his ship left London. Eleanor had received a call to meet the ship in New York Harbor with a doctor and an ambulance.

Eleanor, raised to believe she was hopelessly ugly, compensated by being dutiful and helpful. She dutifully met her husband's ship with the doctor and ambulance and helpfully put her husband to bed in their Manhattan town house. And then, looking around nervously for new ways to be dutiful and helpful, she decided to unpack his valise, hang up his clothes, and see to his laundry.

But somewhere in between her husband's shaving kit and underpants she found something that caused her heart to skitter: a packet of faintly scented letters tied in a soft, blue ribbon, addressed to her husband in a hand she instantly recognized: that of her former social secretary, the beautiful Lucy Mercer. Almost against her will, her hands shaking, Eleanor opened one. Gasping, she read it and then ripped through all of them. They were love letters indicating a hot sexual affair that had gone on for years, letters sent via diplomatic pouch to all the cities Franklin had visited.

"The bottom dropped out of my particular world," Eleanor later said. Her husband's betrayal of her with a beautiful, charming woman brought back all the horrors of Eleanor's childhood. Though born to great wealth—she was the niece of Teddy Roosevelt, president from 1901 to 1909—her early life had been quite grim. Her mother, a New York society beauty, often told her, "Eleanor, I hardly know what's to happen to you. You're so plain that you really have nothing to do except be good." And "You have no looks, so see to it you have manners." Her aunt Edith said, "Poor little soul, she is very plain. Her mouth and teeth seem to have no future."

When Eleanor was eight, diphtheria killed her mother and younger brother. When she was ten, her father, an alcoholic, jumped out of an upstairs window while suffering withdrawal symptoms and died. As an orphan, she entered a surreal world of mixed Dickensian metaphors. She was sent to live at an estate something like Bleak House, presided over by her grandmother, a nasty old lady something like Miss Havisham, and a spinster daughter, the lamentably named Aunt Pussie. Living in seclusion with all the blinds pulled down, Eleanor wore hand-me-down clothes, was served inedible meals, and received harsh discipline, like Oliver Twist. Perhaps worst of all, her relatives constantly told her how ugly she was. Trying to shrink out of sight proved impossible when Eleanor grew to five foot eleven, grotesquely tall for a woman of the time. Yet she was not ugly. Her teeth protruded a bit in that age before orthodontia was common, and her chin was receding. But she had wide, soft blue eyes, thick honey-blond hair, and a flawless, milky complexion.

At fifteen, Eleanor was let out on probation to attend a school outside Paris, where she reveled in light and color and freedom, in friendships with other students, in discussions with brilliant female teachers. After three years, she was forced to return home to make her society debut, a hideously painful experience. Towering over most of the men, she stood, palms clammy, a wallflower, as few of the eligible bachelors asked her to dance. "I often felt that I'd like to have the floor open so that I could sink into it," she recalled.

Shockingly, the one young man who sought her out was the handsomest, most eligible bachelor in society, Eleanor's fifth cousin, Franklin Delano Roosevelt, often called FDR. Not only did he ask her to dance at balls, but he invited her for walks, games of tennis, and sailing. Franklin, two years Eleanor's senior, was the only child of James and Sara Delano Roosevelt. A child of privilege, he was his indomitable mother's obsession and her masterpiece. When his father died in 1900, his will stated that Sara controlled all of Franklin's inheritance until her death, which meant that she could, to a great extent, control him as well. Now, to Sara's alarm, her son was in love for the first time. Sara could hardly complain about the girl's family—it was the family she had married into, after all—but Franklin was still at Harvard. Though Sara tried repeatedly to break up the budding romance, her son refused to obey.

What did FDR see in this ungainly, timid girl? For one thing, Eleanor was different from all the pretty misses with perfect features and empty minds. She was smart, well-read, passionate about helping the less fortunate. It was a relationship something like that of Bill Clinton and Hillary Rodham seventy years later. A handsome, magnetic, popular man—who could marry almost anyone—chooses as his mate a brilliant but rather plain woman.

Franklin's proposal of marriage was like spring after a bitter winter, sunshine after an interminable rain. Eleanor—who thought no one would ever love her because no one ever had—suddenly saw a radiant future. "I am so happy. So very happy in your love dearest, that all the world has changed for me," she wrote him during their courtship. Resigned to the marriage, Sara insisted they wait until Franklin graduated Harvard. They married on March 17, 1905. The groom was twenty-three, the bride twenty-one.

But the first seeds of discord were sown during their three-month European honeymoon. For one thing, Eleanor did not enjoy sex. As she told her daughter, Anna, before her 1925 wedding, "Sex, my dear, is something a woman must learn to endure." Secondly, Franklin flirted with every pretty woman in sight, which

just made Eleanor feel ugly and unloved all over again. The new-
lyweds quarreled. Franklin, always cheerful, would joke about
their disagreements soon afterward. Eleanor, serious as Death
eating an onion, played the silent, wounded martyr. She had not
found a loving soul mate, after all, just a husband she couldn't
connect with and who jumped on her at night, and an interfering
mother-in-law from hell.

When the young couple returned from their honeymoon,
Eleanor found that Sara had bought two contiguous Manhattan
brownstones—one for her, one for them—and knocked down
doors between them on each floor so she could burst into Eleanor's house and see if she was running Franklin's household properly. Sara had also hired all of Eleanor's servants and furnished
her house according to her own taste, without consulting Eleanor
in anything. A few weeks after moving in, FDR found his wife
sobbing uncontrollably that this was not her house, she had not
chosen one thing in it. Franklin told Eleanor she was mad, shook
his head, and left the room. Then there were public embarrass-
ments. At one dinner party, in front of several society guests, Sara
said sweetly to Eleanor, "If you just ran a comb through your hair,
dear, you'd look so much nicer."

There was motherhood, of course, to distract her. But motherhood didn't come easily to Eleanor. As one baby followed another, she realized she had no idea what she was doing. When her
doctor told her that her first baby should be given regular airings,
Eleanor dutifully hoisted the baby's bassinet outside her second-
floor window on a rope until a neighbor, hearing the child's wails,
threatened to call child welfare services. "This was a shock to
me," Eleanor recalled, "as I thought I was a most modern mother."

Though FDR practiced law the first few years of his marriage,
he intended to go into politics. In 1910, he was elected New York

State senator and developed a reputation for standing up to corruption and championing the poor against the powerful. In 1913, President Woodrow Wilson appointed him assistant secretary of the navy, which meant a move to Washington, D.C. Eleanor—who now had three children—was nervous at the social responsibilities expected of a top official's wife: calling on the wives of other administration officials, congressmen, Supreme Court justices, and ambassadors in strict order of precedence, and making charming small talk. Panic-stricken, she wrote her aunt, "I don't know a soul in Washington and am afraid of all kinds of stupid mistakes." She found herself making up to thirty calls a day, usually staying only six minutes as she had no idea what to say. Almost every night, there was a dinner.

One night, Eleanor burst into tears as dinner guests waited downstairs. "What's wrong, dear?" her husband asked. She sobbed, "I'm afraid I cannot face all those people, Franklin." Stunned, he said, "Do pull yourself together."

Insecure and overwhelmed, Eleanor had a hard time keeping track of her schedule and her correspondence—writing thank-you notes, accepting and declining invitations, and issuing her own. What she needed, her aunt said, was a social secretary to relieve her of the pressure, and she knew the perfect girl.

Twenty-two-year-old Lucy Mercer had an impeccable pedigree—she was a descendant of Charles Carroll of Carrollton, a signer of the Declaration of Independence—but her family had fallen on hard times. Her father was a drunk, her mother a spendthrift. Lucy had attended finishing school abroad and knew D.C. society like the back of her hand. Possessed of a regal grace, she remained unbowed by her family's recent misfortunes. She was five foot nine, with thick, dark-blond hair, a flawless complexion, and dreamy blue eyes. One of Lucy's friends later said of her, "I think she was the most beautiful woman I ever saw. It was a beauty the artist and photographer didn't catch. Her beauty was in her expression and in her graceful manner." As her cousin said, "Every man who ever knew her fell in love with her."

Eleanor interviewed Lucy and hired her immediately. Three mornings a week, Lucy competently arranged Eleanor's appointments and handled her correspondence. And when the Roosevelts found they needed a charming woman to liven up their dinner parties, it was Lucy they invited.

When Franklin moved to Washington, he was no longer the cute college boy who had courted the gangly debutante Eleanor. He was now a vital, virile man of thirty-one. A Washington journalist wrote of him, "The face was particularly interesting. Breeding showed there, cleanly cut features, a small, sensitive mouth, tiny lines running from nostrils to the outline of his lips, broad forehead, close cropped brown hair, frank blue eyes, but above all the straight, upstanding set of the head placed on the man." Nigel Law, a secretary at the British embassy, said that Franklin was "the most attractive man whom it was my good fortune to meet during my four years in America." The Roosevelts' son Elliott wrote, "Men and women alike were impressed by the sheer physical magnetism of Father. On meeting anyone, the first impression he gave was of abounding energy and virility. He would leap over a rail rather than open a gate, run rather than walk."

Elliott claimed that after his brother John was born in 1916, Eleanor, who had given birth to six children in ten years (one had died), had had enough of unwelcome sex and even less welcome pregnancies. She announced to Franklin that she had done her part and would do no more. In this case, it is understandable that a virile man like Franklin would look elsewhere for sex. And he did not have to look very far.

For Lucy—lovely, feminine Lucy in her fashionable, feminine clothes—was and would forever be FDR's ideal woman. Like Franklin, she had a playful sense of humor and loved to laugh. Poor Eleanor rarely thought anything was funny. Lucy spoke in low, dulcet tones; hers was a voice that soothed. Eleanor's voice was high-pitched, insistent, each word fraught with earnest significance. Eleanor hectored him, irritated him. Lucy calmed him, made him laugh and enjoy himself. And, as events would prove, Franklin needed the company of cheerful, alluring women to relieve his stress. "Nothing is more pleasing to the eye than a good-looking lady," he later told a friend, "nothing more refreshing to the spirit than the company of one."

We do not know exactly when Franklin and Lucy's affair began, but it was certainly going on by mid-1916. Many of the wealthier men in Washington, D.C., sent their wives and families to the country for the summer to escape the devastating heat, while the men enjoyed "summer wives" in the city. FDR sent his family to the Roosevelt retreat on Campobello Island, in the Canadian province of New Brunswick. To Eleanor's repeated invitations to visit them, he begged off, citing his workload as he enjoyed a romance with Lucy. By June 1917—two months after the U.S. had joined the war—Franklin was once again suggesting Eleanor should take the children and go far, far away for the summer. It seems that by this time Eleanor had heard rumors. She fired Lucy, which just made matters worse because she immediately got a job in the Department of the Navy working directly for Franklin.

When Eleanor and the children were back at Campobello

that summer, Franklin and Lucy grew reckless; they were seen driving and sailing together, and Lucy visited him at his home, servants be damned. Alice Roosevelt Longworth, Teddy Roosevelt's malicious daughter, allowed the two to use her mansion as a trysting place. When a family member reproached her for aiding and abetting adultery, Alice quipped, "Franklin deserved a good time. He was married to Eleanor."

Although Lucy had received a promotion and a perfect job performance evaluation at the Department of the Navy, she was abruptly fired in the fall of 1917, probably because FDR's boss, the puritanical U.S. Navy Secretary Josephus Daniels, had heard rumors of the love affair. Eleanor must have been relieved Lucy would no longer work with FDR. Perhaps she naively assumed they no longer had any contact.

But then, a year later, she discovered his letters. It would prove to be the most calamitous blow of her life. Her devastation indicates she had not been aware of a full-blown sexual affair; maybe she thought it had only been a flirtation heading in that direction, a flirtation that was over. The letters showed her just how wrong she had been. We will never know exactly what was written because Eleanor destroyed them, she later told a library curator. But we can imagine the impassioned avowals of love, the references to ecstatic sex, the times they sneaked away to the houses of friends.

Eleanor's heart broke. All the self-loathing of her childhood came racing back, threatening to engulf her—she was ugly, she would never amount to anything, no man would ever want her. Her mother, her grandmother, Aunt Pussie—they had all been right. Her own friends and relatives in Washington had abetted the affair. They must all think her a fool. Even her servants, knowing FDR had brought Lucy to his bedroom, must have thought her a fool.

At first, Eleanor did nothing other than see to Franklin's recuperation. And then, once he was better, she showed him the letters. Franklin admitted that he loved Lucy and wanted a divorce so he could marry her. And Eleanor, furious and betrayed, agreed to give him his freedom. It was Sara Roosevelt who was aghast. She had never wanted him to marry the unprepossessing Eleanor in the first place, but now she was adamant that they remain together. While many society couples had lovers, divorce was a social stigma. If Franklin wanted to throw away his family and political career for Lucy, Sara couldn't prevent it. But she could cut him off without a dime. And Franklin liked his country clubs and pleasure boats, his first-class cruises to Europe and expensive suits. He had always sent his bills to his mother to pay. Plus, to obtain his divorce he would have to admit betraying his faithful wife, the mother of his five children—poison to his burgeoning political career.

Sadly, Franklin accepted that he could not divorce Eleanor. But now Eleanor had her own conditions for staying in the marriage: that he would never see or contact Lucy Mercer again, and that he would never try to bed Eleanor again. He agreed. But he would keep only one of those promises.

Eleanor must have been relieved he was staying. The gossip and finger-pointing would have been horrible to bear, the comparison of her plain looks and Lucy's beauty, of her humorless personality and Lucy's charming one. And it would have been too painful to see Franklin walk into his future blissfully wedded to Lucy. Still, Eleanor never forgave him. Their son James later said that his parents' marriage was "an armed truce that endured until the day he died."

When Eleanor accepted that her marriage would never be a happy one, she began to feel something growing inside her for the first time ever—strength. She had survived the ruin of all her hopes. She began to take charge of her household affairs, firing all the white servants Sara had hired—Sara said African Americans couldn't be trusted—and replacing them with African Americans.

She wrote, "I think I learned then that practically no one in this world is entirely bad or entirely good . . . I gained a certain assurance as to my ability to run things and the knowledge that there is joy in accomplishing a good job. I knew more about the human heart, which had been somewhat veiled in mystery up to now."

In 1919, Lucy began working for Winthrop Rutherfurd, a wealthy widower in his late fifties known as the "handsomest bachelor in society." Rutherfurd owned a thousand-acre estate in New Jersey, as well as stately homes in Washington, New York, and Paris. Lucy had known Rutherfurd, a fixture in Washington society, for several years, when he was happily married. Now, however, with six motherless young children to raise, the youngest of which was only two, he hired Lucy to help look after them. Predictably, the two were soon engaged. Winthrop "worshipped the ground she walked on," her niece recalled. A friend of Lucy's said, "He was desperately in love with her. He kissed her every time he saw her." Shortly before Lucy's February 1920 wedding, Franklin and Eleanor were having tea with guests when someone mentioned that Eleanor's former social secretary was going to marry Winthrop Rutherfurd. Franklin "started like a horse in fear of a hornet."

Clearly, Rutherfurd's money and social position were attractive to Lucy, who had been mired in genteel poverty for years. She was not in love with him—her heart would always belong to FDR—but she strove to be the best wife, hostess, and stepmother she could possibly be. Lucy's stepson said, "She was never a stepmother. I never considered her anything but my mother. She was a fantastic woman, beautiful and very loving. We all got along very well." Late in 1920, Lucy had her only biological child, Barbara.

Luckily for Franklin, now that Lucy was a wealthy, respectable matron, whispers of their affair would evaporate. Eleanor, too, must have sighed with relief. In the 1920 presidential election, Franklin was the Democratic vice presidential candidate running on the ticket of Ohio governor James Cox. But Republican Warren Harding took nearly twice the popular vote. After the election, FDR accepted a job as vice president of the New York office of the Fidelity and Deposit Company.

It was Eleanor who suggested that FDR temporarily employ a personal secretary to help him deal with the mounds of correspondence he had neglected during the campaign. He hired twenty-four-year-old Marguerite LeHand, a striking young woman whose poise and regal bearing belied her blue-collar Boston background. Missy—as she came to be known by the Roosevelt children who could not pronounce her name—was not beautiful, which must have comforted Eleanor somewhat. Her face was too long, her jaw and nose too prominent, and her thick, dark hair would turn prematurely gray. But she had grace, confidence, and charm. Slender and five foot seven, she wore beautiful, feminine clothing, often in a shade of inky blue that exactly matched her eyes.

One acquaintance described Missy's "lovely throaty voice and quick upturn of the face . . . lips parted in that strange secret smile composed of cunning influence, forever baffling." Missy was discreet, hardworking, competent, and possessed of a delightful sense of humor. She was, in short, exactly the charming female company that soothed and relaxed FDR. After she completed her temporary contract, FDR asked her to stay on.

In August 1921, FDR was vacationing at Campobello when he became ill with a high fever, extreme fatigue, and chills. A couple of days later, he could not move his legs and slipped into delirium. The horrifying diagnosis was polio. Yet FDR remained defiantly optimistic that he would walk again. He developed his upper body strength to an extraordinary degree; his biceps, shoulders, and chest bulged with new muscles even as his withered legs shrank down to bones. Six months after his attack, FDR weighed 182 pounds, almost all of it muscle in his upper body.

He pulled himself out of bed on a bar dangling from the ceiling and lowered himself into his wheelchair. In a sitting position, he pushed himself upstairs backward until he was drenched in sweat, then turned and flashed his concerned family a radiant smile. Instead of using a bulky wheelchair, he had a kitchen chair outfitted with wheels so he could move easily through the brownstone's narrow doors and passageways. He learned to heave himself from the wheelchair to a regular chair and back so swiftly it was barely noticeable. FDR's main fear was burning to death immobilized. Wherever he slept, he planned an escape route in the event of fire.

In 1923, he decided to live on a houseboat in Florida for extended periods of time with a small crew and a cook. Appalled at the laziness of such a life, Eleanor didn't join him, but Missy did. Together they swam, fished, and lay in the sun. When Franklin's friends visited, Missy played the hostess and often sat on the lap of "FD," as she called him, in a bathing suit. His son James said that Missy "filled a need and made him feel a man again, which Mother did not do." Given the total paralysis in his legs, we might wonder if FDR was impotent. But a decade later, three top doctors examined him and reported that his private parts were fully functional.

How could Eleanor, who had been so heartbroken about Lucy, leave her husband with Missy on the houseboat? Eleanor had changed. She no longer defined herself as a wife but as someone who wanted to make a difference in the world helping others. In a magazine article, she wrote, "If anyone were to ask me what I want out of life, I would say the opportunity for doing something useful, for in no other way, I am convinced, can true happiness be attained."

Eleanor was actually relieved that Missy was looking after Franklin. "Missy alleviated Mother's guilt," son Elliott explained years later. "Knowing Missy was always there allowed Mother to come and go as she pleased without worrying about Father or feeling she was neglecting her wifely duties." FDR's wife and mistress were on very friendly terms, frequently shopping together and going for long walks.

Franklin had not given up his dreams of a political life and stayed involved, from a distance, in the Democratic Party, supporting candidates and writing newspaper columns. He wanted to run for public office himself, of course, but he knew no one would vote for a "cripple." But what if they didn't know the extent of it: What if he appeared to be only somewhat lame? FDR practiced for months to develop a kind of pretend walking. He locked his hips and legs into heavy metal braces under his suit pants, leaned on his eldest son, and rotated his wasted legs out from the hips, giving the illusion of slow, awkward walking, but walking nonetheless. FDR accepted the opportunity to speak at the 1924 Democratic convention in Chicago and knew that if he fell on his way to the podium, his political career would be over. Sweat dropped off his chin as he agonizingly made his way forward. Reaching the podium, he flashed his dazzling grin to a cheering crowd. And in that moment of victorious, exhausting sweat equity, his political career was saved.

That autumn, FDR bought a dilapidated resort hotel in Georgia, eighty miles southwest of Atlanta. He dubbed it Warm Springs for the warm thermal pools where handicapped people could swim as physical therapy and where, for the first time in three years, he could move his toes. He renovated the property and created the Georgia Warm Springs Foundation, which would cover the costs of polio victims to visit the resort for treatment. Eleanor hated the place—the abject poverty of local African Americans, along with strict segregation and cruel Jim Crow laws depressed her—so again, FDR stayed there with Missy, apparently living as man and wife. He designed a car he could operate with his hands and found a mechanic to make the changes. Soon he was driving Missy all over the area, a picnic lunch stashed in the back.

Meanwhile, Eleanor had become friends with a lesbian couple, Nancy Cook and Marion Dickerman, who helped her come out of her shell. The three of them went hiking, swimming, and riding. In 1927, they founded Val-Kill Industries, a furniture factory on the Roosevelt Hyde Park estate ninety miles north of New York City to generate income for local farming families. FDR built the three a little cottage near Hyde Park, where the linens were embroidered with the initials "EMN," as if they were some kind of marital trio. Naturally, there was some talk about this unusual relationship. FDR called Nancy and Marion "shemales." Alice Roosevelt Longworth acidly referred to them as "female impersonators." Eleanor didn't care. For the first time in her life, she was having fun.

When she was separated from Nancy and Marion, Eleanor felt their absence keenly. "I feel I'd like to go off with you and forget the rest of the world existed," she wrote. The three of them bought the Todhunter School in New York, a private girls' school, where Eleanor taught U.S. history and English and American literature.

FDR continued to deliver keynote addresses at state and national Democratic conventions, swinging his legs forward across the stage as he leaned on his son's arm. By 1927, he was bored with the houseboat and wanted to get back into politics in a serious way. He soon got his wish: in October 1928, he was chosen as the Democratic candidate for governor of New York.

The main question going into the campaign was whether a person known to be lame could have a political future. When the *New York Post* criticized his selection for this very reason, the outgoing governor and Democratic presidential candidate Al Smith replied, "We do not elect him for his ability to do a double back flip or handspring. The work of the governorship is brain work. Ninety-five percent of it is accomplished sitting at a desk."

On November 6, 1928, Franklin was elected governor of New York by a tiny margin. On New Year's Day, 1929, when the Roosevelts moved into the governor's mansion in Albany, Eleanor assigned Missy LeHand a bedroom off Franklin's room. Elliott Roosevelt wrote, "It was no great shock to discover that Missy shared a familial life in all its aspects with Father. What did surprise us was the later knowledge that Mother knew, too, and accepted the situation as a fact of life like the rest of us."

James Roosevelt, who disagreed with his brother's statement that the two were having an affair, wrote, "Elliott makes a lot of Missy being seen entering or leaving Father's room in her nightclothes, but was she supposed to dress to the teeth every time she was summoned at midnight? None of us thought anything of it." Though we can wonder why FDR summoned Missy at midnight.

Eleanor was not happy about being the first lady of New York State and was often absent, but she began to stay closer to home when she developed a crush on Franklin's handsome bodyguard, State Trooper Earl Miller. They went riding and swimming together and on camping trips with friends. They gave each other back massages at the pool and held hands. Was it a friendship? A flirtation? A sexual affair? Eleanor was a plain woman of forty-four, Earl a gorgeous, muscled thirty-two.

In his memoirs, James Roosevelt wrote, "I believe there may have been one real romance in Mother's life outside of marriage. Mother may have had an affair with Earl Miller . . . Victorian as Mother may have been, she was a woman, too, who suffered from her separation from Father." Franklin, who was no idiot, must have noticed how close Eleanor and Earl had become. But, James said, "He did not seem to mind." In the 1970s, the elderly Marion Dickerman told a historian that Eleanor had written her that she was going to leave Franklin and go off with Earl. Apparently, duty prevailed, or perhaps Earl objected. In 1932, he married a seventeen-year-old.

In two years as governor, Franklin built roads and hospitals and regulated public utilities to put money in the pockets of the public rather than in the pockets of rich industrialists. He gave frequent talks on the radio about the state of New York and what he was doing to improve it. Then, only ten months into office, the stock market crash of October 1929 presaged the Great Depression.

Soon, one American in three was jobless. FDR created a state program, the Temporary Emergency Relief Administration (TERA), to provide food, clothing, and shelter for the destitute, the first time that impoverished people could seek help from the government rather than charitable institutions. He asked the brightest minds at universities for advice in combatting the worsening economic situation. FDR radiated hope, confidence, energy, and new ideas. He was reelected in 1930 by a margin thirty times that of 1928. On July 2, 1932, he was chosen as the Democratic presidential candidate, running against President Herbert Hoover.

When it came to dealing with the Depression, Hoover was the one who was truly paralyzed, unwilling for the federal government to intervene in the nation's precipitous economic slide. By 1932, more than five thousand banks had failed. Bank foreclosures on homes were up to one thousand per day. Thirty-four out of forty-eight states had shut down their banks, meaning the public had no access to their funds. People couldn't buy gas and, when it ran out, just abandoned their cars in the middle of the road. Journalist Joseph Alsop recalled driving along Manhattan's East River and seeing people, "mostly respectable-looking older men and women, climbing precariously about on the enormous dumps in the hope of finding bits of edible garbage." FDR campaigned energetically, offering exciting new ideas to put people back to work. Hoover rejected those ideas, counseling starving, homeless people to be patient. He was heckled and bombarded with eggs and rotten fruit.

Neither FDR's wife nor his mistress wanted him to become president. Missy resigned herself to it. Eleanor, however, was almost hysterical at the thought of becoming "a prisoner in the White House, forced onto a treadmill of formal receptions, openings, dedications, teas, official dinners." Nancy Dickerman was convinced "she won't do it. She'll run away with Earl Miller . . . She'll file for divorce."

Back in 1887, when Franklin was five, his father took him to visit Grover Cleveland in the White House. The president came out of his office, clearly exhausted, patted Franklin on the head and said, "My little man, I am making a strange wish for you. It is that you may never be President of the United States." Grover Cleveland's wish did not come true. FDR won the election with the biggest electoral lead up to that time. He received seven million votes more than Hoover, won 42 of the 48 states, and took 472 electoral college votes while Hoover received only fifty-nine.

That night, as twenty-four-year-old James Roosevelt helped his father into bed, FDR said, "All my life I have only been afraid of one thing—fire. Tonight I am afraid of something else. I'm afraid I may not have the strength to do this job."

But Franklin—bursting with plans to stop the run on banks and the foreclosures of homes and farms—had to cool his heels a frustrating four months between the election and the inauguration. The Founding Fathers had chosen November as the month for presidential elections as the harvest was in and the roads had not yet become icy, which presented a danger for horses and buggies. Starting with George Washington's second inaugural in 1793, inauguration day was always March 4. There were two reasons for this four-month delay between the election and inauguration; the first involved the time it took to hand count the votes and then send messengers with the tabulations riding around the country. By that time, winter was setting in, and everyone wanted to wait for the March thaw to travel to the inauguration. Even with the advent of improved vote tallying and transportation by the early twentieth century, the March 4 date remained because it had become a historic tradition. But in the winter of 1932, Americans literally starved to death on the streets of Washington as Herbert Hoover glided by in his big black limousine, unmoved.

In 1937, FDR would successfully push for the Twentieth Amendment to the Constitution, changing the inaugural date to January 20.

On March 4, 1933, a black limousine picked up Lucy Mercer Rutherfurd from her sister's house on Q Street, NW, in Washington, D.C., and drove her to the inauguration. Sitting next to her husband, Eleanor had no idea that Lucy was in the huge audience, watching the man she still loved become president of the United States.

As soon as he took office, FDR instructed White House switchboard operators to accept calls from a Mrs. Paul Johnson, a code name for Lucy. The two went for long drives when the first lady was out of town. Eleanor was unaware that her husband was breaking his 1918 promise never to contact Lucy again. She was embarking on a love affair of her own. Lorena Hickok—known as Hick—was the nation's top female journalist and covered the presidential campaign in the fall of 1932 for the Associated Press. Foreseeing that Eleanor would be a first lady unlike any other, she worked hard to win her trust. Eleanor's usual reserve melted when she realized that she and Hick had some things in common. Hick, too, had had a Dickensian childhood, though hers had been the truly impoverished version. Abused by her violent father and kicked out of the house by her wicked stepmother at fourteen, Hick scrubbed floors to support herself. She managed to graduate high school with top grades and attend college for two years before joining the *Battle Creek Journal* as a nineteen-year-old cub reporter in 1912.

Most women journalists of the time wrote about society parties and fashion. Those wanting to cover news and politics had to be fiercely competitive and tough as nails. Hick worked her way up to become the AP New York City bureau chief by the time she was thirty-five, writing articles on politics and crime. At five foot eight, Hick weighed two hundred pounds. She had a wide, friendly face, a beautiful complexion, and wore the requisite skirt, makeup, and earrings when on the job. Off the job, however, she wore men's clothes, smoked cigars, played poker, swore like a sailor, and drank the men under the table with bootleg bourbon. Immensely popular, Hick was kindhearted, outspoken, and emotional.

During the campaign, Eleanor would frequently dismiss the other reporters and socialize alone with Hick. They ate dinner together, went to the theater, and spoke on the phone often. The afternoon after the inauguration, White House servants were confused when Eleanor, who had been giving Hick an interview in the sitting room, took her into the bathroom to conclude it. One maid who witnessed it wrote, "It was hardly the kind of thing one would do with an ordinary reporter. Or even with an adult friend." Later, Eleanor explained that they had retired to the bathroom because they kept getting interrupted.

The true nature of Eleanor and Hick's relationship did not come to light until 1979 when former *New York Times* reporter Doris Faber was researching Eleanor Roosevelt's letters at the Roosevelt Library in Hyde Park. There she found some two thousand letters between the women that had just been made available to the public, and apparently Faber was the first researcher to read them. Late in life, Eleanor had returned Hick's letters to her, entrusting her with both sides of the correspondence. Hick apparently destroyed the most sexually explicit letters but gave the rest to the library on the condition they not be released for ten years after her death.

Soon after the inauguration, Hick returned to her job in New York. The same day, Eleanor wrote, "Hick my dearest, I cannot go to bed without a word to you. I felt a little as though part of me was leaving tonight, you have grown so much to be a part of my life . . . Oh! I want to put my arms around you, I ache to hold you close . . . My pictures are nearly all up & I have you in my sitting room where I can look at you most of my waking hours! I can't kiss you so I kiss your picture good night & good morning . . . I miss you so much and I love you so much & please never apologize . . . Oh! I wanted to put my arms around you in reality instead of spirit. I went & kissed your photograph instead & tears were in my eyes."

Hick wrote Eleanor, "I remember your eyes, with a kind of teasing smile in them and the feeling of that soft spot just northeast of the corner of your mouth against my lips. I wonder what we'll do when we meet—what we'll say."

Eleanor wrote, "Dearest, it was a lovely weekend . . . Each time we have together <u>that</u> way—brings us closer, doesn't it."

Separation was painful. Moreover, Hick realized she no longer had journalistic impartiality when covering Eleanor. She resigned from the AP in the summer of 1933 and took a three-week road trip with Eleanor—and no Secret Service—to Quebec in a Plymouth roadster convertible. After the trip, Hick moved into the White House. Eleanor gave her a small bedroom in the second-floor family quarters and arranged a job for her at the Women's Division of the Democratic National Committee. Lillian Parks, now a seamstress in the White House, recalled many occasions when "Hicky, as we all called her behind her back, slept in the First Lady's bedroom suite, on the daybed in her sitting room. Supposedly, the reason was that there were so many guests."

Hick became a source of friction between FDR and Eleanor. Lillian said, "When the Roosevelts first arrived in 1933, there was a short honeymoon stage around the White House when Hick was an open guest, welcomed by the President, joining the family for dinner. But eventually, so the *sub rosa* story went, he got the drift and feared the situation could give the White House a bad reputation. The President was heard raising his voice to Eleanor, telling her, 'I want that woman kept out of this house.' That woman meant too much to Eleanor, and instead of keeping her out of the house, she simply kept her out of FDR's sight."

Franklin, who loved feminine women in pastel chiffon swishing around him in a cloud of delicate perfume, couldn't stand the sight of Hick stomping around in men's clothes chewing on a cigar. He put up with her as much as he did because he knew it made Eleanor happy.

Missy LeHand also lived in the White House, in a room on the third floor. As in the governor's mansion in Albany, servants became accustomed to seeing her in and out of the president's suite at all hours clad only in a nightgown and robe. Initially, White House staff were confused by this four-way living arrangement. "What goes?" one servant asked. "FDR was spending his evenings with Missy LeHand, while Eleanor Roosevelt was spending evenings with Lorena Hickok."

Lillian Parks wrote, "After you accepted the situation, there was no shock in seeing Missy come to FDR's suite at night in her nightgown and robe or sitting on his lap in the Oval study." She added, "A man has no secrets from his valet. The valets knew there was nothing incomplete about FDR's love life." His only concern during sex, she said, was that "he just didn't want anything heavy pushing on his legs."

Odd though the servants found the living arrangements, they soon grew to love Missy LeHand, who was "sunshine and laughter," Lillian Parks recalled. Realizing her significance in the president's life, "When Missy gave an order we responded as if it had come from the First Lady . . . We really had two mistresses in the White House." The servants concluded "that Missy was the substitute wife, and we honored her for it . . . As we saw it at the White House, Missy gave him the companionship, the rapt attention, the ego building boost that men sometimes find in their wives. Mrs. Roosevelt was not the kind of woman who would give blind praise or blanket approval. For that kind of warm support and recognition, no matter what he did, the President turned to Missy."

Eleanor—in a position now to do something truly useful—crusaded for racial justice, decent wages and housing, women's equality, and a host of other social issues. Hick persuaded her to hold regular press conferences—often open only to female reporters to encourage papers to employ more women—and write articles that became a nationally syndicated column, *My Day*. A blur of action, Eleanor would race out of the White House clutching her flower-bedecked hat, tumble into a waiting limo, and ask, "Where am I going?" Often, she burst into her husband's presence with a list of important tasks he must do—immediately—just when he was hoping to relax.

The Roosevelts' daughter, Anna—called Sis by the family—recalled an evening when Missy was mixing cocktails for Franklin and a few friends when Eleanor arrived in high-hectoring mode. "She came in and sat down across the desk from Father. And she had a sheaf of papers this high and she said, 'Now Franklin, I want to talk to you about this.' I just remember, like lightning, that I thought, 'Oh God, he's going to blow.' And sure enough, he blew his top. He took every single speck of that whole pile of papers, threw them across the desk at me and said, 'Sis, you handle these tomorrow morning.' She just got up. She was the most controlled person in the world. And she just stood there half a second and said, 'I'm sorry . . .' Intuitively I understood that here was a man plagued with God knows how many problems and right now he had twenty minutes to have two cocktails . . . He wanted to tell stories and relax and enjoy himself—period. I don't think Mother had the slightest realization. She could pester the hell out of him."

Though he lost his temper with Eleanor's pushiness, Franklin appreciated her efforts to help the less fortunate and often ended up doing exactly what she wanted. Sometimes, when he tried to give her a big old hug, "She would recoil and back away," according to Lillian Parks. White House usher J. B. West said he "never saw Eleanor and Franklin Roosevelt in the same room alone together. They had the most separate relationship I have ever seen between man and wife." James Roosevelt said that there were "several occasions I was to observe in which he in one way or another held out his arms to Mother, and she refused flatly to enter his embrace."

While White House servants were surprised at the Roosevelts' domestic arrangements, they were delighted with their warmth and generosity. The day the Roosevelts moved in, the servants were shocked to see Eleanor carrying chairs and stacks of books, pitching in to help the moving men. That day at lunch, she helped the butlers serve the guests. Lillian recalled, "All the changes Mrs. Roosevelt made were for the comfort of other people—for example, she assigned a nice dining room for the help, and a room to lie down in if you were ill."

Former first lady Lou Hoover had actually used hand signals to instruct servants when to move or not move, when to speak and not speak, as if they were dogs. Strangely, the Hoovers also demanded that servants remain unseen. When the president or first lady was coming, a bell would ring and all the servants would jump into broom closets—maids with mops and buckets, butlers holding trays over their heads—all of them squeezed in together so the Hoovers would not see them. Outside, when the bell rang, gardeners wielding hedge clippers dived into bushes. FDR and Eleanor were mystified to hear bells ring and see servants throwing themselves into closets and bushes. They put a stop to the practice immediately.

Eleanor brought homeless men she found in nearby parks to the White House for dinner. The staff cleaned them up as best they could before they sat down with the president and first lady, and sometimes they stole the silver, but the Roosevelts didn't care. FDR had other worries. Knowing that the White House was a firetrap, he had the Secret Service install special chutes to get him out of his bedroom window and down to the ground in record time. His agents held regular drills.

At first, Eleanor was miserable in her new role. She wrote to Hick, "I know I've got to stick. I know I'll never make an open break & I never tell FDR how I feel. Darling I do take happiness in many ways & I'm never likely to fight with F. I always shut up." In another letter, Eleanor wrote Hick, "I realize FDR is a great man, & he was nice to me but as a person, I'm a stranger and don't want to be anything else."

Franklin and Eleanor were fortunate that the press continued to maintain a patriotic silence about their private lives. In 1933, journalist Raymond Clapper wrote in his diary that gossip about FDR's continuing affair with Lucy Mercer Rutherfurd "buzzed around Washington," yet nary a word was printed. Journalists also heard of just how private a private secretary Missy LeHand was. They reported the almost telepathic closeness of FDR and Missy and stopped there. Additionally, FDR's paralysis was seen as a state secret. Knowing he could control the press, he often said, as cameras rolled when he was being lifted out of his wheelchair and deposited in his car, "No movies of me getting out of the machine, boys."

Those who were clueless enough to take such pictures often found their cameras knocked from their hands, lying broken on the pavement with a roll of exposed film. No newspaper would print such a photograph. A story about the president's love affairs or his paralysis might have derailed his efforts to heave the country out of the Depression. By the time the U.S. joined World War II, it would have been seen as nothing less than treason. When, after his death, the American people learned the extent of FDR's paralysis, they were shocked.

As soon as Franklin was inaugurated, he began issuing legislation that Congress readily passed. The first step was to restore confidence in the banks. His initial bill would reopen the banks under Treasury Department licenses that guaranteed them. If a bank had insufficient cash, the Federal Reserve Board would lend the bank the money it needed. In his first fireside chat on March 12, he said, "I want to talk for a few minutes . . . about banking. When the people find out that they can get their money—that they can get it when they want it—the phantom of fear will soon be laid . . . I can assure you that it is safer to keep your money in a reopened bank than under the mattress." The following morning, the long lines in front of banks had vanished. In fact, people soon formed lines to put their money back into the banks.

He also addressed the crisis of farm mortgages, thousands of which had been foreclosed on, telling Congress, "At the same time that you and I are joining in emergency action to bring order to our banks, I deem it of equal importance to take other and simultaneous steps . . . One of these seeks to increase the purchasing power of our farmers and at the same time greatly relieve the pressure of farm mortgages . . ." Franklin allocated $2 billion for the plan, which utilized federal credit agencies to refinance farm mortgages at 4.5 percent—far lower than what farmers had been paying—with far more time to pay.

Another of FDR's first efforts to lessen the grip of the Depression was to end Prohibition. Only eighteen days after taking office, on March 22, 1933, he signed an act allowing the manufacture of beer and wine. The Eighteenth Amendment enacting Prohibition was repealed entirely in December, allowing the manufacture of hard liquor. In the depths of the Depression, the government needed the revenue from the sale of alcohol, which before Prohibition had been 14 percent of all federal, state, and local revenue. Just as important, repeal stimulated employment and the economy. Breweries, wineries, and bars opened back up. Across the country, restaurants did a booming business again. And, with some booze in them, Americans just generally felt more optimistic.

FDR created many new federal agencies to buoy the American economy: the Federal Deposit Insurance Corporation, the Federal Housing Administration, the Tennessee Valley Authority, the Social Security Administration, the Public Works Administration, and the Securities and Exchange Commission. Public money went to hire the unemployed and build much-needed infrastructure such as schools, hospitals, sewers, roads, parks, and government buildings. In 1933, four thousand banks failed, most before he took office. In 1934, only nine banks failed. Over the course of FDR's first term, the number of unemployed dropped by a third. American businesses, which had lost $2 billion in 1932, made $5 billion in profits in 1936. In the 1936 presidential election, FDR won 46 out of 48 states and swept the electoral college by 523 votes to 8.

Before the reelection, the relationship of Eleanor and Hick had begun to cool as Eleanor became a national figure with less and less time for her personal life. Deeply hurt, Hick became jealous and demanding, which just drove Eleanor further away. "You have a feeling for me that I may not return in kind," Eleanor warned. Hick moved out of the White House and on to other relationships with women. She would move back into her old room from 1941 to 1945 as she wasn't earning much money and had nowhere else to go. Eleanor, though no longer in love with Hick, would always look out for her.

FDR dreamed of buying a Florida Key and opening up a fishing resort after his second term. Yet, when the time came, he felt his work wasn't done, particularly with war raging in Europe. He ran and won an unprecedented third term, defeating the Republican candidate by five million votes. With Eleanor off saving the world, he spent more time with Lucy who, at fifty, was still beautiful. White House staff recalled that FDR would return from their long drives "relaxed and happy." Missy LeHand, who knew what FDR was doing every minute of the day, must have been devastated.

She had devoted her entire life to Franklin Roosevelt. Attractive, personable, and certainly well connected, Missy had received a great deal of male attention over the years and dated a few men. But when a friend asked her if she wanted to marry, Missy replied, "Absolutely not. How could anyone measure up to FD?"

Lucy wasn't Missy's only rival for FDR's love. When the glamorous thirty-seven-year-old Princess Märtha of Norway fled Hitler's takeover of her country in 1940, Franklin offered her and her three young children sanctuary at the White House. The princess joined FDR for cocktails, accompanied him on long drives in the countryside, laughed and flirted with him. When she moved to an estate nearby, FDR visited her there. Then there was Margaret Suckley, known as Daisy, FDR's sixth cousin, who saw him frequently. Nine years his junior, she became a close confidante, possibly more. FDR instructed Daisy to burn his letters, and we can only wonder why.

By 1941, Missy, aged forty-three, had devoted twenty years of her life to Franklin. Now she found herself just one of many women in his life, and not even the favorite. "I don't think she ever felt that she was his great heart's desire," Elliott Roosevelt said. "She was too honest with herself for that."

In 1941, Missy—who had always been so cool, calm, and efficient—uncharacteristically began throwing shocking temper tantrums. On June 10, 1941, at a White House dinner for staff, after FDR rolled himself up to bed Missy fell to the floor with a minor stroke. Seventeen days later she had a major one, paralyzing her entire right side and robbing her of the power of speech forever. Franklin changed his will so Missy would receive half his estate, should he die before her, to pay for her medical care. As it turned out, Missy died on July 31, 1944, aged forty-seven. FDR's grandson Curtis Roosevelt, who grew up in the White House, concluded, "I think it's not entirely speculative to tie Missy's eventual breakdowns to her frustration with the fact that she was in love with somebody who was probably not in love with her."

With Missy out of the picture, FDR saw more of Lucy than ever, in the White House and out, sometimes for two or three hours at a time. His divorced daughter, Anna, moved into the White House to take over Missy's social tasks—mixing drinks and entertaining visitors—and one day walked into the Oval Office to find a strange woman on her knees massaging the president's wasted legs. Franklin grinned at Anna and introduced "my old friend, Mrs. Winthrop Rutherfurd." He made her promise not to tell her mother. She didn't.

On March 19, 1944, Winthrop Rutherfurd died, aged eighty-two, after several years of illness. Lucy told James Roosevelt's first wife that "although she loved Winthrop Rutherfurd and owed him much, FDR had nonetheless been the love of her life."

After the U.S. had entered World War II in 1941, Roosevelt calmed and inspired the country with his frequent radio addresses. But the stress of running a nation in a world war clearly affected his health. By 1943, he was gray-faced and seemed shrunken in oversized clothing. Sometimes his breathing was labored, and he started a sentence only to forget what he was going to say. His doctor discovered he was suffering from severe hypertension; his blood pressure was 210 over 120, his arteries were hardening, and the left ventricle of his heart failing. He was, in short, dying. As with Woodrow Wilson's hypertension forty years earlier, physicians could diagnose high blood pressure, but had no means of treating it other than advising rest and relaxation. And FDR couldn't jaunt off to Bermuda; he was planning the D-Day invasion.

Realizing how ill her father was and the tremendous stress he was under, Anna decided to assist his romance, even if it meant betraying her mother. She facilitated Lucy's visits and often joined her father and his mistress for cocktails and dinner. Anna said that Lucy's visits "were occasions which I welcomed for my father because they were light-hearted and gay, affording a few hours of much needed relaxation for a loved father and world leader in a time of crisis."

By the fall of 1944, FDR knew he was a dying man. He also knew he had to see the war to its end, and then, possibly, he could resign. Announcing his decision to seek a fourth term of office, he said, "All that is within me cries out to go back to my home on the Hudson River, but the future existence of the nation and the future existence of our chosen form of government are at stake."

In early April 1945, FDR arrived in Warm Springs for some rest and relaxation. His cousin Daisy Suckley was there, along with another cousin, Laura Delano. On April 9, Lucy arrived with a portrait painter named Madame Elizabeth Shoumatoff, who was to paint the president, and a photographer, Nicholas Robbins, who would photograph him for Shoumatoff. On the morning of April 12, FDR sat at a card table he used as a desk in his living room, reading documents as the artist painted him. He said, "We have got just about fifteen minutes more to work."

Suddenly, FDR's head slumped forward, and his hands shook violently. He put his left hand to the back of his head and said, "I have a terrific pain in the back of my head." He had just had a massive stroke. Lucy knew she needed to get out of there immediately, before the press arrived. As doctors attended him, she threw her clothes in a bag and, sobbing, raced out of the resort with the artist and photographer. She later learned he was pronounced dead at 3:35 p.m. He was sixty-two.

After his death, Eleanor discovered he had been seeing Lucy all along. In time, she forgave her daughter, Anna, for arranging the meetings, and she came to forgive her husband, as well. "The act of being physically unfaithful seems much less important to the average man," she said, and a man finds it "hard to understand why the woman he loves looks upon it as all important. He might have been happier with a wife who was completely uncritical. That, I was never able to be, and he had to find it in other people." Of Lucy she said, "She deserves forgiveness as much as anyone." Looking back, Eleanor described herself as "pig-headed" and said, "If only I had found the courage to talk to Franklin. I should have said, 'Let's bury this whole matter and begin over again together.'" Recalling how she had badgered him, she said, "I felt akin to a hair shirt."

Daisy Suckley best summed up the Roosevelt marriage. "Poor Eleanor Roosevelt, I believe she loved him more deeply than she knows herself, and his feeling for her was deep & lasting," she said. "That fact that they could not relax together, or play together, is the tragedy of their joint lives, for I believe, from everything that I have seen of them, that they had everything else in common. It was probably a matter of personalities, of a certain lack of humor on her part—I cannot blame either of them."

Eleanor continued to travel, write, and lecture for social justice. She became a delegate for the United Nations General Assembly in December 1945 and chairperson for the UN Commission on Human Rights the following April. She made sure that Hick, who had diabetes and was going blind, had enough money to live on and moved her to a cottage on the Roosevelts' Hyde Park estate to be close to her. In 1947, at sixty-three, Eleanor fell in love one last time with an attractive, forty-five-year-old doctor, Dave Gurewitsch, whom she engaged as her personal physician. He accompanied Eleanor on thirteen international trips she made for the United Nations. Eleanor wrote or called him almost every single day. "I'm glad you love me," she gushed in one missive. "I love you dearly and send you my most devoted thoughts," and "I love you as I have never loved anyone else." She kept his photo on her bedside table, and she insisted that he was "the love of her life." She knew he would eventually marry a young, pretty woman, and he did. The three of them moved into a Manhattan town house where they lived in separate apartments but saw one another often. Eleanor Roosevelt died November 7, 1962, aged seventy-eight. Hick survived her by six years and died at seventy-five.

Lucy Mercer Rutherfurd lost FDR, her mother, and her sister, who committed suicide, in the space of three years. Perhaps it was too much for her to bear. In the spring of 1948, she was diagnosed with leukemia, which quickly advanced. Living her last weeks on morphine, she died in July, at fifty-seven.

"As far as emotions were concerned," Anna Roosevelt said, "Lucy was Father's emotion for life."

8

DWIGHT EISENHOWER OUT OF PRACTICE IN LOVE

A World War II hero who successfully invaded France and Germany, and a two-term president, Eisenhower was known for exuding the quintessential American spirit: optimism, integrity, duty, and determination. The American public had no idea until after his death that during the war, Eisenhower fell deeply in love with his driver and aide.

* * *

Things are never the way you think they'll be. At least, that was what Kay Summersby discovered when she finally found herself in the arms of General Dwight D. Eisenhower in his London town house in January 1944. Their intimacy had grown slowly but surely since the fall of 1942 when she first became his driver. Working twelve- and fourteen-hour days together, seven days a week, to save the Free World had resulted first in mutual respect, then fondness and, finally, love. Ike had confessed his feelings for her eight months earlier, and she had enthusiastically responded, but theirs had remained a chaste relationship, a squeeze of the hand, a stolen kiss.

Now, their passion knew no bounds. "Our ties came off," Kay wrote in her 1975 autobiography. "Our jackets came off. Buttons were unbuttoned. It was as if we were frantic. And we were."

They kissed and groped and moaned, enjoying—finally— the tantalizing sensation of skin against skin. She waited to feel him inside her. And waited. But General Eisenhower—supreme commander of the Allied Forces—couldn't command his penis to rise to the occasion. Perhaps it was age-related erectile dysfunction. After all, he was a chain-smoking, whiskey-belting, fifty-three-year-old bundle of stress upon whose shoulders rested the salvation of mankind. Or perhaps it was his old-fashioned values of honor and integrity. When it came right down to it, he just couldn't betray his wife.

Whatever the case, there they were naked. With nothing to do.

"This was not what I had expected," Kay wrote, and we can imagine that was an understatement. "Wearily, we slowly calmed down. He snuggled his face into the hollow between my neck and shoulder and said, 'Oh, God, Kay, I'm sorry. I'm not going to be any good for you.'

"You're good enough for me," she insisted. "What you need is some sleep."

Perhaps, as Kay looked under the couch for her bra, she reflected on the long, strange path that led her to that moment of unbearable embarrassment. It had all been Hitler's fault. On September 2, 1939, the day after Great Britain declared war on Germany, the thirty-one-year-old decided to forge a new path in life. Daughter of a wealthy Irish landowner, in 1936 she had married a handsome young publisher in London's social set and found a life of constant partying soul-numbing. They soon separated.

Kay became a model for the Worth fashion house and found that equally stultifying. With war in the offing, her family begged her to return to the safety of County Cork, but Kay could not see spending the war "sitting on a horse properly and pouring tea correctly," as she wrote. She wanted to make a difference, to offer something of substance to people in need. An excellent driver in a time when most women didn't have driver's licenses, she decided to become a London ambulance driver. Within months, the Blitz began. And she got more than she bargained for.

She described it as "living, driving, and working in a bomb-made hell where blood and death were as commonplace as a cigarette . . . Driving ambulances loaded with bodies, the stench of burnt flesh, being turned away by morgue after morgue with 'Sorry, we're full' . . . A cinema with the lights on but the front row stalls filled with bodies, all headless . . ." She kept a flask of whiskey with her to mask the taste of dead flesh in her mouth.

Kay was skilled at driving in blackouts and the thick yellow fog which periodically crouched over the city. What's more, all the street signs in Britain had been removed to confuse any German troops who might invade. Ambulance drivers needed a photographic memory of every street in London.

When the United States joined the Allies after Pearl Harbor in December 1941, a host of American military bigwigs arrived in London, and their drivers got hopelessly lost even in the cold, clear light of day. The solution was to provide them with British ambulance drivers. Kay was assigned to drive General Dwight Eisenhower—known as Ike—when he arrived in London in May 1942. She recalled their first meeting when their eyes locked. "Brilliant blue eyes. Sandy hair—but not very much of it. A fair, ruddy complexion. A nice face—not conventionally handsome, but strong, and, I thought, very American. Certainly very appealing. And I succumbed immediately to that grin that was to become so famous."

What did Ike see when he first met his new driver? A trim, shapely brunette five foot eight inches tall, with a wide forehead, high cheekbones, and a strong jaw. Though pretty, to be sure, her most attractive feature was the light in her face, an expression of alert intelligence, competence, and good humor ready to bubble up into laughter.

And laugh she did at the shocking informality of the Americans. When she drove Eisenhower and one of his senior commanders, Major General Mark Clark, they would eat boiled cabbages for lunch, start farting in the car, and roll down the windows as they howled with laughter. Ike often invited her to join him for lunch, something a British senior officer would never do. He even invited her mother. As she waited in his office all day for him to order the car around, she pitched in answering the phone and making his appointments. Soon she became an invaluable aide.

Focused on winning the war, Eisenhower hated wasting time attending social events. As a down-to-earth American, he ridiculed "all that la-di-da" of London's upper crust. After one reception, he slid into the car and told Kay, "I don't think my blood pressure can take it if one more silly woman calls me 'My deeaaah general.' I'm nobody's goddamned 'deeaaah general,' and I'm not fighting this war over teacups."

He hated his hotel suite, too, in the lavish Claridge's. He thought the black-and-gold sitting room "looks like a goddamned fancy funeral parlor," and the bedroom was decorated in "whorehouse pink. Makes me feel as if I'm living in sin." He hated the noise and crowds of London, and whenever he walked outside, people stopped and stared at him. Or asked him about the war. Or saluted. "I'm a captive," he complained. "I can't even go for a walk without starting a parade."

As Eisenhower, stressed and harried, planned the first Allied invasion against Hitler's armies, he needed a homelike atmosphere where he could truly relax. He moved out of the hotel and into Telegraph Cottage, a Victorian five-bedroom, mock-Tudor home in a ten-acre park. Only a forty-minute drive from London and minutes from Bushy Park, the U.S. Army Air Forces headquarters, Telegraph Cottage offered privacy away from the crowds and noise of London. The general and his male aides stayed there three or four nights a week, while Kay had a room with a nearby family. Together, Eisenhower's "family" cooked, drank, played bridge, and practiced their golf swings in the garden.

Kay wrote, "In the middle of a vast world war, the commanding general had managed to establish a happy home in that precarious calm of the eye of the storm."

Kay felt that one thing only was missing to make Telegraph Cottage the perfect home. One day, as she was driving the general, she remarked, "I miss having a dog. We always had dogs around the house." She talked about her favorite, a Scottie named MacTavish.

"Kay, would you like a dog?" Ike asked. "Another Scottie?"

She braked the car suddenly. "Would I like a dog? Oh, General, having a dog would be heaven!"

"Well," he said with a grin, "if you want one, we'll get one. I think I can manage that. I'd like to do something for you for working all these crazy hours and everything." Eisenhower knew tongues would wag if it got out that he had given his attractive female driver a dog, so he pretended it was for him. He named the black Scottie puppy Telek, a combination of Telegraph Cottage and Kay, "two parts of my life that make me very happy," he said.

Telek was presented to Ike at his birthday dinner, wearing a big red bow, as the general's wartime family toasted his health. After dinner, Kay and Ike found themselves alone in front of the fire having a drink, as they so often did, the puppy asleep in Ike's lap. "Thank you, Kay," he said, "for bringing so much gaiety into my life. I don't know what I'd do without you." From that time on, Telek accompanied them almost everywhere.

Kay met numerous celebrities during the war. She dined periodically with Prime Minister Winston Churchill in the basement of 10 Downing Street—the upstairs had been bombed. Churchill was "a menace at the table," Kay recalled. "His manners were atrocious. He would slurp his soup, spill things, pick up food with his fingers. He would pick his nose while listening to the rare person who managed to get a word in edgewise and would quite uninhibitedly unzip his siren suit to scratch his crotch. Make sweeping gestures while telling a story and knock glasses and pitchers to the floor. Pay no attention whatsoever to what he had done and keep talking as servants raced to clean up the mess. All these possibly purposeful gaucheries seemed trivial when he started talking. He had the most fabulous command of the English language. I could have listened to him forever."

One day, Kay gave U.S. general George Patton a tour of London. As she pointed out bombed ruins of a school, an apartment building, or a shop, he would say, "The bastards! The dirty mother-fucking bastards!" and apologize immediately. "Excuse me, Miss Summersby. I beg your pardon. My tongue ran away with me." Seconds later he would erupt in expletives again. "The sonsabitches! The bloody sonsabitches!" And apologize again.

Kay drove King George VI of Great Britain, who usually didn't talk, and later, FDR, who insisted on holding Telek in his lap. When he found a good place for a picnic, the U.S. president asked, "Won't you come back here, child, and have lunch with a dull old man?" She wrote, "FDR was enjoying himself immensely, laughing and telling stories. He had the gift of putting a person completely at ease, and I soon got over my awe of him and was chatting away as if I had known him all my life."

Kay also met entertainers who came to perform for the troops. Vivien Leigh, whom she found more beautiful in person than she had been in *Gone with the Wind*. Bob Hope. Noël Coward. Her hobnobbing with celebrities disturbed her fiancé, U.S. Army Lieutenant Colonel Dick Arnold, who rarely saw her.

"My God," he said one day, "you know all those top generals, the ones the rest of us only hear about. And Winston Churchill calls you Kay."

"It's only because it's my job," she said. "It has nothing to do with me."

Dick shook his head and said, "You know, when the war is over and we are living in the States, you won't be associating with prime ministers and three-star generals."

Kay knew this to be true, but she also found it impossible to envision life after the war. Though she and Dick were wrapping up their divorces and expected to marry the following summer, she "simply could not imagine leading any other life. I was completely caught up in the moment. I loved Dick. I really did. But at the moment, I felt closer to Ike. It was not a time for love, I felt. We all had a mission that was far more important than our personal lives and desires."

Thirty years later, as Kay lay dying of cancer, she looked back on the war and saw things with the twenty-twenty clarity of hindsight. Those fighting the war, she wrote, existed "in their own special dimension. Their preoccupation is so great, their commitment so complete, their energies so all-absorbed that it is as if their days were being lived out in a tunnel . . . They are people apart . . . This knowledge was something that the General and I shared. His own family was far away. He rarely mentioned them. This was not through lack of caring. It was simply that we were in another world. And one could not share it with outsiders. The war was an irresistible catalyst. It overwhelmed everything, forced relationships like a hothouse so that in a matter of days one would achieve a closeness with someone that would have taken months to develop in peacetime."

Soon after Pearl Harbor, President Roosevelt and Prime Minister Churchill had agreed that Americans must carry out a major invasion into Nazi-occupied territory within the year. At first, both believed the invasion should be in northern Europe, envisioning an operation much like D-Day would turn out to be. But FDR quickly realized that the U.S. was not prepared for the conquest of Europe. Civilians were being drafted and trained, tanks and ships built. They would not be up to their full force for some time. The first U.S. operation needed to be smaller, more focused. FDR decided to invade northwest Africa, held by the Vichy government of France, which was cooperating with Hitler. Such a move would surprise the Germans, who were expecting a European attack. The invasion was called Operation Torch.

As Eisenhower prepared to leave for North Africa in early November 1942, Kay believed her months of excitement and glamour were over. She would be transferred back to routine driving duties for whichever military official needed her in London. But Eisenhower asked her to follow him to North Africa once the battle was over and things had settled down. "From that time on, I felt as if there were clouds under my feet instead of pavements or a gas pedal," she recalled.

When Eisenhower's wife, Mamie, heard that Kay would be

joining him in North Africa, she evidently wrote him a scathing letter. For months, she had seethed with outrage whenever she saw the attractive brunette standing next to him in photos and newsreels, even on the cover of *Life* magazine.

"She is terribly in love with a young American colonel," Eisenhower replied, "and is to be married to him come June, assuming both are alive. I doubt that *Life* told you that."

The Eisenhower marriage had gone through many ups and downs. When Ike and Mamie married in 1916—she was twenty, he twenty-six—the young officer told her, "The country will always come first. You will come second." Several months later, the U.S. was in World War I. Ike stayed stateside, much to his frustration. A son born in 1917 died in 1921 from scarlet fever, and suddenly the marriage was different, tarnished, something irrevocably lost, though a second son born in 1922 helped improve the relationship. Mostly, Ike focused on his work, Mamie on being the perfect officer's wife. Though Mamie would move a total of twenty-eight times over the course of her husband's long career, she particularly hated Ike's posting to Panama in the early twenties and the Philippines in the mid-thirties. She spent as much time as possible in the U.S.—often away from Ike—and was now living in Washington, D.C.

At the outbreak of war in 1941, Mamie Eisenhower was a slender forty-five-year-old with merry blue eyes, youthful apple cheeks, and dark hair with inexplicably short curled bangs that would be her signature look until her dying day. Her life in Washington was proving difficult. Unwilling to be seen partying while so many men fought and died, she had poured herself into volunteering for the Red Cross and other organizations to help the war effort. But that, too, would be curtailed due to a lack of balance that had her walking into walls and unable to navigate stairs.

Though she would later be diagnosed with Meniere's disease—an inner ear disorder—word got out that the supreme commander's wife was a raging alcoholic. Often too dizzy to leave her apartment, worried about her husband serving in Europe and her only child, John, who would graduate West Point on D-Day, she grew sleepless and irritable. On top of everything else, she frequently heard about the young, beautiful Kay Summersby always hovering at her husband's side.

Operation Torch began November 8, 1942. More than a hundred ships disgorged a hundred thousand American soldiers onto the coasts of Morocco and Algeria, supported by British warships and aircraft in the largest amphibious landing in U.S. history. Losses were minimal, and the invasion was over by November 11, after which Eisenhower established an Allied headquarters in Algiers.

Five weeks later in her London flat, Kay joyously packed a suitcase with satin nightgowns. Her fiancé, Dick Arnold, was stationed in Algiers, and his divorce had been finalized. Her own divorce papers would arrive soon, and the two would marry. But between Spain and Algiers, Kay's huge troop transport ship, the *Strathallan*, struck a German mine. She made it to a lifeboat—but her nightgowns did not—and she arrived in Algiers the following morning wet and bedraggled.

Though Operation Torch had been a success, Eisenhower still found himself fighting in North Africa as German troops in Tunisia attacked U.S. troops from the east. His stress levels were through the roof. The American Army had not been prepared for the torrential rains; tanks and jeeps sank in the mud. Eisenhower's commanding officer, U.S. Chief of Staff George Catlett Marshall Jr., took one look at the stressed, sleepless, chain-smoking general and ordered him to balance his work with some time off.

Ike decided he needed another Telegraph Cottage, a place where he and his war family could relax. He chose a white stucco farmhouse called Sailor's Delight, only ten miles from his headquarters in Algiers. The property had tennis courts, stables, and a sea view. He and Kay often went riding.

"We would leave the office in the middle of the afternoon several days a week," Kay recalled, "drive out to Sailor's Delight, ride for a couple of hours, shower, have a drink and supper and then drive back to Algiers. Once in a while we would spend Saturday night and all day Sunday, doing all the things we had done at Telegraph Cottage. We played bridge, sat outdoors when it was warm enough, knocked a few golf balls around the grass and practiced target shooting."

In Algiers, one of Eisenhower's closest aides, Colonel Ernest Lee of Texas, called Tex, took Kay aside and said, "I think you ought to know, Kay, that there's a lot of gossip about you and the Boss. People are saying that you—uh-oh . . ." He was too embarrassed to continue. "That we what?" she asked innocently. "That you, uh—well, that you sleep together when you go on trips."

Indeed, many powerful men assumed the two were sleeping together. As soon as Franklin Roosevelt returned to the White House, he roared with laughter about it as he drank cocktails with his staff. Winston Churchill assumed it. Ike's deputy chief of staff, General Everett Hughes, said, "Leave Ike and Kay alone, she's helping Ike win the war." Another aide said the general and his driver were "as close as two coats of paint."

Kay was amused at the gossip. "Don't worry, Tex," she said. "If anyone says anything more, just tell them that I'm engaged to be married and that the General and I are certainly not interested in each other that way. It's ridiculous." Yes, she and Ike had a special relationship. But it wasn't romantic. Theirs was a mutual respect, a kind of telepathy. "He would often look over at me in the course of a conversation and say, 'Kay knows what I'm talking about.' And I did. I did indeed."

The Axis forces in North Africa surrendered on May 8, 1943. Churchill proclaimed, "This is not the end. It is not even the beginning of the end. But it is, perhaps, the end of the beginning." Soon after the victory, Kay's divorce papers arrived. She and Dick could finally get married. But now Dick's regiment was ready to leave Algiers for a few weeks of mine clearing. The wedding would have to wait until he returned sometime in June. And then news came in early June that Dick had been blown up in a minefield.

It was Ike who broke the news to her, after handing her a stiff drink at Sailor's Delight. Then he put his arms around her and guided her to the sofa. "Go ahead," he said. "Go ahead and cry. It's the only way. Just let it out." And she did, crying like a baby as he patted her shoulder and said, "There, there." He handed her a handkerchief to blow her nose. He fixed her a cup of tea and spooned it into her mouth.

Kay soon realized she had known very little about Dick, whom she had seen so rarely. "Each time we met it had been as exciting as a first date," she wrote, "and probably for that very reason our knowledge of each other had not progressed much beyond the first-date stage. Ike knew more about me and had seen more of my family than Dick ever had. I knew very little of Dick's family. It was as if we had met and loved in a vacuum. Now when I tried to mourn him, I discovered that I did not really know the man I was grieving for . . . The realization that I had never really known him was as shocking as the knowledge that now I never would."

Work helped ease her grief; Eisenhower was now planning the invasion of Sicily. Horseback rides on the beach with Ike helped, and listening to music with him after dinner. Dick had served as a kind of wall between them. With him gone, there was nothing to stop their true feelings from rising to the surface. One day, Ike told her he had a surprise—new uniforms, a luxury at the time. "You do so many nice things for me," she said with a smile. "How can I ever thank you?"

"You can't possibly know how much I would like to do for you," he replied, his voice strangled. Then Ike removed his reading glasses and touched her hand. "Kay, you are someone very special to me," he said. Kay wrote:

> We just sat there and looked at each other. I felt overpoweringly shy. We were both silent, serious, eyes searching eyes. It was a communion, a pledging, an avowal of love. And it was an absolutely shocking surprise.
>
> So this is love, I thought. I had been in love before, but it had never been like this—so completely logical, so right. For over a year, Ike and I had spent more time with each other than with anyone else. We had worked, worried and played together. Love had grown so naturally that it was a part of our lives, something precious that I had taken for granted without ever putting a name to it. Yes, I loved this middle-aged man with his thinning hair, his eyeglasses, his drawn, tired face. I wanted to hold him in my arms, to cuddle him, delight him. I wanted to lie on some grassy lawn and see those broad shoulders above me, feel the intensity of those eyes on mine, feel that hard body against mine. I loved this man.

Then one of his aides burst in with some papers for the general. The moment was lost. But the joy was not. Kay recalled,

"That morning, life took on a sweetness that was almost unbearable. I floated on a cloud of happiness, delighting in my secret, exploring the feelings I had hidden from myself for months. I felt peaceful and fulfilled." And later that day, Eisenhower told Kay he loved her. He realized he would probably be transferred to Washington, D.C., to work at the Pentagon once the war was over, and if that happened, he would find a way to take her with him. "I'm never going to let you go," he vowed.

But their physical intimacy was limited to a quick kiss or holding hands a few seconds. While many officers had mistresses during the war, Eisenhower had to maintain a sterling reputation for the sake of morale. He was known as a man of the strictest integrity and the deepest sense of honor. His life had to be seen as above reproach.

He confessed to Kay the agony he felt the night he learned her ship had gone down. "If there was ever any question in my mind as to how deeply I felt about you, that night answered it. I had never let myself realize quite how dear you were to me before. But for God's sake, I never thought that I would be talking to you like this. Never. I was never going to tell you how I felt. And sweet Jesus Christ, I don't know how I ever had the guts to. I'm very out of practice in love, Kay." She didn't understand what he meant. That he didn't love his wife anymore?

General Marshall ordered Ike back to the States for twelve days over Christmas 1943 to spend time with Mamie, whom he hadn't seen in a year and a half. Stewing in Algiers, Kay was fretting with jealousy during the visit, but she needn't have bothered. Ike and Mamie didn't have a happy reunion because he kept calling her Kay.

In early January, Kay returned to London and a few days later picked up Eisenhower at the airport. She took him to his new London town house—she doubted she could find Telegraph Cottage in the thick fog that night—and they drank whiskey by the fire as they always did. Then they found themselves in each other's arms, and their clothes came off. And nothing happened.

One morning soon after, in that same living room of shame, Ike spoke to Kay of his relationship with Mamie. After the death of their three-year-old son, he said, nothing could recapture the love and happiness they had shared. Both had hurt each other over the years.

"Kay," he said, "I guess I'm telling you that I'm not the lover you should have. It killed something in me. Not all at once, but little by little. For years I never thought of making love. And then when I did . . . when it had been on my mind for weeks, I failed. I failed with you, my dearest. Didn't I?"

Kay sat on the arm of his chair, her head against his shoulder. "It's all right," she said. "I love you. It's all right." They couldn't afford to focus on their love affair. Ike was planning D-Day, chain-smoking, nervous, and exhausted. He had headaches and diarrhea. The night of the invasion, he and Kay stood on the roof of the 101st Airborne Division headquarters building in Newbury to watch the bombers take off for Utah Beach in Normandy.

Kay wrote, "The planes were taking off, roaring down the runways and climbing, climbing. Soon there were hundreds circling above us. It was a full moon, so brilliant that it cast shadows. The planes, wheeling like some immense flock of birds, blotted it out from time to time. It was such a gigantic moment! My heart was pounding, and I was practically crying. I knew I had never seen anything like it before and never would see anything like it again. We stayed on the roof a long time watching the planes. Ike stood there with his hands in his pockets, his face tipped toward the sky. The planes kept circling and then they began tailing off and headed toward Normandy."

Ike said, "It's very hard to look a soldier in the eye when you fear that you are sending him to his death."

As they walked to the car, he said, "Well, it's on. No one can stop it now." That night, he could have waited with Winston Churchill or Charles de Gaulle, leader of the French Resistance, or any of his top officers. But he only wanted to wait with Kay. At 6:00 a.m., they received word that despite heavy initial losses, the Germans had been caught by surprise and the invasion was going well. It was the beginning of the end of the war.

Later in June, Ike's son, John, visited his father in England, and Ike sent Kay back to the States with him for a much-needed vacation. Awkwardly, Mamie was waiting at the airport for her son. She greeted Kay pleasantly and invited her to a cocktail party that evening. "It was not much fun," Kay wrote. "I felt very stiff and foreign and military among these women in their fluttery light dresses. No other woman was in uniform. And certainly no other woman was being scrutinized as sharply as I was." Though Kay had heard the rumors of her affair with Eisenhower from friends serving with her in England, in Washington she experienced the outright hostility of other soldiers' wives circling the wagons to defend one of their own. "It was in Washington," Kay added, "that I became aware of the gossip about Ike and me. Of its virulence. No wonder the women at that little cocktail party had been eying me so closely. Wherever I went, I began to feel as if I were on display. I became increasingly sensitive to the whispers. Ike must have been protecting me from a lot of this. Friends told me that there had been several gossip-column mentions of the General's glamorous driver and nastily pointed insinuations about our relationship."

At first, Kay delighted in the luxuries no one in England had seen in years. Soft, feminine dresses. Steaks and chocolate. But after just a few days, she had had enough. She wanted to be back at the center of action, wearing her old uniform, eating canned fish. "I was glad when the holiday was over," she wrote. "I had enjoyed most of it tremendously, and I had fallen in love with the United States, but now I longed to be back where I belonged. I had stepped out of that special dimension in which Ike and I had been living, and I did not like the world I found outside, a world where war was only incidental. Not a crusade against evil things, not a way of life that demanded the best one had to give."

After a thirty-three-hour flight, Kay found herself in London again and was thrilled to learn that Eisenhower—with FDR's support—was getting her a commission in the U.S. Women's Army Corps (WAC) as a second lieutenant. "I'm trying to plan ahead," he said. "We're winning this war, although I'm not always sure of it, and I'm not going to be in Europe forever. I told you once that I was never going to let you go. If you're a WAC, I can keep you on my staff later on." One night, in front of the fire, they spoke about having a child together. When buzz bombs chased them to the shelter in the backyard, they fell asleep on cots, holding hands in the dark.

There were few opportunities for private moments after Ike moved his headquarters to Normandy in early August 1944. Kay told him, "If I ever write you a love letter, you'll have to tear it up and swallow it."

"You don't have to write me, Kay," he replied. "Every time you look at me, I see a love letter in your eyes."

When Kay received her commission as a WAC in October 1944, she could no longer drive the general but sat next to him in the backseat. Ike soon promoted her to first lieutenant and his official aide—the first woman aide to a five-star general in U.S. history. Winston Churchill awarded her the British Empire Medal. On the battlefield, victory followed victory. Things were happening so fast they barely had time to mourn FDR's death on April 12, 1945. Less than a month later, on May 7 at 2:41 a.m., German officers marched into Ike's office in the French city of Reims to sign the surrender. Kay, at her desk with Telek at her feet, watched them stride past and into Ike's office, where they clicked their heels and saluted.

A dozen of Ike's staff went to his quarters in an old castle and popped champagne. But it was a solemn celebration. No one even smiled. "We had won," Kay wrote, "but victory was not anything like what I had thought it would be. There was a dull bitterness about it. So many deaths. So much destruction. And everyone was very, very tired."

Having lived in the micro-bubble of war for so many years, Kay wondered what life would be like now. "For all tunnels come to an end," she mused. "Wars are won. Orgasm achieved; a vision captured. A child is born. The gates of death open—and close. Then one must emerge. Into what?" Ike had been working with FDR to cut through miles of red tape and get American citizenship for Kay; now he was communicating with President Harry Truman; it was urgent because he knew he would be assigned to the Pentagon by the end of the year. He kept mentioning the baby he wanted to have with her. She didn't ask him, but it sounded as if he might ask Mamie for a divorce.

After the surrender, Eisenhower and his staff moved to Frank-furt, Germany, where he took up his position as military governor of the American occupation zone. When his men reported to him the atrocities they discovered at Nazi concentration camps, he instructed them to photograph and film what they found for use in the Nuremberg Trials and to refute future Holocaust deniers.

On the afternoon of October 15, 1945, sitting on the sofa of his living room, Kay and Ike found themselves kissing passionately. "The fire was warm," Kay recalled. "The sofa was soft. We held each other close, closer. Excitedly, I remember thinking, the way one thinks odd thoughts at significant moments, 'Wouldn't it be wonderful if this were the day we conceived the baby—our very first time.' Ike was tender, careful, loving. But it didn't work."

Kay said, "Wait, you're too excited. It will be all right."

"No. It won't," he said bitterly. "It's too late. I can't."

They dressed slowly, sadly. It had happened again, on this second attempt at sex. Or rather, it had not happened again.

Ike ordered supper and the two sat there in companionable silence. "It's not important," Kay said. "It's not the least bit important. It just takes time. That's all. And I'm very stubborn. You've said so yourself."

"I know you are, but I'm not sure that you're right," he said.

Two weeks later, he told her he was going to Washington the following day to work at the Pentagon for a few weeks. Then he would return to Frankfurt, finish up some things, and bring his entire staff back to Washington by the first of the year.

Kay waited and, after a few weeks, learned that Eisenhower would not be returning due to a bad cold. His staff, however, received instructions to join him in Washington in ten days. Shortly thereafter, a telex arrived that Lieutenant Summersby was not to head to Washington. Mystified, Kay wondered if she was supposed to come before the group, or if he had an assignment for her and she would travel later. But there were no more orders.

"I was stunned," she recalled. "It took nearly an hour for the truth to sink in. I was not going to Washington with the others. The General did not want me to come earlier or later. I was here and he was there. I felt like throwing up."

Kay went to her room in the WAC house, threw herself on the bed, and cried for hours, going over their every moment together. Was there a clue, somewhere? What had happened? It was over. That was what had happened. Ike must have realized he would be sacrificing his military career if he divorced Mamie, and the political career he dreamed of might never get off the ground. His decision must have been confirmed by his impotence. A young, vital woman like Kay needed a man who could get it up. Kay finally received a typed letter from Ike.

> *Dear Kay,*
>
> *I am terribly distressed, first because it has become impossible [any] longer to keep you as a member of my personal official family, and secondly because I cannot come back and give you a detailed account of my reasons . . . I am sure you will understand that I am personally much distressed that an association that has been so valuable to me has to be terminated in this particular fashion . . .*

At the bottom he had written, "Take care and retain your optimism."

It was a cold, cowardly brush-off. The man who had faced down Hitler's armies couldn't face the woman he had loved for three years. Kay accepted a posting at an army guesthouse in Berlin, and then one doing public relations in California. Visiting old friends in Washington, she called on Ike at the Pentagon, Telek on a leash.

She was afraid she would cry if she touched him, even shaking hands, so she bent down and fiddled with Telek's leash to avoid it. "It was a strange experience," she wrote. "The General stood up to greet me as I came into the office. I stopped and let Telek off his leash, and he ran straight to Ike after all those months and rolled over on his back, paws in the air, to have his stomach scratched. I could tell that Ike was very much affected. He got all red . . . We chatted for a few minutes about my future plans." He told her to drop in again; busy as he was, he could always find a few minutes for her. She went back twice for equally brief, awkward visits.

In 1947, Kay applied for her discharge from the U.S. Army. For her, the war was truly over now. "What do you do," she asked, "when you have been caught up in the whirlwind of history and, after several years, the whirlwind sets you gently down back where you were? For the first time since I had been a very young woman in London, I spent my days sleeping late, having my hair done, lunching with friends, going to dinner parties and dancing all night. Weekends I would visit friends in the country and play bridge and golf . . . I was happy." She also wrote a book called *Eisenhower Was My Boss*, which left out all hints at romance, of course. It became a bestseller, earning her a fortune.

In 1948, she read in the paper that Eisenhower had become president of Columbia University in New York. Kay, who had been dating several charming men, became obsessed with seeing him again. She started walking around the campus several times a week, hoping to run into him. Finally, she did spot him coming in one of the gates. He was shocked to see her there. She feigned surprise, explaining that she was there to look up an old friend. He didn't believe her. Frowning, he said, "Kay, it's impossible. There's nothing I can do."

Kay knew Ike was being discussed as a U.S. presidential

candidate for the 1952 election. While the wartime gossip about them had faded, he could not afford to be seen with Kay Summersby again. Kay wrote, "I looked at him. There were tears in my eyes. But I tried to smile. 'I understand,' I told him. And I did. We had had a fabulous relationship, but it was over. Completely over."

In 1952, Kay married a stockbroker, whom she divorced six years later. Over the years, she eagerly followed Ike's career in the papers: he became the first head of NATO in 1950 and won the U.S. presidential election as a Republican in 1952. Popular until the end of his second term, he ended the Korean War in 1953, established the Interstate Highway System in 1956, authorized the establishment of NASA, and signed the Civil Rights Act of 1957, sending troops to enforce school desegregation in Little Rock, Arkansas.

Mamie was a popular first lady. Eleanor Roosevelt had been the perfect first lady during the war—rushing about to save the world in sensible lace-up shoes. But after the horrors of the war, the American public wanted a gracious hostess, a traditional wife, mother, and grandmother who never got involved in politics, someone who reminded them of that innocent time before all the death and destruction, and Mamie Eisenhower was all of that. She set foot in the Oval Office just three times in eight years, and only at her husband's invitation. Her love of all things pink popularized a shade known as "Mamie pink" in clothing, bathrooms, and kitchens, and she usually wore large crinoline dresses while holding ladies' tea parties. Though known for her charm, Mamie had a frosty dislike of Ike's personal secretary. Ann Whitman, forty-four when Ike became president, was trim, blond, and happily married. But perhaps she brought with her the sour whiff of Kay Summersby.

Memories of Kay must have haunted Ike, too. According to the White House dog keeper, Traphes Bryant, whenever Eisenhower was watching a movie with "too many women or a romance, he would get up and leave. He would say, 'Let the Secret Service and the rest of the fellows watch it. It's not for me.'" His relationship with Kay may have affected not just his choice of movies, but also his appointment of 175 women to high-level federal posts, including as ambassador to Switzerland and Italy, and delegate to the United Nations. Eisenhower knew firsthand just how efficient women could be.

Over his eight years as president, Eisenhower held more than two hundred press conferences, communicating directly with the American people, which Kay watched avidly. Even when he wasn't in the news, Ike would come suddenly into Kay's thoughts. The haunting melody of a song they used to play on the old Victrola at Telegraph Cottage would instantly take her back to those days, plucking at her heartstrings for the loss of so many beloved things. The saddest day, however, was when Telek died. Her constant companion for seventeen years, one morning the ailing dog could not get up. Tearfully, she took him to the vet.

"I picked Telek up, put him in my lap, and talked to him," she recalled. "I told him how much he had always meant to me, how much I had loved him. I told him that he was an important part of my life, that when I was sitting at home and he was curled up at my feet I never felt alone. I talked to him about Ike, I told that poor tired Scottie how much Ike had liked him. I reminded him of how he used to ride in the car with us, of how he had visited Buckingham Palace, of how President Roosevelt had held him, of all the adorable scampering puppies he had sired. I let my voice and my memories surround him. Then I put him on my bed, buckled his little tartan coat around him and carried him out to a taxi and to the veterinarian."

"Please put him to sleep," she said, sobbing.

"Such a gallant little dog," she wrote. "Such a faithful, loving friend. It hit me very hard. It was not just Telek's death I was mourning. He had been my last link to Ike, the man I had loved more than anyone else in my life. And I was grieving for my own loss. From now on there would always be something missing in my life, the spirit, the gaiety, the devotion of a small dog named Telek."

With great concern, Kay followed Ike's waning health over the years. He finally died of heart failure in 1969 at the age of seventy-eight; Mamie died ten years later at eighty-three. In the 1960s, Kay became a fashion consultant for the CBS network, and her last job was choosing costumes for the Hollywood cult classic film *The Stepford Wives*, released in 1975. A few months before the film's release, in the hospital with liver cancer, she read a newspaper story she could hardly believe.

A few years earlier, biographer Merle Miller had spent hundreds of hours interviewing former President Truman, who died in 1972. Miller reported, "Right after the war was over, he [Eisenhower] wrote a letter to General Marshall saying that he wanted to come back to the United States and divorce Mrs. Eisenhower so that he could marry this English woman."

Truman said, "Marshall wrote him back a letter the like of which I never did see. He said that if Eisenhower even came close to doing such a thing, he'd not only bust him out of the Army, he'd see to it that never for the rest of his life would he be able to draw a peaceful breath . . . and that if he ever again mentioned a thing like that, he'd see to it that the rest of his life was a living hell." Truman added, "One of the last things I did as President,

I got those letters from his file in the Pentagon and I destroyed them." Truman, apparently, did not wish them to leak out, ruining Eisenhower's reputation as a wartime hero.

Reading the article, Kay suddenly understood why Ike had dropped her like a hot potato all those years ago. With Eisenhower, Kay wrote, "Duty would always come first. He told me once that if there are two paths a man can take, both of them honorable, then all things being equal, he should take the path along which he will do the most good and inflict the least hurt. And that, I believe, is what he did."

Most of Eisenhower's family and friends were aghast at Kay's book, which came out soon after she died in January 1975 at the age of sixty-six. Kay's ghostwriter had made up the love affair after Kay's death to sell books, they said, though certainly a nice hard erection would have sold more books than a sad limp pizzle. President Truman's memory was faulty, they said, or maybe Merle Miller lied to sell more of *his* books. And Kay's story had to be a lie because Ike's letters to Mamie during the war were frequent and loving. Moreover, in one of them Eisenhower requested permission for Mamie to join him in Europe after the German surrender. "The strain of the past three years," he wrote General Marshall, "has also been very considerable so far as my wife is concerned and because of the fact that she has had trouble with her general nervous system for many years. I would feel far more comfortable about her if she could be with me." His request was denied.

But many men compartmentalize their relationships with their wives and mistresses, leading each one on. Perhaps, too, Ike was increasingly recognizing the hopelessness of his affair with Kay. We don't know the date of Ike's purported letter "right after the war" to Marshall asking for a divorce. Was his June letter asking permission for Mamie to join him in Frankfurt a response to Marshall's harrowing reply? Far away from Mamie, with Kay constantly at his side, was he uncertain which path to take until his second failed attempt at making love to Kay four months later?

Nor could the family deny the closeness indicated in a note Ike sent Kay during the war which appeared at auction after her death. "How about lunch, tea & dinner today?" he asked. "If yes: Who else do you want, if any? At which time? How are you?"

Eisenhower's son, John, who spent time with Ike and Kay at military headquarters, was less startled at the allegations than his mother, Mamie. In an interview with PBS, John described Kay as "the Mary Tyler Moore of headquarters. She was perky and she was cute. Whether she had any designs on the Old Man and the extent to which he succumbed, I just don't know."

Looking back, Kay wrote, "We were two people caught up in a cataclysm. Two people who shared one of the most tremendous experiences of our time. Two people who gave each other comfort, laughter, love. Now that I am very close to the end of my life, I have a strong sense of being close to Ike again. I can almost hear him say, 'Goddamnit, don't cry.'"

In 1797, the relationship of U.S. treasury secretary Alexander Hamilton with a blackmailing prostitute resulted in the first U.S. political sex scandal. *John Trumball (painter)*

In 1786, Thomas Jefferson served as U.S. ambassador to France where he began a thirty-year relationship with his enslaved woman, Sally Hemings. *Mather Brown (painter)*

Though the American public learned that Grover Cleveland had impregnated a woman in 1873, that didn't stop him from winning the 1884 presidential election. Voters cared more about his honesty in public office. *Library of Congress Prints and Photographs Division*

In 1886, forty-nine-year-old Cleveland married his ward, twenty-one-year-old Frances Folsom. Cleveland was the only U.S. president to marry in the White House, and Frances was the youngest first lady ever. *George "Geo" Prince (photographer), Library of Congress Prints and Photographs Division*

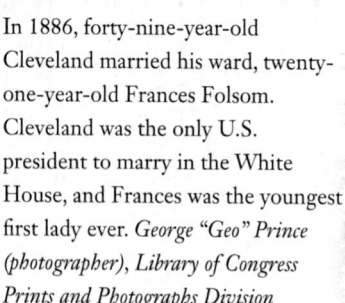

Cleveland's illegitimate child became fodder for political cartoonists, and "Ma, Ma, I want my Pa!" became a rallying cry for his opponents.
Frank Beard (artist), Library of Congress Prints and Photographs Division

Despite his prim appearance, Woodrow Wilson was quite the lady's man, writing steamy letters to his mistresses. *Harris & Ewing, Inc. (photographers), Library of Congress Prints and Photographs Division*

After his wife's death in 1914, Wilson ditched his long-term mistress to marry a wealthy, statuesque widow, Edith Bolling Galt. *Harris & Ewing, Inc. (photographers), Library of Congress Prints and Photographs Division*

The G

Warren Harding had thousands of lovers, several long-term mistresses, and more than one illegitimate child. *Harris & Ewing, Inc. (photographers), Library of Congress Prints and Photographs Division*

Florence Harding often publicly berated her husband for his love affairs. When he died unexpectedly in 1923, many believed she had poisoned him. *Library of Congress Prints and Photographs Division*

Nan Britton was unable to support her daughter with President Harding after his death. In 1927, she wrote the first presidential sex tell-all and earned a fortune. *Alamy Stock Photo*

Though she married a multi-millionaire, Lucy Mercer always remained close to FDR and was with him when he had his fatal stroke in 1945. *Alamy Stock Photo*

Franklin Delano Roosevelt in 1916, the year he began having an affair with his wife Eleanor's social secretary. Lucy Mercer would be the love of his life. *Alamy Stock Photo*

Journalist Lorena Hickok was, almost certainly, the lover of Eleanor Roosevelt, who never got over her husband's betrayal of her with Lucy. *Courtesy of the FDR Library*

FDR's secretary of twenty years, the coolly efficient Missy LeHand, lived with him on a houseboat at times. Servants frequently saw her in the President's bedroom. *Harris & Ewing, Inc. (photographers), Library of Congress Prints and Photographs Division*

Kay Summersby was the driver and right-hand assistant of General Dwight D. Eisenhower during World War II. Their love was doomed to remain unconsummated, despite their best efforts. *Alamy Stock Photo*

Lyndon Baines Johnson in 1934, the year he married Texas heiress Lady Bird Taylor. The rising congressional aide always said he would marry for money. *Courtesy of the LBJ Library*

Lady Bird Johnson learned to accept her husband's many mistresses with such equanimity that she even tidied up their undergarments in her husband's hotel rooms. *Courtesy of the LBJ Library*

Alice Glass, six feet tall with golden red hair, had a steamy affair with young congressman Lyndon B. Johnson. *Courtesy of the LBJ Library*

Good-time girl Judith Campbell had an affair with both President John F. Kennedy and Chicago mob boss Sam Giancana at the same time. *Alamy Stock Photo*

9

JOHN F. KENNEDY'S
TERRIBLE HEADACHES

On November 29, 1963—a week after the assassination of President John F. Kennedy in Dallas—his widow, Jacqueline Bouvier Kennedy, sat down with Theodore White, a writer for *Life* magazine, and invented the myth of Camelot. Her late husband had loved the popular Broadway musical, she said (though many who knew him swore he had not), and loved to sing, "Don't let it be forgot, that once there was a spot, for one brief shining moment, that was known as Camelot."

Jackie was correct that the all-too-brief presidency was full of beautiful people. And, as in an early monarchy, there were many ladies-in-waiting, though none of them in the Kennedy White House had to wait very long. The comparison of Camelot was correct, too, in that adultery infected King Arthur's court like a plague, and his reign ended in bloodshed.

★ ★ ★

When Jackie Kennedy slid between her sheets one evening, her hand touched something odd beneath her pillow. She pulled out a pair of women's panties. While most wives would be perturbed to find such an item wadded up in their bed, the first lady merely dangled them from a finger and asked her husband, "Would you please shop around and see who this belongs to? It's not my size."

By the time she moved to the White House, Jackie was used to her husband's philandering. Given her background, she must have expected a certain amount of infidelity from anyone she married. She was the daughter of a serial adulterer—John "Black Jack" Bouvier—and a member of a privileged society where few saw the need to deny themselves anything. But Jackie had had no idea of Jack Kennedy's pathological need for sex with prostitutes, society matrons, schoolgirls, babysitters, debutantes, employees, actresses, strippers, and strangers picked up in bars, often with two women at once, or with two women and another man with the men swapping partners, some of those men his own brothers. The sex took place in closets, cars, brothels, hotel rooms, the homes of his friends, bathtubs, showers, swimming pools, yachts, and in Jackie's own bed. In 1962, during a summit in the Bahamas, Kennedy told British prime minister Harold Macmillan, "You know, I get a migraine headache if I don't get a strange piece of ass every day."

JFK's best friend from high school, Lem Billings, a frequent participant in those orgies, warned Jackie before the wedding that her fiancé could never settle down with one woman. Not for a moment did she consider canceling. Looking back, she said, "I saw it as a challenge."

Her friend, journalist Charles Bartlett, said that Jackie was not "prepared for the humiliation she would suffer when she found herself stranded at parties while Jack would suddenly disappear with some pretty young girl. Before the marriage, I think she found Jack's appeal to other women tantalizing—I suspect it reminded her of the magic appeal her handsome, rakish father had had with women, but once she was married and once it was happening to her, it was much harder to accept."

Three days before the inauguration, Jackie told a writer for *Life* magazine that she and Jack were "rather like an iceberg, one part fully exposed to public view and most of it quietly submerged."

And what the American people saw of the iceberg above the water was dazzlingly beautiful. For Jack and Jackie were, from the moment of their engagement, the most glamorous, photogenic couple in America. At six feet tall and 165 pounds, Jack was lean muscle, with gray-blue eyes, a thick mane of chestnut hair, and a million-dollar grin. At five foot seven and 120 pounds, Jackie was slender and athletic with a lithe grace. She had a square face with wide hazel eyes and dark hair teased into a kind of helmet. She had gone to the best private schools, spent her junior year of college in Paris, and graduated from George Washington University with a bachelor's in French literature. In 1951 she became an Inquiring Camera Girl for the *Washington Times-Herald*, photographing people on the street and asking them their opinions.

Jack was the scion of Joe Kennedy Sr., a bootlegging, womanizing, filthy rich tycoon who placed pornographic magazines on his son's bed when he was fourteen. Jack graduated from Harvard in 1940 with a bachelor's in government, his education derailed on numerous occasions due to ill health. His first major love affair began in 1941, when he was twenty-four, and the object of his desire was Inga Arvad, four years his senior, a reporter for the *Washington Times-Herald*. The statuesque former beauty queen was a native of Denmark who had written glowing articles about

Adolf Hitler's "kind heart." "The perfect Nordic beauty," according to the führer, Inga had been invited to Hermann Göring's 1935 wedding and was Hitler's personal guest at the Summer Olympics the following year. Suspecting that Inga was a Nazi spy, FBI director J. Edgar Hoover bugged her apartment, tapped her phone, and had her followed, discovering, to his horror, that she was sleeping with Kennedy, who was working in the U.S. Office of Naval Intelligence.

Hoover believed Inga might be wheedling naval secrets out of Kennedy and passing them on to the Germans. JFK and Inga knew they were being followed and recorded and continued to see each other, pure recklessness on Kennedy's part given his military position. Kennedy's superiors wanted to eject him from the navy for consorting with a woman they considered to be a Mata Hari. But because JFK's father was the rich and powerful Joseph Kennedy, who had been U.S. ambassador to Great Britain a year earlier, they merely transferred him to a desk job in South Carolina. Even then, the reckless pair didn't break it off. Inga drove down to Charleston or they met in hotel rooms in D.C. where Hoover presumably would not be listening in.

Soon, Kennedy saw action in the South Pacific. In 1943, he was commander of a PT boat when a Japanese destroyer collided with it, cutting it in half. Kennedy's actions to save his surviving crew—including towing a badly burned man to an island with his life preserver strap between his teeth—made him a war hero. Joe Kennedy was delighted as heroic actions could help propel a man into public office.

Irish Catholic Joe, son of a barkeep, was never really accepted into elite, Protestant Boston society no matter how many millions he made. He insisted on a son of his becoming president just to show them all. Jack's older brother, Joe Jr., had died in the war, so now the weighty mantle of paternal expectations fell on Jack, the second son. His campaign bankrolled by his father, in 1947, at the age of twenty-nine, Jack became a Massachusetts congressman. Handsome, dashing, and politically important, he found himself surrounded by beautiful women, including major Hollywood movie stars like Gene Tierney.

Many young bachelors enjoy sexual liaisons, but Kennedy seemed to have no control over his impulses and dropped his pants whenever the spirit overtook him, which was often. He didn't even bother to learn the names of many of his sex partners, calling them "kiddo" or "sweetie" for the ten or fifteen minutes he used them before they vanished from his life. "No one was off limits to Jack," said Florida senator George Smathers, one of his regular partners in carousing. "Not your wife, your mother or your sister." In 1952, Kennedy caused a ruckus when he locked himself and a woman in a closet at a white-tie benefit in Newport, Rhode Island. Guests had to wait until he was done to get their coats back.

By the beginning of 1953, now a newly minted senator, Kennedy was thirty-five and knew he needed to marry and start a family to remain popular with voters. Friends introduced him to Jacqueline Bouvier at a dinner, and he quickly saw that here was everything he could have asked for: Jackie was Catholic, beautiful, and intelligent. Her style and charm would help him politically. Oleg Cassini, Jackie's friend and dress designer, explained the attraction. "Jack wanted more than looks," he said. "He wanted courage, accomplishment. He wanted a champion, a star."

If Jackie suspected her husband might have an affair after a few years of marriage, she got a rude shock on her Mexican honeymoon. At a cocktail reception, Jack collected phone numbers on slips of paper from a crowd of women hovering around him.

Then, according to Michael Diaz, a lawyer from Mexico City, "At one point he brazenly walked off with one of the better-looking women and headed for a bedroom. They emerged twenty minutes later, looking flushed and spent. You had to feel sorry for Mrs. Kennedy."

In the first years of her marriage, Jackie saw her husband infrequently as he traveled both domestically and internationally without her. In the summer of 1955, Jack spent a week with a gorgeous twenty-three-year-old Swedish aristocrat, Gunilla von Post, at a resort in Sweden. He had met her in the south of France in August 1953, and they had, by her account, fallen in love during an evening of dinner and dancing. She was shattered to hear he would be getting married in a month. "If I had met you one week before," he said, "I would have canceled the whole thing." It was doubtful, given the prize Jackie was, that he would have jilted her, but the story did work in seducing Gunilla after two years of letters, phone calls, and complaints about his "cold" wife. They spent much of their week together in bed. Before leaving, Jack promised Gunilla he would talk to his father about getting a divorce so he could marry her. This comment shocked her, as she couldn't imagine a thirty-eight-year-old United States senator having to ask his father permission for anything.

We will never know if Kennedy actually spoke with his father about a divorce. But he told Gunilla that Joe Sr. said, "You're out of your mind. You're going to be president someday. This would ruin everything. Divorce is impossible . . . Can't you get it into your head that it's not important what you really are? The only important thing is what people think you are!" Jack offered Gunilla a job and financial support if she agreed to move to the U.S. She wisely turned him down and within the year married a wealthy Swedish landowner.

At the same time Jack was begging Gunilla to relocate, he was having a red-hot affair in Washington with a stripper named Tempest Storm. The following year, in a Malibu restaurant, he met twenty-four-year-old Joan Lundberg and began a three-year relationship, arranging for her to meet him in hotels all over the country. When she got pregnant—he refused to wear a condom, perhaps for religious reasons—he sent her money for an abortion.

In the summer of 1956, Jackie was seven months pregnant, having suffered a miscarriage the year before, when Jack went on a European cruise with his brother Teddy and Florida senator George Smathers. Soon after Jackie learned there were also three Scandinavian women on board, she began to hemorrhage and gave birth to a stillborn girl born a month early. When he heard the news, Jack was reluctant to return home, wondering aloud what he could do there. He called his younger brother Bobby, who said, "If you ever want to run for president, you had better haul ass back to your wife." He did, but Jackie nearly divorced him. Something had been irretrievably broken in their marriage.

Later that year, Jackie disconsolately sat for a taped television interview. "You're pretty much in love with him, aren't you?" asked the interviewer. "Oh no," she said, her eyes downcast. Almost surprised at herself, she raised her eyes and asked, "I said no, didn't I?" The director cut and they started over again. When asked if she was in love with her husband, she said carelessly, "I suppose so. I've ruined it, haven't I?"

In January 1957, Jackie and a gay friend, artist Bill Walton, took a trip to Hollywood. There they had dinner with one of the film industry's most popular stars, thirty-nine-year-old William Holden, and his wife. Walton said that Jackie quickly fell into bed with the actor and the affair was "primarily driven by Jackie's desire to seek revenge on Jack." Her desire for revenge increased the following year, according to White House dog keeper Traphes Bryant, when she discovered Jack had impregnated the fifteen-year-old babysitter of their infant daughter, Caroline. The babysitter, according to gossip, got an abortion, while Jackie once more threatened divorce. Rumor had it that her father-in-law bribed her to stay in the marriage.

It must have been an awful lot of money. Because the following year, Jackie, "always cheerful and obliging," according to campaign adviser Kenneth O'Donnell, campaigned hard for Jack's Senate reelection. "The size of the crowd was twice as big" when Jackie accompanied her husband, O'Donnell reported. She was, perhaps, his greatest asset on the campaign trail.

Despite Kennedy's popular wife, some of his friends were worried his women stories would get out when he threw his hat into the ring for the 1960 presidential campaign. Joe Kennedy Sr. ridiculed their fears, growling, "The American people don't care how many times he gets laid." Fred Dutton, a Democratic Party power broker, agreed. "There are more votes in virility than fidelity," he pointed out. Kennedy, he said, "was like a God, fucking anybody he wants to anytime he feels like it." The candidate was someone who, if the stories got out, most American men would envy.

Langdon Marvin, a Kennedy campaign worker, recalled that Kennedy would "dispatch me to a given town or city as a kind of advance man. I'd set things up for him. When he arrived, I'd pick him up at the airport. He'd clamber off the *Caroline*, the campaign plane his father had purchased for him, and he'd say to me, 'Where are the broads?'" Marvin would have several prostitutes lined up that Kennedy picked from. He usually chose two. A speechwriter for the 1960 election recalled, "It was just the way Jack felt—you weren't a man if you let a really incredible piece of ass get away."

On November 8, 1960, Kennedy won the presidential election by some 113,000 votes out of nearly 69 million total votes cast—49.7 percent versus 49.6 percent for Richard Nixon—the smallest victory margin in a century. It was a generational shift in America's power structure. At seventy, Eisenhower, the outgoing president, was the oldest person ever to serve in the office to that point; his wife, Mamie, was sixty-four. The president-elect was the youngest ever, forty-three. Jackie was thirty-one and almost nine months pregnant with their son John F. Kennedy Jr.

Giddy as many Americans were with their handsome young president, they did not know two essential pieces of information about him. One was the alarming state of his health. Sickly as a child, at the age of thirty Kennedy was diagnosed with Addison's disease, a rare endocrine disorder that caused severe lower back pain (which was greatly exacerbated by his war injuries), discoloration of the skin (resulting in his eternal orangey tan), abdominal pain, weight loss, diarrhea, headaches, impaired judgment, and high fevers. Severe stress could trigger an Addisonian crisis, with convulsions and dangerously low blood pressure, resulting in death. Kennedy was given last rites four times before he became president.

He wore a stiff, laced-up corset to stabilize his weak spine, slept on a special firm mattress, and often had his aides bring his rocking chair to private dinners. From time to time, his back was so bad he walked on crutches or with a cane, which, like FDR, he was careful to hide from the public. In the White House movie theater, he lay in a bed propped up on pillows. Kennedy strongly denied rumors that he had Addison's disease, claiming his back pain was solely the result of his heroic acts during the war.

His treatments—by three doctors working separately—involved hormones, steroids, vitamins, enzymes, and amphetamines, with the potential side effects of hyperactivity, impaired judgment, nervousness, and mood swings. Kennedy was treated with cortisone, in the form of pills, injections, and pellets inserted into the skin. His father had the medicine placed in safe-deposit boxes around the world in case Jack suffered a crisis in a foreign country. One of his physicians, Max Jacobson—who would lose his medical license after killing a patient in 1969 with intravenous amphetamine poisoning—was known as Dr. Feelgood. "I don't care if it's horse piss," Kennedy snapped when his brother Bobby warned him about the doctor's mysterious injections. "It works."

The other tidbit Americans didn't know was his reckless, obsessive philandering, much of it done in the White House when Jackie wasn't there, which was often. Traphes Bryant explained, "Usually when he wanted to be alone with his female company, JFK passed the word that the private family quarters on the second floor were off-limits." One night, Bryant pressed the wrong elevator button. "Just as the elevator door opened, a naked blond office girl ran through the hall between the second-floor kitchen and the door leading to the West Hall. Her breasts were swinging as she ran by. There was nothing to do but to get out fast and push the basement buttons."

After JFK had a tryst with a woman in the White House private quarters, either in his bed or—and here we shudder—his wife's, housekeepers and Secret Service agents rushed in to clean up the incriminating evidence before Jackie returned, according to Bryant. This was especially true after the president had bedded a blond, which he usually preferred. In that era, women's bouffant hairstyles were nothing less than extraordinary feats of engineering sustained by relentless teasing, hair spray, and bobby pins. Jackie may not have been suspicious if she found a long, dark hair or dark bobby pin on her pillow. "Why can't he make it easier for us?" the staff asked, cursing under their breath as they sifted the covers and floors on their hands and knees. "Why do we always have to be searching for blond hair and blond bobby pins? Why can't he get himself a steady brunette?"

Perhaps the most troubling aspect of this story is that the staff picked hairs off the sheets instead of changing them. Which leads us to ponder how many sets of sheets the White House possessed. Perhaps not enough to keep up with JFK's constant soiling of them? Fresh sheets would have offered the added advantage of whisking away all those pesky leftover panties, like the ones the first lady found wadded up beneath her pillow.

One evening, Bryant recalled, JFK, Bobby, and several women were swimming nude in the White House pool and knocking back daiquiris soon after Jackie left with the children for her country house in Virginia. Word came she had forgotten something and was at that moment entering the White House. "Suddenly the ushers were sounding the alarm," Bryant said, "and first thing I knew naked bodies were scurrying every which way. It was easy to get rid of bodies, but gathering up the drinks was another matter, and the help had a time clearing away the evidence—like highball glasses. Only the President remained in the pool. As I remember it, Jackie seemed not to notice anything amiss. Soon word came that she was getting back into her car, and then that it had driven off. But just in case, the President swam alone in the pool for a while."

Kennedy's unrestrained sexual appetite infuriated some of the men who were assigned to protect him. Secret Service agent Larry Newman remembered the "morale problems" that the president's indiscretions caused. "You were on the most elite assignment in the Secret Service," he said, "and you were there watching an elevator or a door because the president was inside with two hookers.

It just didn't compute. Your neighbors and everybody thought you were risking your life, and you were actually out there to see that he's not disturbed while he's having an interlude in the shower with two gals from Twelfth Avenue."

Then there was the issue of the president's personal safety. Agent Newman remembered joking with his colleagues about which one of them would testify on Capitol Hill if and when "the president received harm or was killed in the room by these two women." When Jackie was away, young women would show up at the White House unheralded, claiming the president had invited them over. The Secret Service agents had no time to vet the visitors, and Kennedy was in no mood to wait. Any one of these women could have killed the president when they were alone together in the second-floor residence. After sex, he often offered his lovers food his staff had left in his private kitchen, which had plenty of knives lying about. If a woman had attacked Kennedy, help would have been slow in coming as he had exiled all staff, including his Secret Service personnel, to other floors.

JFK's reckless philandering even threatened national security. Sometimes he ditched his Secret Service agents to meet a woman outside the White House, leaving behind the army officer with the nuclear security codes in a black briefcase handcuffed to his wrist. If the Soviets had launched an all-out attack with the president missing in action, America would have been unable to respond.

Though Kennedy probably had sex with hundreds of women while he was president, we only know the stories of a dozen. Two were purported spies. Kennedy's mistress Judith Campbell was a gorgeous good-time girl whose louche life, according to her autobiography, was a never-ending round of parties, dressing up, drinking, dining, swimming, and attending the midnight shows of Dean Martin or Frank Sinatra, after which she would disappear with a rich and famous man. A stunning, shapely brunette with ice-blue eyes, she claimed she was never paid for sex. And yet, reading her book, one wonders where she got all the money for the travel and designer clothing she described, as she had no visible means of support.

On February 7, 1960, one of her regular lovers, Frank Sinatra, introduced her to JFK in the lounge of the Sands Hotel in Las Vegas. There was immediate chemistry between the two. A month later, Kennedy arranged a tryst with her at the Plaza Hotel in New York, the day before the New Hampshire primary. He spent time with her in his Georgetown house, in a friend's home in Palm Beach, and at the Los Angeles Hilton during the Democratic National Convention. She is recorded as having visited the White House on twenty occasions. Judith confessed she was "caught up a little with the intrigue of it. The sneaking around, a mild form of cloak-and-dagger, the anticipation, the 'Boy, we didn't get caught!'"

But they would get caught in a scandal that threatened to derail Kennedy's entire presidency. Because Judith Campbell was also the mistress of the Chicago Mafia boss Sam Giancana, Al Capone's successor, who ran a criminal empire of some fifty thousand bookies, counterfeiters, murderers-for-hire, and assorted wise guys with an annual off-the-books revenue of $2 billion. In March 1962, FBI director J. Edgar Hoover, who eventually learned everything about everybody, informed Kennedy that the affair made him particularly vulnerable to blackmail by the Mafia. The president, who had been trying to reduce Hoover's unlimited power, clearly would not be able to do so now. Even worse, Attorney General Bobby Kennedy, who had been working to crack down on the mob, found his efforts hobbled. While some sources state that Kennedy ceased all contact with Judith after his discussion with Hoover, in a 1997 *Vanity Fair* interview, she claimed they last had sex in December 1962, some nine months after the president knew he was setting himself up for blackmail.

Ellen Rometsch was a gorgeous twenty-seven-year-old with a black beehive hairstyle, an hourglass figure, and a fetching little mole on the side of her pouting red lips. An East German, she had worked briefly as a secretary for Walter Ulbricht, head of the Communist East German government, before she and her family fled to West Germany in 1955. Soon after, she married a West German air force sergeant who was stationed at the embassy in Washington in 1961. She allegedly worked as a high-class prostitute at a hotel next to the Senate office building, servicing politicians. After his first date with Ellen, Kennedy called a friend and said, "That was the best blow job I ever had in my life." The two met for dinner privately several times at the White House.

Naturally, J. Edgar Hoover learned of it. He had his agents interview Rometsch and concluded she was probably a Soviet spy. One of her lovers, in fact, worked at the Soviet embassy in D.C. When Hoover informed Kennedy, for the first time ever he was worried about a sex scandal bringing him down. In June 1963, the British secretary of state for war John Profumo resigned in full-on tabloid disgrace after it came out that he had slept with a call girl—who was sleeping with the Soviet naval attaché—and then lied about it. Rometsch was sent packing back to West Germany. For once in Jack Kennedy's life, reason overcame recklessness.

His other lovers were far less dangerous. Twenty-year-old college junior Diana de Vegh met Kennedy during his 1959 Senate campaign at a political dinner in Boston. He arranged for her to work on Capitol Hill and then, after the inauguration, on the

National Security Council. When Jackie was out of town, he invited Diana to his private quarters in the White House for dinner. Afterward, they would go to the Lincoln Bedroom—Jackie's personal haven where she felt "the kind of peace . . . you feel when going into a church," with a high carved bed "like a cathedral"—and desecrate it. After a year, Diana had had enough of an affair with a married man. She quit her job, moved to Paris, became an actress in the soap opera *All My Children*, earned a master's degree in social work at Columbia, and became a psychotherapist.

Mary Meyer was the sister-in-law of *Newsweek*'s Washington bureau chief, Ben Bradlee, a close friend of JFK who in 1965 would become the editor of the *Washington Post*. Blond, spunky, and in search of a good time, Mary was the divorced mother of two and a painter of minimalist art. Though Mary had known the Kennedys ever since they moved in next door to her Georgetown house in 1954, her affair with Jack didn't start until October 3, 1961, when she arrived at the White House for an intimate dinner. According to White House logbooks, she would have at least thirteen such dinners over the next two years, though some sources say she had more than thirty, entering as the "plus one" of Kennedy's loyal special assistant Dave Powers. At a March 8, 1963, dinner dance, she disappeared for half an hour. Her date later reported, "Finally I went looking for her. She had been upstairs with Jack."

Mary's story had a very dark ending. She told friends she kept a detailed diary of her affair with JFK, including their experiments with LSD, marijuana, and cocaine. On October 12, 1964, while taking her usual walk along the C&O Canal towpath near her Georgetown house, she was fatally shot, and later that day Ben Bradlee found James Angleton, chief of CIA Counterintelligence, breaking into her art studio in Bradlee's backyard, looking for her diary. Bradlee agreed to give it to him, and Angleton burned it. The African American man police tried to pin the crime on was found not guilty, and the murder remains unsolved to this day.

When Helen Chavchavadze's affair with JFK began in 1960, she was a twenty-seven-year-old divorcée with two young children, studying for her master's degree in Russian at Georgetown University. The pretty brunette had met the Kennedys through Jackie's sister, Lee Radziwill, with whom she had gone to school. After the inauguration, when Jackie was traveling, Kennedy invited Helen for private dinners followed by sex.

Helen's affair came back to haunt her when, in the fall of 1962, she couldn't get a security clearance for a job she had been offered at the Foreign Service Institute. She realized that the denial was due to her affair with the president and that she was under surveillance. Falling into a deep depression, she had a nervous breakdown, was committed into a psychiatric hospital, and lost her house and custody of her children. Released from the hospital after a few months, Helen started teaching at American University, reclaimed her home and children, and met the man she would soon marry. She was standing by her ironing board when she heard the news of JFK's death and burst into tears. Yet, "When he was killed a tiny part of me felt freed," she told author Sally Bedell Smith.

Though Helen had suspected Kennedy may have had other lovers, she wasn't sure until it all came out years after his death. Looking back, she said of his rampant adultery, "It was a compulsion, a quirk in his personality. He was out of control. It may have looked like beautiful convertibles and women and sophistication, but it was the shadow destroying the self. For Mary [Meyer] and me it was our shadow too."

Curiously, Jackie invited Diana, Helen, and Mary to White

House luncheons and dinner dances, often sitting one of them next to her husband. An admirer of French ancien régime history, she seemed to have modeled herself on Louis XV's official mistress Madame de Pompadour, who selected young women for the king's enjoyment as a means of maintaining control. "Jackie was in charge choosing his playmates," Helen said. "It was very French."

Jackie even agreed to her husband's suggestion to hire his lover as her press secretary. Pamela Turnure, a fetching brunette, had been having an affair with Kennedy ever since she started working as his secretary in the Senate in 1958. Though Turnure had absolutely no experience handling the press, Jackie hired the twenty-three-year-old as her most visible staff member.

The president had other compliant young females close at hand whenever the urge struck him: two women dubbed Fiddle and Faddle. Fiddle, whose real name was Priscilla Wear, worked for Kennedy's private secretary Evelyn Lincoln; and Fiddle's close friend Faddle—Jill Cowan—was an assistant in the White House press office. They started working on Kennedy's presidential campaign when they were twenty and dropped out of college when he offered them White House jobs.

At lunchtime, both women enjoyed swimming with the president in the White House pool, returning to their offices with wet hair. They didn't do any work on the presidential trips Kennedy included them in. One day, National Security Advisor McGeorge Bundy and White House aide Myer Feldman walked into the Oval Office and saw the young women massaging gel into the president's scalp. Shocked, Bundy said he didn't think this kind of behavior was sufficiently dignified for the Oval Office. The president, looking at the balding heads of his visitors, said, "Well, I'm not sure you two plan your hair very well."

Jackie knew all about her husband's relationships with the girls. Once, while taking a reporter from *Paris Match* on a White House tour, she walked into Evelyn Lincoln's office and saw Fiddle sitting at her desk. Jackie turned to the reporter and said in French, "This is the girl who supposedly is sleeping with my husband."

Kennedy's most famous girlfriend was the immortal goddess of the silver screen, Marilyn Monroe. They met in the late fifties and had begun their affair by the 1960 presidential campaign. When JFK campaigned in Los Angeles, he and Marilyn made love in a bathtub, according to his brother-in-law and pimp, Rat Pack actor Peter Lawford. On the night of Kennedy's acceptance speech for the Democratic nomination, both Marilyn and Kennedy attended a nude swimming party at Lawford's Santa Monica beach house. Other times, the actress met the president on Air Force One, in the Beverly Hills Hilton, and in his two-story apartment in New York's Carlyle Hotel. Marilyn, perhaps the most recognizable woman in the nation, was smuggled in from a nearby apartment building through underground tunnels by Secret Service agents with flashlights. On the weekend of March 24, 1962, while Jackie was enjoying a camel ride in India, her husband had a rendezvous with Marilyn at Bing Crosby's Palm Springs home.

Marilyn had fallen hard for the president and dreamed he would divorce Jackie and marry her. When she called his private number in the White House residence, sometimes Jackie picked up and, hearing who it was, mutely handed the phone to her husband. Jackie wisely stayed away from the May 19, 1962, televised celebration of the president's forty-fifth birthday at Madison Square Garden. Marilyn sang a throaty "Happy Birthday, Mr. President" wearing a skintight, pink silk dress with sequins. One diplomat in attendance described the gown as "skin and beads only I didn't see the beads." The sexual electricity between the president and the actress was clear to the fifteen thousand spectators. Columnist Dorothy Kilgallen called it nothing less than "making love to the President in the direct view of forty million Americans."

After the event, Marilyn and the president spent the night together at the Carlyle Hotel. But five days later when she tried calling Kennedy, White House switchboard operators refused to put her calls through. Kennedy could no longer afford to continue the affair. He had learned from J. Edgar Hoover that the Mafia had bugged their meeting places and had recordings of them in bed. The president asked his brother Bobby to console her, which he did admirably. But after a scorching affair of two months, Bobby stopped taking her calls for the same reason. Hoover informed him that the Mafia would release tapes of him in bed with Marilyn if he continued coming down hard on organized crime. Furious at being dumped by both brothers in two months, Marilyn started speaking with the press. The president asked friends to talk some sense into her.

Her last call was on August 4 to Peter Lawford, who told police she instructed him to say goodbye to Jack and hung up. Lawford may or may not have been telling the truth. There are also reports that Bobby Kennedy was with Lawford that night. A few hours after that call, Marilyn Monroe was found dead of an overdose of barbiturates, a scrap of paper with a White House phone number in her hand. The scrap of paper disappeared, as well as all of her phone records from the offices of General Telephone.

Kennedy began his affair with the voluptuous, platinum blond actress Jayne Mansfield during his presidential campaign, and it lasted until his death. Mansfield had created a lucrative career by imitating Marilyn Monroe. Kennedy told Lawford, "She's so anxious to ape Marilyn, be Marilyn, we'll add to her credentials by giving her a roll in the hay."

"Why, think," Jayne told a friend, "I'll go down in history like that—what was her name—Madame O'Barry." Her friend had to tell her the famous eighteenth-century royal mistress was named Madame du Barry, and she was French, not Irish.

In 1962, Hollywood icon Marlene Dietrich received an invitation from the president to the White House for a drink the evening she was to receive an award for aiding Jewish war refugees. He immediately made it clear he wanted sex, according to film critic Kenneth Tynan, who heard the tale from Dietrich and immediately recorded this priceless pearl in his diary. "I hope you aren't in a hurry," Kennedy said. The sixty-year-old actress explained that two thousand people were waiting to give her an award in half an hour.

Undeterred, Kennedy grabbed her glass and led her to his bedroom. She recalled, "I remembered about his bad back, that wartime injury. I looked at him and he was already undressing. He was unwinding rolls of bandage from around his middle—he looked like Laocoon and that snake, you know? Now I'm an old lady, and I said to myself: I'd like to sleep with the president, sure, but I'll be goddamned if I'm going to be on top!"

After only six minutes, the president climaxed and fell sound asleep. "I looked at my watch and it was 6:50," Dietrich said. "I got dressed and shook him—because I didn't know my way around the place, and I couldn't just call for a cab. I said, 'Jack—wake up! Two thousand Jews are waiting! For Christ's sake get me out of here!' So he grabbed a towel and wrapped it around his waist and took me along this corridor to an elevator. He told the elevator man to get me a car to the Statler Hotel immediately—standing right there in his towel, without any embarrassment, as if it was an everyday event—which in his life it probably was."

There is one story that stands out from the kaleidoscope of sex tales involving movie stars, sophisticated socialites, and lonely divorcées. It is the tale of nineteen-year-old Mimi Beardsley, a fresh-faced college girl from New Jersey, who, on her fourth day as an intern in the White House Press Office in the summer of 1962, found herself thrown onto Jackie Kennedy's bed by the president of the United States and penetrated. On her way home afterward, she asked herself how it had happened and lamented that she would no longer be a virgin on her wedding night.

Mimi had first met Kennedy a little more than a year earlier, when she'd visited the White House for her high school newspaper. He had shaken her hand and asked her about herself. And then, months later, came an unexpected offer for a highly coveted internship. Mimi was a pretty girl who wore no makeup at all, her only adornments a wide white smile and a string of pearls. She had never been popular with boys. She blamed this on her height that, at five foot nine, was unfashionably tall for the time, and her build, thin and athletic rather than the rocket-boobs-hourglass figure women were supposed to have.

On her fourth day working in the Press Office, Kennedy's aide Dave Powers asked her to join him for a swim in the White House pool. Shocked, Mimi assumed this was some kind of White House custom and agreed. She soon found herself swimming with Fiddle, Faddle, and Kennedy and returned to the Press Office reeking of chlorine, her hair wet. And then, a few hours later, Powers suggested she join the president and a few of the staff for drinks up in the residence. Wide-eyed, Mimi guzzled daiquiris with Fiddle, Faddle, Dave Powers, and the president. When she learned that the first lady had taken the children to the

Virginia countryside, Mimi sensed there was something wrong; she shouldn't be there.

Then the president offered to give her a tour of the quarters. In the first lady's bedroom, she wrote in her 2012 autobiography, "He pulled down his pants and then he was above me. He paused briefly when he felt some physical resistance." He was gentler when she told him she was a virgin. Back home soon after, she wondered what she could have done to resist him. "When we were in the bedroom," she wrote, "he had maneuvered me so swiftly and unexpectedly, and with such authority and strength, that short of screaming I doubt if I could have done anything to thwart his intentions."

Mimi's shock and horror soon morphed into "the thrill of being desired. And the fact that I was being desired by the most famous and powerful man in America only amplified my feelings to the point where resistance was out of the question. That's why I didn't say no to the president. It's the best answer I can give. I wouldn't describe what happened that night as making love. But I wouldn't call it nonconsensual, either." It was the beginning of an affair that would last over a year. The president chose Mimi to accompany him on most of his trips, even though she did no work.

Mimi experienced some particularly cruel moments at the hands of the president. When Kennedy instructed her to perform oral sex on Powers, who was sitting on the edge of the pool, she swam up to him and complied. While visiting Bing Crosby's California ranch, Kennedy held out an orange capsule—which Mimi later believed to be poppers, or amyl nitrate—promised it would enhance sex, and asked Mimi to try it. When she refused, he snapped it open under her nose, sending her heart racing and bringing on a raging panic attack. Powers helped calm her as Kennedy had disappeared.

When Mimi returned to college, Kennedy arranged for her to spend some weekends at the White House and got her another internship in the summer of 1963. But by August, she was engaged to a young army reserve officer and stopped sleeping with the president. On the day of Kennedy's assassination, a grieving Mimi told her fiancé about the affair. Hurt, betrayed, but still in love with her, he married her but made her pay every day for betraying him with Kennedy while they were dating. There was no trust in the marriage, just bitterness and pain, and they eventually divorced.

What was in it for the president's women? Jack Kennedy was no Louis XIV, distributing castles, estates, and eye-popping jewels to his mistresses. While his aides paid prostitutes the going rate, women like Diana, Helen, and Mary received no payment. Mimi, a virgin who had practically been raped, came back for more.

Kennedy's women testified to his irresistible charisma, and the glamour and excitement of bedding the most important man in the world. Gunilla von Post wrote, "He cast a spell on people that I've never quite seen before or since . . . He embraced his life with ferocious energy. Jack burned like a brilliant comet in the sky. His grin was incandescent. His eyes were intensely blue, sparkling with joy, a smile that lit up his entire face. He was such a powerful, magnetic man, it was hard to deny my growing attraction to him."

Judith Campbell noticed that he had a knack for seducing people of all ages, male and female. "When he listened, it was as if every nerve and muscle in his whole body was poised at attention . . . When you talked to Jack there was total concentration and absorption. He really wanted to hear what you had to say. He had a habit when he listened of tilting his head slightly toward you, as if to facilitate the process, guarding against the possibility that a word might mischievously try to slip by him."

Mimi Beardsley explained, "He had that politician's gift of making you feel that when you were in his company, you were the most important and interesting person in the world . . . Being with the President and having his undivided attention was like taking this incredibly potent self-esteem drug. And that's a hard habit to kick. Despite the humiliation and uncertainty, I remained enthralled by his charisma and the glamour of traveling with his entourage. My college life of dorms, cafeteria dining, fraternity parties, homework, and moviegoing paled by comparison with Air Force One, Caribbean resorts, the Secret Service, and limos . . . The fact that I was desired by the most famous and powerful man in America merely amplified the thrill. I simply couldn't say no to the President."

While countless women were eager to jump into Kennedy's bed, those who landed there were almost always disappointed. Jackie confessed to her good friend, Dr. Frank Finnerty, that sex with her husband was unsatisfying because "he just goes too fast and falls asleep" and she wondered if she had somehow failed him. She portrayed herself as being "left out" of the sexual experience.

Marilyn Monroe, though hopelessly in love with Jack, lamented to a friend that his sexual performance was horrible. "A minute on and a minute off. Brutal and perfunctory in bed."

"He was in for quantity rather than quality," said his friend George Smathers, with whom Kennedy often engaged in partner swapping. "I don't know how the women ever tolerated it."

Actress Angie Dickinson reportedly said that sex with Kennedy was "the best sixty seconds of my life." Jayne Mansfield told Peter Lawford—who told author Lawrence Quirk—that Jack left something to be desired as a lover, preferring sex while on his back and pressing her to perform oral sex on him. "And once he's done, he's done, it's like you don't exist anymore!"

Judith Campbell, wrote, "When people make love, they should make love to each other. I mention this because, as I was to learn in my relationship with Jack, his attitude was that he was there to be serviced. Partly this was due to his back problem, and partly I think he had been spoiled by women. There is a world of difference between a man who expects to be made love to and two people making love to each other."

Like Roosevelt, Harding, and Wilson before him, Kennedy benefited from the unwritten journalistic rule that no stories of a president's sex life would make the news. This tradition was compounded by the fact that Kennedy served at the height of the Cold War, with emergencies like the Bay of Pigs, the Cuban Missile Crisis, and the building of the Berlin Wall. Diminishing the president's stature would diminish the strength of the entire nation. Journalists frequently saw Kennedy with women not his wife and never reported a word.

The press had protected Kennedy even before he became president. When he ran against Lyndon Johnson for the Democratic nomination in 1960, a Georgetown couple, Leonard and Florence Kater, mailed details of Kennedy's love affair with their former tenant Pamela Turnure to the newspapers. Devout Catholics, they had been disgusted to learn that Kennedy, a married man, had been sneaking into the building. They rigged up a tape recorder to capture sounds of their lovemaking and took pictures of him entering and leaving the apartment. When Kennedy moved into the White House, they protested out front with placards stating that an adulterer lived there. No paper covered the story.

Shortly before his 1961 inauguration, for three days Kennedy reportedly vanished into a Palm Springs vacation cottage with the blond, twenty-nine-year-old actress Angie Dickinson. A *Newsweek* reporter entered the room, saw her stretched out on a bed, and quickly closed the door.

In April 1961, Otto Fuerbringer, the managing editor of *Time* magazine, finished an interview with Kennedy in the White House private quarters and, a few minutes later, returned to retrieve a hat he had left on a chair. He recalled, "There sitting on the sofa was a striking blonde, about thirty-five years old, wearing a short black dress and pearls. Jack handed me my hat, and I left."

In early 1963, a cub reporter for a major newspaper was assigned to patrol the lobby of New York's Carlyle Hotel where President Kennedy was staying. When he saw a top Hollywood star—probably Marilyn Monroe—being hustled up to the president's floor—he told his editor. "No story there" was the reply. Photographs showing a goggle-eyed Kennedy staring at Marilyn's rear end at the "Happy Birthday, Mr. President" event at Madison Square Garden mysteriously disappeared from wire services.

Journalists hoped that staying on good terms with Kennedy would ensure them important scoops and invitations to fabulous White House parties. Not only did they remain silent on his adultery, they went out of their way to portray the Kennedy marriage as idyllic. Reporters and authors often submitted material to him and Bobby for corrections and comments before publication. In some ways, the press were greater prostitutes than the women Kennedy paid for sexual services.

Kennedy was well aware of his invulnerability with the press. "They can't touch me while I'm alive," he boasted to a friend, "and after I'm dead who cares?"

The press protection even extended to Jackie. No photos of her smoking—she had a three-pack-a-day habit—made the newspapers. If her skirt seemed too short in a photo, an artist would make it longer before a paper published it.

Thirty years after the assassination, in an interview with *Washingtonian* magazine, Kennedy's press secretary Pierre Salinger recalled a journalist's question about Kennedy and a woman. "I gave him a 1960s answer, not a 1990s answer. 'Look, he's the president of the United States. He's got to work 14 to 16 hours a day. He's got to run foreign and domestic policy. If he's got time for mistresses after all that, what the hell difference does it make?' The reporter laughed and walked out. That was the end of the story."

Jack's pathological infidelity deeply scarred his marriage. Jackie was trapped; no first lady had ever divorced her husband. To keep scandal from tarnishing the nation, she had to stay. She suffered depression and headaches that were treated by Max Jacobson, Dr. Feelgood, with injections of amphetamines.

While Jackie usually pasted on a smiling face with her husband's women friends, on at least one occasion, she became publicly enraged. Standing in a reception line, her eyes fell on a "blond bimbo" inching her way toward her. Jackie "wheeled around in fury" and scolded one of her husband's aides, "Isn't it bad enough that you solicit this woman for my husband, but then you insult me by asking me to shake her hand!" She managed to quickly compose herself and shake the blond bimbo's hand.

For all her fury and depression about her husband's philandering, Jackie Kennedy had two healthy and rewarding focuses as first lady. The first and foremost was motherhood. Jackie was a devoted mother, keeping her children firmly out of the press and creating a loving, learning environment. She played with them, read to them, insisted they have good manners, and built them their own little zoo on the White House grounds. She created a school on the third floor of the White House where Caroline and John-John were joined by children of White House employees. She told one reporter, "If you bungle raising your children, I don't think whatever else you do matters very much."

Her other focus was redecorating the White House. When the Kennedys moved in, the furnishings were a dumpy mishmash of more than a century of bad taste. Jackie raised funds, hired experts, and tracked down original White House pieces that previous presidents had blithely carted off with them when they left office. She founded the White House Historical Association and the Committee for the Preservation of the White House. Her February 1962 television show giving the viewers a tour of the refurbished White House was watched by 56 million Americans.

Jackie also found solace in punishing her husband in myriad manifestations of passive aggression, taking refuge in wild spending sprees—spending hundreds of thousands of dollars on designer clothing and budget-busting antiques in a year—that sent him into foaming-at-the-mouth rages. He always gave in to her, though. Under the circumstances, he had to.

In addition, she flirted outrageously with male friends in an effort to make her husband jealous. Traphes Bryant wrote, "I remember one particular White House party, Mrs. K. was loaded on champagne and flung her shoes off while dancing under the chandelier in the main lobby . . . Jacqueline seemed to flirt with every guy she danced with—making eyes, throwing her head back love-dovey. All the men danced with her."

One time she commanded Faddle to play tennis with her. When Faddle explained she had no tennis shoes, Jackie made her play on the hot court in bare feet. She knew the value of her style and beauty to her husband's popularity and tortured him with a thousand little cuts by simply not showing up for official events, sometimes at the last minute, embarrassing him deeply. She maintained that she would not be going to Dallas in November 1963 until Texas governor John Connally threw a raging tantrum, insisting he needed her there.

Jackie escaped from the White House at every opportunity, spending many weekends at Glen Ora, an estate an hour west of Washington, where she went riding and fox hunting. In the summer of 1962, she spent three weeks on the Amalfi coast of Italy with her children and her sister, and reportedly had an affair with the wealthy forty-one-year-old Italian industrialist Gianni Agnelli. Newspapers ran photos of the handsome pair joyfully walking through piazzas. Kennedy, alarmed, sent his wife a tersely worded telegram indicating she should be photographed more often with their daughter: "More Caroline, less Agnelli."

During Jack's final sixty-three days of life, he and his wife were apart for forty-two of them. On August 9, 1963, Jackie lost her premature son, Patrick, who survived only thirty-nine hours. Still deeply depressed several weeks later, she accepted an invitation from Greek shipping magnate Aristotle Onassis for an Aegean cruise on his luxurious yacht. Kennedy was aghast; a few years earlier, Onassis had been found guilty of U.S. tax evasion and fined $7 million. How would it look for the grieving first lady to kick up her heels with the playboy tax evader? But Jackie gleefully defied him, arriving in Greece October 3. Her sister Lee, who was having an affair with Onassis, joined her.

But events took a surprising turn when the shipping tycoon started courting the wife of the U.S. president. They flirted and laughed as Lee stewed. Onassis thought Jackie's jewelry was cheap, called Van Cleef & Arpels in Paris, and told them to fly a magnificent piece to the yacht. A few days later, Onassis gave Jackie a diamond-and-ruby necklace that cost $80,000 ($671,000 today). As for Lee, she complained that Onassis had only given her "three dinky little bracelets that Caroline wouldn't wear to her own birthday party." Onassis's friend Constantine Gratsos worried that what had happened on board that yacht would cost a lot more than $80,000. "I kept thinking: this could be the most expensive fuck in the history of the world."

Newspapers around the globe reported on Jackie's disgraceful behavior. Republican National Chairman William E. Miller denounced her "lack of decorum and dignity" carousing at "late night parties in foreign lands." Republican Congressman Oliver Bolton of Ohio condemned the first lady twice on the floor of the House for showing "poor judgment and perhaps impropriety in accepting the lavish hospitality of a man who has defrauded the American public. Why doesn't the first lady see more of her own country instead of gallivanting all over Europe?" Women picketed in front of the White House with signs demanding she return to the U.S. and do her job.

Instead of coming back, however, Jackie added another leg to her journey, visiting Morocco. She finally returned to Washington on October 17. To counter the rumors of problems with their marriage, Jack showed up with their two children to welcome Jackie as she glided off the airplane wearing her new $80,000 necklace.

Jackie would tell her sister Lee when she was upset about her husband's extracurricular activities, and Lee would talk to Jack. He had absolutely no guilt about it. "I love her deeply and have done everything for her," he would say. "I've no feeling of letting her down because I've put her foremost in everything."

According to her friend Dr. Frank Finnerty, Jackie wasn't certain her husband remembered most of his fleeting sex partners. "She was also sure that Jack felt no love or any kind of affection" for these women, he said. Jackie believed "he was just getting rid of some hormonal surge." Jackie said she was helpless to stop her husband's philandering, which was "an intrinsic part of his life," a "vicious trait" that he had "undoubtedly inherited" from his father.

"All Kennedy men are like that," she once told Ted Kennedy's wife, Joan, who was horrified by her own husband's infidelity. "It doesn't mean a thing. You can't let it get to you because you shouldn't take it personally."

In 1962, when a *New York Times* reporter asked her what her husband would do after his presidency, without missing a beat she said, "He'll probably take a job as a headmaster of an exclusive, all-girls prep school."

Still, Jackie considered divorcing her husband once he was out of office. She told U.S. ambassador to the United Nations Adlai Stevenson that she and her sister Lee—unhappily married to a Polish aristocrat—"always talked about divorce as something to look forward to."

And yet her grief was real after the assassination. The photos of her in the bloodstained pink suit on Air Force One, standing next to Lyndon Johnson as he took the oath of office, and her black-draped figure at the funeral suggest stunned disbelief and pain chewing its way through the numbness of shock. Author Truman Capote said, "Their relationship had become an utter farce by the time he became president. I think she fell in love with him again only after the assassination."

Jackie invented the Camelot tale as a gift to her children, the American people, and herself, obliterating adultery, drugs, and lies, creating a new reality—accepted by all—of a brief, shining moment in time with herself as the glorious female lead.

Jackie married Aristotle Onassis in 1968, defying the Kennedy family and the American public who wanted her to remain frozen on the day of the funeral, a beautiful cold statue eternally veiled in black. They soon led separate lives, Onassis dying in 1975. Jackie moved back to New York and became a successful book editor for Doubleday. She enjoyed a relationship with Maurice Tempelsman, her financial adviser, from 1980 until her death from cancer in 1994 at the age of sixty-four. Many Kennedy wives and lovers suffered appalling tragedy, as if infected with a kind of family curse. But Jackie had the strength to pull herself out of the maelstrom and create a new life for herself on her own terms.

10

LYNDON JOHNSON AND HALF
THE PEOPLE IN THE WORLD

*W*hile visiting President Lyndon Johnson's ranch in Texas, a female aide was startled in the middle of the night when a man in a nightshirt appeared at the foot of her bed holding a flashlight. She couldn't make out who it was until she heard a familiar Texas drawl. "Move over," the visitor said. "This is your president."

* * *

It is hard for many of us today to understand the attractiveness of Lyndon Johnson to women. When we look at a photo of him as president, we see a rumpled bulldog face, beady, dark eyes, and thinning gray hair. But many women were fascinated by the young Lyndon's dramatic appearance: his coal-black hair and eyebrows and milky white skin. He used his size—six foot four, with long arms and big hands—to dominate other men, standing a bit too close, wrapping his arm around a shoulder, doling out rib-crushing hugs. His appeal lay mostly in his vitality, his energy, an ability to command and entrance no matter how much like a bulldog he grew to resemble. Add to that a spellbinding eloquence that could wrap his listeners into a story and take them wherever Johnson wanted to go.

"It was his animation that made him good-looking," said the sister of one of his long-term mistresses. "He didn't have power, or money, or anything. He just had this personal force—a huge, unique personal force. He just radiated self-confidence." Another recalled, "He had what they call now a charisma. He was dynamic, and he had this piercing look, and he knew exactly where he was going, and what he was going to do next, and he had you sold down the river on whatever he was telling you. And you had no doubts that he was going to do what he said—no doubts at all . . . You felt the power."

It was that personal power that propelled him from a dirt-poor childhood in the hardscrabble Texas hills to the highest office in the land. The Johnsons were a dilapidated family with pretensions of grandeur. His father was a failed businessman and former state representative who drank too much and owed everyone in town money. His mother was a dreamer who read poetry but didn't wash her children's clothing, nor did she always manage to feed her brood of five. The Johnsons were, in short, the town laughingstocks, and it rankled in the breast of little Lyndon, who hated the sneering, the taunts. At the age of ten, hurt and defiant, he told the other boys in the schoolyard, "Someday I'm going to be president of the United States." Naturally, they laughed at him and said they wouldn't vote for him. But most of them probably did.

Lyndon's political career began in 1930 when the twenty-two-year-old attended a political rally for Pat Neff, a former governor running for reelection. When Neff didn't show, Lyndon stepped forward and made a powerful, persuasive speech promoting him. Lyndon could spin a yarn better than anybody. Filled with self-deprecating good ole boy charm, he grabbed listeners by the heartstrings and didn't release them until he was good and ready. A candidate for state legislature in the crowd that night, astonished by Johnson's impromptu speech, hired him to work on his own campaign. A year later, Johnson was hired by newly elected Texas congressman Richard Kleberg as his secretary. Since Kleberg rarely did any work—spending most of his time playing poker, drinking whiskey, and golfing—it was Johnson who tirelessly ran the office and assisted constituents. He soon became known as the most powerful congressional secretary in Washington at the age of twenty-three.

He relied on the same tried-and-true methods to get ahead in Congress as he had in college at Southwest Texas State Normal School, when he had arrived poor and unknown, an utter nobody. He buttered up older female secretaries and the wives of powerful men, complimenting them on their hairstyles and dresses, bursting into rapture at the cakes and pies they brought him. With influential men, he gazed at them in rapt wonder at their wisdom, a "professional son," as some called him. "He would just drink up what they were saying," a friend of his said, "sit at their knees and drink it up, and they would pour out their hearts to him." When the twenty-eight-year-old was elected to Congress in 1937, he played the same role of adoring son with President Roosevelt, who took quite a shine to the young congressman.

With his colleagues, he was a bully, a liar who always had to be the center of attention. His nickname in college was "Bullshit Johnson." "He'd cut your throat to get what he wanted," said an acquaintance. Yet he inspired unswerving loyalty from some. When he arrived in Washington, he had in tow a clique of young men from his Texas university who would have followed him to hell if he'd asked, and he did. He made them work seven days a week, sometimes fourteen or sixteen hours a day, answering every single letter from a constituent the same day it arrived, and paid them a pittance. He even made them take dictation while he sat on the toilet having a bowel movement—an unfortunate habit he continued throughout his life.

FDR's vast new bureaucracies—the Social Security Administration, the Public Works Administration, the Tennessee Valley Authority—meant many thousands of jobs which, in the heart of the Depression, meant food, housing, even life itself. Wheeling, dealing, and forging alliances, Johnson obtained the right to hand out jobs—not great jobs, but any job was manna from heaven in those days: a postal clerk, an elevator operator, a janitor. One recipient said, "Lyndon didn't make you rich, but he got you a job." He built, job by job, a network of support throughout Texas, people who would vote for him, campaign for him, and convince their friends and family members to do the same.

Now that Lyndon was on his way, he needed a charming wife to entertain and socialize with other congressional wives, a woman to continue building that network of support so crucial to politicians. Moreover, he needed a rich wife to fund his campaigns.

He met twenty-two-year-old Lady Bird Taylor, a reporter for the *Daily Texan*, in 1934. Her real name was Claudia, but soon after birth, her African American nurse gazed at her and said, "She's as purty as a lady bird," and the name stuck. Daughter of a wealthy Alabama businessman who had settled in Texas, Lady Bird was five when she lost her mother. She grew up a shy, lonely child, who wandered for hours at a time in nature, particularly enjoying wildflowers, and often disappeared for much of the day with a book. She was not a classic beauty with her long nose and wide mouth, but she had a distinctive attractiveness, with alert, dark eyes under arched black brows, thick, dark hair, and a beautifully shaped face. She paid scant attention to her appearance, wearing dowdy gray clothes and sensible heels, as if she hoped to fade into the background so no one would notice her.

Beneath her fluttering southern belle charm and drab dresses, Bird, as Lyndon usually called her, was shrewd, determined, and ambitious, a proverbial steel magnolia. She had graduated high school at fifteen and received two university degrees in teaching and journalism.

On their first date over breakfast at an Austin café, Lyndon told her he wanted to marry her. "I thought it was some kind of joke," she said. But she was impressed. "I knew I had met something remarkable, but I didn't know quite what . . . I had a queer sort of moth-and-flame feeling." He introduced her to his parents the following day and acted as if they would soon be engaged.

Lyndon pursued Bird with the same relentless drive and ambition he pursued politics, and within two months, she was somewhat surprised to find herself standing with him in front of a justice of the peace, wearing a $2.50 wedding band bought across the street at Sears Roebuck. The next morning, she called a friend and said, "Lyndon and I committed matrimony last night."

The honeymoon lasted only hours. The next day, while visiting a friend, Lyndon rudely told Bird to change her stockings as one had a run in it. It was a sign of things to come. He criticized her frumpy clothes and bought her more fashionable dresses. He made her wear high heels and red lipstick and have her hair and nails done. He insisted she keep her weight down to 113 pounds and, when they were separated for long stretches, as often happened, instructed her to send him the measurements of her waist and hips in every letter. Whatever orders he shouted at her—and there were many—had to be obeyed immediately.

Every evening, Bird laid out his clothes, polished his shoes, filled his cigarette case, and made sure his fountain pens had ink. Every morning she served him breakfast in bed. Her checkbook was available to help him with his next campaign. And when he yelled and shouted at her at polite dinner parties, and other guests winced, the unflappable Bird just smiled, nodded, and did what he asked. His moods swung wildly from high to low and back again, but she was always stable, always calm, always his anchor in the storm. After her husband became a congressman in a 1937 special election, and a senator in 1948, Bird entered the world of competitive political entertaining, where she never said a bad word about anyone, and made them all love her and, by extension, think better of Lyndon. She went behind him with a figurative dustpan and broom, cleaning up the messes he made, comforting the insulted staff, soothing hurt feelings, telling them he didn't mean it, and they should come by for dinner real soon now.

She accepted all of this because, contrary to appearances, she was actually the stronger, Lyndon the weaker. There were days when his nerves and depression were so bad—the Valley of the Black Pig, he came to call it—he could barely get out of bed, and she was there telling him just to put one foot in front of the other. Bird was so strong she didn't mind appearing weak and bullied. It didn't matter. One issue she had not reckoned with when she married him, however, was his rampant infidelity.

His first serious love affair began in 1938, when he took up with twenty-six-year-old Alice Glass, the gorgeous, six-foot-tall, blue-eyed mistress of Charles Marsh, a wealthy newspaper magnate. Marsh, always bouncing around Capitol Hill, was one of those older, powerful men Johnson so expertly cultivated. Johnson met Alice when Marsh invited him and Bird to spend the weekend at Longlea, his Virginia country estate ninety miles outside of Washington. Marsh had built a replica of an eighteenth-century English manor house Alice had admired, setting it on a thousand acres so she wouldn't have to be bothered with hearing the neighbors.

Born and raised in sleepy Marlin, Texas, Alice was a nineteen-year-old secretary in Austin when she met the forty-four-year-old Marsh at a party. They became lovers that night, and he left his wife and three children soon after. A friend said that Marsh "lavished jewels on her—not only a quarter-of-a-million-dollar necklace of perfect emeralds, but earrings of emeralds and diamonds and rubies." Alice's cousin recalled, "The first time she came back to Marlin and walked down the street in her New York clothes and her jewels, women came running out of the shops to stare at her." Another friend said that "when she walked into a restaurant, between those emeralds and her height and that red-gold hair, the place would go completely silent."

"Her blond hair had a red overlay," said Frank Oltorf, a Washington lobbyist. "Usually it was long enough so that she could sit on it, and it shimmered and gleamed like nothing you ever saw . . . There was something about the way she walked and sat that was elegant and aloof. And with her height, and that creamy skin and that incredible hair, she looked like a Viking princess."

"She was a free spirit, very independent, in an era when women weren't that way," said her sister, Mary Louise. She didn't believe in marriage, and she had refused to marry Marsh, even though she had two children while with him, though one, according to Marsh's daughter, had been sired by Alice's interior designer. Outspoken, highly intelligent, and idealistic, she looked up to politicians who tried to help the less fortunate. When she met Johnson, and he regaled her with tales of Texas poverty, and all he was doing to bring jobs and electricity to his district, she thought that she had met a kindred spirit. Looking back, Mary Louise said, "She thought he was a young man who was going to save the world."

Alice also admired what she believed was Johnson's indifference to money. Marsh and his friends almost always spoke of money, how to make it, how to spend it, how to take it from others. "She was just sick of money, money, money," her sister said. We can picture Alice, sitting at her thirty-foot-long dining room table, sipping champagne her butler offered her, as candlelight glinted off those emeralds, just bursting with rage that everyone was discussing a subject as sordid as money.

"Lyndon was the love of Alice's life," Mary Louise said. "My sister was mad for Lyndon—absolutely mad for him." When Marsh was traveling the country to supervise his countless businesses, Lyndon and Alice met in Marsh's Washington, D.C., apartment or at Longlea, where Lyndon repaired on weekends without Bird.

But sometimes Bird was invited. When she was there, Alice Glass's salon of witty, beautiful, rich, and powerful people ignored the lackluster woman sitting in the corner, dark eyes watchful. Alice's cousin Alice Hopkins recalled, "Everybody was trying to be nice to her, but she was just . . . out of place." Even Bird herself agreed. "I remember Alice in a series of long and elegant dresses," she said, "and me in—well, much less elegant."

Did Bird know her husband was having an affair with Alice Glass? Frank Oltorf said, "Oh, I'm sure she did." Alice's sister, Mary Louise, said, "The thing I could never understand was how she stood it. Lyndon would leave her on weekends, weekend after weekend, just leave her home. I wouldn't have stood it for a minute."

While Alice hoped to marry Johnson, they both knew it to be impossible. For one thing, no matter how he treated Bird, he loved her—he absolutely lit up when she entered a room—and needed her as he did no other. Because no other woman could help him get through the Valley of the Black Pig. Surely, he never told Alice Glass about his serious struggles with depression, about those days when he was helpless and trembling in bed with the covers pulled up over his head. He also needed Bird's money for his campaigns—not just her father's money, but the profits she was making on her own. A shrewd businesswoman who counted every penny, she managed three thousand acres of Alabama cotton- and timberland and would, starting in 1943, become immensely wealthy by owning a chain of Texas radio stations. And then there was his political career. It was believed that no divorced man could ever become president, which was Lyndon's lifelong dream.

In late 1939, Charles Marsh discovered the affair and felt doubly betrayed. He had looked on Johnson as a son, had made sure his newspapers wrote glowing articles about him, and had even helped Johnson financially by selling him nineteen acres of prime Austin real estate ripe for development at a below-market price. Marsh yelled and cursed and threw Johnson out. But Johnson came back the next morning and abjectly apologized—we can picture tears glistening in his eyes—and promised to end the relationship. Surprisingly, Marsh forgave him. Marsh's daughter, Antoinette Marsh Haskell, said, "They didn't let her come between them. Men in power like that don't give a damn about women. They were not that important in the end. They treated women like toys. That's just the way it was."

In early 1940, Alice married Charles Marsh but quickly divorced him. The woman who said she didn't believe in marriage ended up marrying six times. "She never got over Lyndon," Alice Hopkins said. After she divorced Marsh, Lyndon visited her again at Longlea. The relationship lasted on and off until the mid-1960s, when he plunged the nation deeper into the Vietnam War. Alice told friends she had burned Johnson's love letters because she didn't want her granddaughter to know she had been to bed with the man responsible for the worst brutalities of the war.

Lyndon's next long-term affair was with a beautiful new California congresswoman, Helen Gahagan Douglas. A Hollywood star and opera singer married to matinee idol Melvyn Douglas, she took up her office in 1944, while her husband was serving in the army. Johnson virtually lived with the tall, curvy blonde, driving with her to work in the morning and walking hand in hand into the Capitol.

It is likely that in 1949 Johnson began an affair with a twenty-four-year-old Texas advertising saleswoman named Madeleine Brown. At least, that is what she later claimed. Brown was a bit of a grifter—in 1989 she was convicted of forging a will. Moreover, she had no love letters from Johnson, had no eyewitnesses who saw them together, and made a good amount of money from the story. But she did have one document no one could explain away.

Cute and petite with dark hair, sparkling, dark eyes, and a dazzling smile, Madeleine claimed she met Johnson, then a powerful senator, at an Austin social event. He pursued her, and they soon found themselves in a hotel bathtub together. "When he closed his eyes and parted my lips with his tongue, I felt as if I were lost in a whirlpool," she wrote in her steamy 1994 tell-all. "With deliberate slowness, he teased and tasted my lips and tongue. Lyndon's lustful kiss blazed through me with the fire of a thousand suns, withering my reserve and melting my resistance . . . He devoured me with a ferocity that turned me into liquid heat. My body simmered from one end to the other. Every inch of my being was eager for his touch."

She continued, "Lyndon was trembling with agonizing anticipation as he rubbed my breasts and began running his hands over the silky terrain of my hips, thighs, and legs. Suddenly he stood up, scooped me into his arms and carried me soaking wet into the bedroom . . . Lyndon was as thrilling in bed as he was in the public forum of politics—energetic, powerful, and commandeering. He explored all the nuances of my body. I felt nothing but wild pleasure as he entered me effortlessly. Together our ecstasy grew like a roaring tide, overpowering us in its intensity until ultimately my moans rose into an ecstatic cry."

According to Brown, one night Johnson showed up at her hotel room with a brown grocery bag that held "a little black whip along with a string of pearls and a funny-looking big peter." Johnson asked, "Madeleine, you ready for something different?" Oh yes, she was. Sadly, Madeleine didn't describe what he did with these items. She wrote that Johnson loved to watch homemade movies of animals mating, and during sex with her he would imitate the animals' bellows. While we might not believe such tales about, say, Dwight Eisenhower, they do have the ring of truth with Lyndon Johnson.

Madeleine claimed that Johnson was the father of her son born in 1950, Steven Brown, and that Johnson paid for her two-bedroom Austin home, maid service, unlimited charge cards, and a new car every two years. Brown claimed she withheld the truth of her son's paternity until she had a heart attack in 1987 and feared she might go to her grave without him knowing. Soon after, Steven Brown filed a $10.5 million patrimony suit against

Johnson's estate but lost the case when he failed to appear in court. He died of cancer in 1990 and left no children upon whom DNA tests could be conducted.

Indeed, the whole story might be suspect except for a letter a Dallas attorney wrote Madeleine Brown soon after Johnson's death in 1973. Jerome Ragsdale promised to "continue with the financial arrangements that Lyndon provided for you and Steve throughout the past." Though Ragsdale was dead by the time Brown first publicly claimed to be Johnson's son in 1987, the letter was genuine, and we can only wonder why the former president of the United States would be making financial arrangements for a woman he had never met and her son.

By 1954, Johnson was having an affair with his secretary, twenty-two-year-old Mary Margaret Wiley, whose desk was right next to his. A meltingly beautiful honey blonde, Mary Margaret was perfectly in tune with Johnson's moods, often knowing what he wanted before he said it. Their closeness during the day extended to after-hours socializing. Naturally, he had to fly his secretary around with him on business trips.

Many speculated that he might divorce Bird, who had given him two daughters, to marry Mary Margaret and have the son he had always longed for. As it happened, in 1962 she married Johnson aide Jack Valenti—later the longtime president of the Motion Picture Association of America. When she had a daughter, Courtenay, a year later, Johnson was so crazy about the curly-haired little girl—he had never shown any extraordinary fondness for his own daughters—that many in the White House assumed he was her father. The crude, foulmouthed president sat in cabinet meetings with the baby on his lap.

At some point in the early years of their marriage, Bird threatened to divorce Johnson if he continued his infidelity, but she soon managed to make peace with it. Perhaps she realized he couldn't stop, and she didn't really want a divorce. Perhaps, too, there was an advantage that Bird was not the sole recipient of her husband's urgent desires. One of the first things she did after their brief honeymoon was to phone her gynecologist for an appointment to make sure she wasn't internally injured.

More than just accepting her husband's other women, Bird went out of her way to be kind to them, complimenting them on their hair and clothing, inviting them to dinner. If Lyndon got out of hand with a woman at a party, she would say gently, "You're wanted over there, Lyndon. You're neglecting some of your friends." She referred to Lucy Mercer Rutherfurd—Franklin Roosevelt's lifelong lover—as nothing more than "a fly on the wedding cake."

On one occasion, a longtime Johnson secretary, Marie Fehmer, accompanied Lady Bird to Johnson's California hotel room, where they found Mary Margaret Wiley's bras and panties strewn around the room. Bird gathered them up in a tidy little heap and "went on her way to be nice" to Mary Margaret, according to Fehmer. On another occasion, when Lady Bird inadvertently opened a box delivered to the Johnson ranch in Texas and found an impossibly tiny lavender bikini, she handed it to her husband and said sweetly, "It must be for one of your lady friends."

In 1974, a year after Lyndon's death, Barbara Walters of the *Today* show asked, "How did you handle your flirt and ladies' man husband?" Bird replied calmly, "Lyndon was a people lover and that certainly did not exclude half the people of the world, women. He got a lot of solace and happiness and inspiration from women." She agreed that Lyndon was "a flirt and a ladies' man."

Then she added, "I hope that I was reasonable. And if all those ladies had some good points that I didn't have, I hope that I had the good sense to try to learn by it."

Though Bird accepted Lyndon's infidelity, voters might not have. In 1939, when his aide Walter Jenkins expressed concern about his playboy reputation, Johnson replied that he paid close attention to constituents' opinions in all matters but two—the car he drove and the women he slept with. He could afford such equanimity. He would be the last U.S. president whose blatant marital infidelities would be concealed by the press. At the time of Jenkins's warning, news organizations had conspired to hide from the American people the fact that their president was a paraplegic and he was sleeping with his secretary. The affairs of a young Texas congressman would have been far less interesting.

Nor was the press remotely interested in Johnson's public urination. "He would piss in the parking lot of the House Office Building," said Wingate Lucas, a representative from Fort Worth. "Well, a lot of fellows did that. I did it. But the rest of us would try to hide behind a car or something. He just didn't care if someone noticed him." Lucas recalled one occasion where Johnson and some men were walking across the parking lot with female secretaries behind them, and "he just stopped and began to take a piss right in front of them." Perhaps it was Johnson's pride in the size of his member that caused such behavior. Lucas recalled, "In the men's bathrooms in the House Office Building, if a colleague came in, Johnson, after he finished urinating, would wave his penis and ask, 'Have you ever seen anything as big as this?'"

In 1948, Johnson became a senator after having, evidently, stuffed the ballot boxes in the highly contested Democratic primary. He became Senate majority whip in 1951, Senate minority leader in 1953, and, when the Democrats returned to a majority in the Senate in 1955, majority leader. Johnson was, quite possibly, the most powerful Senate majority leader ever. Perhaps he learned a lesson from FBI director J. Edgar Hoover, a good friend, who had files on every politician in Washington, D.C. Johnson, too, accumulated files on all his fellow senators. One Johnson biographer wrote, "He could get up every day and learn what their fears, their desires, their wishes, their wants were, and he could then manipulate, dominate, persuade and cajole them."

Johnson's tactics to persuade a senator to vote yea or nay on a bill came to be called "the Treatment." It involved Johnson dominating with his height, leaning over his victim and causing him to lean backward as their noses almost touched. A colleague of Johnson's described it as "an incredible blend of badgering, cajolery, reminders of past favors, promises of future favors, predictions of gloom if something doesn't happen. When that man started to work on you, all of a sudden, you just felt that you were standing under a waterfall and the stuff was pouring on you."

According to two journalists, "The Treatment could last ten minutes or four hours. It came, enveloping its target, at the Johnson Ranch swimming pool, in one of Johnson's offices, in the Senate cloakroom, on the floor of the Senate itself—wherever Johnson might find a fellow Senator within his reach. Its tone could be supplication, accusation, cajolery, exuberance, scorn, tears, complaint and the hint of threat. It was all of these together. It ran the gamut of human emotions. Its velocity was breathtaking, and it was all in one direction . . . The Treatment was an almost hypnotic experience and rendered the target stunned and helpless." Harvard historian Arthur Schlesinger agreed. "After nearly two hours of hypnosis," he wrote about a 1956 meeting with Johnson, "I staggered away in a condition of exhaustion."

Johnson had hoped to win the Democratic nomination for president in 1960 but saw it going to John F. Kennedy instead. When Kennedy—a Catholic from Massachusetts—offered Johnson the vice presidential slot, it was to balance out the ticket. Johnson was a southerner, a Protestant. Kennedy told his aides that Johnson could deliver the South and take "the Catholic flavor off me." Johnson also boasted far more political experience. He was the second most powerful man in the country after President Eisenhower, having served twenty-three years in Congress, nine of them as a Senate leader. Kennedy had less than half the experience, and none of it in leadership.

There was another huge advantage to having Johnson as vice president. It was a position of no power—other than breaking ties in Senate votes and doing whatever errands the president assigned him. And Kennedy wanted to neutralize Johnson's power in Washington. He could be a formidable enemy in the Senate if he didn't agree with the president. By offering Johnson the position, Kennedy could, in one move, both deliver the South and take this powerful piece off the political chessboard.

Johnson knew he would not be electable in eight years and might not even be alive. Though only fifty-two, he looked much older. It is hard to believe that he was only nine years Kennedy's senior. Johnson had smoked a hundred cigarettes a day until his 1955 heart attack and knew he could quite possibly be living on borrowed time. But did he want to lose his Senate position for a job that John Nance Garner, FDR's unhappy vice president from 1933 to 1941, called "not worth a bucket of warm piss"? The nation's first vice president, John Adams, wrote his wife, "My country in its wisdom has contrived for me the most insignificant office that ever the invention of man contrived or his imagination conceived."

Johnson decided he did. "I looked it up," Johnson told journalist Clare Boothe Luce. "One out of every four presidents has died in office. I'm a gamblin' man, darlin', and this is the only chance I got." Johnson also knew what many in Washington did not. That Kennedy was terribly sick, racked with pain from Addison's disease, a potentially fatal illness. "Here was a young whippersnapper," he said of Kennedy, "malaria-ridden and yellah, sickly, sickly . . . Now I admit that he had a good sense of humor and he looked awfully good on that goddamn television screen, and through it all he was a pretty decent fellow, but his growing hold on the American people was simply a mystery to me."

Kennedy, who would have hated to see Johnson succeed him, told his aide Kenny O'Donnell, "I'm forty-three years old. I'm not going to die in office. So the vice-presidency doesn't mean anything."

It was a union of opposites. Kennedy was four inches shorter, leaner, graceful, a handsome man who listened intently, his few words carefully chosen with a clipped Boston accent. Johnson was huge, lumbering, crude, and grizzled; he could spin out a story for hours in his Texas drawl, and the minute someone else began to tell a story he would fall sound asleep. Johnson called Kennedy "sonny boy" and his brother Bobby—whom he despised—"that little shitass." The Kennedy circle called Lyndon and Lady Bird "Uncle Cornpone and his Little Pork Chop." Kennedy thought Johnson was "uncouth and somewhat of an oaf," but told his aides to "literally kiss his ass from one end of Washington to the other" because he was a "very insecure, sensitive man with a huge ego." The relationship was to be one of stiff formality and elaborate courtesy.

Given Johnson's strong support of civil rights, Kennedy appointed him chairman of the President's Committee on Equal

Employment Opportunity. He also became chairman of the National Aeronautics and Space Council, where he helped select Houston for the new $60 million NASA command center, which would be renamed in his honor after his death. But overall, Lyndon's years as vice president were the unhappiest of his life. Kennedy sent him on ridiculous assignments, such as posing with Miss Muffin at the National Retail Bakers Association. To get him out of Washington, Kennedy arranged for him to visit thirty-three countries where he made one hundred and fifty speeches. Johnson saw it as demeaning busywork to keep him away from the seat of power. A colleague called him "thoroughly, visibly and persistently miserable." He was a "frustrated force of nature," said journalist Joe Alsop. His vice presidency was "gilded impotence," crowed that little shitass Bobby.

"I can't stand Johnson's long face," Kennedy told his friend Florida senator George Smathers. "He just comes in with his face all screwed up, never says anything. He looks so sad." Whenever Johnson was asked his opinion, he would say firmly, "I agree with the president." In February 1963, *Time* magazine ran a story on Johnson titled "Seen, Not Heard." "Power has slipped from his grasp," the article stated. At White House meetings, "He is free to speak up, but nobody really has to heed him anymore." Many people felt sorry for him. Harry McPherson, general counsel of the Democratic Policy Committee, recalled, "It was so moving to think of this massive figure, reduced in his eyes and the eyes of others." Sometimes Johnson was so depressed he would go to his Texas ranch and pull the covers over his head.

The Kennedys and their privileged friends laughed at Johnson's Texan accent, his dirt-poor beginnings, and just about everything else about him. The only one of them Johnson liked was Jackie, who "was always nicer to me than anybody in the Kennedy family," he said. "She just made me feel like I was a human being." As for the rest of the snotty lot, Johnson made fun of them right back, telling the majority leader secretary Bobby Baker, "All those Bostons and Harvards . . . didn't know any more about Capitol Hill than an old maid does about fuckin'."

For Bird, however, the years of her husband's vice presidency were perhaps the happiest of her life. For one thing, she loved the trips to foreign countries as she had never had the opportunity to travel much before. For another, she delighted in interacting with the press and the public. When Jackie was punishing Kennedy for his infidelity by not showing up at an official event—usually once a week—Bird graciously stepped in with a genuine smile. Jackie told Johnson how much she appreciated Lady Bird's "willingness to assume every burden. She assumed so many for me."

By August 1963, Johnson was wondering if he should even stay on Kennedy's ticket for the 1964 election. Maybe he should retire from politics and live at his ranch, away from Kennedy's snobbery, condescension, and demeaning errands. Then, on November 22, 1963, everything changed during a motorcade ride in Dallas. Suddenly Johnson was president. In the midst of national chaos, Johnson stepped into the role with dignity and somber leadership. He "looked carved in bronze those hours," Lady Bird recalled. "Very stern and very grave." Kennedy's secretary of agriculture, Orville Freeman, said, "The frustration seemed gone, he seemed relaxed. The power, the confidence, the assurance of Majority Leader Johnson seemed to be there."

It is an interesting footnote to history that the Constitution makes no provision for what to call a vice president who succeeds a president who dies in office. The first president to die in office was sixty-eight-year-old William Henry Harrison in 1841 from pneumonia contracted during his cold, wet inaugural a month earlier. All agreed that Vice President John Tyler would assume the president's duties, as mandated in the Constitution, but no one knew if he should take the oath of office and become president. Would the Founders have agreed to someone bearing the title of president without having being elected? A son of one of those Founders, former president John Quincy Adams, who hated Tyler, wanted to call him "Mr. Vice-President Acting as President." Many people called him "His Accidency." Tyler insisted on taking the oath and becoming president, a precedent that resulted in the orderly transfer of power on future such occasions.

Under the best of circumstances, the Kennedys would have been a difficult act to follow. But as "Accidencies," the Johnsons had a delicate balancing act with a nation in deep mourning. Lyndon had to show he was following Kennedy's vision for the nation while demonstrating his own able leadership. A week after the assassination, he issued an executive order to rename NASA's Apollo Launch Operations Center and the NASA/Air Force Cape Canaveral launch facilities as the John F. Kennedy Space Center. He pushed hard for Kennedy's Civil Rights Act—which ultimately became law in 1964—against southern politicians vehemently opposed to it by insisting that its passage would be the best way to honor Kennedy's memory. He asked Kennedy's cabinet members to remain in office and even kept that little shitass Bobby as attorney general.

Many Kennedy appointees left in the first months, however, unable to stand the contrast of Kennedy elegance with Johnsonian crudity. The new president farted so much his dogs ran under the furniture to hide. If he didn't like his food, he would spit it out—on the plate of the person sitting next to him. He threatened his own Secret Service agents, saying, "If you don't get away from me, I'm gonna shoot out your tires." His language was often crude, redolent of Texas country sayings. For instance, when someone pressed him to fire J. Edgar Hoover, Johnson replied, "If you've got a skunk around, it's better to have him inside the tent pissing out than outside the tent pissing in." Looking out his window, "It's raining as hard as a cat pissing on a flat rock." And, regarding a Republican senator's speech, he scoffed, "Making a speech on economics is a lot like pissing down your leg. It may seem hot to you, but it never does to anyone else." Camelot it was not.

But the public didn't see this side of Johnson. They saw a noble, skilled politician, unexpectedly president under the most tragic circumstances, rising to the position while following in the footsteps of their martyred leader. After only two months in office, Johnson had an 80 percent approval rating. In 1964, he signed legislation for the Civil Rights Act and the largest reduction of income taxes in the nation's history. Johnson was overwhelmingly elected president in November, receiving 486 electoral votes compared to his Republican opponent's 52, a satisfying confirmation of his leadership.

As for Bird, she knew she could never compete with Jackie's beauty and style and didn't even try. It would be months after becoming first lady before she even bought new clothes. Though Bird was trim and attractive, she was seventeen years older than her predecessor, several inches shorter, and lacked her stunning wide-eyed beauty. When a friend commiserated with her that she would inevitably be compared with Jackie, Bird replied in surprise, "Don't feel sorry for me. I still have my Lyndon."

Lady Bird Johnson offered something far more compelling than Hollywood looks: her approach to the job. A first lady, she stated, should always be available to the press and public and never lie. She instructed her press secretary to reach out to journalists, to befriend and cultivate them in the hopes of positive coverage that would reflect well on her husband's administration. Jackie, on the other hand, had despised reporters as threatening her beloved privacy. She had told her press secretary to keep them away with any lie or excuse possible.

As first lady, Lady Bird initiated a program to beautify Washington, D.C., which Jack Kennedy had jokingly called "a city of Southern efficiency and Northern charm." She created the Society for a More Beautiful National Capital, which planted millions of flowers, many of them along roadways around the city. "Where flowers bloom, so does hope," she said. She pushed for the Highway Beautification Act, which limited unsightly billboards across the country and planted wildflowers along highways. Those flowers we see blooming today on the roadside are there because of Bird Johnson's love of nature.

In the #MeToo era, Lyndon Johnson's treatment of female employees and reporters would make us all cringe and beat a path for HR or the nearest lawyer. Johnson let it be known that he only wanted to hire women with "good behinds" so he could "enjoy" their rear ends as they left his office. Calling all his female staffers "honey," he instructed them to get their "hair fixed real pretty" and "get perfumed up." He gave them expensive jewelry and high-heeled shoes and stole kisses.

His ultimate compliment was to tell a woman, "You're just as pretty as a polecat," which must have puzzled many, especially because it was the same thing he told his dogs. Dog keeper Traphes Bryant recalled, "At White House events, he would fix his eye on an attractive woman, cry, 'Come over here! You're the prettiest little thing I ever saw!' and invite them into a private room where they could have a 'serious conversation.'"

One day Johnson told Bryant, "I can't help it. I put a high

mark on beauty. I can't stand an ugly woman around or a fat one who looks like a cow that's gonna step on her own udder."

His bad behavior went beyond crude flirtation. According to some reports, he was having affairs with four of his six White House secretaries. Before he hired one, he would ask around to determine, "Does she shuck her drawers?" Lady Bird walked into the Oval Office one day to find him having sex with a secretary on a couch and quietly walked back out. After that, the president had a buzzer system installed. The Secret Service was to buzz him when the first lady was on her way so he could pull up his pants before she arrived. His official diary records dozens of forty-five-minute sessions in the Oval Office with only one woman present, many of them with a *Washington Star* reporter. He enjoyed numerous evening trysts on the presidential yacht, the *Sequoia*. On Air Force One, he would lock himself in his private compartment with a secretary, even with his wife aboard.

Naturally, the Washington press knew. In 2012, Hal Wingo, who had been a reporter for *Life* fifty years earlier, recalled spending New Year's Eve 1963 with the newly inaugurated Lyndon Johnson and a group of other reporters. Johnson put his hand on Wingo's knee and said, "One more thing, boys. You may see me coming in and out of a few women's bedrooms while I am in the White House, but just remember, that is none of your business." They remembered, and not a peep made it into the papers.

"I've had more women by accident than Kennedy ever had on purpose," Johnson often bragged to his friends. But there was one difference between these two philandering presidents. Most of Kennedy's women were disposable. He used them, often without even getting their names, and tossed them aside. Lyndon formed lasting relationships and truly cared about his women. And, despite his appalling behavior with female staff, he instructed all his cabinet members to promote fifty women each. He made many women ambassadors.

Johnson's domestic accomplishments were significant. He signed into law legislation creating Medicare and Medicaid, the Head Start program, the Civil Rights Act, the Voting Rights Act, and the National Endowment for the Arts. He supported the space program, declared a "War on Poverty," and established several programs to help the disadvantaged. "Our chief weapons," he said, "will be better schools, and better health, and better homes, and better training, and better job opportunities to help more Americans, and especially young Americans, escape from squalor and misery and unemployment." Decrying the Ku Klux Klan as a "hooded society of bigots," he was the first president to arrest and prosecute members of the Klan since Ulysses S. Grant ninety-three years earlier. Author Robert Gilbert wrote that Johnson's national policies were "perhaps as extraordinary as [those] of Franklin D. Roosevelt, making him one of the most effective legislative leaders in American history."

But the war in Vietnam would tarnish his legacy beyond repair. Casualties mounted—by 1967 more than seventy thousand Americans had been killed or wounded—and U.S. involvement in the conflict became immensely unpopular. Johnson lied to the press about what was going on, and reporters on the ground in Vietnam pointed out his "credibility gap." His approval ratings tanked. Anti-war protests started up all over the country—one involved one hundred thousand people at the Pentagon. Whenever Johnson left the White House, he was met with chants of "Hey, hey, LBJ, how many kids did you kill today?"

Johnson was baffled about Vietnam. Should the U.S. withdraw and let the Communists take over Southeast Asia? Or should he stick it out, despite the high cost, and beat them back? He told his press secretary Bill Moyers that he was accustomed to looking "for the light at the end of the tunnel." But in this case, "Hell, we don't even have a tunnel; we don't even know where the tunnel is." The Valley of the Black Pig returned. Many days the president stayed in bed, Bird at his side, coaxing him to eat something from his tray. Only she could cheer him, cajole him, inspire him to stand up and "put one foot in front of the other."

On other occasions he was paranoid, accusing his staff of being in the pay of Communists or Kennedys, accusing them of treason. One day, when reporters bombarded him with questions about why he was intensifying the American commitment in Vietnam, Johnson pulled out his eight-and-a-half-inch penis, waved it at the stunned journalists, and shouted, "This is why!" Which was as good an explanation as any. Not a word about this unusual response made it into the papers.

Finally, Johnson decided not to run for a second full term. "I tried to make it possible for every child of every color to grow up in a nice house, eat a solid breakfast, to attend a decent school and to get a good and lasting job," he told an aide. "But look what I got instead . . . Young people leaving the university, marching in the streets . . . They shot me down. The only difference between the Kennedy assassination and mine is that I am still alive and feeling it."

After retirement from a political career that had lasted thirty-nine years, Johnson grew restless and frustrated. He went back to his five-pack-a-day smoking habit, gained weight, and drank too much. In 1972, he had another heart attack. His heart was so damaged the nation's top heart specialist refused to perform surgery. On the afternoon of January 22, 1973, Johnson felt another heart attack coming on. Bird was out of the house, so he called the Secret Service. They found him moments later, dead at sixty-four, still gripping the phone.

Lady Bird lived thirty-four years after his death. She traveled a great deal, served on various boards, including that of the National Park Service, and became closer to her daughters and grandchildren. She died in 2007 at the age of ninety-four.

The marriage of Lyndon and Lady Bird was an odd love story. Toward the end of Johnson's life, when a friend reminded him that the best thing he ever did was marry Bird, he replied not a day passed that he did not think of that.

Years after Johnson's death, Bird said, "Lyndon pushed me, he drove me, at times he humiliated me, but he made me become someone bigger and better than I would have been." Her calm acceptance of his infidelities was not because she was weak, but because she was strong. As she explained, "I had a great love affair. No matter what, I knew he loved me best."

GARY HART AND THE MONKEY BUSINESS THAT CHANGED EVERYTHING

*I*n the first part of 1987, Senator Gary Hart of Colorado was the top contender early in the presidential race, crushing all other candidates for the Democratic nomination by double digits and boasting a similar lead over the presumed Republican candidate, Vice President George H. W. Bush. Widely acknowledged as having the finest political mind in the nation, Hart was so confident of his ascent to the White House, he had already prepared a detailed eight-year action plan.

Yet Hart had a blind spot. He was locked into the JFK-era mentality that a politician's private life had nothing to do with his governing ability. No self-respecting journalist would stoop to cover it, and no reputable news organization would think of publishing it. But Gary Hart learned the hard way that times had changed. After Hart was eviscerated, all other politicians knew they had to take precautions.

* * *

At 8:40 p.m. on Saturday, May 2, 1987, fifty-year-old Gary Hart steered his date, twenty-nine-year-old sometime model and full-time pharmaceutical rep Donna Rice, out of his Capitol Hill townhome toward his car. They would meet another couple for dinner: his campaign aide, Bill Broadhurst, and Rice's friend, Lynn Armandt.

Though married for twenty-nine years, Hart—with the tawny mane, blue-gray eyes, and chiseled good looks of the Kennedys—had never let that stop him as far as women were concerned. People in Washington political and society circles were well aware of his reputation as a ladies' man.

Hart had connected with the leggy blonde a month earlier when he and Bill Broadhurst spent a weekend in Miami to relax a bit before they officially announced the campaign two weeks later. One evening, Donna Rice and some friends left a disco and strolled along the piers, admiring the yachts. She noticed Gary Hart on an eighty-three-foot chartered yacht called *Monkey Business*, greeted him, and reminded him that they had met at a New Year's Eve party at the Aspen home of singer Don Henley, whom Rice had been dating. Hart invited Rice and Armandt to join him the next day on a cruise to the isle of Bimini, fifty-seven miles away, where Bill Broadhurst would pick up his own yacht from a repair company. They would be back by nightfall. Under a blue sky, the four enjoyed the cruise and, upon landing in Bimini, Armandt took a picture of Hart, wearing a *Monkey Business* T-shirt, sitting against a piling, a smiling Rice in his lap.

But they soon discovered that Broadhurst could not get his vessel out of customs as the office had closed for the day; they would have to wait until it opened the following morning. Later,

Hart and Rice would claim the women had spent the night on the *Monkey Business*, and the men had slept on Broadhurst's yacht. Hart's friend Armandt, in an article for *People* magazine, would claim she woke up in the middle of the night to find that Donna had vanished, and she assumed she was with Hart on the other boat. After the cruise, Hart and Rice spoke frequently, trying to meet up again, and finally arranged to do so in Washington, D.C., the first weekend in May.

Now, as Hart and Rice left his town house and strode toward his car, the senator noticed something strange. On a warm May night, there was a man wearing dark sunglasses and a hooded parka standing in front of Hart's house. Another man, in a jogging suit, was periodically running up and down the block. Fearing something amiss, Hart ditched his dinner plans and guided Rice back inside, where they peered out the windows.

Hart was right to be alarmed. The five men in front of his home were reporters from the *Miami Herald*. The previous Monday, one of them, Tom Fiedler, had received a call from a woman who refused to identify herself, claiming to have proof that Gary Hart was having an affair with a friend of hers. Fiedler had written a story on rumors of Hart's infidelity, which appeared that morning with the headline "Sex Lives Become an Issue for Presidential Hopefuls." In his article, Fiedler reported that as Hart stood in the aisle of his press plane, reporters peppered him with questions about his rumored love affairs. "Anybody want to talk about ideas?" Hart had asked. They didn't.

The tipster on the phone, who had seen Fiedler's story, told him about two women she refused to name who had been on Hart's cruise to Bimini. She told him about numerous calls Hart had made to the blonde, who was flying to Washington on Friday to spend the weekend with him at his home. Fiedler mulled over the issue. No news organization had ever undertaken a stakeout of a presidential candidate's home to sniff out a sexual affair. The sex, he decided, wasn't important. But if a leading presidential candidate was a liar and a hypocrite, voters should know. Only two weeks earlier, Hart had promised to hold himself to the "very highest possible standards of integrity and ethics." Even though Hart had been talking about integrity in public office—contrasting himself with corrupt Reagan administration officials then embroiled in the Iran-Contra Affair—could the senator claim to be an ethical leader if he lied not only to his wife but to the American public?

Given the hypocrisy angle, Fiedler decided to pursue the story. He assigned a reporter, Jim McGee, to get on the Friday flight that Hart's as-yet-unnamed girlfriend was taking from Miami and stake out the senator's house. The following morning, McGee called in that Hart had left the house the evening before with the blonde, returned two hours later with another couple—evidently after eating dinner out—and no one had left the house all night. Fiedler himself got on a plane and assigned a photographer and editor to meet him near Hart's home.

Whatever misgivings Fiedler had on the plane vanished when he read an advance copy of the *New York Times* set to publish Monday, May 3, provided as a courtesy to other major news organizations. When *Times* reporter E. J. Dionne had pressed Hart on rumors of his infidelities, Hart had snapped, "Follow me around. I don't care. I'm serious. If anybody wants to put a tail on me, go ahead. They'd be very bored."

Hart had *invited* the press to do exactly what Fiedler and his team were doing.

Peering out from his town house at the men below, Hart considered calling the police but thought it would sound stupid to complain that people were standing in front of his home. Instead, he called Broadhurst, who brought dinner over with Armandt and discussed strategy. According to Armandt's subsequent account of that evening in *People*, everyone agreed to deny that Rice had spent the night there. They would say they were planning to talk about possible campaign jobs for the women over dinner. Broadhurst took the two women out the back door and departed.

Angry now, Hart put on a white sweatshirt with a hoodie and got into his car, hoping the reporters would follow him, which they did. When he wrote down the license number of the reporters' car, they realized there was no point in evasion anymore. They trailed him down an alley between the rows of town houses and saw him leaning against a brick wall, sulkily waiting.

"Good evening, Senator," McGee began, "I'm a reporter from the *Miami Herald*. We'd like to talk to you." He then asked about the young woman in Hart's house. Hart denied there was a woman in his house. When McGee asked him about his relationship with the woman, Hart denied that, too. McGee asked about all the phone calls he had made to the woman. Hart claimed they involved discussions about fundraising. When McGee pointed out that they had seen Hart and the woman enter the town house earlier, Hart declared he was being set up.

The reporters continued to pepper Hart with questions about his blond companion, questions he answered evasively. He didn't remember any yachting trip in Miami. Then Fiedler asked, "Have you had sex with the woman in the town house?"

Hart replied, "The answer is no. I'm not going to get into all that."

He walked toward his home and, as the photographer started taking pictures, he spun around to face them, resulting in an unfortunate photo: the leading presidential contender in a hoodie, cornered, guilty, turning away. Hart would later say that he knew, at that moment, something had irrevocably changed, and he felt nothing so much as sadness. The old rules no longer applied. The mainstream media had, at that moment, gone tabloid. A door sealed for nine decades had opened, and he was the first person to hurtle through into the vicious howling maws of the press.

Blazing across the Monday edition of the *Herald* was the headline "Miami Woman Is Linked to Hart" with the photo of Hart in his hoodie. The same morning, the *Times* ran the E. J. Dionne interview with Hart's taunting dare to follow him around.

The *Herald* piece began: "Gary Hart, the Democratic presidential candidate who has dismissed allegations of womanizing, spent Friday night and most of Saturday in his Capitol Hill townhouse with a young woman who flew from Miami to meet him," adding "Hart has denied any impropriety." The article stated that *Herald* reporters had witnessed Hart and the blonde leave his house, return two hours later, and not reemerge until the following evening.

The Hart campaign fought back. Broadhurst claimed to have been in the house Friday night with Armandt and to have taken the two women out the back door to the alley around midnight. They spent the night in his home in spare bedrooms, he said. They returned to the Hart house Saturday evening by the alley door. The *Herald* reporters admitted they had only watched the front door.

With reporters thronging his town house, Hart issued a statement.

Recent accusations about Senator Hart's personal life are preposterous and inaccurate in their entirety. They have taken a casual acquaintance and a simple dinner with three friends and political supporters and attempted to make a story where there is none. The system, when reduced to hiding in bushes, peaking in windows, and personal harassment, has clearly run amok. Senator Hart accepts the scrutiny that comes with his leadership role in the Democratic Party and the country. But scrutiny and questions of character are one thing; character assassinations are entirely another. Those who cover politics have some duty of self-restraint; here the boundaries of journalistic ethics have clearly been crossed.

On Monday, Rice was devastated to learn that her name had been leaked to the press. She gave a hasty press conference in which she denied having a sexual relationship with Hart.

Meanwhile, at the *Washington Post*, the reporter covering the Hart campaign, Paul Taylor, met with editor Ben Bradlee and others to discuss a question that had, in their lifetimes, never been considered by a major newspaper. Taylor, in his own book about the 1988 campaign, *See How They Run: Electing the President in an Age of Mediaocracy*, summed it up as follows:

If a candidate for president is believed to be a womanizer but there's no suggestion that his sexual activities have ever interfered with his public duties, is it even worth investigating, much less publishing? Is there a statute of limitations, or is screwing around in the past tense just as newsworthy as in the present? Is a series of one-night stands more reportable than a single long-term extramarital affair? Does it matter if a candidate has an open-marriage understanding with his spouse?

Is Hart a special case, or if we begin looking into his mating habits, must we do the same with everyone else running for president?

Bradlee, who had known of JFK's countless affairs, including one with Bradlee's own sister-in-law, Mary Meyer, and never written a word about them, decided that times had changed. Hart's sex life had already become a major issue in his campaign for president. The *Post* would cover it. News organizations across the country followed suit.

At a news conference in New Hampshire, Hart said that a man's character should be measured by his fifteen years of public service, not by a single weekend.

The *Washington Post*'s Paul Taylor asked him what later became known as "the Question." "Senator," he began, "in your remarks yesterday you raised the issue of morality, and you raised the issue of truthfulness. Let me ask you what you mean when you talk about morality, and let me be very specific. I have a series of questions about it. When you said you did nothing immoral, did you mean that you had no sexual relationship with Donna Rice last weekend or at any other time that you were with her?"

"That is correct. That's correct," Hart replied.

"Do you believe that adultery is immoral?

"Yes."

"Have you ever committed adultery?" Those in the room couldn't believe what Taylor had just asked. No reporter had ever asked a presidential candidate anything like that. Seconds ticked by like hours.

Finally, Hart said, "Ahhh, I do not think that's a fair question."

"Have you ever committed adultery?" Taylor persisted.

"I do not know—I'm not going to get into a theological definition of what constitutes adultery. In some people's minds, it's people being married and having relationships with other people, so . . ."

"Can I ask you," Taylor pressed, "whether you and your wife have an understanding about whether or not you can have relationships, you can have sexual encounters with—"

"My inclination is to say no, you can't ask me that question. But the answer is no, we don't have any such understanding. We have an understanding of faithfulness, fidelity, and loyalty."

Hart then jumped into a supporter's car and barreled out of there.

After the fiasco of the New Hampshire press conference, Hart learned there was a second woman, a Washington resident, who had confirmed an affair with him. He knew his campaign would tank under another such story. On May 8, just five days after the Donna Rice story broke, he suspended his campaign.

On *Nightline* in September, Hart, interviewed by Ted Koppel, was the first politician to admit on national television that he had committed adultery. But he wouldn't say if it had been with Donna Rice.

"The question should have never been asked," he said, "and I shouldn't have to answer it."

Despite the negative coverage, most Americans didn't care about Hart's adultery. According to a *Time* magazine poll taken at the time, 67 percent disapproved of the press reporting on a candidate's sex life, and 60 percent believed that Hart's relationship with Rice was irrelevant to the presidency. If he had emulated the actions of Alexander Hamilton or Grover Cleveland and admitted his mistakes, he could have remained in the race and possibly become the Democratic nominee. But Hart refused to apologize for what he vehemently believed was nobody's damned business but his and his wife's. His anger seemed like arrogance to many, and his obfuscation was just plain irritating. His haughty, holier-than-thou lectures on responsible journalism offended voters when he was the one caught cheating on his wife. How could they forgive him if he didn't confess, didn't apologize? It was like sitting in a theater, watching the wrong ending to a play. It was unsatisfying. The play's flawed hero—Hart—had proved to be unlikable, stony, with no desire for redemption.

Moreover, the American public didn't like being lied to. What was a fifty-year-old man doing spending the night on a boat on an island with a twenty-nine-year-old blonde? Why did he spend the weekend with her? Did he really expect them to believe they were discussing fundraising all that time before she had left through the back alley? Not bloody likely. And why did these meetings occur when his wife was thousands of miles away, back at the ranch? The American people might be able to embrace adulterers, but not liars and hypocrites. Soon after the story came out, *Time* magazine conducted a poll asking Americans what they disliked more in a politician: engaging in extramarital sex or lying to the public. Sixty-nine percent responded that they disliked being lied to, while only 7 percent said they minded the extramarital sex more.

With Hart's affair the biggest story in the country, Lynn Armandt decided to cash in. She sold the iconic photo of Donna Rice sitting on Hart's lap to the *National Enquirer* for $75,000—it made the cover and would define him the rest of his life—and sold her story to *People* magazine for $150,000. Donna Rice lost her job and turned down a million-dollar offer to pose nude for *Playboy*.

In December, Hart returned to the race, hoping the scandal had died down. It hadn't. He was fodder for raunchy late-night television jokes. *Late Night* host David Letterman quipped, "In, out, in, out, isn't that what got him in trouble in the first place?" Another popular joke was: "Who do you want to be president? Answer: In my heart I want Bush, but in my bush I want Hart." Issues of character—a candidate's sex life—were suddenly fair game for journalists and the public alike. Hart's results were so bad in New Hampshire and on Super Tuesday, he withdrew from the race.

It is no wonder that Hart was caught completely unawares by the full-scale press assault. After all, it had been 103 years since journalists tore into a presidential candidate—Grover Cleveland—for sexual wrongdoing. What happened? By 1987, the history of political sex scandal coverage had come full circle: from the muckraking rags of the eighteenth and nineteenth centuries screaming out headlines about Hamilton's adultery, Thomas Jefferson's enslaved mistress, and Grover Cleveland's illegitimate child, to the dignified, sedate press of the first decades of the twentieth century, right back into shrill muckraking.

Several factors contributed to the profound shift. For one thing, social mores had changed by the late eighties. The *Mad Men* era—when chain-smoking executives slapped their secretaries on the butt and enjoyed three-martini lunches—was over. Adultery, which had been seen as men's prerogative for centuries, was less tolerated. For another thing, high political office was no longer a source of awe so much as it was of disgust due to the government's lies and policies concerning the Vietnam War and the resulting carnage.

In 1969, journalists who protected the bad behavior of the

Kennedy men had no choice but to report Teddy Kennedy's catastrophic car accident in Chappaquiddick. The drunken Massachusetts senator had careened off a bridge, swum to safety, and pretended it never happened while his female companion, a twenty-nine-year-old campaign worker named Mary Jo Kopechne, trapped in the car, slowly drowned over a period of several hours.

Then there was journalistic guilt for not reporting something they probably should have, something which may have saved the young woman's life. Only a few months before Chappaquiddick, Teddy Kennedy had staggered onto a plane full of reporters in Anchorage, Alaska, clearly intoxicated and swigging from a silver flask. He threw a dinner roll at a network correspondent and tossed a pillow at a flight attendant. He lurched down the aisle holding a cup of boiling hot coffee, frightening a woman holding a newborn. A *Newsweek* reporter wrote his editor that Kennedy was "an accident waiting to happen." No one on that plane full of journalists wrote a word about it to the public.

Perhaps most importantly, during the Watergate scandal of the early 1970s, Bob Woodward and Carl Bernstein of the *Washington Post* exposed a corrupt president, further tarnishing the image of the office. Journalists were no longer buddies with the chief executive, hiding his weaknesses in the hopes of a news scoop or an invitation to a great party. They were adversaries *searching* for weaknesses, hoping to be the next Woodward or Bernstein. They were heroes, exposing corruption, hypocrisy, and lies. Journalism schools were flooded with eager students.

After the floodgates were opened, the press covered the next political sex scandal relentlessly—that of sixty-five-year-old, married Congressman Wilbur Mills of Arkansas, one of the most powerful members of Congress, who at 2:00 a.m. on October 9,

1974, was stopped near the Tidal Basin by D.C. Park Police for speeding and driving without his headlights on. Both Mills and his passenger, a thirty-eight-year-old stripper who went by the name of Fanne Foxe, the Argentine Firecracker, were heavily intoxicated and had been beaten brutally in the face, evidently by each other. Much to the officers' surprise, the Firecracker got out of the car and leaped into the water, where one officer jumped in after her and the other threw the two of them a spare tire to climb onto. Given Mills's status, the police declined to pursue the matter. But the press got wind of it and unearthed stories of the congressman's devastating alcoholism, discovering he had spent half his time in Congress in a drunken daze and couldn't remember what had happened in most of his meetings. He was stripped of his chairmanship of the House Ways and Means Committee, his reputation demolished.

No politicians were immune to the new journalism, even a martyred president. The dam around Jack Kennedy's reputation started to crack in 1975 when the Senate Committee on Intelligence Operations, led by Senator Frank Church of Idaho, was looking into an early 1960s CIA plot to hire Chicago mobster Sam Giancana to assassinate Fidel Castro. The Church Committee, as it was called, discovered that Giancana and Kennedy had shared the same girlfriend, Judith Campbell, for eighteen months, that she telephoned Kennedy at the White House seventy times during a fifty-four-week period in 1961 and early 1962, and that many of those calls came from Giancana's home. Sam Giancana was deposed to testify, but he was gunned down in his kitchen while frying sausages the day before he was due to appear. No one knew if the murder was a mob hit or a CIA assassination. The committee left Judith's relationship with the president out of the final report, concluding that the late president's sex life was nobody's business. Perhaps it was no coincidence that the committee member who pushed hardest to keep it out was none other than young Senator Gary Hart of Colorado.

In 1975, Hart didn't see that times were changing after Vietnam, Chappaquiddick, and Watergate; the Kennedy–mob connection story leaked and made national headlines. On December 29, *Time* magazine published an article with the headline "Scandals: JFK and the Mobsters' Moll." Companion articles described "Jack Kennedy's Other Women," detailing Kennedy's countless adulteries in the White House. The same year, Traphes Bryant published his book, *Dog Days at the White House*, in which he recalled Kennedy's orgies. Judith Campbell herself wrote a memoir of her affair with the president in 1977. All the stories of bad Kennedy behavior, dammed up for so many years, came tumbling forth. The gloves were off, the knives were out, and the syrupy nostalgia for Camelot had turned to ash.

In 1976, the *Washington Post* broke the story that sixty-five-year-old Congressman Wayne Hays of Ohio kept a gorgeous, thirty-three-year-old blond mistress named Elizabeth Ray on his staff on the taxpayer dime who couldn't type or file or even take phone messages. The FBI and the House Oversight Committee began investigations, and Hays resigned from office.

The media also began reporting the off-color jokes and statements of prominent politicians. In 1976, Agriculture Secretary Earl Butz said to entertainers Sonny Bono and Pat Boone and former White House counsel John Dean, "I'll tell you what coloreds want. It's three things: first a tight pussy; second, loose shoes; and third, a warm place to shit, that's all." Shocked, John Dean reported the story to the press, and Butz was forced to resign amid general outrage.

Perhaps because he did not drive drunk with a stripper, or

keep a girlfriend who did no work on a public payroll, or share a girlfriend with Al Capone's successor, or make lewd and racist remarks, Gary Hart expected better treatment from this disturbing, dangerous new crop of journalists. Moreover, since well before he was born, the press had never unearthed the illicit sex life of a living president or presidential candidate, and Hart naively thought he was safe. But he was, in fact, rather like the first victim of a serial killer, knocked off balance and taken by surprise. Those adulterous politicians who followed in his footsteps, including a young governor from Arkansas, would be prepared for investigations into their sexual foibles.

In Hart's speech announcing his withdrawal from the race in May, he said,

> In public life, some things may be interesting, but that doesn't necessarily mean they're important . . . We're all going to have to seriously question the system for selecting our national leaders that reduces the press of this nation to hunters and presidential candidates to being hunted, that has reporters in bushes, false and inaccurate stories printed, photographers peeking in our windows, swarms of helicopters hovering over our roofs, and my very strong wife close to tears because she can't even get into her own house at night without being harassed. And then after all that, ponderous pundits wonder in mock seriousness why some of the best people in this country choose not to run for higher office . . . We'd all better do something to make this system work, or we're all going to be soon rephrasing Jefferson to say, I tremble for my country when I think we may, in fact, get the kind of leaders we deserve.

There is a recent twist to this decades-old story. Throughout the scandal, Hart whined that he had been set up. He sounded childish and petulant; a naughty little boy caught with his hand in the cookie jar. At first it seemed that Lynn Armandt had set the sting in motion because she and a friend of hers, Dana Weems, were jealous of Donna Rice. It was Weems, after all, who had called the *Miami Herald*, Armandt straining to listen at her side. But Hart may have been right, and there may have been something far more sinister at work than a pair of catty, envious women.

In 1991, forty-year-old Lee Atwater, who had been the campaign manager for George H. W. Bush in the 1988 election, knew he was dying of an inoperable brain tumor. A savvy political operative, he had numerous confessions and apologies to make before he died, numerous requests for forgiveness. He told Raymond Strother, an aide to Hart, that he had set up Hart by bribing Broadhurst. It was Broadhurst, he said, who arranged for the women to come on the cruise to Bimini, to rent the yacht with the most memorable name, to make sure he showed up too late to get his yacht out of customs, and to plan in advance with Armandt and Rice to take the picture as proof. As for the rest, Broadhurst just needed to step back and let Hart be Hart.

Shocked by the confession, Strother opted to let sleeping dogs lie and keep this information to himself. Atwater died soon after his confession, and Broadhurst died in 2017. But then, a few months later, Strother was diagnosed with possibly fatal prostate cancer and had his own confession to make. He met face-to-face with Gary Hart and told him the story. Hart had always thought someone had set him up for a fall; he had even said he was being set up to the *Miami Herald* reporters who confronted him in front of his town house the night that shattered everything. There was no proof, of course, and he didn't know *who* had set him up. But now, with the Lee Atwater story, it must have all suddenly made sense: Atwater had booted him out of the race in disgrace, clearing the path for George Bush to win.

In retrospect, it was most likely a loss for the nation. We can only imagine the country's trajectory if Hart had become president. "A scandal to me," he said, "is a child living in poverty. An elderly person without medicine. Unemployed workers. Those are scandals. People's sex lives or their personal lives are scandals only in the sense of tabloid journalism, but not in the sense of ethics. They're not bribery. They're not some under-the-table exchange of money, buying votes. Those, I suppose, would be real political scandals."

Donna Rice briefly modeled for No Excuses jeans and kept refusing to answer questions about what had happened between her and Gary Hart. She disappeared from public view for seven years, during which she reconnected with her evangelistic Christian faith.

In 1994, she married a tech entrepreneur in the Washington, D.C., area and raised three stepchildren. The same year, now Donna Rice Hughes, she began working for a nonprofit organization, Enough Is Enough, whose mission is to protect children online, and has been president and CEO since 2002. On the organization's website, she wrote about the Hart scandal, "I have chosen to remain silent, for the most part, about this devastating turning point in my life. Rather than exploit the situation for my own gain, I chose the high road and sought to use my pain to help others. By the grace of God, I found healing and restoration and eventually came full circle . . . I encourage others to seek the high road, as I did, and find hope and purpose in the midst of their life's storms."

After his failed presidential campaign, Hart resumed his law practice and was appointed by President Bill Clinton to lead a commission to study homeland security. In 2014, President Barack Obama named him U.S. special envoy to Northern Ireland, a position he held for three years. Hart is now eighty-three, retired, and still married to the same woman. And yet, he will forever be trapped in amber, sitting on a pier piling, a grinning blonde on his lap.

12

BILL CLINTON DID NOT HAVE SEX WITH THAT WOMAN

Only a few U.S. presidents can boast of statements so memorable they define both their legacy and an era. Franklin Roosevelt said, "We have nothing to fear but fear itself." John F. Kennedy said, "Ask not what your country can do for you, but what you can do for your country." Richard Nixon emphatically stated, "I am not a crook." And Bill Clinton insisted, "I did not have sexual relations with that woman—Miss Lewinsky."

* * *

According to her 2003 memoir, *Living History*, on the morning of Saturday, August 15, 1998, Hillary Clinton was awakened by her husband, President Bill Clinton, pacing agitatedly next to her bed. Bill, it seemed, had a little confession to make. Though he had denied for months to special prosecutors that he had had a sexual relationship with former White House intern Monica Lewinsky, well, that wasn't exactly the truth. Not that he had lied—because blow jobs aren't really sex, everyone knows that—but still, Hillary recalled, he "told me for the first time that the situation was much more serious than he had previously acknowledged. He now realized he would have to testify that there had been an inappropriate intimacy. He told me that what happened between them had been brief and sporadic." In all likelihood, the only reason Bill fessed up was that the FBI had DNA evidence of the affair. Otherwise, it's safe to say Bill would have denied it until he was blue in the face.

"I could hardly breathe," Hillary continued. "Gulping for air, I started crying and yelling at him, 'What do you mean? What are you saying? Why did you lie to me?' I was furious and getting more so by the second. He just stood there saying over and over again, 'I'm sorry. I'm so sorry. I was trying to protect you and [their eighteen-year-old daughter] Chelsea.'" According to Hillary's account, until that morning she'd believed that he was being unfairly attacked. In January, she had even told Matt Lauer of NBC that the whole story was ginned up by "a vast right-wing conspiracy."

Now, upon hearing the truth, Hillary maintained, "I was dumbfounded, heartbroken and outraged that I'd believed him at all." Yes, she was shocked, *shocked*, to find that Bill had been at it with a girl because such behavior was so very unlike him.

The fact is that Hillary Rodham knew Bill was a philanderer well before she married him. They met at Yale Law School in 1971 and immediately became an item, though they were an odd couple from the get-go. Bill was handsome, personable, and funny, a back-slapping good ole Arkansas boy, always flying by the seat of his pants and coming out on top. Hillary, from Chicago, was chilly, calculating, painstakingly prepared, and frumpy. A creature of the mind, she gave no heed to her appearance. She had good features but wore no makeup to bring them out and had thick glasses and limp brown hair in no particular style. Long, unflattering granny dresses hid her figure. According to Jerry

Oppenheimer's 2000 book, *State of a Union: Inside the Complex Marriage of Bill and Hillary Clinton*, when Bill's childhood friend Paul Fray met Hillary, his reaction was, "My God, Bill Clinton, you son of a bitch—you could have any damn woman on the face of the earth, and you brought one that looks like the south end of a mule going north?"

Oppenheimer wrote that Bill leaped to Hillary's defense. "He told me she was the smartest woman he'd ever met," Paul said, "brilliant beyond compare." When Bill's mother, Virginia, first met Hillary, she, too, was unimpressed by the looks, and even more so by the aloofness that hinted of sneering superiority. "I want you to know that I've had it up to here with beauty queens," Bill raged. "I have to have somebody I can talk to. Do you understand that?" And to a woman he'd dated, who asked him what on earth it was about Hillary that fascinated him so, he replied, "She challenges me, every moment of every day, intellectually. She makes me a better person. She gets me started, kicks my butt, and makes me do the things I've got to do."

And, in fact, their differences held them together, like two puzzle pieces of vastly different shapes, interlocking perfectly. Both were highly intelligent and politically ambitious, but she had the cold calculation to maneuver him into political office, while he had the overwhelming charm. Because getting into office— *getting into the White House*—was the goal of their relationship. Both had dreamed of it since childhood. Both had chosen their postgraduate education, their internships and volunteer work for political campaigns based on that single goal. According to Gail Sheehy, author of the 1999 *Hillary's Choice*, Hillary had already dumped one boyfriend for lack of ambition. David Rupert, whom Hillary dated when they both worked as summer interns in Congress, told Sheehy Hillary lost interest in him because he never "stated a burning desire to be president. I believe that was a need for her in a partner."

And because the White House was Hillary's goal, the regular rules of a relationship didn't necessarily apply. According to Oppenheimer, they came to an agreement: Bill could carouse with women all he wanted as long as it didn't rise to the level of interfering with their political future. That would be the only betrayal of significance.

After graduating Yale in 1973, Hillary went to Washington, D.C., where she joined the impeachment inquiry staff of the House Judiciary Committee during the Watergate investigation. Bill went to Little Rock, where he taught law at the University of Arkansas. He ran for the U.S. House of Representatives in 1974, lost narrowly, ran in 1976 for Arkansas attorney general and won.

Though Hillary would periodically swoop into Little Rock to visit Bill, he was dating other women, including one in particular, Marla Crider, a winsome, dark-haired, twenty-one-year-old political science major at the University of Arkansas who volunteered on his first campaign. Marla told Jerry Oppenheimer that one day Bill told her to stop by his house and pick up some things she would need for the campaign trail. He also asked her to retrieve some papers from his desk. On the desk she saw an open letter, clearly meant for her to read. According to her recollection, it went like this:

Dear Bill,

I still do not understand why you do the things you do to hurt me. You left me in tears and not knowing what our relationship was all about. I know all your little girls are around there, if that's what it is, you will outgrow this. They will not be with you when you need them. They are not the ones who can help you achieve your goals. If this is about your feelings for Marla, this too shall pass. Let me remind you it always does. Remember what we talked about. Remember the goals we've set for ourselves. You keep trying to stray away from the plan we've put together. Take some time, think about it, and call me when you're ready.

Hillary

Though Bill had clearly maneuvered Marla into reading Hillary's letter, she didn't understand it. She knew Hillary was possessive of Bill, giving Marla the evil eye during her brief visits. But other than the first couple of lines, this wasn't a letter of love and jealousy, doubt and heartbreak. It was a letter about goals, about a plan. Love, fidelity, and trust were not the main focus of their relationship. There was something else, something Bill wanted Marla to understand.

Looking back years later, Marla said that Hillary "decided the most important thing was that political partnership, that goal they'd set, rather than taking care of their personal life, or being confident, or having a trustworthy relationship. I'm just amazed, as a woman, at her thought process. To be so smart and allow that to happen . . . to go for politics over personal life and love and happiness."

Nightclub singer Gennifer Flowers alleged in her 1995 memoir *Passion and Betrayal* that she had had a twelve-year affair with Bill. She wrote, "Hillary never tried to put a stop to my relationship with Bill. In fact, he told me that after he hung up from talking with me one night, she walked into the room and asked, 'How's Gennifer?' He looked at her carefully and replied, 'Just fine.' And that was the end of it . . . In retrospect, I can see that Bill and Hillary's political career was undoubtedly more important to her than her husband's faithfulness. But back then I couldn't imagine why she would close her eyes to his fooling around."

After Nixon's resignation in August 1974, Hillary gave up the chance for a lucrative job at a D.C. law firm and joined Bill, where she taught at the University of Arkansas and then accepted a position at the Rose Law Firm. She made no effort to adapt to her new environment. She didn't bleach her hair and tease it high, or slather on makeup, or wear more stylish clothing. She didn't try to acquire a bit of southern charm or learn how to bake peach pie. Instead, she was brusque, impatient, giving the impression of disdaining those she spoke to, of not having the time to bother with them. After Bill and Hillary married in 1975, she even kept her maiden name, a shocking break from tradition for the time and place.

In 1978, Bill was elected governor of Arkansas—the youngest governor in the country at thirty-two—a position he held for twelve nonconsecutive years (1979–1981 and 1983–1992). Their only child, Chelsea, was born in 1980. Some, who just didn't understand the dynamics of the Clinton marriage, called it an immaculate conception or the result of artificial insemination. Yet, over the years, there was never any doubt that the Clintons were devoted parents; even their most hostile political opponents agreed to that. Despite hectic schedules, they were there at the soccer games and ballet recitals. They drove their daughter to math programs, music lessons, and slumber parties.

When Bill lost the 1981 governor's race, Hillary realized she needed to make some changes. She took his name—she was now Hillary Rodham Clinton—and did a full-body makeover. With shorter blond hair, tasteful makeup, contact lenses, and more becoming clothing, she was quite attractive and far more appealing to southern voters with strong ideas of how women should look.

As soon as Bill started running for public office, he was more of a babe magnet than ever before. On the campaign trail, women handed him their phone numbers on slips of paper. One campaign aide said every day some twenty-five women would show up at campaign headquarters looking for him. He would later tell Monica Lewinsky that he had slept with hundreds of women before he ran for president.

Bill loved the story of Lyndon Johnson having sex in the Oval Office, and the legendary tales of Kennedy's endless harem of starlets and secretaries. His friend U.S. Senator J. William Fulbright of Arkansas admonished him, "Bill, if you're going to idolize the womanizing side of Jack Kennedy, you're gonna end up turning out that way yourself. You don't need to be putting yourself in that kind of jeopardy. Don't idolize someone who does things that are wrong."

Rumors percolated, mostly in right-wing quarters years later, about Hillary having an affair of her own. At the Rose Law Firm, she developed a close friendship with another lawyer named Vince Foster. Handsome with thick graying hair, courteous and thoughtful, he was married with three children. Vince and Hillary ate lunch together most days, often having a drink after work. Those who suspected an affair couldn't blame Hillary for seeking a little solace outside her own marriage, given Bill's reputation. Others thought she couldn't be having an affair with Foster because she was a lesbian; given her lifelong disinterest in makeup and clothing until political expediency required a trip to the hair salon, Hillary had to be gay.

By 1987, Bill was ready to toss his hat in the ring and run for president. But those plans crumbled after Gary Hart's political meltdown in May of that year. As one of Bill's state troopers said, "Governor, you're gonna make Gary Hart look like a damned saint."

"Yeah," Bill replied. "I do, don't I?"

In his memoir, Clinton wrote, "After the Hart affair, those of us who had not led perfect lives had no way of knowing what the press's standards of disclosure were." By the time he did run, four years after *Monkey Business*, he had a better idea than Hart how to navigate the media onslaught.

For one thing, Clinton learned that it was better to address the issue right off the bat. Republican consultant Eddie Mahe told the *New York Times*, "The press has collectively made a decision that when any information is presented to them and documented, they will publish it. So the new rule on these things is you'd better talk about it, and you'd better talk about it first." When confronted with proof of his infidelity, Gary Hart had hemmed and hawed, obfuscated and denied, and chastised the media for even asking about his private life. By the late eighties, with the rise of cable TV talk shows like *Oprah*, voters wanted gut-wrenching honesty—or what passed for it—along with an apology.

On October 3, 1991, Bill Clinton announced his plans to run for president. His youth, vitality, eloquence, and charm all helped him become the early front-runner in a lackluster field of Democrats. He addressed his infidelity issue with members of the national political press at an off-the-record event in Washington. There had been problems in his marriage, he admitted, but that was in the past. He and Hillary had worked them out and were committed to each other. Bill must have hoped that was all that would be required. It was not.

In February 1992, on the eve of the New Hampshire primary, Bill's long-term mistress, Gennifer Flowers, appeared in the tabloid *Star*, describing their relationship in an article with the headline, "My 12-Year Affair with Bill Clinton." Denial wasn't an option for Bill; Gennifer had recordings of their phone conversations indicating they'd had a relationship. History seemed to be repeating itself. This looked like *Monkey Business*, Part Two.

According to Flowers, their affair began in 1977 when he was the twenty-nine-year-old Arkansas attorney general and she a twenty-seven-year-old reporter for a local Little Rock TV station. "I can still remember the way he had of staring at me," she wrote in her 1995 autobiography. "He did more than just mentally undress me, he was visually seducing me, and he made sure I knew it. He was turning me upside down and inside out just by looking at me, and when he looked away, I almost felt as though we had just made love. I was breathless and more than a little uneasy."

When they ended up making jubilant love in her bed, it was the start of a twelve-year love affair. "As a lover, Bill was great," she wrote. "Though not particularly well-endowed, his desire to please was astounding. He was determined to satisfy me, and boy, did he! I thought my head would explode with the pleasure . . . His stamina amazed me. We made love over and over that night, and he never seemed to run out of energy." In 1977, she wrote, she realized she was pregnant with his child and he gave her money for an abortion.

He suggested she take an apartment not far from the governor's mansion so he could jog over in the morning and spend half an hour in the sack. His driver, waiting outside, would drop him off a block from the governor's mansion, where he would start jogging again and arrive red-faced and sweaty, with an excellent excuse for jumping into the shower immediately. Though their affair had ended in 1989 when she began dating a single man, Gennifer and Bill remained on friendly terms.

As soon as Bill announced his candidacy, reporters came to Little Rock, determined to dig up dirt on him, and soon heard about Flowers. They called her at work and at home and stalked her. She was ambushed by cameramen and lost her nightclub job. But something more sinister was at work than an overzealous press. Her mother got death threats, evidently from Clinton supporters, while Gennifer received a lot of heavy-breathing hang-up calls. Her apartment was ransacked, after which she made recordings of her conversations with Bill.

When Gennifer spoke to Bill about the break-ins and mysterious phone calls, he told her it was Republican harassment and to just deny, deny, deny. But now she wondered if Bill himself was behind it, or at least a group of his wealthy and powerful supporters determined to see him become president. Her neighbor in her apartment building, a lawyer named Gary Johnson, had set up a video camera in the hallway for security purposes with a clear view of Gennifer's door. When rumors got around that Bill had had an affair with her, Johnson let it be known he had videotapes of the governor entering her apartment with his own key. One day, some men forced their way into his apartment, beat him severely, and left him for dead. When he regained consciousness, the videos were missing.

Flowers said that she sold her story to the *Star* as a means of self-defense. It would be out there once and for all; there would be no need to threaten her and her mother or to ransack her apartment.

But Gennifer didn't count on the Clintons' ruthless counterattacks. When the Flowers story broke, Hillary was campaigning for her husband in South Dakota. Gail Sheehy, covering Hillary for *Vanity Fair*, heard her on her phone talking to campaign aides. Hillary was furious, Sheehy said. "Not anger at Bill, but at Flowers, the press and Republicans."

Sheehy heard Hillary ask, "Who's tracking down all the research on Gennifer?"

The research involved a ruthless private investigator named Jack Palladino whose job it was, as he wrote in a memo, to disparage Gennifer's "character and veracity until she is destroyed beyond all recognition . . . Every acquaintance, employer, and past lover should be located and interviewed." Any unflattering information was given to Betsey Wright, Bill's former chief of staff in Arkansas, who was made responsible for dealing with "bimbo eruptions," as she called accusations of infidelity. Wright would release the information to the press. Gennifer Flowers, Wright said in an interview with *Penthouse*, was a liar, out for money, and guilty of "résumé hype, attempted blackmail, manufacturing a self-styled affair with Clinton to salvage a flopola singing career."

It was a brutal response that would be replayed some two dozen times over the next eight years as women came forward with stories about sex with Bill Clinton. Wright's job turned out to be a kind of bimbo whack-a-mole, standing vigilant with a mallet ready to hammer the women back into the holes they popped out of.

The Clinton campaign took their attack a step further by accusing President George H. W. Bush of having a twelve-year affair with his own Jennifer, his aide Jennifer Fitzgerald, who had joined his staff in 1974 when she was forty-two. The divorcée had served as Bush's gatekeeper for his two terms as vice president under Ronald Reagan. *People* magazine reported that in 1984, Ambassador Louis Fields allowed the two to stay at his Geneva home during an official trip while Barbara Bush was off promoting a book on their dog. "It became clear [they] were romantically involved," Fields said, adding that the relationship of the vice president and Fitzgerald made him "very uncomfortable."

An acquaintance of both Bush and Fitzgerald told the London *Times* in 2004 that Jennifer Fitzgerald "wasn't just another woman. She was a woman who came to exert enormous influence over George for many, many years . . . She became, in essence, his other wife . . . his office wife." The acquaintance added that Barbara Bush put up with the relationship mainly because her husband never humiliated her. Yet, as Barbara wrote in her diary, "His eyes really glaze over when you mention her name. She is just what he wants, he says, and says the hell with it all." Friends said Fitzgerald could be charming—but only to Bush. She was so rude to others that many valued staff members quit rather than work with her.

Rumors about Bush and Fitzgerald had bounced around Washington for years and even made a few fairly discreet headlines. The *Washington Post* had the best one: "Fitzgerald has served President-elect Bush in a variety of positions." Now Hillary brought the rumors front and center to media attention.

During Bush's August 11, 1992, press conference with Israeli prime minister Yitzhak Rabin, a CNN reporter asked the president about a front-page *New York Post* story on Fitzgerald titled "The Bush Affair." "I'm not going to take any sleazy questions like that from CNN," the president snapped. "I'm very disappointed that you would ask such a question of me, and I will not respond to it. I think it's—I am outraged. But, nevertheless, in this kind of screwy climate that we're in, why, I expect it. But I don't like it, and I'm not going to respond other than to say it's a lie." When NBC's Stone Phillips asked him about the affair, Bush retorted, "You're perpetuating the sleaze by even asking the question, to say nothing of asking in the Oval Office." Bush clearly thought he was living in a pre–*Monkey Business* world.

The story ended up withering away. Short and stern-faced, her blond hair lacquered into a French twist, the prickly Fitzgerald didn't seem to be the kind of femme fatale capable of turning a president's head. Buttoned-up, plump, and now sixty, she was an uninteresting target of media attention compared to the sexy bleached-blond lounge singer Gennifer Flowers and her audio-tapes.

The twin Clinton strategy of accusing their political opponents of engaging in adultery and disparaging Bill's women would not be enough. If the Clintons learned how not to address the infidelity issue from Gary Hart, perhaps they also learned some pointers from Alexander Hamilton, who made a gut-wrenching public confession of his affair with Maria Reynolds in his hundred-page pamphlet. Two hundred years later, Bill Clinton would choose television as his confessional. Bill and Hillary appeared on *60 Minutes* right after the 1992 Super Bowl, the most watched program in the world.

Bill's confession lacked something that Hamilton's had: the full truth. He denied having an affair with Gennifer Flowers. But, looking chastened and remorseful, he said, "I have acknowledged wrongdoing. I have acknowledged causing pain in my marriage. I think most Americans who are watching this tonight will know what we're saying. They'll get it, and they'll feel we've been more than candid. And I think what the press has to decide is: Are we going to engage in a game of 'gotcha'?" Hillary asked whether people who had experienced marital difficulties should be prevented from running for public office. The two of them looked like a typical married couple who had had problems over the years. An ABC News poll found that 80 percent of those surveyed thought Bill Clinton should stay in the race.

Ironically, the Gennifer Flowers scandal helped Bill Clinton win the Democratic nomination. Primary voters saw that he had the skill, grace, and media savvy to parry attacks by the Republican machine. While it is usually difficult to unseat an incumbent president, Clinton's candidacy was aided and abetted by the U.S. economy, which had fallen into a recession. On November 3, 1992, Clinton received 370 delegates, Bush 168.

If the Clintons believed the scandals were behind them, they were dead wrong. In May 1993, it was Travelgate. Soon after taking office, Clinton had fired seven employees of the White House Travel Office, which he was fully entitled to do as any of his staff could be dismissed at his pleasure. But his political opponents claimed he had sacked efficient career employees to hire his friends and supporters.

In July, Vince Foster, Hillary's good friend from the Rose Law Firm in Little Rock, shot himself in a Virginia park. A sensitive, gentlemanly soul, Foster had come to Washington to work as deputy White House counsel. But almost immediately he disliked his new life. For one thing, Hillary no longer had time for him. "It's just not the same," he told Webb Hubbell, White House liaison to the Department of Justice, another Clinton associate from Little Rock. "She's so busy that we don't ever have any time to talk."

Attacked by the media for botched Justice Department nominations and his handling of Travelgate, Foster soon slipped into a deep depression. In a note, found torn to pieces in the bottom of his briefcase after his death, he wrote, "The WSJ [*Wall Street Journal*] editors lie without consequence . . . I was not meant for the job or the spotlight of public life in Washington. Here, ruining people is considered sport." Although the FBI, the park police, the independent counsel, and two congressional investigations found his death to be suicide, according to conspiracy theories, Hillary had had him murdered.

Another scandal, called the Whitewater controversy, resulted in an investigation into purported illegal activities of the Clintons and another couple, the McDougals, with regards to a failed Arkansas real estate deal. The McDougals were convicted of financial crimes, but the Clintons were never charged.

In December, it was Troopergate, news articles reporting allegations by four Arkansas state troopers that Clinton had forced them to help with his romantic assignations. They claimed Clinton sent them to scout out attractive women, obtain their phone numbers, arrange hotel rooms, drive him there and back, deliver gifts to the women afterward, and lie to Hillary about where he was. One trooper estimated that Clinton had been intimate with hundreds of women. "There would hardly be an opportunity he would let slip to have sex," he said. Bill denied the allegations. It turned out that Troopergate was orchestrated and, in some cases, financially supported by Clinton's political enemies, yet there was never proof that the men were lying. In 1996, the scandal du jour was Filegate—improper access to hundreds of security clearance documents without the individuals' permission, which Clinton explained away as a "bureaucratic snafu."

But there were political successes along with the scandals. On November 30, 1993, Clinton signed into law the Brady Bill, which mandated federal background checks on people who purchase firearms in the United States. He also expanded the earned income tax credit, a subsidy for low-income workers. In 1994, he implemented a directive known as "Don't Ask, Don't Tell," which allowed gay men and women to serve in the armed services as long as they didn't discuss their sexual orientation, which was considered a huge stride forward at the time. In 1997 he proposed—and signed—legislation to create the State Children's Health Insurance Program (SCHIP), which helped pay for medical care for children from low-income families.

Despite Bill Clinton's political achievements, the largest scandal by far, the one that would define his presidency, was Monica Lewinsky. That morning in August 1998, according to Hillary, Bill finally told her the truth after months of vehement denials. He had lied to her, lied to the American people and, most dangerous of all, lied to the independent counsel, Ken Starr.

The affair had started when Monica, a recent twenty-two-year-old college graduate, began working as a White House intern in the summer of 1995. Aimless, smarting from the ending of an affair with her married former high school drama teacher, she thought this position, arranged by an influential family friend, would look good on her résumé. But when she first caught sight of the charismatic Bill Clinton in person, she shifted her obsession to him, arriving for White House ceremonies hours early to have a place up front to catch his eye. At one such event, she was successful. The president not only noticed the voluptuous brunette with a toothy grin and lustrous shoulder-length hair, he gave her "the full Bill Clinton," as she said, and her description is quite similar to that of Gennifer Flowers. "It was this look, it's the way he flirts with women . . . We shared an intense but brief sexual exchange. He undressed me with his eyes."

According to Lewinsky's testimony in the Starr Report, on the evening of November 15, 1995, Monica walked past the inner office of the West Wing and saw the president alone. She lifted the back of her jacket to flash the straps of her thong panties and a sizable amount of firm, round buttock. A few minutes later, Clinton summoned her into his study, and they kissed. Two days later, Lewinsky gave him oral sex as he spoke on the phone with two congressmen. But he never allowed her to bring him to climax and finished himself off over a wastepaper basket. Perhaps he was afraid that DNA might be used as evidence—and rightly so, as events would prove. Or perhaps he had convinced himself that sex wasn't sex without orgasm, and the orgasm he achieved all by himself, so that was actually masturbation, not sex. On one occasion, however, Clinton left two small spots on Monica's navy blue Gap dress. Over the course of a year and a half, during which Lewinsky went from intern to full-time employee, the two engaged in physical encounters nine times—during one he inserted a cigar in her vagina and then put it in his mouth—and in phone sex fifteen times.

The relationship wasn't just sex. "We enjoyed talking with each other and being with each other," Lewinsky said. "We were very affectionate. We would tell jokes. We would talk about our childhoods, talk about current events . . . I think back on it and he always made me smile when I was with him. He was sunshine." A good friend of Bill's told author Jerry Oppenheimer, "I know how he is with women. But she was different. He was literally hooked on her and pursued her with the same level of adolescent obsession that she pursued him. He desperately needed to be loved—I'm not talking just about sex, but a caring kind of love, and Monica probably more than any other woman—except his mother—filled that need. Certainly Hillary never did. From things he has said since, I truly believe that Bill would have run off with that girl if he had the chance, if things had been different." Caught up in the euphoria of secret, forbidden assignations, Bill even suggested he might divorce Hillary after he left the White House. Overjoyed, Monica boasted to a friend that one day she might become the second Mrs. Clinton.

In April 1996, concerned Secret Service agents informed Deputy Chief of Staff Evelyn Lieberman that Monica was spending too much time with the president. Lieberman immediately transferred her to a job at the Pentagon. Monica was devastated at being so distant from her lover, though she did make a few White House visits.

Soon, Clinton's passion for Monica ebbed, rather like helium leaking out of a balloon until all you have left is a limp, sagging memory of better times. He wanted to end the relationship but he feared she would blab if he did. As long as they had a relationship, he believed she would keep quiet about it. Bill promised to find Monica a great job and asked Washington power broker Vernon Jordan to help. By January 1998, Jordan had an exciting job lined up for Monica at Revlon in New York.

Unfortunately for Clinton, Monica couldn't keep her mouth shut even though he was still stringing her along. At the Pentagon, she befriended Linda Tripp, who had worked at the White House for George H. W. Bush and then briefly for Clinton, whom she despised. She was, in fact, planning to write a tell-all book about Bill's sexual dalliances and even had a literary agent, Lucianne Goldberg. When Monica began confiding in Linda about her affair with the president, including details of their sexual encounters, Linda notified her agent, who suggested she tape-record the calls. It was Linda who instructed Monica to put that navy blue dress in the freezer to preserve the DNA.

Linda heard that lawyers for a woman named Paula Jones, who were suing Bill Clinton for sexual harassment, were looking for other women who had worked as his subordinates and been subjected to romantic overtures. Paula's run-in with Clinton occurred on May 8, 1991, at an event in Little Rock's Excelsior Hotel, when Governor Clinton asked a state trooper to invite the twenty-five-year-old, $6.35-an-hour state document examiner to come up to his room. According to Jones, when she arrived, Clinton "began pulling me over like he has done this a million times and grabs me and pulls me over to him to the windowsill and tries to kiss me and just didn't ask me or nothing." Then the governor pulled his pants down, sat down and asked, "Would you kiss it for me?" Paula uttered the immortal words, "I'm not that kind of girl!" and fled.

In 1994, with Clinton now president, Jones filed a lawsuit against Clinton for sexual harassment, as she had been a state employee when he, her ultimate boss as governor, pressed for sex. She wanted $700,000. To prove she was no liar, she said she could identify an unusual bend in his penis. In an affidavit that is considered one of the strangest legal documents ever, she stated that Bill's penis was "five to five and one-half inches, or less, in length . . . a circumference of the approximate size of a quarter, or perhaps very slightly larger" and "was bent or crooked from Mr. Clinton's right to left."

The main question was whether a civil suit could go ahead against a sitting president. For two hundred years, such suits had been dismissed, as judges presumed national security depended on a president completely focused on protecting the nation. But by the time Jones filed her suit, the Cold War and America's arch-enemy, the Soviet Union, were no more. Perhaps the president could handle some distraction without the country going up in smoke. In January 1997, the Supreme Court unanimously ruled that Jones's suit could proceed. The *New York Post* trumpeted the headline "Grin and Bare It" for an article that suggested the best method of proving Jones had seen the president's penis would be for the president to drop his pants in court. Those in the courtroom could study it to see how bent it actually was.

Tripp told Jones's lawyers that her friend—and we use that term loosely—Monica Lewinsky had confided that she had been having an affair with the president for some eighteen months while she was a federal employee. The lawyers subpoenaed Monica, and on January 7, 1998, she signed an affidavit under penalty of perjury that she had never engaged in sexual relations with the president. Foiled and bursting with venom at the thought of losing her book deal, Tripp turned over the tapes of her phone conversations with Monica to Independent Special Counsel Ken Starr, who had been looking into the Whitewater controversy but had the prerogative to investigate any suspicious matters that came his way. Now Starr turned a gimlet eye on Monica Lewinsky. On January 16, Starr wired Tripp for a meeting with Monica and prosecutors listened to their conversation. Minutes later, they swooped in, took her into custody, and told her she could either cooperate or go to jail for twenty-five years for perjury, obstruction of justice, and several other charges.

The following day, January 17, 1998, Bill Clinton was deposed under oath in the Paula Jones case. He didn't remember Jones, he said. He certainly never showed her his penis in a hotel room. He did know Monica but had never had a sexual relationship with her, couldn't even remember being alone with her.

Meanwhile, rumors of the Clinton-Lewinsky affair had reached the press. The same day as Clinton's deposition, the internet news site the Drudge Report first published the story about the affair and, over the next few days, stories about blow jobs in the White House, presidential perjury, and a cushy job in the private sector as a bribe for silence.

What to do? Clinton did what most men do in such a situation: deny, deny, deny. On January 26, he marched into the Roosevelt Room of the White House, looked straight into a TV camera, and said the words that would define his presidency. "I did not have sexual relations with that woman—Miss Lewinsky."

On April 1, 1998, a federal judge dismissed Paula Jones's sexual harassment suit, finding that Clinton's conduct did not constitute sexual assault. Jones's lawyers appealed the dismissal. Given the newer, bigger, and more dangerous mess of Monica Lewinsky, however, Clinton didn't wait for the appeal decision and settled with Jones for $850,000—$150,000 more than she had asked for in her lawsuit—with no acknowledgment of wrongdoing. Costly as it was, he had whacked that mole.

But other moles had popped up during the Paula Jones case. On March 18, 1998, Dallas lawyer Dolly Kyle Browning, who had attended high school with Clinton, testified that they had had an affair starting in the mid-1970s which lasted until January 1992. According to Browning, her own brother, who worked for the Clinton campaign, said, "We think you should deny the story," and, "If you cooperate with the media, we will destroy you."

Fifty-one-year-old White House volunteer aide Kathleen Willey had also been subpoenaed by Paula Jones's lawyers. On March 15, 1998, she went public with her story, telling *60 Minutes* that Clinton had sexually assaulted her on November 29, 1993, in the Oval Office. She had met with him to discuss some personal and professional issues, she said, when he grabbed her crotch and rubbed up against her. In a deposition, Clinton denied Willey's story but did finally admit he'd had sex with Gennifer Flowers. But only once. In 1977. It seems that Bill Clinton couldn't help but lie even when he was telling the truth.

Bill's most important testimony occurred on August 17 when he appeared before a grand jury on a closed-circuit television feed from the White House and conceded that he'd had "inappropriate intimate physical contact" with Monica Lewinsky. But he stubbornly insisted it had not actually been sex as defined by the judge in the Paula Jones deposition, so he had not really perjured himself. The judge had defined sex—and many of us may wonder why he had felt the need to do so—as "contact with the genitalia, anus, groin, breast, or buttocks of any person with an intent to arouse or gratify the sexual desire of any person." Clinton argued that if a woman was performing oral sex on him, he was actually not in contact with her genitalia, anus, groin, breast, or buttocks, but with her lips.

That night, Clinton curtly told the nation, "I know that my public comments and my silence about this matter gave a false impression. I misled people including even my own wife. I deeply regret that." The American public was unimpressed. They wanted breast-beating drama, streaming tears, agonized sobs, guilt, and remorse, not this tight-lipped pseudo-apology. They wanted a poignant performance. They would get it on September 11, when Clinton tried again at a prayer breakfast. "I have sinned," he lamented. The voice cracked. The eyes overflowed with tears. The audience found it far more satisfying.

The same day, Starr released a 452-page report full of disgusting details: the cigar-cum-tampon, the ejaculating into the trashcan, the blow job while he was talking to members of Congress on the phone. The press was horrified. More than sixty-five major newspapers demanded he resign. Worse for Clinton, Starr's findings reported that he had discovered "substantial and credible information that President William Jefferson Clinton committed acts that may constitute grounds for impeachment."

On December 19, the House of Representatives voted to impeach Clinton on two charges of perjury and obstruction of justice. On February 12, 1999, the Senate, however, acquitted him of perjury with a vote of 55 to 45, and of obstruction of justice by 50 to 50.

Oddly, impeachment only served to beef up Clinton's approval ratings. His highest Gallup score ever—73 percent—occurred the week of the impeachment. A *Washington Post* poll found that even though a majority of Americans believed Clinton had lied under oath, the lies didn't bother them as they had only been about sex, and almost everybody lied about sex. If he had lied, say, about stealing taxpayer dollars and putting them in an offshore bank account, it is likely they would have felt quite differently.

The majority of Americans also believed that Clinton was a victim of a political conspiracy. A man playing around with a girlfriend was far less objectionable than a political group plotting to take an opponent down by any means, no matter how ridiculous. Starr's investigation smacked of sexual McCarthyism; his investigation was a kind of House Committee on Unpious Activities, where old white men shrieked with outrage as they examined semen stains under a magnifying glass, but also experienced a prurient thrill.

Time magazine named Bill Clinton and independent counsel Kenneth Starr its 1998 Persons of the Year. Columnist Michael Kinsley wrote, "The most significant political story of the year is that most citizens don't seem to think it's significant that the President had oral sex with a 22-year-old intern. Yes, yes, and he lied about it. Under oath. Blah blah blah. They still don't care. Rarely has such an unexpected popular consensus been so clear. And rarely has such a clear consensus been so unexpected."

Clinton's sex life was unimportant compared to the sky-high stock market, record job creation, low inflation, higher household incomes, a federal budget surplus, reduced crime, and the lowest welfare rolls in thirty years. Gary Langer of ABC News summed up how most Americans felt about Bill Clinton: "You can't trust him, he's got weak morals and ethics—and he's done a heck of a good job."

During the impeachment, the *Los Angeles Times*, which had supported Clinton in the past, declared, "The picture of Clinton that now emerges is that of a middle-aged man with a pathetic inability to control his sexual fantasies." No one could deny that, but it didn't necessarily mean he was a bad president. In fact, Clinton's sexual behavior came to be seen as part and parcel of his political brilliance. The energy, the drive, the impish charm, and the insatiable love of life seemed irrevocably interwoven with his skill for foreign relations and handling of the U.S. economy. A dried-out old stick of a president surely would not have been so successful at governing. Personal morality, Americans of the 1990s figured out, had little to do with leadership capability. It was as if the American public were becoming French.

Many Americans were also disturbed by the hypocrisy angle of the impeachment. How many of those lantern-jawed hanging judges in Congress and the independent counsel's office had had a little sex on the side themselves? Larry Flynt, the publisher of *Hustler* magazine, was determined to find out. In October 1998, as the House initiated impeachment proceedings, he placed an $85,000 full-page ad in the *Washington Post* offering a $1 million reward to anyone who could provide "documentary evidence of illicit sexual relations" involving any senators, congressmen, or other high-ranking government officials. "I feel the people who are going to be sitting in judgment who have not been truthful about similar activities in their own lives should recuse themselves," Flynt said. "What we are talking about is hypocrisy in its highest form."

"That's some very easy money," said one veteran House staffer interviewed by the *Washington Post*, and he was right. More than two thousand calls came into the hotline. Evidence arrived showing that Congressman Henry Hyde, the House leader on impeachment, had been unfaithful to his wife with a hairdresser back in the 1960s. Flynt released transcripts from the 1985 divorce case of Congressman Bob Barr—one of the House managers who presented the Clinton case to the Senate—in which he refused to answer questions about cheating on his second wife with the woman who would become his third. Congressman Bob Livingston, the powerful chairman of the House Appropriations Committee, had had numerous affairs, including one with an employee. When Livingston accused Flynt of being a "bottom feeder," the publisher replied, "Well, that's right. But look what I found when I got down there." As a result of Flynt's inquiry, Livingston resigned from Congress in March 1999. Bill Clinton quipped, "The interesting thing was, Larry Flynt turned out to be a better guy than Ken Starr."

Even after Flynt's stunt, proof of more hypocrisy came rolling in. In 2007, Senator Larry Craig, who had spoken harshly against Clinton's crimes, was accused of soliciting sex from a male undercover cop in an airport men's room. In 2015, Dennis Hastert, who had replaced Newt Gingrich as speaker of the House, pled guilty to charges of illegally structuring cash withdrawals to make blackmail payments to young men he had molested decades earlier while working as a high school wrestling coach.

Two months after Clinton was acquitted, just as things were finally settling down, the most serious accusation of all arose. On February 24, 1999, Juanita Broaddrick told NBC's *Dateline* that Clinton had raped her in 1978 when she was a thirty-five-year-old volunteer on his gubernatorial campaign. She had arranged to meet him in a hotel coffee shop, but Clinton suggested they meet for coffee in her hotel room to avoid the throng of journalists in the hotel lobby. There, she said, he raped her so violently he left her bloody. Her friend Norma Rogers, who shared the hotel room with Broaddrick, said she found her in bed with torn panty hose and a bleeding, swollen lip. Rogers stated that Broaddrick described the rape to her, as did three other friends of Broaddrick's. Yet in 1997, when Juanita was deposed in the Paula Jones case, she denied having any sexual contact with Clinton. A year later, when Ken Starr questioned her, she told the truth, she said, as she was terrified of the harsher criminal penalties for lying to the independent counsel. Yet she ended up as only a footnote in Starr's final report.

By the time her story came out, Americans were exhausted by the Lewinsky scandal, the Starr Report, and the impeachment. Broaddrick's allegation was far worse than the others, as she claimed rape, but still. Broaddrick had no proof to bring a lawsuit against Clinton and had muddied the waters by denying the assault in her original deposition. Scandal fatigue caused most Americans to insert their fingers in their ears, close their eyes, and stick out their tongues. Broaddrick ended up self-publishing her book, *You'd Better Put Some Ice on That: How I Survived Being Raped by Bill Clinton*, in 2019.

The most recent accuser of Bill Clinton behaving badly was Leslie Millwee, who in 2016 came forward to accuse him of sexually assaulting her three times in a small editing room in 1980 when she was working as a reporter at an Arkansas television station. According to Millwee, Governor Clinton came up to her on each occasion, groped her breasts and, on the second and third assaults, rubbed himself against her until he climaxed.

In 2017, public opinion veered in another direction with the #MeToo movement. Unwanted groping, rubbing, and touching was now defined as sexual assault. It was time to reexamine Clinton's bad behavior, even his consensual relationship with Monica Lewinsky.

Lewinsky had been twenty-two when the affair began, an adult, but barely. Most of us with a few more years on us, looking at twenty-two-year-olds, see them as big children with functioning reproductive organs. And who among us hasn't done something illegal, immoral, or just plain idiotic at twenty-two? Luckily for us, our poor judgment was not at the center of a presidential impeachment inquiry, resulting in the global sliming of our names for all time to come. Blushing furiously as we remember foolhardy choices, we can raise a toast to the good fortune of our own obscurity.

In contrast to Lewinsky's youth, Clinton had been forty-nine, her superior in the workplace, and the most important man in the country, arguably in the world. After he left office, he remained an A-list celebrity, earning fortunes in speaking fees, campaigning for Democratic candidates, going to all the best parties. Little if any slime stuck to him, but then again, Teflon skin is usually a male attribute. Lewinsky, reduced to a punchline and a semen-stained dress, struggled to find work and a relationship. Fleeing the U.S., she obtained her Master of Science degree in Social Psychology at the London School of Economics in 2006 but had difficulty getting a job due to her notoriety.

In 2014, she reemerged from a long hibernation to discuss the scandal in an essay in *Vanity Fair* and began to speak out against cyberbullying. "When news of my affair with Bill Clinton broke," she wrote, "I was arguably the most humiliated person in the world. Thanks to the Drudge Report, I was also possibly the first person whose global humiliation was driven by the Internet." In 2105 she joined the anti-bullying organization Bystander Revolution as an ambassador and strategic adviser.

In a March 2018 *Vanity Fair* essay, Lewinsky shifted her position from four years earlier when she had accepted full responsibility for her actions. Now, in the light of #MeToo, she saw her relationship with the president as replete with "inappropriate abuse of authority, station, and privilege . . . Now, at 44, I'm beginning (just beginning) to consider the implications of the power differentials that were so vast between a president and a White House intern. I'm beginning to entertain the notion that in such a circumstance the idea of consent might well be rendered moot."

A few months later, when Bill Clinton was asked in an interview if he owed Lewinsky an apology, he said he did not. Hillary Clinton said Bill had not abused his power as Lewinsky had been an adult.

"What feels more important to me than whether I am *owed* or *deserving* of a personal apology is my belief that Bill Clinton should want to apologize," Lewinsky said. "I'm less disappointed *by* him and more disappointed *for* him. He would be a better man for it . . . and we, in turn, a better society."

In the 2020 Hulu documentary series *Hillary*, Bill finally apologized to Monica, sort of. "I feel terrible about the fact that Monica Lewinsky's life was defined by it, unfairly, I think," he said. "Over the years I watched her try to get a normal life back. But you gotta decide how to define normal." His final remark seemed to indicate she should just accept the spectacular public derailment of her life, suck it up, and move on.

Oddly, Clinton blamed his decision to pursue the affair on the stress of office. "Here's something that will take your mind off it for a while," he explained. "Things I did to manage my anxiety for years." It seems he did indeed emulate his hero, JFK, who used unseemly sex to prevent stress headaches.

Most Democrats stood by the Clintons despite Bill's numerous sex scandals and Hillary's rather chilling reaction to them. But when the Clintons' supporters excoriated another candidate trailing a long list of similar allegations, including rape, Republicans called them out on hypocrisy. That candidate's name was Donald Trump.

13

DONALD TRUMP CAN DO ANYTHING

*O*n October 7, 2016, the *Washington Post* and NBC News released an audio tape of Republican presidential nominee Donald Trump bragging back in 2005 to *Access Hollywood* coanchor Billy Bush about groping and kissing unsuspecting women. "And when you're a star," he said, "they let you do it. You can do anything. Grab them by the pussy. You can do anything."

Such a revelation would have quickly tanked any other candidate, but not Donald, who has enjoyed one of the most highly improbable lives in the history of mankind.

* * *

Most single-name celebrities are entertainers or athletes: Adele, Shaq, Oprah. Trump was a single-name celebrity real estate developer, the world's most shameless and successful self-promoter, a barking Ringling Bros. and Barnum & Bailey ringmaster, whose blustering hyperbole praised the greatest, most spectacular, most amazing show on earth, with himself as the only act. He was, by turns, brash, irritable, childish, deceitful, and a marketing genius. A man whose over-the-top buildings combined Buckingham Place with Caesar's Palace. And, since 2017, a man whose presidential power has put hubris syndrome on the world stage.

Born in 1946 in Queens, New York, Donald was the son of Fred Trump, a successful real estate developer. Though Donald dutifully graduated from the Wharton School of the University of Pennsylvania with a degree in economics, as his father wished, he was itching to run his own real estate business. Fred Trump had focused on developing Queens and Coney Island, eventually building some 27,000 apartments and rowhouses in the New York area for the working class in the postwar housing shortage. Young Donald gazed across the river at Manhattan, where glittering skyscrapers rose above a city devastated by crime and tottering on the brink of bankruptcy. "I'm basically an optimist," he wrote in *The Art of the Deal*, "and frankly, I saw the city's trouble as a great opportunity for me. Because I grew up in Queens, I believed, perhaps to an irrational degree, that Manhattan was always going to be the best place to live—the center of the world."

He started off in 1978 by buying the run-down Commodore Hotel, next to Grand Central Terminal, refurbishing it, and renaming it the Grand Hyatt. The same year he began building Trump Tower, a fifty-eight-story, mixed-use building in Midtown, which opened in 1983. He acquired the Plaza Hotel in 1988 for $400 million and spent another $50 million renovating it. Then came Atlantic City casinos: Trump Plaza, Trump's Castle, the Trump Taj Mahal, for hundreds of millions of dollars each. Trump was always betting big while rolling the dice, acquiring properties in a real-life Monopoly game. He started developing resorts and golf courses in countries around the world, and licensed his name for a variety of products: hotels, wine, menswear, vodka, steaks, water, deodorant, eyeglasses, coffee, mattresses, home furnishings, adult learning courses, and a board game, most of which did not last long. His real estate projects bounced in and out of bankruptcy restructuring, and several times he was forced to give up his interest to those who'd assumed his debt. Often, Father Fred came through, pledging his own equity toward his son's success. Undaunted by bankruptcy, undeterred by investor takeovers, and unembarrassed at accepting his father's help when he was in his thirties, Donald Trump proclaimed himself a giant success and moved on to the next big deal. According to a Gallup poll conducted in December 1988, he was the tenth most admired man in America.

Trump's mind-set has always been a rather simple one: the world is composed of winners and losers, and he wants to be a winner every single time. If he admitted defeat—even a single, minor mistake—he would be a loser. He also has a rather negative view of his fellow humans. In a 1981 article in *People*, he said, "Man is the most vicious of all animals, and life is a series of battles ending in victory or defeat. You just can't let people make a sucker out of you." And in a 2011 speech at the National Achievers Congress in Sydney, Australia, he said, "When a person screws you, you screw them back ten times harder!"

In 1977, Trump married a blond, six-foot-tall Czech model named Ivana Zelnickova, three years his junior. His marriage proposal was unique: "If you don't marry me, you'll ruin your life." Ivana agreed that she did not want to ruin her life. They had three children: Donald Jr. in 1977, Ivanka in 1981, and Eric in 1984. Trump has always made it clear who was boss in his marriages. He and Ivana never had "tremendous fights" because, he said, "ultimately, Ivana does exactly what I tell her to do." Though Ivana often acquiesced to his bidding, she was no Stepford wife and played an active role in her husband's businesses as vice president for interior design. Her projects included the Trump Tower, the Plaza Hotel, and the Trump Plaza Hotel and Casino in Atlantic City, supervising a budget of tens of millions of dollars for each property.

Perhaps he sent his wife to Atlantic City in 1985 for personal rather than business reasons. That same year, Trump began an affair with a twenty-two-year-old, five-foot-eight model from Georgia named Marla Maples, stashing her on his yacht and at his various hotels. He'd lost interest in Ivana—and told her so— even though she bought herself bigger breasts, wider cheekbones, a softer face, and fuller lips to please him, emerging from her bandages looking a lot like a young Brigitte Bardot. But her efforts were futile. Marla boasted something unattainable to Ivana— youth—and somewhat resembled her idol, Farrah Fawcett, with a wild mane of feathery blond locks.

Donald bemoaned to Marla the state of his loveless marriage for years and promised he would get a divorce one day soon—as most unfaithful married men do. Finally, Marla grew sick of waiting. In December 1989, she marched up to Ivana, Donald, and the three kids at a restaurant in Aspen, where they had been enjoying a ski vacation, and said, "I'm Marla and I love your husband. Do you?" Specific accounts differ, but Ivana told her something like "You bitch, leave my husband alone," followed by a string of Slavic profanities.

The ski-slope face-off soon made the headlines. It was the perfect tabloid story in that era of excess, a time of huge hair and linebacker shoulder pads and record Wall Street numbers. It was a real-life version of one of the biggest TV shows of the eighties— *Dynasty*, where money was no object and the ex-wife and the current wife and the mistress all bitch-slapped each other in public to the cheers of onlookers. As the Trumps' marriage quickly crumbled, New York tabloids slavered after the story, splashing photos and headlines of the love triangle on their covers for months.

The average man would be horrified by a public confrontation between his wife and his mistress—in front of the children, no less—and its breathless coverage in the New York papers, but not Donald Trump. He reveled in it. There he was for all to see, the object of lustful desire of two beautiful blondes fighting over him. The infamous *New York Post* headline "Marla Boasts to Her Friends: Best Sex I've Ever Had" was one that Trump himself convinced the paper to run, according to Jill Brooke, a *Post* reporter.

He scoured the papers every day, pleased that his divorce was getting far more coverage than the high-profile split of director Steven Spielberg and actress Amy Irving, and claimed the press increased his casino profits. "A divorce is never a pleasant thing," he explained, and indeed, his elder son didn't speak to him for a year, "but from a business standpoint, it's had a very positive effect." In a 1991 interview with *Esquire* magazine, he said, "You know it doesn't really matter what they write as long as you've got a young and beautiful piece of ass."

It is curious that of the two dozen or so accusations women have made against Trump for sexual assault, unwanted kissing, and dressing-room leering, the very first one came from his wife, and it was nothing less than an accusation of rape. In a divorce deposition obtained by Harry Hurt, author of the 1993 *Lost Tycoon: The Many Lives of Donald J. Trump*, Ivana stated under oath that she had recommended a cosmetic surgeon to treat her husband's bald spot, and he came home furious because the procedure was not only painful, but ineffective. According to Hurt, Ivana stated that he pinned back her arms, yanked handfuls of hair from her scalp so she, too, would have a sore bald spot, tore off her clothes, and raped her. The following morning, Ivana awoke sore and bruised, and gazed at clumps of her hair all over the bed. As she examined her own bald spots in the mirror, Trump glared at her and asked casually, "Does it hurt?" She told several friends about it soon after.

Once she reached a generous divorce settlement, however, and signed a gag order, she changed her tune. Her lawyers insisted that new editions of Hurt's book include a statement from Ivana on the flyleaf. "During a deposition given by me in connection with my matrimonial case, I stated that my husband had raped me," the statement said. "On one occasion during 1989, Mr. Trump and I had marital relations in which he behaved very differently toward me than he had during our marriage. As a woman, I felt violated, as the love and tenderness which he normally exhibited towards me, was absent. I referred to this as a 'rape' but I do not want my words to be interpreted in a literal or criminal sense." Trump denied the rape, but perhaps he was more concerned about the allegations of scalp surgery. His hair was so naturally thick, he never would have needed such a thing.

But if the story of the angry, balding rapist faded away, the fable of the celebrity playboy was just getting started. Now that he was getting divorced, beautiful women would only burnish his brand, the brand of a regular guy—setting aside for the moment that his father was worth hundreds of millions of dollars—who worked hard and obtained amazing success. *You too*, he was saying, in what was perhaps the world's most brilliant marketing ploy, *could be like me if you stay in my hotels and buy my wine and fly my airline and wear my ties*. He gave consumers—for a price—the cachet of Trump fabulousness, dreams of a life of private jets and Bond girls and gilded penthouse apartments.

When in 1991 a reporter from *People* magazine named Sue

Carswell called Trump's office to confirm or refute the rumor that he had dumped Marla Maples for Italian model and future first lady of France Carla Bruni, she quickly got a return call from a man who identified himself as Trump's publicist, John Miller. Miller confirmed that Trump had dumped Marla and had numerous beautiful women hoping he would pick them as his next girlfriend, including Bruni. "Important, beautiful women call him all the time," Miller said. He listed several names, including Madonna. "He mentioned basically every hot woman in Hollywood," Carswell said. Miller told her, "Actresses just call to see if they can go out with him and things." He boasted that in addition to living with Marla, Trump had "three other girlfriends." For her part, Bruni denied dating Trump, calling him "the king of Tacky" and "obviously a lunatic."

John Miller sounded eerily similar to Trump himself. When Carswell called Marla and played the tape, she began to cry and confirmed John Miller was none other than Trump. Sometimes Trump said he was John Barron, a vice president of the Trump Organization, when he called major newspapers and magazines to tell journalists how dozens of gorgeous women were panting to go to bed with Trump.

In January 1993, an event occurred that would lead to the second sexual assault allegation made against Trump. According to a lawsuit filed four years later, a woman named Jill Harth and her boyfriend George Houraney dined with Trump at his opulent Florida estate, Mar-a-Lago, to celebrate a business deal. During the meal, Harth got more than she bargained for when Trump tried to slip his hands between her legs. After dinner, Trump gave her a tour of the mansion and, in his daughter Ivanka's bedroom, Harth claimed in a 2016 interview with the *Guardian*, "He pushed me up against the wall, and had his hands all over me and tried to get up my dress again, and I had to physically say, 'What are you doing? Stop it.' It was a shocking thing to have him do this because he knew I was with George, he knew they were in the next room. And how could he be doing this when I'm there for business?"

She and George, who had planned to spend the night, left. After Jill and George became engaged, Trump began to stalk her, Harth stated in her suit claiming sexual assault and relentless sexual harassment. New York tabloids trumpeted the suit, but it was withdrawn after George Houraney settled with Trump for an undisclosed amount in a lawsuit that claimed Trump had backed out of a business deal.

Marla Maples traveled frequently with Donald, perhaps to keep her eye on him, and always packed a wedding dress, just in case he changed his mind and decided to marry her on the spot. "You've got to be prepared," she explained. She was supposed to be on the pill but, curiously, got pregnant anyway. When relating the story to Howard Stern, Trump said he asked her, "What are we going to do about this?" which seemed to indicate abortion was an option. But it was not an option for Marla, who in October 1993 gave birth to his daughter Tiffany—named after the jewelry store—and still he didn't marry her. Circumstances, however, pushed the reluctant groom toward the altar. Trump's reputation for instability—financial and personal—would reduce the price of his casino stock offering early in 1994. But a newly married man, settled down with an infant, would likely increase his revenue. The final shove came on December 7, 1993; a mass shooting on the Long Island Rail Road made Trump realize that "life is short," as he later explained it, so they might as well get married. Perhaps it's not surprising Marla cooked up a lavish wedding with a thousand of their closest friends in the Grand Ballroom of the Plaza in just days, because she was prepared.

Delighted as Marla was with the nuptials, Trump was less so. "I was bored when she was walking down the aisle," Trump later said. "I kept thinking, 'What the hell am I doing here?'"

O. J. Simpson was among the guests watching the radiant bride come down the aisle. "I think everybody in the country believes if *their* relationship can work, then anyone's relationship can work," he said, six months before he was charged with stabbing his wife and a friend of hers to death in her front yard.

Ivana was a strong-minded, independent woman, which is why she quickly divorced her husband once she realized he was a philanderer. She had held important positions in the Trump Organization, made her own schedule, and spoke her mind. Not so Marla, a delicate southern belle who let Trump run the show. Maureen Orth of *Vanity Fair* wrote, "Getting to know Marla Maples is akin to pressing your thumb on an aerosol can and watching mountains of Reddi-wip flow out."

Marla knew she didn't fit into Trump World. "Once we started going out in public, an image was expected," she recalled. "The hair and makeup and the designer dresses, and you become a caricature of yourself. And I think what he loved about me the most was that I wasn't part of that world. But once we were together publicly, he wanted to change me into that social animal . . . Putting on gowns and going out hosting events and having Harry Winston put jewelry on my hands was always uncomfortable for me—that was me playing a role. I felt that's what the job called for." Indeed, her primary job as Trump's wife was to make men jealous of Trump.

Marla did what she was told, but it wasn't enough. A little

more than a year after the wedding, in an interview with *Vanity Fair* in 1995, Trump looked back on his bachelor days between wives with longing. "I had been in Europe fucking every model in the world. My life was wild," he lamented. As could be expected, while Marla stayed home with the baby, Trump resumed his playboy ways, traveling around the world in his private jet with gorgeous models. Marla grew lonely and sad.

She had signed a prenup capping her divorce settlement at a measly $1 million if they separated within five years, with another million for a house and $100,000 a year child support for Tiffany that would end when she turned twenty-one or before that if, oddly enough, she joined the army or the Peace Corps. But Trump dumped Marla well before the deadline. At 4:00 a.m. on April 16, 1996, police caught her with Trump's bodyguard, a thirty-five-year-old hunk named Spencer Wagner, under a lifeguard stand on a beach not far from Mar-a-Lago while Trump was out of town. The *National Enquirer* crowed, "Shock for Trump! Marla Caught with Hunk/Cops Interrupt Late Night Beach Frolic."

Trump and Marla both denied the story. She and the bodyguard had gone for a walk, they said—as many people do at 4:00 a.m.—and when she had to pee, the only place offering a modicum of privacy was under the lifeguard stand. But Trump was livid. This time the screaming tabloid headlines weren't burnishing his image but tarnishing it. This time *he* was the cuckold, the dupe, the fool, while his sexy young wife was making love in the sand with a younger, buffer, more handsome man. Serving her with divorce papers immediately would have validated the story. It is stunning that a man known for impatience and outbursts of anger didn't fire the bodyguard until four months later. He bided his time even longer with Marla, informing her of the divorce a year later by leaving a copy of the *New York Post* outside their bedroom door with the headline "Donald Is Divorcing Marla."

Under the terms of their prenuptial agreement and divorce settlement, Maples is bound by a confidentiality agreement regarding their marriage which has rendered her as mute as a zombie whose mouth has been filled up with salt and whose lips have been sewn together. She got a contract from HarperCollins in 2001 for her memoirs, to be called *All That Glitters Is Not Gold*. But the book was never published. At the time, Trump refused to comment whether he invoked the confidentiality agreement to scotch the deal. Either way, her story, such as it is, looks lost to history.

Trump was overjoyed to be a bachelor again, to publicly surround himself with beautiful women. In his bestselling 1997 memoir, *Trump: The Art of the Comeback*, he recalled—or, more likely, invented—stories of women wild to have sex with him. "If I told the real stories of my experiences with women," he wrote, "often seemingly very happily married and important women, this book would be a guaranteed bestseller (which it will be anyway!)" He told of a certain "lady of great social pedigree and wealth," whose husband was also at the dinner table. "All of a sudden, I felt her hand on my knee, then on my leg. She started petting me in all different ways." Then, in language from a 1940s film noir starring Bette Davis, language no woman in real life would *ever* utter, she cried, "Donald, I don't care. I just don't care. I have to have you, and I have to have you now." When Trump gave a limo ride to another "truly great-looking and sexy" wealthy woman who was about to get married, "within five seconds after the door closed, she would be jumping on top of me wanting to get screwed."

In 1998, Trump arrived at New York's Kit Kat Club with a

beautiful Norwegian heiress named Celina Midelfart as his date. There he spotted twenty-eight-year-old Slovenian model Melania Knauss. At five foot eleven, slender and shapely with wide cheekbones, catlike blue eyes, and a tumble of gleaming brown hair, she enchanted him immediately. "She's incredible," he told a friend. "I want this woman." While Midelfart powdered her nose, Trump asked Melania for her phone number. Having seen Trump with a date, she turned him down, but he persisted. They married in a million-dollar ceremony in 2005. A year later, they had a son, Barron. Trump's older children called Melania "the Portrait" because she was beautiful and spoke so little. Indeed, each of Trump's wives has grown more silent than the one before.

In 2003, Trump began filming *The Apprentice*, a reality TV show in which aspiring businesspeople competed for a one-year, $250,000 contract at one of Trump's companies. Trump proved a natural; easy to work with, fascinating to watch, memorizing direction so well the crew often needed only one take. It was he who came up with the famous line, "You're fired!" Over fourteen seasons, the show made Trump a household name nationally, paving the way for his entry onto the political stage.

Trump had long been interested in politics and in 1987 took out several full-page ads in major newspapers promoting a reduced budget deficit, peace in Central America, nuclear disarmament with the Soviet Union, and renegotiating the money the U.S. spent supporting global organizations. He changed his party several times, from Republican to Reform to Democrat back to Republican. Starting in 2010, he helped fuel the Obama "birther" movement, the false belief that President Barack Obama had been born in Kenya, not Hawaii, and was therefore constitutionally prohibited from becoming president. The theory was trumpeted by the *National Enquirer*, owned by Trump's good friend David Pecker, and appealed to many Americans who didn't like Obama.

After Obama released his long-form birth certificate on April 27, 2011, Trump put a self-congratulatory spin on the fact that he had been wrong. "I am really honored, and I am really proud, that I was able to do something that nobody else could do," he said.

On June 16, 2015, a Republican again, Trump announced his candidacy for president at Trump Tower in Manhattan. He was one of seventeen candidates vying for the 2016 Republican nomination; the largest presidential field in American history. Political analysts scoffed at Trump's campaign. *Chicago Tribune* columnist Clarence Page wrote, "Let's not treat Donald Trump like a serious candidate. He's a marketing genius, and that's what he's doing." CNN political analyst Jeffrey Toobin said, "Donald Trump is engaging in one of his fictional presidential campaigns." Yet this darkest of dark horse candidates quickly rose to the top of opinion polls. On May 3, 2016, he became the presumptive Republican nominee.

Why did he run for president? Was it because he reveled in publicity? Was it to sell Trump-branded consumer products—those that hadn't gone bankrupt—and Trump hotel rooms and Trump condos? Was he planning on having his own Fox News TV show, the *Trump Hour*, after he dropped out of the race? Did he actually think he could win running against Republican favorites like Ted Cruz, Jeb Bush, and Marco Rubio? Journalist Michael Wolff, who interviewed numerous people involved with Trump's campaign for his book *Fire and Fury: Inside the Trump White House*, offers us insight into this question: Trump didn't really want or expect to win. "Losing would work out for everybody," he reportedly said. "Losing was winning." Because, according to Wolff, "Once he lost, Trump would be both insanely famous and a martyr to Crooked Hillary. His daughter Ivanka and son-in-law Jared would be international celebrities . . . Melania Trump, who had been assured by her husband that he wouldn't become president, could return to inconspicuously lunching."

When Trump threw his hat in the ring, there had been only two allegations of sexual misconduct, that of Ivana in 1990, which she recanted after her divorce settlement, and the sexual harassment lawsuit of Jill Harth in 1996, which she dropped when her boyfriend's lawsuit was settled. Now that his name was everywhere, however, new reports surfaced. In May 2016, the *New York Times* reported allegations by Temple Taggart McDowell, who had been twenty-one and Miss Utah USA in 1997. McDowell accused Trump, who owned the pageant, of kissing and embracing her in such an alarming manner that one of the pageant chaperones told her not to remain in a room alone with him.

Also in May, Bridget Sullivan, who was crowned Miss New Hampshire 2000, spoke publicly about how Trump came into the Miss USA pageant changing room while the contestants were naked, ostensibly to wish them good luck. "The time that he walked through the dressing rooms was really shocking. We were all naked," she told BuzzFeed in May 2016. Mariah Billado, Miss Vermont Teen USA 1997, said, "I remember putting on my dress really quick, because I was like, 'Oh my God, there's a man in here.'" Trump, she recalled, said something like, "Don't worry, ladies, I've seen it all before." Billado said she brought the matter to the attention of Trump's daughter Ivanka, who responded, "Yeah, he does that." Another contestant, Victoria Hughes, Miss New Mexico Teen USA, agreed that Trump marched into their dressing room, where the youngest contestant was fifteen.

In June, former Miss Washington Cassandra Searles posted a photo on Facebook of several Miss USA contestants from 2013, Trump grinning in the center. "This one guy treated us like cattle," she wrote. "I forgot to mention that guy will be running to become the next President of the United States . . . He probably doesn't want me telling the story about that time he continually grabbed my ass and invited me to his hotel room."

In October, Tasha Dixon, Miss Arizona USA 2001, told a CBS affiliate in Los Angeles that in 2001, Trump "just came strolling right in. There was no second to put a robe on or any sort of clothing or anything. Some girls were topless, other girls were naked." The same month, Ninni Laaksonen, Miss Finland 2006, claimed that Trump squeezed her rear end after posing for a photo before an appearance on the *Late Show with David Letterman* that year. "Trump stood right next to me and suddenly he squeezed my butt. He really grabbed my butt. I don't think anybody saw it but I flinched and thought: 'What is happening?'"

Trump's 2016 campaign team denied the pageant contestants' allegations, though they seemed to be substantiated by a 2005 interview Trump gave to radio host Howard Stern in which he talked about going backstage at pageants when the contestants were changing clothes. "No men are anywhere," Trump said, "and I'm allowed to go in, because I'm the owner of the pageant and therefore I'm inspecting it . . . 'Is everyone OK?' You know, they're standing there with no clothes. 'Is everybody OK?' And you see these incredible looking women, and so I sort of get away with things like that. But no, I've been very good."

The pageant contestants' accusations seemed like a mere hiccup in the campaign. Because one faux pas followed the other. Trump mocked a handicapped reporter, twisting his arms and hands. He called many Mexican immigrants rapists, criminals, and drug dealers. He attacked Senator John McCain's record as a prisoner of war, while Trump got a draft deferral four times due to bone spurs in his feet. He encouraged his supporters at rallies to knock the crap out of hecklers. Bizarrely, he even suggested Ted Cruz's father was involved in the assassination of John F. Kennedy. He said he could shoot somebody on Fifth Avenue and get away with it. His supporters ate it up as yet more proof that he had the strength to stand up for them, to change things.

And then, on October 7, came the release of the pussy tape, more politely called the *Access Hollywood* tape. In the tumultuous aftermath of the tape's release, Trump declared he had never sexually assaulted anyone and called the conversation mere "locker room talk." Political pundits believed that Trump's candidacy was toast.

In the second presidential debate on October 9, CNN anchor Anderson Cooper asked Trump if he understood that he had bragged about sexually assaulting women. Trump denied he had ever grabbed women, repeating that his statement was merely "locker room talk." Anderson asked him three times whether he had ever kissed or groped any woman without her consent. Finally, Trump said, "No, I have not."

As seventy-four-year-old Jessica Leeds watched the debate, her anger rose. The next day, she informed the *New York Times* about an experience she had had on a flight in 1980 from the Midwest to New York, when she was seated next to Trump. According to Leeds, about forty-five minutes after takeoff, Trump raised the armrest and began touching her breasts and trying to slip his hand up her skirt. "He was like an octopus," she said. "His hands were everywhere. It was an assault."

In 1980, Leeds was a slender thirty-eight-year-old with tousled short brown hair and a wide white grin. In 2016, she was still trim and attractive, with short white hair and round black glasses. But Trump indicated that her current appearance—rather than any other reservations he might have had—was proof that he had never sexually assaulted her. "Believe me—she would not be my first choice," Trump told a rally of cackling supporters. "That I can tell you."

Other women watching the debate had the same reaction as Leeds and told similar stories, resulting in an avalanche of sexual assault accusations over the next week. Kristin Anderson stated that in the early 1990s, when she was a young, aspiring model, Trump sexually assaulted her in a New York nightclub. They were sitting next to each other—she recognized him—when she felt his hand slide between her legs and touch her private parts through her underpants.

Cathy Heller claimed that Trump had grabbed and kissed her against her will back in 1997, when the forty-four-year-old and her family attended a Mother's Day brunch at the Mar-a-Lago estate. Karena Virginia, a New York–area yoga instructor, said Trump approached her outside the 1998 U.S. Open tennis tournament in New York. While the twenty-seven-year-old was awaiting a car service, he made unseemly comments about her appearance, grabbed her arm, and groped her breast. "Don't you know who I am?" he asked. She said she blamed herself for years for wearing a dress that was too short.

Mindy McGillivray said that Trump grabbed her rear end when she was twenty-three and working as a photographer's assistant at a 2003 event at Mar-a-Lago. The photographer corroborated that she had told him, "Donald just grabbed my ass!" Rachel Crooks, a secretary who worked in Trump's building, was twenty-two and first met Trump in 2005 outside an elevator at Trump Tower in New York City. He shook her hand, she said, and kissed her on the cheeks and then on the lips. "It was so inappropriate," Crooks recalled in an interview. "I was so upset that he thought I was so insignificant that he could do that."

Natasha Stoynoff, a writer for *People* magazine, said Trump inappropriately touched her in 2005 when she was at Mar-a-Lago for an interview timed to be published on the first anniversary of his marriage to Melania. Stoynoff, forty at the time of the encounter, claimed that he pushed her against a wall and forced his tongue into her mouth. "We're going to have an affair, I'm telling you," he said. *People* produced six witnesses who corroborated that Stoynoff had told them about the event soon afterward. Jennifer Murphy, a twenty-six-year-old contestant on the fourth season of *The Apprentice*, claimed that Trump kissed her on the lips after a job interview in 2005.

Adult film star Jessica Drake said Trump kissed her and two other women without their consent in 2006 in his suite at a golf tournament in Lake Tahoe. "When we entered the room, he grabbed each of us tightly in a hug and kissed each one of us without asking permission," said Drake, who was thirty-two at the time of the alleged assault. According to Drake, Trump offered her $10,000 to sleep with him, which she turned down.

Summer Zervos, a contestant in her early thirties on the fifth season of *The Apprentice*, which had filmed in 2005, met with Trump in 2007 in his suite at the Beverly Hills Hotel to discuss a job. She claimed that Trump kissed her open-mouthed, groped her breasts, and thrust his genitals against her. In January 2017, Trump publicly called Zervos a liar. In response, she sued him for defamation, though only for damages of three thousand dollars, a sign that the suit is not about getting rich but about clearing her name. Amid legal scrambling, appeals, hearings, and objections, the case crawls forward.

Lisa Boyne claimed that when she was twenty-five, in 1996, she attended a dinner with Trump, modeling agent John Casablancas, and five or six models, where Trump made the models walk across the table, looked under their skirts, and noted whether they were wearing underwear.

Many Trump supporters wondered aloud why none of these women reported the events earlier. Maybe not the quick kiss on the mouth—inappropriate as that is—but the breast, butt, and genital groping. Were these women paid by the Hillary Clinton campaign to come forward weeks before the presidential election? Were they Clinton supporters? In fact, the accusers held a variety of political affiliations from right-wing Republicans to Democrats who gave the maximum legal amount to Hillary Clinton's campaign.

One accusation that came in early 2019 seemed to validate Trump supporters' suspicions. A former Trump campaign employee named Alva Johnson filed a lawsuit against him alleging gender and pay discrimination against women and African Americans, as well as claiming that he had forcibly kissed her at a rally in Florida in August 2016. Cellphone video surfaced showing Trump giving her a peck on the cheek as she smiled broadly. The judge dismissed the suit, calling it "a political lawsuit."

A more damning accusation surfaced in June 2019 when advice columnist E. Jean Carroll accused Trump of raping her in a Bergdorf Goodman dressing room in 1995 or 1996, when she was fifty-two. She claimed she ran into him at the store's entrance, and he said, "Hey, you're that Advice Lady!" He then asked her for advice on buying a present for "a girl." The two went to the lingerie department where, Carroll claimed, Trump asked her to try on a see-through bodysuit. Inside the dressing room, Carroll alleges that Trump lunged at her, pushed her against the wall, causing her to hit her head "quite badly," placed his mouth on her lips, and reached under her coatdress and pulled down her tights. Carroll recalled, "The next moment, still wearing correct business attire, shirt, tie, suit jacket, overcoat, he opens the overcoat, unzips his pants, and, forcing his fingers around my private area, then thrusts his penis halfway—or completely, I'm not certain—inside me. It turns into a colossal struggle."

She said she escaped from the dressing room and left the store, the whole incident having lasted no more than three minutes. Carroll said she never reported the incident to the police, but that she confided in two friends soon thereafter. One told Carroll that she had been raped and must report it to the police. The other advised, "Tell no one. Forget it! He has 200 lawyers. He'll bury you." Carroll's friends confirmed those conversations to *New York* magazine and ABC News. Trump denied the rape, accusing her of lying to sell her upcoming book, and adding, "She's not my type."

Even if some of the allegations are true, why would Donald Trump grope unknown women and force them to kiss him? Why would he think it was okay to stick his fingers up the underwear of a stranger sitting next to him on a plane or on a barstool? Is it because with his wealth and fame—and the power that comes with them—he can? In terms of self-discipline and emotional development, is he like a naughty six-year-old who can't help himself grabbing a fistful of birthday cake before the party? Does he act wholly on impulse? He sees a nice pair of breasts or buttocks and, without giving it much consideration, marches up and squeezes them? Trump himself seems to confirm it. In *The Art of the Deal*, he wrote, "When I look at myself in the first grade and I look at myself now, I'm basically the same. The temperament is not that different."

The hashtag #WhyWomenDontReport started trending on Twitter in response to the Trump campaign's statements that the accusers were lying. Many women tweeted that they waited months and even years to report a sexual assault, often until other women came forward to accuse the same perpetrator. Many worried that no one would believe them or that a powerful man would make their lives miserable. In Trump's case, the women, like E. Jean Carroll, feared his battery of threatening lawyers would sue them into bankruptcy. They also worried—and were right to do so, as events proved—that they would be accused of lying to get attention and money.

Trump vehemently denied all the claims and called the allegations "a conspiracy against you, the American people." A vast, left-wing conspiracy, no doubt. In the third presidential debate of 2016, Trump said, "I think they want either fame or her [Hillary's] campaign did it and I think it's her campaign."

While we will probably never know exactly what happened between Trump and his many accusers, there are other clues to Trump's outlook on women in general. In the 1990s, he tried to get *Playboy* to do a spread called "The Girls of Trump," and encouraged those he considered his best-looking female employees to pose for the magazine nude or at least topless.

"Women have one of the great acts of all time," he wrote in his 1997 book, *The Art of the Comeback*. "The smart ones act very feminine and needy, but inside they are real killers . . . I have seen women manipulate men with just a twitch of their eye—or perhaps another body part . . ."

In a 1992 story that appeared in *New York* magazine, writer Marie Brenner claimed that Trump said, "Women, you have to treat 'em like shit." Trump was so furious at Brenner for writing that he treated women poorly, that the next time he saw her at a social event, he poured a glass of wine down her back. When asked about Brenner's statement, Trump responded, "I didn't say that. The woman's a liar, extremely unattractive, lots of problems because of her looks."

Then, in 1994, in a *Primetime Live* interview, Trump made a statement oddly similar to what Marie Brenner reported: "I tell friends who treat their wives magnificently, get treated like crap in return, 'Be rougher and you'll see a different relationship.'"

Even before the release of the pussy tape and the resulting onslaught of women coming forward alleging sexual assault, most reputable pollsters and pundits had never expected Trump to win. And yet, he did, on November 8, 2016, winning 304 electoral votes to Hillary Clinton's 227. He lost the popular vote—the fifth elected president to do so—by nearly three million votes, 65,853,514 votes (48.18 percent) to 62,984,828 votes (46.09 percent). It was an election between two candidates who both had more baggage than LAX. And yet, after the pussy tape, how could he have won? What happened?

Sick and tired of career politicians, many voters saw Trump as a no-nonsense businessman who would straighten out the country, hiring the best people, making the U.S. more prosperous than ever before, bringing his brand of sweet success to the entire nation. The economy had left many behind. A large segment of the American population wanted a change, a breath of fresh air, someone to shake up Washington, not someone like Hillary Clinton, who had been in a scandal-plagued White House twenty years before, albeit as first lady. They wanted a man who they saw as having common sense to take them back to a safer time where they understood the world and fit seamlessly into it, before good blue-collar jobs drained away to other countries; before men married men and women could marry women; before people could change the gender on their driver's licenses based on how they identified rather than what was on their birth certificates. Many saw Trump's rhetoric—crude, insulting, and self-aggrandizing—as proof that he was the one to take on the establishment and shake things up. They had been hurting, picked on, scorned, and Donald Trump seemed to be the only politician who understood, the only one who stood with them and vowed to fight for them.

Those election experts who consigned Trump's campaign to the rubbish heap because of his history with women failed to consider his historic persona. While most American male politicians cultivate an image as pious, churchgoing family men, Trump never made the slightest attempt to do so. On the contrary, long before the election, Donald Trump had carefully crafted an image more akin to that of Hugh Hefner, surrounded by adoring, long-legged Playmates in skimpy clothing, though his own costume was a business suit and tie instead of a satin bathrobe.

In other words, Trump's supporters, who had lifted him out of a crowded field of experienced Republican candidates, knew he was no monk and didn't care. Of course, the allegations of sexual assault were clearly far more disturbing than consensual affairs, and most registered voters believed them. A poll showed that only 14 percent believed Trump innocent, while 68 percent believed he was guilty, and the rest weren't sure. It turns out, many who believed him guilty still voted for him. And many of those were evangelical Christians, who had been so horrified to have a Slick Willie Clinton soiling the dignity of the White House yet didn't much care about a "grab them by the pussy" Donald Trump. A poll conducted by the nonpartisan Public Religion Research Institute taken right after the *Access Hollywood* tape release found that 72 percent of white evangelicals believed a politician could be immoral in his private life and still govern well. In 2011, the same poll had the figure at only 30 percent.

What had happened in only five years? For one thing, conservatives found a candidate whose policies they could rally behind, and policy has always been far more powerfully attractive to voters than personal sanctitude. Trump's victory had something in common with Grover Cleveland's in 1884. When a pastor asked, "Do the American people want a common libertine for their president?" the answer was yes, as long as he would reduce taxes.

Second, Trump supporters likely found solace in the fact that his sex stories, consensual and otherwise, had all taken place years before the 2016 election. There had been no examples of bad behavior since then that anyone had heard of. Perhaps he had changed. Once Trump was ensconced in the White House—one that initially leaked like a sieve—there were no stories of naked women running around with "breasts swinging," as in JFK's day, or of interns doing strange things with cigars in the Oval Office, as during Bill Clinton's tenure.

And lastly, it is likely that the 24/7 coverage of scandal—sex, lies, and the bad behavior of governors, senators, and congressmen—has inured us to it all. Just to mention a few scandals leading up to the 2016 election: In 2007, North Carolina senator John Edwards impregnated a campaign employee while his wife was dying of breast cancer, denied it, enlisted his friend in a cover-up, and finally admitted it. In 2008, Elliott Spitzer, the New York governor tough on prostitution, resigned after investigators discovered he had spent as much as $80,000 on prostitutes. Mark Sanford, the married governor of South Carolina, seemed to have disappeared from the planet for six days in 2009, his aides unable to locate him. When he reemerged, he held a press conference to explain that he had fallen in love with a woman in Argentina.

In 2011, New York Democratic congressman Anthony Weiner tweeted photos of his private parts, lied about it, told the truth, found redemption with his wife and the American public, and then did it again, this time with a minor, earning himself a prison sentence. We are exhausted. Numb. Desensitized. We are now a very hard nation to shock, and sexual assault claims have become business as usual. When E. Jean Carroll accused the president of the United States of rape in June 2019, most newspapers didn't put it on their front page, and it was mentioned on only one of the many Sunday morning talk shows.

As for Trump's supporters, a *USA Today* Trump voter panel reported respondents as collectively shrugging about the sex and the lies. "We're human. We all sin," said one. "And he tried to cover it up." "We know he's no angel, and he didn't become a multi-billionaire because he's a nice guy," said another. "I got over the shock of presidential affairs after Kennedy and Clinton."

Given the national prostration regarding political sex stories, when two women Trump had slept with a decade earlier seemed ready to sell their stories shortly before the 2016 election, he should have simply let the tawdry tales unspool. Trump's lawyer and fixer, Michael Cohen, arranged to pay both for their silence.

Karen McDougal, the 1998 *Playboy* Playmate of the Year, first met Trump at the Playboy Mansion in June 2006 when he was filming an episode of *Celebrity Apprentice*. He was stunned by the gorgeous, blue-eyed brunette, and they soon began an affair. Trump would arrange for her to meet him at various hotels or in his homes. Karen told Anderson Cooper of CNN that she loved Trump and "He always told me he loved me." But Karen felt guilty about her affair with a married man and after ten torrid months called it off. "The excitement took over for a while, but I started feeling so bad about myself. . . . It was tearing me apart in the long run. I knew I needed to get out," she said.

Some of Trump's behavior made it easier for Karen to leave. For instance, when she mentioned her mother's disapproval of him, Trump scoffed, "What, that old hag?" even though Trump and Karen's mother were quite close in age. On another occasion, as Karen and a female friend rode in a limo with Trump, her friend mentioned she was dating an African American man. Multiple sources said that Trump said the friend liked "the big black dick." Then he started talking about her good looks and breast size. The friend was outraged, McDougal horrified. The affair was over.

As Trump continued to beat down his opponents for the Republican nomination, a friend of Karen's began posting about the affair on social media. Karen, who would have preferred the story to remain secret, decided that since it was going to come out, she might as well tell it herself to make sure it was, at least, accurate. And, of course, there would be money involved.

On August 16, 2016, she signed a $150,000 contract with AMI, the parent company of the *National Enquirer*, whose CEO, David Pecker, was a close friend of Trump's. AMI agreed to publish one hundred columns written by McDougal on fitness and put her on at least two covers. The contract also stipulated that she would never discuss her relationship with Donald Trump. There's a term for this kind of contract: "catch and kill."

McDougal was delighted with the deal. She had never wanted to tank Trump's chance at the presidency—she had truly cared for him and was a devout Republican—and she was excited about rebranding herself from nude model to fitness guru. But AMI did not live up to its side of the bargain, putting her on only one cover and publishing only a handful of columns.

In March 2018, McDougal filed a lawsuit against AMI in Los Angeles Superior Court, aiming to invalidate the nondisclosure agreement. A month later, just four days after the FBI raided Michael Cohen's homes and office looking for evidence of bank fraud, wire fraud, and campaign finance violations and seizing 3.7 million documents including emails, AMI settled with McDougal, which allowed her to speak about the alleged affair. In the years since her entanglement with Trump, she has returned to her roots and faith. "I'm going to church. I'm involved in ministry," she said. The White House has denied her story.

The other woman paid to keep her mouth shut about Trump in the weeks leading up to the election was Stormy Daniels, a buxom blonde, blue-eyed porn star with an intelligent face whose real name is Stephanie Clifford. According to Stormy, she had met Trump at a celebrity golf tournament in Lake Tahoe in 2006, where they had a one-night stand. In October 2016, she signed a contract for $130,000, in return for which she agreed never to discuss her affair with Trump. Yet the *Wall Street Journal* got hold of the story, resulting in denials by Michael Cohen and Donald Trump that they had paid her. Although Trump never admitted to the affair, he eventually said he'd repaid Cohen from his personal account, not the campaign account.

Though Michael Cohen is currently serving a three-year jail term, Trump's culpability remains debatable. Did he pay Stormy "for the principal purpose of influencing an election," as Cohen's lawyer claimed? If so, that would be a campaign finance violation. Or did he silence the women to save himself personal embarrassment with his wife and family, which would not have been breaking the law?

In March 2018, Stormy Daniels sued to break her nondisclosure agreement, claiming it was invalid because Trump himself had never signed it. But in September of that year, Trump's lawyers stated he would not enforce the agreement, nor would he dispute Stormy's claim that it was invalid. Naturally, she wrote a book, including the only description we have of sex with Donald Trump.

Having accepted an invitation to dinner at his penthouse suite, Stormy found Trump was not at all suggestive or vulgar, and pleasant company initially. Then he talked and talked about himself, bragging and boasting while her stomach grumbled in rage at the absence of the promised dinner. When he showed her a magazine—it might have been *Forbes*—with his face on the cover, she finally lost her temper.

"Are you so insecure that you have to brag about yourself or are you just a fucking asshole? Which is it?" she asked. "Someone should take that magazine and spank you."

"You wouldn't," he said quietly. She ordered him to drop his pants and bend over—which, oddly enough, he did—and swatted him a couple of times. As he stood to pull up his pants, he said, "I like you. You remind me of my daughter." His daughter, he explained, was smart, beautiful, and a woman to be reckoned with. Trump then offered to get Stormy a role on his hit show *The Apprentice*.

Three hours after she had arrived, still with no food in sight— she went to attend a call of nature. When she emerged from the bathroom, she was shocked to find him sitting on the bed, waiting for her, wearing only his briefs, an undershirt, and socks. "I sighed inwardly," she recalled. The ever-practical Stormy figured sex was just the price she had to pay to get on his show. And it might help to finally get her dinner.

"I was lying down on the bed with him on top of me, naked," she wrote. "I was just there, my head on the pillow. There was no foreplay and it was one position. Missionary. We kissed, and his hard, darting tongue pushed in and out of my mouth. *He's even a terrible kisser.*"

Her description certainly dampens our expectations that sex with a man dynamic enough to win the U.S. presidency would rock our world, but it gets worse. "I lay there as he fumbled his dick into me," she continued. "I was surprised he didn't even mention a condom. I didn't have one with me anyway because I wasn't meeting him for sex . . . He was a little verbal, but nothing dirty. 'That's great,' he said. 'That's great. Oh, you're so beautiful.' I certainly didn't do any kind of performance. I just kind of lay there . . ." She added that during the sex act, she replayed the past three hours in her mind to figure out how she had gotten herself in that position. We can picture her frowning up at the ceiling as she went over events, paying no more attention to Trump thrusting and groaning over her than if she had been having a manicure.

With the frankness that only a porn star could muster, Stormy described his private parts. "The world is waiting to hear about his penis," she wrote, which might be the only lie in her entire autobiography. "I am sorry to report that it is not freakishly small. It is smaller than average—below the true average, not the porn average. I didn't take out a measuring stick." She added that it had a "huge mushroom head like a toadstool." The sex, she said, lasted two or three minutes and, after his orgasm, he rolled off her, sighed, and said, "We're so good together, honey bunch."

Stormy didn't agree, saying that it might have been "the least impressive sex" she'd ever had. Though Trump pursued her, and she met him a couple of times over the course of the next year to discuss her appearance on *The Apprentice*—which never came to fruition—there was no sex. Stormy never wanted to see that mushroom of his again.

It is possible that the payoffs to Karen McDougal and Stormy Daniels were just the tip of the iceberg. Michael Wolff reported a comment made by Steve Bannon, CEO of Trump's campaign, regarding Marc Kasowitz, another of Trump's longtime fixer attorneys. "Kasowitz has gotten him out of all kinds of jams," Bannon allegedly said. "Kasowitz on the campaign—what did we have, a hundred women? Kasowitz took care of all of them."

The Trump of decades ago—the funny, irreverent, boisterous showman—has taken on a darker, angrier tone since he became president. While narcissistic personality disorder and hubris syndrome have some common symptoms, it is fair to say he has slipped into the latter, especially in August 2019 when he said he was the "second coming of God" and "the Chosen One." Hubris syndrome symptoms include using power for self-glorification; an almost obsessive focus on personal image; contempt for others; excessive self-confidence; refusal to listen to the advice of others; refusal to admit even minor mistakes; loss of contact with reality; reckless and impulsive actions; and incompetence due to supreme overconfidence, leading to inattention to details.

Trump's three wives have had very different reactions to his infidelity. Outspoken, independent Ivana divorced his ass and got a large settlement. She went on to become the queen of the home-shopping channels, making millions hawking her clothing, skincare products, and jewelry. A successful, globe-trotting entrepreneur and tabloid fixture, she married twice after her divorce from Trump. The second one was to a man twenty-three years her junior, and neither marriage lasted much more than a year. She has houses around the world and often chooses to stay in Saint-Tropez with a handsome young lover. In her seventies, she is often seen tottering around in a miniskirt and four-inch heels, still sporting her signature blond beehive, a small dog in tow.

Sweet little Reddi-wip Marla had an affair of own. Dumped with chump change, she moved with Tiffany to California to escape the screaming tabloids of New York City. She ditched her glass slippers, which had pinched rather severely, lived modestly, and never remarried. Her Trump trauma awakened an interest in spirituality; she goes to church, keeps Shabbat, eats kosher, explores her past lives, and does a lot of yoga. Her primary focus, however, has been raising her daughter, which is just as well because Tiffany grew up without her father—reportedly seeing him only four times between his separation from Marla in 1997 and the start of his campaign in 2015. Indeed, Tiffany was treated by Trump something like the bastard child of an eighteenth-century English duke. In August 2019, Trump's personal assistant, Madeleine Westerhout, lost her job after she told reporters the president didn't like being photographed with Tiffany because he thought she was fat and joked that he couldn't pick her out of a crowd.

A joyless sphinx, Melania appears at his side now and then for official functions, though she reportedly spends much of her time at her parents' house in Potomac, Maryland, with her son, Barron, whose school is nearby. When staying at the White House, she sleeps in a separate bedroom. This is not so unusual; all U.S. presidents and their wives have separate White House bedrooms, though whether they choose to sleep separately or together is up to them. Former White House aide Omarosa Manigault Newman wrote that Melania plans to divorce Trump as soon as he leaves the White House. Formerly sparkling and animated, Melania looks as if she has gazed on cursed, snake-headed Medusa— and perhaps, in a way, she has—and her face is slowly turning to stone.

Certainly, Melania wasn't happy when Donald won the election. She valued, above all things, her privacy and that of her son. According to Michael Wolff, when returns began to show that Trump would, in fact, win, Melania, sitting on the couch, began to cry. She didn't even move to the White House from New York for six months after the inauguration, saying she wanted Barron to finish the school year.

Reports indicated that Melania was "blindsided" and "furious" about her husband's affairs with McDougal and Daniels, according to anonymous sources who spoke with the *New York Times*. These reports make us scratch our collective head. It smacks of Hillary Clinton claiming to be shocked by Bill's diddling the intern. Though perhaps Melania was surprised that her husband had had unprotected sex with a porn star. That would pretty much shock even the most hardened betrayed wife.

But unlike Hillary Clinton, Melania didn't spring into action to defend her husband and attack his accusers. On the contrary, she canceled several public appearances with him and drove to his 2018 State of the Union address separately. "It is not a concern and focus of mine," she sniffed, when asked about press reports of Trump's infidelities. "I'm a mother and a First Lady and I have much more important things to think about and to do."

Even before Stormy's story took the nation by storm, Melania wasn't all that thrilled with Donald. Perhaps her feelings are best summed up in the hand swat seen round the world, that unforgettable moment on May 22, 2017, when the first couple deplaned Air Force One at Ben Gurion Airport in Tel Aviv and, walking down the red carpet, the president reached out for his wife's hand. With a disdainful flick of the wrist, she pushed him away in a small gesture that screamed, *Don't you even touch my fingers.*

14

FROM OOH-LA-LA TO BUNGA BUNGA: THE POLITICAL SEX SCANDALS OF OTHER NATIONS

*I*n Europe, because love affairs between married people are considered normal, fewer stories of presidential adultery make it out of the bedroom and into the public eye compared to the puritanical republic of the United States. The French, weaned on stories of riotous kings and fragrant royal mistresses, are titillated by modern scandals, to be sure, but almost never horrified. Their reaction to the love affairs of their political leaders is a smirk, in between a swig of espresso and a puff of a cigarette. According to a 2006 survey in the popular newspaper *Le Figaro*, only 17 percent of French voters would vote against a candidate for president if he'd had an affair.

In France, a lusty sex life is seen as evidence of good health. They want their leaders to be virile, bold, and radiantly confident. The Latin root of the word "impotent" literally means "lack of power," and in the French view, the limp penis of a president or prime minister might signify he cannot effectively run the country. Such beliefs were epitomized by poor Louis XVI, unable to make love to his luscious young wife, Marie Antoinette, for seven years after marriage. Cartoonists portrayed him as a giant flaccid penis with one testicle—his head—lying helpless and inert on the ground. Seen as impotent in bed and on the throne, he was guillotined in 1793, and no French leader wants to follow in his footsteps. On the other hand, many Americans might see a limp presidential penis as a bonus.

In the 1990s, while many Americans expressed disgust at Bill Clinton's unending stories of adulterous dalliances, a top French politician, Christine Boutin, said, "He loves women, this man? It is a sign of good health!" The French were utterly baffled by the Lewinsky scandal, which they called Le Zippergate. French journalist Anne-Elisabeth Moutet wrote, "It looked pretty ridiculous to Europeans, who asked, 'Why doesn't he have a normal relationship with a nice, elegant, clever mistress who won't talk?' We do not talk about politicians' private lives. President François Mitterrand had lots of mistresses, and two regular mistresses, and every journalist in town, myself included, knew all about them, and we had the telephone numbers and we knew about the kids and everything. And we never wrote it. It was perfectly understood that nobody will back you up. The public will hate you to kingdom come. Do not talk about politicians' love lives." She added, "Besides, the French like their leaders to have a sex drive."

In 1992, when Bill Clinton's adulteries dominated his campaign, a reporter asked French politicians whether they had ever betrayed their wives, apparently the first time in French history that a member of the press had ever done so. One senator said, "This concept doesn't make any sense to me." A minister of health replied, "Betrayed, no. Had various relationships, yes." Another senator boasted, "I adore women. I have been a very, very, very big womanizer." A leading national politician said, "No. But I just got married two days ago."

In January 2018, iconic actress Catherine Deneuve and more than a hundred other well-known Frenchwomen in entertainment, business, and academia signed a letter to the newspaper *Le Monde* newspaper denouncing the #MeToo movement for hampering the fine art of seduction in the workplace. The movement, they claimed, repressed the sexual freedom of men who only tried to touch a knee, steal a kiss, or speak about pornographic matters at a business dinner, as well as the sexual freedom of women who might like it.

The most shocking story of a French president and his mistress is that of Félix Faure who, in 1895 at the age of fifty-four, began an affair with a twenty-five-year-old society hostess, Marguerite Steinheil. Though Marguerite was not beautiful—she had heavy features and no neck—she was dazzlingly sexy. Society meant everything to her, and she reveled in the swirl of balls and concerts, of revolving lovers and bitter feuds. She wrote, "This is Parisian life. And when you have tasted its exquisite poison you cannot do without it." To earn money to keep up her social pretensions, she convinced her numerous wealthy lovers to buy paintings from her artist husband, the timid, feeble Adolphe Steinheil. Out of guilt, many did.

Marguerite visited the presidential palace once or twice a week, where she and Faure closeted themselves in his office behind locked doors to work on his memoirs, as she explained. On one such occasion in 1899, the president had an unusual reaction to her tender ministrations. He cried out in pain rather than passion and locked his hands into rigid fists in her hair, an iron grip from which Marguerite could not extricate herself. She screamed for the guards, who broke down the door and, summing up the situation, grabbed a pair of scissors and cut off the hair on the top of her head to free her.

As the palace descended into an uproar and the first lady made her way rapidly to her moribund husband, Marguerite threw on her clothes and, sporting an unattractive new hairstyle, raced from the palace. Unfortunately, in her haste she had forgotten her corset, which the first lady found on the floor. A French newspaper reported, "Félix Faure passed away in good health, indeed from the excess of good health." It can also be said that he was one of the few political leaders who came and went at the same time.

Oddly, the fact that President Faure died while receiving oral sex from Marguerite enhanced her reputation greatly in Parisian society. Many suitors, believing she could drive men so wild their hearts stopped, bravely wanted to give it a try, especially after her hair grew back. One of her lovers, Aristide Briand, became prime minister in 1909. Others included rich industrialists, the Prince of Wales, and the king of Cambodia.

Most French presidents have continued to embody the tradition of Gallic lustiness. In 1974, President Valéry Giscard d'Estaing, having told his Secret Service agents to clear off, was driving a Ferrari on the Champs-Élysées at 5:00 a.m. when he collided with a milk truck. Clearly, the president had been returning from a romantic tryst. The police were called, the milk bottles swept up, and when the story appeared in the press, d'Estaing's poll ratings soared.

It shocks American sensibilities to imagine the future president of France, François Mitterrand, his wife, Danielle, and her lover, Jean Balenci, companionably dipping croissants into their café au lait at their communal Paris home and reading *Le Figaro*. We cannot picture, for instance, Bill and Hillary Clinton inviting Monica Lewinsky to live with them and the three buttering their toast together at breakfast. Or Stormy Daniels passing a bowl of scrambled eggs to Melania Trump. But such a situation seems perfectly reasonable to the French, and in Mitterrand's case, it lasted for many years.

Though Mitterrand was faithful to none, he fell deeply in love with one, a love that would last until death. In 1964 at the age of forty-seven, he began an affair with twenty-year-old Anne Pingeot, who became his lifelong companion and gave him a daughter, Mazarine, ten years later.

On November 3, 1994, the magazine *Paris Match* published a photo spread showing President Mitterrand and his secret daughter, then twenty, leaving a restaurant together. The French public was outraged—not at their president for having a second family, but at the press for invading his privacy, and closed ranks behind the old fellow. Many journalists agreed, calling it a sign of creeping Anglo-Saxon puritanism infecting French joie de vivre. "It's a pity I don't have one or two more daughters in reserve," Mitterrand said wryly. "It would have helped me climb back further in the opinion polls."

When Mitterrand was dying of cancer in 1995, the seventy-nine-year-old instructed his bodyguards to drop him off at the apartment of a pretty, young brunette who had just turned twenty. Sometimes he had her picked up and taken to the presidential palace to spend the night. His staff believed it was another secret daughter. It was not.

He did, however, have a secret son in Sweden with a journalist named Christine Forsne, with whom he had a thirteen-year relationship ending only when he became fatally ill in 1994. The son, Hravn, was born in 1988, when Mitterrand was an impressive seventy-two years old. Hravn revealed the identity of his father in 2014 when he ran for public office.

Mitterrand's successor, Jacques Chirac, was just as much a philanderer, though with less aplomb. The night of August 30–31, 1997, when Diana, Princess of Wales, died in a car accident in a Paris tunnel, Chirac had gone AWOL. No one—not his wife, not his security detail—had any idea where he was, and the British prime minister was desperately trying to reach him. At least President D'Estaing, twenty years earlier, had had the foresight to leave a note with his whereabouts in a sealed letter on his presidential desk so that security could contact him if nuclear war broke out. But Jacques Chirac often just wandered off without a trace. Having spent the night with a well-known Italian actress, he reappeared at seven o'clock in the morning—nearly seven hours after Diana's accident—to a presidential palace plunged into crisis.

Chirac's wife, Bernadette, put on a brave face when asked about her husband's countless love affairs. "He's a handsome man, and very charming, very gay. Girls are always galloping by," she said in a 2002 interview. When, in 2006, a reporter from the French magazine *L'Express* asked her if she suffered from her husband's reputation as a serial seducer, she replied, "No, I'm rather proud of it! It is necessary for a politician to be able to seduce."

Yet according to Chirac's chauffeur of twenty-five years, Jean-Claude Laumond, in private Bernadette was far less understanding. After depositing the president at a mistress's apartment, Laumond would return to the presidential palace, see the curtains of Bernadette's window twitch, and glimpse her disapproving face staring out at him. Then she would throw the window open and yell for all the world to hear, "And my husband, Monsieur Laumond, where is he?"

Despite his reputation as a ladies' man, Chirac was not a satisfying lover. His women friends—journalists, government employees, actresses—called him, "Chirac, three minutes shower included."

Italy, home of the prototypical Latin lover, has an unbroken tradition of virile leaders going back to ancient times. In 49 BCE, Julius Caesar's legions marched from Gaul to Rome singing,

> *Home we bring our bald whoremonger;*
> *Romans, lock your wives away!*
> *All the bags of gold you lent him*
> *Went his Gallic tarts to pay.*

It was a boast. Fast-forward two thousand years and Italians elected a thirty-six-year-old porn star to Parliament. Ilona Staller, known as La Cicciolina, won the 1987 election, according to the Italian press, because voters "appreciated her revealing talent and biological actions." To forestall the Gulf War breaking out, the congresswoman generously offered to have sex with Iraqi leader Saddam Hussein in return for peace. Ironically, the American press reported on Staller's background far more often than their Italian counterparts, which didn't find her election all that odd.

The multibillionaire media tycoon Silvio Berlusconi, prime minister of Italy for nine years between 1994 and 2011, entered politics not to help the nation but to avoid going to jail. His empire of television stations and newspapers was so corrupt that he needed the protection of high political office and, when he got it, immediately set about passing laws to protect himself. Out of thirty-two criminal cases against him, he was convicted in only one, and that was after he left office.

As prime minister, Berlusconi had much in common with Donald Trump. His skin a preternatural shade of orange, his scalp a mass of hair plugs, he had never held any public office before running for prime minister. He committed an unending stream of jaw-dropping social and diplomatic gaffes, befriending Russian president Vladimir Putin and calling German Chancellor Angela Merkel "an unfuckable lard-arse." With federal prosecutors hard on his trail pretty much all the time, he decried their investigations as a "witch hunt." At a Holocaust memorial ceremony in Milan, at the spot from which thousands of Italian Jews were sent to death camps, he said that Mussolini hadn't been all that bad and had done some "good things." One Italian journalist moaned, "What else could he have done? Snore? Fart noisily during the minutes of silence? Piss in the corner?"

Berlusconi's romantic life was even more colorful than his political one, though there are no reports of any women actually falling in love with him. His partners were in it for the cash, lots of it. In 2011 alone, he had handed out $15 million to those who indulged in his orgies, most of them held in his private palace on the island of Sardinia. His bodyguards and female employees pimped for him, inviting attractive young women to his parties, promising them three thousand euros each. Those whom he slept with—often as many as a dozen in one night—received twice as much. He also promised them jobs as weather girls on the many television stations he owned or high-level political jobs. A topless model and dancer on one of his TV shows became equal opportunities minister. His buxom dental hygienist who performed explicit lesbian floorshows in a naughty nun's costume became a regional councilor. An eighteen-year-old girlfriend said in an interview that she wanted to become an underwear model, a showgirl, or a member of Parliament, whatever Berlusconi decided. One journalist called Berlusconi's regime a "tartocracy."

He was the epitome of the *uomo forte*, the charismatic strong man considered single-handedly capable of leading the nation to greatness. Berlusconi's unending stream of amatory escapades—

such as keeping highly paid harems of very young women in his island palace well into his seventies and holding extreme lap-dancing competitions he called "bunga bunga"—served not to detract from his popularity but to increase it. Even his affairs with seventeen-year-old prostitutes failed to rattle Italian voters who, according to opinion polls, believed it to be a private matter.

Berlusconi routinely boasted about his sexual prowess pub-licly, saying it was "better to be passionate about beautiful women than to be gay." In 2011, he joked that pollsters asked women if they would have sex with him. "Thirty percent said yes," he ex-plained, "while seventy percent replied, 'What, again?'"

In one conversation recorded by government investigators seeking evidence of the prime minister's financial corruption, Berlusconi told a friend about a party the night before. "I had a queue outside my door, there were eleven of them. I only man-aged to do eight of them, I couldn't manage any more. You just can't get around to all of them. But this morning I feel great, I'm pleased with my stamina." As any man in his seventies should be.

Considering the constant stream of scandal Berlusconi trailed in his wake, his continued popularity—he was elected three times—may surprise us. But stories of his romantic dalliances just made him more likable to many, and even corruption stories didn't upset many voters, who supported him for not bothering to collect their taxes.

Losing support in Parliament, Berlusconi resigned in Octo-ber 2011, as large crowds sang the hallelujah chorus from George Frideric Handel's *Messiah* outside Rome's Parliament building. In 2013, he received a four-year prison sentence for tax fraud but was exempt from incarceration because he was over seventy. Instead, he was sentenced to serve food in old age homes where he was the most popular server ever. Because of his conviction, he was barred from running for public office for six years. In July 2019, at the age of eighty-three, he ran for European Parliament. And won.

It is likely that Berlusconi's wife, Veronica Lario, never expected him to be faithful. After all, their relationship began in 1980 when the married Berlusconi saw her topless in a stage play. With sublime dignity, Veronica put up with his infidelities and unexplained absences. Then, in 2009, she discovered that he had been sleeping with underaged girls. On May 3, 2009, she published a letter in *La Repubblica* newspaper informing him of her decision to seek a divorce. "I cannot stay with a man who frequents minors," she wrote. "I've tried to help my husband; I've implored those he's with to change things, as you would with a person who's not well. But it was useless. Now I say 'enough.'"

Knowledge of the love affairs of Great Britain's prime ministers has, for the most part, evaporated due to upper-crust discretion. William Ewart Gladstone, who served as British prime minister for twelve years at different times between 1868 and 1894, said that he had known twelve British prime ministers, and all but one were adulterers. We are not certain where he put himself on that list as nothing is known of most of these affairs. True, adultery among Britain's elite was rampant at the time—even among women, once they had given their husbands an heir and a spare, as long as it didn't become public knowledge. Journalists refused to cover their leaders' love lives, unless, ending up in divorce court, they were already a matter of public record.

The love affair of the fifty-seven-year-old Prime Minister William Lamb, 2nd Viscount Melbourne, and the novelist, twenty-eight-year-old Caroline Norton, exploded into the press in 1836 because it was the centerpiece of a public trial. Caroline's husband, the Honorable George Norton, sued Melbourne for "criminal conversation" with Norton's wife, demanding ten thousand pounds (close to a million pounds in today's money) for depriving him of her body. According to contemporary descriptions of Caroline's beauty, it was worth every penny.

Melbourne called on Caroline Norton three or four times a week when her husband was at work. During the visits, she would lock the parlor door and instruct her servants not to disturb her. Servants testified that, on rare occasions when the door was not locked, they had entered to find Mrs. Norton on her knees in front of Melbourne or lying on the floor with "her clothes in a position to expose her person."

After much tawdry testimony, the jury found the prime minister not guilty. Though it seemed clear he was guilty as sin, the jurors believed that Melbourne's political enemies had manipulated the scandal to remove him from office, and they weren't going to be used as pawns in such a scheme. He remained prime minister, his reputation burnished rather than tarnished by dallying with a famous beauty thirty years his junior. (We can only assume he would have been pleased to see Rufus Sewell's devastatingly rakish portrayal of him in ITV's *Victoria* series.) But Caroline Norton's reputation was ruined. Her husband confiscated their three young sons, refusing to grant her visitation. For decades, she campaigned tirelessly to bring about legislation to protect the legal rights of separated and divorced mothers.

British Prime Minister David Lloyd George, a Welshman by birth, guided the nation through much of World War I. Dubbed "the Welsh goat" for his relentless pursuit of women, he usually had discreet affairs with married society ladies, much to the consternation of his wife, Margaret. He fathered so many illegitimate children that one day his son Dick ventured into a pub and saw a man who could have been his twin. The two realized they were brothers. Lloyd George's daughter Olwen thought it wasn't entirely his fault. She said, "Many of his friends felt he should be protected against women; they flocked round him and often threw themselves at him."

In 1913, at the age of fifty, Lloyd George began an affair with his private secretary, twenty-five-year-old Frances Stevenson. When his wife left one of their many residences by one door, Frances would be coming in another, like something out of a French farce. After having two abortions, Frances had his daughter in 1929 at the age of forty and pretended she had adopted an orphan. In 1943, two years after Lloyd George's wife died, Frances finally married him after waiting thirty years. The dashing groom was eighty, and Frances was relegated to nursing him for the remaining eighteen months of his life. While one might wonder if it was worth the wait, Frances did seem quite satisfied that she had outlasted the wife and gotten him in the end.

True to form, the British press reported on various lawsuits against Lloyd George over the years naming him corespondent in adultery cases—all of which he successfully defended. But journalists refused to publish anything on Frances Stevenson who, everyone in government circles knew, was a kind of second wife. It would have been unworthy of English gentlemen to tarnish the reputation of the public servant who had steered Britain through the perils of a world war.

Most Australians, too, believe that a politician's sex life should remain private, and journalists Down Under have followed that lead. But in 2018, the married, fifty-year-old Deputy Prime Minister Barnaby Joyce resigned over a relationship with his thirty-three-year-old press secretary, whom he had impregnated. Joyce admitted he was the father of the unborn child and had been having a relationship with the woman.

In the #MeToo era, it wasn't Joyce's extramarital affair that led to his resignation but the fact that the woman in question worked for him, and their relationship could be seen as sexual harassment on the job. Prime Minister Malcolm Turnbull introduced a rule prohibiting sexual relations between ministers and their staff, which social media immediately dubbed the "bonk ban." Now Australia is wrestling with the ethics of exposing the sex lives of politicians.

"It licenses the press to investigate politicians' private lives," said the director of an Australian think tank, the Center for Independent Studies. "It's an invasion of privacy."

Japan has long had the tradition of the *uwaki mono*—the frivolous womanizer—which sounds like a bad thing to us but was seen as a good thing by them. In 1952, during a public forum, an opponent accused political party leader Bukichi Miki of keeping four mistresses. "I must strive for accuracy," Miki retorted angrily. "I will go ahead and correct the mathematical errors of the aforementioned weak candidate right now. It was said that I have four mistresses, but actually I have five. Confusing four with five ought to be considered shameful even for a first grader . . . However, all these women have now become old maids and aren't of use to me anymore. Even so, Bukichi Miki could never do something so inhumane as abandon them! Even today I care for them all." The crowd roared with laughter, applauding Miki's generosity, and Miki's party won the election.

It was a lack of generosity that toppled sixty-six-year-old Prime Minister Sosuke Uno in 1989. Uno resigned from office after only sixty-nine days due to a sex scandal with a geisha. His crime was not the sex—no one cared about that—but his stinginess. Though Uno was one of Japan's wealthiest politicians, he had only given his thirty-five-year-old lover, Mitsuko Nakanishi, about $2,300 a month over their five-month affair—meager indeed for a geisha—and no traditional goodbye present when he dumped her. Incensed at the injustice, when Uno was suddenly appointed prime minister four years later, the geisha contacted a Japanese magazine because, she said, "A man who treats women so shabbily shouldn't be allowed to lead a nation."

Many Japanese citizens, however, felt the scandal unworthy of press coverage. As one politician said on TV, "What's below the navel isn't personal character."

CONCLUSION

*W*ith regards to political sex scandals, Americans have historically gasped in outrage as the cultural descendants of Puritans are bound to do. But then we forgave Alexander Hamilton, who had done so much for the economy and told the truth about his affair, and Thomas Jefferson, who doubled the size of the nation. And we voted for rapist Grover Cleveland, who saved the taxpayers a boatload of money. True, we were upset at Gary Hart's lies more than his affair. But these days we don't even care about the lies anymore. Bill Clinton had a 73 percent approval rating the week he was impeached for lying about sex. Compared to the constant chaos of all his other scandals involving the coronavirus, national security, and the Constitution, Trump's lies about sex are trivial.

Still, some illicit affairs are more dignified than others. There is a difference between Woodrow Wilson's years'-long relationship with Mary Peck and JFK's three-whore-a-day habit. Between FDR's thirty-year affair with the love of his life, Lucy Mercer Rutherfurd, and Trump grabbing unsuspecting women by the genitals.

There is also a difference—at the moment—between how

Democrats and Republicans treat sex scandals. Democrat Al Franken, a senator since 2009 and a comedian before that, was forced to resign by his fellow Democrats in 2017 after several women came forward with various allegations of inappropriate touching and kissing. Perhaps most damning, during a 2006 USO tour Franken was photographed appearing to place his hands above a woman's breasts while she was asleep wearing body armor and a helmet. In his resignation speech, Franken pointed out that President Trump remained in office despite his grab-'em-by-the-pussy tape and accusations of sexual assault, and that the Republican Party supported accused child molester Roy Moore in his 2017 Senate campaign. This is, of course, the polar opposite of 1998, when Republicans were aghast at Bill Clinton's disgraceful amatory antics while Democrats shook their heads at all the uproar over a little sex and several unproven allegations.

Given that so many men who seek high office suffer from hubris syndrome, bipolar disorder, narcissistic personality disorder, and a superfluity of testosterone, it is likely many of them will continue to seek sex on the side, in ways both dignified and sordid. Perhaps a Trump voter best summed up the likelihood of change during an interview in 2016 after the release of the *Access Hollywood* tape. "That's what powerful men do," he said.

But what about powerful women? In November 2018, 121 women won House and Senate seats, a record number. It is quite difficult to unearth sex scandals involving female politicians, which could be rooted in the fact that, according to political science experts, such as University of Washington professor Amanda Clayton, women become politicians in order to *do something*—get behind a cause such as good schools or gun control—while men become politicians in order to *be somebody*, which is where the hubris and narcissism kick in, often trailing naked women in their wake. Most likely, as the number of female politicians increases, the number of sex scandals will decrease.

Because, quite frankly, it is inconceivable that U.S. speaker of the House of Representatives Nancy Pelosi, German chancellor Angela Merkel, former British prime minister Theresa May, or a future female U.S. president would have sex with interns and porn stars, or brag about grabbing unsuspecting men's penises, or tweet images of their nether regions to minors. In other words, girls won't be boys.

Which, certainly, will be a good thing.

BIBLIOGRAPHY

Alford, Mimi. *Once Upon a Secret: My Affair with President John F. Kennedy and Its Aftermath.* New York: Random House, 2012.

Ambrose, Stephen. *Eisenhower: Soldier, General of the Army, President-Elect, 1890–1952.* Volume I. New York: Simon & Schuster, 1983.

Anthony, Carl Sferrazza. *Florence Harding: The First Lady, the Jazz Age, and the Death of America's Most Scandalous President.* New York: William Morrow, 1998.

Atkinson, Diane. *The Criminal Conversation of Mrs. Norton: Victorian England's "Scandal of the Century" and the Fallen Socialite Who Changed Women's Lives Forever.* Chicago: Chicago Review Press, 2012.

Bai, Matt. *All the Truth Is Out: The Week Politics Went Tabloid.* New York: Vintage, 2014.

Benes, Ross. *The Sex Effect: Baring Our Complicated Relationship with Sex.* Naperville, IL: Sourcebooks, 2017.

Bly, Nellie. *The Kennedy Men: Three Generations of Sex, Scandal and Secrets.* New York: Kensington, 1996.

Britton, Nan. *The President's Daughter.* New York: Elizabeth Ann Guild, 1927.

Brown, Madeleine Duncan. *Texas in the Morning: The Love Story of Madeleine Brown and President Lyndon Baines Johnson.* Baltimore: Conservatory Press, 1997.

Bryant, Traphes. *Dog Days at the White House: The Outrageous Memoirs of the Presidential Kennel Keeper.* New York: Macmillan, 1975.

Burleigh, Nina. *Golden Handcuffs: The Secret History of Trump's Women.* New York: Simon & Schuster, 2018.

Caro, Robert A. *The Years of Lyndon Johnson: Master of the Senate*. New York: Alfred A. Knopf, 2002.

———. *The Years of Lyndon Johnson: Means of Ascent*. New York: Alfred A. Knopf, 1990.

———. *The Years of Lyndon Johnson: Passage of Power*. New York: Alfred A. Knopf, 2012.

———. *The Years of Lyndon Johnson: The Path to Power*. New York: Alfred A. Knopf, 1982.

Caroli, Betty Boyd. *Lady Bird and Lyndon: The Hidden Story of a Marriage that Made a President*. New York: Simon & Schuster, 2015.

Cawthorne, Nigel. *Sex Lives of the U.S. Presidents*. London: Prion, 1996.

Chernow, Ron. *Alexander Hamilton*. New York: Penguin, 2004.

Daniels, Stormy. *Full Disclosure*. New York: St. Martin's Press, 2018.

Day, Michael. *Being Berlusconi: The Rise & Fall from Cosa Nostra to Bunga Bunga*. New York: Palgrave Macmillan, 2015.

Deloire, Christophe, and Christophe Dubois. *Sexus Politicus*. Paris: Albin Michel, 2006.

Flowers, Gennifer. *Passion and Betrayal*. Del Mar, CA: Emery Dalton, 1995.

Flynt, Larry, and David Eisenbach. *One Nation Under Sex: How the Private Lives of Presidents, First Ladies, and Their Lovers Changed the Course of American History*. New York: Palgrave Macmillan, 2011.

Gordon-Reed, Annette. *The Hemingses of Monticello: An American Family*. New York: W. W. Norton, 2008.

Hague, Ffion. *The Pain and the Privilege: The Women in Lloyd George's Life*. London: Harper Perennial, 2008.

Holt, Marilyn Irvin. *Mamie Doud Eisenhower: The General's First Lady*. Wichita, KS: University Press of Kansas, 2007.

Hunter, Rielle. *What Really Happened: John Edwards, Our Daughter, and Me*. Dallas, TX: Benbella Books, 2012.

Kaminski, John P., editor. *Jefferson in Love: The Love Letters Between Thomas Jefferson & Maria Cosway*. Madison, WI: Madison House, 1999.

Kranish, Michael, and Marc Fisher. *Trump Revealed: The Definitive Biography of the 45th President*. New York: Scribner, 2016.

Lachman, Charles. *A Secret Life: The Lies and Scandals of President Grover Cleveland*. New York: Skyhorse, 2012.

Laumond, Jean-Claude. *Vingt-Cinq Ans Avec Lui*. Paris: Ramsay, 2001.

Longford, Ruth. *Frances, Countess Lloyd-George: More Than a Mistress.* London: Gracewing, 1996.

Means, Gaston B., and May Dixon Thacker. *The Strange Death of President Harding.* New York: Gold Label, 1930.

Miller, Kristie. *Ellen and Edith: Woodrow Wilson's First Ladies.* Wichita, KS: University Press of Kansas, 2014.

Morgan, Kay Summersby. *Past Forgetting: My Love Affair with Dwight D. Eisenhower.* New York: Simon & Schuster, 1976.

Oppenheimer, Jerry. *State of a Union: Inside the Complex Marriage of Bill and Hillary Clinton.* New York: HarperCollins, 2000.

Owen, David. *In Sickness and in Power: Illness in Heads of Government during the Last 100 Years.* London: Methuen, 2008.

Parks, Lillian Rogers, and Frances Spatz Leighton. *My Thirty Years Backstairs at the White House.* Bronx, NY: Ishi Press International, 2009.

Persico, Joseph E. *Franklin & Lucy: President Roosevelt, Mrs. Rutherfurd, and the Other Remarkable Women in His Life.* New York: Random House, 2008.

Phillips-Schrock, Patrick. *The White House: An Illustrated Architectural History.* Jefferson, NC: McFarland, 2013.

Quinn, Susan. *Eleanor and Hick: The Love Affair That Shaped a First Lady.* New York: Penguin Random House, 2016.

Robenalt, James David. *The Harding Affair: Love and Espionage During the Great War.* New York: St. Martin's Press, 2009.

Ross, Shelley. *Fall from Grace: Sex, Scandal, and Corruption in American Politics from 1702 to the Present.* New York: Ballantine, 1988.

Sciacca, Tony. *Kennedy and His Women.* New York: Manor Books, 1976.

Sheehy, Gail. *Hillary's Choice.* New York: Penguin Random House, 1999.

Short, Philip. *Mitterrand: A Study in Ambiguity.* London: Bodley Head, 2013.

Sloan, Sam. *Mafia Moll: The Judith Exner Story, The Life of the Mistress of John F. Kennedy.* Bronx, NY: Ishi Press International, 2008.

Smith, Jean Edward. *Eisenhower in War and Peace.* New York: Random House, 2013.

Smith, Kathryn. *The Gatekeeper: Missy LeHand, FDR, and the Untold Story of the Partnership that Defined a Presidency.* New York: Touchstone, 2016.

Smith, Sally Bedell. *Grace and Power: The Private World of the Kennedy White House.* New York: Random House, 2004.

Taylor, A. J. P., editor. *My Darling Pussy: The Letters of Lloyd George and Frances Stevenson 1913–41.* London: Weidenfeld and Nicolson, 1975.

Von Post, Gunilla. *Love, Jack.* New York: Crown, 1997.

Witcover, Jules. *The American Vice Presidency: From Irrelevance to Power.* Washington, D.C.: Smithsonian Books, 2014.

About the author

About the book

Insights,
Interviews
& More...

Meet Eleanor Herman

Sigrid Estrada

ELEANOR HERMAN is the *New York Times* bestselling author of *Sex with Kings, Sex with the Queen*, and several other works of popular history. She has hosted *Lost Worlds* for the History Channel, *The Madness of Henry VIII* for National Geographic Channel, and *America: Facts vs. Fiction* for the American Heroes Channel. Herman lives with her husband, their yellow Lab, and her three very dignified cats in McLean, Virginia. ◠

The Other Side of the Mattress: Happy Presidential Marriages

I don't know about you, but I'm tired of marital dysfunction. Not my own, of course. My husband is perfect. He has the patience of Job (as any husband of mine would have to, putting up with my collection of rescue cats; thousands of dusty old books; dozens of nightmare-inducing, antique paintings of grimacing people in ruffs and white wigs; and the baffling manic-depressive mood swings of an author).

What I'm tired of is *presidential* marital dysfunction. Because writing *Sex with Presidents* was emotionally taxing. Yes, there were times when I was shrieking with laughter (so loud, apparently, that my husband, whose home office is right below mine, would tiptoe upstairs, poke his head into the room, and gently ask if everything was okay). But really, spending a couple of years researching and writing about these guys with chronic broken-zipper syndrome can take a psychological toll. Probably because it reminds me of my first marriage.

True, wallowing in delicious schadenfreude over rich and powerful people in dysfunctional marriages offers us a perverse gratification (yes, they have power, glamor, and luxury, ▶

but just look at how *miserable* they are!). However, we can take even greater pleasure in heartwarming, uplifting, you're-weeping-from-joy love stories.

So let's take a journey backward in time.

"She Gave Me Back My Life"

I don't think you could find two men as different as Donald Trump and Joe Biden if you searched the world over. One of those countless differences is how they treat their wives. Adultery aside, there is the more important issue of basic courtesy. I can't get out of my mind the image of Donald racing up the steps of Air Force One in something like a typhoon, holding an umbrella the size of Rhode Island over his perfectly coiffed golden head, leaving his wife and eleven-year-old son to plod through the torrential downpour as best they could.

Then there was another unforgettable Air Force One moment in May 2017 when they landed in Rome. As Donald and Melania started to descend, he reached for her hand. She decided it was the exact right moment to brush her hair out of her face with that ever-elusive hand, *so he put his hand on her rear end instead.* Yup, with all the cameras rolling. Right before the happy couple met the pope.

Oh, and there was that smack-your-head weird handshake he gave her after she introduced him at Joint Base Andrews in September 2017 (who *shakes their wife's hand?*), after which he told her, "You go sit down." But at least she let him touch her hand that time, which was something of an achievement for him.

Compare those moments with this one: Inauguration Day 2021, the newly sworn-in forty-sixth president, Joe Biden, and First Lady Dr. Jill Biden stand awkwardly on the White House front porch staring at a closed door. In a final act of petty nastiness, outgoing President Trump had fired the chief usher hours earlier so that no one was there to open it. What does a spanking new presidential couple do while waiting for a butler to open the damned White House door? They cuddle, Jill snuggling up against Joe in the chill January wind, his arm firmly around her back.

Jill is so fiercely protective of Joe that she has literally thrown herself into the line of fire to protect him. At a March 4, 2020, campaign event, when a vegan protester bearing a "Let Dairy Die" sign rushed onstage, Jill placed herself squarely in front of her husband. After the woman was dragged off, another protester ran up, and Jill grabbed her wrist and flung her away. She was magnificent, exuding all the ferocity of a tigress protecting her young. Slender, seventy-year-old Jill Biden is a total badass you just don't want to mess with. Joe joked, "I'm probably the only candidate running for president whose wife is my Secret Service."

Now, if a protester came running toward Donald Trump, Melania, still smiling her frozen smile, would probably step deftly out of the way in her four-inch Manolo Blahniks to give the assailant a clear path.

Jill and Joe met on a blind date in 1975, set up by Joe's brother Frank, who had met her in college. Jill was a twenty-three-year-old senior at the University of Delaware going through a bruising divorce. Joe was a thirty-two-year-old U.S. senator and widower. Three years earlier, he had lost his wife, Neilia, in a tragic car accident, along with their infant daughter, and found himself a single parent to two young sons.

In a 2016 interview with *Vogue*, Jill recalled their first meeting. "I was a senior, and I had been dating guys in jeans and clogs and T-shirts," she said, "and he came to the door and he had a sport coat and loafers, and I thought, 'God, this is never going to work, not in a million years.' He was nine years older than I am! But we went out to see *A Man and a Woman* at the movie theater in Philadelphia, and we really hit it off. When we came home . . . he shook my hand good night. I went upstairs and called my mother at 1:00 a.m. and said, 'Mom, I finally met a gentleman.'"

After their second date, Joe asked her not to see any other men. His office shrine of dozens of photos of Neilia started to ▸

disappear. After a few months of dating, Joe introduced Jill to his sons, who adored her. In his 2007 memoir *Promises to Keep*, Biden recalled one morning when his sons, then seven and six, were watching him shave. Hunter said, "Beau thinks we should get married." Beau explained, "We think we should marry Jill. What do you think, Dad?"

"I think that's a pretty good idea," Joe told them. "I'll never forget how good I felt at that moment."

Jill, however, was hesitant, perhaps because her first marriage had soured so quickly. "By that time, of course, I had fallen in love with the boys, and I really felt that this marriage had to work," she told *Vogue*. "Because they had lost their mom, and I couldn't have them lose another mother. So I had to be 100 percent sure."

Jill turned Joe down four times. When he proposed for the fifth time, he said, "Look, this is the last time I'm asking you. I don't care when we get married. But I want a commitment." Beau and Hunter stood with them at the altar in June 1977. Then they all went off on a honeymoon.

"The way they thought of it, the four of us were getting married," Joe wrote. "She gave me back my life. She made me start to think my family might be whole again." The family was complete in June 1981 when they welcomed a daughter. Her brothers got to choose her name: Ashley.

Jill earned two master's degrees and a doctorate in education. Joe made an unsuccessful bid for the presidency in 1987 and continued to serve in the U.S. Senate until 2009, when he was selected as Barack Obama's vice president. There is a lasting memento of the Bidens' time as second couple on the grounds of the vice president's residence, a plaque Joe had installed on a tree as a Valentine's surprise: *Joe Loves Jilly, Valentine's Day 2010.*

In an August 2020 CBS interview, Joe said of his wife, "I adore her. I'm gonna sound so stupid—I was saying the other day, when she comes down the steps and I look at her, my heart still skips a beat."

"First of All, How Good-Looking Is My Wife?"

In 1989, twenty-seven-year-old Barack Obama met Michelle Robinson, twenty-five, when he worked as a summer associate in her Chicago law office, Sidley & Austin. Barack had just finished his first year at Harvard Law School; Michelle had graduated from the same school a year earlier and was assigned as his mentor. Barack was smitten at first sight. He told Oprah that he was "struck by how tall and beautiful [Michelle] was," adding that working with her was "the luckiest break of my life."

Michelle, however, dismissed him as a "good-looking, smooth-talking guy" in an interview with Obama biographer David Mendell. Serious by nature, she was focusing intently on her career and not dating.

Barack asked her out repeatedly and was just as often turned down. Michelle said dating would be inappropriate, as she was his mentor. Barack offered to quit if that would make her go out with him. Worn down, exhausted, and interested in spite of herself, she agreed to see him.

Michelle found him likable and fun, but she wasn't all that impressed. Her family had struggled financially, and she worried that Barack, who seemed unconcerned about money, would never amount to much. Which is pretty funny, considering. Barack "was really broke," she told the *Hyde Park Herald*. He had a "cruddy" wardrobe and a rusted-out car. "I thought, 'This brother is not interested in ever making a dime.'" But on a date at a Chicago church where Barack spoke as a community organizer, she was deeply moved by his passion for creating a brighter future for African Americans.

At the end of the summer, Barack returned to Harvard Law while Michelle continued to work in Chicago. The two continued to see each other as often as possible. Michelle wanted to get married, to emulate her parents' strong and happy relationship. But Barack, though head over heels in love with Michelle, told her that he didn't believe in marriage, calling it a "meaningless institution." After two years, Michelle was getting fed up. ▶

The Other Side of the Mattress: Happy Presidential Marriages
(*continued*)

Then, on July 31, 1991, the two went to dinner to celebrate Barack's passing the bar exam. As Michelle recalled in her book *Becoming*: "As we were reaching the end of the meal, Barack smiled at me and raised the subject of marriage. He reached for my hand and said that as much as he loved me with his whole being, he still didn't really see the point."

The waiter served them a dessert plate with a silver lid and removed the cover. Michelle was so angry she didn't even want to look down. But when she did, she saw there was no chocolate cake, just a small, dark velvet box. Inside was a diamond ring.

They had a huge wedding in October 1992, and two daughters, Malia in 1998, and Sasha in 2001. Barack became an Illinois state senator in 1998 and, six years later, a U.S. senator. His elegant, inspirational oratory, combined with his passion to help the less fortunate, propelled him to become the nation's forty-third president, and its first Black one.

At a 2009 inaugural ball, the first couple entered to roars of approval. Barack quieted the crowd and said, "First of all, how good-looking is my wife?" Moments later, the new president swept his wife into his arms to dance to "At Last," performed live by Beyoncé. As they danced, they whispered and nuzzled. It was more like the first dance of a bride and groom than a couple who had been married sixteen years.

After eight years of stress and vicious politics, leaving the White House was probably more exhilarating for the couple than moving in. Michelle "has been more relaxed and more joyful since we left office," Barack told *People* magazine. "That allowed us to just enjoy the deep love that comes with a marriage this long."

"The Greatest Love Affair in the History of the American Presidency"
It's a funny thing and not at all well known, but Nancy Reagan became the first lady of the United States because of the infamous Communist-chasing Senator Joseph McCarthy.

In 1951, the thirty-year-old actress—then Nancy Davis—had a serious problem. Another Hollywood actress with her name had ended up on McCarthy's Hollywood blacklist of Communist sympathizers, and the non-Communist Nancy kept getting passed over for roles. She decided to visit the president of the Screen Actors Guild to help her sort out the problem, a handsome forty-year-old actor named Ronald Reagan.

Sparks flew between the two, and Ronald asked her to dinner, where he impressed her further. "He had a broad knowledge of a lot of different things," she recalled in her 2002 book *I Love You, Ronnie: The Letters of Ronald Reagan to Nancy*. "I loved to listen to him talk. I loved his sense of humor. I saw it clearly that very first night: He was everything that I wanted." The two soon became an item.

Nancy knew she wanted to spend her life with him and hoped for children. But Ronald, who had divorced actress Jane Wyman a few years earlier, was hesitant to remarry. In January 1952, Nancy "decided to give things a push," as she said, and mentioned that she was trying to get a role in New York. Horrified, he replied, "I think we ought to get married." He would have no regrets.

For their twenty-eighth wedding anniversary in 1980, Ronald wrote her a letter. "Beginning in 1951," he began, "Nancy Davis [*sic*] seeing the plight of a lonely man who didn't know how lonely he really was, determined to rescue him from a completely empty life. Refusing to be rebuffed by a certain amount of stupidity on his part she ignored his somewhat slow response. With patience and tenderness she gradually brought the light of understanding to his darkened, obtuse mind and he discovered the joy of loving someone with all his heart."

Ronald and Nancy had two children together, as well as Ronald's two children from his previous marriage. In 1957, they both appeared in a movie called *Hellcats of the Navy*. By the mid-sixties, Nancy had left acting and Ronald entered politics. He was elected governor of California in 1966 and ▶

again in 1970. Nancy was such a popular first lady of California that the *Los Angeles Times* named her its Woman of the Year.

In 1981, when Ronald became the fortieth president of the United States, the American public was delighted that their first couple idolized each other. When Ronald spoke, Nancy would gaze at him with such ecstatic adoration one might think she was watching Jesus deliver the Sermon on the Mount. Ronald's face lit up when Nancy entered a room, and he left little love notes around the White House for her to find. The two often held hands. Their courtship, it seemed, continued even after decades of marriage. Actor Charlton Heston, who had known the couple in Hollywood, described their relationship as "the greatest love affair in the history of the American Presidency."

On their thirty-first wedding anniversary, Ronald wrote her, "I more than love you, I'm not whole without you. You are life itself to me. When you are gone I'm waiting for you to return so I can start living again." Many years later, Nancy wrote of their marriage, "If either of us ever left the room, we both felt lonely. People don't always believe this, but it's true. Filling the loneliness, completing each other—that's what it still meant to us to be husband and wife."

Soon after he left office in 1989, Ronald was diagnosed with Alzheimer's disease, and Nancy saw to his needs even as he slowly slipped away from her. She read his old letters over and over again to remember the man she loved. He finally died in 2004 at the age of ninety-three. In a 2009 interview with *Vanity Fair*, Nancy said, "I miss Ronnie a lot, an awful lot. People say it gets better. No, it does not."

"She's the One I'm Going to Marry"

The longest-lasting presidential love story is that of Jimmy and Rosalynn Carter, who have been married for seventy-five years, longer than most U.S. presidents have been alive. They were next-door neighbors in the tiny town of Plains, Georgia, and Carter literally knew Rosalynn Smith since the day she was born. At thirteen, Rosalynn developed quite a crush on him. Once

Jimmy went off to the U.S. Naval Academy, her sister—best friends with Jimmy's sister Ruth—tried to set the two up when he visited, but it never worked out.

It looked hopeless once more during his month-long leave in 1945, when Jimmy was seeing a beauty pageant winner, Miss Georgia Southwestern State, almost every night. But on his last night of leave, the beauty queen had other plans. Cruising around town with his sister and her boyfriend, Jimmy spotted Rosalynn coming out of church and invited her to go to the movies with them. "She was remarkably beautiful, almost painfully shy, obviously intelligent, and yet unrestrained in our discussion on the rumble seat of the Ford Coupe," he wrote in his 2015 memoir, *A Full Life: Reflections at Ninety*.

The next morning, Jimmy's mother asked him how he felt about Rosalynn.

"She's the one I'm going to marry," he replied. They saw each other again when he returned home for Christmas break. When she visited him at the academy for Presidents' Day, he asked her to marry him. She turned him down.

She had made a deathbed promise to her father six years earlier that she would complete college before marrying. She was still in her second year of junior college and insisted on dating other men.

Jimmy kept up the pressure, calling and writing, letting her know how much he wanted to get married. By the time summer rolled around, she had finished junior college and he had graduated from the academy. When they married on July 7, 1946, he was twenty-one; Rosalynn was eighteen.

After he left the navy in 1953, Jimmy focused on making his peanut farm profitable while Rosalynn learned accounting to manage the books. Jimmy was a popular Georgia state senator from 1963 through 1967 and served as governor from 1971 through 1975. In 1976, running for president as a Washington outsider against Nixon's successor, Gerald Ford, Carter won by a narrow margin.

After they left the White House, the Carters focused on ▶

The Other Side of the Mattress: Happy Presidential Marriages
(*continued*)

helping the less fortunate, particularly through the nonprofit Habitat for Humanity. In 2002, Jimmy won the Nobel Peace Prize "for his decades of untiring effort to find peaceful solutions to international conflicts, to advance democracy and human rights, and to promote economic and social development."

In August 2015, ninety-year-old Jimmy was diagnosed with brain and liver cancer. After radiation and drug therapy, he was declared cancer-free in December of that year. The couple still holds hands when they walk.

"The best thing I ever did was marry Rosalynn," Carter said in a C-SPAN interview at the Carter Center in 2015. "That's the pinnacle of my life."

"The Mother-in-Law from Hell"

The Trumans, who moved into the White House in 1945, looked like a typical gray-haired couple in their sixties. But their appearances belied their fierce passion for each other. One morning, a shamefaced first lady had to ask the chief butler to replace the slats on their bed. They had broken them.

Harry S. Truman was born a poor farm boy; Elizabeth (Bess) Virginia Wallace lived in a big house on the best street in Independence, Missouri. They met in Sunday school in 1890, when he was six and she was five, and attended the same schools through high school, after which Harry moved to his grandfather's farm, twenty miles outside of town. When Bess was eighteen, her alcoholic father committed suicide. Bess gave up any thought of college and focused on getting her three younger brothers educated and away from their mother, who, many modern historians agree, had some sort of horrifying personality disorder. Harry, too, had lost his father, and devoted himself to running the farm and bringing up his younger siblings.

One day, when the two were in their mid-twenties, Harry was visiting relatives in town when one of them mentioned that a pie plate needed to be returned to Mrs. Wallace. Harry volunteered to take it and was smitten when he saw Bess again. They dated sporadically as Harry tried to earn more money to support a wife. But Mrs. Wallace tried hard to break it up. Harry was poor; he had the occasional drink; he would never amount to anything.

When Bess finally agreed to marry him, World War I intervened and Harry signed up. By the time they wed in 1919, they were in their mid-thirties. Bess insisted they move in with her mother—"the mother-in-law from hell," according to his friends—as Mrs. Wallace needed someone to take care of her and no one else would go near her. It is surely a sign of Harry's love for Bess that he agreed to live with such a disagreeable old shrew. He never invited a single friend over, fearful that Mother Wallace might spit nails at them. The couple had one child, Margaret, in 1924.

In 1934, Truman was elected to the U.S. Senate. To his great surprise, ten years later President Franklin Roosevelt chose him as his candidate for vice president. Only three months after FDR's fourth inauguration in 1945, the president had a fatal stroke. Harry S. Truman, the farm boy who would never amount to much, quite unexpectedly found himself the thirty-third president of the United States.

Mother Wallace moved into the White House with them, of course, where she terrorized the staff. (She would live to be ninety, probably because venom doesn't decay as quickly as flesh and blood.) Her low opinion of her son-in-law never improved, and she still called him "Farmer Truman" until her dying day.

And Harry, with the patience of Job, never said a word against her to anybody because of his great love for Bess.

"A Plain Little Wife"

In 1844, Frederick Dent invited his former West Point roommate, Ulysses S. Grant, to visit his home ten miles away from their regiment in Jefferson Barracks, Missouri. It was there that the twenty-one-year-old Ulysses—handsome, rugged, and lean— first met Miss Julia Dent, Frederick's sister. He was entranced by her and soon started visiting daily with marriage in mind. ▶

The Other Side of the Mattress: Happy Presidential Marriages
(continued)

Perhaps no one was more surprised by his courtship than Julia herself. The eighteen-year-old knew that she was not the type to attract men: short, cross-eyed, her head placed right on top of her shoulders with no evidence of a neck. But Ulysses recognized in her a warmth, a kindness, a gentle self-awareness that stole his heart. In his opinion, no willowy sylph-like girl with big wide eyes could compare to Julia's loveliness. They rode horses and read poetry to each other. When her pet canary died, Grant built a tiny yellow coffin and asked eight fellow officers to serve as an honor guard for the funeral.

Soon Ulysses had to leave for war with Mexico. He took off his West Point ring and handed it to Julia as an engagement ring; she gave him a lock of her hair. Their engagement remained secret, as both sets of parents disapproved of the match. The Dents were slaveholders. The Grants were abolitionists. The secretly engaged couple wrote loving letters. In one, Julia enclosed two dried wildflowers. When Ulysses opened it outside, the petals scattered in the wind as he raced hither and yon trying to catch just one. He was unsuccessful.

After a separation of four years, Ulysses returned to marry his beloved Julia. His parents were conspicuously absent from the wedding; they liked Julia well enough but didn't want to be soiled by the company of her slaveholding family. Her parents, however, had fallen on hard times and now welcomed the match.

Ulysses's military service resulted in long separations from Julia that upset him so much he drowned his sorrow in drink. In 1854, he resigned from the army due to his problematic inebriation. But even sober as a judge, he could barely support Julia and their four children. He built a log cabin, farmed, chopped wood, and peddled it on the streets of St. Louis. Ill with malaria, he lost his farm, moved his family in with Julia's parents, and bounced from job to job.

Then, in April 1861, when he was thirty-eight, Southerners fired on Fort Sumter. Ulysses snapped into action, organizing volunteers and taking command of Illinois troops. One military victory followed another, and he was promoted to brigadier general, then major general. But being away from Julia caused him to hit the bottle again. He sent for her. She foisted the children onto relatives, and—highly unusual for an army wife at the time—she accompanied him across ten thousand miles, bouncing in a carriage from one bloody battlefield to the next. The drinking stopped. In this way, Julia helped save the Union.

In 1868, three years after Ulysses accepted Confederate General Robert E. Lee's surrender, he was elected the eighteenth president of the United States. Julia decided it might be time to get surgery on her eyes to correct her condition, an operation she had put off for years. "I never had the courage to consent," she wrote in her memoirs, "but now that my husband had become so famous, I really thought it behooved me to try to look as well as possible." The surgeon, however, told her it was too late. As first lady, she would pose for her photographs in profile.

When she apologized to her husband for waiting too long for surgery, he was shocked. "What in the world put such a thought in your head, Julia?" he asked.

"Why, you are getting to be such a great man, and I am such a plain little wife," she replied. "I thought if my eyes were as others' are, I might not be so very, very plain."

Grant put his arms around her. "Did I not see you and fall in love with you with these same eyes?" he asked. "I like them just as they are, and now, remember, you are not to interfere with them. They are mine, and let me tell you, Mrs. Grant, you had better not make any experiments, as I might not like you half so well with any other eyes."

"Your Letter Makes My Heart Throb"

We've all heard of John and Abigail Adams's amazing marriage, the enduring partnership that helped forge a nation. What most people don't know is that their first meeting was disastrous.

It was 1759, and twenty-four-year-old John Adams had ridden with his friend Richard Cranch to visit Rev. William Smith of ▶

Weymouth, Massachusetts, as Richard was courting the reverend's oldest daughter, Mary. There John met the middle daughter, fifteen-year-old Abigail, a mere slip of a girl, with dark brown hair and bright brown eyes. It is likely that witty, lively Abigail was not impressed by the rather plump man, already losing his hair, who seemed quite full of himself.

Harshly critical by nature, John wrote in his diary that he didn't like any of the daughters, all three of whom he described as "not fond, not frank, not candid." Their father, John decided, was "a crafty designing man." Nor did Abigail's mother like John very much; she found him a country bumpkin lacking in manners.

But over the course of the next few years, John continued to visit the horrible Smiths as his friend pursued his courtship and eventually married Mary. During that time, John realized that Abigail was perhaps the most fond, frank, and candid person he would ever meet.

They wed on October 25, 1764, and rode off together to the nearby farm John had inherited. John became a leading figure in the American Revolution and helped draft the Declaration of Independence. He was often away from home, serving in the Continental Congress in Philadelphia and later in diplomatic missions in Europe. Back in Massachusetts, Abigail ran the farm, enlarged the house, profitably managed the family's finances, and raised their four children, one of whom, John Quincy Adams, would become America's sixth president in 1825.

Because of John's long absences from home on government service, we have a treasure trove of nearly 1,200 letters between the two, letters that demonstrate their abiding love and powerful partnership.

On April 28, 1776, John wrote to Abigail from the Continental Congress in Philadelphia, "Is there no Way for two friendly Souls, to converse together, altho the Bodies are 400 Miles off?—Yes by Letter.—But I want a better Communication. I want to hear you think, or see your Thoughts. The Conclusion of your Letter makes my Heart throb, more than a Cannonade would."

Abigail's engaging letters are the product of her omnivorous reading rather than any formal education. Perhaps her most famous missive is the one she wrote him on March 31, 1776:

I long to hear that you have declared an independency. And, by the way, in the new code of laws which I suppose it will be necessary for you to make, I desire you would remember the ladies and be more generous and favorable to them than your ancestors. Do not put such unlimited power into the hands of the husbands. Remember, all men would be tyrants if they could. If particular care and attention is not paid to the ladies, we are determined to foment a rebellion, and will not hold ourselves bound by any laws in which we have no voice or representation.

Unfortunately, her husband did not act on her suggestion.

A year later she wrote: "Not ten minutes pass without thinking of you. 'Tis four months wanting three days since we parted. Every day of the time I have mourned the absence of my friend, and felt a vacancy in my heart which nothing, nothing can supply. In vain the spring blooms or the birds sing. Their music has not its former melody, nor the spring its usual pleasures. I look around with a melancholy delight and sigh for my absent partner. I fancy I see you worn down with cares, fatigued with business, and solitary amidst a multitude."

On February 16, 1780, John wrote Abigail from a diplomatic mission in Paris:

I am, as I ever was and ever shall be,
Yours, yours, yours.

John served as George Washington's vice president from 1789 through 1797, "the most insignificant Office that ever the Invention of Man contrived or his imagination conceived," as he wrote. As the nation's second president from 1797 through 1801, ▶

The Other Side of the Mattress:
Happy Presidential Marriages *(continued)*

he was often so upset that he cursed his cabinet with four-letter words while "dashing and trampling his wig on the floor."

When they moved into the White House in 1800, it was damp, cold, and still under construction. Abigail famously hung her laundry to dry in the unfinished East Room. Usually, though, she served as John's most trusted adviser, so much so that many in government circles called her "Mrs. President."

"Abigail was his best ally, and because she was intelligent, well-informed and totally sympathetic with him, she was devoted to his politics," said Edith B. Gelles, author of *Abigail & John: Portrait of a Marriage.* "She probably was the best-informed and most reliable advisor to a president until Eleanor Roosevelt in the 20th century."

Abigail Adams died on October 28, 1818, of typhoid fever, aged seventy-three, her devastated husband holding her hand. "Do not grieve, my friend, my dearest friend," she said, as she gasped out her final breaths. "I am ready to go. And John, it will not be long." ∼

	Dallas	N.Y. Giants	Philadelphia	St. Louis	Washington	Chicago	Detroit	Green Bay	Minnesota	Tampa Bay	Atlanta	L.A. Rams	New Orleans	San Francisco
Buffalo	1-3-0	1-2-0	1-3-0	1-3-0	2-2-0	1-2-0	1-1-1	2-1-0	1-4-0	1-2-0	2-2-0	1-3-0	2-1-0	2-1-0
Indianapolis	3-6-0	7-3-0	5-5-0	4-5-0	15-6-0	21-14-0	17-16-2	17-18-1	12-5-1	2-1-0	8-0-0	20-14-2	3-0-0	21-14-0
Miami	3-2-0	1-0-0	3-2-0	5-0-0	4-2-0	4-0-0	2-1-0	4-0-0	4-1-0	2-1-0	4-0-0	3-1-0	3-1-0	4-1-0
New England	0-5-0	1-1-0	2-3-0	1-4-0	1-3-0	2-3-0	2-2-0	2-1-0	2-1-0	2-0-0	2-2-0	4-0-0	2-1-0	1-3-0
N.Y. Jets	0-3-0	2-2-0	0-3-0	1-2-0	0-3-0	1-2-0	2-2-0	4-1-0	3-1-0	3-1-0	1-2-0	2-2-0	3-1-0	1-3-0

	Dallas	N.Y. Giants	Philadelphia	St. Louis	Washington	Chicago	Detroit	Green Bay	Minnesota	Tampa Bay	Atlanta	L.A. Rams	New Orleans	San Francisco
Cincinnati	1-2-0	3-0-0	4-0-0	2-1-0	1-3-0	2-0-0	1-2-0	3-2-0	2-2-0	2-1-0	4-1-0	3-2-0	3-2-0	1-4-0
Cleveland	15-9-0	26-16-2	29-11-1	30-10-3	31-8-1	6-2-0	3-12-0	5-7-0	1-7-0	3-0-0	6-1-0	8-7-0	8-1-0	8-4-0
Houston	1-4-0	0-3-0	0-3-0	1-3-0	2-2-0	2-1-0	2-1-0	2-2-0	1-2-0	2-1-0	1-4-0	1-3-0	2-2-1	2-3-0
Pittsburgh	12-11-0	26-41-3	25-42-3	29-20-3	27-40-3	4-13-0	8-13-1	10-16-0	4-5-0	3-0-0	6-1-0	4-12-2	4-4-0	6-6-0

	Dallas	N.Y. Giants	Philadelphia	St. Louis	Washington	Chicago	Detroit	Green Bay	Minnesota	Tampa Bay	Atlanta	L.A. Rams	New Orleans	San Francisco
Denver	1-3-0	2-1-0	1-3-0	1-0-1	1-2-0	3-4-0	3-2-0	3-1-0	2-2-0	2-0-0	3-3-0	2-3-0	4-0-0	3-2-0
Kansas City	1-2-0	1-4-0	0-1-0	3-0-1	2-1-0	1-2-0	2-2-0	1-1-1	2-2-0	3-2-0	2-0-0		2-2-0	1-3-0
L.A. Raiders	2-1-0	3-0-0	3-1-0	1-1-0	4-1-0	3-2-0	3-2-0	4-1-0	5-1-0	2-0-0	4-1-0	4-1-0	3-0-1	3-2-0
San Diego	1-2-0	2-2-0	2-1-0	2-1-0	1-2-0	4-1-0	2-3-0	1-3-0	3-3-0	2-0-0	0-2-0	4-1-0	3-0-0	3-1-0
Seattle	0-3-0	1-3-0	0-2-0	0-2-0	1-2-0	3-1-0	2-1-0	1-3-0	2-1-0	2-0-0	3-0-0	0-3-0	2-1-0	1-2-0

	Dallas	N.Y. Giants	Philadelphia	St. Louis	Washington	Chicago	Detroit	Green Bay	Minnesota	Tampa Bay	Atlanta	L.A. Rams	New Orleans	San Francisco
Dallas		32-13-2	34-17-0	29-17-1	30-20-2	8-4-0	6-3-0	5-8-0	10-5-0	6-0-0	8-1-0	10-10-0	11-1-0	8-8-1
N.Y. Giants	13-32-2		56-45-2	53-31-2	58-46-3	16-27-2	11-18-1	18-25-2	1-6-0	6-3-0	5-6-0	8-16-0	6-5-0	10-7-0
Philadelphia	17-34-0	45-56-2		34-40-4	39-57-5	4-19-1	9-12-2	5-17-0	4-9-0	2-1-0	6-6-1	9-15-1	8-6-0	4-10-1
St. Louis	17-29-1	31-53-2	40-34-4		32-49-2	25-50-6	15-25-5	21-38-4	7-3-0	1-3-0	6-3-0	15-20-2	9-4-0	7-6-0
Washington	20-30-2	46-58-3	57-39-5	49-32-2		11-20-1	19-8-0	11-14-1	4-5-0	2-0-0	9-2-1	14-5-1	7-4-0	6-8-1

	Dallas	N.Y. Giants	Philadelphia	St. Louis	Washington	Chicago	Detroit	Green Bay	Minnesota	Tampa Bay	Atlanta	L.A. Rams	New Orleans	San Francisco
Chicago	4-8-0	27-16-2	19-4-1	50-25-6	20-11-1		64-44-5	70-55-6	22-25-2	12-4-0	5-9-0	43-27-3	7-4-0	24-23-1
Detroit	3-6-0	18-11-1	12-9-2	25-15-5	8-19-0	44-64-5		47-57-7	17-30-2	9-7-0	12-4-0	34-36-1	4-4-1	26-23-1
Green Bay	8-5-0	25-18-2	17-5-0	38-21-4	14-11-1	55-70-6	57-47-7		24-24-1	8-6-1	8-6-0	34-39-2	10-2-0	22-20-1
Minnesota	5-10-0	6-1-0	9-4-0	3-7-0	5-4-0	25-22-2	30-17-2	24-24-1		11-5-0	9-6-0	15-12-2	8-4-0	13-12-1
Tampa Bay	0-6-0	3-6-0	1-2-0	3-1-0	0-2-0	4-12-0	7-9-0	6-8-1	5-11-0		3-2-0	2-5-0	3-5-0	1-5-0

	Dallas	N.Y. Giants	Philadelphia	St. Louis	Washington	Chicago	Detroit	Green Bay	Minnesota	Tampa Bay	Atlanta	L.A. Rams	New Orleans	San Francisco
Atlanta	1-8-0	6-5-0	6-6-1	3-6-0	2-9-0	9-5-0	4-12-0	6-8-0	6-9-0	2-3-0		8-28-2	23-11-0	17-21-0
L.A. Rams	10-10-0	16-8-0	15-9-1	20-15-2	5-14-1	27-43-3	36-34-1	39-34-2	12-15-2	5-2-0	28-8-2		23-9-0	44-26-2
New Orleans	1-11-0	5-6-0	6-8-0	4-9-0	4-7-0	4-7-0	4-4-1	2-10-0	4-8-0	5-3-0	11-23-0	9-23-0		9-22-2
San Francisco	8-8-1	7-10-0	10-4-1	6-7-0	8-6-1	23-24-1	23-26-1	20-22-1	12-13-1	5-1-0	21-17-0	26-44-2	22-9-2	

INTERPRETING THE ALL-TIME TEAM RECORDS CHART (See inside cover)

The numbers in the boxes represent the all-time won-lost-tied record of the team in the left (vertical) column against the team in the top (horizontal) row. Thus, Buffalo have won seven, lost thirty-two and tied one game in the series against Miami.
The colour of the box indicates the current status.

A blue box indicates that the team is leading in the series.

A red box indicates that the team is behind in the series.

A yellow box indicates that the series is tied. Thus, Buffalo is tied with Indianapolis, trailing Miami and leading the New York Jets.

THE AMERICAN FOOTBALL

BOOK 4

THE AMERICAN FOOTBALL

BOOK 4

KEN THOMAS

Macdonald   Queen Anne Press
In association with
Channel Four Television Company Limited

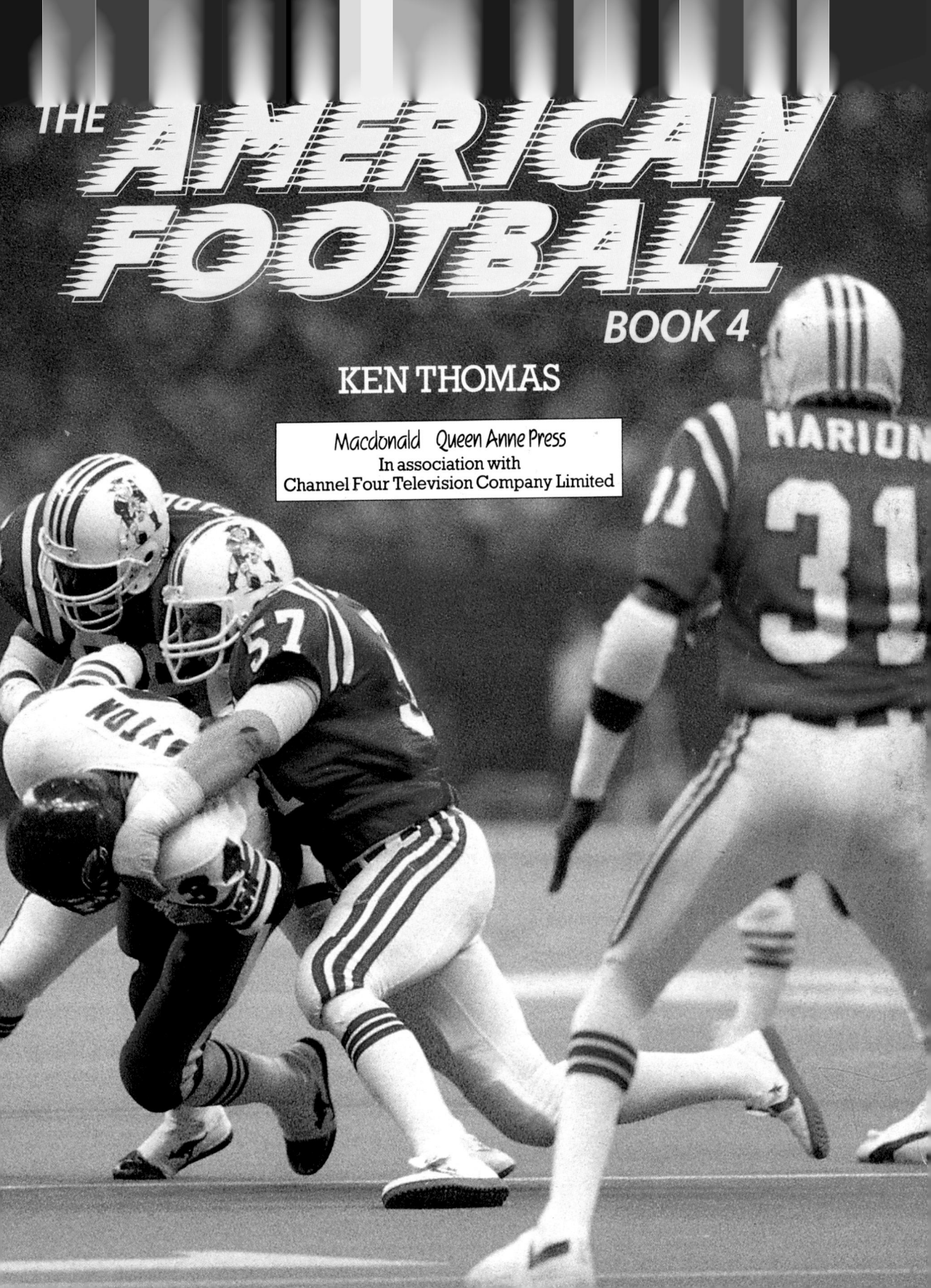

ACKNOWLEDGEMENTS

Once again, the time has come when I take great pleasure in expressing my gratitude to the team of people who have been of incalculable assistance in the preparation of this book. Nick Wridgway, the assistant editor of Touchdown magazine, has played a key part from the beginning, researching the clubs, correcting text and, even as I write, proof-reading the final article. Thanks mate. As usual, Roger Smith, the first British fan of the Dallas Cowboys, has ploughed his way painstakingly through the all-time statistics, for which he has my sincere thanks.

When he said, 'Sure Ken, any time,' Burgh Riffenbaugh, of NFL Properties, Inc., Los Angeles, can hardly have realised that he would be receiving a daily telephone call for assistance. It is testimony both to his kindness and his resilience that we're still on speaking terms. Thanks Burgh I'll be calling you tomorrow – but I guess you knew that anyway.

From that same office came the bulk of the photographic material, and, for their swiftness and efficiency, I should like to thank Sharon Kuthe and Paul Tsuchiya. The balance came from Mike Niblock and Peter Eaton, the publishers of *Touchdown* magazine. Thank you gentlemen.

The Orbis lads do a good job. I shall not forget that it was that company which was the only one to take a chance by publishing 'A Guide To American Football'. They now operate under a different title but the people are the same. So, to the editor and designer, 'Thanks lads'.

Yet again, my thanks go to the charming Mrs Susanna Yager, the Publishing and Merchandising Manager of Channel Four Television, who sees to the paper work and keeps me on an even keel.

Finally, there's a certain Minnesota Vikings fan who plays a special part in the whole production. The lady happens to be my wife, Janie, who puts up with a house-full of hairy men talking of 'traps', 'sweeps' and 'zone defenses', for most of the autumn and early winter. Thanks love.

K.T. June 1986

PHOTOGRAPHS

All photographs have been supplied by courtesy of the NFL, with the exception of the title page, supplied by courtesy of All-Sport/Mike Powell. In addition the following photographers took the pictures on the pages indicated: John Biever, facing Introduction, 9, 19B, 42; Vernon Biever 61, 63, 145, 155; David Boss Contents page, 10, 32, 62, 70B, 157; Peter Brouillet 88; Rob Brown 13T, 20, 115; Jim Chaffin 33; Alvin Chung 13B; Ian Christy 94; Scott Cunningham 151; Jay Dickman 17; Brian Drake 78; Malcolm Emmons 34, 48, 51T, 65; L.D. Fullerton 25C; George Gojkovich 30, 109; Jon Hayt 86; Paul Jasienski 35L, 107, 113; D. Johnson 121; Ali Jorge 105; Levy 46-7; Richard Mackson, half title, 48-9; Ed Mahan 16L, 29; Al Messerschmidt 29 inset, 39, 72B 99, 103, 131, 143, 149; Vic Milton 18; Bill Mount 37, 41B; Darryl Norenberg 64; Peter Read Miller 28, 50T, 95, 97; PRM 93, 128-9; Kevin Reece 16R; George Rose 35R, 45, 82, 84, 119; Ron Ross 15R, 135; Manny Rubio 46T, 83, 127, 139; Alan Schwartz 101; Robert Shaver 147; Robert L. Smith 8R; Chuck Solomon 137; Paul Spinelli 23, 70T, 72T; Dave Stock 22; Steve Swope 25B; Tony Tomsic 11, 19T, 44, 75, 79, 91, 111, 125, 133, 141; Corky Trewin 89, 123; Greg Trott 27, 31T; Jim Turner 8L, 15L, 21, 26, 41T, 43, 85, 87; Herb Weitman 31B, 38-9; Hank Young 117; Michael Zagaris 14, 36, 51B.

CONTENTS

INTRODUCTION

'For yet another year,' the chairman of the board might report, 'there has been significant improvement on all fronts. Our product has attracted much greater media attention and sales have increased dramatically. We anticipate continued growth at an accelerated rate.' Of course, the speaker is the head of a company which imports American Football.

He might well have added that, on the domestic front, the year has seen a consolidation of the game's infrastructure, referring specifically to the two organizations, firstly BAFL, and subsequently, the Budweiser League, which have done so much to bring into focus the energies of thousands of enthusiasts. If, in the early days, it was little more than a flirtation with this most glamorous of diversions, it is now a serious matter. The teams, which frequently attract gates of more than two thousand, are well-drilled – they know what they are doing.

However, the main thrust of the movement still lies in Channel Four's coverage of the National Football League. In excess of four million people now settle down on Sunday evenings to see a package put together by Gary Franses and his intrepid band, under the heading of Cheerleader Productions. The Super Bowl has a special place in the British sporting calendar.

It is entirely possible that there may come to be another annual event, and here one refers to the American Bowl. The NFL could have given no more definitive a seal of approval than by sending two of its finest emissaries, the Bears and the Cowboys, to our shores. And had they needed confirmation of our commitment, it came with the first postbag of ticket applications. Way back in May, the game was a sell-out.

Speaking of sell-outs, last year's Book was one of the hottest items around. Long before Christmas, there were none to be had. It meant two things, firstly, that I had to go to work for another year and, secondly, that the print run has been increased significantly. I hope that the veterans of three previous efforts will notice an improvement, not least in the number of colour pictures and their more generous distribution. As for the informational side of things, the analyses of the clubs have been enlarged and the presentation of statistical detail modified slightly. Hopefully, the readers, many of whom I have come to know as friends and whose comments I value, will find it acceptable. It represents my best attempts to share my love of this remarkable game.

49ers running back Roger Craig last year became the first player in league history to go over 1,000 yards in both rushing and pass receiving.

CHAPTER ONE

A REVIEW OF THE 1985 SEASON

Prologue

'It's going to be a difficult act to follow,' they said, referring to the 1984 season. And what a season it had been. Almost every major individual record, career and regular-season, had been re-written. And there was a certain club which had set a new all-time best with fifteen regular-season wins, before bringing down the curtain with as comprehensive a display as you'd like to see (unless you were a Miami fan), in Super Bowl XIX.

More than just establishing records, that club, the San Francisco 49ers, had set new standards by the style and efficiency with which they went about the business of winning football games. How could they be stopped? In late January, 1985, then, there was

much head-shaking around the league.

Of 1984's individual record breakers, Chicago running back Walter Payton, the new NFL career-rushing leader, was not yet ready to settle for simply putting the icing on the cake – he was bent on making a bigger cake. Having established a new NFL career record for pass receptions, San Diego wide receiver Charlie Joiner now had his sights set on Don Maynard's all-time mark for yards receiving. For Joiner, another 1,061 yards would do the trick. Minnesota placekicker Jan Stenerud, the league's oldest active player, was returning for a nineteenth year and would be adding to the league record for field goals (358) with every successful kick. Of the younger men who had made 1984 such a memor-

Left: Owen Gill (#44) playing for the Colts

Below: Bruce Smith celebrates selection with his family

able year, Eric Dickerson, Dan Marino and Mark Clayton each spent some or all of the 1985 preseason operating at different levels of brinkmanship, as they sought to reach contractual agreement with their clubs. Come opening day, the Miami pair was back in harness, but Dickerson's return to action would be delayed until Week Three.

Even before the day of the formal collegiate draft, the Buffalo Bills, who held the rights to select first overall, had picked Virginia Tech defensive end Bruce Smith. Following Buffalo's lead, on draft day a further eight clubs would show a preference for beef on the hoof, as two more defensive ends, four tackles and two linebackers were snapped up before the name of Wisconsin wide receiver Al Toon was called by the New York Jets. In what was considered a good year for wide receivers, Eddie Brown (Cincinnati), Jerry Rice (San Francisco) and Jessie Hester (L.A. Raiders) also went in the first round. In twenty-second position, the Bears sprang a surprise by selecting the enormous Clemson defensive tackle, William Perry. The critics argued that he'd need every bit of his undoubted talent, just to move his weight around, and questioned his ability to perform in the pros. Before long, they would get their answer.

In the days leading up to the draft there had been much speculation, on our side of the Atlantic, concerning the destination of the British-born Iowa running back, Owen Gill. As the 53rd selection overall, he went to Seattle, but it was in the colours of the Indianapolis Colts that he would begin his pro career.

The Colts were one of four teams to start out the season under a new head coach. Their man, Rod Dowhower, had gained wide experience in the colleges as an assistant to three future NFL head coaches, Don Coryell (San Diego State, St Louis and the Chargers), Dick Vermeil (UCLA and Philadelphia) and Bill Walsh (Stanford and San Francisco), succeeding the latter at Stanford. After three years as offensive co-ordinator of the Broncos and a further two in the same capacity with St Louis, he was ready to direct his own show. Darryl Rogers, the new head coach at Detroit, was entering his first year in the pros. However, over twenty years in college football, he had earned his spurs at Hayward State, Fresno State, San Jose State, Michigan State and, most recently, Arizona State. His would be the task of revitalising a Lions team which had relinquished its NFC Central division title to Chicago. Leeman Bennett, who took over at Tampa Bay, was no stranger to the NFL's higher echelons. During his tenure as the head coach at Atlanta (1977-82), the Falcons went to the playoffs as a wild card (1978), won their one and only division title (1980) and, in his

William Perry limbers up

final year, they had the best record of any NFC West team (they were 5-4 in the strike-shortened 1982 season). That kind of performance would suit the Buccaneers nicely. Finally, there was Bud Grant, a man's man and a legend in his own time. After coaching the Minnesota Vikings to eleven NFC Central division titles and four Super Bowls, he retired at the end of the 1983 season. During his absence, the Vikings had gone through an unhappy time – he was coming back to put matters right.

When it came to prediction time, few people looked beyond the 49ers, but those who did saw the Rams as a threat in the NFC West. The Bears, who had fallen just short in 1984, seemed to have control of the NFC Central. Over in the NFC East, it was going to be tough all the way from gun to tape. One could imagine every intradivisional game being decided by a field goal. As for the AFC clubs, the Raiders' defense seemed to give them a slight edge in the West, whilst the Dolphins were fancied to hold off the Patriots in the East. The title in the Central always looked likely to go to the club which could win nine games.

And when it came to Super Bowl XX, it would have surprised few people to see San Francisco and Miami taking up where they'd left off.

WEEK ONE

American Football Conference
Indianapolis 3 at Pittsburgh 45
Miami 23 at Houston 26
New York Jets 0 at Los Angeles Raiders 31
San Diego 14 at Buffalo 9
Seattle 28 at Cincinnati 24

National Football Conference
Detroit 28 at Atlanta 27
Philadelphia 0 at New York Giants 21
San Francisco 21 at Minnesota 28
Tampa Bay 28 at Chicago 38
Washington 14 at Dallas 44

Interconference Games
Denver 16 at Los Angeles Rams 20
Green Bay 20 at New England 26
Kansas City 47 at New Orleans 27
St Louis 27 at Cleveland 24 (OT)

Interconference Play
AFC 2, NFC 2

One had the feeling that it was going to be one of those seasons, when, on opening day, both San Francisco and Miami lost to teams, each of whom had managed only three wins in 1984.

Despite having turned the ball over five times on three fumbles and two pass interceptions, the 49ers appeared to have banished the gremlins from their system, and they seemed on the way to victory when running back Roger Craig caught Joe Montana's 19-yard pass for his third touchdown of the day. That gave them a 21-14 lead with 6:06 remaining in the game. However, two more fumble recoveries by the Vikings, on the 49ers one- and 34-yard lines respectively, were converted into touchdowns, the winner coming on a ten-yard run by Ted Brown with just 1:49 to go. The Houston Oilers left it even later – their winning score against Miami came with only 25 seconds to go. Earlier, Miami quarterback Dan Marino had clearly been out of touch and was replaced by Don Strock in the fourth quarter. Strock passed 67 yards to wide receiver Mark Duper for a touchdown to give Miami a 23-19 lead which, surely, would be enough. But Houston quarterback Warren Moon, showing great composure, moved the Oilers 79 yards as the clock wound down, to set up rookie running back Mike Rozier's one-yard plunge. The Cardinals left it later still, as quarterback Neil Lomax brought them into a tie against Cleveland, passing five yards for a touchdown to wide receiver Pat Tilley with only four seconds of regulation time left. Neil O'Donoghue kicked the winner in overtime.

Elsewhere, the Raiders registered ten sacks when scoring their first shutout victory in the 25-game series with the Jets. The Giants did their bit to restore the honour of the city of New York, by sacking Philadelphia quarterback Ron Jaworski eight times. They, too, had a shutout victory, their tenth in that series. The Bears got off to a slow start against Tampa Bay, falling behind 21-7 and trailing, 28-17, at half time. But cornerback Leslie Frazier's 29-yard interception return for a touchdown began a 21-point rally, which was completed when quarterback Jim McMahon, now fully recovered from injury, sneaked one yard for his second rushing touchdown of the game.

ABC TV's Monday Night Game, between Dallas and Washington, was expected to be one of those hand-to-hand combat affairs. And it was, but in the sense that five Joe Theismann passes fell into the hands of Dallas defensive players. Out of a total of six passes picked off by Dallas, two were returned for touchdowns as they romped to a 44-14 victory.

Nick Lowery (Kansas City) kicked field goals of 48, 52, 52 and 34 yards

Mark Malone equalled the Steelers' club record with five touchdown passes and rushed for a touchdown

STANDINGS

AFC East	W	L	T	PF	PA	NFC East	W	L	T	PF	PA
New England	1	0	0	26	20	Dallas	1	0	0	44	14
Buffalo	0	1	0	9	14	N.Y. Giants	1	0	0	21	0
Indianapolis	0	1	0	3	45	St Louis	1	0	0	27	24
Miami	0	1	0	23	26	Philadelphia	0	1	0	0	21
N.Y. Jets	0	1	0	0	31	Washington	0	1	0	14	44
AFC Central						**NFC Central**					
Houston	1	0	0	26	23	Chicago	1	0	0	38	28
Pittsburgh	1	0	0	45	3	Detroit	1	0	0	28	27
Cincinnati	0	1	0	24	28	Minnesota	1	0	0	28	21
Cleveland	0	1	0	24	27	Green Bay	0	1	0	20	26
AFC West						Tampa Bay	0	1	0	28	38
Kansas City	1	0	0	47	27	**NFC West**					
L.A. Raiders	1	0	0	31	0	L.A. Rams	1	0	0	20	16
San Diego	1	0	0	14	9	Atlanta	0	1	0	27	28
Seattle	1	0	0	28	24	New Orleans	0	1	0	27	47
Denver	0	1	0	16	20	San Francisco	0	1	0	21	28

Outstanding Individual Performances

Bill Kenney (Kansas City) completed 22 of 34 passes for 397 yards and three touchdowns.

Louis Lipps (Pittsburgh) caught nine passes for 154 yards and scored three touchdowns.

Carlos Carson (Kansas City) caught eight passes for 173 yards and scored two touchdowns.

Dokie Williams (L.A. Raiders) caught five passes for 131 yards and scored one touchdown.

James Wilder (Tampa Bay) rushed for 166 yards on 27 carries and scored one touchdown.

Gerald Riggs (Atlanta) rushed for 131 yards on 31 carries and scored one touchdown.

Joey Browner (Minnesota) equalled the NFL record with three fumble recoveries in one game.

WEEK TWO

American Football Conference
Buffalo 3 at New York Jets 42
Indianapolis 13 at Miami 30
Los Angeles Raiders 20 at Kansas City 36
Pittsburgh 7 at Cleveland 17
Seattle 49 at San Diego 35

National Football Conference
Atlanta 16 at San Francisco 35
Dallas 21 at Detroit 26
Los Angeles Rams 17 at Philadelphia 6
Minnesota 31 at Tampa Bay 16
New York Giants 20 at Green Bay 23

Interconference Games
Cincinnati 27 at St Louis 41
Houston 13 at Washington 16
New England 7 at Chicago 20
New Orleans 23 at Denver 34

Interconference Play
AFC 3, NFC 5

Yet another shock result, a couple of surprises, a shootout and no little controversy, made for an interesting Week Two.

The shock came in Detroit, where the Lions used two fumble recoveries and two interceptions in opening up a 26-0 lead over Dallas, and then held on in the face of a determined fourth-quarter rally, engineered by replacement quarterback Gary Hogeboom. Hogeboom, who passed for two touchdowns and rushed for another, was not the only disappointed player on the losing team, for whom wide receiver Tony Hill and tight end Doug Cosbie

each caught eleven passes for a combined total of 340 yards.

The surprises came in Green Bay and Kansas City, where the home teams beat the Giants and the Raiders respectively. The Packers needed a late one-yard touchdown run by Eddie Lee Ivery to re-establish a lead they'd held for most of the game. In Kansas City, five field goals from Nick Lowery kept the Chiefs in contact, before they eased away on touchdown receptions by wide receivers Carlos Carson and Stephone Paige.

In San Diego, both quarterbacks loaded up with buckshot and blasted away for an hour, at the end of which, San Diego's Dan Fouts had equalled Sonny Jurgensen's NFL career record of five 400-yards-passing games. Seattle quarterback Dave Krieg's 307 yards looked modest by comparison, but he threw five touchdown passes, four of which were to wide receiver Daryl Turner. And Seattle running back Curt Warner confirmed his return to full fitness in the best possible way, rushing for 169 yards and two touchdowns.

The controversy arose in Washington, where the Houston Oilers saw two touchdowns nullified by officials' decisions which, after the game, were acknowledged as incorrect by Art McNally, the NFL's supervisor of officials. Completing a frustrating day for Houston, placekicker Tony Zendejas failed with a late 33-yard field goal attempt which could have brought them level. And it was a relieved Washington team which held on for a 16-13 win.

There was relief, too, in Miami, where Dan Marino answered the derision from the home crowd with a masterly display in the Dolphins' 30-13 victory over the Colts.

STANDINGS

AFC East	W	L	T	PF	PA	NFC East	W	L	T	PF	PA
Miami	1	1	0	53	39	St Louis	2	0	0	68	51
New England	1	1	0	33	40	Dallas	1	1	0	65	40
N.Y. Jets	1	1	0	42	34	N.Y. Giants	1	1	0	41	23
Buffalo	0	2	0	12	56	Washington	1	1	0	30	57
Indianapolis	0	2	0	16	75	Philadelphia	0	2	0	6	38
AFC Central						**NFC Central**					
Cleveland	1	1	0	41	34	Chicago	2	0	0	58	35
Houston	1	1	0	39	39	Detroit	2	0	0	54	48
Pittsburgh	1	1	0	52	20	Minnesota	2	0	0	59	37
Cincinnati	0	2	0	51	69	Green Bay	1	1	0	43	46
AFC West						Tampa Bay	0	2	0	44	69
Kansas City	2	0	0	83	47	**NFC West**					
Seattle	2	0	0	77	59	L.A. Rams	2	0	0	37	22
Denver	1	1	0	50	43	San Francisco	1	1	0	56	44
L.A. Raiders	1	1	0	51	36	Atlanta	0	2	0	43	63
San Diego	1	1	0	49	58	New Orleans	0	2	0	50	81

Outstanding Individual Performances

Dave Krieg (Seattle) completed 22 of 32 passes for 307 yards and five touchdowns.

Wes Chandler (San Diego) caught 13 passes for 243 yards and scored one touchdown.

Tony Hill (Dallas) caught 11 passes for 181 yards and scored two touchdowns.

Doug Cosbie (Dallas) caught 11 passes for 159 yards.

Freeman McNeil (N.Y. Jets) rushed for 192 yards on 18 carries and scored two touchdowns.

Curt Warner (Seattle) rushed for 169 yards on 28 carries and scored two touchdowns.

Charles White (L.A. Rams) rushed for 144 yards on 36 carries and scored one touchdown.

Left: Dan Fouts (San Diego) completed 29 of 43 passes for 440 yards and four touchdowns

Below: Daryl Turner (Seattle) beats Wayne Davis of San Diego to catch one of his four touchdown passes in the game

WEEK THREE

American Football Conference
Houston 0 at Pittsburgh 20
Kansas City 0 at Miami 31
New England 17 at Buffalo 14
San Diego 44 at Cincinnati 41

National Football Conference
Chicago 33 at Minnesota 24
Philadelphia 19 at Washington 6
St Louis 17 at New York Giants 27
Tampa Bay 13 at New Orleans 20

Intercorerence Games
Cleveland 7 at Dallas 20
Denver 44 at Atlanta 28
Detroit 6 at Indianapolis 14
Los Angeles Rams 35 at Seattle 24
New York Jets 24 at Green Bay 3 (played in Milwaukee)
San Francisco 34 at Los Angeles Raiders 10

Interconference Play
AFC 6, NFC 8

It was more like a normal week in the NFL, with Eric Dickerson returning to rush for 150 yards in the Rams' 35-24 victory over Seattle. The 49ers, too, were at their 1984 best in beating the Raiders for whom, sadly, quarterback Jim Plunkett was lost for the season with a shoulder dislocation. The Dolphins banished the memory of their hesitant start with a 31-0 shutout over Kansas City, and the Cowboys were virtually flawless in defeating a Cleveland team which was coming off a good victory over its traditional rival, the Pittsburgh Steelers. Yes, it was all taking shape, even to the extent of a 'normal' show from the Chargers offense.

The fans in San Diego will tell you that the Chargers don't regroup, they simply reload, and on Week Three they slipped a mini-cartridge into the breech. Lionel James's 290-yard performance, the previous week, had been somewhat masked by the thunder of the big guns. But nothing could hide his multi-offensive display against Cincinnati, which ranks alongside the finest of all time. Rushing, catching passes, and returning kickoffs and punts, he clocked up a total of 316 yards. He scored touchdowns on a 56-yard run and a 60-yard pass reception, and was robbed of having the biggest offensive day in league history when a 100-yard kickoff return was called back for an infringement. James, all 5ft 6in and 170 pounds of him, and a four-touchdown performance from quarterback Dan Fouts, swept the Chargers to a 44-41 victory.

Before that game, on Thursday evening, a national TV audience had been given a treat by those old

Dwaine Board (San Francisco) registered four quarterback sacks

rivals, Minnesota and Chicago. With quarterback Tommy Kramer filling the air with passes, the Vikings went out to a 17-9 lead, halfway through the third quarter. It was then that Bears quarterback Jim McMahon, who had been troubled with neck spasms and an infected leg, came off the bench. On his first play from scrimmage, he hit wide receiver Willie Gault with a 70-yard touchdown pass. On his second play, he passed 25 yards for a touchdown to wide receiver Dennis McKinnon. His third score took a little longer – he warmed up with five plays from scrimmage, before passing 43 yards, again to McKinnon, for a touchdown. It was enough for a victory which left Chicago and the Rams as the only unbeaten teams going into Week Four.

Left: George Wonsley (Indianapolis) rushed for a career-best 170 yards on 27 carries

Below: Tommy Kramer (Minnesota) completed 28 of 55 passes for 436 yards and three touchdowns

STANDINGS

AFC East	W	L	T	PF	PA
Miami	2	1	0	84	39
New England	2	1	0	50	54
N.Y. Jets	2	1	0	66	37
Indianapolis	1	2	0	30	81
Buffalo	0	3	0	26	73
AFC Central					
Pittsburgh	2	1	0	72	20
Cleveland	1	2	0	48	54
Houston	1	2	0	39	59
Cincinnati	0	3	0	92	113
AFC West					
Denver	2	1	0	94	71
Kansas City	2	1	0	83	78
San Diego	2	1	0	93	99
Seattle	2	1	0	101	94
L.A. Raiders	1	2	0	61	70

NFC East	W	L	T	PF	PA
Dallas	2	1	0	85	47
N.Y. Giants	2	1	0	68	40
St Louis	2	1	0	85	78
Philadelphia	1	2	0	25	44
Washington	1	2	0	36	76
NFC Central					
Chicago	3	0	0	91	59
Detroit	2	1	0	60	62
Minnesota	2	1	0	83	70
Green Bay	1	2	0	46	70
Tampa Bay	0	3	0	57	89
NFC West					
L.A. Rams	3	0	0	72	46
San Francisco	2	1	0	90	54
New Orleans	1	2	0	70	94
Atlanta	0	3	0	71	107

Outstanding Individual Performances

Dan Fouts (San Diego) completed 25 of 43 passes for 344 yards and four touchdowns.

Boomer Esiason (Cincinnati) completed 26 of 44 passes for 320 yards and three touchdowns.

Cris Collinsworth (Cincinnati) caught ten passes for 161 yards and scored two touchdowns.

Willie Gault (Chicago) caught six passes for 146 yards, including a 70-yard touchdown reception.

Dennis McKinnon (Chicago) caught four passes for 133 yards and scored two touchdowns.

Lionel James (San Diego) rushed for 127 yards on 12 carries, caught five passes for 118 yards and scored touchdowns with a 56-yard run and a 60-yard pass reception.

Eric Dickerson (L.A. Rams) rushed for 150 yards on 31 carries and scored three touchdowns.

WEEK FOUR

American Football Conference
Cincinnati 37 at Pittsburgh 24
Cleveland 21 at San Diego 7
Indianapolis 20 at New York Jets 25
Los Angeles Raiders 35 at New England 20
Miami 30 at Denver 26
Seattle 7 at Kansas City 28

National Football Conference
Atlanta 6 at Los Angeles Rams 17
Green Bay 28 at St Louis 43
New Orleans 20 at San Francisco 17
New York Giants 16 at Philadelphia 10 (OT)
Tampa Bay 9 at Detroit 30
Washington 10 at Chicago 45

Intercoference Games
Dallas 17 at Houston 10
Minnesota 27 at Buffalo 20

Interconference Play
AFC 6, NFC 10

On Week Four, the Bears entertained Washington, though a 45-10 thrashing would hardly come under any definition of hospitality. In the early going the Redskins had looked solid, easing to a 10-0 lead. But a 99-yard kickoff return for a touchdown by Willie Gault signalled the beginning of a 31-point second-quarter avalanche, which buried the Redskins for good. In the game, McMahon threw three touchdown passes and caught a touchdown pass from Walter Payton (it was the eighth touchdown pass of Payton's career). The Rams were less expressive but nonetheless, impressive, in a 17-6 victory which maintained their own unbeaten record and kept the Falcons as one of three teams without a win on the season. San Francisco's upset defeat, at home to New Orleans, left the Rams with a two-game margin on top of the NFC West.

With running back James Brooks dodging for 133 yards, the Cincinnati Bengals broke their duck against Pittsburgh. But they had to withstand a bombardment from Steelers quarterback Mark Malone, who threw for 374 yards, 151 of them to wide receiver John Stallworth. And it was when Malone attempted a late pass to Stallworth that a hobbling Cincinnati cornerback, Ray Horton, nipped in for an interception to kill the threat and help preserve the win.

Up in Mile High Stadium, as expected, quarterbacks Dan Marino and John Elway traded missile for missile, before Marino found wide receiver Vince

Below: Deron Cherry (Kansas City) equalled the NFL record with four interceptions in one game

Philadelphia's Reggie White registered 2.5 quarterback sacks on his NFL debut

Heflin with a 46-yard touchdown pass to put the Dolphins ahead to stay. Against the Seattle Seahawks, the Chiefs were outgained but they took their chances and, rightly, went into Week Five as leaders of the AFC West. In that game, Kansas City's Deron Cherry had equalled an NFL record with four interceptions. 'Remarkable,' one might say, but it was not entirely unexpected – in their last three meetings Seattle and Kansas City have picked off twenty-one passes. The Cowboys sacked Houston quarterback Warren Moon twelve times (it equalled the NFL record), but needed a late touchdown pass from Danny White to tight end Fred Cornwell to break a 10-10 deadlock. The Giants kept pace in the NFC East with an overtime win against Philadelphia, and the Cardinals matched them, step-for-step, by beating Green Bay 43-28.

A late touchdown by Minnesota's Ted Brown broke a 20-20 tie with Buffalo, whose head coach, Kay Stephenson was released after the game.

Outstanding Individual Performances

Dan Marino (Miami) completed 25 of 43 passes for 390 yards and three touchdowns.

Mark Malone (Pittsburgh) completed 26 of 44 passes for 374 yards and three touchdowns.

John Stallworth (Pittsburgh) caught 11 passes for 151 yards and scored one touchdown.

Henry Ellard (L.A. Rams) caught five passes for 123 yards including a 64-yard touchdown reception.

Tony Nathan (Miami) caught ten passes for 120 yards..

James Brooks (Cincinnati) rushed for 133 yards on 18 carries and scored two touchdowns.

Kevin Mack (Cleveland) rushed for 130 yards on 16 carries and scored touchdowns in both rushing and pass receiving.

Tony Dorsett (Dallas) rushed for 159 yards on 22 carries

STANDINGS					
AFC East	**W**	**L**	**T**	**PF**	**PA**
Miami	3	1	0	114	65
N.Y. Jets	3	1	0	91	57
New England	2	2	0	70	89
Indianapolis	1	3	0	50	106
Buffalo	0	4	0	46	100
AFC Central					
Cleveland	2	2	0	69	61
Pittsburgh	2	2	0	96	57
Cincinnati	1	3	0	129	137
Houston	1	3	0	49	76
AFC West					
Kansas City	3	1	0	111	85
Denver	2	2	0	120	101
L.A. Raiders	2	2	0	96	90
San Diego	2	2	0	100	120
Seattle	2	2	0	108	122
NFC East	**W**	**L**	**T**	**PF**	**PA**
Dallas	3	1	0	102	57
N.Y. Giants	3	1	0	84	50
St Louis	3	1	0	128	106
Philadelphia	1	3	0	35	60
Washington	1	3	0	46	121
NFC Central					
Chicago	4	0	0	136	69
Detroit	3	1	0	90	71
Minnesota	3	1	0	110	90
Green Bay	1	3	0	74	113
Tampa Bay	0	4	0	66	119
NFC West					
L.A. Rams	4	0	0	89	52
New Orleans	2	2	0	90	111
San Francisco	2	2	0	107	74
Atlanta	0	4	0	77	124

WEEK FIVE

American Football Conference
Buffalo 17 at Indianapolis 49
Houston 20 at Denver 31
Kansas City 10 at Los Angeles Raiders 19
New England 20 at Cleveland 24
New York Jets 29 at Cincinnati 20
Pittsburgh 20 at Miami 24
San Diego 21 at Seattle 26

National Football Conference
Chicago 27 at Tampa Bay 19
Dallas 30 at New York Giants 29
Detroit 10 at Green Bay 43
Minnesota 10 at Los Angeles Rams 13
Philadelphia 21 at New Orleans 23
San Francisco 38 at Atlanta 17
St Louis 10 at Washington 27

Interconference Play
AFC 6, NFC 10

Joe Montana (San Francisco) completed 37 of 57 passes for 429 yards and five touchdowns

It was time to renew a few domestic squabbles on Week Five, when there were no interconference matchups. The Raiders gained revenge for their earlier loss to Kansas City and nudged the Chiefs along a losing path which would not, as it turned out, change direction until Week Twelve. Denver beat Houston and Seattle beat San Diego (they were without the injured Dan Fouts), producing a four-way tie on top of the AFC West, with the Chargers only one game adrift. Cleveland's 24-20 victory over New England, coupled with Pittsburgh's loss to Miami, gave the Browns a one-game lead in the AFC Central. With the one-two punch provided by Earnest Byner and Kevin Mack, the Browns were now recognised as a solid rushing club – and that's usually an indicator of future prosperity. The Dolphins were settling into their normal position, on top of the AFC East, but they shared that spot with the Jets who, without much fuss, had erased the memory of their opening-day shutout. Over the last four games, they'd conceded only 46 points, and their top

STANDINGS

AFC East	W	L	T	PF	PA	NFC East	W	L	T	PF	PA
Miami	4	1	0	138	85	Dallas	4	1	0	132	86
N.Y. Jets	4	1	0	120	77	N.Y. Giants	3	2	0	113	80
Indianapolis	2	3	0	99	123	St Louis	3	2	0	138	133
New England	2	3	0	90	113	Washington	2	3	0	73	131
Buffalo	0	5	0	63	149	Philadelphia	1	4	0	56	83
AFC Central						**NFC Central**					
Cleveland	3	2	0	93	81	Chicago	5	0	0	163	88
Pittsburgh	2	3	0	116	81	Detroit	3	2	0	100	114
Cincinnati	1	4	0	149	166	Minnesota	3	2	0	120	103
Houston	1	4	0	69	107	Green Bay	2	3	0	117	123
AFC West						Tampa Bay	0	5	0	85	146
Denver	3	2	0	151	121	**NFC West**					
Kansas City	3	2	0	121	104	L.A. Rams	5	0	0	102	62
L.A. Raiders	3	2	0	115	100	New Orleans	3	2	0	113	132
Seattle	3	2	0	134	143	San Francisco	3	2	0	145	91
San Diego	2	3	0	121	146	Atlanta	0	5	0	94	162

Above: New England's Stanley Morgan (#86) missed this one but caught six passes for 140 yards and a touchdown

James Lofton (Green Bay) caught ten passes for 151 yards

running back, Freeman McNeil, was warming up.

As if to demonstrate that there's not much difference between top and bottom, the Tampa Bay Buccaneers gave Chicago the runaround for much of a game in which, at one time, they led 12-0. Both Jimmie Giles and Kevin House caught passes for 100 or more yards. But the Bucs couldn't quite stay the pace against a Bears club which, for the fourth time in the season, came from behind to win. The Rams, too, preserved their unbeaten record, but it was only after a decision, uncharacteristic of Minnesota head coach Bud Grant. On first down at the Rams one-yard line, with one second remaining in the game, Grant discarded the safe option of an easy field goal which would have levelled the scores. Somebody was going to be a hero. As it turned out, the glory went to Rams' linebacker Jim Collins, who stopped Minnesota's Darrin Nelson short of the goal line. Against the Cowboys, quarterback Phil Simms went to the air and brought the Giants back to lead 26-14, with touchdown passes of 51 and 23 yards to wide receiver Lionel Manuel, and a 70-yard scoring pass to rookie running back George Adams. However, a touchdown reception by Mike Renfro and three subsequent Rafael Septien field goals against the Giants' one, gave Dallas both a one-point victory and a one-game lead on top of the NFC East.

Outstanding Individual Performances

Phil Simms (N.Y. Giants) completed 18 of 36 passes for 432 yards and three touchdowns.

Steve DeBerg (Tampa Bay) completed 23 of 43 passes for 346 yards and one touchdown.

Mark Herrmann (San Diego) completed 26 of 35 passes for 344 yards and three touchdowns.

Roger Craig (San Francisco) caught 12 passes for 167 yards and scored one touchdown.

Wes Chandler (San Diego) caught nine passes for 150 yards and scored two touchdowns.

Marcus Allen (L.A. Raiders) rushed for 126 yards on 29 carries.

WEEK SIX

American Football Conference
Buffalo 3 at New England 14
Cleveland 21 at Houston 6
Denver 15 at Indianapolis 10
Kansas City 20 at San Diego 31
Miami 7 at New York Jets 23

National Football Conference
Chicago 26 at San Francisco 10
Detroit 3 at Washington 24
Los Angeles Rams 31 at Tampa Bay 27
Minnesota 17 at Green Bay 20 (played in Milwaukee)
St Louis 7 at Philadelphia 30 (venue switched because of World Series clash)

Interconference Games
Atlanta 26 at Seattle 30
New Orleans 13 at Los Angeles Raiders 23
New York Giants 30 at Cincinnati 35
Pittsburgh 13 at Dallas 27

Interconference Play
AFC 9, NFC 11

It was against San Francisco on Week Six that the Bears faced their first really serious test – until then they'd beaten only one former playoff club, the Redskins. And they went on to gain revenge for their loss in the 1984 NFC Championship Game, in a style which would set the pattern for the remainder of the season. Sacking 49ers quarterback Joe Montana seven times and allowing only three yards rushing in the second half, they won fair and square. Increasingly, the Rams were relying on defense for their victories and the trend continued against Tampa Bay, when it took two second-half touchdowns on interception returns to overhaul the winless Buccaneers. This week, Minnesota did the smart thing, going for a game-tying 18-yard field goal with 1:24 remaining against Green Bay. But the Packers won, 20-17, on a field goal with seven seconds left – maybe the 'Vikes' should have gone for the touch-

Phil Simms (N.Y. Giants) completed 40 of 62 passes for 513 yards and one touchdown, while Seattle's Dave Krieg (inset) completed 33 of 51 passes for 405 yards and four touchdowns

Freeman McNeil (N.Y. Jets) rushed for 173 yards on 28 carries

down. For the second week in a row, it was a bitter-sweet day for Giants quarterback Phil Simms, who passed for 513 yards, the second-best total in league history, and yet finished on the losing side. The Giants had fought back to trail by only one point, after the unpredictable Bengals had jumped out to a 21-0 lead. But two big defensive plays, firstly a pass interception which Cincinnati's Ray Griffin returned directly for a touchdown, and then a Reggie Williams fumble return to set up another touchdown, took the Bengals clear.

In the AFC's major confrontation, the Jets beat Miami with some ease. Led by Freeman McNeil, who rushed for 173 yards, they rolled up 476 net yards offense and, in restricting the Dolphins to just 200 net yards, it was confirmed that they also had a defense. The win took the Jets one game clear in the AFC East, ahead of the Dolphins, who now had to keep an eye on New England. The Patriots had made a modest start, and they were trailing Buffalo 3-0 in the second quarter, when starting quarter-back Tony Eason was forced out with an injured shoulder. Eason's replacement, Steve Grogan, proceeded to fumble his first snap from scrimmage. But then he gave us a glimpse of that old free-wheeling style, passing for 282 yards and the touchdown which set the Patriots on the road to victory. The Patriots were now on the move.

Outstanding Individual Performances

Mark Bavaro (N.Y. Giants) caught 12 passes for 176 yards.

Clarence Weathers (Cleveland) caught three passes for 146 yards, including a 68-yard touchdown reception.

Irving Fryar (New England) caught six passes for 132 yards and scored one touchdown.

Gerald Riggs (Atlanta) rushed for 139 yards on 23 carries.

Walter Payton (Chicago) rushed for 132 yards on 24 carries and scored two touchdowns.

Herman Hunter (Philadelphia) caught six passes for 120 yards and scored one touchdown.

STANDINGS

AFC East	W	L	T	PF	PA	NFC East	W	L	T	PF	PA
N.Y. Jets	5	1	0	143	84	Dallas	5	1	0	159	99
Miami	4	2	0	145	108	N.Y. Giants	3	3	0	143	115
New England	3	3	0	104	116	St Louis	3	3	0	145	163
Indianapolis	2	4	0	109	138	Washington	3	3	0	97	134
Buffalo	0	6	0	66	163	Philadelphia	2	4	0	86	90
AFC Central						**NFC Central**					
Cleveland	4	2	0	114	87	Chicago	6	0	0	189	98
Cincinnati	2	4	0	184	196	Detroit	3	3	0	103	138
Pittsburgh	2	4	0	129	108	Green Bay	3	3	0	137	140
Houston	1	5	0	75	128	Minnesota	3	3	0	137	123
AFC West						Tampa Bay	0	6	0	112	177
Denver	4	2	0	166	131	**NFC West**					
L.A. Raiders	4	2	0	138	113	L.A. Rams	6	0	0	133	89
Seattle	4	2	0	164	169	New Orleans	3	3	0	126	155
Kansas City	3	3	0	141	135	San Francisco	3	3	0	155	117
San Diego	3	3	0	152	166	Atlanta	0	6	0	120	192

WEEK SEVEN

American Football Conference
Cincinnati 27 at Houston 44
Indianapolis 9 at Buffalo 21
Los Angeles Raiders 21 at Cleveland 20
New York Jets 13 at New England 20
Seattle 10 at Denver 13 (OT)

National Football Conference
Dallas 14 at Philadelphia 16
Green Bay 7 at Chicago 23
New Orleans 24 at Atlanta 31
San Francisco 21 at Detroit 23
Washington 3 at New York Giants 17

Interconference Games
Los Angeles Rams 16 at Kansas City 0
St Louis 10 at Pittsburgh 23
San Diego 17 at Minnesota 21
Tampa Bay 38 at Miami 41

Interconference Play
AFC 11, NFC 13

Above: Kenny Jackson (Philadelphia) caught six passes for 134 yards and scored one touchdown

Opposite: Jimmie Giles (Tampa Bay) returned to his best form, catching seven passes for 116 yards and four touchdowns

On Week Seven, there was competition for the headlines. Atlanta and Buffalo each scored their first victories of the campaign, Tampa Bay almost joined them, Philadelphia beat Dallas, Detroit beat San Francisco and New England beat the Jets. But they were all relegated to the small print by a large figure, indeed a very large figure, Chicago's rookie defensive tackle, William Perry. 'The Refrigerator', as he was already known, not least for his consumption of things normally contained therein, came on as a fullback and went off as the media's darling. In the former capacity he saw action three times but, twice, he delivered crushing blocks, clearing the way for Walter Payton touchdowns. Inbetween those, he rushed for one himself. From now on, he would never be out of the spotlight. That victory over Green Bay left the Bears at 7-0 and though they weren't saying much about the prospects of a perfect season, lots of people were. The Rams, too, continued in the same vein, though still on the strength of their defense. They intercepted quarterback Todd Blackledge six times in holding the Chiefs scoreless.

Against the Jets it wasn't Steve Grogan the 'bomber' but rather, Grogan the crafty bootlegger, who ran three yards for the touchdown which broke a 13-13 tie. Spare a thought for Tampa Bay. They'd given Chicago two tough games and now, they clawed back into a 38-38 tie with Miami, only to lose on a Fuad Reveiz field goal in the dying seconds of the game. In other close finishes around the league, just 29 seconds remained when tight end Todd

Christensen caught an eight-yard, fourth-down pass from Marc Wilson, giving the Raiders a 21-20 win over Cleveland. In Minnesota, a mere nineteen seconds remained when quarterback Tommy Kramer passed to Leo Lewis for the winning touchdown against San Diego. Denver's Rich Karlis is one of those placekickers to whom the responsibility for winning the game seems to fall more often than normal. And against Seattle he obliged with a 24-yard effort in overtime. Curiously, with just one minor alteration, the AFC's playoff teams were now in position, and astonishingly, the same was also true of the NFC.

Outstanding Individual Performances

Boomer Esiason (Cincinnati) completed 30 of 52 passes for 381 yards and three touchdowns.

Ron Jaworski (Philadelphia) completed 22 of 35 passes for 380 yards and one touchdown.

Steve DeBerg (Tampa Bay) completed 19 of 32 passes for 365 yards and four touchdowns.

Gary Clark (Washington) caught 11 passes for 193 yards.

Billy Johnson (Atlanta) caught 11 passes for 153 yards.

Wesley Walker (N.Y. Jets) caught six passes for 140 yards.

Curt Warner (Seattle) rushed for 136 yards on 27 carries.

James Jones (Detroit) rushed for 116 yards on 30 carries and scored one touchdown.

STANDINGS

AFC East	W	L	T	PF	PA
Miami	5	2	0	186	146
N.Y. Jets	5	2	0	156	104
New England	4	3	0	124	129
Indianapolis	2	5	0	118	159
Buffalo	1	6	0	87	172
AFC Central					
Cleveland	4	3	0	134	108
Pittsburgh	3	4	0	152	118
Cincinnati	2	5	0	211	240
Houston	2	5	0	119	155
AFC West					
Denver	5	2	0	179	141
L.A. Raiders	5	2	0	159	133
Seattle	4	3	0	174	182
Kansas City	3	4	0	141	151
San Diego	3	4	0	169	187

NFC East	W	L	T	PF	PA
Dallas	5	2	0	173	115
N.Y. Giants	4	3	0	160	118
Philadelphia	3	4	0	102	104
St Louis	3	4	0	155	186
Washington	3	4	0	100	151
NFC Central					
Chicago	7	0	0	212	105
Detroit	4	3	0	126	159
Minnesota	4	3	0	158	140
Green Bay	3	4	0	144	163
Tampa Bay	0	7	0	150	218
NFC West					
L.A. Rams	7	0	0	149	89
New Orleans	3	4	0	150	186
San Francisco	3	4	0	176	140
Atlanta	1	6	0	151	216

WEEK EIGHT

American Football Conference
Denver 30 at Kansas City 10
Pittsburgh 21 at Cincinnati 26
San Diego 21 at Los Angeles Raiders 34
Seattle 14 at New York Jets 17

National Football Conference
Atlanta 10 at Dallas 24
Minnesota 9 at Chicago 27
New York Giants 21 at New Orleans 13
San Francisco 28 at Los Angeles Rams 14

Interconference Games
Buffalo 17 at Philadelphia 21
Green Bay 10 at Indianapolis 37
Houston 20 at St Louis 10
Miami 21 at Detroit 31
New England 32 at Tampa Bay 14
Washington 14 at Cleveland 7

Interconference Play
AFC 14, NFC 16

Approaching the halfway stage, the 49ers were in danger of being written off, having gone down to Detroit the previous week and now facing a game in which a loss would put them out of serious contention. But they came back in the best possible way, mounting a show of flawless football in handing the Rams their first defeat of the season. San Francisco quarterback Joe Montana passed for 306 yards and three touchdowns, before retiring with a bruised sternum. By then, they led the Rams 28-0 and it was just a matter of coasting home. The Bears, however, continued their march, this time at the expense of Minnesota, whose quarterbacks were

Opposite, top: Todd Christensen (L.A. Raiders) caught seven passes for 134 yards

intercepted five times. In the NFC East, St Louis was the only loser, despite moving out to a first-quarter 10-0 lead over Houston. In a division they had been fancied to win, the Cardinals now occupied bottom place and there they would remain for the rest of the season. Led by wide receiver Tony Hill, who caught ten passes for 161 yards and a touchdown, and a 60-yard touchdown run by Tony Dorsett, Dallas overcame a ten-point deficit against Atlanta, for whom placekicker Mick Luckhurst saw a sequence of successful field goal attempts end at 17.

In the AFC, the West was becoming a two-horse race, with both Denver and the Raiders scoring victories over divisional opponents. And the Jets disposed of the Seahawks – so what, wasn't that a true reflection of the 1985 formline? Much more – it was the Jets' first victory over Seattle at the eighth attempt. Underpinned by a 151-yards-rushing performance from Freeman McNeil, who also caught a 16-yard touchdown pass, the Jets overcame a 14-0 half-time deficit and erased a trivia question from the quiz books. The win was all the more significant in the light of Miami's loss to the Detroit Lions, who thus claimed their third big scalp of the season.

In the Central, Cincinnati's win over Pittsburgh gave them a valuable 'double' which might, just might, come in handy when it came to the end-of-season sorting out.

Opposite, centre: Robert Jackson (Cincinnati) intercepted two passes, one of which he returned 57 yards for a touchdown

Opposite, below: The Colts' Eugene Daniel (#38) returning one of his three interceptions against Green Bay

STANDINGS

AFC East	W	L	T	PF	PA	NFC East	W	L	T	PF	PA
N.Y. Jets	6	2	0	173	118	Dallas	6	2	0	197	125
Miami	5	3	0	207	177	N.Y. Giants	5	3	0	181	131
New England	5	3	0	156	143	Philadelphia	4	4	0	123	121
Indianapolis	3	5	0	155	169	Washington	4	4	0	114	158
Buffalo	1	7	0	104	193	St Louis	3	5	0	165	206
AFC Central						**NFC Central**					
Cleveland	4	4	0	141	122	Chicago	8	0	0	239	114
Cincinnati	3	5	0	237	261	Detroit	5	3	0	157	180
Houston	3	5	0	139	165	Minnesota	4	4	0	167	167
Pittsburgh	3	5	0	173	144	Green Bay	3	5	0	154	200
AFC West						Tampa Bay	0	8	0	164	250
Denver	6	2	0	209	151	**NFC West**					
L.A. Raiders	6	2	0	193	154	L.A. Rams	7	1	0	163	117
Seattle	4	4	0	188	199	San Francisco	4	4	0	204	154
Kansas City	3	5	0	151	181	New Orleans	3	5	0	163	207
San Diego	3	5	0	190	221	Atlanta	1	7	0	161	240

Outstanding Individual Performances

Danny White (Dallas) completed 27 of 47 passes for 362 yards, passed for one touchdown and rushed for another.

Dieter Brock (L.A. Rams) completed 35 of 51 passes for 344 yards and two touchdowns.

Tony Hill (Dallas) caught ten passes for 161 yards and scored one touchdown.

Leonard Thompson (Detroit) caught six passes for 133 yards and scored one touchdown.

Roger Craig (San Francisco) caught six passes for 132 yards, rushed for 63 yards on 14 carries and scored two touchdowns.

Drew Hill (Houston) caught six passes for 132 yards and scored one touchdown.

Freeman McNeil (N.Y. Jets) rushed for 151 yards on 22 carries and caught a touchdown pass.

Stump Mitchell (St Louis) rushed for 148 yards on 21 carries and caught four passes for 63 yards.

WEEK NINE

American Football Conference
Cincinnati 23 at Buffalo 17
Cleveland 9 at Pittsburgh 10
Denver 10 at San Diego 30
Kansas City 20 at Houston 23
Los Angeles Raiders 3 at Seattle 33
Miami 13 at New England 17
New York Jets 35 at Indianapolis 17

National Football Conference
Chicago 16 at Green Bay 10
Dallas 10 at St Louis 21
Detroit 13 at Minnesota 16
New Orleans 10 at Los Angeles Rams 28
Philadelphia 13 at San Francisco 24
Tampa Bay 20 at New York Giants 22
Washington 44 at Atlanta 10

Interconference Play
AFC 14, NFC 16

The Raiders usually write off one game each year against Seattle, and the pen was out long before the end of a 33-3 hammering. Even so, it counted as one of the four upsets to which, also, San Diego, Minnesota and St Louis could lay claim. With Dan Fouts back to full fitness, the Chargers had little trouble handling Denver. And the Cardinals moved serenely to an eleven-point win after giving Dallas a ten-point start. Minnesota left it until late, in fact as late as possible, with Jan Stenerud kicking a 28-yard field goal to beat Detroit as the clock ran out.

But you can always rely on Cleveland losing away from home to Pittsburgh, at least, they did just that for the sixteenth time in a row. That result, together with wins by Cincinnati and Houston, brought all four AFC Central teams into a tie for first place, or bottom

Outstanding Individual Performances

Mike Quick (Philadelphia) caught six passes for 146 yards, including an 82-yard touchdown reception.

Mark Clayton (Miami) caught seven passes for 122 yards.

Walter Payton (Chicago) rushed for 192 yards on 28 carries and scored one touchdown.

Keith Griffin (Washington) rushed for 164 yards on 16 carries and scored two touchdowns.

Freeman McNeil (N.Y. Jets) rushed for 149 yards on 26 carries and scored one touchdown.

Joe Morris (N.Y. Giants) rushed for 132 yards on 26 carries and scored one touchdown.

Larry Kinnebrew (Cincinnati) rushed for 128 yards on 30 carries and scored one touchdown.

Eric Schubert (N.Y. Giants) kicked five field goals on his NFL debut

STANDINGS

AFC East	W	L	T	PF	PA	NFC East	W	L	T	PF	PA
N.Y. Jets	7	2	0	208	135	Dallas	6	3	0	207	146
New England	6	3	0	173	156	N.Y. Giants	6	3	0	203	151
Miami	5	4	0	220	194	Washington	5	4	0	158	168
Indianapolis	3	6	0	172	204	Philadelphia	4	5	0	136	145
Buffalo	1	8	0	121	216	St Louis	4	5	0	186	216
AFC Central						**NFC Central**					
Cincinnati	4	5	0	260	278	Chicago	9	0	0	255	124
Cleveland	4	5	0	150	132	Detroit	5	4	0	170	196
Houston	4	5	0	162	185	Minnesota	5	4	0	183	180
Pittsburgh	4	5	0	183	153	Green Bay	3	6	0	164	216
AFC West						Tampa Bay	0	9	0	184	272
Denver	6	3	0	219	181	**NFC West**					
L.A. Raiders	6	3	0	196	187	L.A. Rams	8	1	0	191	127
Seattle	5	4	0	221	202	San Francisco	5	4	0	228	167
San Diego	4	5	0	220	231	New Orleans	3	6	0	173	235
Kansas City	3	6	0	171	204	Atlanta	1	8	0	171	284

place, depending on how you look at it.

The William Perry Road Show stopped over in Green Bay, and the star attraction obliged the customers with a touchdown, this time on a four-yard pass reception. But the Bears needed 192 yards rushing from Walter Payton and a fourth-quarter comeback to beat the Packers. The Rams bounced back from their defeat with yet another awesome defensive show, as they sacked the Saints' quarterbacks nine times and picked off three passes.

For the Giants, running back Joe Morris underlined his 104-yard rushing performance on Week Eight, with a 132-yard effort against Tampa Bay. He'd take some watching from now on. But for the moment, all eyes were upon the Giants' kicker, Eric Schubert. He was called into the squad only on the Friday before the game and, in a unique NFL debut, kicked five field goals. The win took the Giants into a first-place tie with Dallas, one win ahead of Washington, who had outrushed Atlanta to win 44-10. In that game, Washington's pair of Keith Griffin and George Rogers rushed for 164 and 124 yards respectively, and Atlanta's Gerald Riggs rushed for 127 yards – lovely stuff.

At the end of Week Nine, there could be no doubting the authenticity of the Patriots' surge which had brought them four straight victories. Again, Steve Grogan had occupied centre stage, throwing a 28-yard touchdown pass on fourth down, after surviving the intricacies of a flea-flicker, and then rushing for the winner. The defeated Dolphins were left with a few matters over which to ponder.

Ron Jaworski (Philadelphia) completed 24 of 48 passes for 394 yards and one touchdown

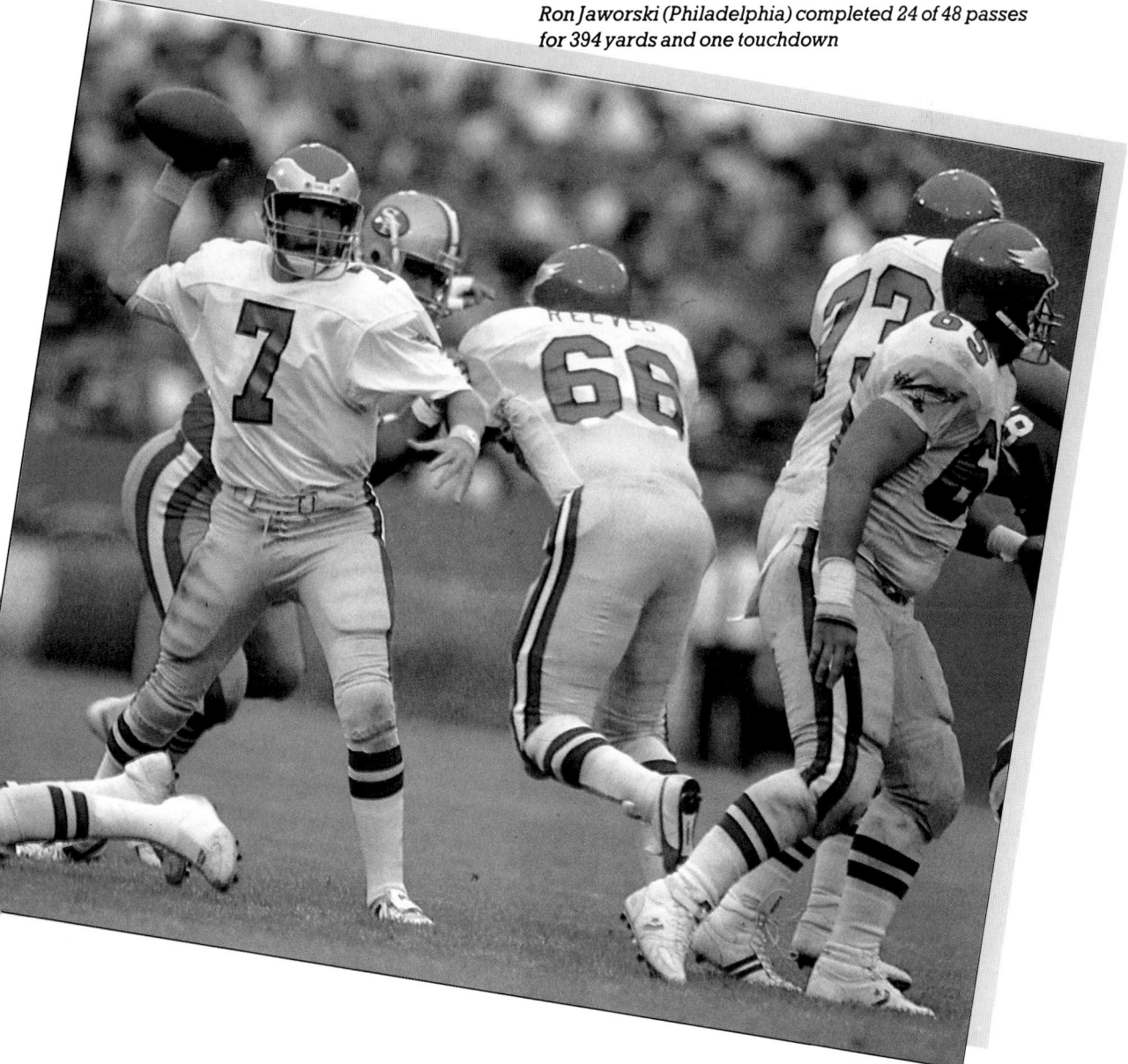

WEEK TEN

American Football Conference
Cleveland 10 at Cincinnati 27
Houston 0 at Buffalo 20
Indianapolis 15 at New England 34
Los Angeles Raiders 34 at San Diego 40 (OT)
New York Jets 17 at Miami 21
Pittsburgh 36 at Kansas City 28

National Football Conference
Atlanta 17 at Philadelphia 23 (OT)
Dallas 13 at Washington 7
Detroit 3 at Chicago 24
Green Bay 27 at Minnesota 17
Los Angeles Rams 19 at New York Giants 24
St Louis 0 at Tampa Bay 16

Interconference Games
San Francisco 16 at Denver 17
Seattle 27 at New Orleans 3

Interconference Play
AFC 16, NFC 16

San Diego's Lionel James (#26) caught 11 passes for 168 yards, rushed for 51 yards, returned five kickoffs for 126 yards, and scored two touchdowns

Week Ten saw the day of the individual as several players turned in performances of extravagant proportions. But firstly let's give pride of place to the Tampa Bay Buccaneers who, at last, had something to show for their efforts. And it is a convenient place to start on the individual feats, with Buccaneers' tight end Jimmie Giles catching passes for a career-best 134 yards.

Ron Brown returned a kickoff 89 yards to set up a field goal, but it only served to lessen the margin of the Rams' defeat against the Giants. On the other hand, Irving Fryar's 77-yard punt return for a touchdown certainly helped in a New England victory which was their fifth in a row. It took them into a tie for first place on top of the AFC Eastern division, following Miami's victory over the Jets. In that game, wide receiver Mark Duper established a Dolphins club record with 217 yards receiving and, after opening with a 60-yard touchdown reception, he closed out with a 50-yarder for the touchdown which brought a last-minute victory. Louis Lipps, who returned a punt 71 yards for a touchdown, urged the Steelers on to greater things in a win against Kansas City. For the Cowboys, defensive end Jim Jeffcoat took advantage of Washington's first-year left tackle, Dan McQuaid, to register five solo sacks in the Cowboys' 13-7 win. The Philadelphia Eagles stayed in touch with an overtime victory which came in fine style. They'd been driven back to their own one-yard line by an Atlanta punt and were 'just looking for a little breathing space,' said Mike Quick. The same player then took a modest 20-yard pass from

Ron Jaworski and became the sixth player in league history to score on a 99-yard touchdown reception. In San Diego's overtime victory against the Raiders, Dan Fouts became the first man in league history to pass for 400 yards in a game on six occasions, and Lionel James put on another one-man show, gaining 345 all-purpose yards and scoring two touchdowns, including the winner from seventeen yards out.

Outstanding Individual Performances

Dan Fouts (San Diego) completed 26 of 41 passes for 436 yards and four touchdowns.

Ken O'Brien (N.Y. Jets) completed 26 of 43 passes for 393 yards and two touchdowns.

Dan Marino (Miami) completed 21 of 37 passes for 362 yards and three touchdowns.

Mark Duper (Miami) caught eight passes for 217 yards, including touchdown receptions of 60 and 50 yards.

Tony Hill (Dallas) caught seven passes for 136 yards.

Cris Collinsworth (Cincinnati) caught eight passes for 135 yards.

Jimmie Giles (Tampa Bay) caught six passes for 134 yards.

Darrin Nelson (Minnesota) rushed for 146 yards on 21 carries and scored one touchdown.

Philadelphia's Mike Quick (#82) caught three passes for 145 yards, including a 99-yard touchdown reception

Inset: Al Toon (N.Y. Jets) caught ten passes for 156 yards

STANDINGS

AFC East	W	L	T	PF	PA	NFC East	W	L	T	PF	PA
New England	7	3	0	207	171	Dallas	7	3	0	220	153
N.Y. Jets	7	3	0	225	156	N.Y. Giants	7	3	0	227	170
Miami	6	4	0	241	211	Philadelphia	5	5	0	159	162
Indianapolis	3	7	0	187	238	Washington	5	5	0	165	181
Buffalo	2	8	0	141	216	St Louis	4	6	0	186	232
AFC Central						**NFC Central**					
Cincinnati	5	5	0	287	288	Chicago	10	0	0	279	127
Pittsburgh	5	5	0	219	181	Detroit	5	5	0	173	220
Cleveland	4	6	0	160	159	Minnesota	5	5	0	200	207
Houston	4	6	0	162	205	Green Bay	4	6	0	191	233
AFC West						Tampa Bay	1	9	0	200	272
Denver	7	3	0	236	197	**NFC West**					
L.A. Raiders	6	4	0	230	227	L.A. Rams	8	2	0	210	151
Seattle	6	4	0	248	205	San Francisco	5	5	0	244	184
San Diego	5	5	0	260	265	New Orleans	3	7	0	176	262
Kansas City	3	7	0	199	240	Atlanta	1	9	0	188	307

WEEK ELEVEN

American Football Conference
Buffalo 7 at Cleveland 17
Cincinnati 6 at Los Angeles Raiders 13
Miami 34 at Indianapolis 20
New England 20 at Seattle 13
Pittsburgh 30 at Houston 7
San Diego 24 at Denver 30 (OT)

National Football Conference
Chicago 44 at Dallas 0
Los Angeles Rams 14 at Atlanta 30
Minnesota 21 at Detroit 41
New Orleans 14 at Green Bay 38 (played in Milwaukee)
New York Giants 21 at Washington 23
Philadelphia 24 at St Louis 14 (venue switched)

Interconference Games
Kansas City 3 at San Francisco 31
Tampa Bay 28 at New York Jets 62

Interconference Play
AFC 17, NFC 17

Ken O'Brien (N.Y. Jets) completed 23 of 30 passes for 367 yards and five touchdowns

One thing was settled on Week Eleven, when the Bears thrashed the Cowboys to clinch the NFC Central division title. The Cowboys were unlucky to fall behind when an attempted pass was tipped at the line of scrimmage and picked off by Chicago defensive end Richard Dent, who strolled in for a touchdown. And the harder they tried to fight their way back, the more they were punished by a Chicago defense at its best. The defeat was the worst in Dallas history. The Redskins suffered the tragedy of Joe Theismann's broken leg but discovered a new hero in Jay Schroeder, and the entire team rallied round to beat the Giants 23-21. In a losing cause, the Giants' Joe Morris rushed for three touchdowns. The Rams came a real cropper at Atlanta, where Gerald Riggs rushed for two touchdowns as the Falcons established a 23-0 lead, and then he scored a third to snuff out a Rams comeback. With Wendell Tyler rushing for 111 yards, San Francisco won easily against Kansas City and drew to within two games of the lead. Pittsburgh's victory at Houston raised them to the top in the AFC Central for the first time since Week Three.

Tampa Bay will remember Week Eleven as 'the day the lights went out'. The start of their game against the Jets was delayed because of a power failure, but it didn't seem to bother the Buccaneers, who went out to a 14-0 lead after only 3:11 of the first quarter. But then the lights really went out as the Jets poured it on to the tune of a club-record 62 points. In the first quarter Miami trailed the Colts 10-0, but then Dan Marino put on one of his characteristic shows, in total passing for 330 yards and a touchdown. The Patriots, too, looked in danger of losing to Seattle, whom they trailed 13-7 entering the final quarter. However, with the Seahawks pressing, Patriots safety Fred Marion picked off a pass and raced 83 yards to set up the Irving Fryar touchdown reception which broke a 13-13 tie.

Against Denver, the Chargers started out in dramatic fashion when Gary Anderson returned the opening kickoff 98 yards for a touchdown. But Denver's finish, in overtime, was equally memorable. Firstly, Dennis Smith (he had blocked a 47-yard field goal attempt in the first quarter) charged down a 41-yard field goal attempt only to see his efforts wasted because his teammate, Mike Harden, had called a timeout. Astonishingly, Smith blocked the retaken kick and, this time, cornerback Louis Wright recovered the ball before racing 60 yards for the winning touchdown.

Outstanding Individual Performances

Dan Marino (Miami) completed 22 of 37 passes for 330 yards and one touchdown.

Steve Largent (Seattle) caught eight passes for 138 yards.

Al Toon (N.Y. Jets) caught six passes for 133 yards, including a 78-yard touchdown reception.

Art Monk (Washington) caught seven passes for 130 yards.

Marcus Allen (L.A. Raiders) rushed for 135 yards on 31 carries and caught a touchdown pass.

Walter Payton (Chicago) rushed for 132 yards on 22 carries.

Gary Anderson (San Diego) returned the opening kickoff 98 yards for a touchdown.

Above: Earnest Jackson (Philadelphia) carried 34 times for 162 yards and scored a touchdown on a 51-yard run

Below: Stump Mitchell (St Louis) rushed for 179 yards and two touchdowns

STANDINGS					
AFC East	**W**	**L**	**T**	**PF**	**PA**
New England	8	3	0	227	184
N.Y. Jets	8	3	0	287	184
Miami	7	4	0	275	231
Indianapolis	3	8	0	207	272
Buffalo	2	9	0	148	233
AFC Central					
Pittsburgh	6	5	0	249	188
Cincinnati	5	6	0	293	301
Cleveland	5	6	0	177	166
Houston	4	7	0	169	235
AFC West					
Denver	8	3	0	266	221
L.A. Raiders	7	4	0	243	233
Seattle	6	5	0	261	225
San Diego	5	6	0	284	295
Kansas City	3	8	0	202	271
NFC East	**W**	**L**	**T**	**PF**	**PA**
Dallas	7	4	0	220	197
N.Y. Giants	7	4	0	248	193
Philadelphia	6	5	0	183	176
Washington	6	5	0	188	202
St Louis	4	7	0	200	256
NFC Central					
†Chicago	11	0	0	323	127
Detroit	6	5	0	214	241
Green Bay	5	6	0	229	247
Minnesota	5	6	0	221	248
Tampa Bay	1	10	0	228	334
NFC West					
L.A. Rams	8	3	0	224	181
San Francisco	6	5	0	275	187
New Orleans	3	8	0	190	300
Atlanta	2	9	0	218	321

†Division Champions

WEEK TWELVE

American Football Conference
Cincinnati 6 at Cleveland 24
Denver 28 at Los Angeles Raiders 31 (OT)
Indianapolis 7 at Kansas City 20
Miami 23 at Buffalo 14
New England 13 at New York Jets 16 (OT)
San Diego 35 at Houston 37

National Football Conference
Atlanta 0 at Chicago 36
Detroit 16 at Tampa Bay 19 (OT)
Green Bay 17 at Los Angeles Rams 34
New Orleans 30 at Minnesota 23
New York Giants 34 at St Louis 3
Philadelphia 17 at Dallas 34

Interconference Games
Seattle 6 at San Francisco 19
Washington 30 at Pittsburgh 23

Interconference Play
AFC 17, NFC 19

It was expected to be a tense game when the Raiders and Denver met for the first time this season, and it was not surprising that they needed overtime to settle the matter. But before then, 56 points had been scored. Three times, the Raiders drew level after touchdown passes by Denver quarterback John Elway. And after the Raiders had nosed ahead, Denver's Steve Sewell scored from three yards out to take the game into an extra period. The Raiders' Marcus Allen rushed for a regular-season career-best 173 yards (he rushed for 191 yards in Super Bowl XVIII), but it was wide receiver Dokie Williams who hauled in a short pass and turned it into a 42-yard gain to set up Chris Bahr's winning field goal. It was also in overtime that New England's run of wins was halted at six by the Jets, who moved into first place in the AFC East. Sadly, New England's Steve Grogan went out with damaged knee ligaments. In the AFC Central, the teams continued to shuffle around, with Cleveland, directed by Gary Danielson in place of rookie quarterback Bernie Kosar, moving into a tie for first place alongside Pittsburgh.

Earl Campbell (New Orleans) rushed for 160 yards on 35 carries and scored one touchdown

In the NFC, the Eastern division leaders continued their steady march with, still, no obvious champion emerging. The Cowboys did themselves a bit of good by beating Philadelphia, and the Giants reduced the Cardinals' chances of reaching the playoffs to one of those mathematical possibilities that no-one can ever work out.

Tampa Bay gave their home fans a second treat, with the bonus of overtime excitement, in putting a dent into Detroit's playoff hopes. For the Buccaneers, rookie quarterback Steve Young was making his first start. As usual the Bears won, and the manner of their 36-0 victory over Atlanta made it clear that there would be no letting up – they were going for that elusive perfect season. The 49ers survived an untidy first-half performance by Joe Montana and defeated Seattle to stay two games adrift of the Rams, who had been helped by two big kickoff returns for touchdowns by Ron Brown. 'Bum' Phillips resigned. After seeing his protege, Earl Campbell, rush for 160 yards in a victory over Minnesota, the Saints' head coach handed the job to his son, Wade, for the remainder of the season. A genuine character and nice guy, it was sad to see him go.

STANDINGS

AFC East	W	L	T	PF	PA
N.Y. Jets	9	3	0	303	197
Miami	8	4	0	298	245
New England	8	4	0	240	200
Indianapolis	3	9	0	214	292
Buffalo	2	10	0	162	256
AFC Central					
Cleveland	6	6	0	201	172
Pittsburgh	6	6	0	272	218
Cincinnati	5	7	0	299	325
Houston	5	7	0	206	270
AFC West					
Denver	8	4	0	294	252
L.A. Raiders	8	4	0	274	261
Seattle	6	6	0	267	244
San Diego	5	7	0	319	332
Kansas City	4	8	0	222	278
NFC East	**W**	**L**	**T**	**PF**	**PA**
Dallas	8	4	0	254	214
N.Y. Giants	8	4	0	282	196
Washington	7	5	0	218	225
Philadelphia	6	6	0	200	210
St Louis	4	8	0	203	290
NFC Central					
†Chicago	12	0	0	359	127
Detroit	6	6	0	230	260
Green Bay	5	7	0	246	281
Minnesota	5	7	0	244	278
Tampa Bay	2	10	0	247	350
NFC West					
L.A. Rams	9	3	0	258	198
San Francisco	7	5	0	294	193
New Orleans	4	8	0	220	323
Atlanta	2	10	0	218	357

†Division Champions

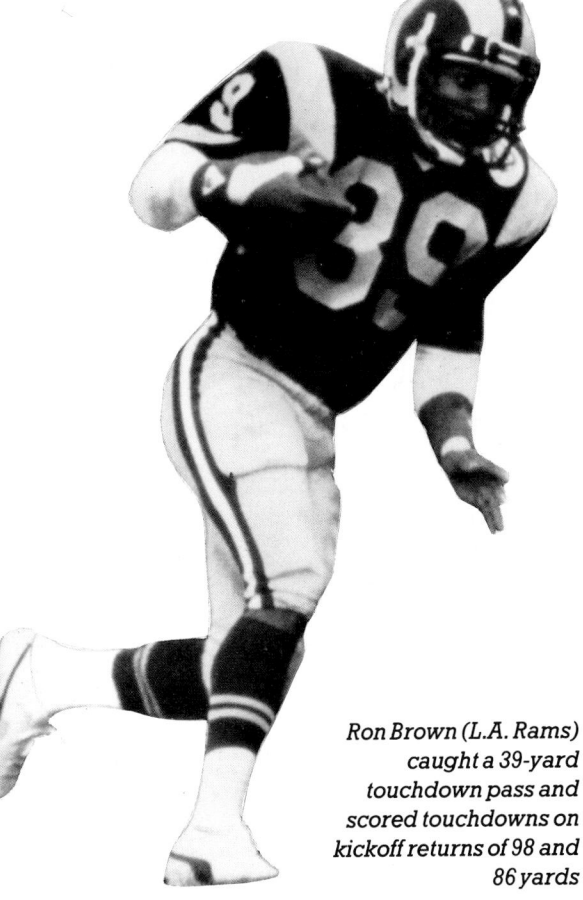

Ron Brown (L.A. Rams) caught a 39-yard touchdown pass and scored touchdowns on kickoff returns of 98 and 86 yards

Outstanding Individual Performances

Dan Fouts (San Diego) completed 24 of 36 passes for 343 yards and two touchdowns.

Wesley Walker (N.Y. Jets) caught six passes for 168 yards, including an 88-yard touchdown reception.

Louis Lipps (Pittsburgh) caught five passes for 121 yards and scored one touchdown.

Marcus Allen (L.A. Raiders) rushed for 173 yards on 24 carries and scored a 61-yard touchdown.

Eric Dickerson (L.A. Rams) rushed for 150 yards on 31 carries and scored one touchdown.

Ken Jenkins (Washington) returned a kickoff 95 yards.

George Martin (N.Y. Giants) recovered a fumble, returned an interception 56 yards for a touchdown and registered three sacks.

WEEK THIRTEEN

American Football Conference
Buffalo 7 at San Diego 40
Denver 31 at Pittsburgh 23
Houston 27 at Cincinnati 45
Kansas City 6 at Seattle 24
New England 38 at Indianapolis 31

National Football Conference
St Louis 17 at Dallas 35
Los Angeles Rams 3 at New Orleans 29
Minnesota 28 at Philadelphia 23
San Francisco 35 at Washington 8
Tampa Bay 0 at Green Bay 21

Interconference Games
New York Jets 20 at Detroit 31
Cleveland 35 at New York Giants 33
Los Angeles Raiders 34 at Atlanta 24
Chicago 24 at Miami 38

Interconference Play
AFC 20, NFC 20

Denver's Karl Mecklenburg (#77) logged four quarterback sacks for the second time in the season

Wade Phillips will not forget his debut as head coach of the Saints. His team put on a show of over-powering defense, with nine sacks, three fumble recoveries and an interception, as they beat the Rams 29-3. Against Washington, the 49ers' Carl Monroe returned the opening kickoff 95 yards for a touchdown in what turned out to be a 35-8 drubbing. It now meant that only one victory separated the two NFC West contenders – and they were to meet on Week Fourteen. In the AFC West, both the Raiders and Denver won to remain locked in a tie on top of the division. But they, too, would be in a showdown in one week's time.

Over in the NFC East, the clubs were beginning to form some kind of order. The Cowboys had beaten St Louis on Thanksgiving Day, the previous Thursday, and could sit back and watch the Giants go down to Cleveland. Only 1:52 remained of a seesaw battle when the Browns went into a 35-33 lead, and there were seconds to go when Giants' kicker Eric Schubert missed from 34 yards out after a poor snap from scrimmage. Pittsburgh's loss to Denver meant that Cleveland went to the top in the AFC Central – but they would now have to keep an eye on Cincinnati, who had beaten Houston 45-27.

Chicago's hopes for a perfect season came to an end against the only team ever to have achieved that feat, the Miami Dolphins. Dan Marino found a way to beat the notorious '46 Defense', constantly rolling out of the pocket and throwing quick passes. And the gods threw in a bit of good fortune to help out when the ball was tipped. Nonetheless, the Dolphins were

worthy winners and moved into a three-way tie for the division lead, having seen the Jets lose to Detroit three days earlier. By way of consolation for Walter Payton, he became the first man in league history to rush for eight consecutive 100-yard games.

The comeback of the week, perhaps the season, happened in Philadelphia, where the Minnesota Vikings overcame a 23-point deficit with four fourth-quarter touchdowns. The winner came on a fourth-and-five, 42-yard touchdown reception by wide receiver Anthony Carter.

Outstanding Individual Performances

Jay Schroeder (Washington) completed 30 of 58 passes for 348 yards.

Art Monk (Washington) caught eight passes for 150 yards.

Billy Johnson (Atlanta) caught six passes for 136 yards and scored one touchdown.

Marcus Allen (L.A. Raiders) rushed for 156 yards on 28 carries and caught a touchdown pass.

Joe Morris (N.Y. Giants) rushed for 131 yards on 22 carries and scored three touchdowns.

Walter Payton (Chicago) rushed for 121 yards on 23 carries.

John Hendy (San Diego) intercepted two passes, one of which he returned 75 yards for a touchdown.

STANDINGS

AFC East	W	L	T	PF	PA	NFC East	W	L	T	PF	PA
Miami	9	4	0	336	269	Dallas	9	4	0	289	231
New England	9	4	0	278	231	N.Y. Giants	8	5	0	315	231
N.Y. Jets	9	4	0	323	228	Washington	7	6	0	226	260
Indianapolis	3	10	0	245	330	Philadelphia	6	7	0	223	238
Buffalo	2	11	0	169	296	St Louis	4	9	0	220	325
AFC Central						**NFC Central**					
Cleveland	7	6	0	236	205	†Chicago	12	1	0	383	165
Cincinnati	6	7	0	344	352	Detroit	7	6	0	261	280
Pittsburgh	6	7	0	295	249	Green Bay	6	7	0	267	281
Houston	5	8	0	233	315	Minnesota	6	7	0	272	301
AFC West						Tampa Bay	2	11	0	247	371
Denver	9	4	0	325	275	**NFC West**					
L.A. Raiders	9	4	0	308	285	L.A. Rams	9	4	0	261	227
Seattle	7	6	0	291	250	San Francisco	8	5	0	329	201
San Diego	6	7	0	359	339	New Orleans	5	8	0	249	326
Kansas City	4	9	0	228	302	Atlanta	2	11	0	242	391

†Division Champions

Left: Jack Del Rio (New Orleans) recovered two fumbles, one of which he returned for a touchdown

San Francisco's Carl Monroe (#32) returned the opening kickoff 95 yards for a touchdown

WEEK FOURTEEN

American Football Conference
Cleveland 13 at Seattle 31
Los Angeles Raiders 17 at Denver 14 (OT)
New York Jets 27 at Buffalo 7
Pittsburgh 44 at San Diego 54

National Football Conference
New Orleans 16 at St Louis 28
Tampa Bay 7 at Minnesota 26
Washington 17 at Philadelphia 12
Los Angeles Rams 27 at San Francisco 20

Interconference Games
Atlanta 10 at Kansas City 38
Dallas 24 at Cincinnati 50
Detroit 6 at New England 23
Indianapolis 10 at Chicago 17
Miami 34 at Green Bay 24
New York Giants 35 at Houston 14

Interconference Play
AFC 24, NFC 22

Jerry Rice (San Francisco) caught ten passes for 241 yards, including a 66-yard touchdown reception

The 49ers did nearly everything right, the Rams hung on and rode their luck and, at the end, they were in the playoffs (they were now assured of a wild card berth). With the Rams trailing by the score of 20-13 and 5:08 remaining, wide receiver Henry Ellard caught a tipped pass and scored on a 39-yard play. And on the 49ers' next possession, Rams' cornerback Gary Green intercepted a pass before rambling 41 yards for the winner. Earlier, the Rams had been torn apart by Joe Montana, who threw for three touchdowns, and rookie wide receiver Jerry Rice, who caught ten passes for 241 yards. Nonetheless, the 49ers were left to figure their prospects of becoming a wild card. The battle for the outright leadership in the AFC West went into overtime, with the winner coming from the boot of Chris Bahr, on the next play after a fumble by Denver quarterback John Elway had been recovered by the Raiders' Greg Townsend. The Raiders, who trailed 14-0 at half time, drew level on a 15-yard touchdown run by Marcus Allen, who also rushed for over 100 yards for the seventh consecutive game. Throughout the season, almost without exception, Allen had been truly outstanding. Having rushed for 1,527 yards thus far, he had a lock on the AFC rushing title and, by a margin of 21 yards, trailed only Atlanta's Gerald Riggs in the entire NFL. Defeat for Denver meant that they would have to keep a nervous eye on the AFC East contenders, each of whom won and, at the very least, enhanced their prospects of gaining a wild card spot. For Miami, Dan Marino had thrown five touchdown passes against the Packers, and in the Jets-Buffalo game, New York quarterback Ken O'Brien passed for 370 yards, 96 of which came in combination with wide receiver Wesley Walker for a touchdown.

Cincinnati's astonishing 50-24 win against Dallas, combined with losses by Cleveland and Pittsburgh, gave the Bengals a share of the lead in the AFC Central. In that 54-44 San Diego-Pittsburgh game, the two teams had combined for the fourth-highest single-game points total in league history.

The Giants took advantage of the Cowboys' loss to go joint first in the NFC East. In their 35-14 victory over Houston, running back Joe Morris rushed for three touchdowns for the third time in the season, raising his total to seventeen. After the game, Houston head coach Hugh Campbell was fired.

STANDINGS

AFC East	W	L	T	PF	PA
Miami	10	4	0	370	293
New England	10	4	0	301	237
N.Y. Jets	10	4	0	350	235
Indianapolis	3	11	0	255	347
Buffalo	2	12	0	176	323
AFC Central					
Cincinnati	7	7	0	394	376
Cleveland	7	7	0	249	236
Pittsburgh	6	8	0	339	303
Houston	5	9	0	247	350
AFC West					
L.A. Raiders	10	4	0	325	299
Denver	9	5	0	339	292
Seattle	8	6	0	322	263
San Diego	7	7	0	413	383
Kansas City	5	9	0	266	312

NFC East	W	L	T	PF	PA
Dallas	9	5	0	313	281
N.Y. Giants	9	5	0	350	245
Washington	8	6	0	243	272
Philadelphia	6	8	0	235	255
St Louis	5	9	0	248	341
NFC Central					
†Chicago	13	1	0	400	175
Detroit	7	7	0	267	303
Minnesota	7	7	0	298	308
Green Bay	6	8	0	291	315
Tampa Bay	2	12	0	254	397
NFC West					
*L.A. Rams	10	4	0	288	247
San Francisco	8	6	0	349	228
New Orleans	5	9	0	265	354
Atlanta	2	12	0	252	429

†Division Champions
* Qualified for playoffs

Gerald Riggs (Atlanta) rushed for 197 yards on 26 carries and scored one touchdown

Outstanding Individual Performances

Dan Fouts (San Diego) completed 21 of 33 passes for 372 yards and three touchdowns.

Ken O'Brien (N.Y. Jets) completed 25 of 40 passes for 370 yards and three touchdowns.

Wes Chandler (San Diego) caught five passes for 154 yards and scored two touchdowns, one of which covered 75 yards.

Wesley Walker (N.Y. Jets) caught four passes for 129 yards, including a 96-yard touchdown reception.

Stump Mitchell (St Louis) rushed for 158 yards on 28 carries and scored three touchdowns, two rushing and one by pass reception.

George Rogers (Washington) rushed for 150 yards on 36 carries and scored one touchdown.

Dennis Smith (Denver) intercepted three passes.

WEEK FIFTEEN

American Football Conference
Buffalo 24 at Pittsburgh 30
Houston 21 at Cleveland 28
Kansas City 13 at Denver 14
New England 27 at Miami 30
Seattle 3 at Los Angeles Raiders 13

National Football Conference
Green Bay 26 at Detroit 23
Minnesota 13 at Atlanta 14
New York Giants 21 at Dallas 28
St Louis 14 at Los Angeles Rams 46
San Francisco 31 at New Orleans 19

Interconference Games
Cincinnati 24 at Washington 27
Chicago 19 at New York Jets 6
Indianapolis 31 at Tampa Bay 23
Philadelphia 14 at San Diego 20

Interconference Play
AFC 26, NFC 24

Dieter Brock (L.A. Rams) completed 13 of 20 passes for 216 yards and four touchdowns

On Week Fifteen, the mists began to clear as the destination of three division championships became known. Dallas won its first division title in four years with a heroic victory over the Giants. The Cowboys had gone ahead on Mike Renfro's 58-yard touchdown reception, but they were trailing 14-7 and looked in imminent danger of falling further behind, as Phil Simms had the Giants pressing in Dallas territory. But his pass was batted into the air and subsequently intercepted by the Cowboys' Jim Jeffcoat, who ran 65 yards for a touchdown. Less than a minute later, they were seven points ahead. Giants' punter Sean Landeta had been forced into attempting a pass which had fallen incomplete, and Danny White rammed home the advantage with a 12-yard pass for Renfro's second touchdown. The drama came later, when both White and his backup, Gary Hogeboom, were sidelined with injuries. On came second-year Steve Pelluer, who hadn't even been able to elbow his way into a practice scrimmage. Nonetheless, showing great composure, he handed off when he was told to and completed a key pass to rookie wide receiver Karl Powe when he had to. The drive produced a touchdown by Timmy Newsome and was enough to keep the Giants at bay, despite their late rally.

The Raiders won a bad-tempered, defensive struggle with the Seahawks, to clinch the AFC Western division title. The Rams secured their division title without undue bother against St Louis, whom they defeated by the score of 46-14. Rams quarterback Dieter Brock was clinically efficient, passing for four touchdowns without an interception, and Eric Dickerson, who had been out of the limelight for most of the season, rushed for 124 yards and a pair of touchdowns. The big game in the AFC East went to Miami, but only after a few tense moments. Though the Patriots never led, they moved into a 27-27 tie, halfway through the final quarter, with two touchdowns in the space of fifteen seconds. Fuad Reveiz regained the lead for Miami with a 47-yard field goal, but the Patriots were moving into range for their own field goal attempt when Miami's Glenn Blackwood intercepted to kill the drive. With the Jets also losing, Miami had one foot in the playoffs. Cleveland, too, took a giant step towards the AFC Central division title. They weren't there yet, but a win over Houston gave them the inside lane. Philadelphia head coach Marion Campbell was released after his team's loss to San Diego.

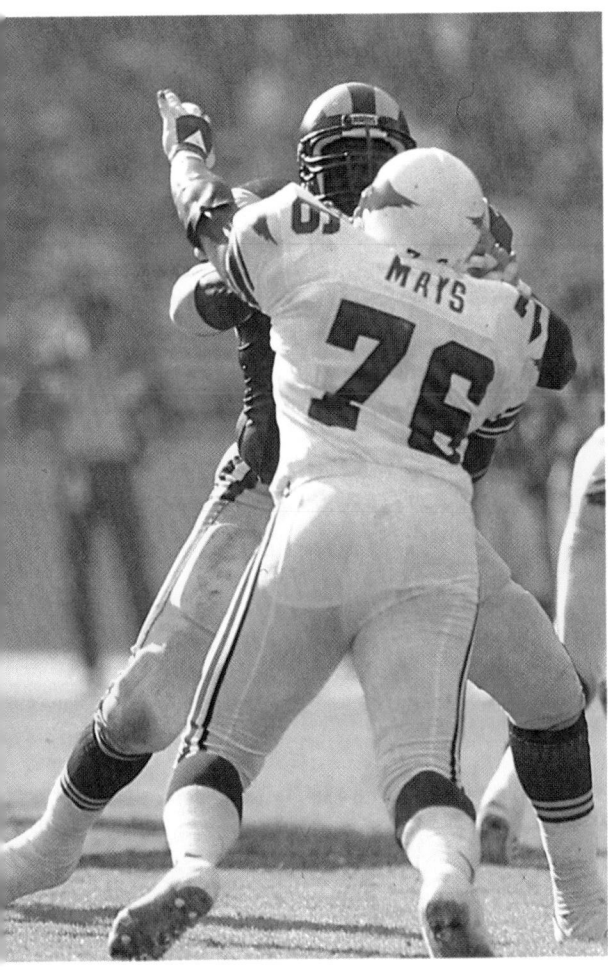

Art Monk (Washington)
caught 13 passes for 230 yards and scored one touchdown

Outstanding Individual Performances

Boomer Esiason (Cincinnati) completed 22 of 39 passes for 357 yards and two touchdowns.

Joe Montana (San Francisco) completed 25 of 38 passes for 354 yards and three touchdowns.

Anthony Carter (Minnesota) caught seven passes for 144 yards and scored one touchdown.

Eugene Goodlow (New Orleans) caught five passes for 135 yards, including a 76-yard touchdown reception.

Kevin House (Tampa Bay) caught four passes for 131 yards and scored one touchdown.

Eric Dickerson (L.A. Rams) rushed for 124 yards on 20 carries and scored two touchdowns.

Greg Bell (Buffalo) rushed for 123 yards on 19 carries and scored a 77-yard touchdown.

Jim Jeffcoat (Dallas) registered two quarterback sacks and returned an interception 65 yards for a touchdown.

Mike Douglass (Green Bay) returned an interception 80 yards for a touchdown.

STANDINGS

AFC East	W	L	T	PF	PA
†Miami	12	4	0	428	320
*N.Y. Jets	11	5	0	393	264
*New England	11	5	0	362	290
Indianapolis	5	11	0	320	386
Buffalo	2	14	0	200	381
AFC Central					
†Cleveland	8	8	0	287	294
Cincinnati	7	9	0	441	437
Pittsburgh	7	9	0	379	355
Houston	5	11	0	284	412
AFC West					
†L.A. Raiders	12	4	0	354	308
Denver	11	5	0	380	329
Seattle	8	8	0	349	303
San Diego	8	8	0	467	435
Kansas City	6	10	0	317	360
NFC East	W	L	T	PF	PA
†Dallas	10	6	0	357	333
*N.Y. Giants	10	6	0	399	283
Washington	10	6	0	297	312
Philadelphia	7	9	0	286	310
St Louis	5	11	0	278	414
NFC Central					
†Chicago	15	1	0	456	198
Green Bay	8	8	0	337	355
Minnesota	7	9	0	346	359
Detroit	7	9	0	307	366
Tampa Bay	2	14	0	294	448
NFC West					
†L.A. Rams	11	5	0	340	277
*San Francisco	10	6	0	411	263
New Orleans	5	11	0	294	401
Atlanta	4	12	0	266	452

†Division Champions * Wild Card

WEEK SIXTEEN

American Football Conference
Buffalo 0 at Miami 28
Denver 27 at Seattle 24
Cincinnati 23 at New England 34
Cleveland 10 at New York Jets 37
Houston 16 at Indianapolis 34
San Diego 34 at Kansas City 38

National Football Conference
Atlanta 16 at New Orleans 10
Chicago 37 at Detroit 17
Dallas 16 at San Francisco 31
Green Bay 20 at Tampa Bay 17
Philadelphia 37 at Minnesota 35
Washington 27 at St Louis 16

Interconference Games
Los Angeles Raiders 16 at Los Angeles Rams 6
Pittsburgh 10 at New York Giants 28

Interconference Play
AFC 27, NFC 25

Denver began the final-week programme with a win over Seattle on Friday evening. Now they could only wait for one of the three AFC East teams to slip. The Redskins, too, would have to sweat it out, after beating the Cardinals on Saturday. Earlier, on the same day, the Giants had beaten Pittsburgh to earn a wild card berth. It meant that Washington's fate would be decided on Sunday, when the Cowboys travelled to play San Francisco. For the Redskins to go into the playoffs, the 49ers would have to lose. Imagine that – Washington rooting for Dallas! And for a time, it looked as if their prayers would be answered, as Dallas went out to a 13-0 lead. But the margin was steadily eroded by a 49ers team which gained in strength as it neared its goal. Victory and a wild card spot came by the score of 31-16. San Francisco running back Roger Craig became the first player in NFL history to go over 1,000 yards, in both rushing and pass receiving, in the same season.

Now let's look back at the AFC Central where, curiously, Pittsburgh's loss had decided the title for one of Cleveland or Cincinnati. Though the Steelers could not, under any circumstances, have won the division title, the combination of their victory, a win by Cincinnati and a loss by Cleveland, would have produced a three-way tie on top of the division. Cincinnati would have won that tie-breaker on the basis of head-to-head games between the three teams. However, following Pittsburgh's loss, only the Bengals and the Browns could be involved in a tie-breaker, and in this, the Browns would come out ahead because of their better intraconference record. Hey Presto! the Browns had already won the title in the AFC Central. Still, both teams could have an influence in the AFC East. And for much of Sunday's Cincinnati-New England game, the Bengals had the Patriots worried. Rookie wide receiver Eddie Brown caught five passes for 129 yards and a touchdown as the Bengals clung on. But New England's Robert Weathers had the final say, extending a slim four-point margin to eleven with his 42-yard touchdown run. Both Miami and the Jets won easily, as all three AFC East teams went into the playoffs, with Miami as division champions. Poor Denver became the first 11-5 team ever to miss out. On Monday night, the Raiders beat the Rams, thus earning both home-field advantage for the playoffs and the bragging rights to the City of Los Angeles.

STANDINGS

AFC East	W	L	T	PF	PA	NFC East	W	L	T	PF	PA
†Miami	12	4	0	428	320	†Dallas	10	6	0	357	333
*N.Y. Jets	11	5	0	393	264	*N.Y. Giants	10	6	0	399	283
*New England	11	5	0	362	290	Washington	10	6	0	297	312
Indianapolis	5	11	0	320	386	Philadelphia	7	9	0	286	310
Buffalo	2	14	0	200	381	St Louis	5	11	0	278	414
AFC Central						**NFC Central**					
†Cleveland	8	8	0	287	294	†Chicago	15	1	0	456	198
Cincinnati	7	9	0	441	437	Green Bay	8	8	0	337	355
Pittsburgh	7	9	0	379	355	Minnesota	7	9	0	346	359
Houston	5	11	0	284	412	Detroit	7	9	0	307	366
AFC West						Tampa Bay	2	14	0	294	448
†L.A. Raiders	12	4	0	354	308	**NFC West**					
Denver	11	5	0	380	329	†L.A. Rams	11	5	0	340	277
Seattle	8	8	0	349	303	*San Francisco	10	6	0	411	263
San Diego	8	8	0	467	435	New Orleans	5	11	0	294	401
Kansas City	6	10	0	317	360	Atlanta	4	12	0	282	452

†Division Champions   *Wild Card

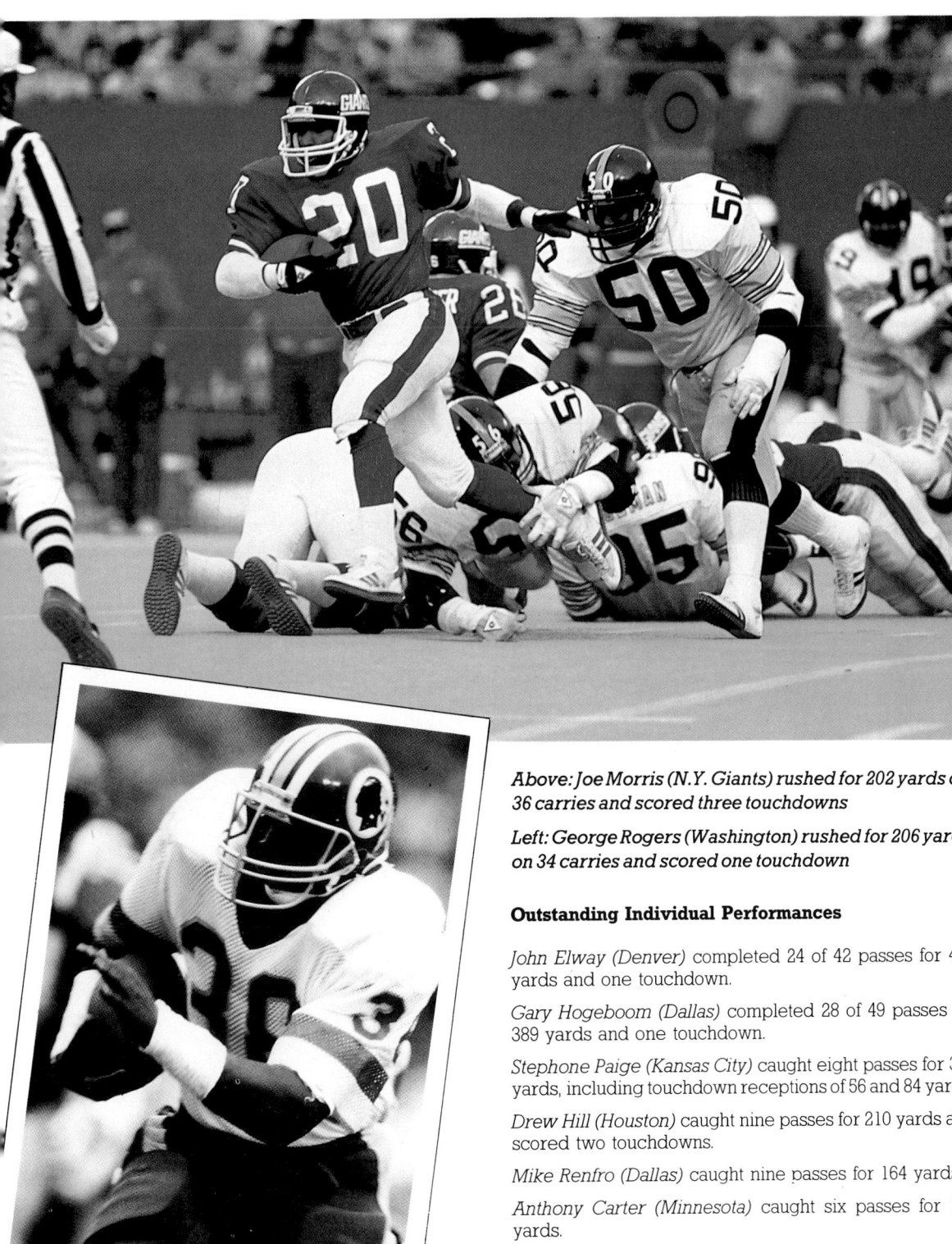

Above: Joe Morris (N.Y. Giants) rushed for 202 yards on 36 carries and scored three touchdowns

Left: George Rogers (Washington) rushed for 206 yards on 34 carries and scored one touchdown

Outstanding Individual Performances

John Elway (Denver) completed 24 of 42 passes for 432 yards and one touchdown.

Gary Hogeboom (Dallas) completed 28 of 49 passes for 389 yards and one touchdown.

Stephone Paige (Kansas City) caught eight passes for 309 yards, including touchdown receptions of 56 and 84 yards.

Drew Hill (Houston) caught nine passes for 210 yards and scored two touchdowns.

Mike Renfro (Dallas) caught nine passes for 164 yards.

Anthony Carter (Minnesota) caught six passes for 132 yards.

Gerald Riggs (Atlanta) rushed for 158 yards on 39 carries and scored one touchdown.

Dennis Gentry (Chicago) returned a kickoff 94 yards for a touchdown.

WEEK SEVENTEEN –
WILD CARD WEEKEND

AFC   New England 26 at New York Jets 14

The Patriots built on a solid performance from quarterback Tony Eason, and took advantage of turnovers, to beat the Jets in Giants Stadium. Tony Franklin kicked a 33-yard field goal and was again on target, with a 41-yard effort, after the Jets' Johnny Hector had caught an 11-yard touchdown pass from Ken O'Brien. Towards the end of the second quarter, the Jets were driving when O'Brien's pass was intercepted by New England safety Fred Marion and returned 26 yards. Subsequently, a five-play drive put Eason in position for a 36-yard

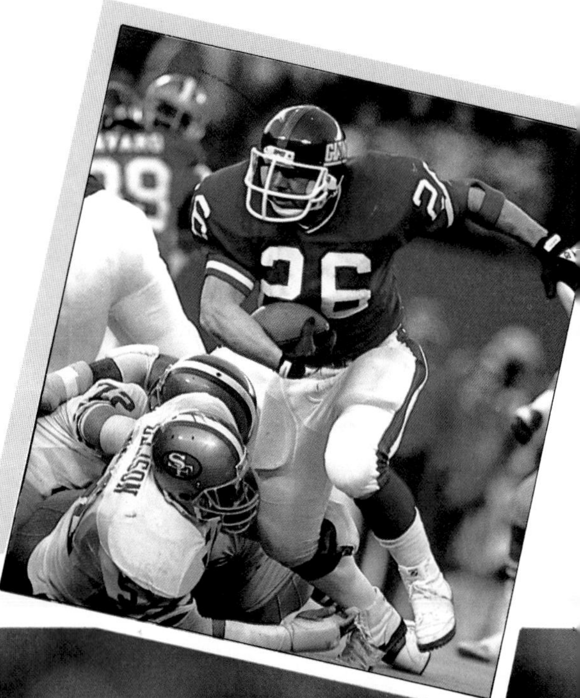

Right: Rob Carpenter rips off some yards against the 49ers

Below: Joe Morris (#20) rushed for 141 yards on 28 carries

touchdown pass to wide receiver Stanley Morgan, giving the Patriots a 13-7 lead which they took into half time. By now, O'Brien was off the field with concussion. When Franklin kicked his third field goal, the game was still not out of reach for the Jets but, on the ensuing kickoff, disaster struck. Hector's fumble was recovered by New England's Johnny Rembert and returned directly for a touchdown. A 12-yard touchdown pass, from replacement quarterback Pat Ryan to tight end Mickey Shuler, brought the Jets to within nine points with just over one quarter of the game to go. But less than five minutes remained when a Ryan pass was intercepted by Patriots rookie defensive end Garin Veris. His 18-yard return set up Franklin's fourth field goal to end the scoring.

NFC   San Francisco 3 at New York Giants 17

The 49ers were faced with a tall order when they travelled to New York. Quarterback Joe Montana was playing with strained rib muscles, cornerback Eric Wright was injured, Ronnie Lott had a suspect right hand, and neither of the two running backs, Wendell Tyler and Roger Craig, were fit to handle the rigours of a full game. They had to face one of the league's most aggressive defenses, led by everybody's All-Pro, linebacker Lawrence Taylor. The end was predictable and the Giants might well have won by a larger margin had not Eric Schubert missed on field goal attempts from 43, 36 and 39 yards. The Giants took a 10-0 lead on Schubert's 47-yard field goal and rookie tight end Mark Bavaro's one-handed touchdown reception, the latter which was no less astonishing for the ease with which it was made. On another day, Ray Wersching's 21-yard field goal might have sparked a revival, but, under unremitting pressure from the Giants' pass rush, Montana could never establish any kind of platform to do what he normally does with ease – even the short passes went to ground. Giants tight end Don Hasselbeck was unmarked in the end zone when he caught a three-yard touchdown pass to make the score 17-3, and though the 49ers briefly flickered to life, that's how the score remained. Joe Morris warmed up for the Bears, rushing for an impressive 141 yards on 28 carries.

Outstanding Individual Performances

Dwight Clark (San Francisco) caught eight passes for 120 yards.

Freeman McNeil looks for an opening in the Patriots' defense

Garin Veris (#60) logging one of his three sacks in the game against the Jets

WEEK EIGHTEEN – DIVISIONAL PLAYOFFS

American Football Conference

Cleveland 21 at Miami 24

Here was just the club to exploit Miami's known weakness against the run. In Earnest Byner and Kevin Mack, the Browns have the best young backfield pair in the league. Miami scored first, on a Fuad Reveiz 51-yard goal, but then the Cleveland runners cranked into gear. Punishing thrusts by Mack and Byner set up the field position for Bernie Kosar's 16-yard scoring pass to tight end Ozzie Newsome. Further touchdowns covering 21 and 66 yards, both of them by Byner, who rushed for 161 yards on the day, gave Cleveland a 21-3 lead after 3:38 of the third quarter. But the Browns couldn't quite complete the job – another score would surely have done it. Mixing his passes well, Miami quarterback Dan Marino slowly brought the Dolphins back into contention, firstly passing six yards for a touchdown to wide receiver Nat Moore. Rookie running back Ron Davenport broke more than one tackle and thundered in from the 31-yard line to make the score 21-17. Returning to the air, Marino passed 39 yards to Tony Nathan and then 14 yards to Bruce Hardy to leave the Dolphins knocking on the door. And from one yard out, Davenport knocked the same door off its hinges to give Miami a 24-21 win.

New England 27 at Los Angeles Raiders 20

The Patriots could not have chosen a better opponent against which to answer those who questioned their right to be in the big time. They travelled to the cauldron of the Los Angeles Coliseum and won playing Raiders-type football. In other words, they didn't roll over when the going was tough – at one time they trailed 17-7 – and they punished the other guy's mistakes. The comeback was inspired by running back Craig James, who became the first player to rush for 100 yards in a game against the Raiders on the year. James scored from the two-yard line. Two Tony Franklin field goals kept the Patriots level and then came the knockout punch. The Raiders' Sam Seale fumbled a kickoff and Jim Bowman, who had recovered a fumble to set up the Patriots' first touchdown, fell on the ball inside the end zone for the winning points.

National Football Conference

New York Giants 0 at Chicago 21

The week before, the Giants had done it to San Francisco, and now the Bears did it to the Giants. For 'it' read 'dominate by defense'. Quarterback Phil Simms was sacked six times as the Giants were held to minus net yardage until their brief, but fruitless, late-game flurry. The tone was set when the Giants' Sean Landeta, attempting to punt in a swirling wind, addressed the ball but didn't post it. The Bears' Shaun Gayle gathered in the free ball and ran five

Earnest Byner (#44) sets off against Miami

Jim McMahon (#9) finds the way barred by the Giants' Lawrence Taylor (#56)

yards for the opening touchdown. With running back Joe Morris still feeling the effects of an early collision with 'The Refrigerator', the Giants lost the key part of their offense. Their defense, too, appeared to have left its fury at home – not once did they collar Chicago quarterback Jim McMahon. Seemingly not bothered by the weather conditions either, the same player calmly threw for a brace of third-quarter touchdowns to wide receiver Dennis McKinnon. The Giants were out and the Bears were into their second NFC Championship Game in two years.

Dallas 0 at Los Angeles Rams 20

Rams running back Eric Dickerson rushed for an NFL playoff-record 248 yards and scored on touchdown runs of 55 and 40 yards to help his team into the NFC Championship Game for the first time since 1979 (it was the Rams' sixth since the 1970 merger). And when the Cowboys were on offense, they came up against a marauding Rams defense which registered five sacks, grabbed three pass interceptions and recovered three fumbles. Tragically, for the Cowboys, even the slightest error was punished. Mike Saxon was hurriedly drafted in to kick off for

Eric Dickerson (#29) blows through a gap on his 40-yard touchdown run

the second half, after Rafael Septien had injured himself. Saxon made a hash of the unfamiliar job and Dickerson scored his first touchdown on the very next play. Rams placekicker Mike Lansford was on target from 34 yards out after the Cowboys had fumbled the ensuing kickoff. Even the Rams' final score came after yet another Dallas error. Punt returner Gordon Banks fumbled on the Dallas 49-yard line and, four plays later, Dickerson streaked into the end zone.

Outstanding Individual Performances

Marcus Allen (L.A. Raiders) rushed for 121 yards on 22 carries and scored one touchdown.

Craig James (New England) rushed for 104 yards on 23 carries and scored one touchdown.

Tony Nathan (Miami) caught ten passes for 101 yards.

Richard Dent (Chicago) registered 3.5 quarterback sacks.

Gary Jeter (L.A. Rams) registered three quarterback sacks.

WEEK NINETEEN – CONFERENCE CHAMPIONSHIPS

American Football Conference

New England 31 at Miami 14

The New England Patriots faced more than just an outstanding opponent when they travelled to Miami – 'travel' was one of the key words. They'd lost on their last eighteen visits, most recently by the score of 30-27 on Week Fifteen. Also, they would be aware that the Dolphins had been in the AFC Championship Game five times previously, and they'd won the lot. Another key word was 'momentum', which the Dolphins certainly had established over their previous eight games (seven in the 1985 regular season and against Cleveland in the playoffs), all of which they'd won. The final key word, though it would become apparent only as the game progressed, was 'fumble'.

The Patriots went out to a 3-0 lead after recovering a Tony Nathan fumble, but then saw Miami respond with an 80-yard touchdown drive – Uh Uh, get ready for it. But it would be in the fourth quarter before Miami's next success. By then, the Patriots had scored on a commanding 66-yard drive and had taken advantage of fumbles by Dan Marino and Lorenzo Hampton to move out into a 24-7 lead. And even after Miami's final statement (it came after the Patriots had spilled the ball), yet another Dolphins fumble gave New England the opportunity to drive 45 yards for the game-clinching touchdown. Between them, running backs Craig James, Robert Weathers and Tony Collins, had rushed for 253 yards. Tony Eason had passed sparingly and yet effectively for three touchdowns, and Dan Marino's output had been restricted to fairly manageable proportions.

National Football Conference

Los Angeles Rams 0 at Chicago 24

'Intimidating' is a description that has been freely acknowledged by the Bears throughout their history. Perhaps 'intimidation by perfection' would be more appropriate of the 1985 defense, which threw down the gauntlet on every play. They could be beaten – Miami's Dan Marino had shown that to be true – but, with respect to Dieter Brock, the Rams simply did not possess that kind of quarterback. But they did have Eric Dickerson, who was coming off a record-breaking game, and the great man would exploit every opportunity provided by an offensive line which was one of the league's best. Furthermore, there would be an alert defense waiting to pounce on the slightest Chicago mistake – and it was

ough enough to force a few.

Right from the start, however, Chicago quarterback Jim McMahon went to the air with abandon, completing passes to Emery Moorehead and Willie Gault, before bootlegging 16 yards for the opening touchdown. On the Bears' next possession, three more pass completions set up Kevin Butler's 34-yard field goal. And it was a measure of McMahon's confidence that, in the third quarter, on fourth-and-six at the Rams 33-yard line, he scampered into space before firing a 13-yard pass to Walter Payton.

Left: Tony Eason winding up to pass against Miami

Below: Craig James (#32) rushing against Miami

That kept the drive alive, and it was rounded off two plays later with a 22-yard touchdown pass to Willie Gault. The Rams had their chances and were on the wrong end of one or two doubtful official judgements, but Wilber Marshall's 52-yard touchdown return, after Brock had been forced to fumble the ball, underlined the Bears' superiority which, rightly, took them to their first Super Bowl.

Outstanding Individual Performances

Craig James (New England) rushed for 105 yards on 22 carries.

Tony Eason (New England) completed ten of twelve passes, three of which were for touchdowns.

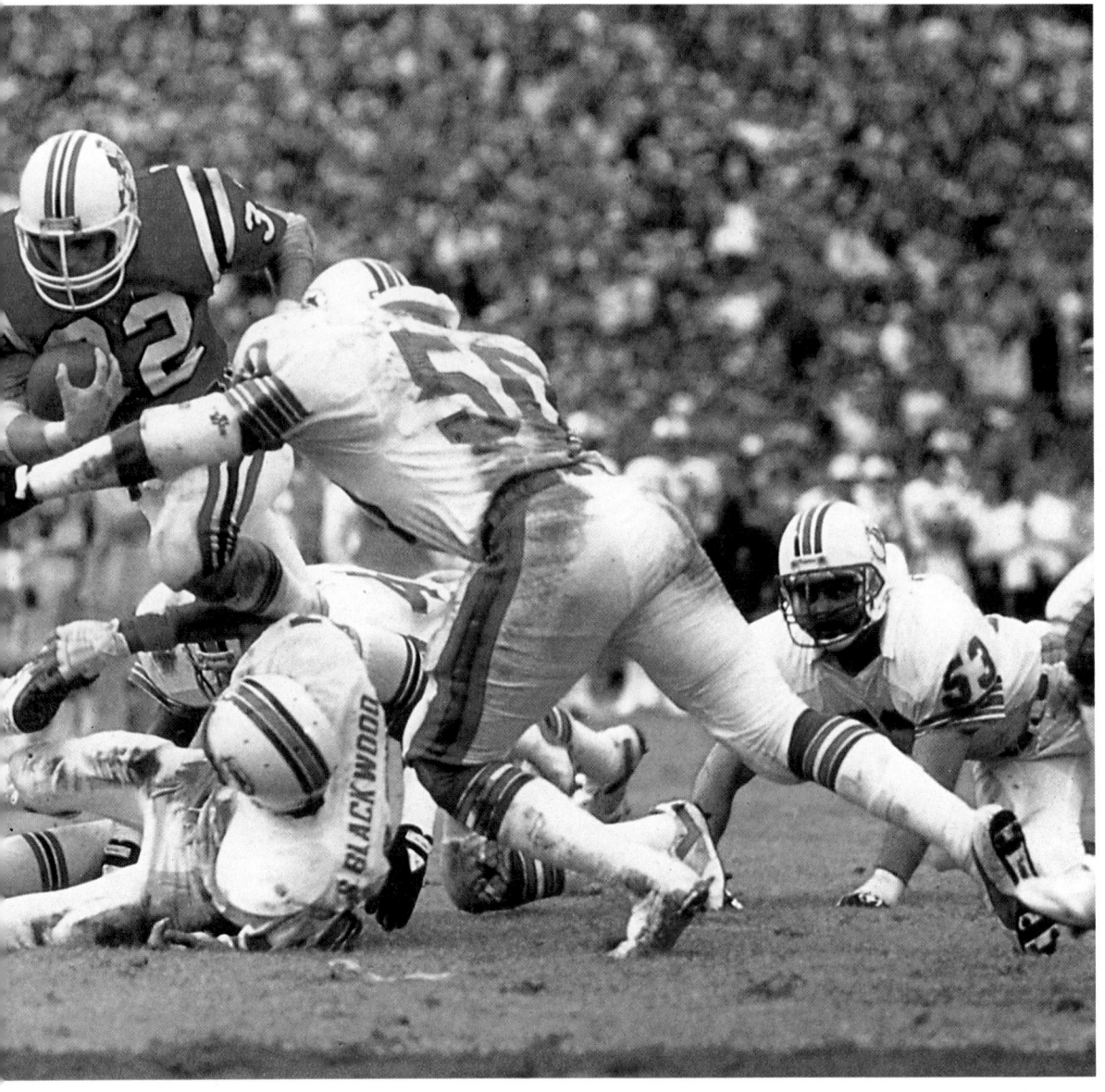

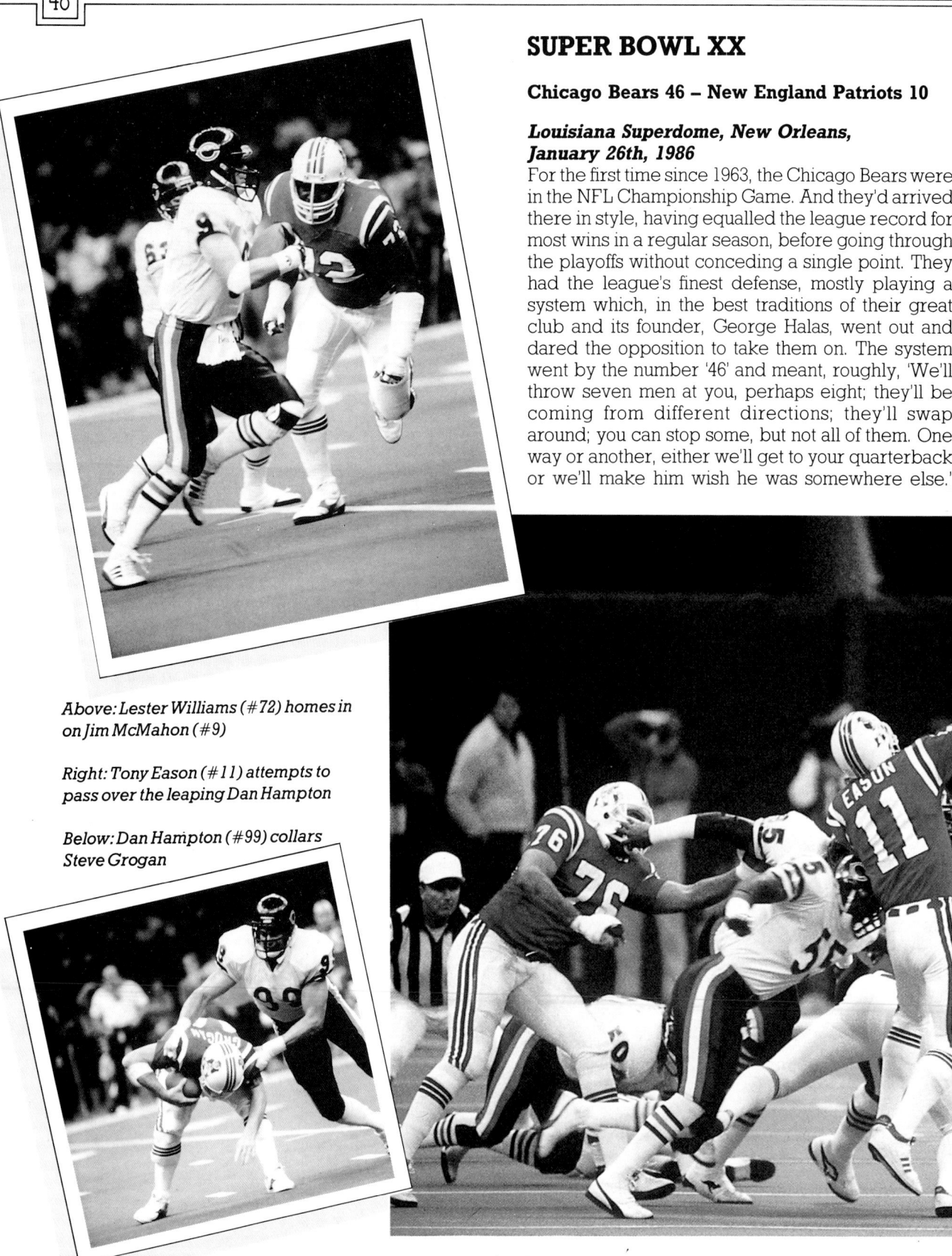

SUPER BOWL XX

Chicago Bears 46 – New England Patriots 10

Louisiana Superdome, New Orleans, January 26th, 1986

For the first time since 1963, the Chicago Bears were in the NFL Championship Game. And they'd arrived there in style, having equalled the league record for most wins in a regular season, before going through the playoffs without conceding a single point. They had the league's finest defense, mostly playing a system which, in the best traditions of their great club and its founder, George Halas, went out and dared the opposition to take them on. The system went by the number '46' and meant, roughly, 'We'll throw seven men at you, perhaps eight; they'll be coming from different directions; they'll swap around; you can stop some, but not all of them. One way or another, either we'll get to your quarterback or we'll make him wish he was somewhere else.'

Above: Lester Williams (#72) homes in on Jim McMahon (#9)

Right: Tony Eason (#11) attempts to pass over the leaping Dan Hampton

Below: Dan Hampton (#99) collars Steve Grogan

Names such as Dan Hampton, Richard Dent, Mike Singletary, Otis Wilson, Wilber Marshall, Leslie Frazier and Gary Fencik, had occupied the Patriots' coaches, day and night, for two weeks. Another name would come to mind every time they reached for a can of cold beer. When it came to stopping the Bears' offense, those same coaches would be thinking of a tough young offensive line which was sending Jim Covert and Jay Hilgenberg to start in the Pro Bowl. Quarterback Jim McMahon, a dashing figure who didn't give a damn, was improving by the game – they weren't sure just how good he was, but they knew he was good. His prime target, wide receiver Willie Gault, is amongst the fastest around, and no-one makes a better adjustment to the ball during its flight. At the heart of their offense lay the quintessential football player, Walter Payton.

But the Patriots could walk into the Superdome with their heads held high. They'd knocked off Chicago's AFC equivalent, the Raiders, even in their own backyard. Subsequently, they'd seen off Miami

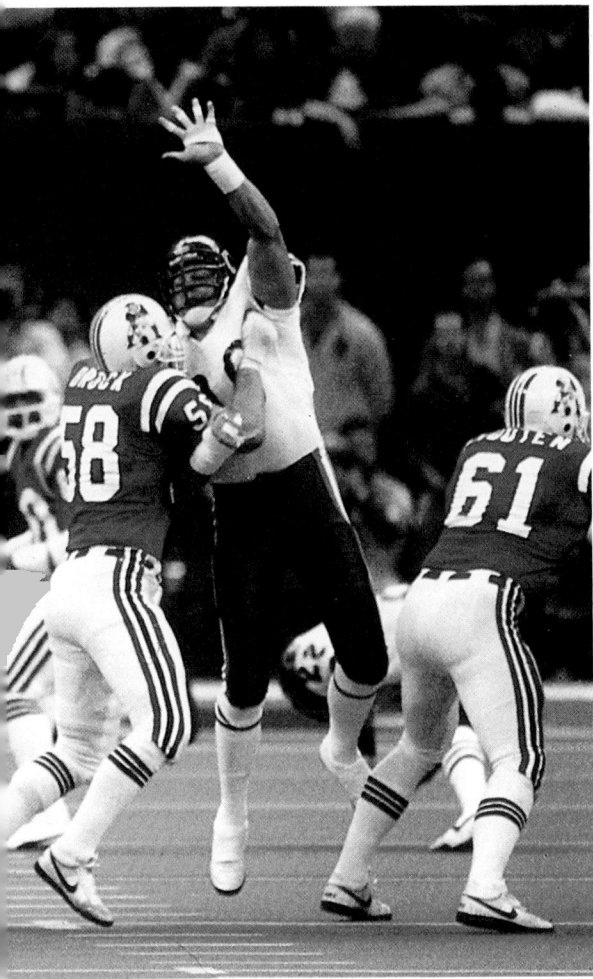

– and that's something that the Bears hadn't been able to do. In Tony Eason, the Patriots, too, had a quarterback of high class. He would be protected by a big offensive line featuring the incomparable guard, John Hannah, supported by a cast which included tackle Brian Holloway and center Pete Brock. Running back Craig James had clocked up the only century conceded by the Raiders all year – he would need careful watching. The mercurial Stanley Morgan was at wide receiver. His usual partner, Irving Fryar, was not expected to play. But he might possibly be returning the punts – and that would spell trouble. Their defense could mount a solid pass rush. The form of rookie defensive end Garin Veris had been a revelation – he'd logged ten sacks in the regular season – and, in that category, outside linebacker Andre Tippett had led the entire AFC with 16.5. Inside linebacker Steve Nelson is a notorious run-stuffer. Their secondary was alert, fast and had developed a nose for the ball. Indeed, the whole defensive unit had become adept in the art of grand larceny – in the three-game playoff series, they had converted eleven turnovers into a total of 61 points.

THE GAME
Scoring By Quarters

1st Quarter
New England: Franklin, 36-yard field goal (1:19)
Chicago 0 – New England 3
Chicago: Butler, 28-yard field goal (5:40)
Chicago 3 – New England 3
Chicago: Butler, 24-yard field goal (13:39)
Chicago 6 – New England 3
Chicago: Suhey, 11-yard run; Butler kick (14:37)
Chicago 13 – New England 3

2nd Quarter
Chicago: McMahon, 2-yard run; Butler kick (7:36)
Chicago 20 – New England 3
Chicago: Butler, 25-yard field goal (15:00)
Chicago 23 – New England 3

3rd Quarter
Chicago: McMahon, 1-yard run; Butler kick (7:38)
Chicago 30 – New England 3
Chicago: Phillips, 29-yard interception return; Butler kick (8:44)
Chicago 37 – New England 3
Chicago: Perry, 1-yard run; Butler kick (11:38)
Chicago 44 – New England 3

4th Quarter
New England: Fryar, 8-yard pass from Grogan; Franklin kick (1:46)
Chicago 44 – New England 10
Chicago: Waechter safety (9:24)
Chicago 46 – New England 10

Above: The Patriots pass rush nails Jim McMahon (#9)

Below: William Perry jostles with John Hannah (#73)

For the Patriots, it all went according to plan, at least, it did for just over a minute. Veris forced a fumble by Payton on the Bears' second play from scrimmage and, of course, the Patriots established possession. Had Morgan held onto a pass over the middle, a touchdown would have been a formality. But he didn't, and the Patriots had to settle for the field goal which, incidentally, was the earliest time any team had scored in a Super Bowl. On Chicago's very next play from scrimmage, New England linebacker Don Blackmon did get a hand to the ball, on an errant McMahon pass, but it didn't stick. Again, there was a clear path into the end zone. At this stage in a Super Bowl, after a hesitant start, most quarterbacks would proceed with a little circumspection. But not McMahon, who dropped back and unloaded a 43-yard pass to Gault. With just a little more mustard on the ball, Gault would have been off to the races, as they say. Still, the Bears were on the move and, shortly afterwards, they drew level on Butler's 28-yard field goal. Four minutes later, Hampton recovered an Eason fumble to set up another field goal. The roof hadn't yet caved in but the rafters were beginning to creak. Less than a minute later, Matt Suhey darted into the New England end zone from 11 yards out, two plays after Singletary had recovered a fumble by Craig James on the Patriots' 13-yard line. It made the tally 13-3 and precipitated a scoring orgy.

When the Patriots were in possession, either they punted or fumbled the ball away. Each time, the Bears came roaring back with a fury which did not abate until after William Perry had plunged in for the touchdown which took their total to 44 points. Even then, and fielding many backup players, they topped up with a two-point safety.

The Bears were never going to match their 73-point romp of 1940, but their points total was good enough for a new Super Bowl record, as was the margin of their victory. Defensive end Richard Dent was voted the game's Most Valuable Player, though, in this and most other years, both McMahon and Gault would have been good candidates. Let's end with a few words of consolation for New England, who had the misfortune to come up against one of the finest defenses of all time. Poor Eason did not complete a pass. But no-one can erase the club name from the list of AFC Champions. And that's how the 1985 Patriots should be remembered.

Outstanding Individual Performances

Willie Gault (Chicago) caught four passes for 129 yards.

Jim McMahon (Chicago) completed 12 of 20 passes for 256 yards and rushed for two touchdowns.

Richard Dent (Chicago) registered 1.5 quarterback sacks and forced two fumbles.

Above: Jim McMahon (#9) pitches to Matt Suhey (#26)

Below: Richard Dent, the Super Bowl MVP

ANATOMY OF SUPER BOWL XX QUARTER BY QUARTER

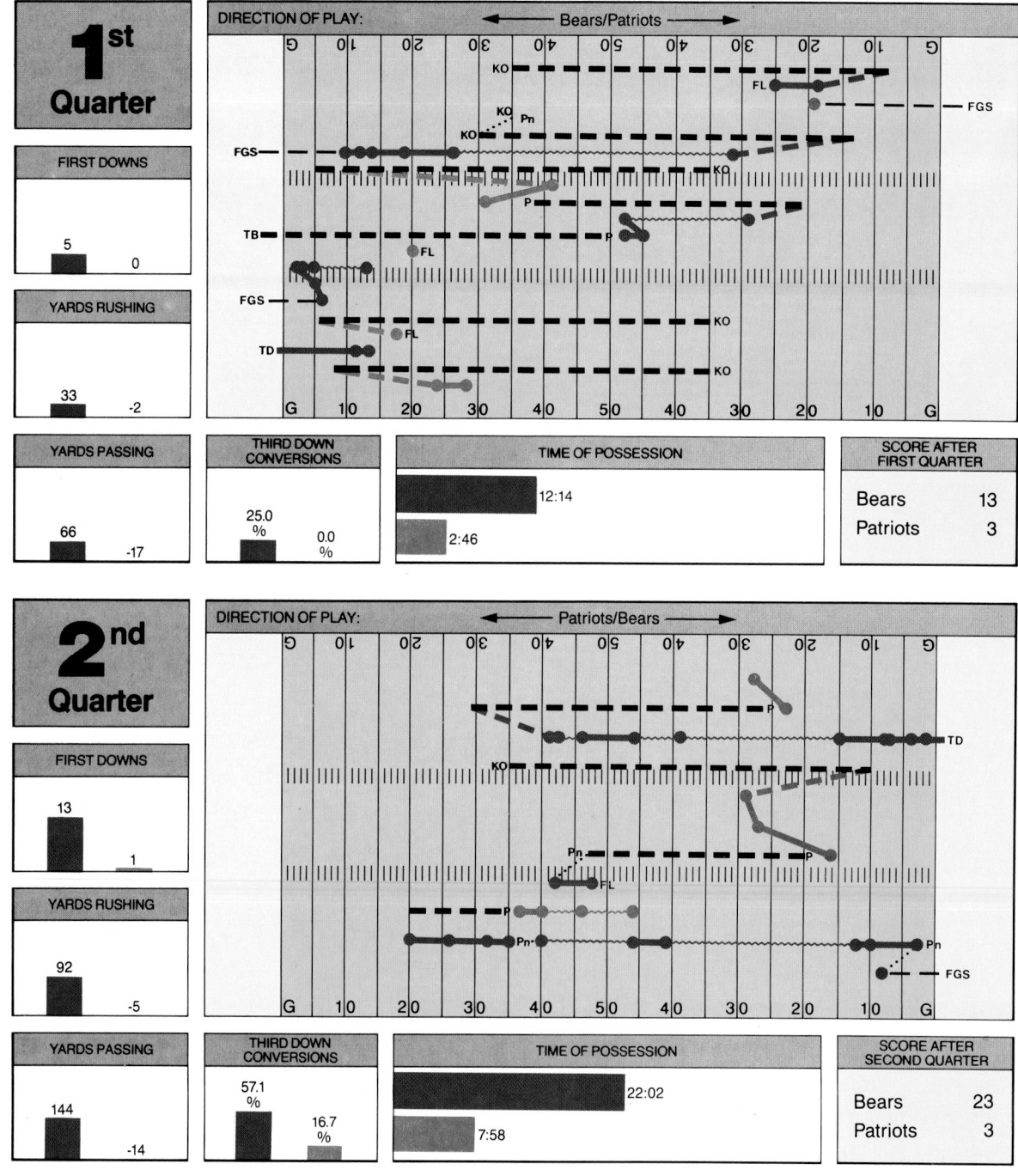

1st Quarter

DIRECTION OF PLAY: ← Bears/Patriots →

FIRST DOWNS	
5	0

YARDS RUSHING	
33	-2

YARDS PASSING	
66	-17

THIRD DOWN CONVERSIONS	
25.0 %	0.0 %

TIME OF POSSESSION
12:14
2:46

SCORE AFTER FIRST QUARTER	
Bears	13
Patriots	3

2nd Quarter

DIRECTION OF PLAY: ← Patriots/Bears →

FIRST DOWNS	
13	1

YARDS RUSHING	
92	-5

YARDS PASSING	
144	-14

THIRD DOWN CONVERSIONS	
57.1 %	16.7 %

TIME OF POSSESSION
22:02
7:58

SCORE AFTER SECOND QUARTER	
Bears	23
Patriots	3

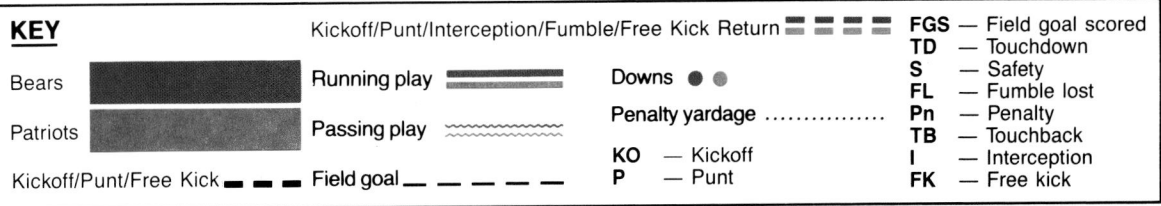

KEY

Bears

Patriots

Kickoff/Punt/Free Kick ▬ ▬ ▬

Kickoff/Punt/Interception/Fumble/Free Kick Return

Running play

Passing play

Field goal

Downs ● ●

Penalty yardage ⋯⋯⋯

KO — Kickoff
P — Punt

FGS — Field goal scored
TD — Touchdown
S — Safety
FL — Fumble lost
Pn — Penalty
TB — Touchback
I — Interception
FK — Free kick

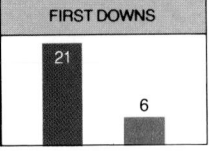

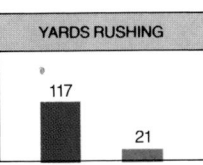

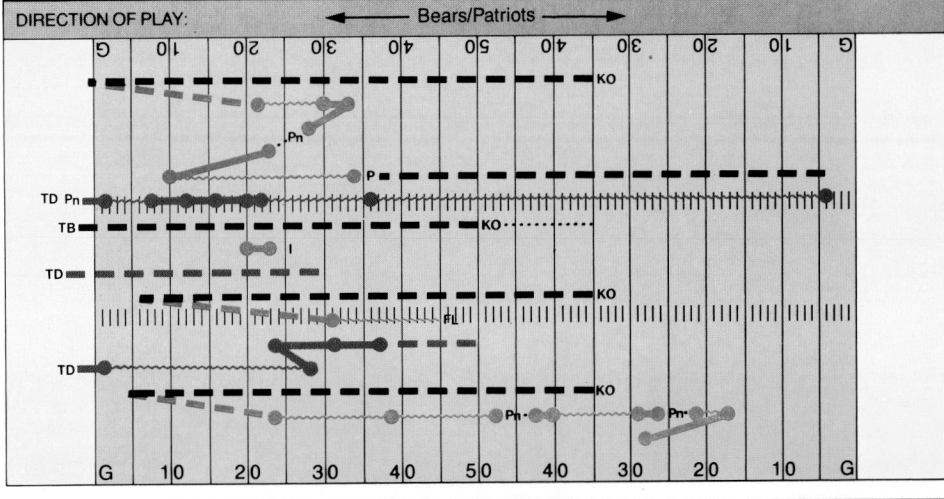

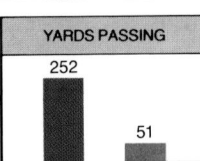

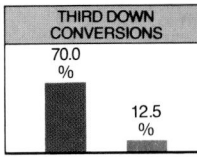

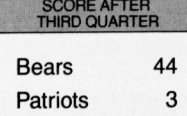

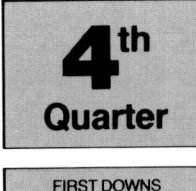

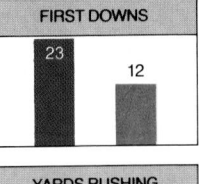

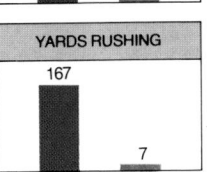

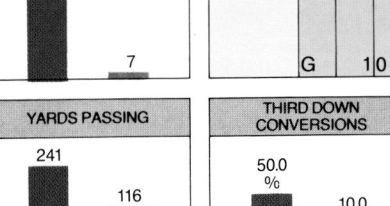

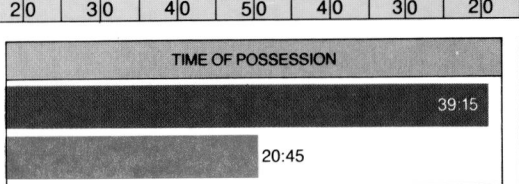

SCORE AFTER THIRD QUARTER

Bears 44
Patriots 3

FINAL SCORE

Bears 46
Patriots 10

CHAPTER TWO

A HISTORY OF THE CHICAGO BEARS

This is a tale which begins, before the 'Twenties had started to roar, when A.E. Staley, a manufacturer of starch, hit upon the idea of sponsoring a football team to boost the sales of his product. Within a short time, that team became known as the Chicago Bears. Theirs is a story interwoven with that of George Stanley Halas, sportsman and visionary, who would later be recognised as the Father of the NFL. Under Halas, pro football's men of iron were alloyed with the precious metal of the game's superstars, in a formula which would produce eight league championships. Halas and twenty-three of his players are now enshrined in the Pro Football Hall of Fame. But there would, too, be the dark days – days stretching into years of disappointment. And there would be times for shedding a tear.

Halas was not prowling the sideline when the 1985 Bears gave new meaning to the word 'dominance' as they destroyed New England in Super Bowl XX. He died on October 31st, 1983. But he would be watching from somewhere, no doubt castigating the officials for every close call which went the wrong way. And when it was all over, he'd be smiling quietly as he chalked up championship number nine.

Back in 1920, Mr Staley's company was based in Decatur, Illinois. Already, he had a semi-pro baseball team but it's not clear if he knew much about pro football. And it's unlikely that he recognised its full potential. But then, not many did at that time, when the pro game was treated with no little measure of circumspection by an American public which saw football as an amateur game, played by college heroes. However, Staley knew a good man when he saw one, and he hired George Halas, both to play on his baseball team and see to the pro football side of things. At twenty-five years old, Halas had a good track record. He had been a star in college football at Illinois and later, playing at 'end', he was named player of the game on the Great Lakes (Navy) team which defeated Mare Island (Marines) 17-0 in the 1919 Rose Bowl. Recently, he had been playing major league baseball for the New York Yankees, no less, until losing his place to a combination of hip injury and the arrival of George H. (Babe) Ruth, none greater.

Some things, it seems, are meant to happen – Halas turned up in Decatur at precisely the right time. There was serious talk of forming a professional football league, and he was one of the figures who attended the preliminary meeting in Canton on August 20th, 1920. The details were ironed out a month later (on September 17th), and the Decatur Staleys duly joined the other eleven clubs which embarked on the great adventure.

There's little of substance which remains of that first season, when the clubs played under the title of the American Professional Football Association (APFA). There was no formal schedule and a team standing (league table) was either not kept or, simply, was lost. Come the end of the season, Decatur was one of four clubs which laid claim to the championship – and a strong claim it was. They had shut out eleven of their thirteen opponents en route to a 10-1-2 record. Their only loss was a 7-6 squeaker against the Racine Cardinals (they are now better known as the St Louis Cardinals) who, it is described, scored their touchdown with the blocking assistance of a bunch of fans who had invaded the field. The other claimants, Akron, Buffalo and Canton, played an ad hoc postseason round-robin (excluding the Staleys), but that, too, failed to decide the issue.

The Staleys were one of the few clubs which showed a profit in that first year of operation – each man on the squad received $1,900 for the season. But Mr Staley was soon to find himself in financial trouble and he was forced to withdraw his sponsorship. He struck a deal with Halas, handing over ownership of the club, together with a $5,000 cash payment, and, in return, Halas agreed to retain the team nickname for one year. Subsequently, Halas gave a half share to his friend and teammate, Dutch Sternaman, in lieu of future salaries. Together, they moved the club north to the city of Chicago, taking the best of the original Decatur squad with them. Included amongst these was George Trafton, a future Hall of Famer, who played center on offense and tackled everything which moved when he played on defense. (At that time, they all played 'both ways'.) He was everybody's villain, noted for his 'physical' approach. Yet he was much more than just a rough-house, indeed, it is said that he never made a bad snap in thirteen years of pro football.

By hiring Joe Carr as president in 1921, the APFA had

The 1920 Decatur Staleys

taken a significant step to put its house in order. Carr was a sound administrator and knew just when to wield the big stick. In his very first season he was called to use his executive authority when, again, there was a major dispute over the destination of the league title. It involved the Staleys and the Buffalo All-Americans. The Staleys ended the season at 10-1-1, shading the 9-1-2 All-Americans by 90.9% to 90% (tied games did not count in the calculation). But the All-Americans charged the Staleys with having included victories over non-league clubs in their record. Without much hesitation, Carr ruled in favour of the Staleys, who thus became the first official league champions.

Though it would be eleven years before the club again tasted championship success, they were often in contention. In each of the next three seasons they were the runners-up behind the Bulldogs (the Bulldogs moved from Canton to Cleveland after the 1923 season). It was when playing against the Oorang Indians, in 1923, that Halas gathered in a fumble by the legendary Jim Thorpe and raced 98 yards for a touchdown, to establish a league record which stood until Oakland's Jack Tatum went 104 yards in 1972. Again, in 1926, they trailed only the Frankford Yellowjackets.

Halas was a dominant figure at league meetings. It was at his suggestion that the league be renamed the National Football League, beginning in the 1922 season. He'd renamed his club the Chicago Bears in the same year. Later, in 1926, it was Halas at his persuasive best who coaxed the other club owners into agreeing not to sign any college player whose class had not graduated. This was a

really major act of fence-mending between the colleges and the pros, and marked the origins of a partnership whose unruffled smoothness we now take for granted.

Unlike other clubs, many of whom had difficulty paying for the team bus, the Bears consistently made profits. It meant that Halas could go out and buy the best, as he had done when acquiring the services of a future Hall of Famer, tackle Ed Healey, from the Rock Island Independents in 1922. At the end of the 1924 season, Halas and Sternaman shared a profit reported to be $20,000. It was all heady stuff and yet, it did not even begin to compare with what was just around the corner – in November, 1925, Halas signed Harold 'Red' Grange.

Without doubt, Grange was the most exciting college football player of his era. The 6-0, 185-pound Illinois tailback had been All-America in 1923 and 1924, and would shortly make it three in a row. He did things in style. In 1924, against a Michigan team which had not lost for the last twenty straight games, he returned the opening kickoff 95 yards for a touchdown and, on his next three possessions, ran 67, 56 and 44 yards for three more scores. The first quarter was not yet over – he would later return to throw for a fifth touchdown and rush for a sixth. It was the kind of performance that earned him the nickname, 'The Galloping Ghost'.

There was wide consternation over the manner and timing of Grange's signing, which came immediately after completion of the Illinois schedule (it could not happen these days). But Grange was now under the wing of an agent, C.C. 'Cash and Carry' Pyle, and there was no time to waste. The Bears still had seven regular-season games to play and it was the intention to squeeze in three extra games to capitalise on Grange's nationwide appeal. Astonishingly, those ten games were played in the space of eighteen days. After pausing for eight days' rest, Grange and the Bears (they were bolstered by a few guest players from other NFL clubs) were off again, this time on a nine-game exhibition tour from which only the northeast of the United States was excluded.

At the end of it all (the last game was in Seattle on January 31st), Grange was richer to the tune of over $100,000 and that was just for starters – there would be endorsements and even movies to boost his bank balance.

And what of Grange the rookie pro football player? He certainly had his moments, scoring touchdowns by passing, rushing and even by intercepting enemy passes (he also played on defense). He ripped off a few big plays. Also, he came through well after taking terrible physical punishment. Yet, as a player, only rarely did he make the kind of impact we'd expect from the modern-day franchise running back such as Eric Dickerson, to say nothing of Walter Payton.

But it didn't matter – throughout the tour the fans flocked in their tens of thousands just to catch a glimpse of the great man. More than 70,000 packed into the New York Polo Grounds and an even greater number was on hand to see him score twice in the Los Angeles Coliseum. But more than just helping the Bears, in the space of a few weeks he had given pro football the launching pad it had needed.

Ironically, it was Grange's celebrity value which brought an end to his first brief tenure with the Bears. Pyle's demands (he and Grange each wanted a one-third share of the ownership) were too much for Halas and Sternaman and, together with Grange, he went off to New York City to form a new league. It lasted just one year, after which Grange's team, the New York Yankees, was absorbed into the NFL. In 1927, playing for the Yankees against the Bears, Grange suffered a non-contact knee injury which greatly reduced his effectiveness. The injury kept him out of football until 1929, when he rejoined the Bears, and it was mostly as a defensive player that he played out the remainder of his career.

By 1930, the relationship between Halas and Sternaman had begun to sour and it was time for a change. Halas retired from playing and handed over the position of head coach to Ralph Jones, who had been the head coach at Lake Forest (Illinois) Academy. Jones promised a championship within three years and made a start to that end by signing Bronko Nagurski, a 6-2, 230-pound freight train of a running back. The following year, he picked up Keith Molesworth, a classy halfback, and then, in 1932, the versatile end, Bill Hewitt.

By the beginning of 1932, the list of NFL clubs which would endure had risen to six. Both the Cardinals and the New York Giants had won championships, and the Green Bay Packers were on a roll – they'd won the last three. (The other clubs were the Boston Braves and the Portsmouth (Ohio) Spartans, who later took root in Washington and Detroit respectively.) Now it was the Bears' turn.

In the final game of the 1932 season, against Green Bay, Nagurski's 56-yard touchdown run helped the Bears to a 9-0 victory and brought them level with Portsmouth on top of the league. (Chicago and Portsmouth were 6-1-6 and 6-1-4 respectively, but tied games still did not count in the calculation of percentage.) There would have to be a playoff game which, because of inclement weather in the Chicago area, was held indoors at Chicago Stadium. The Bears won the game, 9-0, and their second NFL Championship, though, as with their first title, it was the subject of controversy. The two teams had played three quarters of scoreless football, when Nagurski threw a fourth-and-goal touchdown pass to Grange, who was standing in the end zone. At the time the rule was that a forward pass could be made only from at least five yards behind the line of scrimmage. The Spartans angrily claimed that Nagurski had violated the rule – but nobody listened.

Even though they won the championship, the Bears lost $18,000 in 1932, and Sternaman decided that it was time to go. He sold his half-share to Halas for $38,000, $5,000 of which Halas had borrowed from Charles Bidwill who, in that same year, purchased the Cardinals. (Charles Bidwill was the father of William V. Bidwill, the current owner of the St Louis Cardinals.) Halas also resumed as head coach following the departure of Jones who, incidentally, had indeed kept his promise of winning a championship within three years.

The 1932 playoff game had proved so popular that the idea was incorporated as a permanent feature, beginning in 1933, and would involve the champion teams of the two, newly-created, Eastern and Western divisions. At the end of the regular season, the Bears were on top in the West by a four-game margin over Portsmouth. They were now into the first of two periods when they totally dominated the league. (It was in the 1930s that the Bears were nicknamed 'the Monsters of the Midway'.) Entering the 1933 championship game against the Giants, they had won their last four games, and they duly made it five with a 23-21 victory.

Bronko Nagurski is tackled by New York's Ed Danowski in the 1934 NFL Championship Game

The winning points came in the fourth quarter, when Hewitt took a forward pass from Nagurski and lateralled to Bill Karr, who ran 19 yards for a touchdown.

On through 1934 they swept everyone aside, pausing only briefly to count their sequence of successes which, by the end of the regular season, numbered a league-record 18 (including the 1933 championship game). They had acquired rookie Beattie Feathers, an extraordinary halfback. Behind the blocking of the indestructible Nagurski, Feathers carried the ball 101 times for 1,004 yards in thirteen games. The sceptic might point out that, in those days, the statisticians weren't quite as hot as they are now – they did make mistakes. Nonetheless, the name of Feathers went into the record books as the first player in league history to rush for over 1,000 yards in a regular season.

However, it was the name of the New York Giants, who had been the last team to beat the Bears (they won 3-0 on November 19th, 1933), which was added to the list of NFL Champions. Playing on a frozen pitch, the Bears led 10-3 at half time and 13-3 after three quarters, and seemed well on the way to retaining their title. But the crafty Giants came out for the second half wearing basketball shoes which, as it turned out, gave them extra traction. The Bears slithered around while the Giants motored to 27 fourth-quarter points, and their second NFL Championship by the score of 30-13. At the time, it was dubbed the 'Sneakers Game', 'sneakers' being the general term for sports shoes.

It was 1937 before the Bears had another tilt at the championship and this time they came up against one of the league's all-time great quarterbacks (many old-timers say he was the greatest), Washington's Sammy Baugh. (Baugh was listed as a halfback but played the role that we now understand as that of quarterback.) Though still a rookie, Baugh logged championship-game figures which would be astounding even in the modern era, as he passed for 335 yards and touchdowns covering 55, 78 and 35 yards. It was too good for the Bears, who lost 28-21 – but wait until next time!

That 'next time' came in the 1940 championship game when, again, they faced Baugh and the Redskins. With six future Hall of Famers in the starting lineup, that 1940 Bears team was probably the best in their history.

George Halas and the Bears celebrate their 73-0 victory over Washington in the 1940 NFL Championship Game

1940 NFL Championship Game Starting Lineups
(Hall of Famers in **bold**)

Chicago	Position	Washington
Bob Nowaskey	LE	Bob Masterson
Joe Stydahar	LT	Willie Wilkin
Danny Fortmann	LG	Dick Farman
Clyde 'Bulldog' Turner	C	Bob Titchenal
George Musso	RG	Steve Slivinski
Lee Artoe	RT	Jim Barber
George Wilson	RE	Charley Malone
Sid Luckman	QB	Max Krause
Ray Nolting	LHB	**Sammy Baugh**
George McAfee	RHB	Ed Justice
Bill Osmanski	FB	Jim Johnston

Just three weeks before the championship game, during the regular season, Washington had beaten the Bears 7-3. Subsequently, Redskins owner George Preston Marshall had labelled the Bears as 'crybabies' for having disputed an official's decision. There is no record of Marshall's comments after the championship game, when his team was slaughtered by the score of 73-0. Ten different Chicago players scored touchdowns.

The reasons for the Bears' astonishing victory are not clear. Some historians point to the effectiveness of their T-formation, which they had been perfecting for more than a decade. It featured a man-in-motion and compared much more closely with the modern style of play than did the 'Single Wing' formation, which was popular with most NFL clubs. But the Bears weren't in the T-formation – they

were on defense – when they grabbed eight pass interceptions (three were returned directly for touchdowns) and restricted the Redskins to just 22 net yards rushing. Nonetheless, the formation was quickly adopted by teams around the league.

That 1940 encounter fuelled a rivalry which had been simmering for some time and would last for another decade.

The following year, 1941, the Bears' only loss was against Green Bay, with whom they were tied at 10-1-0 at the end of the regular season. In the playoff game to decide the Western division title, the Bears won easily, 33-14, and had even less difficulty beating the Giants, 37-9, to earn their fifth NFL Championship.

Halas's team went on to dominate the NFL throughout the 1942 regular season, winning all eleven of its games and matching the 18-game winning streak established in the seasons spanning 1933 and 1934. But it all came to an abrupt halt in the championship game, where they lost 14-6 to the Redskins. By then, Halas and two of the Bears' backfield starters, George McAfee and Norm Standlee, had left to fight in the Second World War – the Bears were down to their fourth-string fullback, Gary Famiglietti. Even so they had their chances to win. Twice in the first quarter, they failed to capitalise on good field position, and a fourth-quarter touchdown run by Hugh Gallarneau was called back for an infringement in the Chicago backfield. A 50-yard fumble return for a touchdown by tackle Lee Artoe was all they could muster.

In 1943, it was becoming a regular feature when, for the

Action from the Bears' 33-14 NFC Western Division Playoff victory over Green Bay in 1941

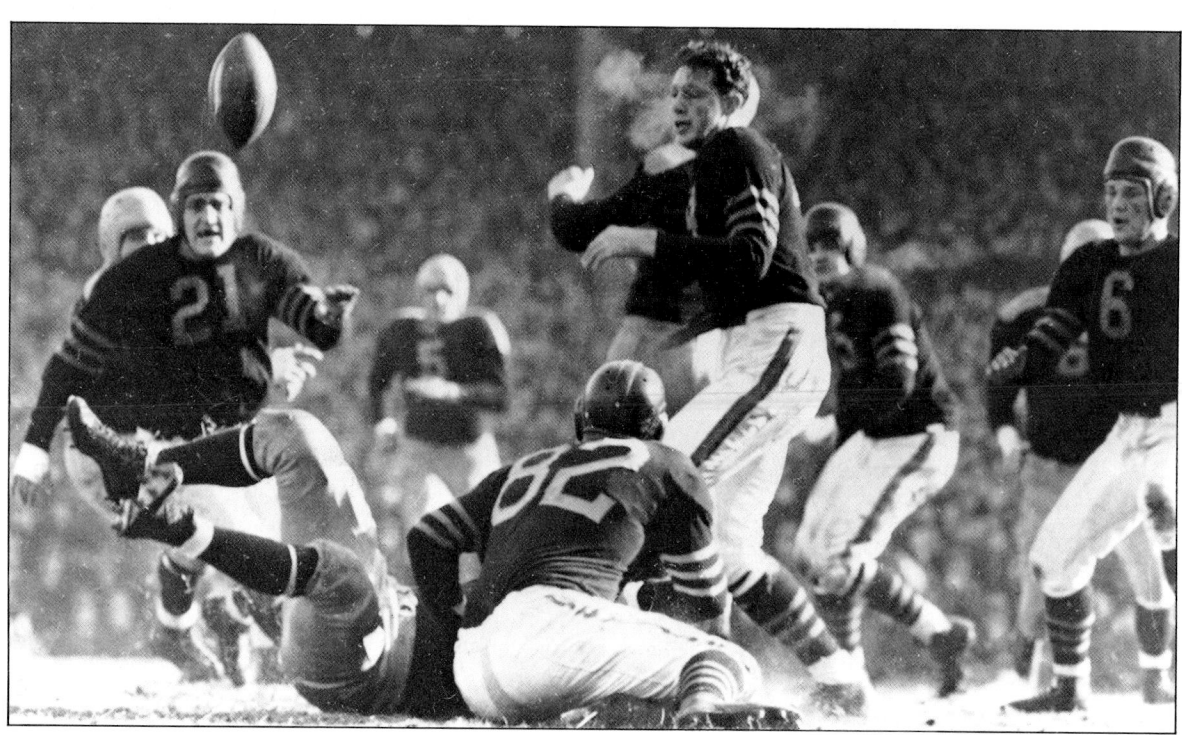

fourth year in a row, Chicago went to the NFL Championship Game – it was their third title game against Washington over the same period. Sid Luckman had developed into a big-play quarterback. Against the Giants on November 14th, he established two league records, passing for 433 yards (he was the first in league history to go over 400 yards) and seven touchdowns. Nagurski had come out of retirement to help the club, which was still missing several starters because of the war. In the big game, the Redskins scored first, on a touchdown by Andy Farkas. Fittingly, Nagurski brought the Bears back on equal terms with his last touchdown in the NFL, and they had nosed ahead on the first of Sid Luckman's five touchdown passes when Redskins owner Marshall was ejected from the playing field, after trying to gain access to the Washington players' bench. He was still complaining after the game whilst the Chicago players were celebrating a 41-21 victory.

The two fierce rivals did not meet again in the playoffs until the 1984 season, by which time any last traces of bitterness had evaporated.

In 1946, the Bears were back in the championship game, with many of their former starters who had returned from the armed services. McAfee returned in late 1945 and, being somewhat out of tune, asked Halas to go easy on him. And Halas did, using him for only twelve minutes, but he still managed to score three touchdowns.

With Luckman at quarterback, the Bears went 8-2-1 in the 1946 regular season, losing 14-0 to the Giants and 35-28 to their local rivals, the Cardinals. But they had a great deal of trouble in the championship game where, for the fourth time, they came up against the Giants. The scores were level at 14-14 in the final quarter, when Luckman ran

Left: George Halas with quarterback Sid Luckman

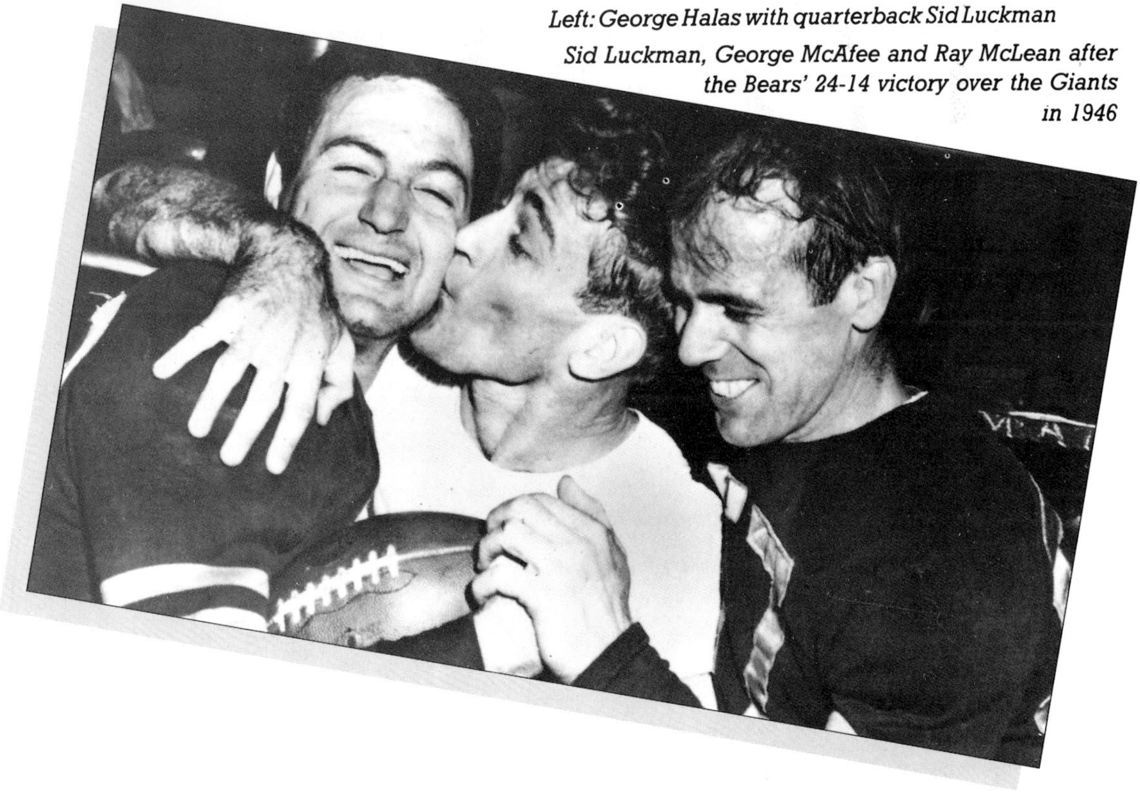

Sid Luckman, George McAfee and Ray McLean after the Bears' 24-14 victory over the Giants in 1946

19 yards for a touchdown on a surprise play. In the Bears' playbook it was known as '97 Bingo, keep it', and keep it is what Luckman did after faking a handoff. The Bears ran out winners by the score of 24-14.

Not until 1956 did the Bears again contest the championship game. Over the intervening period, though their wanderings were not always aimless, they felt the weight of two emerging NFL powers, the Detroit Lions and the Rams. (In 1950, they were beaten 24-14 by the Rams in a playoff for the conference title.) That period saw the retirement of those players who had made the name of the Bears synonymous with greatness. They were replaced by the new stars, notably future Hall of Famer Bill George, who was drafted in 1951 (he reported in 1952) and is widely considered to have been the game's first great middle linebacker. George Blanda, who was a backup quarterback and did the placekicking, also would find his way into the Hall of Fame – but one feels it was more for his subsequent achievements with Houston and the Raiders. Another future Hall of Famer, defensive end Doug Atkins, joined the Bears from Cleveland in 1955. In 1956, second-year running back Rick Casares became the second Bears player (he was the fifth man in NFL history) to rush for over 1,000 yards, as he led the league with 1,126. But Halas hadn't always made the right decisions – he fought a costly bidding war to sign quarterback Bobby Layne in 1948, but sold him to the New York Bulldogs in 1949. Layne, too, is now in the Hall of Fame. In the 1956 championship game, against the Giants, both teams wore sneakers but it didn't help the Bears at all – they were well-and-truly licked, 47-7, with Frank Gifford (ABC TV's Monday Night Football commentator) scoring the final touchdown.

In 1958, Halas, who had stepped down after the 1955 season, resumed as head coach for a fourth time. In consecutive years, his team finished second in the Western conference behind the powerful Baltimore Colts. Later, as the Colts faded, it was not Chicago but Green Bay who established a conference domination lasting three seasons. And the Packers would go further than that, but in 1963 they were momentarily halted by the Bears. Looking at the final standings, the Bears won the Western conference title by the narrowest of margins (Chicago and Green Bay were 11-1-2 and 11-2-1 respectively). But both of the Packers' losses had been in games against the Bears, who had indeed won the conference title fair and square. In that 1963 regular season, a third-year tight end by the name of Mike Ditka caught 59 passes for 794 yards (he led the club in both categories) and eight touchdowns. Ditka and wide receiver Johnny Morris gave quarterback Bill Wade two first-class targets. Seventh-year man Willie Galimore was still one of the game's most elusive running backs. In addition, with assistant coach George Allen as the architect, the Bears had put together an asphyxiating defense which allowed an average of only 10.3 points per game. And it was the defense which was largely responsible for the 14-10 championship game victory which gave Chicago its eighth NFL title. Of course, they played the Giants – who else?

Of the five Y.A. Tittle passes intercepted by the Bears, two were on attempted screen passes and both of them

Above: Willie Galimore, Chicago's star running back of the late '50s and early '60s

Opposite: Chicago's great middle linebacker, Dick Butkus (#51)

led to touchdowns. Linebacker Larry Morris returned the first 61 yards to the New York five-yard line, setting up Wade's two-yard run, and Wade went in from the one-yard line, five plays after defensive end Ed O'Bradovich had intercepted and returned ten yards down to the New York 14-yard line.

As Halas left the field, swamped with the congratulations which came after his sixth NFL Championship as a head coach, he can hardly have imagined that his club would struggle through the next twenty years without a title of any kind. After Baltimore had nipped in for a final fling, Green Bay resumed its dominance. And when the Packers faded, the Vikings stepped in for a sequence of eleven division titles in thirteen years. The Packers won a further title and even Tampa Bay, an expansion club, had a couple. Chicago went to the playoffs as a wild card in both 1977 and 1979, but on each occasion they fell at the first hurdle. Detroit's division championship, in 1983, left the Bears as the only NFC Central club with nothing to show for a lot of sweat and no little heartbreak.

Over that twenty years, there were tragedies. In the preseason of 1964, Galimore and the starting left end, John Farrington, were killed in a car accident. Halfback Brian Piccolo was becoming a force in the Bears' backfield when he died of cancer, at the age of 26, in 1970. In 1979, Halas's son, George Jr., died of a heart attack at the age of 54. There were, too, serious injuries to many starters, and none more devastating than the one suffered by Gale Sayers.

jokingly, but looking over his shoulder nonetheless. Had Butkus been playing in 1986, he'd surely have been nicknamed 'The Terminator'. Or maybe they'd have titled the movie, 'Butkus'.

Gale Sayers, the rookie running back, was nicknamed the 'Kansas Comet' – and that was just a warning. Words, such as 'sensational', are reserved for lesser mortals – they do not even begin to describe a man with that unique combination of vision, speed and moves. He did not possess the raw power of Jim Brown; he was more like Hugh McElhenny, but better. McElhenny was a cavalier – Sayers was a man with a purpose. In his rookie year he established an NFL record with 22 touchdowns, six of them coming in a 61-20 thrashing of San Francisco. In 1966, he was the NFL leading rusher, with 1,231 yards at an average of 5.4 per carry. Also, in that same year, he led the league with 718 yards on kickoff returns, helping himself to the league all-purpose yardage record (he had a total of 2,440). His troubles began with a serious knee injury against San Francisco, halfway through the 1968 season. In 1969, he came back from surgery to win the league rushing title with 1,032 yards, and that on a team which went 1-13. But his knee problems returned, halfway through the 1970 season, and he was never the same again. In 1971, after one final attempt to come back, he retired to await his invitation to the Hall of Fame, which duly came in 1977. Two years later, he was joined in that august body by Butkus.

The Bears' slow and tortuous climb back to the top has its origins in the 1975 collegiate draft. In round one, Halas selected a running back who had been a phenomenon in college and would be even more in the pros. His name is Walter Payton. After eleven years, in many of which he fought a lone battle on a Bears' squad which was slow to develop, Payton holds virtually every league rushing record worth having. Here's just a sample – there are more records under different headings.

Career Rushing Yardage	14,860
Single-Game Rushing Yardage	275
100-Yards-Rushing Games	73
1,000-Yards-Rushing Seasons	9

His, too, are the unofficial records for humanity, heart and commitment.

Along with Payton came Mike Hartenstine, a solid defensive end. Another future All-Pro, defensive end Dan Hampton, arrived in 1979. In 1980, Payton got a future partner in Matt Suhey, and the linebacking corps got speed in Otis Wilson. With the selections of tackle Keith Van Horne and linebacker Mike Singletary, in 1981, the squad was taking shape. In 1982, Halas obtained his field marshall by hiring Mike Ditka – the lads would now be in good hands. Also in that year, came an aggressive rookie quarterback, Jim McMahon. An outstanding draft in 1983 produced five future starters in tackle Jim Covert, wide receiver Willie Gault, cornerback Mike Richardson, safety Dave Duerson and defensive end Richard Dent. Along the way, safety Gary Fencik, cornerback Leslie

Above: Running back Gale Sayers, the 'Kansas Comet'

Opposite: Linebacker Larry Morris, a key member of the Bears' defense over the period 1959-65

Once in every decade, an NFL club just might draft a superman – in the first round of the 1965 collegiate draft, the Bears got two. The first, Dick Butkus, would become the most dominating linebacker in the history of the game. There have been some great ones – Bill George (Chicago), Joe Schmidt (Detroit), Sam Huff (the New York Giants and Washington), Ray Nitschke (Green Bay), Willie Lanier (Kansas City) and Lawrence Taylor, the latter who is currently active with the Giants. But none quite compares with the awe-inspiring, the demonic, the terrifying man who wore jersey number 51. 'He just hated anybody wearing a different shirt,' reflected Green Bay running back Paul Hornung, from a safe distance. 'Is there somewhere to hide?' pleaded the fabled O.J. Simpson, perhaps

Frazier, center Jay Hilgenberg and wide receiver Dennis McKinnon, had all been signed from the free agent list.

The Bears were ready in 1984 when, at last, the Central division title became theirs. But they could not overcome the loss of the injured McMahon and went down to San Francisco, without scoring a single point, in the NFC Championship Game.

But there was to be no stopping the 1985 squad. Even playing without linebacker Al Harris and safety Todd Bell, both of whom held out in the hope of improved contracts, they equalled the league record of fifteen regular-season victories, set by San Francisco in 1984. In the entire playoff series, they conceded only ten points, seven of those coming late in Super Bowl XX, when the issue had been decided.

The Bears, then, sit proudly atop the league, which, without their involvement, might never have survived. But that same league, which Halas helped create and subsequently nurtured for sixty years, is not made of fainthearted men. None of them plays for second place, and the Bears know only too well that they have it all to do again in 1986.

Staleys-Bears Players in the Pro Football Hall of Fame

George Halas, End-Coach-Owner (1920-83) 1963*
Guy Chamberlin, End (1920-21) 1965*
Jimmy Conzelman, Quarterback (1920) 1964*
George Trafton, Center (1920-32) 1964*
Ed Healey, Tackle (1922-27) 1964*
John L. 'Paddy' Driscoll, Quarterback (1920, 1926-29) 1965*
Roy 'Link' Lyman, Tackle (1926-28, 1930-31, 1933-34) 1964*
Harold 'Red' Grange, Halfback (1925, 1929-34) 1963*
Bronko Nagurski, Fullback-Tackle (1930-37, 1943) 1963*
Bill Hewitt, End (1932-36) 1971*
George Musso, Tackle-Guard (1933-44) 1982*
Walt Kiesling, Guard (1934) 1966*
Danny Fortmann, Guard (1936-43) 1965*
Joe Stydahar, Tackle (1936-42, 1945-46) 1967*
Sid Luckman, Quarterback (1939-50) 1965*
George McAfee, Halfback (1940-41, 1945-50) 1966*
Clyde 'Bulldog' Turner, Center-Linebacker (1940-52) 1966*
Bobby Layne, Quarterback (1948) 1967*
George Connor, Tackle-Linebacker (1948-55) 1975*
George Blanda, Quarterback-Kicker (1949-58) 1981*
Bill George, Linebacker (1952-65) 1974*
Doug Atkins, Defensive End (1955-66) 1982*
Dick Butkus, Linebacker (1965-73) 1979*
Gale Sayers, Running Back (1965-71) 1977*

* Indicates year of induction

Staleys-Bears Head Coaches

George Halas	1920-29, 1933-42, 1946-55, 1958-67
Ralph Jones	1930-32
Hartley 'Hunk' Anderson	1942-45*
Luke Johnsos	1942-45*
John L. 'Paddy' Driscoll	1956-57
Jim Dooley	1968-71
Abe Gibron	1972-74
Jack Pardee	1975-77
Neill Armstrong	1978-81
Mike Ditka	1982-

* Co-Head Coach (Anderson and Johnsos took over from Halas after November 1st, 1942)

Left: Current head coach Mike Ditka, pictured here in his playing days

Opposite: Mike Ditka talks things over with his two quarterbacks, Jim McMahon (#9) and Steve Fuller (#4)

STALEYS-BEARS RECORD 1920-85

Year	Won	Lost	Tied	PF	PA
1920	10	1	2	166	14
1921 (a)	10	1	1	163	53
1922	9	3	0	123	44
1923	9	2	1	123	35
1924	6	1	4	122	44
1925	9	5	3	158	96
1926	12	1	3	216	63
1927	9	3	2	149	98
1928	7	5	1	182	85
1929	4	9	2	119	227
1930	8	4	1	157	71
1931	8	5	0	145	92
1932 (b)	7	1	6	160	44
1933 (c)(b)	10	2	1	133	82
1934 (c)	13	0	0	286	86
1935	6	4	2	192	106
1936	9	3	0	222	94
1937 (c)	9	1	1	201	100
1938	6	5	0	194	148
1939	8	3	0	298	157
1940 (c)(b)	8	3	0	238	152
1941 (c)(b)	10	1	0	396	147
1942 (c)	11	0	0	376	84
1943 (c)(b)	8	1	1	303	157
1944	6	3	1	258	172
1945	3	7	0	192	235
1946 (c)(b)	8	2	1	289	193
1947	8	4	0	363	241
1948	10	2	0	375	151
1949	9	3	0	332	218
1950	9	3	0	279	207
1951	7	5	0	286	282
1952	5	7	0	245	326
1953	3	8	1	218	262
1954	8	4	0	301	279
1955	8	4	0	294	251
1956 (d)	9	2	1	363	246
1957	5	7	0	203	211
1958	8	4	0	298	230
1959	8	4	0	252	196
1960	5	6	1	194	299
1961	8	6	0	326	302
1962	9	5	0	321	287
1963 (d)(b)	11	1	2	301	144
1964	5	9	0	260	379
1965	9	5	0	409	275
1966	5	7	2	234	272
1967	7	6	1	239	218
1968	7	7	0	250	333
1969	1	13	0	210	339
1970	6	8	0	256	261
1971	6	8	0	185	276
1972	4	9	1	225	275
1973	3	11	0	195	334
1974	4	10	0	152	279
1975	4	10	0	191	379
1976	7	7	0	253	216
1977 (e)	9	5	0	255	253
1978	7	9	0	253	274
1979 (e)	10	6	0	306	249
1980	7	9	0	304	264
1981	6	10	0	253	324
1982	3	6	0	141	174
1983	8	8	0	311	301
1984 (f)	10	6	0	325	248
1985 (f)(g)(h)	15	1	0	456	198

(a) APFA (NFL) Champion
(b) NFL Champion
(c) Western Division Champion
(d) Western Conference Champion
(e) NFC Wild Card
(f) NFC Central Division Champion
(g) NFC Champion
(h) Super Bowl (NFL) Champion

☆☆☆☆☆☆☆☆ CHAPTER THREE ☆☆☆☆☆☆☆☆

HOW THE SEASON WORKS

The National Football League consists of twenty-eight teams divided into two **Conferences,** the American Football Conference (AFC) and the National Football Conference (NFC). Each conference has fourteen teams, and is subdivided into two five-team **Divisions** and one four-team **Division.** These are essentially based on sensible geographical considerations but also take into account the traditional rivalries which were in existence when the expanded NFL was restructured in 1970. The teams are listed below in order of their final 1985 division standings since this is of importance in arriving at a team's schedule (fixture list) for 1986.

AMERICAN FOOTBALL CONFERENCE

Eastern Division

	W	L	T
Miami	12	4	0
New York Jets	11	5	0
New England	11	5	0
Indianapolis	5	11	0
Buffalo	2	14	0

Central Division

	W	L	T
Cleveland	8	8	0
Cincinnati	7	9	0
Pittsburgh	7	9	0
Houston	5	11	0

Western Division

	W	L	T
Los Angeles Raiders	12	4	0
Denver	11	5	0
Seattle	8	8	0
San Diego	8	8	0
Kansas City	6	10	0

NATIONAL FOOTBALL CONFERENCE

Eastern Division

	W	L	T
Dallas	10	6	0
New York Giants	10	6	0
Washington	10	6	0
Philadelphia	7	9	0
St Louis	5	11	0

Central Division

	W	L	T
Chicago	15	1	0
Green Bay	8	8	0
Minnesota	7	9	0
Detroit	7	9	0
Tampa Bay	2	14	0

Western Division

	W	L	T
Los Angeles Rams	11	5	0
San Francisco	10	6	0
New Orleans	5	11	0
Atlanta	4	12	0

THE SCHEDULE

When considering a team's schedule, it's best to set aside the four teams who each finished the 1985 season in fifth place in their divisions. Looking at the remaining twenty-four, every team plays twelve games against others from its own conference.

Again, excluding the four fifth-placed teams, every team will play four games against teams from the rival conference (known as Interconference games), specifically to allow fans in the cities of one conference the opportunity of seeing the star players and teams of the other conference. The structure of a team's schedule depends on whether it plays in a four-team or a five-team division.

Four-Team Division

A typical schedule, e.g. for the Cleveland Browns, appears below. It is set out, deliberately not in chronological order, to emphasise that the schedule has a quite definite structure.

CLEVELAND BROWNS (AFC Central)

Cincinnati Bengals	AFC Central	Home
Cincinnati Bengals	AFC Central	Away
Houston Oilers	AFC Central	Home
Houston Oilers	AFC Central	Away
Pittsburgh Steelers	AFC Central	Home
Pittsburgh Steelers	AFC Central	Away
Miami Dolphins	AFC East	Home
Buffalo Bills	AFC East	Away
Indianapolis Colts	AFC East	Away
Kansas City Chiefs	AFC West	Home
San Diego Chargers	AFC West	Home
Los Angeles Raiders	AFC West	Away
Detroit Lions	NFC Central	Home
Green Bay Packers	NFC Central	Home
Chicago Bears	NFC Central	Away
Minnesota Vikings	NFC Central	Away

The Browns will always play their division rivals, Cincinnati, Houston and Pittsburgh, both home and away. The flavour of intraconference competition is maintained by six games, every year, against teams from outside their division but within their conference. There will always be three games against the AFC East and three against the AFC West. Again, every year, there will be four games against teams from a particular division of the rival conference, based on a three-year cycle. In 1986, they play against the NFC Central; in 1987 they will play teams from the NFC West and in 1988, the NFC East. For every team in the NFL, a complete list of opponents, other than those within a team's own division, is arrived at by applying the following formula. The letters and numbers refer to Conference, Division and final standing in that division. Thus the Dallas Cowboys, who are in the National Conference Eastern Division and finished first in that division, are identified as NE-1. Equally, the Houston Oilers, who are in the American Conference Central Division and finished fourth in that division, are labelled AC-4.

AFC EAST-AE

AE-1		AE-2		AE-3		AE-4		AE-5	
H	**A**	**H**	**A**	**H**	**A**	**H**	**A**	**H**	**A**
NW-2	NW-1	NW-1	NW-2	NW-2	NW-1	NW-1	NW-2	AC-1	AC-2
NW-4	NW-3	NW-3	NW-4	NW-4	NW-3	NW-3	NW-4	AC-3	AC-4
AC-4	AC-1	AC-3	AC-2	AC-2	AC-3	AC-1	AC-4	NE-5	NC-5
AW-1	AW-4	AW-2	AW-3	AW-3	AW-2	AW-4	AW-1	AW-5	AW-5

AFC CENTRAL-AC

AC-1		AC-2		AC-3		AC-4	
H	**A**	**H**	**A**	**H**	**A**	**H**	**A**
NC-2	NC-1	NC-1	NC-2	NC-2	NC-1	NC-1	NC-2
NC-4	NC-3	NC-3	NC-4	NC-4	NC-3	NC-3	NC-4
AE-1	AE-4	AE-2	AE-3	AE-3	AE-2	AE-4	AE-1
AW-4	AW-1	AW-3	AW-2	AW-2	AW-3	AW-1	AW-4
AW-5	AE-5	AE-5	AW-5	AW-5	AE-5	AE-5	AW-5

AFC WEST-AW

AW-1		AW-2		AW-3		AW-4		AW-5	
H	**A**	**H**	**A**	**H**	**A**	**H**	**A**	**H**	**A**
NE-2	NE-1	NE-1	NE-2	NE-2	NE-1	NE-1	NE-2	NC-5	NE-5
NE-4	NE-3	NE-3	NE-4	NE-4	NE-3	NE-3	NE-4	AE-5	AE-5
AE-4	AE-1	AE-3	AE-2	AE-2	AE-3	AE-1	AE-4	AC-2	AC-1
AC-1	AC-4	AC-2	AC-3	AC-3	AC-2	AC-4	AC-1	AC-4	AC-3

NFC EAST-NE

NE-1		NE-2		NE-3		NE-4		NE-5	
H	**A**	**H**	**A**	**H**	**A**	**H**	**A**	**H**	**A**
AW-1	AW-2	AW-2	AW-1	AW-1	AW-2	AW-2	AW-1	AW-5	AE-5
AW-3	AW-4	AW-4	AW-3	AW-3	AW-4	AW-4	AW-3	NC-5	NC-5
NC-1	NC-4	NC-2	NC-3	NC-3	NC-2	NC-4	NC-1	NW-1	NW-2
NW-4	NW-1	NW-3	NW-2	NW-2	NW-3	NW-1	NW-4	NW-3	NW-4

NFC CENTRAL-NC

NC-1		NC-2		NC-3		NC-4		NC-5	
H	**A**	**H**	**A**	**H**	**A**	**H**	**A**	**H**	**A**
AC-1	AC-2	AC-2	AC-1	AC-1	AC-2	AC-2	AC-1	AE-5	AW-5
AC-3	AC-4	AC-4	AC-3	AC-3	AC-4	AC-4	AC-3	NE-5	NE-5
NE-4	NE-1	NE-3	NE-2	NE-2	NE-3	NE-1	NE-4	NW-2	NW-1
NW-1	NW-4	NW-2	NW-3	NW-3	NW-2	NW-4	NW-1	NW-4	NW-3

NFC WEST-NW

NW-1		NW-2		NW-3		NW-4	
H	**A**	**H**	**A**	**H**	**A**	**H**	**A**
AE-1	AE-2	AE-2	AE-1	AE-1	AE-2	AE-2	AE-1
AE-3	AE-4	AE-4	AE-3	AE-3	AE-4	AE-4	AE-3
NE-1	NE-4	NE-2	NE-3	NE-3	NE-2	NE-4	NE-1
NC-4	NC-1	NC-3	NC-2	NC-2	NC-3	NC-1	NC-4
NC-5	NE-5	NE-5	NC-5	NC-5	NE-5	NE-5	NC-5

Five-Team Division (Top Four Teams Only)

In the AFC West, the schedules for the top four teams have identical structure and include home and away games against the other four teams in the division. Each of the top four teams plays two games against AFC Central teams and two against the AFC East. Also, they play the four teams in the NFC East as part of their three-year cycle of interconference games. In 1987, they will play teams from the NFC Central and, in 1988, the NFC West. Below is the schedule structure for the Seattle Seahawks.

SEATTLE SEAHAWKS (AFC West)

Denver Broncos	AFC West	Home
Denver Broncos	AFC West	Away
Kansas City Chiefs	AFC West	Home
Kansas City Chiefs	AFC West	Away
Los Angeles Raiders	AFC West	Home
Los Angeles Raiders	AFC West	Away
San Diego Chargers	AFC West	Home
San Diego Chargers	AFC West	Away
New York Jets	AFC East	Home
New England Patriots	AFC East	Away
Pittsburgh Steelers	AFC Central	Home
Cincinnati Bengals	AFC Central	Away
New York Giants	NFC East	Home
Philadelphia Eagles	NFC East	Home
Dallas Cowboys	NFC East	Away
Washington Redskins	NFC East	Away

Fifth-Placed Teams

In the AFC, the two fifth-placed teams will each play eight games against teams from their own divisions and will always play single games against each of the four AFC Central division teams. In the NFC, the two fifth-placed teams each play eight games against teams within their own divisions and will always play single games against the four NFC West teams. Each of the four fifth-placed teams is guaranteed home and away games against the other fifth-placed team in its own conference, and single games against the two fifth-placed teams from the rival conference. The schedule structures for all four teams are set out as follows:

Buffalo (AFC East)

AFC East		8 games
AFC Central		4 games
Kansas City	(AFC)	Home
Kansas City	(AFC)	Away
St Louis	(NFC)	Home
Tampa Bay	(NFC)	Away

Kansas City (AFC West)

AFC West		8 games
AFC Central		4 games
Buffalo	(AFC)	Home
Buffalo	(AFC)	Away
Tampa Bay	(NFC)	Home
St Louis	(NFC)	Away

St Louis (NFC East)

NFC East		8 games
NFC West		4 games
Tampa Bay	(NFC)	Home
Tampa Bay	(NFC)	Away
Kansas City	(AFC)	Home
Buffalo	(AFC)	Away

Tampa Bay (NFC Central)

NFC Central		8 games
NFC West		4 games
St Louis	(NFC)	Home
St Louis	(NFC)	Away
Buffalo	(AFC)	Home
Kansas City	(AFC)	Away

THE PLAYOFFS

On completion of the regular season, each conference holds an elimination competition known as the Playoffs. The teams involved are the three division winners and two Wild Card teams, namely those two, other than the division winners, who have the best won-lost-tied records. The two Wild Card teams play each other to decide which one advances to join the three division winners in the Divisional Playoffs (conference semi-final games). The results of the 1985 American Football Conference playoffs are set out as follows:

Wild Card Game
New England 26 at New York Jets 14

Divisional Playoffs
Cleveland 21 at Miami 24
New England 27 at Los Angeles Raiders 20

AFC Championship Game
New England 31 at Miami 14
New England advanced to Super Bowl XX as AFC Champions.

Home-Field Advantage in the Playoffs
For the Wild Card game, the team with the better regular-season record is given the home-field advantage. Again, in the Divisional Playoffs, the home-field advantage goes to the team with the better regular-season record except in so far as the Wild Card winner can never play at home. For the AFC playoffs then, the pecking order was as follows:

	W	L	T
Los Angeles Raiders*	12	4	0
Miami*	12	4	0
Cleveland*	8	8	0
New York Jets†	11	5	0
New England†	11	5	0

* Division champions
† Wild Card teams

TIE-BREAKING PROCEDURES

Ties are broken by the following list of criteria:

Teams in the same division
A: *Two teams*
1. Head-to-head (best record in games played between the two teams)
2. Best record in games played within the division
3. Best record in games played within the conference
4. Best record in common games
5. Best net points scored in division games (just like goal difference in soccer)
6. Best net points in all games

B: *Three or More Teams* (if two teams remain tied after all other teams are eliminated, the tie-breaking procedure reverts to A:1.)
1. Head-to-head (best record in games played between the teams)
2. Best record in games played within the division
3. Best record in games played within the conference
4. Best record in common games
5. Best net points in division games
6. Best net points in all games

Wild Card places and Home-Field Advantage
(a) If the teams are from the same division, the division tie-breaker is applied.
(b) If the teams are from different divisions, the following procedure is adopted:
C: *Two Teams*
1. Head-to-head (if they have played each other)
2. Best record in games played within the conference
3. Best record in common games (minimum of four)
4. Best average net points in conference games
5. Best net points in all games

D: *Three or More Teams* (If two teams remain tied after all other teams are eliminated, the tie-breaking procedure reverts to A:1, or C:1, whichever is applicable.)
1. Head-to-head sweep (this applies only if one team has either beaten or lost to all the others)
2. Best record in games played within the conference
3. Best record in common games (minimum of four)
4. Best average net points in conference games
5. Best net points in all games

1985 Tie-Breakers
Raiders-Dolphins (Home-field advantage):
C:3; Raiders (5-1), Miami (4-2)
Jets-Patriots-Broncos (Wild Cards):
D:2; Jets (9-3), Patriots (8-4), Broncos (8-4)
Patriots-Broncos (Wild Cards):
C:3; Patriots (4-2), Broncos (3-3)
The Denver Broncos were eliminated.
Cowboys-Giants-Redskins (NFC East title):
B:1; Cowboys (4-0), Giants (1-3), Redskins (1-3)
Giants-49ers-Redskins (Wild Cards):
D:2; Giants (8-4), 49ers (7-5), Redskins (6-6)
The Washington Redskins were eliminated.

THE SUPER BOWL

Though the obvious comparison is with the FA Cup Final, the Super Bowl is best seen as the culmination of an end-of-season knockout competition, involving the champions of six mini leagues together with the Wild Card teams, the latter being considered, perhaps, as potential giant killers. (Only one team, the Oakland Raiders, has won the Super Bowl Championship starting out as a Wild Card.) Unlike for the FA Cup Final, the Super Bowl venue changes from year to year and, since the site is chosen some three years in advance, it is possible for one team to be playing 'at home'. This has never occurred, though both the Los Angeles Rams and the San Francisco 49ers were close to home when they played in Super Bowls XIV and XIX respectively. In selecting the venue, great importance is placed on the likelihood of good weather. Consequently, with the exception of the Pontiac Silverdome (this is a domed stadium), all past Super Bowl stadia have been in the 'sunshine belt', stretching from Florida to California. Super Bowl XXI will be played in the Rose Bowl and XXII in San Diego's Jack Murphy Stadium.

THE PRO BOWL

At the end of the season, the best players from each conference fly off to Hawaii to give the fans out there a treat. The teams are selected by a ballot of head coaches and players in each conference. Each team has two equal votes, those being the head coach's and a consensus of the players' selections. Coaches and players vote only for players in their own conference and may not vote for players from their own teams. Last year, three touchdown passes by Phil Simms brought the NFC from behind to win 28-24.

Above: Roger Craig in action in the 1986 Pro Bowl

Below: Joe Klecko (#72)

AFC-NFC Pro Bowl Results – NFC leads series 10-6

YEAR	DATE	WINNER	LOSER	SITE	ATTENDANCE
1986	Feb. 2	NFC 28	AFC 24	Honolulu	50,101
1985	Jan. 27	AFC 22	NFC 14	Honolulu	50,385
1984	Jan. 29	NFC 45	AFC 3	Honolulu	50,445
1983	Feb. 6	NFC 20	AFC 19	Honolulu	49,883
1982	Jan. 31	AFC 16	NFC 13	Honolulu	50,402
1981	Feb. 1	NFC 21	AFC 7	Honolulu	50,360
1980	Jan. 27	NFC 37	AFC 27	Honolulu	49,800
1979	Jan. 29	NFC 13	AFC 7	Los Angeles	46,281
1978	Jan. 23	NFC 14	AFC 13	Tampa	51,337
1977	Jan. 17	AFC 24	NFC 14	Seattle	64,752
1976	Jan. 26	NFC 23	AFC 20	New Orleans	30,546
1975	Jan. 20	NFC 17	AFC 10	Miami	26,484
1974	Jan. 20	AFC 15	NFC 13	Kansas City	66,918
1973	Jan. 21	AFC 33	NFC 28	Dallas	37,091
1972	Jan. 23	AFC 26	NFC 13	Los Angeles	53,647
1971	Jan. 24	NFC 27	AFC 6	Los Angeles	48,222

PRO BOWL ROSTERS
(Original selections – starters in Capitals)

OFFENSE	American Football Conference		National Football Conference	
Wide Receivers	LOUIS LIPPS	Pittsburgh	MIKE QUICK	Philadelphia
	STEVE LARGENT	Seattle	ART MONK	Washington
	Wes Chandler	San Diego	James Lofton	Green Bay
	Mark Clayton	Miami	Tony Hill	Dallas
Tight Ends	OZZIE NEWSOME	Cleveland	DOUG COSBIE	Dallas
	Todd Christensen	L.A. Raiders	Jimmie Giles	Tampa Bay
Tackles	ANTHONY MUNOZ	Cincinnati	JIM COVERT	Chicago
	BRIAN HOLLOWAY	New England	JACKIE SLATER	L.A. Rams
	Chris Hinton	Indianapolis	Joe Jacoby	Washington
Guards	JOHN HANNAH	New England	RUSS GRIMM	Washington
	MIKE MUNCHAK	Houston	KENT HILL	L.A. Rams
	Roy Foster	Miami	Dennis Harrah	L.A. Rams
Centers	DWIGHT STEPHENSON	Miami	JAY HILGENBERG	Chicago
	Mike Webster	Pittsburgh	Doug Smith	L.A. Rams
Quarterbacks	DAN MARINO	Miami	JOE MONTANA	San Francisco
	Dan Fouts	San Diego	Phil Simms	N.Y. Giants
Running Backs	MARCUS ALLEN	L.A. Raiders	WALTER PAYTON	Chicago
	FREEMAN McNEIL	N.Y. Jets	ROGER CRAIG	San Francisco
	Craig James	New England	Gerald Riggs	Atlanta
	Kevin Mack	Cleveland	Joe Morris	N.Y. Giants

DEFENSE				
Defensive Ends	MARK GASTINEAU	N.Y. Jets	RICHARD DENT	Chicago
	HOWIE LONG	L.A. Raiders	LEONARD MARSHALL	N.Y. Giants
	Rulon Jones	Denver	Dan Hampton	Chicago
Nose Tackles	JOE KLECKO	N.Y. Jets	RANDY WHITE	Dallas
	Bob Golic	Cleveland	Michael Carter	San Francisco
Outside Linebackers	ANDRE TIPPETT	New England	LAWRENCE TAYLOR	N.Y. Giants
	CHIP BANKS	Cleveland	RICKEY JACKSON	New Orleans
	Mike Merriweather	Pittsburgh	Otis Wilson	Chicago
Inside Linebackers	STEVE NELSON	New England	MIKE SINGLETARY	Chicago
	KARL MECKLENBURG	Denver	HARRY CARSON	N.Y. Giants
	Lance Mehl	N.Y. Jets	E.J. Junior	St Louis
Cornerbacks	MIKE HAYNES	L.A. Raiders	EVERSON WALLS	Dallas
	LOUIS WRIGHT	Denver	ERIC WRIGHT	San Francisco
	Ray Clayborn	New England	LeRoy Irvin	L.A. Rams
Safeties	KENNY EASLEY	Seattle	WES HOPKINS	Philadelphia
	DERON CHERRY	Kansas City	CARLTON WILLIAMSON	San Francisco
	Dennis Smith	Denver	Dave Duerson	Chicago

SPECIAL TEAMS				
Placekicker	GARY ANDERSON	Pittsburgh	MORTEN ANDERSEN	New Orleans
Punter	ROHN STARK	Indianapolis	DALE HATCHER	L.A. Rams
Kick Returner	IRVING FRYAR	New England	RON BROWN	L.A. Rams
Specialist	FREDD YOUNG	Seattle	JOEY BROWNER	Minnesota
Head Coach	Don Shula	Miami	John Robinson	L.A. Rams

Above: Ken O'Brien (#7) poised to pass in the Pro Bowl

Below: All-Pro defensive end Howie Long (#75)

THE ALL-PRO TEAM

Anyone can pick his or her own All-Pro team and just about everyone does. Here's the list of my heroes.

Wide Receivers	James Lofton	Green Bay
	Mike Quick	Philadelphia
Tight End	Kellen Winslow	San Diego
Tackles	Anthony Munoz	Cincinnati
	Joe Jacoby	Washington
Guards	John Hannah	New England
	Kent Hill	L.A. Rams
Center	Dwight Stephenson	Miami
Quarterback	Dan Marino	Miami
Running Backs	Eric Dickerson	L.A. Rams
	Walter Payton	Chicago
Defensive Ends	Mark Gastineau	N.Y. Jets
	Howie Long	L.A. Raiders
Defensive Tackles	Dan Hampton	Chicago
	Randy White	Dallas
Outside Linebackers	Lawrence Taylor	N.Y. Giants
	Andre Tippett	New England
Inside Linebackers	Mike Singletary	Chicago
	E.J. Junior	St Louis
Safeties	Kenny Easley	Seattle
	Wes Hopkins	Philadelphia
Cornerbacks	Mike Haynes	L.A. Raiders
	Eric Wright	San Francisco
Placekicker	Morten Andersen	New Orleans
Punter	Reggie Roby	Miami
Punt Returner	Henry Ellard	L.A. Rams
Kickoff Returner	Ron Brown	L.A. Rams
Special-team Specialist	Bill Bates	Dallas
Head Coach	Dan Reeves	Denver

CHAMPIONS 1921-1985

National Football League 1921-1969
(Until 1933 based solely on regular-season play)

1921	Chicago Staleys
1922	Canton Bulldogs
1923	Canton Bulldogs
1924	Cleveland Bulldogs
1925	Chicago Cardinals
1926	Frankford Yellowjackets
1927	New York Giants
1928	Providence Steamroller
1929	Green Bay Packers
1930	Green Bay Packers
1931	Green Bay Packers
1932	Chicago Bears 9 – Portsmouth Spartans 0 (Championship Playoff)
1933	Chicago Bears 23 – New York Giants 21
1934	New York Giants 30 – Chicago Bears 13
1935	Detroit Lions 26 – New York Giants 7
1936	Green Bay Packers 21 – Boston Redskins 6
1937	Washington Redskins 28 – Chicago Bears 21
1938	New York Giants 23 – Green Bay Packers 17
1939	Green Bay Packers 27 – New York Giants 0
1940	Chicago Bears 73 – Washington Redskins 0
1941	Chicago Bears 37 – New York Giants 9
1942	Washington Redskins 14 – Chicago Bears 6
1943	Chicago Bears 41 – Washington Redskins 21
1944	Green Bay Packers 14 – New York Giants 7
1945	Cleveland Rams 15 – Washington Redskins 14
1946	Chicago Bears 24 – New York Giants 14
1947	Chicago Cardinals 28 – Philadelphia Eagles 21
1948	Philadelphia Eagles 7 – Chicago Cardinals 0
1949	Philadelphia Eagles 14 – Los Angeles Rams 0
1950	Cleveland Browns 30 – Los Angeles Rams 28
1951	Los Angeles Rams 24 – Cleveland Browns 17
1952	Detroit Lions 17 – Cleveland Browns 7
1953	Detroit Lions 17 – Cleveland Browns 16
1954	Cleveland Browns 56 – Detroit Lions 10
1955	Cleveland Browns 38 – Los Angeles Rams 14
1956	New York Giants 47 – Chicago Bears 7
1957	Detroit Lions 59 – Cleveland Browns 14
1958	Baltimore Colts 23 – New York Giants 17
1959	Baltimore Colts 31 – New York Giants 16
1960	Philadelphia Eagles 17 – Green Bay Packers 13
1961	Green Bay Packers 37 – New York Giants 0
1962	Green Bay Packers 16 – New York Giants 7
1963	Chicago Bears 14 – New York Giants 10
1964	Cleveland Browns 27 – Baltimore Colts 0
1965	Green Bay Packers 23 – Cleveland Browns 12
1966	Green Bay Packers 34 – Dallas Cowboys 27
1967	Green Bay Packers 21 – Dallas Cowboys 17
1968	Baltimore Colts 34 – Cleveland Browns 0
1969	Minnesota Vikings 27 – Cleveland Browns 7

American Football League 1960-1969

1960	Houston Oilers 24 – Los Angeles Chargers 16
1961	Houston Oilers 10 – San Diego Chargers 3
1962	Dallas Texans 20 – Houston Oilers 17
1963	San Diego Chargers 51 – Boston Patriots 10
1964	Buffalo Bills 20 – San Diego Chargers 7
1965	Buffalo Bills 23 – San Diego Chargers 0
1966	Kansas City Chiefs 31 – Buffalo Bills 7
1967	Oakland Raiders 40 – Houston Oilers 7
1968	New York Jets 27 – Oakland Raiders 23
1969	Kansas City Chiefs 17 – Oakland Raiders 7

Conference Champions 1970-1985

NFC

1970	Dallas Cowboys 17 – San Francisco 49ers 10
1971	Dallas Cowboys 14 – San Francisco 49ers 3
1972	Washington Redskins 26 – Dallas Cowboys 3
1973	Minnesota Vikings 27 – Dallas Cowboys 10
1974	Minnesota Vikings 14 – Los Angeles Rams 10
1975	Dallas Cowboys 37 – Los Angeles Rams 7
1976	Minnesota Vikings 24 – Los Angeles Rams 13
1977	Dallas Cowboys 23 – Minnesota Vikings 6
1978	Dallas Cowboys 28 – Los Angeles Rams 0
1979	Los Angeles Rams 9 – Tampa Bay Buccaneers 0
1980	Philadelphia Eagles 20 – Dallas Cowboys 7
1981	San Francisco 49ers 28 – Dallas Cowboys 27
1982	Washington Redskins 31 – Dallas Cowboys 17
1983	Washington Redskins 24 – San Francisco 49ers 21
1984	San Francisco 49ers 23 – Chicago Bears 0
1985	Chicago Bears 24 – Los Angeles Rams 0

Above: Pittsburgh head coach Chuck Noll with his Vince Lombardi Trophies

Right: Ollie Matson (#33)

AFC

1970	Baltimore Colts 27 – Oakland Raiders 17
1971	Miami Dolphins 21 – Baltimore Colts 0
1972	Miami Dolphins 21 – Pittsburgh Steelers 17
1973	Miami Dolphins 27 – Oakland Raiders 10
1974	Pittsburgh Steelers 24 – Oakland Raiders 13
1975	Pittsburgh Steelers 16 – Oakland Raiders 10
1976	Oakland Raiders 24 – Pittsburgh Steelers 7
1977	Denver Broncos 20 – Oakland Raiders 17
1978	Pittsburgh Steelers 34 – Houston Oilers 5
1979	Pittsburgh Steelers 27 – Houston Oilers 13
1980	Oakland Raiders 34 – San Diego Chargers 27
1981	Cincinnati Bengals 27 – San Diego Chargers 7
1982	Miami Dolphins 14 – New York Jets 0
1983	Los Angeles Raiders 30 – Seattle Seahawks 14
1984	Miami Dolphins 45 – Pittsburgh Steelers 28
1985	New England Patriots 31 – Miami Dolphins 14

Super Bowl 1966-1985

Season	SB	Winner		Loser		Stadium	Attendance
1966	I	Green Bay	35	Kansas City	10	Los Angeles Coliseum	61,946
1967	II	Green Bay	33	Oakland	14	Miami Orange Bowl	75,546
1968	III	N.Y. Jets	16	Baltimore	7	Miami Orange Bowl	75,389
1969	IV	Kansas City	23	Minnesota	7	New Orleans Tulane Stadium	80,562
1970	V	Baltimore	16	Dallas	13	Miami Orange Bowl	79,204
1971	VI	Dallas	24	Miami	3	New Orleans Tulane Stadium	81,023
1972	VII	Miami	14	Washington	7	Los Angeles Coliseum	90,182
1973	VIII	Miami	24	Minnesota	7	Houston Rice Stadium	71,882
1974	IX	Pittsburgh	16	Minnesota	6	New Orleans Tulane Stadium	80,997
1975	X	Pittsburgh	21	Dallas	17	Miami Orange Bowl	80,187
1976	XI	Oakland	32	Minnesota	14	Pasadena Rose Bowl	103,438
1977	XII	Dallas	27	Denver	10	New Orleans Superdome	75,583
1978	XIII	Pittsburgh	35	Dallas	31	Miami Orange Bowl	79,484
1979	XIV	Pittsburgh	31	L.A. Rams	19	Pasadena Rose Bowl	103,985
1980	XV	Oakland	27	Philadelphia	10	New Orleans Superdome	76,135
1981	XVI	San Francisco	26	Cincinnati	21	Pontiac Silverdome	81,270
1982	XVII	Washington	27	Miami	17	Pasadena Rose Bowl	103,667
1983	XVIII	L.A. Raiders	38	Washington	9	Tampa Stadium	72,920
1984	XIX	San Francisco	38	Miami	16	Stanford Stadium	84,059
1985	XX	Chicago	46	New England	10	New Orleans Superdome	73,818

ALL-TIME INDIVIDUAL RECORDS
(Regular Season only – New Records and Records tied are in bold type)

Career Best

SEASONS PLAYED	26	George Blanda
GAMES PLAYED	340	George Blanda
POINTS	2,002	George Blanda (9-TD, 943-EP, 335-FG)
EXTRA POINTS	943	George Blanda
FIELD GOALS	**373**	**Jan Stenerud**
TOUCHDOWNS		
Rushing and Pass Receiving	126	Jim Brown (106-R, 20-P)
Rushing	106	Jim Brown
Pass Receiving	99	Don Hutson
Passes Thrown	342	Fran Tarkenton
By Interception Return	9	Ken Houston
By Punt Return	8	Jack Christiansen
		Rick Upchurch
By Kickoff Return	6	Ollie Matson
		Gale Sayers
		Travis Williams
By Fumble Recovery Return	4	Bill Thompson
YARDAGE		
Rushing	**14,860**	**Walter Payton**
Pass Receiving	11,834	Don Maynard
Passing	47,003	Fran Tarkenton
HOW MANY TIMES		
Pass Receptions	**716**	**Charlie Joiner**
Passes Completed	3,686	Fran Tarkenton
Interceptions	81	Paul Krause
100-Yards-Rushing Games	**73**	**Walter Payton**
100-Yards-Pass Receiving Games	50	Don Maynard
1,000-Yards-Rushing Seasons	**9**	**Walter Payton**

The peerless Jim Brown (#32)

MOST SEASONS LEADING LEAGUE		
Points	5	Don Hutson, Green Bay 1940-44
		Gino Cappelletti, Boston 1961, 1963-66
Extra Points	8	George Blanda, Chicago Bears 1956, Houston 1961-62, Oakland 1967-69, 1972, 1974
Field Goals	5	Lou Groza, Cleveland Browns 1950, 1952-54, 1957
Touchdowns	8	Don Hutson, Green Bay 1935-38, 1941-44
Touchdowns, Rushing	5	Jim Brown, Cleveland Browns 1957-59, 1963, 1965
Touchdowns, Pass Receiving	9	Don Hutson, Green Bay 1935-38, 1940-44
Touchdowns, Passes Thrown	4	Johnny Unitas, Baltimore 1957-60
		Len Dawson, Dallas Texans 1962, Kansas City 1963, 1965-66
Yards, Rushing	8	Jim Brown, Cleveland Browns 1957-61, 1963-65
Yards, Pass Receiving	7	Don Hutson, Green Bay 1936, 1938-39, 1941-44
Yards, Passing	5	Sonny Jurgensen, Philadelphia 1961-62, Washington 1966-67, 1969
Pass Receptions	8	Don Hutson, Green Bay 1936-37, 1939, 1941-45
Passes Completed	5	Sammy Baugh, Washington 1937, 1943, 1945, 1947-48
Pass Interceptions	**3**	**Everson Walls, Dallas 1981-82, 1985**

Season Best

POINTS	176	Paul Hornung, Green Bay 1960 (15-TD, 41-EP, 15-FG)
EXTRA POINTS	66	Uwe von Schamann, Miami 1984
FIELD GOALS	35	Ali Haji-Sheikh, N.Y. Giants 1983
TOUCHDOWNS		
Rushing and Pass Receiving	24	John Riggins, Washington 1983 (24-R)
Rushing	24	John Riggins, Washington 1983
Pass Receiving	18	Mark Clayton, Miami 1984

ALL-TIME INDIVIDUAL RECORDS (Regular Season)—cont.

Passes Thrown	48	Dan Marino, Miami 1984
By Interception Return	4	Ken Houston, Houston 1971
		Jim Kearney, Kansas City 1972
By Punt Return	4	Jack Christiansen, Detroit 1951
		Rick Upchurch, Denver 1976
By Kickoff Return	4	Travis Williams, Green Bay 1967
		Cecil Turner, Chicago 1970
By Fumble Recovery Return	2	By many players
YARDAGE		
Rushing	2,105	Eric Dickerson, L.A. Rams 1984
Pass Receiving	1,746	Charley Hennigan, Houston 1961
Passing	5,084	Dan Marino, Miami 1984
HOW MANY TIMES		
Pass Receptions	106	Art Monk, Washington 1984
Passes Completed	362	Dan Marino, Miami 1984
Interceptions	14	Dick 'Night Train' Lane, L.A. Rams 1952

Game Best

POINTS	40	Ernie Nevers (6-TD, 4-EP), Chicago Cardinals v Chicago Bears 1929
EXTRA POINTS	9	Pat Harder, Chicago Cardinals v N.Y. Giants 1948
		Bob Waterfield, L.A. Rams v Baltimore 1950
		Charley Gogolak, Washington v N.Y. Giants 1966
FIELD GOALS	7	Jim Bakken, St Louis v Pittsburgh 1967
TOUCHDOWNS		
All methods of scoring	6	Ernie Nevers (6-R), Chicago Cardinals v Chicago Bears 1929
		Dub Jones (4-R, 2-P), Cleveland v Chicago Bears 1951
		Gale Sayers (4-R, 1-P, 1-Ret) Chicago Bears v San Francisco 1965
Rushing	6	Ernie Nevers, Chicago Cardinals v Chicago Bears 1929
Pass Receiving	5	Bob Shaw, Chicago Cardinals v Baltimore 1950
		Kellen Winslow, San Diego v Oakland 1981
Passes Thrown	7	Sid Luckman, Chicago Bears v N.Y. Giants 1943
		Adrian Burk, Philadelphia v Washington 1954
		George Blanda, Houston v N.Y. Titans 1961
		Y.A. Tittle, N.Y. Giants v Washington 1962
		Joe Kapp, Minnesota v Baltimore 1969
YARDAGE		
Rushing	275	Walter Payton, Chicago Bears v Minnesota 1977
Pass Receiving	**309**	**Stephone Paige, Kansas City v San Diego 1985**
Passing	554	Norm Van Brocklin, L.A. Rams v N.Y. Yanks 1951
HOW MANY TIMES		
Rushing Attempts	43	Butch Woolfolk, N.Y. Giants v Philadelphia 1983
		James Wilder, Tampa Bay v Green Bay 1984 (OT)
Pass Receptions	18	Tom Fears, L.A. Rams v Green Bay 1950
Passes Completed	42	Richard Todd, N.Y. Jets v San Francisco 1980
Interceptions	4	By many players
LONGEST		
Touchdown Rushing	99 yds	Tony Dorsett, Dallas v Minnesota 1982
Touchdown Pass Receiving	99 yds	Andy Farkas (from Filchock), Washington v Pittsburgh 1939
		Bobby Mitchell (from Izo), Washington v Cleveland 1963
		Pat Studstill (from Sweetan), Detroit v Baltimore 1966
		Gerry Allen (from Jurgensen), Washington v Chicago 1968
		Cliff Branch (from Plunkett), L.A. Raiders v Washington 1983
		Mike Quick (from Jaworski), Philadelphia v Atlanta 1985
Field Goal	63 yds	Tom Dempsey, New Orleans v Detroit 1970
Punt Return (All TDs)	98 yds	Gil LeFebvre, Cincinnati v Brooklyn 1933
		Charlie West, Minnesota v Washington 1968
		Dennis Morgan, Dallas v St Louis 1974

Kickoff Return (All TDs)	106 yds	Al Carmichael, Green Bay v Chicago Bears 1956
		Noland Smith, Kansas City v Denver 1967
		Roy Green, St Louis v Dallas 1979
Interception Return (All TDs)	102 yds	Bob Smith, Detroit v Chicago Bears 1949
		Erich Barnes, N.Y. Giants v Dallas 1961
		Gary Barbaro, Kansas City v Seattle 1977
		Louis Breeden, Cincinnati v San Diego 1981
Fumble Recovery Return (TD)	104 yds	Jack Tatum, Oakland v Green Bay 1972

TEAM RECORDS

Most Championships	11	Green Bay, 1929-31, 1936, 1939, 1944, 1961-62, 1965-67
	9	**Chicago Bears, 1921, 1932-33, 1940-41, 1943, 1946, 1963, 1985**
	4	N.Y. Giants, 1927, 1934, 1938, 1956
		Detroit, 1935, 1952-53, 1957
		Cleveland Browns, 1950, 1954-55, 1964
		Baltimore, 1958-59, 1968, 1970
		Pittsburgh, 1974-75, 1978-79
		Oakland/L.A. Raiders, 1967, 1976, 1980, 1983
Most Consecutive Games Won (inc. playoffs)	18	Chicago Bears, 1933-34 and 1941-42; Miami, 1972-73
Most Consecutive Games Won (exc. playoffs)	17	Chicago Bears, 1933-34
Most Consecutive Games Lost	26	Tampa Bay, 1976-77
Most Points in a Season	541	Washington, 1983
Fewest Points in a Season (Since 1932)	37	Cincinnati-St Louis, 1934
Most Points in a Game	72	Washington v N.Y. Giants, 1966
Most Points (Both Teams) in a Game	113	Washington v N.Y. Giants, 1966
Fewest Points (Both Teams) in a Game	0	Many teams; last time N.Y. Giants v Detroit, 1943

ALL-TIME TOP TWENTY
(1985 Active players in capitals)

All-Time Leading Rushers

		Yrs.	Att.	Yards	Ave.	TDs
1.	WALTER PAYTON	11	3,371	14,860	4.4	98
2.	Jim Brown	9	2,359	12,312	5.2	106
3.	Franco Harris	13	2,949	12,120	4.1	91
4.	JOHN RIGGINS	14	2,916	11,352	3.9	104
5.	O.J. Simpson	11	2,404	11,236	4.7	61
6.	TONY DORSETT	9	2,441	10,832	4.4	66
7.	EARL CAMPBELL	8	2,187	9,407	4.3	74
8.	Jim Taylor	10	1,941	8,597	4.4	83
9.	Joe Perry	14	1,737	8,378	4.8	53
10.	Larry Csonka	11	1,891	8,081	4.3	64
11.	OTTIS ANDERSON	7	1,807	7,843	4.3	44
12.	Leroy Kelly	10	1,727	7,274	4.2	74
13.	MIKE PRUITT	10	1,705	6,930	4.1	49
14.	John Henry Johnson	13	1,571	6,803	4.3	48
15.	WILBERT MONTGOMERY	9	1,540	6,789	4.4	45
16.	Chuck Muncie	9	1,561	6,702	4.3	71
17.	Mark Van Eeghen	10	1,652	6,650	4.0	37
18.	Lawrence McCutcheon	10	1,521	6,578	4.3	26
19.	Lydell Mitchell	9	1,675	6,534	3.9	30
20.	Floyd Little	9	1,641	6,323.	3.8	43

All-Time Leading Receivers

		Yrs.	No.	Yards	Ave.	TDs
1.	CHARLIE JOINER	17	716	11,706	16.3	63
2.	Charley Taylor	13	649	9,110	14.0	79
3.	Don Maynard	15	633	11,834	18.7	88
4.	Raymond Berry	13	631	9,275	14.7	68
5.	STEVE LARGENT	10	624	10,059	16.1	78
6.	Harold Carmichael	14	590	8,985	15.2	79
7.	Fred Biletnikoff	14	589	8,974	15.2	76
8.	Harold Jackson	15	579	10,372	17.9	76
9.	Lionel Taylor	10	567	7,195	12.7	45
10.	Lance Alworth	11	542	10,266	18.9	85
11.	Bobby Mitchell	11	521	7,954	15.3	65
12.	Billy Howton	12	503	8,459	16.8	61
13.	OZZIE NEWSOME	8	502	6,281	12.5	39
14.	CLIFF BRANCH	14	501	8,685	17.3	67
15.	Tommy McDonald	12	495	8,410	17.0	84
	Ahmad Rashad	10	495	6,831	13.8	44
17.	Drew Pearson	11	489	7,822	16.0	48
18.	Don Hutson	11	488	7,991	16.4	99
19.	Jackie Smith	16	480	7,918	16.5	40
20.	Art Powell	10	479	8,046	16.8	81

Charlie Joiner, currently top of the All-Time Receivers list

All-Time Leading Scorers

		Yrs.	TDs	EPs	FGs	Total
1.	George Blanda	26	9	943	335	2,002
2.	JAN STENERUD	19	0	580	373	1,699
3.	Jim Turner	16	1	521	304	1,439
4.	Jim Bakken	17	0	534	282	1,380
5.	Fred Cox	15	0	519	282	1,365
6.	Lou Groza	17	1	641	234	1,349
7.	MARK MOSELEY	15	0	457	288	1,321
8.	Gino Cappelletti*	11	42	350	176	1,130
9.	Don Cockroft	13	0	432	216	1,080
10.	Garo Yepremian	14	0	444	210	1,074
11.	Bruce Gossett	11	0	374	219	1,031
12.	Sam Baker	15	2	428	179	977
13.	Lou Michaels**	13	1	386	187	955
14.	RAY WERSCHING	13	0	371	184	923
15.	Roy Gerela	11	0	351	184	903
16.	PAT LEAHY	12	0	349	184	901
17.	Bobby Walston	12	46	365	80	881
18.	RAFAEL SEPTIEN	9	0	377	165	872
19.	Pete Gogolak	10	0	344	173	863
20.	CHRIS BAHR	10	0	361	166	859

* Includes four two-point conversions
** Includes a safety recorded in 1965 when Michaels played as a defensive end.

All-Time Passer Ratings (Minimum 1,500 attempts)

		Yrs.	Att.	Comp.	Yards	TDs	Int.	Rating
1.	JOE MONTANA	7	2,571	1,627	19,262	133	67	92.4
2.	Roger Staubach	11	2,958	1,685	22,700	153	109	83.4
3.	Len Dawson	19	3,741	2,136	28,711	239	183	82.6
	Sonny Jurgensen	18	4,262	2,433	32,224	255	189	82.6
5.	NEIL LOMAX	5	1,826	1,047	13,406	79	55	82.3
	DANNY WHITE	10	2,393	1,422	17,911	130	107	82.3
7.	KEN ANDERSON	15	4,452	2,643	32,667	196	158	82.0
8.	DAN FOUTS	13	4,810	2,839	37,492	228	205	81.8

9.	Bart Starr	16	3,149	1,808	24,718	152	138	80.5
10.	Fran Tarkenton	18	6,467	3,686	47,003	342	266	80.4
11.	BILL KENNEY	7	1,735	957	12,699	77	61	78.7
12.	Otto Graham	6	1,565	872	13,499	88	94	78.2
	Bert Jones	10	2,551	1,430	18,190	124	101	78.2
	Johnny Unitas	18	5,186	2,830	40,239	290	253	78.2
15.	Frank Ryan	13	2,133	1,090	16,042	149	111	77.6
16.	JOE THEISMANN	12	3,602	2,044	25,206	160	138	77.4
17.	Bob Griese	14	3,429	1,926	25,092	192	172	77.1
18.	STEVE BARTKOWSKI	11	3,330	1,871	23,470	154	141	76.0
19.	GARY DANIELSON	9	1,847	1,049	13,159	77	77	75.6
20.	Ken Stabler	15	3,793	2,270	27,938	194	222	75.3

Quarterback Neil Lomax (#15) leapt into the all-time passer ratings

PASSES COMPLETED	No.	YARDS PASSING	Yards	TOUCHDOWN PASSES	No.
1. Fran Tarkenton	3,686	1. Fran Tarkenton	47,003	1. Fran Tarkenton	342
2. DAN FOUTS	2,839	2. Johnny Unitas	40,239	2. Johnny Unitas	290
3. Johnny Unitas	2,830	3. DAN FOUTS	37,492	3. Sonny Jurgensen	255
4. KEN ANDERSON	2,643	4. Jim Hart	34,665	4. John Hadl	244
5. Jim Hart	2,593	5. John Hadl	33,503	5. Len Dawson	239
6. John Brodie	2,469	6. KEN ANDERSON	32,667	6. George Blanda	236
7. Sonny Jurgensen	2,433	7. Sonny Jurgensen	32,224	7. DAN FOUTS	228
8. Roman Gabriel	2,366	8. John Brodie	31,548	8. John Brodie	214
9. John Hadl	2,363	9. Norm Snead	30,797	9. Terry Bradshaw	212
10. Norm Snead	2,276	10. Roman Gabriel	29,444	Y.A. Tittle	212
11. Ken Stabler	2,270	11. Len Dawson	28,711	11. Jim Hart	209
12. JOE FERGUSON	2,219	12. Y.A. Tittle	28,339	12. Roman Gabriel	201
13. Len Dawson	2,136	13. Terry Bradshaw	27,989	13. KEN ANDERSON	196
14. Y.A. Tittle	2,118	14. JOE FERGUSON	27,954	Norm Snead	196
15. Craig Morton	2,053	15. Ken Stabler	27,938	Bobby Layne	196
16. JOE THEISMANN	2,044	16. Craig Morton	27,908	16. Ken Stabler	194
17. Terry Bradshaw	2,025	17. Joe Namath	27,663	17. Bob Griese	192
18. RON JAWORSKI	2,014	18. George Blanda	26,920	18. Sammy Baugh	187
19. Archie Manning	2,011	19. Bobby Layne	26,768	19. JOE FERGUSON	183
20. Brian Sipe	1,944	20. RON JAWORSKI	26,277	Craig Morton	183

CHAPTER FIVE

OUTSTANDING PLAYERS OF 1985

MARCUS ALLEN

Entering last season, his fourth in the NFL, Marcus Allen could make a strong claim to be the best dual-purpose backfield player in football. In 1982, he became the first non-kicker to lead the league in scoring since 1975, and, again excluding kickers, the first rookie since 1965 (Gale Sayers). He completed an outstanding 1983 season by helping the Raiders to victory in Super Bowl XVIII. In that game, he was voted MVP after setting a Super Bowl record by rushing for 191 yards and, at a stroke, carving out two more by rushing 74 yards for a touchdown (longest rush and longest rushing touchdown). The Raiders came up short in 1984, but Allen had done his bit, having shared the NFL lead for touchdowns (18) and finishing second behind Earnest Jackson for the AFC rushing title. In each of his first three years, he had led all AFC running backs in pass receptions, and, in 1983, had even passed for three touchdowns. But deep down, he was a rusher – he wanted to run more often. However, when he approached club owner Al Davis on that subject, the response was, 'Go jogging!'. It's not clear why, but someone on the Raiders' coaching staff had a change of heart and, in the 1985 season, Allen responded by becoming the first Raiders player ever to win the NFL rushing title. Of equal significance, despite his increased workload, he caught 67 passes, raising his combined-yardage total to a new NFL single-season record of 2,314. In the latter category, he surpassed the previous best marks established by Eric Dickerson (2,244) and O.J. Simpson (2,243). As a measure of his sheer rushing consistency, he now shares, with Walter Payton, the NFL regular-season record for consecutive 100-yards-rushing games. However, unlike Payton, he carries his sequence of nine into the 1986 season, and it will take the best efforts of a tough Denver defense to prevent him making it ten in the opening game.

Marcus Allen in action against New England in the playoffs

Game by Game – 1985

Opponent	Rushing			Receiving			Comb.
	Att	Yds	TD	No	Yds	TD	Yds
N.Y. Jets	20	76	2	2	30	0	106
at Kansas City	14	50	0	6	27	0	77
San Francisco	12	59	0	8	53	0	112
at New England	21	98	0	3	30	0	128
Kansas City	29	126	0	3	24	0	150
New Orleans	28	107	2	3	51	0	158
at Cleveland	20	81	0	3	41	1	122
San Diego	30	111	3	3	24	0	135
at Seattle	19	101	0	5	49	0	150
at San Diego	28	119	1	5	30	0	149
Cincinnati	31	135	0	6	54	1	189
Denver	24	173	1	4	49	0	222
at Atlanta	28	156	0	2	42	1	198
at Denver	25	135	1	5	21	0	156
Seattle	27	109	1	1	5	0	114
at L.A. Rams	24	123	0	8	25	0	148
Totals	**380**	**1,759**	**11**	**67**	**555**	**3**	**2,314**

GERALD RIGGS

'He doesn't get anywhere near the recognition he deserves – he's definitely one of the two or three best backs in the league.' (Rich Milot – Redskins).

'The guy's over 1,000 yards for a 4-12 team. That's amazing. He's the new model of the John Riggins "Diesel".' (Howie Long – Raiders).

'. . . he runs so low to the ground and he's so powerful in the thighs. Unless you cut him really low, he's going to get four or five yards after the contact.' (Johnnie Johnson – Rams).

'He's simply a great back.' (former head coach Bud Grant – Vikings).

Milot, Long, Johnson and Grant, none of whom is noted for dishing out compliments with abandon, were speaking of Gerald Riggs, who has taken over from the likes of his teammate, William Andrews, and John Riggins, as the league's most punishing runner. Riggs took responsibility for the Falcons' rushing offense when Andrews went down with a severe knee injury in August, 1984. And he did well, rushing for 1,486 yards to rank fourth in the NFL. But that was the year when Eric Dickerson occupied centre stage (he gained 2,105 yards). However, it was Riggs who dominated the league for most of 1985, as he slashed and pounded to 1,719 yards and the NFC rushing title. He's a running back in the game's best traditions – reliable, brave, tough – and when he has the ball, he intends to keep it. It was around the halfway stage in 1985 when someone started to look back for his previous fumble and, before the season was over, he extended his sequence to an astonishing 483 possessions since he last spilled the ball. He is the key man in a Falcons offense which could produce a resurgence in 1986.

Gerald Riggs uncoils for another big gain

Game by Game – 1985

Opponent	Att	Rushing Yds	TD
Detroit	31	131	1
at San Francisco	21	92	0
Denver	21	77	1
at L.A. Rams	18	61	0
San Francisco	13	43	0
at Seattle	23	139	0
New Orleans	26	97	1
at Dallas	24	127	0
Washington	22	127	0
at Philadelphia	27	129	1
L.A. Rams	41	123	3
at Chicago	30	110	0
L.A. Raiders	25	95	1
at Kansas City	26	197	1
Minnesota	10	13	0
at New Orleans	39	158	1
Totals	**397**	**1,719**	**10**

LIONEL JAMES

In 1985, the name of Lionel 'Little Train' James was added to the top of a list which had its beginnings in 1960, when Abner Haynes became the first player in pro football history to register more than 2,000 all-purpose yards in a season. It is a catalogue of men, not all of them star players, who, in addition to rushing and catching passes, have done the groundwork. They're the inbetween men who supplement their earnings, often even having to justify their places on the team, by returning kickoffs and punts. Every play which gains the last few yards for a touchdown is chronicled in the annals of the game, but only rarely do we think of the price paid by the returner who has provided the platform for the scoring drive. And last year, eight times James finished off the drive with a touchdown. Almost single-handedly, he was responsible for two victories. The first came on Week Three against Cincinnati, when he sped for 316 all-purpose yards. The second was on Week Ten, as he took the Raiders by storm, dodging for 345 yards (it was the second-highest total in league history behind Billy Cannon's 373 yards) and scoring the winning touchdown on a 17-yard run in overtime. All told, James quarried out 2,535 all-purpose yards to set the new NFL single-season record. He led the AFC with 86 pass receptions and his receiving yardage total was the highest ever by a running back, exceeding the previous best of 938 set by Lenny Moore in 1958. Astonishingly, he led San Diego in all the four categories of rushing (yards), receiving (passes caught), and both punt and kickoff returns (yards). It was less surprising that his teammates voted him the Chargers' Most Valuable Player.

Lionel 'Little Train' James in imminent danger from Seattle's Fredd Young

Game by Game – 1985

Opponent	Rushing Att	Yds	TD	Receiving No	Yds	TD	Punt Ret. No	Yds	Kickoff Ret. No	Yds	Total Comb. Yds
at Buffalo	1	−4	0	3	23	0	2	22	0	0	41
Seattle	8	41	0	6	96	1	3	19	6	134	290
at Cincinnati	12	127	1	5	118	1	1	24	2	47	316
Cleveland	10	27	0	10	68	0	0	0	2	38	133
at Seattle	4	1	0	4	44	0	2	19	1	36	100
Kansas City	6	9	0	6	71	0	3	19	0	0	99
at Minnesota	3	20	0	4	30	0	0	0	2	39	89
at L.A. Raiders	4	18	0	1	7	0	2	9	4	86	120
Denver	4	15	0	3	64	0	1	3	0	0	82
L.A. Raiders	7	51	1	11	168	1	0	0	5	126	345
at Denver	15	64	0	11	93	1	2	13	0	0	170
at Houston	9	69	0	4	99	1	1	11	0	0	179
Buffalo	2	7	0	4	34	0	4	46	0	0	87
Pittsburgh	7	25	0	3	22	0	0	0	5	96	143
Philadelphia	3	3	0	3	48	0	2	12	2	36	99
at Kansas City	10	43	0	8	42	1	2	16	7	141	242
Totals	105	516	2	86	1,027	6	25	213	36	779	2,535

KEN O'BRIEN

In the opinion of several preseason analysts, 1985 was not going to be the Jets' year – they would be hard pressed to reach par. And many of the same people doubted that Ken O'Brien could do much about it. Even his head coach, Joe Walton, was guarded when he stated, 'Ken made good progress last year, but he still has a lot to learn.' It was with Walton that O'Brien spent a great deal of the off-season in the classroom and, whatever they discussed, it worked. As the NFL's Leading Passer, O'Brien took the Jets into the playoffs after directing the team to eleven regular-season wins, the most since 1968 when they won the Super Bowl. O'Brien began the season cautiously, and it was in the style of the artisan that, just after the halfway stage, he had established the platform for the final assault – the Jets were 7-2. However, as injuries were beginning to take their toll of running back Freeman McNeil and a host of defensive players, O'Brien blossomed, bringing the best out of tight end Mickey Shuler and establishing a big-play relationship with wide receivers Wesley Walker and Al Toon. O'Brien played beautifully controlled football – he threw only eight interceptions in sixteen games – as the Jets' offense took to the air. Without any of the fuss of a mad bomber, he coaxed and feathered the ball for 3,888 yards – only Dan Marino and John Elway passed for more. Entering the season, he was known as a player of intelligence and precision. Right now, he's respected and you have the feeling that, before long, he'll be feared.

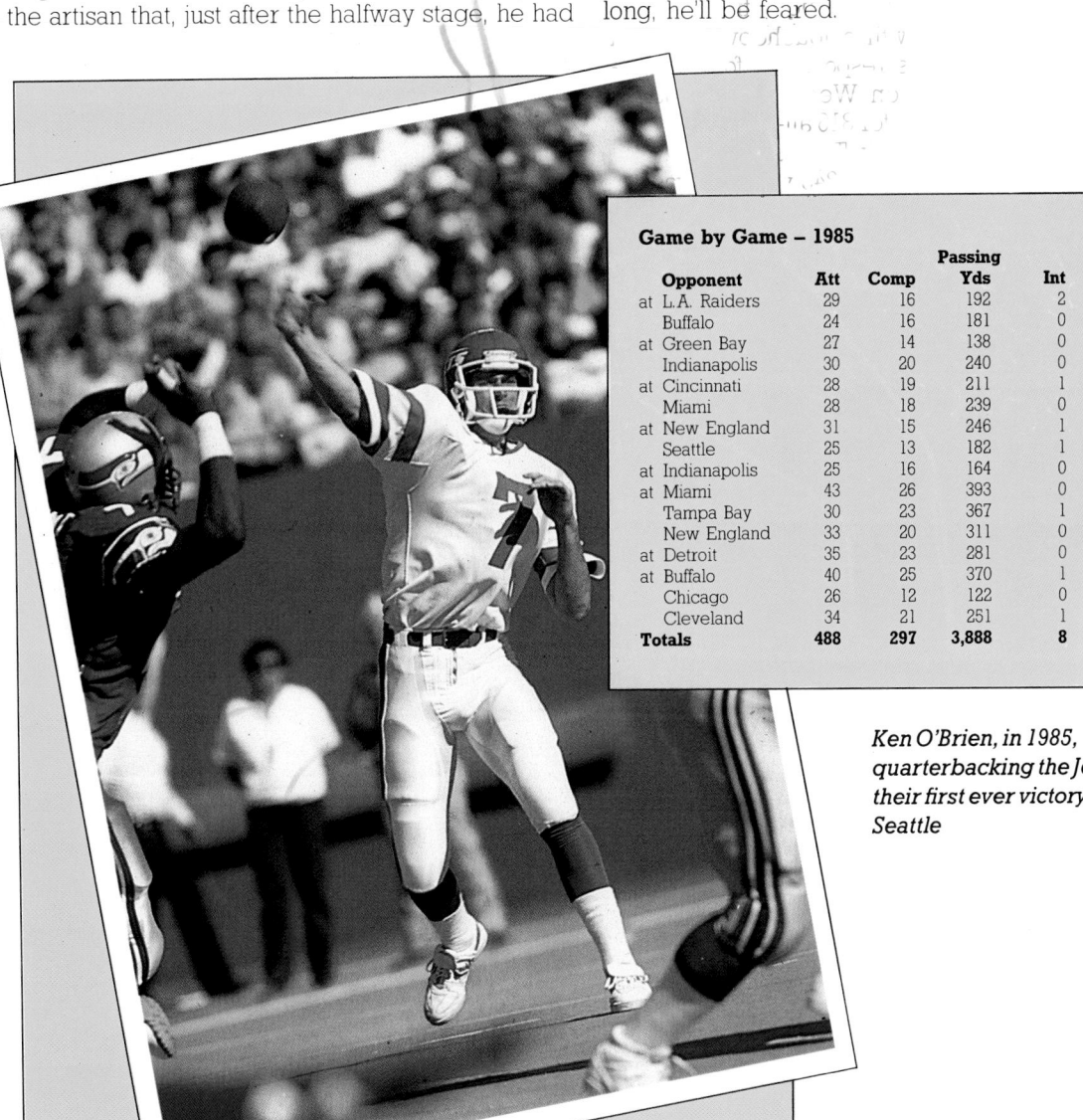

Game by Game – 1985

Opponent	Att	Comp	Passing Yds	Int	TD
at L.A. Raiders	29	16	192	2	0
Buffalo	24	16	181	0	2
at Green Bay	27	14	138	0	1
Indianapolis	30	20	240	0	1
at Cincinnati	28	19	211	1	1
Miami	28	18	239	0	1
at New England	31	15	246	1	0
Seattle	25	13	182	1	2
at Indianapolis	25	16	164	0	3
at Miami	43	26	393	0	2
Tampa Bay	30	23	367	1	5
New England	33	20	311	0	1
at Detroit	35	23	281	0	2
at Buffalo	40	25	370	1	3
Chicago	26	12	122	0	0
Cleveland	34	21	251	1	1
Totals	**488**	**297**	**3,888**	**8**	**25**

Ken O'Brien, in 1985, quarterbacking the Jets to their first ever victory over Seattle

JOE MONTANA

Joe Montana went into the NFC Wild Card Game, suffering with pulled rib-cage muscles and knowing that he could not count on the players (Wendell Tyler and Roger Craig) who, throughout the season, had given him a rushing offense and many of his passing options. And even though he rose only slowly each time after those fearsome Giants pass rushers had knocked him dowm, rise he did. Alas, it was all to no avail and the misery of a 17-3 defeat was a sad way to end the season. In common with most of his teammates, Montana had shown signs of the Super Bowl Championship jinx in the early part of the campaign – the team never did put together more than three consecutive wins. But it was largely by his efforts that, after appearing to be out of contention, they fought their way back and, subsequently, clinched a wild card spot with a come-from-behind victory over Dallas on the final weekend. His personal reward was the NFC passing title, gained with a quarterback rating (91.3) which kept him on top of the all-time list of leading passers. Quite rightly, he deserves a place amongst our Players of the Year.

Game by Game – 1985			Passing		
Opponent	Att	Comp	Yds	Int	TD
at Minnesota	39	24	265	2	2
Atlanta	26	19	204	1	1
at L.A. Raiders	24	14	255	0	2
New Orleans	26	12	120	2	0
at Atlanta	57	37	429	0	5
Chicago	29	17	160	0	0
at Detroit	26	15	97	1	0
at L.A. Rams	30	22	306	0	3
Philadelphia	Injured – did not play				
at Denver	40	17	222	0	1
Kansas City	34	23	235	0	2
Seattle	33	17	237	3	2
at Washington	22	11	119	0	1
L.A. Rams	36	26	328	2	3
at New Orleans	38	25	354	1	3
Dallas	34	24	322	1	2
Totals	**494**	**303**	**3,653**	**13**	**27**

STEVE LARGENT

Steve Largent is another truly great player who continues to defy most of the odds to come out on top in the high-speed NFL. He is not one of those thoroughbred athlete types and, by pro wide receiver standards, is slow. But he does use everything he's got, and that includes an intense concentration, superb hands and an uncanny ability to wrong-foot a defender. Most of the league's cornerbacks can stay in touch with the out-and-out flyers but, as they openly admit, 'How do you outrun a player when you don't know where he's going?' In 1985, they went one way, whilst he went another and enjoyed the best season of his ten-year career, with 79 receptions for 1,287 yards. The latter figure was good for the lead in the NFL. He is now within striking distance of the NFL career records for both receptions and yardage, and, after San Diego's Charlie Joiner has called it a day, two more good seasons should be enough to take him to the top.

Steve Largent thrusting for extra yards

Game by Game – 1985		Receiving	
Opponent	No	Yds	TD
at Cincinnati	5	81	0
at San Diego	6	99	1
L.A. Rams	6	88	0
at Kansas City	6	92	0
San Diego	5	69	1
Atlanta	8	103	1
at Denver	1	9	1
at N.Y. Jets	2	44	0
L.A. Raiders	3	47	0
at New Orleans	5	110	0
New England	8	138	0
at San Francisco	4	91	0
Kansas City	7	101	1
Cleveland	5	89	1
at L.A. Raiders	4	61	0
Denver	4	65	0
Totals	**79**	**1,287**	**6**

Left: Joe Montana rolling right and primed to fire

AMERICAN FOOTBALL CONFERENCE

TEAM RANKINGS

OFFENSE / DEFENSE

	Total Yds. (Off)	Rushing (Off)	Passing (Off)	Points For	%Intercepted	%Sacked	Total Yds. (Def)	Rushing (Def)	Passing (Def)	Points Against	%Interceptions	%Sacks
Buffalo	14	12	12	14	14	7	8	13	4	10	8	14
Cincinnati	2	6	3	2	2	6	11	9	13	14	10	9
Cleveland	11	4	13	12	3	11	5	5	5	3	11	6
Denver	6	8	t4	5	5	2	7	8	6	7	4	7
Houston	13	13	11	13	8	13	13	14	9	12	13	5
Indianapolis	10	1	14	10	7	5	9	10	10	11	14	11
Kansas City	12	14	6	11	9	8	10	11	11	9	3	13
L.A. Raiders	7	5	10	8	10	9	1	2	2	5	12	1
Miami	4	9	2	3	4	1	12	12	12	6	2	8
New England	5	2	9	7	12	10	3	3	3	2	5	3
N.Y. Jets	3	3	5	4	1	14	4	1	7	1	7	4
Pittsburgh	8	7	8	6	13	4	2	6	1	8	9	10
San Diego	1	10	1	1	11	3	14	7	14	13	6	12
Seattle	9	11	7	9	6	12	6	4	8	4	1	2

AFC PASSERS

	Att	Comp	% Comp	Yards	Ave Gain	TD	% TD	Long	Int	% Int	Rating Points
O'Brien, Ken, Jets	488	297	60.9	3888	7.97	25	5.1	t96	8	1.6	96.2
Esiason, Boomer, Cin.	431	251	58.2	3443	7.99	27	6.3	t68	12	2.8	93.2
Fouts, Dan, S.D.	430	254	59.1	3638	8.46	27	6.3	t75	20	4.7	88.1
Danielson, Gary, Clev.	163	97	59.5	1274	7.82	8	4.9	t72	6	3.7	85.3
Herrmann, Mark, S.D.	201	132	65.7	1537	7.65	10	5.0	59	10	5.0	84.5
Grogan, Steve, N.E.	156	85	54.5	1311	8.40	7	4.5	56	5	3.2	84.1
Marino, Dan, Mia.	567	336	59.3	4137	7.30	30	5.3	73	21	3.7	84.1
Kenney, Bill, K.C.	338	181	53.6	2536	7.50	17	5.0	t84	9	2.7	83.6
Krieg, Dave, Sea.	532	285	53.6	3602	6.77	27	5.1	54	20	3.8	76.2
Malone, Mark, Pitt.	233	117	50.2	1428	6.13	13	5.6	t45	7	3.0	75.5
Elway, John, Den.	605	327	54.0	3891	6.43	22	3.6	t65	23	3.8	70.2
Kosar, Bernie, Clev.	248	124	50.0	1578	6.36	8	3.2	t68	7	2.8	69.3
Moon, Warren, Hou.	377	200	53.1	2709	7.19	15	4.0	t80	19	5.0	68.5
Eason, Tony, N.E.	299	168	56.2	2156	7.21	11	3.7	t90	17	5.7	67.5
Pagel, Mike, Ind.	393	199	50.6	2414	6.14	14	3.6	t80	15	3.8	65.8
Wilson, Marc, Raiders	388	193	49.7	2608	6.72	16	4.1	59	21	5.4	62.7
Woodley, David, Pitt.	183	94	51.4	1357	7.42	6	3.3	69	14	7.7	54.8
Mathison, Bruce, Buff.	228	113	49.6	1635	7.17	4	1.8	t60	14	6.1	53.5
Ferragamo, Vince, Buff.	287	149	51.9	1677	5.84	5	1.7	48	17	5.9	50.8

t = Touchdown
Leader based on rating points, minimum 130 attempts

AFC RECEIVERS – Most Receptions

	No	Yards	Ave	Long	TD
James, Lionel, *S.D.*	86	1027	11.9	t67	6
Christensen, Todd, *Raiders*	82	987	12.0	48	6
Woolfolk, Butch, *Hou.*	80	814	10.2	t80	4
Largent, Steve, *Sea.*	79	1287	16.3	43	6
Shuler, Mickey, *Jets*	76	879	11.6	35	7
Stallworth, John, *Pitt.*	75	937	12.5	41	5
Nathan, Tony, *Mia.*	72	651	9.0	73	1
Clayton, Mark, *Mia.*	70	996	14.2	45	4
Chandler, Wes, *S.D.*	67	1199	17.9	t75	10
Allen, Marcus, *Raiders*	67	555	8.3	44	3
Collinsworth, Cris, *Cin.*	65	1125	17.3	71	5
Hill, Drew, *Hou.*	64	1169	18.3	t57	9
Newsome, Ozzie, *Clev.*	62	711	11.5	38	5
Watson, Steve, *Den.*	61	915	15.0	60	5
Lipps, Louis, *Pitt.*	59	1134	19.2	51	12
Joiner, Charlie, *S.D.*	59	932	15.8	t39	7
Bell, Greg, *Buff.*	58	576	9.9	49	1
Brooks, James, *Cin.*	55	576	10.5	t57	5
Brown, Eddie, *Cin.*	53	942	17.8	t68	8
Collins, Tony, *N.E.*	52	549	10.6	49	2
Johnson, Vance, *Den.*	51	721	14.1	t63	3
Moore, Nat, *Mia.*	51	701	13.7	t69	7
Williams, Dokie, *Raiders*	48	925	19.3	55	5
Reed, Andre, *Buff.*	48	637	13.3	32	4
Carson, Carlos, *K.C.*	47	843	17.9	t37	4
Warner, Curt, *Sea.*	47	307	6.5	t27	1
Toon, Al, *Jets*	46	662	14.4	t78	3
Smith, Tim, *Hou.*	46	660	14.3	33	2
Byner, Earnest, *Clev.*	45	460	10.2	31	2

t = Touchdown

AFC RECEIVERS – Most Yards

	Yards	No	Ave	Long	TD
Largent, Steve, *Sea.*	1287	79	16.3	43	6
Chandler, Wes, *S.D.*	1199	67	17.9	t75	10
Hill, Drew, *Hou.*	1169	64	18.3	t57	9
Lipps, Louis, *Pitt.*	1134	59	19.2	51	12
Collinsworth, Cris, *Cin.*	1125	65	17.3	71	5
James, Lionel, *S.D.*	1027	86	11.9	t67	6
Clayton, Mark, *Mia.*	996	70	14.2	45	4
Christensen, Todd, *Raiders*	987	82	12.0	48	6
Paige, Stephone, *K.C.*	943	43	21.9	t84	10
Brown, Eddie, *Cin.*	942	53	17.8	t68	8
Stallworth, John, *Pitt.*	937	75	12.5	41	5
Joiner, Charlie, *S.D.*	932	59	15.8	t39	7
Williams, Dokie, *Raiders*	925	48	19.3	55	5
Watson, Steve, *Den.*	915	61	15.0	60	5
Shuler, Mickey, *Jets*	879	76	11.6	35	7
Carson, Carlos, *K.C.*	843	47	17.9	t37	4
Woolfolk, Butch, *Hou.*	814	80	10.2	t80	4
Butler, Jerry, *Buff.*	770	41	18.8	t60	2
Morgan, Stanley, *N.E.*	760	39	19.5	t50	5
Walker, Wesley, *Jets*	725	34	21.3	t96	5
Johnson, Vance, *Den.*	721	51	14.1	t63	3
Newsome, Ozzie, *Clev.*	711	62	11.5	38	5
Moore, Nat, *Mia.*	701	51	13.7	t69	7
Fryar, Irving, *N.E.*	670	39	17.2	56	7
Turner, Daryl, *Sea.*	670	34	19.7	54	13

t = Touchdown

Ozzie Newsome (#82) became the first tight end in history to catch over 500 passes in a career

AFC RUSHERS

	Att	Yards	Ave	Long	TD
Allen, Marcus, *Raiders*	380	1759	4.6	t61	11
McNeil, Freeman, *Jets*	294	1331	4.5	69	3
James, Craig, *N.E.*	263	1227	4.7	t65	5
Mack, Kevin, *Clev.*	222	1104	5.0	61	7
Warner, Curt, *Sea.*	291	1094	3.8	38	8
Byner, Earnest, *Clev.*	244	1002	4.1	36	8
Pollard, Frank, *Pitt.*	233	991	4.3	56	3
Brooks, James, *Cin.*	192	929	4.8	39	7
Bell, Greg, *Buff.*	223	883	4.0	t77	8
McMillan, Randy, *Ind.*	190	858	4.5	38	7
Abercrombie, Walter, *Pitt.*	227	851	3.7	t32	7
Wonsley, George, *Ind.*	138	716	5.2	36	6
Kinnebrew, Larry, *Cin.*	170	714	4.2	29	9
Winder, Sammy, *Den.*	199	714	3.6	42	8
Nathan, Tony, *Mia.*	143	667	4.7	22	5
Collins, Tony, *N.E.*	163	657	4.0	28	3
Heard, Herman, *K.C.*	164	595	3.6	33	4
Hector, Johnny, *Jets*	145	572	3.9	22	6
James, Lionel, *S.D.*	105	516	4.9	t56	2
Spencer, Tim, *S.D.*	124	478	3.9	24	10
Rozier, Mike, *Hou.*	133	462	3.5	30	8
Anderson, Gary, *S.D.*	116	429	3.7	27	4
Cribbs, Joe, *Buff.*	122	399	3.3	16	1
Woolfolk, Butch, *Hou.*	103	392	3.8	43	1
Pruitt, Mike, *Buff.-K.C.*	112	390	3.5	54	2
Moriarty, Larry, *Hou.*	106	381	3.6	18	3
Davenport, Ron, *Mia.*	98	370	3.8	33	11
Hampton, Lorenzo, *Mia.*	105	369	3.5	15	3
Lang, Gene, *Den.*	84	318	3.8	26	5
Bentley, Albert, *Ind.*	54	288	5.3	t26	2
Sewell, Steve, *Den.*	81	275	3.4	16	4
Hawkins, Frank, *Raiders*	84	269	3.2	t21	4
Gill, Owen, *Ind.*	45	262	5.8	67	2
Bennett, Woody, *Mia.*	54	256	4.7	17	0
Elway, John, *Den.*	51	253	5.0	22	0
Willhite, Gerald, *Den.*	66	237	3.6	14	3
Morris, Randall, *Sea.*	55	236	4.3	21	0
Mathison, Bruce, *Buff.*	27	231	8.6	22	1
McGee, Buford, *S.D.*	42	181	4.3	44	3
Weathers, Robert, *N.E.*	41	174	4.2	t42	1
Pagel, Mike, *Ind.*	25	160	6.4	29	2
Paige, Tony, *Jets*	55	158	2.9	30	8
Alexander, Charles, *Cin.*	44	156	3.5	18	2
Tatupu, Mosi, *N.E.*	47	152	3.2	11	2
Horton, Ethan, *K.C.*	48	146	3.0	t19	3
Moon, Warren, *Hou.*	39	130	3.3	17	0
Brown, Eddie, *Cin.*	14	129	9.2	35	0
Hughes, David, *Sea.*	40	128	3.2	9	0
Danielson, Gary, *Clev.*	25	126	5.0	28	0
Krieg, Dave, *Sea.*	35	121	3.5	17	1
Smith, Jeff, *K.C.*	30	118	3.9	27	0
Bligen, Dennis, *Jets*	22	107	4.9	t28	1
Wilson, Marc, *Raiders*	24	98	4.1	17	2

t = Touchdown

AFC SCORING – Kickers

	XP	XPA	FG	FGA	PTS
Anderson, Gary, *Pitt.*	40	40	33	42	139
Leahy, Pat, *Jets*	43	45	26	34	121
Breech, Jim, *Cin.*	48	50	24	33	120
Reveiz, Fuad, *Mia.*	50	52	22	27	116
Franklin, Tony, *N.E.*	40	41	24	30	112
Karlis, Rich, *Den.*	41	44	23	38	110
Lowery, Nick, *K.C.*	35	35	24	27	107
Thomas, Bob, *S.D.*	51	55	18	28	105
Bahr, Chris, *Raiders*	40	42	20	32	100
Zendejas, Tony, *Hou.*	29	31	21	27	92
Allegre, Raul, *Ind.*	36	39	16	26	84
Johnson, Norm, *Sea.*	40	41	14	25	82
Bahr, Matt, *Clev.*	35	35	14	18	77
Norwood, Scott, *Buff.*	23	23	13	17	62

AFC SCORING – Touchdowns

	TD	TDR	TDP	TDM	PTS
Lipps, Louis, *Pitt.*	15	1	12	2	90
Allen, Marcus, *Raiders*	14	11	3	0	84
Davenport, Ron, *Mia.*	13	11	2	0	78
Turner, Daryl, *Sea.*	13	0	13	0	78
Brooks, James, *Cin.*	12	7	5	0	72
Byner, Earnest, *Clev.*	10	8	2	0	60
Chandler, Wes, *S.D.*	10	0	10	0	60
Fryar, Irving, *N.E.*	10	1	7	2	60
Kinnebrew, Larry, *Cin.*	10	9	1	0	60
Mack, Kevin, *Clev.*	10	7	3	0	60
Paige, Stephone, *K.C.*	10	0	10	0	60
Paige, Tony, *Jets*	10	8	2	0	60
Spencer, Tim, *S.D.*	10	10	0	0	60

AFC KICKOFF RETURNERS

	No	Yards	Ave	Long	TD
Young, Glen, *Clev.*	35	898	25.7	63	0
Bentley, Albert, *Ind.*	27	674	25.0	48	0
Drewrey, Willie, *Hou.*	26	642	24.7	50	0
Johnson, Vance, *Den.*	30	740	24.7	39	0
Martin, Mike, *Cin.*	48	1104	23.0	45	0
Spencer, Todd, *Pitt.*	27	617	22.9	40	0
Hampton, Lorenzo, *Mia.*	45	1020	22.7	46	0
Walker, Fulton, *Raiders*	21	467	22.2	57	0
James, Lionel, *S.D.*	36	779	21.6	46	0
Wilson, Don, *Buff.*	22	465	21.1	37	0
Starring, Stephen, *N.E.*	48	1012	21.1	53	0
Erenberg, Rich, *Pitt.*	21	441	21.0	35	0
Seale, Sam, *Raiders*	23	482	21.0	36	0
Morris, Randall, *Sea.*	31	636	20.5	58	0
Martin, Robbie, *Ind.*	32	638	19.9	36	0
Smith, Jeff, *K.C.*	33	654	19.8	39	0
Steels, Anthony, *S.D.-Buff.*	30	561	18.7	54	0

t = Touchdown
Leader based on average return, minimum 20 returns

Above: Louis Lipps

*Opposite: Curt Warner came back after injury to rush
for over 1,000 yards on the season*

AFC PUNTERS

	No	Yards	Long	Ave	Total Punts	TB	Blk	Opp Ret	Ret Yds	In 20	Net Ave
Stark, Rohn, *Ind.*	78	3584	68	45.9	80	14	2	43	572	12	34.2
Roby, Reggie, *Mia.*	59	2576	63	43.7	59	8	0	27	371	19	34.7
Camarillo, Rich, *N.E.*	92	3953	75	43.0	92	13	0	56	598	16	33.6
Mojsiejenko, Ralf, *S.D.*	68	2881	67	42.4	68	9	0	36	274	15	35.7
McInally, Pat, *Cin.*	57	2410	64	42.3	58	7	1	41	535	8	29.9
Johnson, Lee, *Hou.*	83	3464	65	41.7	83	8	0	45	345	22	35.7
Kidd, John, *Buff.*	92	3818	67	41.5	92	4	0	49	438	33	35.9
Arnold, Jim, *K.C.*	93	3827	62	41.2	95	11	2	48	530	15	32.4
Norman, Chris, *Den.*	92	3764	61	40.9	94	12	2	38	325	16	34.0
Guy, Ray, *Raiders*	89	3627	68	40.8	89	12	0	26	159	32	36.3
Finzer, David, *Sea.*	68	2766	61	40.7	68	6	0	38	295	12	34.6
Gossett, Jeff, *Clev.*	81	3261	64	40.3	81	8	0	36	304	18	34.5
Jennings, Dave, *Jets*	74	2978	66	40.2	74	8	0	36	319	23	33.8
Newsome, Harry, *Pitt.*	78	3088	59	39.6	79	7	1	43	380	17	32.5

Leader based on gross average, minimum 40 punts

AFC PUNT RETURNERS

	No	FC	Yards	Ave	Long	TD
Fryar, Irving, *N.E.*	37	15	520	14.1	t85	2
Lipps, Louis, *Pitt.*	36	2	437	12.1	t71	2
Walker, Fulton, *Raiders*	62	6	692	11.2	32	0
Martin, Robbie, *Ind.*	40	7	443	11.1	t70	1
Willhite, Gerald, *Den.*	16	5	169	10.6	18	0
Skansi, Paul, *Sea.*	31	7	312	10.1	32	0
Wilson, Don, *Buff.*	16	5	161	10.1	30	0
Sohn, Kurt, *Jets*	16	5	149	9.3	46	0
Drewrey, Willie, *Hou.*	24	10	215	9.0	23	0
Vigorito, Tom, *Mia.*	22	5	197	9.0	21	0
Lane, Garcia, *K.C.*	43	7	381	8.9	57	0
Johnson, Vance, *Den.*	30	6	260	8.7	38	0
James, Lionel, *S.D.*	25	8	213	8.5	24	0
Martin, Mike, *Cin.*	32	8	268	8.4	26	0
Brennan, Brian, *Clev.*	19	4	153	8.1	t37	1

t = Touchdown
Leader based on average return, minimum 15 returns

AFC INTERCEPTORS

	No	Yards	Ave	Long	TD
Lewis, Albert, *K.C.*	8	59	7.4	16	0
Daniel, Eugene, *Ind.*	8	53	6.6	29	0
Marion, Fred, *N.E.*	7	189	27.0	83	0
Griffin, James, *Cin.*	7	116	16.6	33	1
Cherry, Deron, *K.C.*	7	87	12.4	t47	1
Romes, Charles, *Buff.*	7	56	8.0	21	0
Harris, John, *Sea.*	7	20	2.9	17	0
Jackson, Robert, *Cin.*	6	100	16.7	t57	1
Clayborn, Ray, *N.E.*	6	80	13.3	38	1
Brown, Dave, *Sea.*	6	58	9.7	t28	1
Blackwood, Glenn, *Mia.*	6	36	6.0	17	0
Gross, Al, *Clev.*	5	109	21.8	t37	1
Harden, Mike, *Den.*	5	100	20.0	t42	1
Woodruff, Dwayne, *Pitt.*	5	80	16.0	33	0
Walters, Danny, *S.D.*	5	71	14.2	30	0
Wright, Louis, *Den.*	5	44	8.8	24	0
Brown, Steve, *Hou.*	5	41	8.2	22	0
Hendy, John, *S.D.*	4	139	34.8	t75	1
Judson, William, *Mia.*	4	88	22.0	t61	1
Taylor, Terry, *Sea.*	4	75	18.8	t75	1
James, Roland, *N.E.*	4	51	12.8	39	0
Williams, Eric, *Pitt.*	4	47	11.8	29	0
Shell, Donnie, *Pitt.*	4	40	10.0	26	0
Hayes, Lester, *Raiders.*	4	27	6.8	t27	1
Glenn, Kerry, *Jets*	4	15	3.8	t15	1
Lankford, Paul, *Mia.*	4	10	2.5	6	0

t = Touchdown

Above: Irving Fryar, who led the NFL on punt return average, seen here scoring the Patriots' only touchdown in Super Bowl XX

Opposite: The outstanding Denver cornerback, Louis Wright, intercepting a pass against the Raiders

BUFFALO BILLS

Address One Bills Drive, Orchard Park, New York 14127.
Stadium Rich Stadium, Orchard Park.
 Capacity 80,290 *Playing Surface* AstroTurf.
Team Colours Royal Blue, Scarlet Red and White.
Head Coach Hank Bullough – second year.
Championships Division 1980; AFL 1964, '65.
History AFL 1960-69, AFC 1970-

Offense

There's not much point in dwelling on last season, when the Bills laboured through their second 2-14 campaign in a row, except to look for features of their play which could bring them back into contention. One clear message to emerge is that second-year running back Greg Bell is a player of real class. He led the club both in rushing and pass receptions and, for the second consecutive year, had the AFC's longest run from scrimmage (he scored on a 77-yarder against Pittsburgh). With the return of running back Joe Cribbs, who had played two years in the USFL, the Bills could have had a backfield pair to match most in the league. However, Cribbs took time to resettle and there are some indications that he would prefer to play for another club. That being the case, it was a sensible move when the Bills drafted Ronnie Harmon, a quick-footed player, and the hefty Carl Byrum. Also, in the collegiate draft, they took steps to reinforce the offensive line, selecting tackle Will Wolford with their second option in round one, and center Leonard Burton in round three. Wolford, one imagines, could be an instant starter, perhaps relegating Ken Jones to the role of backup. All of center Will Grant, guards Tim Vogler and Jim Ritcher, and tackle Joe Devlin, have given good service for several years. And with last year's second-round draftee, guard Mark Traynowicz, in reserve, the Bills begin to look solid. Quarterback Bruce Mathison was out of a job last September and, apparently, going nowhere. However, he took over for the last seven games and did well enough to retain his position, ahead of Frank Reich, the latter who was Buffalo's third-round pick in 1985. There is reason for optimism at wide receiver, where Jerry Butler has shaken off the effects of injury and the rookie, Andre Reed, played unexpectedly well. Reed's performance was on a par with that of the Jets' first-round pick, Al Toon. It is really good to see Butler back, playing almost up to the standards of his first three years in the league. He'll be looking to make up for lost time. Chris Burkett and Eric Richardson are two backups, each of whom presents a deep threat. At tight end, Eason Ramson is not a prolific receiver, but he is solid enough.

Defense

Only in the later rounds of the collegiate draft did the Bills seek help for the defense, and it is unlikely that any of the newcomers will find a starting place. As expected, last year's premier pick, defensive end Bruce Smith, became a dominant figure and led the team with 6.5 quarterback sacks. However, as a group, the remaining defensive linemen and linebackers could manage only 14 between them. One has to believe that perhaps a change in defensive philosophy might help for, certainly, there are one or two really good players who could go after the quarterback with confidence. Don Smith, a versatile reserve, was excellent as a starter for Atlanta and may see more action after a year learning the system. And Sean McNanie could play a big part, were they to turn him loose more often. Buffalo's weakness against the run – they ranked 26th in the league – continues to be a worry. It's also surprising since, in linebackers Jim Haslett (he led the club with 143 tackles) and Eugene Marve, they have two heavy hitters. The defense might expect to improve with the development of outside linebacker Darryl Talley, a second-round pick in 1983. The secondary can take the credit for a pass defense which ranked 11th in the league. Cornerback Charles Romes, who led the team with seven interceptions, is a fine player, and the Bills have found him a starting partner in last year's first-round pick, Derrick Burroughs. Safety Steve Freeman is never far away from the action and his partner, Don Wilson, is looking better and better after coming to Buffalo as a 1984 free agent.

Special Teams

The Bills made improvements last year, particularly in closing down on opposing kickoff and punt returners. First-year placekicker Scott Norwood kicked ten consecutive field goals and missed only four. John Kidd helps his special-team tacklers by hanging his punts really high and should retain his place. Several players had a go at returning kickoffs, with Don Wilson and Rod Hill sharing the punt returns. Back in 1982, cornerback Hill was the Cowboys' first-round pick, not least for his ability as a returner. However, he has not developed as anticipated. Free safety Wilson, on the other hand, is an excellent punt returner and does a reasonable job returning kickoffs.

1986 SCHEDULE OF GAMES	September	
	7 NEW YORK JETS	4:00
	14 at Cincinnati	1:00
	21 ST LOUIS	1:00
	28 KANSAS CITY	1:00
	October	
	5 at New York Jets	4:00
	12 at Miami	1:00
	19 INDIANAPOLIS	1:00
	26 NEW ENGLAND	1:00
	November	
	2 at Tampa Bay	1:00
	9 PITTSBURGH	1:00
	16 MIAMI	1:00
	23 at New England	1:00
	30 at Kansas City	12:00
	December	
	7 CLEVELAND	1:00
	14 at Indianapolis	1:00
	21 at Houston	12:00

1986 DRAFT

Round	Name	Pos.	Ht.	Wt.	College
1.	Harmon, Ronnie	RB	5-11	185	Iowa
1.	Wolford, Will	T	6-5	274	Vanderbilt
3.	Burton, Leonard	C	6-4	255	South Carolina
5.	Byrum, Carl	RB	6-0	234	Mississippi Valley State
7.	Williams, Bob	TE	6-3	226	Penn State
7.	Pike, Mark	NT	6-5	253	Georgia Tech
7.	Rolle, Butch	TE	6-3	241	Michigan State
8.	Furjanic, Tony	LB	6-2	228	Notre Dame
9.	Bynum, Reggie	WR	6-1	189	Oregon State
10.	Teafatiller, Guy	NT	6-2	256	Illinois
11.	Garbarczyk, Tony	NT	6-4	239	Wake Forest
11.	Witt, Billy	DE	6-5	258	North Alabama
12.	McClure, Brian	QB	6-6	226	Bowling Green
12.	Christian, Derek	LB	6-4	235	West Virginia

VETERAN ROSTER

No.	Name	Pos.	Ht.	Wt.	NFL Year	College
	Babyar, Chris	G	6-4	264	1	Illinois
43	Bayless, Martin	S	6-2	195	3	Bowling Green
28	Bell, Greg	RB	5-10	210	3	Notre Dame
36	Bellinger, Rodney	CB	5-8	189	3	Miami
81	Brookins, Mitchell	WR	5-11	196	3	Illinois
85	Burkett, Chris	WR	6-4	198	2	Jackson State
29	Burroughs, Derrick	CB	6-1	180	2	Memphis State
80	Butler, Jerry	WR	6-0	178	7	Clemson
69	Christy, Greg	T	6-4	279	2	Pittsburgh
20	Cribbs, Joe	RB	5-11	193	6	Auburn
63	Cross, Justin	T	6-6	263	5	Western State, Colo.
59	David, Stan	LB	6-3	210	2	Texas Tech
70	Devlin, Joe	T	6-5	267	10	Iowa
58	Dickerson, Anthony	LB	6-2	222	7	Southern Methodist
52	Frazier, Guy	LB	6-2	217	6	Wyoming
22	Freeman, Steve	S	5-11	185	12	Mississippi State
99	Garner, Hal	LB	6-4	219	2	Utah State

No.	Name	Pos.	Ht.	Wt.	NFL Year	College
53	Grant, Will	C	6-3	264	9	Kentucky
	Hamby, Mike	NT	6-4	253	1	Utah State
	Harris, Bo	LB	6-3	226	9	Louisiana State
55	Haslett, Jim	LB	6-3	228	8	Indiana, Pa.
71	Hellestrae, Dale	T	6-5	261	2	Southern Methodist
25	Hill, Rod	CB	6-0	188	4	Kentucky State
30	Hutchison, Anthony	RB	5-10	186	4	Texas Tech
48	Johnson, Lawrence	CB	5-11	202	7	Wisconsin
72	Jones, Ken	T	6-5	279	11	Arkansas State
4	Kidd, John	P	6-3	208	3	Northwestern
90	Maidlow, Steve	LB	6-2	238	4	Michigan State
54	Marve, Eugene	LB	6-2	240	5	Saginaw Valley State
7	Mathison, Bruce	QB	6-3	205	4	Nebraska
95	McNanie, Sean	DE	6-5	265	3	San Diego State
88	Metzelaars, Pete	TE	6-7	243	5	Wabash
34	Moore, Booker	RB	5-11	222	5	Penn State
11	Norwood, Scott	K	6-0	205	2	James Madison
23	Perryman, Jim	S	6-0	175	2	Millikin
	Pitts, Ron	CB	5-10	175	1	UCLA
79	Prater, Dean	DE	6-4	256	5	Oklahoma State
87	Ramson, Eason	TE	6-2	234	7	Washington State
83	Reed, Andre	WR	6-0	186	2	Kutztown State, Pa.
14	Reich, Frank	QB	6-3	208	2	Maryland
82	Richardson, Eric	WR	6-1	185	2	San Jose State
40	Riddick, Robb	RB	6-0	195	5	Millersville State, Pa.
51	Ritcher, Jim	G	6-3	285	7	North Carolina State
26	Romes, Charles	CB	6-1	188	10	North Carolina Central
57	Sanford, Lucius	LB	6-2	220	9	Georgia Tech
	Seawright, James	LB	6-2	219	1	South Carolina
76	Smerlas, Fred	NT	6-3	268	8	Boston College
78	Smith, Bruce	DE	6-4	279	2	Virginia Tech
74	Smith, Don	DE	6-5	262	8	Miami
45	Steels, Anthony	RB	5-9	200	2	Nebraska
56	Talley, Darryl	LB	6-4	227	4	West Virginia
86	Teal, Jimmy	WR	5-10	170	2	Texas A&M
62	Traynowicz, Mark	G	6-5	272	2	Nebraska
	Virkus, Scott	DE	6-5	279	4	San Francisco C.C.
65	Vogler, Tim	G	6-1	267	8	Ohio State
77	Williams, Ben	DE	6-3	266	11	Mississippi
21	Wilson, Don	S	6-2	190	3	North Carolina State

Greg Bell led the Bills in both rushing and pass receiving

INDIANAPOLIS COLTS

Address P.O. Box 54000 Indianapolis, Indiana 46254.
Stadium Hoosier Dome, Indianapolis.
    Capacity 60,127 *Playing Surface* AstroTurf.
Team Colours Royal Blue, White and Silver.
Head Coach Rod Dowhower – second year.
Championships Division 1970,'75,'76,'77; Conference 1970;
    NFL 1958,'59,'68; Super Bowl 1970.
History NFL 1953-69, AFC 1970-
    (Until 1984, they were known as the Baltimore Colts. A
    team of the same name played in the AAFC, from 1947
    to 1949, and in the NFL in 1950, at the end of which they
    went out of business.)

Offense

Last year, there was every sign that the Colts were emerging from the doldrums and, though they're not quite ready to challenge the likes of Miami, those fans who regularly fill the Hoosier Dome to capacity may not have to wait much longer for a winner. Their heroes now have a terrific rushing game featuring four players who, collectively, gave the Colts the league's best average gain per attempt (5.0 yards). In terms of total yardage, they ranked 5th. Just prior to the 1986 collegiate draft, owner Robert Irsay was reported as having turned down a trade which would have sent Randy McMillan to Houston in exchange for the Oilers' first-round draft option. McMillan is a punishing runner, supported by George Wonsley, Albert Bentley and Owen Gill, the latter who was selected in last year's second round by Seattle but was subsequently released. It is in the passing game that improvement is needed. For the fourth year, quarterback Mike Pagel gave a gritty performance without the option of passing to a thoroughbred wide receiver. However, he has been traded to Cleveland, leaving Gary Hogeboom (he was acquired in a trade with Dallas) as the favourite to start, ahead of Matt Kofler and second-round draftee Jack Trudeau. Of the receivers, last year, tight end Pat Beach caught the most passes, though at a modest 10.4-yard average. Wide receiver Wayne Capers has potential and can go the distance (he scored on an 80-yard reception in 1985), but Matt Bouza has yet to pose that kind of threat – his 40-yard reception in 1985 was his longest after four years in the pros. Fourth-round draftee Bill Brooks could find a place on the roster. On the offensive line, the Colts will start the two players, Chris Hinton and Ron Solt, who came as the major parts in the trade which sent quarterback John Elway to Denver. Hinton, who crossed over with Elway, is an outstanding player, able to play at both guard and tackle and having been elected to two Pro Bowls (he was unavailable through injury in 1984). Solt was subsequently drafted with the first-round option which, originally, belonged to Denver. Ben Utt at left guard, center Ray Donaldson and right tackle Karl Baldischwiler should retain their starting spots.

Defense

The defensive line could just make a quantum leap in improvement if two former starters, nose tackle Leo Wisniewski and defensive end Blaise Winter, can recover from injuries. Also, the Colts drafted the enormous Jon Hand in the first round. Hand played at nose tackle in college but is said to be versatile enough to play at defensive end. Brad White and Chris Scott would then join the reserves. Donnell Thompson, an aggressive player who was a first-round pick in 1981, will continue to start at defensive left end. Speaking of former first-round picks, the Colts have three starting at linebacker and all came high in that round. Duane Bickett is the latest to join Johnie Cooks and Barry Krauss. Even in his first season, Bickett emerged as a dominating player, leading the team with six sacks, ahead of defensive ends Scott and Virkus (he has been released), who each had five. Bickett, who came to prominence in his senior year at USC, is destined for greatness. Inside linebacker Cliff Odom was discarded by both Cleveland and the Raiders but, in his fourth season with the Colts, he led the team with 192 tackles. In the secondary, strong safety Nesby Glasgow continued to give value for money, and rookie Anthony Young was a revelation, matching Glasgow tackle for tackle. Reserve defensive back Leonard Coleman, a 1984 first-round pick, joined the team after a flirtation with the USFL and has great potential. Right cornerback Eugene Daniel has become recognised as a real ball-hawker, having added eight interceptions (he shared the lead in the AFC) to his six of 1984. However, left cornerback Preston Davis may be challenged by any one or all of Keith Lee, Don Anderson and Coleman.

Special Teams

The Colts now have one of the league's best special teams. Returning kickoffs, Bentley averaged 25.0 yards to come second in the AFC and sixth in the NFL. Robbie Martin averaged a big-time 11.1 yards returning punts to rank

1986 SCHEDULE OF GAMES	September	
	7 at New England	4:00
	14 at Miami	4:00
	21 LOS ANGELES RAMS	12:00
	28 NEW YORK JETS	3:00
	October	
	5 at San Francisco	1:00
	12 NEW ORLEANS	12:00
	19 at Buffalo	1:00
	26 MIAMI	1:00
	November	
	2 CLEVELAND	1:00
	9 NEW ENGLAND	1:00
	16 at New York Jets	4:00
	23 at Houston	12:00
	30 SAN DIEGO	1:00
	December	
	7 at Atlanta	1:00
	14 BUFFALO	1:00
	21 at Los Angeles Raiders	1:00

fourth in the AFC and fifth overall. Punter Rohn Stark was way ahead of the lot, averaging 45.9 with his rainmakers, and went to the Pro Bowl. Raul Allegre was a little off form, after two good seasons, but anyone who has kicked seven field goals of over 50 yards is unlikely to be replaced.

1986 DRAFT

Round	Name	Pos.	Ht.	Wt.	College
1.	Hand, Jon	DE	6-6	283	Alabama
2.	Trudeau, Jack	QB	6-3	211	Illinois
4.	Brooks, Bill	WR	6-1	187	Boston University
5.	Kellar, Scott	DE	6-2	260	Northern Illinois
5.	Walker, Gary	C	6-3	269	Boston University
7.	O'Malley, Steve	NT	6-2	257	Northern Illinois
7.	White, Chris	K	5-11	168	Illinois
7.	Sims, Tommy	CB	6-0	190	Tennessee
8.	Hooper, Trell	DB	5-11	190	Memphis State
9.	Brotzki, Bob	T	6-4	266	Syracuse
10.	Anderson, Pete	G	6-3	254	Georgia
12.	Wade, Steve	NT	6-3	270	Vanderbilt
12.	Williams, Isaac	NT	6-1	260	Florida State

VETERAN ROSTER

No.	Name	Pos.	Ht.	Wt.	NFL Year	College
57	Ahrens, Dave	LB	6-3	245	6	Wisconsin
2	Allegre, Raul	K	5-10	167	4	Texas
36	Anderson, Don	CB	5-10	197	2	Purdue
61	Bailey, Don	C	6-4	268	3	Miami
72	Baldischwiler, Karl	T	6-5	276	8	Oklahoma
	Barnes, Roosevelt	LB	6-2	228	5	Purdue
81	Beach, Pat	TE	6-4	244	4	Washington State
97	Benson, Charles	DE	6-3	267	3	Baylor
20	Bentley, Albert	RB	5-11	207	2	Miami
50	Bickett, Duane	LB	6-5	241	2	Southern California
85	Bouza, Matt	WR	6-3	212	5	California
84	Boyer, Mark	TE	6-4	233	2	Southern California
68	Broughton, Willie	DE	6-5	245	2	Miami
	Bryant, Steve	WR	6-2	197	5	Purdue
71	Call, Kevin	T	6-7	283	3	Colorado State
87	Capers, Wayne	WR	6-2	193	4	Kansas
74	Caron, Roger	T	6-5	270	2	Harvard
47	Coleman, Leonard	CB	6-2	208	2	Vanderbilt
98	Cooks, Johnie	LB	6-4	241	5	Mississippi State
38	Daniel, Eugene	CB	5-11	181	3	Louisiana State
27	Davis, Preston	CB	5-11	173	3	Baylor
53	Donaldson, Ray	C	6-4	274	7	Georgia
44	Gill, Owen	RB	6-1	230	2	Iowa
25	Glasgow, Nesby	S	5-10	188	8	Washington
	Harbour, James	WR	6-0	192	1	Mississippi
75	Hinton, Chris	T-G	6-4	289	4	Northwestern
	Hogeboom, Gary	QB	6-4	207	7	Central Michigan
	Holston, Michael	WR	6-3	191	6	Morgan State
56	Hunley, LaMonte	LB	6-2	232	2	Arizona
63	Kirchner, Mark	T	6-3	274	3	Baylor
12	Kofler, Matt	QB	6-3	192	5	San Diego State
55	Krauss, Barry	LB	6-3	246	8	Alabama
42	Lee, Keith	DB	5-11	193	6	Colorado State
59	Lowry, Orlando	LB	6-4	234	2	Ohio State
88	Martin, Robbie	WR	5-8	177	6	Cal Poly-SLO
	McGregor, Keli	TE	6-6	250	1	Colorado State
32	McMillan, Randy	RB	6-0	212	6	Pittsburgh
80	Nichols, Ricky	WR	5-10	180	2	East Carolina
93	Odom, Cliff	LB	6-2	236	6	Texas-Arlington
21	Radachowsky, George	S	5-11	178	2	Boston College
35	Randle, Tate	S	6-0	199	5	Texas Tech
95	Scott, Chris	DE	6-5	271	3	Purdue
83	Sherwin, Tim	TE	6-6	243	6	Boston College
91	Smith, Byron	DE	6-5	272	3	California
66	Solt, Ron	G	6-3	273	3	Maryland
3	Stark, Rohn	P	6-3	202	5	Florida State
99	Thompson, Donnell	DE	6-5	262	6	North Carolina
64	Utt, Ben	G	6-5	276	5	Georgia Tech
92	White, Brad	NT	6-2	253	6	Tennessee
86	Williams, Oliver	WR	6-3	191	2	Illinois
96	Winter, Blaise	DE	6-3	262	2	Syracuse
69	Wisniewski, Leo	NT	6-1	259	4	Penn State
34	Wonsley, George	RB	6-0	217	3	Mississippi State
37	Young, Anthony	S	5-11	187	2	Temple

Duane Bickett (#50) continued from where he had left off at USC, leading the Colts with six quarterback sacks in his rookie year

MIAMI DOLPHINS

Address 4770 Biscayne Boulevard, Suite 1440, Miami, Florida 33137.

Stadium Orange Bowl, Miami.
Capacity 75,206 *Playing Surface* Grass.

Team Colours Aqua, Coral, and White.

Head Coach Don Shula – seventeenth year.

Championships Division 1971,'72,'73,'74,'79,'81,'83,'84,'85; Conference 1971,'72,'73,'82,'84'; Super Bowl 1972,'73.

History AFL 1966-69, AFC 1970-

Offense

The Dolphins were not at their best for much of 1985, but they held off two good teams, the Jets and New England, to retain the AFC Eastern division title which has been theirs for the last five years (they had the best record in the nine-game 1982 season). The signs are that they may have less difficulty keeping it for a sixth year. Ed Newman missed the entire campaign with a knee injury, but he should be back to play at right guard in a line which has exceptional talent. With Newman, left guard Roy Foster and center Dwight Stephenson, the Dolphins have three Pro Bowlers operating in the thick of things, flanked by two fine tackles, Jon Giesler and Cleveland Green. Even without Newman's pass blocking, they gave up an NFL low of just 19 quarterback sacks. Mark Dennard, Larry Lee, Jeff Toews and Steve Clark, the latter who started in place of Newman, will function as solid backups. Two new players, rookies Lorenzo Hampton and Ron Davenport, joined the rushing offense. And it was the less-fancied of the two, Davenport, who made the bigger impact, scoring eleven rushing touchdowns. He'd already made a name for himself as a goal-line specialist before he showed a remarkable turn of foot against Cleveland in the playoffs. Running back Tony Nathan holds down one of the two starting positions and whilst the name of Woody Bennett is pencilled in for the second spot, he could be challenged by either of the second-year players and even Joe Carter. There'll be no challenging Dan Marino, who now rates alongside San Diego's Dan Fouts and San Francisco's Joe Montana – he may even be the best. Last year, he became the fourth quarterback in league history to throw for 30 or more touchdowns in consecutive seasons. Only a fool would assess the limits of the quarterback manual which he has been re-writing for the last three years. At his disposal, Marino has an outstanding trio of wide receivers in the 'Mark Brothers', Clayton and Duper, and Nat Moore. It is a measure of Clayton's ability that a 1985 haul of 70 receptions for 996 yards was considered a touch below par. Duper missed seven full games and most of an eighth, but he came back on Week Ten and caught eight passes for a huge 217 yards. Moore just keeps adding to his Dolphins club records. Coming out of the backfield, Nathan led the club with a personal-best 72 catches and now must be regarded as a dangerous dual-purpose player. When the offense stalls, any one of three good tight ends, Bruce Hardy, Joe Rose and Dan Johnson, can strip away from the line for the clutch reception.

Defense

It is on defense, particularly against the run, where the Dolphins have been inexplicably weak for the last four seasons. Head coach Don Shula took the obvious move by selecting John Offerdahl, a linebacker, and nose tackle T.J. Turner, with his first two options in the draft. During the 1985 campaign, he sent the club's only first-round option and a second-round option to Tampa Bay in exchange for the ubiquitous outside linebacker, Hugh Green. Defensive ends Doug Betters and Kim Bokamper clearly missed their teammate, All-Pro nose tackle Bob Baumhower, who viewed the entire season from the sideline because of injury. Betters, who had 16 and 14 sacks in 1983 and 1984 respectively, dropped to 6.5 in 1985. Mike Charles, standing in for Baumhower, had a club-leading seven sacks. He'll be a more-than-useful reserve should Baumhower return, as is expected. At linebacker, Green made a fine contribution, despite having to learn a new system, and he should be making headlines in the coming season. The other likely starters are Bob Brudzinski, Mark Brown and either of Jackie Shipp and Jay Brophy. Strong safety Glenn Blackwood repeated his 1984 total of six pass interceptions and is one of two very firm tacklers in the secondary. The other is Bud Brown, who was waived by Miami in August, 1984, but came back to win a starting spot at free safety ahead of Lyle Blackwood. William Judson and Paul Lankford, each of whom had four interceptions in 1985, are secure on the corners. Mike Smith, a rookie in 1985, and Don McNeal, a former starter who has been troubled with injuries, are the reserves.

1986 SCHEDULE OF GAMES	September	
	7 at San Diego	1:00
	14 INDIANAPOLIS	4:00
	21 at New York Jets	1:00
	28 SAN FRANCISCO	1:00
	October	
	5 at New England	1:00
	12 BUFFALO	1:00
	19 LOS ANGELES RAIDERS	1:00
	26 at Indianapolis	1:00
	November	
	2 HOUSTON	1:00
	10 at Cleveland (Mon.)	9:00
	16 at Buffalo	1:00
	24 NEW YORK JETS (Mon.)	9:00
	30 ATLANTA	1:00
	December	
	7 at New Orleans	12:00
	14 at Los Angeles Rams	1:00
	22 NEW ENGLAND (Mon.)	9:00

Special Teams

Punter Reggie Roby makes a spectacle out of not the most exciting aspect of football. With good distance and excellent hang time, he is a key part of the Dolphins' game. Rookie placekicker Fuad Reveiz did well on his debut and failed on only two field goal attempts inside the 50-yard range. Tommy Vigorito made a useful contribution, returning punts at an average of 9.0 yards, but Lorenzo Hampton, a first-round pick, was no more than adequate returning kickoffs.

1986 DRAFT

Round	Name	Pos.	Ht.	Wt.	College
2.	Offerdahl, John	LB	6-2	225	Western Michigan
3.	Turner, T.J.	NT	6-4	282	Houston
4.	Pruitt, James	WR	6-2	199	Cal State-Fullerton
5.	Wyatt, Kevin	CB	5-9	188	Arkansas
6.	Sowell, Brent	NT	6-5	256	Alabama
7.	Kolic, Larry	LB	6-1	242	Ohio State
8.	Stuart, John	T	6-5	277	Texas
9.	Thompson, Reyna	CB	6-0	185	Baylor
10.	Wickersham, Jeff	QB	6-2	195	Louisiana State
11.	Franklin, Arnold	TE	6-3	244	North Carolina
12.	Isom, Rickey	RB	5-10	235	North Carolina State

VETERAN ROSTER

No.	Name	Pos.	Ht.	Wt.	NFL Year	College
70	Barnett, Bill	DE	6-4	260	7	Nebraska
73	Baumhower, Bob	NT	6-5	265	9	Alabama
34	Bennett, Woody	RB	6-2	225	8	Miami
75	Betters, Doug	DE	6-7	265	9	Nevada-Reno
47	Blackwood, Glenn	S	6-0	190	8	Texas
42	Blackwood, Lyle	S	6-1	190	14	Texas Christian
58	Bokamper, Kim	DE	6-6	255	10	San Jose State
56	Bowser, Charles	LB	6-3	235	5	Duke
53	Brophy, Jay	LB	6-3	233	3	Miami
43	Brown, Bud	S	6-0	194	3	Southern Mississippi
51	Brown, Mark	LB	6-2	225	4	Purdue
59	Brudzinski, Bob	LB	6-4	223	10	Ohio State
23	Carter, Joe	RB	5-11	198	3	Alabama
71	Charles, Mike	DE-NT	6-4	285	4	Syracuse
76	Clark, Steve	G	6-4	255	5	Utah
83	Clayton, Mark	WR	5-9	175	4	Louisville
	Corker, John	LB	6-5	240	4	Oklahoma State
30	Davenport, Ron	RB	6-2	230	2	Louisville
65	Dellenbach, Jeff	T	6-6	280	2	Wisconsin
	Dennard, Mark	C	6-1	262	8	Texas A&M
85	Duper, Mark	WR	5-9	187	5	N.W. State, Louisiana
61	Foster, Roy	G-T	6-4	275	5	Southern California
79	Giesler, Jon	T	6-5	260	8	Michigan
74	Green, Cleveland	T	6-3	262	8	Southern
55	Green, Hugh	LB	6-2	225	6	Pittsburgh
27	Hampton, Lorenzo	RB	6-0	212	2	Florida
24	Hanks, Duan	WR	6-0	180	1	Stephen F. Austin
84	Hardy, Bruce	TE	6-5	232	9	Arizona State
88	Heflin, Vince	WR	6-0	185	5	Central State, Ohio
11	Jensen, Jim	WR	6-4	215	6	Boston University
87	Johnson, Dan	TE	6-3	240	4	Iowa State
49	Judson, William	CB	6-1	190	5	South Carolina State
40	Kozlowski, Mike	S	6-1	198	7	Colorado
44	Lankford, Paul	CB	6-2	184	5	Penn State
63	Lee, Larry	G-C	6-2	263	6	UCLA
72	Lee, Ronnie	G	6-4	265	8	Baylor
99	Little, George	NT	6-4	278	2	Iowa State
13	Marino, Dan	QB	6-4	214	4	Pittsburgh
28	McNeal, Don	CB	5-11	192	6	Alabama
91	Moore, Mack	DE	6-4	258	2	Texas A&M
89	Moore, Nat	WR	5-9	188	13	Florida
54	Moyer, Alex	LB	6-1	221	2	Northwestern
22	Nathan, Tony	RB	6-0	206	8	Alabama
64	Newman, Ed	G	6-2	255	13	Duke
9	Pisarcik, Joe	QB	6-4	220	9	New Mexico State
7	Reveiz, Fuad	K	5-11	222	4	Tennessee
4	Roby, Reggie	P	6-2	243	4	Iowa
80	Rose, Joe	TE	6-3	230	7	California
52	Sendlein, Robin	LB	6-3	225	6	Texas
50	Shipp, Jackie	LB	6-2	236	3	Oklahoma
18	Smith, Mike	CB	6-0	171	2	Texas-El Paso
45	Sowell, Robert	CB	5-11	175	4	Howard
57	Stephenson, Dwight	C	6-2	255	7	Alabama
10	Strock, Don	QB	6-5	220	13	Virginia Tech
60	Toews, Jeff	G-C	6-3	255	8	Washington
32	Vigorito, Tom	WR	5-10	190	4	Virginia

Ron Davenport, the Dolphins' power runner, who led the team with eleven rushing touchdowns and caught two touchdown passes

NEW ENGLAND PATRIOTS

AFC EASTERN DIVISION

Address Sullivan Stadium, Route 1, Foxboro, Mass. 02035.
Stadium Sullivan Stadium, Foxboro.
  Capacity 60,890 *Playing Surface* Super Turf.
Team Colours Red, White, and Blue.
Head Coach Raymond Berry – third year.
Championships Division 1978; Conference 1985.
History AFL 1960-69, AFC 1970-
  (Until 1971, they were known as the Boston Patriots.)

Offense

After watching the Patriots manhandled in Super Bowl XX, it would be easy to overlook their achievements of the 1985 season, during which they answered those who questioned their ability to take on the AFC's powerhouses. In the playoffs, when it mattered, they beat them all. Either of two good quarterbacks, Tony Eason and Steve Grogan, are able to run the offense. And though Grogan was the more effective in terms of passer-rating points, it's probable that Eason, the younger of the two, will be given the opportunity to open the season. The starter will be operating behind one of the AFC's better offensive lines which, as usual, is expected to be strong on the left side where the two Pro Bowlers, guard John Hannah and tackle Brian Holloway, have formed such a good partnership. When speaking of Hannah, it is difficult not to reel off his string of personal awards – All-Pro selections, Pro Bowl appearances and the like. Let's leave it that he's one of the greatest guards ever to play the game. On the right side, tackle Steve Moore and guard Ron Wooten went without much acclaim but did all that was asked of them. Moore came to the rescue when the expected starter, Darryl Haley, was injured. Haley, who missed the entire season, will be back at full strength and should reassert his seniority. Also missing for eleven games was Trevor Matich, who was the Patriots' first-round pick. He'll make a bid to displace Pete Brock at center. Head coach Raymond Berry already had enough running backs but added another when he chose SMU's Reggie Dupard in the first round. That was an intriguing move and it remains to be seen how he juggles the talent around. It would be a real shock if Craig James did not start, after a season in which he rushed for 1,227 yards at an average of 4.7, and was the only player to rush into three figures against the Raiders. Tony Collins, too, staked a claim, by gaining 657 yards and leading the club with 52 pass receptions. Mosi Tatupu is a good short-yardage specialist. Of the pure wide receivers, Stanley Morgan and Irving Fryar are the likely starters. Neither man would be expected to catch lots of passes but they are very fast and provide a constant deep threat, as do reserves Stephen Starring and Derwin Williams. In the tight end position, Lin Dawson, who is the better blocker, will probably share time with Derrick Ramsey.

Defense

There will be severe competition for starting places on the three-man defensive line. Two former starting defensive ends, Ken Sims and Toby Williams, will be returning after injury, and whilst Williams may step into the spot vacated by the retired Julius Adams, it is by no means certain that Sims can displace Garin Veris, who logged ten sacks and was a key figure in the latter part of the season. The solution may be to play Sims, who is better against the run, on the first two downs, and then turn Veris loose. Draftee Mike Ruth will challenge Lester Williams and his backup, Dennis Owens, for playing time at nose tackle. The linebackers are first class. Left outside linebacker Andre Tippett led the AFC with 16.5 sacks whilst Don Blackmon, on the right side, had eight. Inside linebacker Steve Nelson was the leading tackler and lined up together with Tippett to start in the Pro Bowl. Larry McGrew has made the conversion from outside to inside with no loss in effectiveness and completes the quartet which should begin the new season. Further good news for the Patriots is that former starting inside linebacker Clayton Weishuhn, who has missed two full seasons, is expected to be fully fit to resume. From the secondary, both free safety Fred Marion and cornerback Ray Clayborn went to the Pro Bowl, not just for grabbing seven and six interceptions respectively, but for all-round quality play. Two solid performers, cornerback Ronnie Lippett and strong safety Roland James, complete a starting lineup which has Rod McSwain, Ernest Gibson and Jim Bowman in reserve.

Special Teams

Irving Fryar is arguably the best of a few breathtaking punt returners in the league. There's an expectancy every time he fields the ball. Rich Camarillo's 43.0-yard punting average earned him fifth position in the league for gross average. 'If there's a mean kicker, it's Tony Franklin,' says head coach Berry, speaking of a player who, in 1985, scored a personal-best 112 points, including two field goals of 50 yards. Stephen Starring has the speed to go all the way on kickoff returns but, in Berry's words, 'he needs a bit more blocking to spring him into the open field.'

1986 SCHEDULE OF GAMES		
September		
7 INDIANAPOLIS		4:00
11 at New York Jets (Thurs.)		8:00
21 SEATTLE		1:00
28 at Denver		2:00
October		
5 MIAMI		1:00
12 NEW YORK JETS		1:00
19 at Pittsburgh		1:00
26 at Buffalo		1:00
November		
2 ATLANTA		1:00
9 at Indianapolis		1:00
16 at Los Angeles Rams		1:00
23 BUFFALO		1:00
30 at New Orleans		12:00
December		
7 CINCINNATI		1:00
14 SAN FRANCISCO		1:00
22 at Miami (Mon.)		9:00

1986 DRAFT

Round	Name	Pos.	Ht.	Wt.	College
1.	Dupard, Reggie	RB	5-11	201	Southern Methodist
2.	Ruth, Mike	NT	6-2	249	Boston College
2.	Glenn, Vencie	S	6-0	179	Indiana State
4.	Gieselman, Scott	TE	6-6	240	Boston College
5.	Robinson, Greg	G	6-5	286	Cal State-Sacramento
7.	McDonald, Ray	WR	5-11	185	Florida
7.	Williams, Brent	DE	6-4	265	Toledo
8.	Baty, Greg	TE	6-5	230	Stanford
9.	Colton, George	G	6-4	260	Maryland
10.	Jones, Cletis	RB	5-11	217	Florida State
11.	Thomas, Gene	WR	6-1	160	Pacific
12.	McAulay, Donald	K	5-10	198	Syracuse

VETERAN ROSTER

No.	Name	Pos.	Ht.	Wt.	NFL Year	College
55	Blackmon, Don	LB	6-3	235	6	Tulsa
28	Bowman, Jim	S	6-2	210	2	Central Michigan
58	Brock, Pete	C	6-5	275	11	Colorado
3	Camarillo, Rich	P	5-11	185	6	Washington
26	Clayborn, Ray	CB	6-0	186	10	Texas
33	Collins, Tony	RB	5-11	212	6	East Carolina
92	Creswell, Smiley	DE	6-4	251	2	Michigan State
87	Dawson, Lin	TE	6-3	240	6	North Carolina State
11	Eason, Tony	QB	6-4	212	4	Illinois
66	Fairchild, Paul	G	6-4	270	3	Kansas
1	Franklin, Tony	K	5-8	182	8	Texas A&M
80	Fryar, Irving	WR	6-0	200	3	Nebraska
43	Gibson, Ernest	CB	5-10	185	3	Furman
14	Grogan, Steve	QB	6-4	210	12	Kansas State
68	Haley, Darryl	T	6-4	265	4	Utah
73	Hannah, John	G	6-3	265	14	Alabama
27	Hawthorne, Greg	WR-RB	6-2	225	8	Baylor
76	Holloway, Brian	T	6-7	288	6	Stanford
51	Ingram, Brian	LB	6-4	235	5	Tennessee

No.	Name	Pos.	Ht.	Wt.	NFL Year	College
32	James, Craig	RB	6-0	215	3	Southern Methodist
38	James, Roland	S	6-2	191	7	Tennessee
83	Jones, Cedric	WR	6-1	184	5	Duke
42	Lippett, Ronnie	CB	5-11	180	4	Miami
31	Marion, Fred	S	6-2	191	5	Miami
64	Matich, Trevor	C	6-4	270	2	Brigham Young
50	McGrew, Larry	LB	6-5	233	6	Southern California
23	McSwain, Rod	CB	6-1	198	3	Clemson
67	Moore, Steve	T	6-4	285	4	Tennessee State
86	Morgan, Stanley	WR	5-11	181	10	Tennessee
75	Morriss, Guy	C-G	6-4	255	14	Texas Christian
57	Nelson, Steve	LB	6-2	230	13	North Dakota State
98	Owens, Dennis	NT	6-1	258	5	North Carolina State
18	Phelan, Gerard	WR	6-0	190	1	Boston College
70	Plunkett, Art	T	6-7	260	6	Nevada-Las Vegas
88	Ramsey, Derrick	TE	6-5	235	9	Kentucky
12	Ramsey, Tom	QB	6-1	189	2	UCLA
52	Rembert, Johnny	LB	6-3	234	4	Clemson
95	Reynolds, Ed	LB	6-5	230	4	Virginia
41	Robinson, Bo	RB	6-2	225	7	West Texas State
77	Sims, Ken	DE	6-5	271	5	Texas
81	Starring, Stephen	WR-KR	5-10	172	4	McNeese State
30	Tatupu, Mosi	RB	6-0	227	9	Southern California
99	Thomas, Ben	DE	6-4	280	2	Auburn
56	Tippett, Andre	LB	6-3	241	5	Iowa
74	Toth, Tom	T	6-5	275	1	Western Michigan
60	Veris, Garin	DE	6-4	255	2	Stanford
24	Weathers, Robert	RB	6-2	222	5	Arizona State
53	Weishuhn, Clayton	LB	6-1	218	3	Angelo State
82	Williams, Derwin	WR	6-0	170	2	New Mexico
54	Williams, Ed	LB	6-4	244	3	Texas
44	Williams, Jon	RB	5-9	190	2	Penn State
72	Williams, Lester	NT	6-3	272	5	Miami
90	Williams, Toby	DE	6-3	254	4	Nebraska
61	Wooten, Ron	G	6-3	273	5	North Carolina

Brian Holloway, the Patriots' left tackle, who has been selected to the last three Pro Bowls

NEW YORK JETS

AFC EASTERN DIVISION

Address 598 Madison Avenue, New York, N.Y. 10022.
Stadium Giants Stadium, East Rutherford, N.J. 07073.
  Capacity 76,891 *Playing Surface* AstroTurf.
Team Colours Kelly Green and White.
Head Coach Joe Walton – fourth year.
Championships AFL 1968; Super Bowl 1968.
History AFL 1960-69, AFC 1970-
  (Until 1963, they were known as the New York Titans.)

Offense

In a year when the Jets were not expected to be a force, they went out and equalled the club record for regular-season victories established by the 1968 squad which won the Super Bowl. Quarterback Ken O'Brien may not have the charisma and media appeal of Joe Namath, the quarterback in that momentous victory over Baltimore, but he became the first Jets player ever to win the NFL passing title – and it is entirely possible that we have not yet seen the best of him. With both starting wide receivers, Wesley Walker and Johnny 'Lam' Jones, suffering injuries, the Jets have not had a consistent passing offense for a while. However, even though Walker was again bothered with knocks (he missed the first four games), he was right on top of his form, catching 34 passes at an average of 21.3 yards (in this respect he shared second place among the NFL's leading receivers with Willie Gault, behind Stephone Paige) and scored five touchdowns, two of which came on plays covering 96 and 88 yards. There's no doubt that the arrival of the majestic Al Toon was a factor in the Jets' resurgence. With both Toon and Walker posing a deep threat on every passing down, tight end Mickey Shuler had his most productive season, catching more passes for more yards and scoring more touchdowns than in any of his previous seven years as a pro. Wide receiver Kurt Sohn was a pleasant surprise, coming in on first-aid duty early in the season. Running back Freeman McNeil is the jewel in the crown. We just have to expect that he will be injured somewhere along the way but, thankfully, he stayed on the field long enough to have big days of 192, 173, 151 and 149 yards, en route to establishing a club single-season rushing record of 1,331 yards. Two of the Jets' five losses came when he did not play. Johnny Hector and Tony Paige are solid players but, in truth, McNeil is the rushing offense. He's worth protecting and that's perhaps why the club selected big offensive tackles, Mike Haight and Doug Williams, with their first two draft options. One of the rookies should start in place of Marvin Powell, who has been released. The returning starters are tackle Reggie McElroy, guards Jim Sweeney and Dan Alexander, and center Joe Fields, the latter who is a former Pro Bowler. However, their reserve strength is modest and they might be in trouble should injuries strike.

Defense

The Jets made a great improvement on defense, lifting themselves to 8th in the NFL compared with 21st in 1984. Before the season, their intention to switch from 4-3 to 3-4 had surprised a few people. 'Why would they tamper with the "Sack Exchange"?' one mused. In the event, there was hardly a hiccup. They gave up the fewest points in the AFC and set a club record by conceding an average of 16.5 points per game. Despite not starting until the fifth game because of an injured thumb, defensive end Mark Gastineau had 13.5 sacks, coming equal second in the AFC, and started in the Pro Bowl. Remarkably, Gastineau has now had 94 sacks in 86 career starts. Joe Klecko became the first man to be selected to the Pro Bowl in three different positions, defensive end, defensive tackle and now, nose tackle. Both Klecko and defensive end Barry Bennett had 7.5 sacks. Two useful reserves, Marty Lyons and Tom Baldwin have started in the past. It was thought that the Jets would feel the pressure at linebacker, but it never materialised. Lance Mehl, Bob Crable, Kyle Clifton and Charles Jackson, the latter who started after arriving via a trade with Kansas City, buckled down to the job. Clifton took over from Mehl as the leading tackler. However, by way of consolation, Mehl was elected to his first Pro Bowl. In the search for insurance, linebackers were drafted in rounds three, four, five and ten. In the secondary, the Jets had a rash of serious injuries, in particular those to safety Ken Schroy, who has subsequently retired, and cornerback Russell Carter, who missed eight games. There were others, several, who missed at least four games. Left cornerback Bobby Jackson survived long enough to grab four interceptions to tie for the club lead with nickel back Kerry Glenn. Doubtless they'll all be glad to have put their feet up.

1986 SCHEDULE OF GAMES	September	
	7 at Buffalo	4:00
	11 NEW ENGLAND (Thurs.)	8:00
	21 MIAMI	1:00
	28 at Indianapolis	3:00
	October	
	5 BUFFALO	4:00
	12 at New England	1:00
	20 DENVER (Mon.)	9:00
	26 NEW ORLEANS	1:00
	November	
	2 at Seattle	1:00
	9 at Atlanta	1:00
	16 INDIANAPOLIS	4:00
	24 at Miami (Mon.)	9:00
	30 LOS ANGELES RAMS	1:00
	December	
	7 at San Francisco	1:00
	13 PITTSBURGH (Sat.)	12:30
	21 at Cincinnati	1:00

Special Teams

Pat Leahy is a solid placekicker who doesn't miss many of the easy ones and, last year, landed field goals of 55, 53 and 52 yards. Punter Dave Jennings came from the Giants after going through two modest seasons, and, after having a third with the Jets, he will be challenged in camp. All of Kurt Sohn, Kirk Springs and JoJo Townsell can and do return the punts with telling effect, and Johnny Hector might return more kickoffs after averaging 24.9 yards on eleven attempts in 1985.

Joe Klecko (#73), a four-time Pro Bowler, is as solid as a rock at nose tackle

VETERAN ROSTER

No.	Name	Pos.	Ht.	Wt.	NFL Year	College
60	Alexander, Dan	G	6-4	260	10	Louisiana State
95	Baldwin, Tom	NT	6-4	275	3	Tulsa
63	Banker, Ted	G-T	6-2	255	3	Southeast Missouri
31	Barber, Marion	RB	6-2	224	5	Minnesota
78	Bennett, Barry	DE	6-4	260	9	Concordia, Minn.
54	Benson, Troy	LB	6-2	227	1	Pittsburgh
64	Bingham, Guy	C-G	6-3	255	7	Montana
23	Bligen, Dennis	RB	5-11	209	3	St. John's
27	Carter, Russell	CB-S	6-2	195	3	Southern Methodist
59	Clifton, Kyle	LB	6-4	233	3	Texas Christian
67	Collins, Scott	LB	6-1	220	1	Oregon Tech
	Corley, Anthony	RB	6-0	210	3	Nevada-Reno
50	Crable, Bob	LB	6-3	228	5	Notre Dame
86	Dennison, Glenn	TE	6-3	225	2	Miami
37	Elder, Donnie	CB	5-9	175	2	Memphis State
65	Fields, Joe	C	6-2	253	12	Widener
38	Flowers, Larry	S	6-1	190	6	Texas Tech
99	Gastineau, Mark	DE	6-5	265	8	E. Central Oklahoma
35	Glenn, Kerry	CB	5-9	175	2	Minnesota
81	Griggs, Billy	TE	6-3	230	2	Virginia
94	Guilbeau, Rusty	LB	6-4	237	5	McNeese State
61	Gunter, Greg	C	6-3	265	2	C.W. Post
39	Hamilton, Harry	S	6-0	193	3	Penn State
34	Hector, Johnny	RB	5-11	197	4	Texas A&M
28	Howard, Carl	CB	6-3	177	3	Rutgers
84	Humphery, Bobby	WR-KR	5-10	180	3	New Mexico State
55	Jackson, Charles	LB	6-2	224	9	Washington
13	Jennings, Dave	P	6-4	200	13	St Lawrence
80	Jones, Johnny 'Lam'	WR	5-11	180	6	Texas
73	Klecko, Joe	NT	6-3	263	10	Temple
89	Klever, Rocky	TE	6-3	225	4	Montana
5	Leahy, Pat	K	6-0	193	13	St Louis University
90	Luft, Brian	T	6-6	263	1	Southern California
26	Lyles, Lester	S	6-3	209	2	Virginia
29	Lynn, Johnny	CB-S	6-0	198	7	UCLA
93	Lyons, Marty	DE	6-5	269	8	Alabama
68	McElroy, Reggie	T	6-6	270	4	West Texas State
24	McNeil, Freeman	RB	5-11	212	6	UCLA
56	Mehl, Lance	LB	6-3	233	7	Penn State
36	Miano, Rich	S	6-0	200	2	Hawaii
58	Monger, Matt	LB	6-1	235	2	Oklahoma State
20	Mullen, Davlin	CB	6-1	177	4	Western Kentucky
7	O'Brien, Ken	QB	6-4	208	4	Cal-Davis
49	Paige, Tony	RB	5-10	220	3	Virginia Tech
76	Rudolph, Ben	DE	6-5	271	6	Long Beach State
10	Ryan, Pat	QB	6-3	210	9	Tennessee
82	Shuler, Mickey	TE	6-3	231	9	Penn State
87	Sohn, Kurt	WR	5-11	180	5	Fordham
21	Springs, Kirk	S-PR	6-0	197	6	Miami, Ohio
53	Sweeney, Jim	G	6-4	266	3	Pittsburgh
88	Toon, Al	WR	6-4	200	2	Wisconsin
83	Townsell, JoJo	WR	5-9	180	2	UCLA
70	Waldemore, Stan	G	6-4	269	8	Nebraska
85	Walker, Wesley	WR	6-0	182	10	California

1986 DRAFT

Round	Name	Pos.	Ht.	Wt.	College
1.	Haight, Mike	T	6-4	270	Iowa
2.	Williams, Doug	T	6-5	290	Texas A&M
3.	Crawford, Tim	LB	6-4	230	Texas Tech
4.	Alexander, Rogers	LB	6-3	219	Penn State
5.	Hadley, Ron	LB	6-2	241	Washington
7.	White, Bob	T	6-5	255	Rhode Island
8.	Ducksworth, Robert	DB	5-11	200	Southern Mississippi
9.	Faaola, Nuu	RB	5-11	215	Hawaii
10.	Carr, Carl	LB	6-3	228	North Carolina
11.	Amoia, Vince	RB	5-11	220	Arizona State
12.	Cesario, Sal	T	6-5	260	Cal Poly-SLO

CINCINNATI BENGALS

AFC CENTRAL DIVISION

Address 200 Riverfront Stadium, Cincinnati, Ohio 45202.
Stadium Riverfront Stadium, Cincinnati.
   Capacity 59,754 *Playing Surface* AstroTurf.
Team Colours Black, Orange, and White.
Head Coach Sam Wyche – third year.
Championships Divison 1970, '73, '81; Conference 1981.
History AFL 1968-69, AFC 1970-

Offense

If only the Bengals could make a good start to the season – if. In each of the last two years, they have been in contention for the AFC Central division title right down to the final weekend, despite having lost the first five games in 1984 and the first three games in 1985. They have started out in 1986 well enough by having a good draft – don't they always? One scouting combine rated linebacker Joe Kelly as the second-best available, behind Kevin Murphy. Again, wide receiver Tim McGee, who was their second pick in the first round, was considered to be only slightly inferior to the top-rated Mike Sherrard. And the Michigan nose tackle, Mike Hammerstein, could turn out to have been a 'steal' in the third round. Looking at the existing veterans, the starting offensive line is as good as most in the conference, perhaps even in the league. Left tackle Anthony Munoz, a perennial All-Pro, sets the standard by which others are measured. Right tackle Mike Wilson has been up with the best since joining the Bengals in 1978. Right guard Max Montoya, too, has been a highly-respected starter for several years. Both center Dave Rimington and left guard Brian Blados are former first-round picks. The offensive line paved the way for a strike force which, last year, ranked third in the NFL. Quarterback Boomer Esiason made remarkable progress in his first full year as the starter, and, with the veteran Ken Anderson in reserve, the Bengals felt able to trade Turk Schonert. Esiason, who ranked second to the Jets' Ken O'Brien in the NFL, is a player with both the style and presence to bring the best out of two really fine wide receivers, Cris Collinsworth and Eddie Brown. Collinsworth, who has just logged his third 1,000-yards-receiving season, has been a Pro Bowler in three of his five NFL years, and Brown's excellent NFL debut in 1985 earned him the title of NFL Rookie of the Year. Backups Steve Kreider and Mike Martin ease smoothly into the lineup as circumstances demand. At tight end, Rodney Holman had a good year, scoring seven touchdowns, and M.L. Harris is one of the better reserves in the conference. With James Brooks and Larry Kinnebrew as the starting running backs, the Bengals have the ideal combination of speed and power. Two young players, Stanford Jennings and Bill Johnson, await their opportunities.

Defense

It is to the defense that the Bengals look for an improvement which will be necessary if they are to mount a serious challenge in 1986. Last year, they gave up more than 40

points in each of three games. The three-man line, consisting of defensive ends Ross Browner and Eddie Edwards, and nose tackle Tim Krumrie, is solid enough. Browner and Edwards led with 9 and 8.5 sacks respectively, and Krumrie, who led the club with 96 tackles, plays like a future Pro Bowler. However, they could use a little more fire at linebacker and, in this context, draftee Joe Kelly could make an impact. There would have to be some positional adjustment since Kelly is a specialist on the outside, where, already, Reggie Williams and Jeff Schuh are established starters. Ron Simpkins holds down the spot at left inside linebacker. Carl Zander, Emanuel King and Leo Barker will be in the competition for places. The secondary is well stocked with veterans who have played together for some time. Unfairly, in the opinion of head coach Sam Wyche, they have been blamed for the team's defensive shortcomings. Cornerbacks Louis Breeden and Ray Horton, and three safeties, Bobby Kemp, James Griffin and Robert Jackson, will be out to prove him right. Griffin, who shared the free safety position with Jackson, led the club with seven interceptions, had 55 tackles, a sack and a fumble recovery. Jackson came second in tackles, had six interceptions and he, too, recovered a fumble.

Special Teams

Placekicker Jim Breech established a Bengals record with 120 points in 1985, and punter Pat McInally had yet another good year, his tenth with the club. However, both men will be challenged in training camp by three players, Jeff Partridge, Ricky Anderson and Rick Ward, all of whom are dual-purpose kickers with a slight bias towards punting. Martin returned all the punts, at a steady 8.4-yard average, and the majority of kickoffs to similar effect. It is when trying to stop opposing punt returners that the Bengals have trouble – they gave up an average of 13.2 yards per return. One of those mad frontier types, the sort who'd tackle a moose, would suit them nicely.

1986 SCHEDULE OF GAMES		
September		
7	at Kansas City	3:00
14	BUFFALO	1:00
18	at Cleveland (Thurs.)	8:00
28	CHICAGO	1:00
October		
5	vs. Green Bay at Milwaukee	12:00
13	PITTSBURGH (Mon.)	9:00
19	HOUSTON	1:00
26	at Pittsburgh	1:00
November		
2	at Detroit	1:00
9	at Houston	12:00
16	SEATTLE	1:00
23	MINNESOTA	1:00
30	at Denver	2:00
December		
7	at New England	1:00
14	CLEVELAND	1:00
21	NEW YORK JETS	1:00

1986 DRAFT

Round	Name	Pos.	Ht.	Wt.	College
1.	Kelly, Joe	LB	6-2	219	Washington
1.	McGee, Tim	WR	5-10	181	Tennessee
2.	Billups, Lewis	CB	5-11	178	North Alabama
3.	Skow, Jim	DE	6-3	245	Nebraska
3.	Hammerstein, Mike	NT	6-3	250	Michigan
3.	Fulcher, David	S	6-2	220	Arizona State
4.	Kattus, Eric	TE	6-6	224	Michigan
4.	Gaynor, Doug	QB	6-1	207	Cal State-Long Beach
5.	White, Leon	LB	6-2	221	Brigham Young
6.	Hunt, Gary	CB	5-10	172	Memphis State
7.	Franklin, Pat	RB	6-0	234	Southwest Texas State
8.	Douglas, David	G	6-4	266	Tennessee
9.	Whittingham, Cary	LB	6-2	236	Brigham Young
10.	Shaw, Jeff	NT	6-1	280	Salem, West Virginia
11.	Stone, Tim	T	6-6	296	Kansas State
11.	Flaherty, Tom	LB	6-4	235	Northwestern
12.	Bradley, Steve	QB	6-2	224	Indiana

VETERAN ROSTER

No.	Name	Pos.	Ht.	Wt.	NFL Year	College
40	Alexander, Charles	RB	6-1	226	8	Louisiana State
14	Anderson, Ken	QB	6-3	212	16	Augustana, Ill.
53	Barker, Leo	LB	6-2	227	3	New Mexico State
74	Blados, Brian	G	6-4	295	3	North Carolina
61	Boyarsky, Jerry	NT	6-3	290	6	Pittsburgh
3	Breech, Jim	K	5-6	161	8	California
34	Breeden, Louis	CB	5-11	185	9	North Carolina Central
21	Brooks, James	RB	5-10	182	6	Auburn
81	Brown, Eddie	WR	6-0	185	2	Miami
79	Browner, Ross	DE	6-3	265	9	Notre Dame
80	Collinsworth, Cris	WR	6-5	192	6	Florida

No.	Name	Pos.	Ht.	Wt.	NFL Year	College
73	Edwards, Eddie	DE	6-5	256	10	Miami
7	Esiason, Boomer	QB	6-4	220	3	Maryland
22	Griffin, James	S	6-2	197	4	Middle Tennessee St.
83	Harris, M.L.	TE	6-5	238	7	Kansas State
82	Holman, Rodney	TE	6-3	232	5	Tulane
20	Horton, Ray	CB	5-11	190	4	Washington
37	Jackson, Robert	S	5-10	186	5	Central Michigan
36	Jennings, Stanford	RB	6-1	205	3	Furman
30	Johnson, Bill	RB	6-2	230	2	Arkansas State
26	Kemp, Bobby	S	6-0	191	6	Cal State-Fullerton
89	Kern, Don	TE	6-4	225	3	Arizona State
90	King, Emanuel	LB	6-4	245	2	Alabama
28	Kinnebrew, Larry	RB	6-1	255	4	Tennessee State
64	Kozerski, Bruce	C	6-4	275	3	Holy Cross
86	Kreider, Steve	WR	6-3	192	8	Lehigh
69	Krumrie, Tim	NT	6-2	262	4	Wisconsin
88	Martin, Mike	WR	5-10	186	4	Illinois
87	McInally, Pat	P	6-6	212	11	Harvard
65	Montoya, Max	G	6-5	275	8	UCLA
78	Munoz, Anthony	T	6-6	278	7	Southern California
42	Pickering, Clay	WR	6-5	215	2	Maine
75	Reimers, Bruce	T	6-7	280	3	Iowa State
52	Rimington, Dave	C	6-3	288	4	Nebraska
59	Schuh, Jeff	LB	6-3	234	6	Minnesota
25	Simmons, John	CB	5-11	192	6	Southern Methodist
56	Simpkins, Ron	LB	6-1	235	6	Michigan
62	Smith, Gary	G	6-2	265	2	Virginia Tech
35	Turner, Jimmy	CB	6-0	187	4	UCLA
63	Walter, Joe	T	6-6	290	2	Texas Tech
41	Washington, Sam	CB	5-9	180	5	Mississippi Valley State
57	Williams, Reggie	LB	6-0	228	11	Dartmouth
77	Wilson, Mike	T	6-5	271	9	Georgia
91	Zander, Carl	LB	6-2	235	2	Tennessee

Wide receiver Eddie Brown (#81) had an outstanding debut and was voted the NFL Rookie of the Year

CLEVELAND BROWNS

Address Tower B, Cleveland Stadium, Cleveland, Ohio 44114.

Stadium Cleveland Stadium, Cleveland.
Capacity 80,098 *Playing Surface* Grass.

Team Colours Seal Brown, Orange, and White.

Head Coach Marty Schottenheimer – third year.

Championships Division 1971,'80,'85; AAFC 1946,'47,'48,'49; NFL 1950,'54,'55,'64.

History AAFC 1946-49, NFL 1950-69, AFC 1970-

Offense

Cleveland's lingering memory of the 1985 season must be that of the loss to Miami in the last two minutes of the AFC divisional playoff game. Just a couple of pass completions, at the right time, might have made the difference. Nonetheless, they enter 1986 as a club which knows that it can win games, and there's little doubt that the squad is just that bit better than it was at the same stage last year. The big decision falls to head coach Schottenheimer, who will have to identify his starting quarterback. Clearly, last year's highly-touted rookie, Bernie Kosar, represents the future. But, for the present, more than a few Cleveland fans would like to see Gary Danielson at the controls. Danielson's rough edges were smoothed off a long time ago, and there can't be many defensive alignments and shifts that he hasn't seen over his nine NFL years, the first eight of which were spent with Detroit. It would make sense to be a little conservative and start with Danielson, since it is not as if the Browns need to hurry the younger man along – already, they have the components of a steady offense and need take no unnecessary risks. The stability and potential productivity lies in the offensive backfield from which, in 1985, Earnest Byner and Kevin Mack became only the third pair in league history each to rush for over 1,000 yards. Curtis Dickey, who was picked up late in the year from Indianapolis, has breakaway speed and could provide a dangerous option. If the rushing offense stalls, Ozzie Newsome will be on hand for the clutch receptions. Last year, Newsome became the first tight end in NFL history to catch over 500 career passes. Newsome is a pro's pro. The offensive line is unlikely to demolish anybody, but it kept the Browns competitive, despite the fact that only two players, left guard George Lilja and center Mike Baab, were fit to start in every game. All of left tackle Paul Farren, right tackle Cody Risien and rookie right guard Dan Fike missed at least three games. Fortunately they can whistle up the versatile Rickey Bolden, who started in three different positions. The experienced veteran, Robert Jackson, has retired. There is a need for consistent productivity at wide receiver, where several young players will be competing for places. Brian Brennan, Fred Banks and the two flyers, Clarence Weathers and Glen Young, will be involved in the scramble. They are joined by draftee Webster Slaughter and the Canadian Football League imports, Terry Greer and Jeff Boyd, both of whom are said to be sensational – we'll see.

Defense

As a whole, in 1985, the defense was a little less effective than expected. Even so, they did make life difficult for the opposition and have no obvious weaknesses. On the defensive line, nose tackle Bob Golic had an excellent year, earning his first Pro Bowl election. He'll be starting, with Reggie Camp on the left side and, most probably, Carl Hairston on the right. Defensive end Keith Baldwin is a former starter but has been troubled with injuries. The heavy pressure comes from four aggressive linebackers, led by Chip Banks. A Pro Bowler in three of his four NFL years, Banks seemed bound for another club as part of the complicated dealings which brought Kosar to the Browns. Nonetheless, he stayed around and underlined his worth by leading the club with eleven sacks. The other outside linebacker, Clay Matthews, is highly respected and has just made his first Pro Bowl appearance, albeit as a late replacement. On the inside, Scott Nicolas will compete with Tom Cousineau to start alongside Eddie Johnson, with Curtis Weathers and Anthony Griggs (ex-Philadelphia) providing depth. The secondary, featuring cornerbacks Frank Minnifield and Hanford Dixon, and safeties Al Gross and Don Rogers, remained intact throughout 1985 and was one of the league's better outfits. Tragically, Rogers died during the close-season. The Browns will miss this inspirational player who was on the verge of greatness.

Special Teams

Placekicker Matt Bahr does not have the leg strength of several others in the league, but he is otherwise reliably successful – and that's good enough. The lack of distance in punting is more significant, and it means that the incumbent, Jeff Gossett, who averaged just 40.3 gross

1986 SCHEDULE OF GAMES	September	
	7 at Chicago	12:00
	14 at Houston	12:00
	18 CINCINNATI (Thurs.)	8:00
	28 DETROIT	1:00
	October	
	5 at Pittsburgh	1:00
	12 KANSAS CITY	1:00
	19 GREEN BAY	1:00
	26 at Minnesota	12:00
	November	
	2 at Indianapolis	1:00
	10 MIAMI (Mon.)	9:00
	16 at Los Angeles Raiders	1:00
	23 PITTSBURGH	1:00
	30 HOUSTON	1:00
	December	
	7 at Buffalo	1:00
	14 at Cincinnati	1:00
	21 SAN DIEGO	1:00

yards last year, will always be faced with competition in training camp. There's a shortage of yardage, too, on punt returns, in which Clarence Weathers and Brennan combined for a ranking of 13th in the AFC. However, the Browns are certainly given an edge by Glen Young, who returned 35 kickoffs for an AFC-leading 25.7-yard average.

1986 DRAFT

Round	Name	Pos.	Ht.	Wt.	College
2.	Slaughter, Webster	WR	6-0	170	San Diego State
5.	Miller, Nick	LB	6-2	229	Arkansas
7.	Meyer, Jim	T	6-5	298	Illinois State
7.	Norseth, Mike	QB	6-2	200	Kansas
9.	Taylor, Danny	CB	5-9	176	Texas-El Paso
10.	Smith, Willie	TE	6-2	225	Miami
11.	Dausin, Randy	G	6-4	260	Texas A&M
12.	Simmons, King	DB	6-2	199	Texas Tech

VETERAN ROSTER

No.	Name	Pos.	Ht.	Wt.	NFL Year	College
80	Adams, Willis	WR-TE	6-2	200	7	Houston
26	Allen, Greg	RB	5-11	200	2	Florida State
61	Baab, Mike	C	6-4	270	5	Texas
9	Bahr, Matt	K	5-10	175	8	Penn State
99	Baldwin, Keith	DE	6-4	270	5	Texas A&M
56	Banks, Chip	LB	6-4	233	5	Southern California
83	Banks, Fred	WR-KR	5-10	177	2	Liberty Baptist
77	Bolden, Rickey	T	6-6	280	3	Southern Methodist
	Boyd, Jeff	WR	6-2	180	R	Chapman College
47	Braziel, Larry	CB	6-0	184	8	Southern California
86	Brennan, Brian	WR	5-9	178	3	Boston College
44	Byner, Earnest	RB	5-10	215	3	East Carolina
96	Camp, Reggie	DE	6-4	270	4	California
91	Clancy, Sam	DE	6-7	260	3	Pittsburgh
39	Colson, Eddie	RB	5-10	228	1	North Carolina
75	Contz, Bill	T	6-5	270	4	Penn State
50	Cousineau, Tom	LB	6-3	225	5	Ohio State
18	Danielson, Gary	QB	6-2	196	10	Purdue
38	Davis, Johnny	RB	6-1	235	9	Alabama
33	Dickey, Curtis	RB	6-1	220	7	Texas A&M
29	Dixon, Hanford	CB	5-11	186	6	Southern Mississippi
74	Farren, Paul	T	6-5	270	4	Boston University
69	Fike, Dan	G-T	6-7	280	2	Florida
28	Fontenot, Herman	RB	66-0	206	2	Louisiana State
79	Golic, Bob	NT	6-2	260	7	Notre Dame
7	Gossett, Jeff	P	6-2	200	5	Eastern Illinois
	Greer, Terry	WR	6-2	180	R	Alabama State
	Griggs, Anthony	LB	6-3	232	5	Ohio State
27	Gross, Al	S	6-3	195	4	Arizona
78	Hairston, Carl	DE	6-4	260	11	Maryland East. Shore
	Hill, Troy	CB-S	5-11	174	1	Pittsburgh
	Hoggard, D.D.	CB	6-0	188	1	North Carolina State
81	Holt, Harry	TE	6-4	230	4	Arizona
51	Johnson, Eddie	LB	6-1	225	6	Louisville
19	Kosar, Bernie	QB	6-5	210	2	Miami
88	Langhorne, Reginald	WR	6-2	195	2	Elizabeth City State
62	Lilja, George	G	6-4	270	5	Michigan
34	Mack, Kevin	RB	6-0	212	2	Clemson
57	Matthews, Clay	LB	6-2	235	9	Southern California
16	McDonald, Paul	QB	6-2	185	7	Southern California
31	Minnifield, Frank	CB	5-9	180	3	Louisville
97	Morrill, David	DE	6-2	260	1	Ohio State
82	Newsome, Ozzie	TE	6-2	232	9	Alabama
58	Nicolas, Scott	LB	6-3	226	5	Miami
	Pagel, Mike	QB	6-2	207	5	Arizona State
72	Puzzuoli, Dave	NT	6-3	260	4	Pittsburgh
63	Risien, Cody	T	6-7	280	7	Texas A&M
37	Rockins, Chris	S	6-0	195	3	Oklahoma State
24	Shakespeare, Stan	WR	6-0	180	1	Miami
87	Tucker, Travis	TE	6-3	227	2	South Connecticut St.
85	Weathers, Clarence	WR-PR	5-9	170	4	Delaware State
55	Weathers, Curtis	LB	6-5	230	8	Mississippi
70	Williams, Larry	G	6-5	269	1	Notre Dame
22	Wright, Felix	CB-S	6-2	190	2	Drake
84	Young, Glen	WR-KR	6-2	205	4	Mississippi State

Second-year player Bernie Kosar has all the tools to become a great quarterback

HOUSTON OILERS

Address Box 1516, Houston, Texas 77001.
Stadium Astrodome, Houston.
   Capacity 50,496 *Playing Surface* AstroTurf.
Team Colours Columbia Blue, Scarlet, and White.
Head Coach Jerry Glanville – second year.
Championships AFL 1960,'61.
History AFL 1960-69, AFC 1970-

Offense

Including and since the 1982 draft, the Oilers have had more picks in the first five rounds than any other NFL club and, of the 30 players selected, over half have become starters. Their latest blue-chipper, draftee quarterback Jim Everett, is unlikely to start right away unless, of course, the existing starter, Warren Moon, goes into precipitous decline. The offensive line is beginning to look tough. Last year, left guard Mike Munchak went to his second Pro Bowl and the durable right tackle, Bruce Matthews (he played on every offensive down), was a non-travelling reserve. Dean Steinkuhler has been troubled with injuries but, when fit, will challenge John Schuhmacher for the starting position at right guard. Jim Romano is solid at center, backed up by Mike Kelley. The rushing offense has yet to crank into gear, though there is good talent on the squad. Mike Rozier was the 1983 Heisman Trophy winner (he spent two seasons in the USFL) and must surely improve on his modest output of last year, when he appeared somewhat tentative. Butch Woolfolk, who came in a trade with the Giants, is not a prolific rusher but he is becoming a major component in the passing offense – in 1985 he finished third in the AFC with 80 receptions, including 80-, 67- and 46-yarders for touchdowns. Draftee Allen Pinkett is small but has top-class speed. Wide receiver Drew Hill came cheaply from the Rams – he cost a 7th-round pick in 1986 and a 4th-round pick in 1987. Clearly enjoying the responsibility of starting, he came fifth in the league with 1,169 yards receiving, and rounded off the season with nine receptions for 210 yards and two touchdowns against the Colts. Hill's starting partner, Tim Smith, caught passes for over 1,000 yards in each of 1983 and 1984, and provides Moon with a fine optional target. Tight end Jamie Williams hasn't yet broken into the top bracket but is settling down as a steady performer. Moon was erratic in 1985, but he finished off with three consecutive 300-yards-passing games and just might be on the verge of something big.

Defense

Houston now has a good three-man defensive line. Both right defensive end Jesse Baker and middle guard Mike Stensrud have spent seven years learning the trade. Baker, who shared the team lead with 5.5 sacks, is one of the most underrated players in the league. At defensive left end, 1985 first-round pick Ray Childress (he was the third player selected overall) was 'quietly outstanding'. Thankfully, also, he looks the durable type, having started in all sixteen games. With Richard Byrd and Doug Smith hovering in reserve, the Oilers are well set for the future. At linebacker, Avon Riley is becoming a dominant force. Before the 1985 season, he had started on the outside since the beginning of the 1982 season, having joined the Oilers as a rookie in 1981. However, last year, he shifted to the inside, his old college position, teaming up with another sound veteran, Robert Abraham. Riley was the leading tackler with a total of 147, and Abraham led the club with four fumble recoveries. Left outside linebacker Robert Lyles made great progress over a season in which he started in every game. There will be competition to start on the right side, where all three of Johnny Meads and rookies Frank Bush and Tom Briehl showed promise. Meads, in particular, has a nose for the ball – against Pittsburgh on Week Three, he had sixteen tackles. Free safety Bo Eason is another uncompromising hitter and is now established alongside strong safety Keith Bostic. Cornerbacks Patrick Allen and Steve Brown, the latter who led the club with five pass interceptions, may find it more difficult to hold off the challenge of last year's rookie, Richard Johnson, who was the second of two first-round picks. With Johnson, Rod Kush (ex-Buffalo) and Jeff Donaldson in reserve, the Oilers have strength in depth.

Special Teams

Four rookies were at the sharp end of a good special-teams squad. Placekicker Tony Zendejas came from Washington as a free agent and landed 21 field goals to equal the club record. Punter Lee Johnson was a fifth-round pick and averaged a steady 41.7 yards. Willie Drewrey did well as a dual-purpose returner, but he may have to yield a greater share of the kickoff returns to Steve Tasker, who averaged 26.3 yards on 17 attempts, and draftee Ernest Givins, the latter who, for much of last year, led the nation in that category.

1986 SCHEDULE OF GAMES		
September		
7	at Green Bay	12:00
14	CLEVELAND	12:00
21	at Kansas City	3:00
28	PITTSBURGH	12:00
October		
5	at Detroit	1:00
12	CHICAGO	12:00
19	at Cincinnati	1:00
26	LOS ANGELES RAIDERS	12:00
November		
2	at Miami	1:00
9	CINCINNATI	12:00
16	at Pittsburgh	1:00
23	INDIANAPOLIS	12:00
30	at Cleveland	1:00
December		
7	at San Diego	1:00
14	MINNESOTA	3:00
21	BUFFALO	12:00

Wide receiver Drew Hill was an excellent acquisition from the Rams

1986 DRAFT

Round	Name	Pos.	Ht.	Wt.	College
1.	Everett, Jim	QB	6-5	208	Purdue
2.	Givins, Ernest	WR	5-10	170	Louisville
3.	Pinkett, Allen	RB	5-8	181	Notre Dame
5.	Parks, Jeff	TE	6-3	233	Auburn
6.	Wallace, Ray	RB	6-0	215	Purdue
8.	Griffin, Larry	DB	6-1	197	North Carolina
9.	Sebring, Bob	LB	6-2	235	Illinois
10.	Sommer, Don	G	6-4	259	Texas-El Paso
11.	Cochran, Mark	T	6-5	281	Baylor
12.	Banks, Chuck	RB	6-0	219	West Virginia Tech

VETERAN ROSTER

No.	Name	Pos.	Ht.	Wt.	NFL Year	College
56	Abraham, Robert	LB	6-1	230	5	North Carolina State
86	Akiu, Mike	WR	5-9	185	2	Hawaii
29	Allen, Patrick	CB	5-10	185	3	Utah State
75	Baker, Jesse	DE	6-5	271	8	Jacksonville State
25	Bostic, Keith	S	6-1	210	4	Michigan
92	Briehl, Tom	LB	6-3	247	2	Stanford
24	Brown, Steve	CB	5-11	189	4	Oregon
94	Bush, Frank	LB	6-1	218	2	North Carolina State
71	Byrd, Richard	MG	6-3	255	2	Southern Mississippi
79	Childress, Ray	DE	6-6	267	2	Texas A&M
42	Crutchfield, Dwayne	RB	6-0	245	4	Iowa State
31	Donaldson, Jeff	S	6-0	193	3	Colorado
88	Dressel, Chris	TE	6-4	238	4	Stanford
82	Drewrey, Willie	WR-KR	5-7	158	2	West Virginia
21	Eason, Bo	S	6-2	200	3	Cal-Davis
32	Edwards, Stan	RB	6-0	210	5	Michigan
68	Golic, Mike	DE	6-5	265	1	Notre Dame
59	Grimsley, John	LB	6-2	232	3	Kentucky
85	Hill, Drew	WR	5-9	170	8	Georgia Tech
66	Howell, Pat	G	6-6	265	8	Southern California
	Jefferson, John	WR	6-1	204	9	Arizona State

No.	Name	Pos.	Ht.	Wt.	NFL Year	College
11	Johnson, Lee	P	6-1	204	2	Brigham Young
97	Johnson, Mike	DE	6-5	253	2	Illinois
23	Johnson, Richard	CB	6-1	195	2	Wisconsin
58	Kelley, Mike	C-G	6-5	266	2	Notre Dame
37	Kush, Rod	S	6-1	195	7	Nebraska-Omaha
10	Luck, Oliver	QB	6-2	196	5	West Virginia
28	Lyday, Allen	S	5-10	186	3	Nebraska
93	Lyles, Robert	LB	6-1	223	3	Texas Christian
	Madsen, Lynn	NT	6-3	270	R	Washington
74	Matthews, Bruce	T	6-4	280	4	Southern California
89	McCloskey, Mike	TE	6-5	246	4	Penn State
26	McMillian, Audrey	DB	6-0	190	2	Houston
91	Meads, Johnny	LB	6-2	225	3	Nicholls State
1	Moon, Warren	QB	6-3	208	3	Washington
76	Moran, Eric	T	6-5	282	3	Washington
30	Moriarty, Larry	RB	6-1	240	4	Notre Dame
63	Munchak, Mike	G	6-3	286	5	Penn State
53	Riley, Avon	LB	6-3	236	6	UCLA
55	Romano, Jim	C	6-3	255	5	Penn State
33	Rozier, Mike	RB	5-10	198	2	Nebraska
73	Salem, Harvey	T	6-6	285	4	California
	Schellen, Mark	RB	5-9	233	1	Nebraska
62	Schuhmacher, John	G	6-3	277	7	Southern California
99	Smith, Doug	MG	6-4	285	2	Auburn
83	Smith, Tim	WR	6-2	206	7	Nebraska
72	Sochia, Brian	MG	6-3	254	3	Northwest Oklahoma
70	Steinkuhler, Dean	G	6-3	273	3	Nebraska
67	Stensrud, Mike	MG	6-5	280	8	Iowa State
80	Tasker, Steve	PR-KR	5-9	185	2	Northwestern
84	Walls, Herkie	WR-KR	5-8	160	4	Texas
87	Williams, Jamie	TE	6-4	232	4	Nebraska
40	Woolfolk, Butch	RB	6-1	212	5	Michigan
7	Zendejas, Tony	K	5-8	160	2	Nevada-Reno

PITTSBURGH STEELERS

AFC CENTRAL DIVISION

Address Three Rivers Stadium, 300 Stadium Circle,
 Pittsburgh, Pa. 15212.
Stadium Three Rivers Stadium, Pittsburgh.
 Capacity 59,000 *Playing Surface* AstroTurf.
Team Colours Black and Gold.
Head Coach Chuck Noll – eighteenth year.
Championships Division 1972,'74,'75,'76,'77,'78,'79,'83,'84;
 Conference 1974,'75,'78,'79; Super Bowl 1974,'75,'78,'79.
History NFL 1933-69, AFC 1970-
 (Until 1940, they were known as the Pittsburgh Pirates.)

Offense

Here's a club which has lots of really fine players, and a few genuine stars, but lacks the catalyst which would spark the combination to greatness. Even though playing in a division which, currently, is the league's weakest, the Steelers are coming off their first net losing season since 1971. Way back then, the catalyst was defensive tackle Joe Greene – and we all know what happened over the next nine years. (For those who don't know, the Steelers won four Super Bowl Championships.) It could just be that draftee guard John 'Rhino' Rienstra could play the key part in launching the running backs across the gain line, much as did Sam Davis for Franco Harris in the old days. Each of the current running backs, Frank Pollard and Walter Abercrombie, has just had his best season in the league, with Pollard rushing for 991 yards and Abercrombie exceeding his previous best by a whopping 241 yards. A few solid nudges in open field could send both men over 1,000 in a season. Rienstra's potential is added to the existing line which, already, boasts center Mike Webster, guards Craig Wolfley and Terry Long, and tackles Ray Pinney and Tunch Ilkin. Webster, an outstanding veteran who has not missed a game in twelve consecutive years, and New England's John Hannah, are the only two offensive linemen who have been voted to the last eight consecutive Pro Bowls. Of the three quarterbacks, Mark Malone is the probable starter, ahead of David Woodley (he is considering retirement). But when neither was available, the young Scott Campbell showed a great deal of promise. The starter could hardly wish for a better pair of wide receivers than John Stallworth and Louis Lipps. Entering his thirteenth NFL campaign, Stallworth still has the range and moves he had in the late 1970s and, if anything, is now a better clutch receiver. In just two years, Lipps has become one of the AFC's most productive offensive players. Of his AFC-leading fifteen touchdowns in 1985, twelve were scored in his role as a receiver, and his 1,134 yards came at the excellent average of 19.2. Calvin Sweeney and Weegie Thompson are steady reserves, though not in the same class as the starters. If the passing offense has a weakness, it is at tight end, and, from what was a modest crop of college seniors, a top-class

player was never likely to emerge. Bennie Cunningham, a former starter, has been released.

Defense

The Steelers have a powerful group of linemen and linebackers, which pressures opposing quarterbacks but doesn't make as many collars as it ought to (they ranked 12th= in the AFC for sacks). Even so, they came second in the league (behind Washington) for pass defense – and it is that list which gives the true picture. Draftee defensive end Gerald Williams was considered to be the third best available, behind Leslie O'Neal and Jon Hand, and he must surely help the pass rush. He will fit in well with the Steelers, who are not averse to using even five defensive linemen on occasion. The normal three-man line uses two fine young defensive ends, Keith Willis and Keith Gary, with the nine-year veteran, Gary Dunn, at nose tackle. The backups include John Goodman, who can play anywhere on the line, and the 1985 first-round pick, defensive end Darryl Sims. Bryan Hinkle should be fully fit to start at right outside linebacker, rejoining Robin Cole, David Little and Mike Merriweather. It is a quartet which is respected throughout the conference. Encouragingly, the 1985 rookies, Gregg Carr and Fred Small, made the final roster, with Carr performing well as a substitute for Hinkle. The useful veteran, Dennis Winston, returned to Pittsburgh after a spell with New Orleans. The secondary is a blend of experience and speed. With four pass interceptions last season, strong safety Donnie Shell raised his career total to 47 and continues as the NFL's active leader in this category. Left cornerback Dwayne Woodruff, who is one of the fastest defensive backs in the league, led the club with five interceptions. The starting quartet should remain unchanged, with John Swain at right cornerback and Rick Woods at free safety.

1986 SCHEDULE OF GAMES	September	
	7 at Seattle	1:00
	15 DENVER (Mon.)	9:00
	21 at Minnesota	12:00
	28 at Houston	12:00
	October	
	5 CLEVELAND	1:00
	13 at Cincinnati (Mon.)	9:00
	19 NEW ENGLAND	1:00
	26 CINCINNATI	1:00
	November	
	2 GREEN BAY	1:00
	9 at Buffalo	1:00
	16 HOUSTON	1:00
	23 at Cleveland	1:00
	30 at Chicago	12:00
	December	
	7 DETROIT	1:00
	13 at New York Jets (Sat.)	12:30
	21 KANSAS CITY	1:00

Special Teams

Returning punts, Lipps is on a par with New England's Irving Fryar and was preferred by his peers to represent the AFC in the Pro Bowl. Placekicker Gary Anderson led the AFC in scoring and he, too, went to the Pro Bowl. Rookie punter Harry Newsome had a disappointing season and may be replaced. Todd Spencer and Rich Erenberg returned the kickoffs at a respectable level but may hand over the job to draftee Erroll Tucker, who, in his senior year, led the nation in returning both kickoffs and punts, scoring two touchdowns in each capacity.

*The great John Stallworth
remains at the top of his game*

1986 DRAFT

Round	Name	Pos.	Ht.	Wt.	College
1.	Rienstra, John	G	6-5	277	Temple
2.	Williams, Gerald	DE	6-3	262	Auburn
3.	Brister, Walter	QB	6-2	192	Northeast Louisiana
4.	Callahan, Bill	S	6-0	200	Pittsburgh
5.	Tucker, Erroll	CB-KR	5-8	171	Utah
5.	Jones, Brent	TE	6-4	235	Santa Clara
6.	Bryant, Domingo	S	6-3	178	Texas A&M
7.	Carter, Rodney	RB	6-0	206	Purdue
8.	Boso, Cap	TE	6-4	228	Illinois
9.	Henton, Anthony	LB	6-1	218	Troy State
10.	Seitz, Warren	WR	6-4	220	Missouri
11.	Station, Larry	LB	5-11	227	Iowa
12.	Williams, Mike	LB	6-2	215	Tulsa

VETERAN ROSTER

No.	Name	Pos.	Ht.	Wt.	NFL Year	College
34	Abercrombie, Walter	RB	6-0	210	5	Baylor
1	Anderson, Gary	K	5-11	170	5	Syracuse
	Behning, Mark	T	6-6	290	1	Nebraska
71	Boures, Emil	G-C	6-1	257	5	Pittsburgh
10	Campbell, Scott	QB	6-0	195	3	Purdue
91	Carr, Gregg	LB	6-1	217	2	Auburn
78	Catano, Mark	NT-DE	6-3	265	3	Valdosta State
33	Clayton, Harvey	CB	5-9	179	4	Florida State
56	Cole, Robin	LB	6-2	229	10	New Mexico
67	Dunn, Gary	NT	6-3	265	10	Miami
42	Edwards, Dave	S	6-0	196	2	Illinois
24	Erenberg, Rich	RB-KR	5-10	200	3	Colgate
92	Gary, Keith	DE	6-3	264	4	Oklahoma
95	Goodman, John	DE-NT	6-6	255	6	Oklahoma
86	Gothard, Preston	TE	6-4	235	2	Alabama
53	Hinkle, Bryan	LB	6-2	220	5	Oregon
62	Ilkin, Tunch	T	6-3	265	7	Indiana State
	Jacobs, Cam	LB	6-1	218	1	Kentucky
90	Kohrs, Bob	LB	6-3	238	6	Arizona State
83	Lipps, Louis	WR-PR	5-10	186	3	Southern Mississippi
50	Little, David	LB	6-1	240	6	Florida
74	Long, Terry	G	5-11	260	3	East Carolina
16	Malone, Mark	QB	6-4	222	7	Arizona State
57	Merriweather, Mike	LB	6-2	215	5	Pacific
47	Morse, Steve	RB	5-11	214	2	Virginia
64	Nelson, Edmund	DE-NT	6-3	278	5	Auburn
18	Newsome, Harry	P	6-0	187	2	Wake Forest
65	Pinney, Ray	T-C	6-4	265	8	Washington
80	Pokorny, Frank	WR	6-0	198	2	Youngstown State
30	Pollard, Frank	RB	5-10	223	7	Baylor
60	Rasmussen, Randy	G-C	6-1	253	3	Minnesota
63	Rostosky, Pete	T	6-4	263	3	Connecticut
31	Shell, Donnie	S	5-11	197	13	South Carolina State
99	Sims, Darryl	DE	6-3	264	2	Wisconsin
54	Small, Fred	LB	5-11	227	2	Washington
36	Spencer, Todd	RB-KR	6-0	217	3	Southern California
82	Stallworth, John	WR	6-2	202	13	Alabama A&M
26	Swain, John	CB	6-1	195	6	Miami
85	Sweeney, Calvin	WR	6-2	190	7	Southern California
87	Thompson, Weegie	WR	6-6	211	3	Florida State
25	Tuggle, Anthony	DB	6-1	211	2	Nicholls State
51	Turk, Dan	C	6-4	259	2	Wisconsin-Milwaukee
52	Webster, Mike	C	6-1	258	13	Wisconsin
21	Williams, Eric	S	6-1	187	4	North Carolina State
93	Willis, Keith	DE	6-1	254	5	Northeastern
55	Winston, Dennis	LB	6-0	244	10	Arkansas
73	Wolfley, Craig	G	6-1	260	7	Syracuse
19	Woodley, David	QB	6-2	210	7	Louisiana State
49	Woodruff, Dwayne	CB	6-0	197	8	Louisville
22	Woods, Rick	DB	6-1	195	5	Boise State

DENVER BRONCOS

Address 5700 Logan Street, Denver, Colorado 80216.
Stadium Denver Mile High Stadium.
   Capacity 75,100 *Playing Surface* Grass (Prescription Athletic Turf).
Team Colours Orange, Royal Blue, and White.
Head Coach Dan Reeves – sixth year.
Championships Division 1977, '78, '84; Conference 1977.
History AFL 1960-69, AFC 1970-

Offense

'Almost but not quite,' is the description of the 1985 Broncos, who became the first team, since the wild card playoff format was adopted, to win eleven regular-season games and yet not make the playoffs. Of their five defeats, four were against subsequent division champions by a total of 14 points. This is a really tough football club. Quarterback John Elway, the player who was drafted first overall in 1983, the year that Dan Marino went to Miami, still lacks the consistency as a passer which goes with greatness, but he made good progress as a leader of the offense. His rifle arm sent the ball whistling 3,891 yards on 605 attempts, many of which were into the teeth of an unforgiving Colorado blizzard. He ended the season on a high note, passing for 432 yards when overcoming a 17-point deficit in a 27-24 victory over Seattle. The senior wide receiver, Steve Watson, failed to gain over 1,000 yards for the first time since 1982. But there is no doubting his right to be considered amongst the league's best and, as usual, he'll be double-teamed on most downs in 1986. Vance Johnson enjoyed a fine rookie season and moved ahead of Butch Johnson to start on the left side. The expressive Butch must be one of the best reserves around the league and, together with Clint Sampson, gives the Broncos sound insurance. There may be a little more productivity than usual at tight end, with the introduction of Mike Barber. He is another, like Johnson, whose lot it has been to play behind top-class performers. After arriving from the Rams, midway through the season, he caught only one pass, but may be given greater opportunities in the Broncos offense which uses two tight ends. Barber will compete with the current starters, Clarence Kay and James Wright. Of the running backs, Sammy Winder is the starter, ahead of Gerald Willhite, Steve Sewell and Gene Lang. Winder, a former Pro Bowler, is a gutsy runner, and rookie Steve Sewell showed some style towards the end of the season. However, they could make use of the break-away speed which has arrived with rookie free agent Joe Dudek. The offensive line is solid. Even though a figure of 38 sacks conceded looks modest, in percentage terms (this is related to the number of passes attempted) it was good enough for second place in the AFC behind the great Miami line. Billy Bryan, who has 62 consecutive starts, is a rock at center, flanked by guards Keith Bishop

and Paul Howard, and two good tackles, Dave Studdard and Ken Lanier.

Defense

The Broncos could be on the verge of having the best defense in their history. Two crafty veterans, defensive end Barney Chavous and nose tackle Rubin Carter, were starters on the original 'Orange Crush' which played in Super Bowl XII. Defensive right end Rulon Jones has just been to his first Pro Bowl after registering ten sacks in 1985. Andre Townsend came on well as a pass rusher. Behind the three-man front, four linebackers maintain the Denver tradition of quality and competitiveness. Karl Mecklenburg is coming off a sensational season in which, twice, he had four sacks in a game and set a club record with 13 in total. His partner, Steve Busick, is tough against the run and came second on the team with 81 tackles. Jim Ryan will continue to start on the left side but Ken Woodard may press Tom Jackson, a three-time Pro Bowler who was injured for much of the season, for more playing time on the right side. The secondary, too, has always been a Denver strength, and their commitment to maintaining that status was confirmed when, in the close-season, they traded with the Giants for cornerback Mark Haynes. He's a blue-chipper who has been elected to three Pro Bowls and usually finds a place in one of the All-Pro squads. However, the incumbent at right corner-back, Mike Harden, will not be displaced easily after grabbing five interceptions and leading the club in tackles and passes defensed (18) in 1985. On the other corner, the great Louis Wright, who also had five interceptions, is the man the quarterbacks fear. And they're not too keen on challenging the safeties, Dennis Smith and Steve Foley, a pair of aggressive tacklers who each had three interceptions.

Special Teams

Placekicker Rich Karlis has had a few encounters with the uprights but can point to a steady 73.1 career success rate

1986 SCHEDULE OF GAMES	September	
	7 LOS ANGELES RAIDERS	2:00
	15 at Pittsburgh (Mon.)	9:00
	21 at Philadelphia	1:00
	28 NEW ENGLAND	2:00
	October	
	5 DALLAS	2:00
	12 at San Diego	1:00
	20 at New York Jets (Mon.)	9:00
	26 SEATTLE	2:00
	November	
	2 at Los Angeles Raiders	1:00
	9 SAN DIEGO	2:00
	16 KANSAS CITY	2:00
	23 at New York Giants	1:00
	30 CINCINNATI	2:00
	December	
	7 at Kansas City	12:00
	13 WASHINGTON (Sat.)	2:00
	20 at Seattle (Sat.)	1:00

on field goal attempts. Punter Chris Norman could do with a couple of extra yards on his 40.9 average and may have to fight off a challenger in training camp. Vance Johnson doubles as a productive dual-purpose returner, particularly on kickoffs in which he ranked equal third in the AFC.

1986 DRAFT

Round	Name	Pos.	Ht.	Wt.	College
4.	Juriga, Jim	G-T	6-6	269	Illinois
5.	Colorito, Tony	NT	6-5	260	Southern California
6.	Mobley, Orson	TE	6-5	256	Salem, West Virginia
6.	Jackson, Mark	WR	5-9	174	Purdue
7.	Phillips, Raymond	LB	6-3	240	North Carolina State
8.	Klostermann, Bruce	LB	6-4	225	South Dakota State
9.	Thomas, Joe	WR	5-11	167	Mississippi Valley State
10.	Hall, Victor	TE	6-3	234	Jackson State
11.	Dendy, Thomas	RB	5-10	187	South Carolina

VETERAN ROSTER

No.	Name	Pos.	Ht.	Wt.	NFL Year	College
85	Barber, Mike	TE	6-3	237	11	Louisiana Tech
54	Bishop, Keith	C-G	6-3	265	6	Baylor
64	Bryan, Billy	C	6-2	255	9	Duke
58	Busick, Steve	LB	6-4	227	6	Southern California
68	Carter, Rubin	NT	6-0	256	12	Miami
79	Chavous, Barney	DE	6-3	258	14	South Carolina State
59	Comeaux, Darren	LB	6-1	227	5	Arizona State
63	Cooper, Mark	G	6-5	267	4	Miami
55	Dennison, Rick	LB	6-3	220	5	Colorado State
	Dudek, Joe	RB	6-1	190	R	Plymouth State
7	Elway, John	QB	6-3	210	4	Stanford
73	Fletcher, Simon	DE	6-5	240	2	Houston
43	Foley, Steve	S	6-3	190	10	Tulane
62	Freeman, Mike	G	6-3	256	2	Arizona
72	Graves, Marsharne	T	6-3	272	2	Arizona
31	Harden, Mike	CB	6-1	192	7	Michigan
	Haynes, Mark	CB	5-11	195	7	Colorado
13	Hill, Al	WR	6-3	205	1	Arizona
51	Hinson, Billy	G	6-1	278	1	Florida
74	Hood, Winford	T	6-3	262	3	Georgia
60	Howard, Paul	G	6-3	260	13	Brigham Young
98	Hunley, Ricky	LB	6-2	238	3	Arizona
25	Hunter, Daniel	CB	5-11	175	2	Henderson State
57	Jackson, Tom	LB	5-11	220	14	Louisville
86	Johnson, Butch	WR	6-1	187	11	Cal-Riverside
82	Johnson, Vance	WR	5-11	174	2	Arizona
75	Jones, Rulon	DE	6-6	260	7	Utah State
3	Karlis, Rich	K	6-0	180	5	Cincinnati
88	Kay, Clarence	TE	6-2	237	3	Georgia
71	Kragen, Greg	NT	6-3	245	2	Utah State
8	Kubiak, Gary	QB	6-0	192	4	Texas A&M
33	Lang, Gene	RB	5-10	196	3	Louisiana State
76	Lanier, Ken	T	6-3	269	6	Florida State
22	Lilly, Tony	S	6-0	199	3	Florida
77	Mecklenburg, Karl	LB-DE	6-3	250	4	Minnesota
	Mills, Jim	T	6-9	281	3	Hawaii
67	Miraldi, Dean	T	6-5	285	5	Utah
1	Norman, Chris	P	6-2	198	3	South Carolina
34	Poole, Nathan	RB	5-9	212	6	Louisville
21	Riley, Eric	CB	6-0	170	1	Florida State
48	Robbins, Randy	CB	6-2	189	3	Arizona
50	Ryan, Jim	LB	6-1	218	8	William and Mary
84	Sampson, Clint	WR	5-11	183	4	San Diego State
83	Sawyer, John	TE	6-2	230	10	Southern Mississippi
30	Sewell, Steve	RB	6-3	210	2	Oklahoma
56	Smith, Aaron	LB	6-2	225	2	Utah State
49	Smith, Dennis	S	6-3	200	6	Southern California
70	Studdard, Dave	T	6-4	260	8	Texas
61	Townsend, Andre	DE	6-2	265	3	Mississippi
81	Watson, Steve	WR	6-4	195	8	Temple
47	Willhite, Gerald	RB	5-10	200	5	San Jose State
10	Willis, Larry	WR	5-10	170	1	Fresno State
45	Wilson, Steve	CB	5-10	195	8	Howard
23	Winder, Sammy	RB	5-11	203	5	Southern Mississippi
52	Woodard, Ken	LB	6-1	218	5	Tuskegee Inst.
87	Wright, James	TE	6-3	240	7	Texas Christian
20	Wright, Louis	CB	6-3	200	12	San Jose State

Wide receiver Steve Watson is Denver's premier deep threat

KANSAS CITY CHIEFS

AFC WESTERN DIVISION

Address One Arrowhead Drive, Kansas City, Missouri 64129.

Stadium Arrowhead Stadium, Kansas City.
Capacity 78,067 *Playing Surface* AstroTurf-8.

Team Colours Red, Gold, and White.

Head Coach John Mackovic – fourth year.

Championships Division 1971; AFL 1962, '66, '69; Super Bowl 1969.

History AFL 1960-69, AFC 1970-
(Until 1963, they were known as the Dallas Texans.)

Offense

It is worthy of note that, last year, the Chiefs shared victories with all three of the Raiders, San Diego and Seattle. And it is not difficult to imagine them improving on their 6-10 record in the coming season, when their schedule outside the division promises to be a little less demanding. In 1985, they were not helped when the system was disrupted by injuries to key offensive linemen. Guard Brad Budde missed the final nine games, tackle Matt Herkenhoff was out for six in mid-season and tackle John Alt was fit to start in only six games. Elsewhere, center Bob Rush and right tackle Dave Lutz started all season, and rookie right guard Bob Olderman did well, starting in 14 games. The pool is enriched by the arrival of first-round draftee Brian Jozwiak, a 303-pound monster of a tackle, and center Rick Donnalley (ex-Washington). Playing behind the line, however, there could be changes, the most surprising being the possible replacement of quarterback Bill Kenney by Todd Blackledge. (At least, that was the 'paper talk during the close-season.) Kenney has been a good quarterback in an era of great ones – he has been voted to one Pro Bowl. And he would appear to retain an edge over his younger partner, who has been given the opportunity to start but has yet to go out and burn the opposition. When it comes to wide receivers, however, there's not the slightest problem, except that of picking the best out of four real flyers. Carlos Carson and Stephone Paige are projected to strike the first blows. Carson led the club with 47 receptions and had big days on Weeks One and Two, when he caught passes for 173 and 118 yards against New Orleans and the Raiders respectively. On the final weekend, Paige had the biggest day in league history, when he caught eight passes for 309 yards. The ten-year veteran, Henry Marshall, was leading the club in receptions before being injured on Week Nine, and Anthony Hancock has caught his 69 career passes at an average of 17.4 yards. At tight end, Willie Scott has not yet played up to the standard expected of a former first-round pick, but Walt Arnold chips in with a few useful receptions and should retain his starting spot. It is at running back where the main weakness lies. Last year, Herman Heard was the most productive yet rushing for only 595 yards. Rookie Ethan Horton, who was the

Chiefs' first-round selection, must regard 146 yards as disappointing and may be challenged by Boyce Green, who has arrived from Cleveland.

Defense

All three potential starters on the defensive line are former first-round picks and, when healthy, can match most around the league. They were going well last year before defensive end Art Still was injured (he missed the last seven games) and Mike Bell, who was leading the team in sacks, missed the last five games for personal reasons. Bill Maas is a super player, operating either in his preferred position of nose tackle or at defensive end, where he played out of necessity for the final five games whilst Eric Holle took over at nose tackle. In Bell's absence, Bob Hamm was a solid replacement. Dave Lindstrom, Pete Koch and third-round draftee Leonard Griffin complete the pool of reserves. Gary Spani is the most experienced of the linebacking corps and will continue to start with, probably, Calvin Daniels, Scott Radecic and Ken Jolly making up the quartet. Ken McAlister has had big games in the past and Jeff Paine started four games in relief of the injured Jolly. However, the club could make use of someone who likes the sound of clattering helmets and here, draftee Dino Hackett could fit the bill. There is a settled group in the secondary, which focusses around the great free safety, Deron Cherry, who equalled the league record with four interceptions in one game against Seattle. Cherry went to his third consecutive Pro Bowl. Cornerback Albert Lewis tied for first place in the AFC with eight interceptions and made fine progress, starting in all sixteen games. Right cornerback Kevin Ross has now started in 32 consecutive games and must be respected, whilst strong safety Lloyd Burruss was voted the club's MVP by his teammates. Both Greg Hill and Sherman Cocroft had three interceptions, playing as the nickel and dime backs respectively.

1986 SCHEDULE OF GAMES	September	
	7 CINCINNATI	3:00
	14 at Seattle	1:00
	21 HOUSTON	3:00
	28 at Buffalo	1:00
	October	
	5 LOS ANGELES RAIDERS	12:00
	12 at Cleveland	1:00
	19 SAN DIEGO	3:00
	26 TAMPA BAY	12:00
	November	
	2 at San Diego	1:00
	9 SEATTLE	12:00
	16 at Denver	2:00
	23 at St Louis	3:00
	30 BUFFALO	12:00
	December	
	7 DENVER	12:00
	14 at Los Angeles Raiders	1:00
	21 at Pittsburgh	1:00

Special Teams

Nick Lowery is an excellent placekicker. His 88.9% success rate for field goal attempts was the third-best in league history and included an NFL season-longest 58-yarder. However, Jim Arnold's gross punting average slipped, from the huge 44.9 yards of 1984, down to 41.2. Rookie cornerback Garcia Lane gained experience returning all the punts, and averaged a good 8.9 yards, but another rookie, running back Jeff Smith, was well down the list of AFC kickoff returners.

1986 DRAFT

Round	Name	Pos.	Ht.	Wt.	College
1.	Jozwiak, Brian	T	6-6	303	West Virginia
2.	Hackett, Dino	LB	6-4	225	Appalachian State
3.	Griffin, Leonard	DE	6-5	243	Grambling State
4.	Baugh, Tom	C	6-3	270	Southern Illinois
4.	Fox, Chas	WR	6-0	185	Furman
6.	Hagood, Kent	RB	5-11	224	South Carolina
8.	Colbert, Lewis	P	5-11	179	Auburn
9.	Baldinger, Gary	DE	6-2	260	Wake Forest
10.	Readon, Ike	NT	6-2	285	Hampton Institute
11.	Pearson, Aaron	LB	6-1	237	Mississippi State

VETERAN ROSTER

No.	Name	Pos.	Ht.	Wt.	NFL Year	College
	Adickes, Mark	T	6-4	280	R	Baylor
76	Alt, John	T	6-7	278	3	Iowa
6	Arnold, Jim	P	6-2	220	4	Vanderbilt
87	Arnold, Walt	TE	6-3	221	7	New Mexico
68	Auer, Scott	G-T	6-4	255	3	Michigan State
77	Baldinger, Rich	G-T	6-4	281	5	Wake Forest
99	Bell, Mike	DE	6-4	250	7	Colorado State
14	Blackledge, Todd	QB	6-3	225	4	Penn State
57	Blanton, Jerry	LB	6-1	229	8	Kentucky
66	Budde, Brad	G	6-4	260	7	Southern California
34	Burruss, Lloyd	S	6-0	209	6	Maryland
88	Carson, Carlos	WR	5-11	182	7	Louisiana State
20	Cherry, Deron	S	5-11	196	6	Rutgers
22	Cocroft, Sherman	S	6-1	188	2	San Jose State
55	Cooper, Louis	LB	6-2	235	2	Western Carolina
50	Daniels, Calvin	LB	6-3	241	5	North Carolina
	Donnalley, Rick	C-G	6-2	257	5	North Carolina
65	Fada, Rob	G	6-2	259	4	Pittsburgh
	Green, Boyce	RB	5-11	215	4	Carson-Newman
90	Hamm, Bob	DE	6-4	263	4	Nevada-Reno
82	Hancock, Anthony	WR-KR	6-0	204	5	Tennessee
85	Hayes, Jonathan	TE	6-5	234	2	Iowa
44	Heard, Herman	RB	5-10	182	3	Southern Colorado
23	Hill, Greg	CB	6-1	199	4	Oklahoma State
93	Holle, Eric	DE-NT	6-4	258	3	Texas
32	Horton, Ethan	RB	6-3	228	2	North Carolina
52	Jolly, Ken	LB	6-2	220	3	Mid-America Nazarene
9	Kenney, Bill	QB	6-4	211	8	Northern Colorado
46	King, Bruce	RB	6-1	219	2	Purdue
74	Koch, Pete	DE	6-6	265	3	Maryland
41	Lane, Garcia	CB-KR	5-9	180	2	Ohio State
29	Lewis, Albert	CB	6-2	192	4	Grambling State
71	Lindstrom, Dave	DE	6-6	258	9	Boston University
62	Lingner, Adam	C-G	6-4	260	4	Illinois
8	Lowery, Nick	K	6-4	189	7	Dartmouth
72	Lutz, David	T	6-5	287	4	Georgia Tech
63	Maas, Bill	NT	6-4	259	3	Pittsburgh
89	Marshall, Henry	WR	6-2	213	11	Missouri
94	McAlister, Ken	LB	6-5	220	4	San Francisco
64	Olderman, Bob	G	6-4	262	2	Virginia
83	Paige, Stephone	WR	6-2	191	4	Fresno State
95	Paine, Jeff	LB	6-2	224	3	Texas A&M
43	Pruitt, Mike	RB	6-0	225	11	Purdue
97	Radecic, Scott	LB	6-3	246	3	Penn State
30	Robinson, Mark	S	5-10	206	3	Penn State
31	Ross, Kevin	CB	5-9	182	3	Temple
53	Rush, Bob	C	6-5	270	9	Memphis State
81	Scott, Willie	TE	6-4	254	6	South Carolina
70	Shields, Billy	T	6-8	284	12	Georgia Tech
80	Shorthose, George	WR-KR	6-0	198	2	Missouri
42	Smith, Jeff	RB-KR	5-9	201	2	Nebraska
59	Spani, Gary	LB	6-2	229	9	Kansas State
92	Stephens, Hal	DE	6-4	252	2	East Carolina
67	Still, Art	DE	6-7	254	9	Kentucky

Albert Lewis tied for the AFC lead with eight pass interceptions

LOS ANGELES RAIDERS

Address 332 Center Street, El Segundo, California 90245.
Stadium Los Angeles Memorial Coliseum.
  Capacity 92,516 *Playing Surface* Grass.
Team Colours Silver and Black.
Head Coach Tom Flores – eighth year.
Championships Division 1970,'72,'73,'74,'75,'76,'83,'85;
  Conference 1976,'80,'83; AFL 1967;
  Super Bowl 1976,'80,'83.
History AFL 1960-69, AFC 1970-
  (Until 1982, they were known as the Oakland Raiders.)

Offense

In recent years it has been easy to assess the Raiders and conclude that, 'they aren't as good as they used to be', particularly on offense. But this club, which Al Davis took by the scruff of the neck in 1963, is coming off yet another title-winning season, and promises to be competitive, as usual, in 1986. There was the feeling that the club might draft one of several good offensive linemen available, but, instead, they kept faith with their collection of solid veterans. And it is true that they could perm any five from eight and it would make little difference. Tackles Bruce Davis and Henry Lawrence, and guards Charley Hannah and Mickey Marvin, started in Super Bowl XVIII and will probably resume with Don Mosebar at center. Tackle Shelby Jordan, guard Curt Marsh and center Dave Dalby, who has played in 205 consecutive regular-season games, could come in with no loss of effectiveness. Their efforts are rewarded, week after week, by the superb Marcus Allen, who, in the 1985 season, became the first Raiders player ever to win the NFL rushing title. With Allen in full flow, Frank Hawkins and Kenny King aren't called into action very often, but a quick glance back to the 1983 season shows Hawkins rushing for 526 yards at an average of 4.8. King could so easily slip back into the gear which accelerated him to 761 (average 4.4) and 828 (average 4.9) yards in 1980 and 1981 respectively. In starting wide receivers Dokie Williams and last year's rookie, Jessie Hester, the Raiders have the deep threat which forms such an essential part of their game. Another 1985 rookie, Tim Moffett, has similar range and may be given more opportunities in the coming year. At the business of catching passes, there's no player in the league who can match the consistency of tight end Todd Christensen, who is the only man to have 80 or more receptions in the last three consecutive regular seasons. Earl Cooper (ex-49ers) could turn out to be a useful dual-purpose acquisition. It would appear, still, that the position of starting quarterback will belong to either Jim Plunkett or Marc Wilson, with Rusty Hilger as the successor in the long term. Plunkett, whose season ended with a dislocated shoulder in the Week Three loss to San Francisco, may just retain an edge in field generalship over Wilson, but no doubt they'll each see plenty of playing time.

Defense

It is the Raiders defense which can take the lion's share of credit for the team's success in the last two years. In the AFC, they gave up the fewest yards, came second against both the rush and the pass, and registered the most sacks (65). Defensive end Lyle Alzado has retired, but Sean Jones made good progress, logging 8.5 sacks. Bill Pickel has rapidly become one of the league's best nose tackles – he led the team with 12.5 sacks. Both players are helped enormously by the league's premier defensive end, Howie Long, who consistently attracts multiple teaming. In the manner of the Giants' Lawrence Taylor, Long can often dictate things to the opposition – teams have to adopt special tactics just to contain him within reasonable limits. Both Long and Greg Townsend, the latter who comes in on passing downs, had ten sacks. First-round draftee Bob Buczkowski arrives highly recommended. The Raiders love to show the opposition a variety of complex defensive formations and, in this, several fine linebackers, some awesome, play a key part. Rod Martin, Matt Millen, Brad Van Pelt and rookie Reggie McKenzie, ended the season as the starters. But inside linebacker Jerry Robinson, a former Pro Bowler who came via a trade with Philadelphia, must surely press for greater playing time this year. In 1985, the secondary came in for some criticism, much of it directed at cornerback Lester Hayes, who missed out on selection for the Pro Bowl for the first time after five consecutive appearances. He may have been below his best but he's still a good one and, looking over to the other corner, no-one questions the pre-eminence of Mike Haynes. Both Hayes and Haynes intercepted four passes, Mike Davis continues to be one of the game's most underrated strong safeties, and Vann McElroy has few equals when it comes to cleaning up in the free safety position. Stacey Toran, James Davis and Sam Seale are useful backups, whilst Brad Cochran represents a sound investment for the future.

1986 SCHEDULE OF GAMES		
September		
7 at Denver	2:00	
14 at Washington	1:00	
21 NEW YORK GIANTS	1:00	
28 SAN DIEGO	1:00	
October		
5 at Kansas City	12:00	
12 SEATTLE	1:00	
19 at Miami	1:00	
26 at Houston	12:00	
November		
2 DENVER	1:00	
9 at Dallas	3:00	
16 CLEVELAND	1:00	
20 at San Diego (Thurs.)	5:00	
30 PHILADELPHIA	1:00	
December		
8 at Seattle (Mon.)	6:00	
14 KANSAS CITY	1:00	
21 INDIANAPOLIS	1:00	

Special Teams

The former Dolphins player, Fulton Walker, turned out to be a fine acquisition, coming fourth in the NFL with an 11.2-yard punt return average. In company with Seale, he returned the kickoffs with moderate success. Placekicker Chris Bahr was a touch below his best, but Ray Guy continues both to produce and excite as one of the best punters of all time.

Jessie Hester impressed as a big-play wide receiver in his rookie season

1986 DRAFT

Round	Name	Pos.	Ht.	Wt.	College
1.	Buczkowski, Bob	DE	6-4	270	Pittsburgh
3.	Cochran, Brad	S	6-2	200	Michigan
4.	Wise, Mike	DE	6-6	270	Cal-Davis
4.	Mueller, Vance	RB	6-0	210	Occidental
4.	McCallum, Napoleon	RB	6-2	215	Navy
6.	Marrone, Doug	T	6-5	270	Syracuse
7.	Lewis, Bill	C	6-6	275	Nebraska
8.	Mauntel, Joe	LB	6-4	235	Eastern Kentucky
9.	Lee, Zeph	RB	6-3	215	Southern California
10.	Reinke, Jeff	DE	6-5	270	Mankato State
11.	Webster, Randell	LB	6-2	220	Southwestern Oklahoma
12.	Shepherd, Larry	WR	6-2	185	Houston

VETERAN ROSTER

No.	Name	Pos.	Ht.	Wt.	NFL Year	College
59	Adams, Stanley	LB	6-2	215	2	Memphis State
32	Allen, Marcus	RB	6-2	205	5	Southern California
10	Bahr, Chris.	K	5-10	170	11	Penn State
56	Barnes, Jeff	LB	6-2	225	10	California
76	Belcher, Kevin	T	6-5	280	1	Wisconsin
21	Branch, Cliff	WR	5-11	170	15	Colorado
81	Casper, Dave	TE	6-4	241	12	Notre Dame
46	Christensen, Todd	TE	6-3	230	8	Brigham Young
	Cooper, Earl	TE-RB	6-2	232	7	Rice
50	Dalby, Dave	C	6-3	255	15	UCLA
79	Davis, Bruce	T	6-6	285	8	UCLA
45	Davis, James	CB	6-0	195	5	Southern
36	Davis, Mike	S	6-3	205	9	Colorado
94	Franks, Elvis	DE	6-4	270	7	Morgan State
8	Guy, Ray	P	6-3	205	14	Southern Mississippi
	Haden, Nick	C	6-2	270	1	Penn State
73	Hannah, Charley	G	6-5	260	10	Alabama
27	Hawkins, Frank	RB	5-9	210	6	Nevada-Reno
37	Hayes, Lester	CB	6-0	200	10	Texas A&M
22	Haynes, Mike	CB	6-2	190	11	Arizona State
84	Hester, Jessie	WR	5-11	170	2	Florida State
12	Hilger, Rusty	QB	6-4	200	2	Oklahoma State
31	Jensen, Derrick	RB	6-1	220	8	Texas-Arlington
	Jensen, Russ	QB	6-2	215	1	Cal-Lutheran
99	Jones, Sean	DE	6-7	275	3	Northeastern
74	Jordan, Shelby	T	6-7	280	11	Washington, Mo.
87	Junkin, Trey	TE	6-2	225	4	Louisiana Tech
	Kimmel, Jamie	LB	6-3	240	1	Syracuse
33	King, Kenny	RB	5-11	205	8	Oklahoma
70	Lawrence, Henry	T	6-4	275	13	Florida A&M
75	Long, Howie	DE	6-5	270	6	Villanova
60	Marsh, Curt	G	6-5	275	5	Washington
53	Martin, Rod	LB	6-2	225	10	Southern California
65	Marvin, Mickey	G	6-4	265	10	Tennessee
26	McElroy, Vann	S	6-2	195	5	Baylor
54	McKenzie, Reggie	LB	6-1	240	2	Tennessee
23	McKinney, Odis	S	6-2	190	9	Colorado
55	Millen, Matt	LB	6-2	245	7	Penn State
83	Moffett, Tim	WR	6-1	175	2	Mississippi
28	Montgomery, Cle	WR	5-8	180	6	Abilene Christian
72	Mosebar, Don	C	6-6	270	4	Southern California
	Myres, Albert	S	6-0	195	1	Tulsa
51	Nelson, Bob	LB	6-4	235	9	Nebraska
81	Parker, Andy	TE	6-5	240	3	Utah
	Pattison, Mark	WR	6-2	190	1	Washington
71	Pickel, Bill	NT	6-5	260	4	Rutgers
16	Plunkett, Jim	QB	6-2	220	16	Stanford
57	Robinson, Jerry	LB	6-2	225	8	UCLA
43	Seale, Sam	CB	5-9	180	3	Western State, Co.
58	Squirek, Jack	LB	6-4	235	5	Illinois
	Strachan, Steve	RB	6-1	215	2	Boston College
30	Toran, Stacey	S	6-2	200	3	Notre Dame
93	Townsend, Greg	DE	6-3	250	4	Texas Christian
91	Van Pelt, Brad	LB	6-5	235	14	Michigan State
41	Walker, Fulton	PR-KR	5-11	200	6	West Virginia
85	Williams, Dokie	WR	5-11	180	4	UCLA
98	Willis, Mitch	NT	6-7	280	2	Southern Methodist
6	Wilson, Marc	QB	6-6	205	7	Brigham Young

SAN DIEGO CHARGERS

Address San Diego Jack Murphy Stadium, P.O. Box 20666, San Diego, California 92120.

Stadium San Diego Jack Murphy Stadium. *Capacity* 60,100 *Playing Surface* Grass.

Team Colours Blue, Gold, and White.

Head Coach Don Coryell – ninth year.

Championships Division 1979,'80,'81; AFL 1963.

History AFL 1960-69, AFC 1970-
(For 1960 only, they were known as the Los Angeles Chargers.)

Offense

San Diego is what you might call a 1-20s club. The figure '1' is for offense, meaning that they've been ranked first in the league in five of the last six years. The '20s' is the region in which they've ranked for defense over the past five years. In fact, they have not been placed higher than 25th overall and, in four of those years, they have ranked 28th on pass defense. Obviously, they have no shortage of strike players. And they usually have an effective offensive line. Nonetheless, just to be on the safe side, they drafted tackles James FitzPatrick and Jeff Walker in the early going. They struck gold with last year's first-round pick, left tackle Jim Lachey, who started in all sixteen games. The other starters, center Don Macek, right guard Dennis McKnight and right tackle Sam Claphan, are experienced but none more so than left guard Ed White, who holds the NFL record for most games played by an offensive lineman (241) and is entering his eighteenth season. The line came third in the AFC in percentage sacks yielded and, in the final six games, they allowed just eight. Quarterback Dan Fouts continued in the vein which has earned six Pro Bowl selections, and is now within reach of the retired Fran Tarkenton's career records which, until recently, were considered to be beyond the grasp of mere mortals. Fouts' backup, Mark Herrmann, has found San Diego to his liking and he, too, is perfectly capable of scrambling the 'Air Force'. In that squadron (the wide receivers), the dazzling Wes Chandler is coming off his best full season in the pros, whilst the seventeen-year veteran, Charlie Joiner, equalled his previous single-season best of seven touchdown receptions. Joiner needs only 129 yards to surpass Don Maynard's NFL career record of 11,834 — in other words, just one more good game. The peerless tight end, Kellen Winslow, made a miraculous recovery from a serious knee injury suffered in the 1984 season, and, after easing back gently last year, he should be approaching his best form. Even so, he'll have to beat out two excellent competitors, Pete Holohan and Eric Sievers, for the starting job. At running back, last year's rookies, Gary Anderson and Tim Spencer, are ready to explode. The detonator will be Lionel 'Little Train' James, who, in 1985, led the club in both rushing and pass receptions.

Defense

The Chargers have sought help for the line by drafting two defensive ends, Leslie O'Neal and Terry Unrein, in the first and third rounds respectively. Last year, defensive end Lee Williams made great progress, registering a club-leading nine quarterback sacks, whilst Fred Robinson had seven sacks, playing as the extra man when the Chargers adopt the 4-3 formation. Chuck Ehin made the successful move from defensive end to nose tackle, his position in college, and held up well against the run. Earl Wilson started on the right side of the three-man line and completes an interesting group of young players which could play a key part in stiffening the defense as a whole. Linebacking is another area in which the younger players are beginning to shape up. Two in particular, inside linebackers Billy Ray Smith and Mike Green, got through a great deal of work, coming first and second in tackles with 131 and 112 respectively. On the outsides, two veterans, Linden King and Woodrow Lowe, are steady without ever dominating the show. The club would be helped enormously by the rehabilitation of Mike Guendling, who, as a rookie in 1984, was looking extremely good in training camp before suffering a severe knee injury. One can see perhaps two of the four rookies, Ty Allert, Tommy Taylor, Doug Landry and Fred Smalls, making the final roster. The secondary, too, is well stocked with young players. Rookies John Hendy and Jeff Dale started at left cornerback and free safety respectively, and both the right cornerback, Danny Walters, and the strong safety, Gill Byrd, are veterans of only three years. As a group, they were responsible for 12 of the club total of 26 interceptions (Walters led with five) and could well cause a few problems for those who would take them too lightly.

1986 SCHEDULE OF GAMES	September	
	7 MIAMI	1:00
	14 at New York Giants	1:00
	21 WASHINGTON	1:00
	28 at Los Angeles Raiders	1:00
	October	
	6 at Seattle (Mon.)	6:00
	12 DENVER	1:00
	19 at Kansas City	3:00
	26 at Philadelphia	1:00
	November	
	2 KANSAS CITY	1:00
	9 at Denver	2:00
	16 DALLAS	1:00
	20 LOS ANGELES RAIDERS (Thurs.)	5:00
	30 at Indianapolis	1:00
	December	
	7 HOUSTON	1:00
	14 SEATTLE	1:00
	21 at Cleveland	1:00

Special Teams

The astonishing Lionel James led the team on both punt and kickoff returns, topping up his all-purpose yardage haul to an NFL single-season record of 2,535. It must be said, though, that his effectiveness, in terms of average gain and big-play threat, would not compare with the real speedsters around the NFL. Placekicker Bob Thomas was no better than par and it seems certain that Rolf Benirschke will regain the job he lost because of injury. However, rookie punter Ralf Mojsiejenko should be retained after averaging a good 42.4 yards.

Fred Robinson developed into a good pass rusher in his second NFL season

VETERAN ROSTER

No.	Name	Pos.	Ht.	Wt.	NFL Year	College
42	Adams, Curtis	RB	5-11	198	1	Central Michigan
40	Anderson, Gary	RB	6-0	190	2	Arkansas
6	Benirschke, Rolf	K	6-1	183	9	Cal-Davis
59	Bingham, Craig	LB	6-2	220	4	Syracuse
50	Bradley, Carlos	LB	6-0	222	6	Wake Forest
22	Byrd, Gill	S	5-10	201	4	San Jose State
89	Chandler, Wes	WR	6-0	182	9	Florida
77	Claphan, Sam	T	6-6	282	6	Oklahoma
37	Dale, Jeffery	S	6-3	214	2	Louisiana State
61	Dallafior, Ken	G	6-4	269	2	Minnesota
20	Davis, Wayne	CB	5-11	175	2	Indiana State
65	Doerger, Jerry	C-T	6-5	270	3	Wisconsin
12	Dufek, Joe	QB	6-4	215	4	Yale
78	Ehin, Chuck	NT	6-4	265	4	Brigham Young
84	Faulkner, Chris	TE	6-4	250	3	Florida
79	Faurot, Ron	DE	6-7	262	2	Arkansas
52	Fellows, Mark	LB	6-1	222	2	Montana State
14	Fouts, Dan	QB	6-3	205	14	Oregon
92	Garnett, Scott	NT	6-2	271	3	Washington
58	Green, Mike	LB	6-0	239	4	Oklahoma State
53	Guendling, Mike	LB	6-3	238	2	Northwestern
29	Hendy, John	CB	5-10	196	2	Long Beach State
9	Herrmann, Mark	QB	6-4	209	6	Purdue
88	Holohan, Pete	TE	6-4	244	6	Notre Dame
26	James, Lionel	RB-KR	5-6	170	3	Auburn
83	Johnson, Trumaine	WR	6-1	196	2	Grambling State
18	Joiner, Charlie	WR	5-11	177	18	Grambling State
30	King, David	CB	5-8	176	1	Auburn
57	King, Linden	LB	6-4	247	9	Colorado State
68	Kowalski, Gary	T	6-5	290	3	Boston College
74	Lachey, Jim	T	6-6	288	2	Ohio State
63	Leonard, Jim	C	6-3	260	6	Santa Clara
96	Lockette, James	DE	6-4	260	1	Missouri
51	Lowe, Woodrow	LB	6-0	229	11	Alabama
62	Macek, Don	C	6-2	260	11	Boston College
21	McGee, Buford	RB	6-0	203	3	Mississippi
60	McKnight, Dennis	C-G	6-3	273	5	Drake
24	McPherson, Miles	S	5-11	186	5	New Haven, Conn.
47	Micho, Bobby	TE	6-3	240	2	Texas
2	Mojsiejenko, Ralf	P	6-3	198	2	Michigan State
55	Nelson, Derrie	LB	6-2	234	4	Nebraska
59	Nelson, Shane	LB	6-0	238	8	Baylor
27	O'Bard, Ronnie	CB	5-9	190	2	Brigham Young
56	Osby, Vince	LB	5-11	221	3	Illinois
90	Robinson, Fred	DE	6-5	242	3	Miami
64	Searcey, Bill	G	6-1	281	1	Alabama
85	Sievers, Eric	TE	6-3	236	6	Maryland
97	Simmons, Tony	DE	6-4	270	2	Tennessee
54	Smith, Billy Ray	LB	6-3	231	4	Arkansas
33	Smith, Lucious	CB	5-10	190	7	Cal State-Fullerton
43	Spencer, Tim	RB	6-1	220	2	Ohio State
66	Umphrey, Rich	C-G	6-3	270	5	Colorado
23	Walters, Danny	CB	6-1	180	4	Arkansas
67	White, Ed	G	6-2	284	18	California
99	Williams, Lee	DE	6-6	273	3	Bethune-Cookman
93	Wilson, Earl	DE	6-4	267	2	Kentucky
80	Winslow, Kellen	TE	6-5	242	8	Missouri

1986 DRAFT

Round	Name	Pos.	Ht.	Wt.	College
1.	O'Neal, Leslie	DE	6-4	245	Oklahoma State
1.	FitzPatrick, James	T	6-8	273	Southern California
3.	Unrein, Terry	DE	6-5	275	Colorado State
3.	Walker, Jeff	T	6-4	283	Memphis State
4.	Allert, Ty	LB	6-2	225	Texas
4.	Taylor, Tommy	LB	6-1	235	UCLA
5.	Landry, Doug	LB	6-1	220	Louisiana Tech
5.	Brown, Donald	DB	5-11	189	Maryland
5.	Johnson, Matt	CB	6-2	200	Southern California
6.	Pardridge, Curt	WR	5-10	169	Northern Illinois
7.	Smalls, Fred	LB	6-1	213	West Virginia
8.	Perrino, Mike	T	6-5	274	Notre Dame
9.	Zordich, Mike	DB	5-11	207	Penn State
11.	Sanders, Chuck	RB	6-1	224	Slippery Rock
11.	Smetana, Drew	T	6-7	286	Oregon
12.	Sprowls, Jeff	DB	6-1	175	Brigham Young
12.	Travis, Mike	CB	6-0	190	Georgia Tech

SEATTLE SEAHAWKS

Address 5305 Lake Washington Boulevard, Kirkland, Wa. 98033.

Stadium Kingdome, Seattle.

Capacity 64,984 *Playing Surface* AstroTurf.

Team Colours Blue, Green, and Silver.

Head Coach Chuck Knox – fourth year.

Championships None.

History NFC 1976, AFC 1977-

Offense

It would be most unwise to take the Seahawks' 1985 record of 8-8 as an indication that they were slipping back. Far from it – they have an extremely talented squad and can face any team in the NFL with confidence. The offensive line, however, will hope to improve on its pass protection after giving up a club-record 53 sacks last year. Tackles Ron Essink and Bob Cryder, guard Edwin Bailey and center Blair Bush, are the returning starters. Robert Pratt has retired and will probably be replaced by Bryan Millard, who had four of his nine 1985 starts at right guard. Jon Borchardt and Ron Mattes are expected to challenge for playing time. The really good news for Seattle fans is that star running back Curt Warner came through the campaign without any recurrence of the knee injury which kept him out for all but a few minutes of the 1984 season. Warner was one of sixteen backs in the league to rush for over 1,000 yards, a figure he would be expected to eclipse in 1986, not least because the Seahawks used their first-round option to find him a perfect backfield partner, John L. Williams. The blend of speed and power is a recipe which most clubs look for, and whilst Warner has the speed, the power will come from Williams. At quarter-back, Dave Krieg has settled into a style which is tailor-made for the strike players. He's smart and has the arm to go deep in search of a pair of individual wide receivers who become potentially devastating when operating in tandem. Steve Largent is consistency personified. Having caught at least one pass in his last 123 regular-season games, he needs to continue for just five more games to beat the NFL record, which is held by the retired Harold Carmichael. Last year, the combination of positional sense, great moves and super hands, brought Largent the NFL title for most yards receiving. His partner, Daryl Turner, is the burner who caught four touchdown passes against San Diego on Week Two, and went on to lead the league's receivers with thirteen touchdowns for the season. Wide receivers Byron Walker, Paul Skansi, Ray Butler (ex-Colts) and Byron Franklin (ex-Buffalo), are useful backups. Tight end Dan Ross is seeking to rebuild a career which reached a high point in 1981, when, playing for Cincinnati, he caught 71 passes for 910 yards and five touchdowns in the regular season, and established a record with eleven receptions in Super Bowl XVI.

Defense

Seattle has a first-class defense. In 1985, the defensive line led a charge which produced a club-record 61 quarter-back sacks. Since 1982, when quarterback sacks first became an official statistic, defensive left end Jacob Green has had 45.5, a total second only to that of the Jets' Mark Gastineau (he has had 60.5). Nose tackle Joe Nash, who was a Pro Bowler in 1985, and Jeff Bryant, complete the starting three-man line. Coming in as a pass rusher, Randy Edwards had 10.5 sacks, second best in the club behind Green's 13.5. Fredd Young, a ferocious tackler, has moved ahead of Shelton Robinson to start at inside linebacker alongside Keith Butler, with Bruce Scholtz and Michael Jackson on the outsides. It is an excellent four-some in which Jackson, who has learned to harness his enthusiasm, plays a full part. Young led the club with 118 tackles, ahead of Butler's 108. The secondary has more pure ball-hawking talent than any other group in the league. Among active AFC players, Dave Brown (45), John Harris (41), Terry Jackson (28) and Kenny Easley (26), rank 2nd, 4th, 8th and 9th= in career pass interceptions. Jackson is the backup to Brown at right cornerback, whilst Terry Taylor, a 1984 first-round pick, starts at left corner-back. Keith Simpson, who is Taylor's backup, has 19 career interceptions. Easley and Harris are the safeties. Easley is a dominant force and, without doubt, is the best strong safety in the AFC, whom he has represented in the Pro Bowl four times. Free safety Harris must be con-sidered unlucky never to have played in the Pro Bowl. He, too, is the uncompromising type.

Special Teams

Placekicker Norm Johnson was successful on only one of eight field goal attempts in the range from 40 to 49 yards. And though he kicked a 51-yarder, one would have to think that he would be challenged in training camp. Again, punter Dave Finzer was below par – he came 11th in the

1986 SCHEDULE OF GAMES	September	
	7 PITTSBURGH	1:00
	14 KANSAS CITY	1:00
	21 at New England	1:00
	28 at Washington	1:00
	October	
	6 SAN DIEGO (Mon.)	6:00
	12 at Los Angeles Raiders	1:00
	19 NEW YORK GIANTS	1:00
	26 at Denver	2:00
	November	
	2 NEW YORK JETS	1:00
	9 at Kansas City	12:00
	16 at Cincinnati	1:00
	23 PHILADELPHIA	1:00
	27 at Dallas (Thanksgiving)	3:00
	December	
	8 LOS ANGELES RAIDERS (Mon.)	6:00
	14 at San Diego	1:00
	20 DENVER (Sat.)	1:00

AFC with a gross average of 40.7. Paul Skansi, on the other hand, returned 31 punts at an average of 10.1 yards, a figure good enough for fifth place in the AFC. However, neither Skansi nor backup running back Randall Morris was effective returning kickoffs, and one wonders if Danny Greene, who broke for a 52-yarder, will be given a chance when he returns to full fitness.

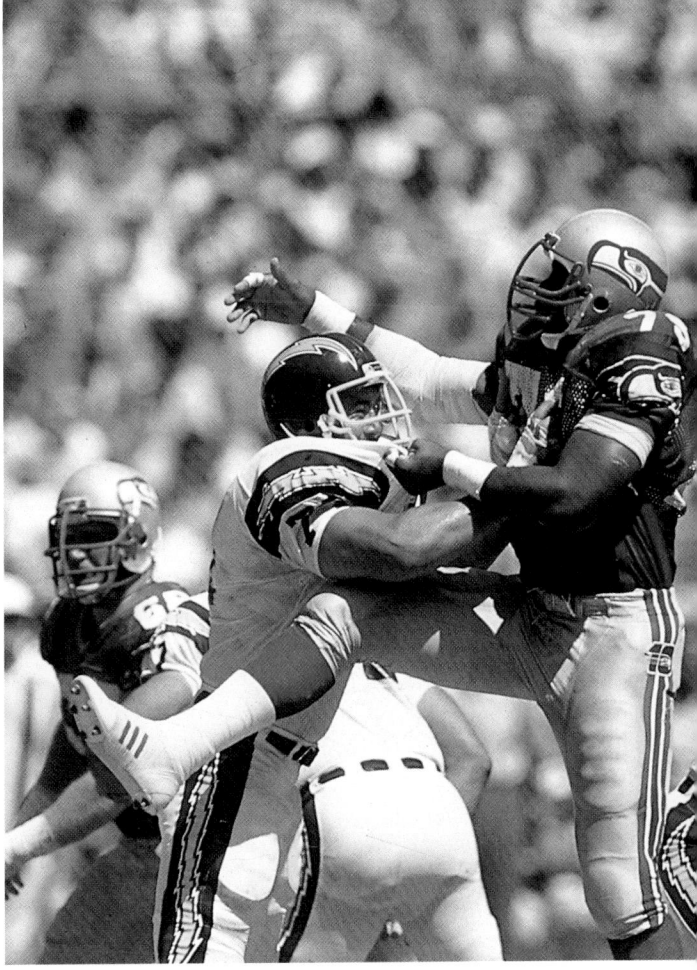

Defensive end Jacob Green (#79) has been the Seahawks' sack leader in five of his six NFL years

VETERAN ROSTER

No.	Name	Pos.	Ht.	Wt.	NFL Year	College
65	Bailey, Edwin	G	6-5	265	6	South Carolina State
76	Borchardt, Jon	G	6-5	265	8	Montana State
22	Brown, Dave	CB	6-1	195	12	Michigan
77	Bryant, Jeff	DE	6-5	270	5	Clemson
59	Bush, Blair	C	6-3	252	9	Washington
53	Butler, Keith	LB	6-4	238	9	Memphis State
83	Butler, Ray	WR	6-3	197	7	Southern California
92	Caldwell, Tony	LB	6-1	225	4	Washington
78	Cryder, Bob	T	6-4	282	9	Alabama
33	Doornink, Dan	RB	6-3	210	9	Washington State
45	Easley, Ken	S	6-3	206	6	UCLA
68	Edwards, Randy	DE	6-4	255	3	Alabama
64	Essink, Ron	T	6-6	275	7	Grand Valley State
15	Finzer, Dave	P	6-1	195	3	DePauw
88	Franklin, Byron	WR	6-1	185	5	Auburn
56	Gaines, Greg	LB	6-3	220	5	Tennessee
7	Gilbert, Gale	QB	6-3	215	2	California
79	Green, Jacob	DE	6-3	255	7	Texas A&M
84	Greene, Danny	WR	5-11	195	7	Washington
44	Harris, John	S	6-2	200	9	Arizona State
91	Hudson, Gordon	TE	6-3	230	R	Brigham Young
46	Hughes, David	RB	6-0	220	6	Boise State
55	Jackson, Michael	LB	6-1	220	8	Washington
24	Jackson, Terry	CB	5-11	197	9	San Diego State
9	Johnson, Norm	K	6-2	193	5	UCLA
54	Kaiser, John	LB	6-3	221	3	Arizona
62	Kauahi, Kani	C	6-2	260	5	Hawaii
63	Kinlaw, Reggie	NT	6-2	245	7	Oklahoma
17	Krieg, Dave	QB	6-1	185	7	Milton, Wis.
37	Lane, Eric	RB	6-0	195	6	Brigham Young
80	Largent, Steve	WR	5-11	184	11	Tulsa
70	Mattes, Ron	T	6-6	290	1	Virginia
51	Merriman, Sam	LB	6-3	225	4	Idaho
71	Millard, Bryan	T	6-5	282	3	Texas
43	Morris, Randall	RB-KR	6-0	190	3	Tennessee
21	Moyer, Paul	S	6-1	201	4	Arizona State
72	Nash, Joe	NT	6-3	250	5	Boston College
29	Parros, Rick	RB	5-11	200	6	Utah State
41	Robinson, Eugene	CB	6-0	180	2	Colgate
57	Robinson, Shelton	LB	6-3	233	5	North Carolina
85	Ross, Dan	TE	6-4	235	7	Northeastern
58	Scholtz, Bruce	LB	6-6	240	5	Texas
42	Simpson, Keith	CB	6-1	195	9	Memphis State
82	Skansi, Paul	WR-PR	5-11	190	4	Washington
20	Taylor, Terry	CB	5-10	188	3	Southern Illinois
86	Tice, Mike	TE	6-7	250	6	Maryland
81	Turner, Daryl	WR	6-3	198	3	Michigan State
89	Walker, Byron	WR	6-4	190	5	Citadel
28	Warner, Curt	RB	5-11	205	3	Penn State
40	Williams, John	RB	5-11	213	2	Wisconsin
50	Young, Fredd	LB	6-1	220	3	New Mexico State

1986 DRAFT

Round	Name	Pos.	Ht.	Wt.	College
1.	Williams, John L.	RB	5-11	219	Florida
3.	Hunter, Patrick	CB	5-11	180	Nevada-Reno
5.	Edmonds, Bobby Joe	WR	5-11	175	Arkansas
6.	Anderson, Eddie	DB	6-1	191	Fort Valley State
7.	Miles, Paul	RB	5-10	198	Nebraska
8	Mitz, Alonzo	DE	6-3	270	Florida
9.	Black, Mike	T	6-4	290	Cal State-Sacramento
10.	Fairbanks, Don	DE	6-3	260	Colorado
11.	Norrie, David	QB	6-4	211	UCLA
12.	McVeigh, John	LB	6-1	226	Miami

NATIONAL FOOTBALL CONFERENCE

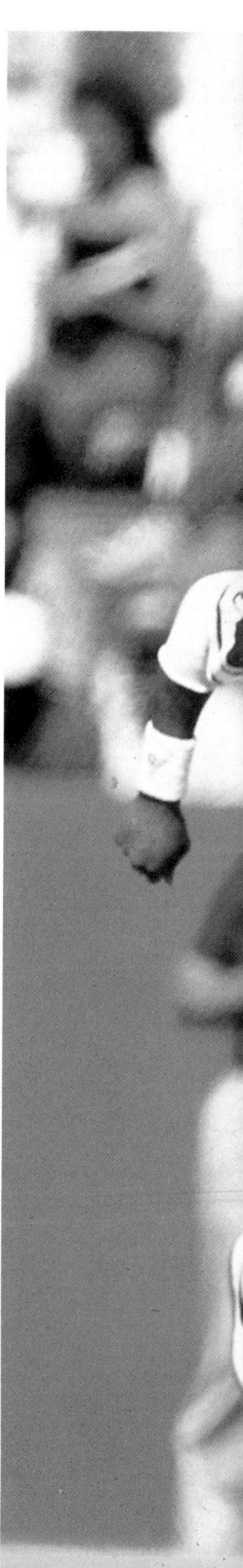

TEAM RANKINGS

	OFFENSE						DEFENSE					
	Total Yds.	Rushing	Passing	Points For	%Intercepted	%Sacked	Total Yds.	Rushing	Passing	Points Against	%Interceptions	%Sacks
Atlanta	10	3	14	13	8	14	13	8	14	14	7	11
Chicago	3	1	9	1	4	7	1	1	2	1	1	2
Dallas	4	9	1	4	7	1	11	6	13	7	2	3
Detroit	14	13	10	8	10	11	10	14	4	10	=9	9
Green Bay	5	6	6	7	14	6	6	7	8	8	12	8
L.A. Rams	12	7	14	6	3	13	4	3	7	3	3	6
Minnesota	8	14	3	5	12	3	9	11	9	9	5	14
New Orleans	13	10	12	=10	9	10	12	9	11	11	8	10
N.Y. Giants	2	4	5	3	5	9	2	2	3	4	6	1
Philadelphia	7	12	4	12	11	5	5	10	5	5	=9	5
St Louis	9	8	8	14	2	12	8	12	6	12	14	12
San Francisco	1	5	2	2	1	2	7	4	10	2	13	7
Tampa Bay	11	11	7	=10	13	4	14	13	12	13	11	13
Washington	6	2	11	9	6	8	3	5	1	6	4	4

NFC PASSERS

	Att	Comp	% Comp	Yards	Ave Gain	TD	% TD	Long	Int	% Int	Rating Points
Montana, Joe, *S.F.*	494	303	61.3	3653	7.39	27	5.5	73	13	2.6	91.3
McMahon, Jim, *Chi.*	313	178	56.9	2392	7.64	15	4.8	t70	11	3.5	82.6
Brock, Dieter, *Rams*	365	218	59.7	2658	7.28	16	4.4	t64	13	3.6	82.0
White, Danny, *Dall.*	450	267	59.3	3157	7.02	21	4.7	t56	17	3.8	80.6
Lomax, Neil, *St.L.*	471	265	56.3	3214	6.82	18	3.8	47	12	2.5	79.5
Simms, Phil, *Giants*	495	275	55.6	3829	7.74	22	4.4	t70	20	4.0	78.6
Hebert, Bobby, *N.O.*	181	97	53.6	1208	6.67	5	2.8	t76	4	2.2	74.6
Schroeder, Jay, *Wash.*	209	112	53.6	1458	6.98	5	2.4	53	5	2.4	73.8
Hipple, Eric, *Det.*	406	223	54.9	2952	7.27	17	4.2	56	18	4.4	73.6
DeBerg, Steve, *T.B.*	370	197	53.2	2488	6.72	19	5.1	57	18	4.9	71.3
Dickey, Lynn, *G.B.*	314	172	54.8	2206	7.03	15	4.8	63	17	5.4	70.4
Jaworski, Ron, *Phil.*	484	255	52.7	3450	7.13	17	3.5	t99	20	4.1	70.2
Kramer, Tommy, *Minn.*	506	277	54.7	3522	6.96	19	3.8	t57	26	5.1	67.8
Wilson, Dave, *N.O.*	293	145	49.5	1843	6.29	11	3.8	50	15	5.1	60.7
Theismann, Joe, *Wash.*	301	167	55.5	1774	5.89	8	2.7	55	16	5.3	59.6
Young, Steve, *T.B.*	138	72	52.2	935	6.78	3	2.2	59	8	5.8	56.9
Archer, David, *Atl.*	312	161	51.6	1992	6.38	7	2.2	t62	17	5.4	56.5

t = Touchdown
Leader based on rating points, minimum 130 attempts

Minnesota's rookie wide receiver, Anthony Carter, had a fine year, averaging 19.1 yards on 43 pass receptions

NFC RECEIVERS – Most Receptions

	No	Yards	Ave	Long	TD
Craig, Roger, *S.F.*	92	1016	11.0	73	6
Monk, Art, *Wash.*	91	1226	13.5	53	2
Hill, Tony, *Dall.*	74	1113	15.0	t53	7
Quick, Mike, *Phil.*	73	1247	17.1	t99	11
Clark, Gary, *Wash.*	72	926	12.9	55	5
Lofton, James, *G.B.*	69	1153	16.7	t56	4
Jordan, Steve, *Minn.*	68	795	11.7	32	0
Cosbie, Doug, *Dall.*	64	793	12.4	42	6
Spagnola, John, *Phil.*	64	772	12.1	35	5
Johnson, Billy, *Atl.*	62	830	13.4	t62	5
Renfro, Mike, *Dall.*	60	955	15.9	t58	8
Ellard, Henry, *Rams*	54	811	15.0	t64	5
Clark, Dwight, *S.F.*	54	705	13.1	t49	10
Wilder, James, *T.B.*	53	341	6.4	20	0
Thompson, Leonard, *Det.*	51	736	14.4	48	5
Green, Roy, *St.L.*	50	693	13.9	47	5
Hunter, Tony, *Rams*	50	562	11.2	t47	4
Rice, Jerry, *S.F.*	49	927	18.9	t66	3
Manuel, Lionel, *Giants*	49	859	17.5	t51	5
Tilley, Pat, *St.L.*	49	726	14.8	t46	6
Coffman, Paul, *G.B.*	49	666	13.6	32	6
Payton, Walter, *Chi.*	49	483	9.9	65	2
Mitchell, Stump, *St.L.*	47	502	10.7	46	3
Jones, Mike, *Minn.*	46	641	13.9	t44	4
Dorsett, Tony, *Dall.*	46	449	9.8	t56	3
Newsome, Tim, *Dall.*	46	361	7.8	24	1
Jones, James, *Det.*	45	334	7.4	36	3
House, Kevin, *T.B.*	44	803	18.3	59	5
Epps, Phillip, *G.B.*	44	683	15.5	63	3
Francis, Russ, *S.F.*	44	478	10.9	25	3
Carter, Anthony, *Minn.*	43	821	19.1	t57	8
Giles, Jimmie, *T.B.*	43	673	15.7	44	8
Smith, J.T., *St.L.*	43	581	13.5	34	1

t = Touchdown

NFC RECEIVERS – Most Yards

	Yards	No	Ave	Long	TD
Quick, Mike, *Phil.*	1247	73	17.1	t99	11
Monk, Art, *Wash.*	1226	91	13.5	53	2
Lofton, James, *G.B.*	1153	69	16.7	t56	4
Hill, Tony, *Dall.*	1113	74	15.0	t53	7
Craig, Roger, *S.F.*	1016	92	11.0	73	6
Renfro, Mike, *Dall.*	955	60	15.9	t58	8
Rice, Jerry, *S.F.*	927	49	18.9	t66	3
Clark, Gary, *Wash.*	926	72	12.9	55	5
Manuel, Lionel, *Giants*	859	49	17.5	t51	5
Johnson, Billy, *Atl.*	830	62	13.4	t62	5
Carter, Anthony, *Minn.*	821	43	19.1	t57	8
Ellard, Henry, *Rams*	811	54	15.0	t64	5
House, Kevin, *T.B.*	803	44	18.3	59	5
Jordan, Steve, *Minn.*	795	68	11.7	32	0
Cosbie, Doug, *Dall.*	793	64	12.4	42	6
Spagnola, John, *Phil.*	772	64	12.1	35	5
Thompson, Leonard, *Det.*	736	51	14.4	48	5
Tilley, Pat, *St.L.*	726	49	14.8	t46	6
Clark, Dwight, *S.F.*	705	54	13.1	t49	10
Gault, Willie, *Chi.*	704	33	21.3	t70	1
Green, Roy, *St.L.*	693	50	13.9	47	5
Jackson, Kenny, *Phil.*	692	40	17.3	54	1
Epps, Phillip, *G.B.*	683	44	15.5	63	3
Giles, Jimmie, *T.B.*	673	43	15.7	44	8
Coffman, Paul, *G.B.*	666	49	13.6	32	6

t = Touchdown

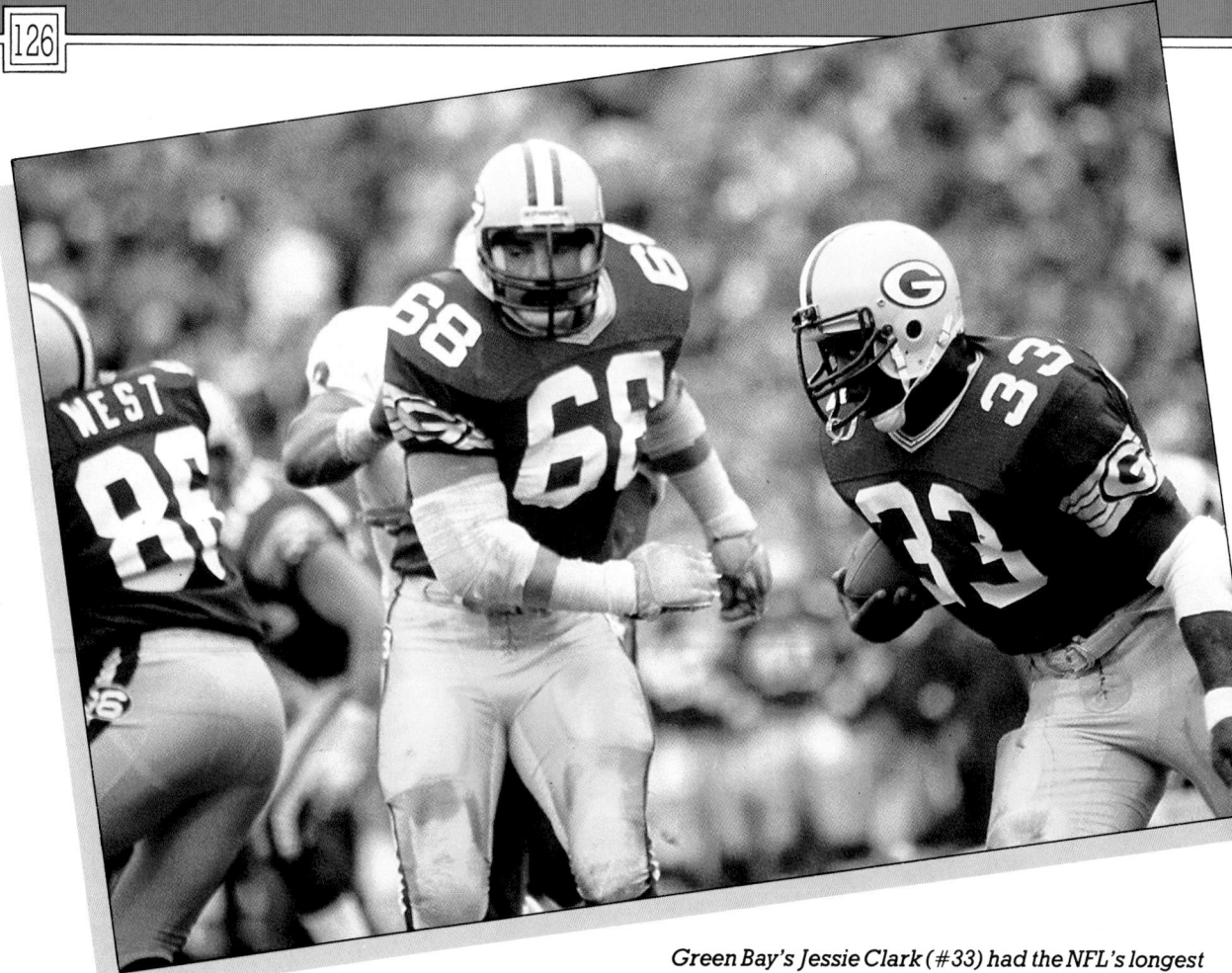

Green Bay's Jessie Clark (#33) had the NFL's longest run from scrimmage

NFC RUSHERS

	Att	Yards	Ave	Long	TD		Att	Yards	Ave	Long	TD
Riggs, Gerald, *Atl.*	397	1719	4.3	50	10	Gajan, Hokie, *N.O.*	50	251	5.0	26	2
Payton, Walter, *Chi.*	324	1551	4.8	t40	9	Montgomery, Wilbert, *Det.*	75	251	3.3	22	0
Morris, Joe, *Giants*	294	1336	4.5	t65	21	Young, Steve, *T.B.*	40	233	5.8	20	1
Dorsett, Tony, *Dall.*	305	1307	4.3	t60	7	Moore, Alvin, *Det.*	80	221	2.8	18	4
Wilder, James, *T.B.*	365	1300	3.6	28	10	Haddix, Michael, *Phil.*	67	213	3.2	12	0
Dickerson, Eric, *Rams*	292	1234	4.2	43	12	Washington, Joe, *Atl.*	52	210	4.0	14	1
Rogers, George, *Wash.*	231	1093	4.7	35	7	Ferrell, Earl, *St.L.*	46	208	4.5	30	2
Craig, Roger, *S.F.*	214	1050	4.9	t62	9	Cunningham, Randall, *Phil.*	29	205	7.1	37	0
Jackson, Earnest, *Phil.*	282	1028	3.6	59	5	Ellerson, Gary, *G.B.*	32	205	6.4	t37	2
Mitchell, Stump, *St.L.*	183	1006	5.5	64	7	Carpenter, Rob, *Giants*	60	201	3.4	46	0
Nelson, Darrin, *Minn.*	200	893	4.5	37	5	Galbreath, Tony, *Giants*	29	187	6.4	18	0
Jones, James, *Det.*	244	886	3.6	29	6	Gentry, Dennis, *Chi.*	30	160	5.3	21	2
Tyler, Wendell, *S.F.*	171	867	5.1	30	6	Montana, Joe, *S.F.*	42	153	3.6	16	3
Riggins, John, *Wash.*	176	677	3.8	51	8	Simms, Phil, *Giants*	37	132	3.6	28	0
Wilson, Wayne, *N.O.*	168	645	3.8	t41	1	Lomax, Neil, *St.L.*	32	125	3.9	23	0
Campbell, Earl, *N.O.*	158	643	4.1	45	1	Thomas, Calvin, *Chi.*	31	125	4.0	17	4
Ivery, Eddie Lee, *G.B.*	132	636	4.8	34	2	Anderson, Alfred, *Minn.*	50	121	2.4	10	4
Clark, Jessie, *G.B.*	147	633	4.3	80	5	Hunter, Herman, *Phil.*	27	121	4.5	t74	1
Ellis, Gerry, *G.B.*	104	571	5.5	t39	5	Theismann, Joe, *Wash.*	25	115	4.6	25	2
Adams, George, *Giants*	128	498	3.9	39	2	Austin, Cliff, *Atl.*	20	110	5.5	17	0
Anderson, Ottis, *St.L.*	117	479	4.1	38	4	Rice, Allen, *Minn.*	31	104	3.4	15	3
Griffin, Keith, *Wash.*	102	473	4.6	t66	3	Sanders, Thomas, *Chi.*	25	104	4.2	28	1
Suhey, Matt, *Chi.*	115	471	4.1	17	1	Epps, Phillip, *G.B.*	5	103	20.6	34	1
Redden, Barry, *Rams*	87	380	4.4	41	0	Harmon, Derrick, *S.F.*	28	92	3.3	17	0
Archer, David, *Atl.*	70	347	5.0	t29	2	Hipple, Eric, *Det.*	32	89	2.8	26	2
Brown, Ted, *Minn.*	93	336	3.6	30	7	Fuller, Steve, *Chi.*	24	77	3.2	13	5
White, Charles, *Rams*	70	310	4.4	32	3	Carthon, Maurice, *Giants*	27	70	2.6	12	0
McMahon, Jim, *Chi.*	47	252	5.4	19	3						
Newsome, Tim, *Dall.*	88	252	2.9	15	2	t = Touchdown					

NFC SCORING – Kickers

	XP	XPA	FG	FGA	PTS
Butler, Kevin, *Chi.*	51	51	31	37	144
Andersen, Morten, *N.O.*	27	29	31	35	120
Murray, Ed, *Det.*	31	33	26	31	109
Lansford, Mike, *Rams*	38	39	22	29	104
McFadden, Paul, *Phil.*	29	29	25	30	104
Luckhurst, Mick, *Atl.*	29	29	24	31	101
Septien, Rafael, *Dall.*	42	43	19	28	99
Moseley, Mark, *Wash.*	31	33	22	34	97
Igwebuike, Donald, *T.B.*	30	32	22	32	96
Del Greco, Al, *G.B.*	38	40	19	26	95
Wersching, Ray, *S.F.*	52	53	13	21	91
Stenerud, Jan, *Minn.*	41	43	15	26	86
Schubert, Eric, *Giants*	26	27	10	13	56
Atkinson, Jess, *Giants-St.L.*	17	18	10	18	*53
O'Donoghue, Neil, *St.L.*	19	19	10	18	49

*Includes six points for a touchdown

NFC SCORING – Touchdowns

	TD	TDR	TDP	TDM	PTS
Morris, Joe, *Giants*	21	21	0	0	126
Craig, Roger, *S.F.*	15	9	6	0	90
Dickerson, Eric, *Rams*	12	12	0	0	72
Payton, Walter, *Chi.*	11	9	2	0	66
Quick, Mike, *Phil.*	11	0	11	0	66
Brown, Ted, *Minn.*	10	7	3	0	60
Clark, Dwight, *S.F.*	10	0	10	0	60
Dorsett, Tony, *Dall.*	10	7	3	0	60
Mitchell, Stump, *St.L.*	10	7	3	0	60
Riggs, Gerald, *Atl.*	10	10	0	0	60
Wilder, James, *T.B.*	10	10	0	0	60

NFC KICKOFF RETURNERS

	No	Yards	Ave	Long	TD
Brown, Ron, *Rams*	28	918	32.8	t98	3
Gault, Willie, *Chi.*	22	577	26.2	t99	1
Gentry, Dennis, *Chi.*	18	466	25.9	t94	1
Monroe, Carl, *S.F.*	28	717	25.6	t95	1
Rhymes, Buster, *Minn.*	53	1345	25.4	88	0
Jenkins, Ken, *Wash.*	41	1018	24.8	95	0
Hall, Alvin, *Det.*	39	886	22.7	54	0
Freeman, Phil, *T.B.*	48	1085	22.6	58	0
Hunter, Herman, *Phil.*	48	1047	21.8	51	0
Austin, Cliff, *Atl.*	39	838	21.5	t94	1
Anthony, Tyrone, *N.O.*	23	476	20.7	52	0
Tullis, Willie, *N.O.*	23	470	20.4	62	0
Harmon, Derrick, *S.F.*	23	467	20.3	37	0
Lavette, Robert, *Dall.*	34	682	20.1	34	0
Duncan, Clyde, *St.L.*	28	550	19.6	34	0

t = Touchdown
Leader based on average return, minimum 18 returns

Placekicker Morten Andersen failed on only four field goal attempts

NFC PUNTERS

	No	Yards	Long	Ave	Total Punts	TB	Blk	Opp Ret	Ret Yds	In 20	Net Ave
Donnelly, Rick, *Atl.*	59	2574	68	43.6	59	5	0	33	260	18	37.5
Hatcher, Dale, *Rams*	87	3761	67	43.2	88	6	1	43	297	32	38.0
Landeta, Sean, *Giants*	81	3472	68	42.9	81	14	0	29	247	20	36.4
Coleman, Greg, *Minn.*	67	2867	62	42.8	67	4	0	36	328	12	36.7
Hansen, Brian, *N.O.*	89	3763	58	42.3	89	6	0	45	397	14	36.5
Buford, Maury, *Chi.*	68	2870	69	42.2	69	14	1	23	203	18	34.6
Garcia, Frank, *T.B.*	77	3233	61	42.0	79	6	2	47	519	12	32.8
Saxon, Mike, *Dall.*	81	3396	57	41.9	82	10	1	44	286	20	35.5
Black, Mike, *Det.*	73	3054	60	41.8	73	5	0	44	420	17	34.7
Cox, Steve, *Wash.*	52	2175	57	41.8	52	13	0	22	228	14	32.4
Birdsong, Carl, *St.L.*	85	3545	67	41.7	87	8	2	51	456	20	33.7
Horan, Mike, *Phil.*	91	3777	75	41.5	91	10	0	41	462	20	34.2
Runager, Max, *S.F.*	86	3422	57	39.8	87	9	1	33	294	30	33.9
Prokop, Joe, *G.B.*	56	2210	66	39.5	56	6	0	30	265	9	32.6

Leader based on gross average, minimum 40 punts

NFC PUNT RETURNERS

	No	FC	Yards	Ave	Long	TD
Ellard, Henry, *Rams*	37	9	501	13.5	t80	1
Green, Darrell, *Wash.*	16	0	214	13.4	37	0
Smith, J.T., *St.L.*	26	10	283	10.9	31	0
Mandley, Pete, *Det.*	38	5	403	10.6	t63	1
Jenkins, Ken, *Wash.*	26	9	272	10.5	28	0
Epps, Phillip, *G.B.*	15	3	146	9.7	46	0
Ortego, Keith, *Chi.*	17	2	158	9.3	23	0
Cooper, Evan, *Phil.*	43	10	364	8.5	56	0
McConkey, Phil, *Giants*	53	18	442	8.3	37	0
Tullis, Willie, *N.O.*	17	6	141	8.3	17	0
Nelson, Darrin, *Minn.*	16	3	133	8.3	21	0
Taylor, Ken, *Chi.*	25	8	198	7.9	21	0
Bates, Bill, *Dall.*	22	6	152	6.9	21	0
McLemore, Dana, *S.F.*	38	14	258	6.8	22	0
Allen, Anthony, *Atl.*	21	8	141	6.7	23	0

t = Touchdown
Leader based on average return, minimum 15 returns

NFC INTERCEPTORS

	No	Yards	Ave	Long	TD
Walls, Everson, *Dall.*	9	31	3.4	19	0
Castille, Jeremiah, *T.B.*	7	49	7.0	20	0
Frazier, Leslie, *Chi.*	6	119	19.8	33	1
Patterson, Elvis, *Giants*	6	88	14.7	t29	1
Green, Gary, *Rams*	6	84	14.0	t41	1
Irvin, LeRoy, *Rams*	6	83	13.8	t34	1
Lott, Ronnie, *S.F.*	6	68	11.3	25	0
Waymer, Dave, *N.O.*	6	49	8.2	28	0
Hopkins, Wes, *Phil.*	6	36	6.0	t24	1
Junior, E.J., *St.L.*	5	109	21.8	53	0
Kinard, Terry, *Giants*	5	100	20.0	31	0
Johnson, Johnnie, *Rams*	5	96	19.2	46	1
Jordan, Curtis, *Wash.*	5	88	17.6	36	0
Turner, John, *Minn.*	5	62	12.4	25	0
Duerson, Dave, *Chi.*	5	53	10.6	20	0
Fencik, Gary, *Chi.*	5	43	8.6	22	0
Thurman, Dennis, *Dall.*	5	21	4.2	t21	1
Greenwood, David, *T.B.*	5	15	3.0	7	0
Watkins, Bobby, *Det.*	5	15	3.0	8	0
Dean, Vernon, *Wash.*	5	8	1.6	8	0
Butler, Bobby, *Atl.*	5	−4	−0.8	0	0
Richardson, Mike, *Chi.*	4	174	43.5	90	1
Hoage, Terry, *N.O.*	4	79	19.8	t52	1
Case, Scott, *Atl.*	4	78	19.5	47	0
Hicks, Dwight, *S.F.*	4	68	17.0	25	0
Fellows, Ron, *Dall.*	4	52	13.0	29	0
Ellis, Ray, *Phil.*	4	32	8.0	18	0
Marshall, Wilber, *Chi.*	4	23	5.8	14	0
Bates, Bill, *Dall.*	4	15	3.8	8	0
Lewis, Tim, *G.B.*	4	4	1.0	4	0
Williamson, Carlton, *S.F.*	3	137	45.7	82	1
Lee, Carl, *Minn.*	3	68	22.7	35	0
Poe, Johnnie, *N.O.*	3	63	21.0	t40	1
Johnson, Demetrious, *Det.*	3	39	13.0	19	0
Wilson, Otis, *Chi.*	3	35	11.7	t23	1
Cason, Wendell, *Atl.*	3	30	10.0	22	0
Taylor, Ken, *Chi.*	3	28	9.3	18	0
Graham, William, *Det.*	3	22	7.3	22	0
Newsome, Vince, *Rams*	3	20	6.7	20	0
Clinkscale, Dextor, *Dall.*	3	16	5.3	11	0
Downs, Michael, *Dall.*	3	11	3.7	11	0
Kaufman, Mel, *Wash.*	3	10	3.3	10	0
Edwards, Herman, *Phil.*	3	8	2.7	t3	1
Teal, Willie, *Minn.*	3	6	2.0	6	0
Young, Lonnie, *St.L.*	3	0	0.0	0	0

t = Touchdown

Cowboys cornerback Everson Walls (#24) intercepting a pass in the Divisional Playoffs.

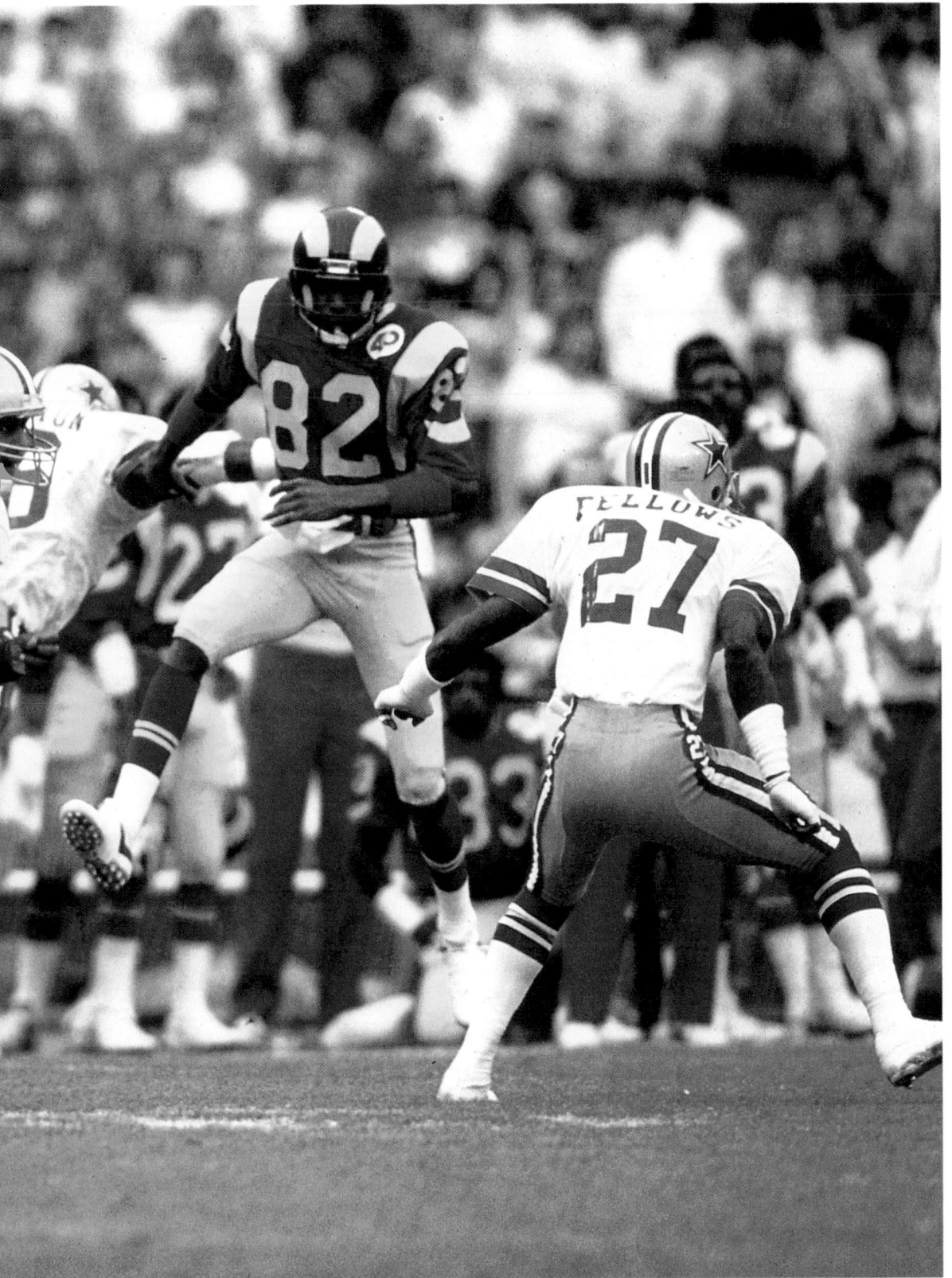

DALLAS COWBOYS

Address One Cowboy Parkway, Irving, Texas 75063.
Stadium Texas Stadium, Irving.
  Capacity 63,749 *Playing Surface* Texas Turf.
Team Colours Royal Blue, Metallic Silver Blue, and White.
Head Coach Tom Landry – twenty-seventh year.
Championships Division 1970,'71,'73,'76,'77,'78,'79,'81,'85;
  Conference 1970,'71,'75,'77,'78; Super Bowl 1971,'77.
History NFL 1960-69, NFC 1970-

Offense

They may have lost a little of their gloss, but the Dallas Cowboys went to the playoffs for the eighteenth time in the last twenty years and, what's more, they made the trip as champions of possibly the toughest division in the league. As usual, their offense could always count on the lightning-quick Tony Dorsett to lead the way – other than in the strike-shortened 1982 campaign, Dorsett can point to a sequence of 1,000-yards-rushing seasons stretching all the way back to high school. With 10,832 career rushing yards, Dorsett retained his place of sixth in the all-time list but, with the players just ahead of him either retired or contemplating that happy prospect, he has a good chance of ending the 1986 season in second place behind Walter Payton. Beyond Dorsett on the Cowboys' squad, though, there was no sign of an obvious successor. Accordingly, they used a second-round option to draft Darryl Clack, who is projected as Dorsett's backup in the short term and will be given the chance to show his paces on passing downs. Victory for Danny White in the quarterback battle was confirmed when Gary Hogeboom was traded to Indianapolis. Even though White was carrying injuries for much of the time, the Cowboys ranked first in the NFC for passing offense. In wide receivers Tony Hill and Mike Renfro, and tight end Doug Cosbie, they had three players who each caught 60 or more passes on the year. Hill established a Dallas club record with 74 receptions. First-round draftee Mike Sherrard was rated as the best wide receiver by some scouts, but he will find it difficult to displace Renfro, who is coming off his best season in the pros. Cosbie is now a regular Pro Bowler and might be the best third-and-long passing target in the business. The offensive line is very solid from center Tom Rafferty out to the right, through guard Kurt Petersen and tackle Jim Cooper. An iron man, Rafferty has never missed a game in his ten-year career. There are the makings, too, of a good combination on the left side, where guard Glen Titensor and tackle Chris Schultz are becoming established.

Defense

The Cowboys persist with their own brand of 4-3 defense (it has many subtleties) and begin with a terrorizing pass rush which, in 1985, registered a Dallas club-record 62 quarterback traps. Defensive left end Ed 'Too Tall' Jones was supposed to be past his best, but he answered his critics by logging 13 traps, the highest total of his eleven-year career, and knocking down seven passes. Right defensive end Jim Jeffcoat, also who had a career-best with 12 traps, is now to be regarded as an outstanding player even in this, an era of great defensive ends. Defensive right tackle Randy White was elected to the Pro Bowl for the ninth consecutive year. And in this company, it would be easy to overlook left tackle John Dutton, a former All-Pro, who's still a battler. In reserve, the Cowboys have Don Smerek and Kevin Brooks, the latter who was a first-round draft pick in 1985 and may stand in for Dutton more often. Linebacking is an area of relative weakness even though, last year, middle linebacker Eugene 'The Hitting Machine' Lockhart underlined his nickname (he led the team with 126 tackles) and, on the outside, Mike Hegman was his usual reliable self. Jeff Rohrer will probably be challenged by 1985 second-round pick Jesse Penn. 'Thurman's Thieves', as the secondary is nicknamed, is challenged often and loses out too many times for comfort. But they rapped a few knuckles, with cornerback Everson Walls grabbing nine of a club-total 33 pass interceptions. Walls became the first man in league history to lead the league in interceptions for the third time. Walls and Ron Fellows will continue on the corners, with Dextor Clinkscale and Michael Downs in the safety positions. Dennis Thurman, Victor Scott and Bill Bates are solid backups.

Special Teams

Placekicker Rafael Septien represents traditional Dallas quality but first-year punter Mike Saxon, though sometimes good, was inconsistent. As a club, the Cowboys ranked surprisingly low in the NFC, 12th and 14th returning kickoffs and punts respectively. Rookie running back Robert Lavette was unable to break for a long kickoff return, and Bill Bates could manage an average of only 6.9 yards on 22 punt returns. Bates is at his best when stopping the other guy – he was the special-team tackler on the 1985 NFC Pro Bowl squad.

1986 SCHEDULE OF GAMES	September	
	8 NEW YORK GIANTS (Mon.)	8:00
	14 at Detroit	1:00
	21 ATLANTA	12:00
	29 at St Louis (Mon.)	8:00
	October	
	5 at Denver	2:00
	12 WASHINGTON	12:00
	19 at Philadelphia	1:00
	26 ST LOUIS	3:00
	November	
	2 at New York Giants	1:00
	9 LOS ANGELES RAIDERS	3:00
	16 at San Diego	1:00
	23 at Washington	1:00
	27 SEATTLE (Thanksgiving)	3:00
	December	
	7 at Los Angeles Rams	6:00
	14 PHILADELPHIA	12:00
	21 CHICAGO	3:00

VETERAN ROSTER

No.	Name	Pos.	Ht.	Wt.	Year	College
36	Albritton, Vince	S-LB	6-2	213	3	Washington
76	Aughtman, Dowe	G	6-2	259	2	Auburn
62	Baldinger, Brian	C-G	6-4	261	4	Duke
87	Banks, Gordon	WR	5-10	173	4	Stanford
40	Bates, Bill	S	6-1	199	4	Tennessee
99	Brooks, Kevin	DE	6-6	270	2	Michigan
47	Clinkscale, Dextor	S	5-11	195	6	South Carolina State
61	Cooper, Jim	T	6-5	274	10	Temple
85	Cornwell, Fred	TE	6-6	233	3	Southern California
84	Cosbie, Doug	TE	6-6	245	8	Santa Clara
55	DeOssie, Steve	LB	6-2	245	3	Boston College
33	Dorsett, Tony	RB	5-11	185	10	Pittsburgh
26	Downs, Michael	S	6-3	204	6	Rice
86	Duckett, Kenny	WR-KR	5-11	183	5	Wake Forest
78	Dutton, John	DT	6-7	268	13	Nebraska
27	Fellows, Ron	CB	6-0	180	6	Missouri
46	Fowler, Todd	RB	6-3	218	2	Stephen F. Austin
83	Gonzalez, Leon	WR	5-10	162	2	Bethune-Cookman
58	Hegman, Mike	LB	6-1	228	11	Tennessee State
80	Hill, Tony	WR	6-2	202	10	Stanford
77	Jeffcoat, Jim	DE	6-5	263	4	Arizona State
72	Jones, Ed	DE	6-9	287	12	Tennessee State
23	Jones, James	RB	5-10	203	6	Mississippi State
68	Ker, Crawford	G	6-3	293	2	Florida
29	Lavette, Robert	RB	5-11	199	2	Georgia Tech
56	Lockhart, Eugene	LB	6-2	234	3	Houston
	Miller, Junior	TE	6-4	244	6	Nebraska
30	Newsome, Timmy	RB	6-1	237	7	Winston-Salem State
16	Pelluer, Steve	QB	6-4	208	3	Washington
59	Penn, Jesse	LB	6-3	217	2	Virginia Tech
65	Petersen, Kurt	G	6-4	278	7	Missouri
98	Ploeger, Kurt	DE	6-5	259	1	Gustavus Adolphus
81	Powe, Karl	WR	6-2	175	2	Alabama State
75	Pozderac, Phil	T	6-9	282	5	Notre Dame
64	Rafferty, Tom	C	6-3	264	11	Penn State
82	Renfro, Mike	WR	6-0	189	9	Texas Christian
70	Richards, Howard	G-T	6-6	262	6	Missouri
50	Rohrer, Jeff	LB	6-2	230	5	Yale
89	Salonen, Brian	TE-LB	6-3	226	3	Montana
4	Saxon, Mike	P	6-3	187	2	San Diego State
66	Schultz, Chris	T	6-8	288	3	Arizona
22	Scott, Victor	CB	6-0	196	3	Colorado
1	Septien, Rafael	K	5-10	179	10	Southwest Louisiana
60	Smerek, Don	DT	6-7	265	5	Nevada-Reno
43	Story, Ronald	RB	5-8	201	1	California
67	Thompson, Broderick	T	6-5	280	2	Kansas
32	Thurman, Dennis	S	5-11	179	9	Southern California
63	Titensor, Glen	G	6-4	261	6	Brigham Young
71	Tuinei, Mark	C	6-5	270	4	Hawaii
24	Walls, Everson	CB	6-1	194	6	Grambling State
94	Waltman, Chris	TE	6-7	255	1	Oregon State
11	White, Danny	QB	6-3	196	11	Arizona State
54	White, Randy	DT	6-4	272	12	Maryland

1986 DRAFT

Round	Name	Pos.	Ht.	Wt.	College
1.	Sherrard, Mike	WR	6-2	185	UCLA
2.	Clack, Darryl	RB	5-10	207	Arizona State
3.	Walen, Mark	DT	6-5	265	UCLA
4.	Zendejas, Max	K	5-11	184	Arizona
6.	Chandler, Thornton	TE	6-5	238	Alabama
6.	Gelbaugh, Stan	QB	6-3	207	Maryland
6.	Yancey, Lloyd	G	6-4	275	Temple
7.	Holloway, Johnny	WR	5-11	181	Kansas
8.	Clemons, Topper	RB	5-11	205	Wake Forest
9.	Ionata, John	G	6-2	280	Florida State
10.	Chester, Bryan	G	6-4	260	Texas
11.	Jax, Garth	LB	6-2	225	Florida State
12.	Duliban, Chris	LB	6-2	216	Texas
12.	Flack, Tony	DB	6-1	184	Georgia

Tony Hill needs 60 pass receptions to become the Cowboys' all-time leader

NEW YORK GIANTS

Address Giants Stadium, East Rutherford, New Jersey
07073.
Stadium Giants Stadium, East Rutherford.
Capacity 76,891 *Playing Surface* AstroTurf.
Team Colours Blue, Red, and White.
Head Coach Bill Parcells – fourth year.
Championships NFL 1927,'34,'38,'56.
History NFL 1925-69, NFC 1970-

Offense

The Giants have had a sound squad for some time but now they have joined the other clubs which have that necessary ingredient, a great running back. Coming into the year, Joe Morris was known to be a quick-footed, dangerous runner, who needed careful watching – he was a shock weapon. But in 1985, he exploded onto the scene, establishing a Giants single-season club record for rushing yardage (1,336) and dodging for 21 rushing touchdowns, the second-best total in league history. He was the difference. His backfield partners were some way adrift, but rookie George Adams, who was a first-round pick, made a good start to his career, both as a runner and as a receiver. Included amongst his 31 receptions was a 70-yarder for a touchdown. Adams is likely to continue for a while as understudy to Morris, with Rob Carpenter starting at fullback. Quarterback Phil Simms does not play the kind of game which earns a high passer rating (his 1985 rating of 78.6 was his career best). But when he's in tune, he's devastating – on Weeks Five and Six, he passed for 432 and 513 yards respectively. Furthermore, he's respected by his NFC colleagues, who voted him to the Pro Bowl, where he engineered a 21-point comeback victory. (Morris and Simms were the first Giants offensive players to play in the Pro Bowl since quarterback Norm Snead and running back Ron Johnson made the trip in 1973.) When Simms goes long, he looks for wide receivers Lionel Manuel and Bob Johnson, two young flyers who have enormous potential. Byron Williams is the third pure wide receiver but, unexpectedly, was used sparingly. The real find for the receiving corps was the 1985 fourth-round pick, tight end Mark Bavaro, who caught his 37 passes at the impressive average of 13.8 yards. He'll be in a battle with Zeke Mowatt, who is returning after a season-long absence. If the Giants need improvement, it is on an offensive line which gave up 52 sacks. Both tackle Bill Roberts, a 1984 first-round pick who started as a rookie, and former starting center Kevin Belcher, should be back after injuries to challenge the incumbents. Roberts could displace Brad Benson at left tackle, but Belcher may have a more difficult task ousting Bart Oates, who is one of several class players to arrive after playing in the USFL.

Defense

With the league's second-best defense, the Giants are one of the few outfits which managed to out-do the Bears in the subsidiary categories, as they led the entire NFL with 68 sacks. It is astonishing to think that, going into last season, the modesty of their pass rush appeared to be a problem (in 1984, they had only 48 sacks). In 1985, playing at defensive right end in the three-man line, third-year man Leonard Marshall led the club, collaring opposing quarterbacks 15.5 times. Hovering just behind Marshall, at right outside linebacker, the predatory Lawrence Taylor had 13.5 successes, with George Martin and Jerome Sally, both of whom come in on obvious passing downs, registering ten and 7.5 respectively. If those are just clear statistical examples, there are many more reasons why the Giants might even surpass the Bears in 1986. Nose tackle Jim Burt and defensive left end Curtis McGriff, together with linebackers Byron Hunt, Gary Reasons and the great veteran, Harry Carson, mount a stifling defense against the run. Behind them, in the secondary, free safety Terry Kinard is a crunching tackler and took advantage of errant passes to log five interceptions. Second-year cornerback Elvis Patterson led the club with six interceptions. He's a fireball and made up for the absence of former All-Pro Mark Haynes, who has subsequently been traded. Perry Williams started in all sixteen games at right cornerback but may be challenged by second-round draftee Mark Collins. Another rookie, second-round pick Greg Lasker, will make a bid to start at strong safety ahead of Kenny Hill. Ted Watts and Herb Welch are useful reserves.

Special Teams

Despite a remarkable debut, when he kicked five field goals, placekicker Eric Schubert will probably step down in favour of Ali Haji-Sheikh, who is returning after injury. If punter Sean Landeta can maintain the excellent form of his rookie year (his gross average was 42.9 yards), the Giants need have no worries over their kicking game. But they could do with a little help returning kickoffs, in which, as a club, they ranked dead last in the league. Wide receiver Phil McConkey doubles as a respectable punt returner but doesn't present a big-play threat.

1986 SCHEDULE OF GAMES		
September		
8 at Dallas (Mon.)		8:00
14 SAN DIEGO		1:00
21 at Los Angeles Raiders		1:00
28 NEW ORLEANS		1:00
October		
5 at St Louis		12:00
12 PHILADELPHIA		4:00
19 at Seattle		1:00
27 WASHINGTON (Mon.)		9:00
November		
2 DALLAS		1:00
9 at Philadelphia		4:00
16 at Minnesota		12:00
23 DENVER		1:00
December		
1 at San Francisco (Mon.)		6:00
7 at Washington		1:00
14 ST LOUIS		1:00
20 GREEN BAY (Sat.)		12:30

VETERAN ROSTER

No.	Name	Pos.	Ht.	Wt.	NFL Year	College
33	Adams, George	RB	6-1	225	2	Kentucky
67	Ard, Bill	G	6-3	270	6	Wake Forest
58	Banks, Carl	LB	6-4	235	3	Michigan State
89	Bavaro, Mark	TE	6-4	245	2	Notre Dame
73	Belcher, Kevin	C	6-3	276	3	Texas-El Paso
60	Benson, Brad	T	6-3	270	9	Penn State
64	Burt, Jim	NT	6-1	260	6	Miami
26	Carpenter, Rob	RB	6-1	226	10	Miami (Ohio)
53	Carson, Harry	LB	6-2	240	11	South Carolina State
44	Carthon, Maurice	RB	6-1	225	2	Arkansas State
24	Daniel, Kenny	CB	5-10	180	2	San Jose State
39	Davis, Ty	CB	6-1	190	2	Clemson
30	Galbreath, Tony	RB	6-0	228	11	Missouri
61	Godfrey, Chris	G	6-3	265	4	Michigan
62	Goode, Conrad	T	6-6	285	3	Missouri
6	Haji-Sheikh, Ali	K	6-0	170	3	Michigan
79	Hardison, Dee	DE	6-4	274	9	North Carolina
85	Hasselbeck, Don	TE	6-7	245	10	Colorado
54	Headen, Andy	LB	6-5	242	4	Clemson
48	Hill, Kenny	S	6-0	195	6	Yale
15	Hostetler, Jeff	QB	6-3	212	3	West Virginia
57	Hunt, Byron	LB	6-5	242	6	Southern Methodist
88	Johnson, Bob	WR	5-11	171	3	Kansas
77	Johnson, Damian	T	6-5	290	1	Kansas State
	Johnston, Brian	C	6-3	275	1	North Carolina
51	Jones, Robbie	LB	6-2	230	3	Alabama
69	Jordan, David	G	6-6	276	3	Auburn
82	Kab, Vyto	TE	6-5	240	5	Penn State
43	Kinard, Terry	S	6-1	200	4	Clemson
72	King, Gordon	T	6-6	275	9	Stanford
5	Landeta, Sean	P	6-0	200	2	Towson State
86	Manuel, Lionel	WR	5-11	175	3	Pacific
70	Marshall, Leonard	DE	6-3	285	4	Louisiana State
75	Martin, George	DE	6-4	255	12	Oregon
80	McConkey, Phil	WR	5-10	170	3	Navy
76	McGriff, Curtis	DE	6-5	276	7	Alabama
71	Merrill, Casey	DE	6-4	258	8	Cal-Davis
20	Morris, Joe	RB	5-7	195	5	Syracuse
84	Mowatt, Zeke	TE	6-3	240	3	Florida State
63	Nelson, Karl	T	6-6	285	3	Iowa State
65	Oates, Bart	C	6-3	265	2	Brigham Young
34	Patterson, Elvis	CB	5-11	188	3	Kansas
55	Reasons, Gary	LB	6-4	234	3	N.W. State, Louisiana
66	Roberts, Bill	T	6-5	280	2	Ohio State
81	Robinson, Stacy	WR	5-11	186	2	North Dakota State
22	Rouson, Lee	RB	6-1	210	2	Colorado
17	Rutledge, Jeff	QB	6-1	195	8	Alabama
78	Sally, Jerome	NT	6-3	270	5	Missouri
3	Schubert, Eric	K	5-8	193	2	Pittsburgh

No.	Name	Pos.	Ht.	Wt.	NFL Year	College
11	Simms, Phil	QB	6-3	214	8	Morehead State
56	Taylor, Lawrence	LB	6-3	243	6	North Carolina
38	Tuggle, John	RB	6-1	210	2	California
21	Watts, Ted	CB	6-0	190	6	Texas Tech
27	Welch, Herb	DB	5-11	180	2	UCLA
87	Williams, Byron	WR	6-2	183	4	Texas-Arlington
23	Williams, Perry	CB	6-2	203	3	North Carolina State
28	Winters, Larry	DB	6-1	210	2	St Paul's

1986 DRAFT

Round	Name	Pos.	Ht.	Wt.	College
1.	Dorsey, Eric	DE	6-5	280	Notre Dame
2.	Collins, Mark	CB	5-10	190	Cal State-Fullerton
2.	Howard, Erik	NT	6-4	268	Washington State
2.	Johnson, Thomas	LB	6-3	248	Ohio State
2.	Lasker, Greg	S	6-0	200	Arkansas
3.	Washington, John	DE	6-4	275	Oklahoma State
5.	Warren, Vince	WR	6-0	180	San Diego State
6.	Brown, Ron	WR	5-10	186	Colorado
6.	Miller, Solomon	WR	6-1	185	Utah State
7.	Francis, Jon	RB	5-11	205	Boise State
8.	Cisowski, Steve	T	6-6	275	Santa Clara
9.	Luebbers, Jim	DE	6-5	246	Iowa State
10.	Kimmel, Jerry	LB	6-2	250	Syracuse
11.	Lynch, Len	G	6-2	269	Maryland

Defensive end Leonard Marshall (#70) made astonishing progress to lead the Giants with 15.5 quarterback sacks

PHILADELPHIA EAGLES

Address Philadelphia Veterans Stadium, Broad St. and
  Pattison Ave., Philadelphia, Pa. 19148.
Stadium Veterans Stadium, Philadelphia.
  Capacity 71,640 *Playing Surface* AstroTurf.
Team Colours Kelly Green, Silver, and White.
Head Coach Buddy Ryan – first year.
Championships Division 1980; Conference 1980;
  NFL 1948,'49,'60.
History NFL 1933-69, NFC 1970-

Offense

New head coach Buddy Ryan is not a man to hang about waiting for something to happen. On arrival, his first acts were to release starting center Mark Dennard, leaving Gerry Feehery and rookie Matt Darwin as the only specialists. Next, he acquired San Francisco's reserve quarterback, Matt Cavanaugh. The latter is an interesting move since Ron Jaworski still has a great deal to offer. Perhaps Ryan was looking at Jaworski's passer rating which, over the last six years, has eased down from a career-high of 90.9 to 70.2. Equally, it is true that Cavanaugh has looked impressive when standing in for Joe Montana. Certainly, he has the know-how and the precision passing to find two of the league's big-play wide receivers. Mike Quick may even be the best in the business – he has caught passes for over 1,000 yards in each of the last three seasons and has a career average of 18.1 yards. The other is Kenny Jackson, a former first-round pick, who has shown great potential playing second fiddle. Over the medium range, tight end John Spagnola has become a distinct threat. Last year, statistically speaking, there was little which separated Spagnola from the Pro Bowl starter, Doug Cosbie, and one has to think that it was only a dramatic return to form by Tampa Bay's Jimmie Giles which kept Spagnola out of the interconference showpiece. It was a shrewd move when former head coach Marion Campbell acquired running back Earnest Jackson from San Diego. Jackson, the AFC leading rusher in 1984, became only the third player in Eagles history to rush for over 1,000 yards in a season. He will be helped by draftees Keith Byars and Anthony Toney. At 244 pounds and very fast, Byars was rated the second-best prospect behind Bo Jackson and, in his own right, could easily be a franchise running back provided he has recovered completely from the foot injury he suffered in college. Running back Herman Hunter may retain a roster spot for his additional value as a receiver – last year, he filtered out of the backfield for 405 yards on 28 pass receptions. In guards Ron Baker and Steve Kenney, and tackle Leonard Mitchell, there is the nucleus of veteran quality for the offensive line. Mitchell is finally beginning to look the part after making the conversion from defense.

Defense

The Eagles have all the talent necessary to go out looking for the opposition, and it is most likely that they will do just that. Defensive ends Reggie White and Greg Brown each had 13 quarterback sacks last year, and specialist pass rusher Thomas Strauthers had 5.5. Strauthers may see greater playing time as the fourth defensive lineman. Nose tackle Ken Clarke is good against the run and he, too, has a taste for quarterbacks – he had seven sacks. There could be significant changes at linebacker where, already, former starters Reggie Wilkes and Anthony Griggs have been traded. Alonzo Johnson, an outside specialist, was the first of three linebackers taken in the draft. They will compete with two good players, former Detroit starter Garry Cobb and Mike Reichenbach, both of whom started last year, and the reserves, Rich Kraynak and Dwayne Jiles. The Eagles secondary is traditionally strong. Free safety Wes Hopkins, who started in the Pro Bowl, led the team in both interceptions (6) and tackles (136). He's a terrier playing in partnership with strong safety Ray Ellis. Herman Edwards has been the starter at right cornerback ever since joining the Eagles as a free agent in 1977. And the only break in left cornerback Roynell Young's sequence of starts came in 1984, when he was injured. Both Brenard Wilson (safety) and Elbert Foules (cornerback) are excellent backups.

Special Teams

Paul McFadden is a placekicker of high class. He missed no extra points and was successful on every field goal attempt up to 41 yards, failing on only two inside 50 yards. There will be a training-camp battle between the existing punter, Mike Horan, and rookie Ray Criswell, the latter who was considered to be the best of the college seniors. On punt returns, Evan Cooper maintained a respectable 8.5 yards per attempt, and gave a glimpse of his speed on his longest return of 56 yards. Hunter showed his versatility by returning 48 kickoffs and gives coach Ryan an extra reason for keeping him in the squad.

1986 SCHEDULE OF GAMES		
September		
7 at Washington	1:00	
14 at Chicago	12:00	
21 DENVER	1:00	
28 LOS ANGELES RAMS	1:00	
October		
5 at Atlanta	1:00	
12 at New York Giants	4:00	
19 DALLAS	1:00	
26 SAN DIEGO	1:00	
November		
2 at St Louis	12:00	
9 NEW YORK GIANTS	4:00	
16 DETROIT	1:00	
23 at Seattle	1:00	
30 at Los Angeles Raiders	1:00	
December		
7 ST LOUIS	1:00	
14 at Dallas	12:00	
21 WASHINGTON	1:00	

VETERAN ROSTER

No.	Name	Pos.	Ht.	Wt.	NFL Year	College
72	Allen, Kevin	T	6-5	284	2	Indiana
63	Baker, Ron	G	6-4	274	9	Oklahoma State
98	Brown, Greg	DE	6-5	265	6	Kansas State
	Cavanaugh, Matt	QB	6-2	212	9	Pittsburgh
71	Clarke, Ken	NT	6-2	272	9	Syracuse
50	Cobb, Garry	LB	6-2	228	8	Southern California
21	Cooper, Evan	DB-KR	5-11	184	3	Michigan
12	Cunningham, Randall	QB	6-4	192	2	Nevada-Las Vegas
94	Darby, Byron	DE	6-4	262	4	Southern California
99	Drake, Joe	NT	6-2	290	2	Arizona
46	Edwards, Herman	CB	6-0	194	10	San Diego State
24	Ellis, Ray	S	6-1	196	6	Ohio State
39	Everett, Major	RB	5-11	218	4	Mississippi College
67	Feehery, Gerry	C	6-2	270	4	Syracuse
29	Foules, Elbert	CB	5-11	185	4	Alcorn State
86	Garrity, Gregg	WR	5-10	169	4	Penn State
84	Goode, John	TE	6-2	243	3	Youngstown State
26	Haddix, Michael	RB	6-2	227	4	Mississippi State
48	Hopkins, Wes	S	6-1	212	4	Southern Methodist
2	Horan, Michael	P	5-11	190	3	Long Beach State
36	Hunter, Herman	RB-KR	6-1	193	2	Tennessee State
41	Jackson, Earnest	RB	5-9	208	4	Texas A&M
81	Jackson, Kenny	WR	6-0	177	3	Penn State
7	Jaworski, Ron	QB	6-2	199	13	Youngstown State
77	Jelesky, Tom	T	6-6	275	2	Purdue
53	Jiles, Dwayne	LB	6-4	242	2	Texas Tech
85	Johnson, Ron	WR	6-3	190	2	Long Beach State
73	Kenney, Steve	G	6-4	274	7	Clemson
52	Kraynak, Rich	LB	6-1	230	4	Pittsburgh
89	Little, Dave	TE	6-2	232	3	Middle Tennessee St.
	Mackey, Kyle	QB	6-2	220	2	East Texas State
8	McFadden, Paul	K	5-11	163	3	Youngstown State
74	Mitchell, Leonard	T	6-7	295	6	Houston
69	Morris, Dwaine	NT	6-2	260	2	Southwestern Louisiana
76	Naron, Greg	G	6-4	270	1	North Carolina
	Oubre, Louis	G	6-4	272	4	Oklahoma
38	Penaranda, Jairo	RB	6-0	218	3	UCLA
57	Polley, Tom	LB	6-3	235	1	Nevada-Las Vegas
82	Quick, Mike	WR	6-2	190	5	North Carolina State
66	Reeves, Ken	T-G	6-5	268	2	Texas A&M
55	Reichenbach, Mike	LB	6-2	238	3	East Stroudsburg State
95	Schulz, Jody	LB	6-3	235	3	East Carolina
88	Spagnola, John	TE	6-4	238	7	Yale
93	Strauthers, Thomas	DE	6-4	264	4	Jackson State
20	Waters, Andre	CB	5-11	185	3	Cheyney State
91	White, Reggie	DE	6-5	285	2	Tennessee
22	Wilson, Brenard	CB-S	6-0	185	8	Vanderbilt
83	Woodruff, Tony	WR	6-0	185	4	Fresno State
43	Young, Roynell	CB	6-1	185	7	Alcorn State

1986 DRAFT

Round	Name	Pos.	Ht.	Wt.	College
1.	Byars, Keith	RB	6-1	244	Ohio State
2.	Toney, Anthony	RB	5-11	227	Texas A&M
2.	Johnson, Alonzo	LB	6-3	217	Florida
4.	Darwin, Matt	C	6-4	263	Texas A&M
5.	Criswell, Ray	P	6-0	182	Florida
5.	McMillen, Dan	DE	6-4	237	Colorado
6.	Landsee, Bob	C	6-4	269	Wisconsin
7.	Redick, Corn	WR	5-11	182	Cal State-Fullerton
7.	Lee, Byron	LB	6-2	230	Ohio State
8.	Joyner, Seth	LB	6-2	210	Texas-El Paso
9.	Simmons, Clyde	DE	6-6	235	Western Carolina
10.	Tautalatasi, Junior	RB	5-11	201	Washington State
11.	Bogdalek, Steve	G	6-4	243	Michigan State
12.	Singletary, Reggie	DE	6-3	255	North Carolina State
12.	Howard, Bobby	RB	6-0	212	Indiana

Wes Hopkins is one of the league's premier safeties

ST LOUIS CARDINALS

Address Busch Stadium, Box 888, St Louis, Missouri 63188.
Stadium Busch Stadium, St Louis.
   Capacity 51,392 *Playing Surface* AstroTurf.
Team Colours Cardinal Red, Black, and White.
Head Coach Gene Stallings – first year.
Championships Division 1974,'75; NFL 1925,'47.
History NFL 1920-69, NFC 1970-
   (Until 1960, they were known as the Chicago Cardinals.)

Offense

In the eyes of many, the Cardinals would be the team to fear in 1985. And they started out well enough, winning three of their first four games. Beyond those, however, they won only twice more. They were not helped by injuries to several key players, amongst them running back Ottis Anderson and wide receiver Roy 'Jetstream' Green. Even so, the play of their offensive line was not good – they gave up 65 quarterback sacks – and it was felt behind the line of scrimmage, where only rarely did quarterback Neil Lomax have the kind of platform from which to cut loose. Still, new head coach Gene Stallings is apparently satisfied with his existing players, since he picked only two rookies for that area. Center Gene Chilton is not likely to displace the current starter, Randy Clark, who will line up inside the guards, Doug Dawson and Joe Bostic, with Luis Sharpe and James 'Tootie' Robbins at tackle. Elsewhere, the Cardinals are in excellent shape with Anderson, a player who would be expected to rush for over 1,000 yards for the sixth time in his career, operating in combination with the mercurial Stump Mitchell, who became a 1,000-yard rusher for the first time in 1985. Mitchell really is a coach's dream. His 2,177 career yards have come at the tremendous average of 5.4, he is a fine pass receiver and can return both kickoffs and punts. At wide receiver, Green, who too is a remarkably versatile athlete, will be hoping to rediscover the momentum of his 1984 season, when he led the NFL with 1,555 yards receiving. His probable starting partner, Pat Tilley, is a neat receiver and has an edge over Earnest Gray, who came to the Cardinals last season after spending some time in dispute with the Giants ownership. Gray is no mean performer, having caught passes for a career-best 1,139 yards in 1983. Clyde Duncan has not shown much form and, even though he was the Cardinals' first-round pick in 1984, he will have to battle with the veteran, J.T. Smith, for the spot behind Green. Doug Marsh, the starting tight end, keeps plugging away, but lacks the productivity of others around the league.

Defense

Back in 1983, the Cardinals had three defensive linemen amongst the top ten NFC sackers – the club led the entire NFL with 59 sacks. In that year, defensive ends Curtis Greer and Al 'Bubba' Baker had 16 and 13 respectively, and defensive tackle David Galloway had 12. In 1985, the whole defensive unit produced only 32 sacks, a number which is surprisingly low since the same three players started regularly. Clearly, the club has the talent available, and they can be pleased with the form of defensive tackle Mark Duda, who stood in for the injured starter, Elois Grooms. As backups, they have defensive end Stafford Mays, defensive tackle Scott Bergold and draftee Jeff Tupper. At middle linebacker, E.J. Junior rates behind only Chicago's Mike Singletary in the NFC. He does everything at the heart of the defense – he is the heart of the defense. He can expect help with the return to full fitness of Charlie Baker, a veteran who has had trouble with injuries for the last few years, and Thomas Howard, a former Kansas City player who came to St Louis in a 1984 trade. With those two unavailable, rookie Freddie Joe Nunn saw plenty of action at right outside linebacker and underlined his status as a first-round pick. As a sign of their commitment to strengthening the defense, the Cardinals took Anthony Bell in the first round. Leonard Smith, who too is a former first-rounder, has really blossomed after making a slow start to his career and is now established at strong safety. Free safety Lonnie Young began his pro career from the other end of the list – he was a twelfth-round pick in 1985 – but, even as a rookie, he was able to make the transition from cornerback and ended the season as the starter. Draftee Carl Carter and the veterans, Cedric Mack and Jeff Griffin, will challenge Wayne Smith and Lionel Washington for starting places at cornerback.

Special Teams

As widely expected, the Cardinals used a high draft option to select placekicker John Lee, whom they hope will give them an edge in those close games. Punter Carl Birdsong will doubtless be challenged in training camp but should retain his roster spot. Returning punts, J.T. Smith showed all his veteran savvy, picking his way through the bodies, and ranked second in the NFC. Duncan was the main kickoff returner but, apart from one covering 34 yards, he had a difficult time.

1986 SCHEDULE OF GAMES		
September		
7	LOS ANGELES RAMS	12:00
14	at Atlanta	1:00
21	at Buffalo	1:00
29	DALLAS (Mon.)	8:00
October		
5	NEW YORK GIANTS	12:00
12	at Tampa Bay	1:00
19	at Washington	1:00
26	at Dallas	3:00
November		
2	PHILADELPHIA	12:00
9	at San Francisco	1:00
16	NEW ORLEANS	12:00
23	KANSAS CITY	3:00
30	WASHINGTON	12:00
December		
7	at Philadelphia	1:00
14	at New York Giants	1:00
21	TAMPA BAY	12:00

1986 DRAFT

Round	Name	Pos.	Ht.	Wt.	College
1.	Bell, Anthony	LB	6-3	231	Michigan State
2.	Lee, John	K	5-11	182	UCLA
3.	Chilton, Gene	C	6-3	271	Texas
4.	Carter, Carl	CB	5-11	180	Texas Tech
5.	Tupper, Jeff	DE	6-5	263	Oklahoma
7.	Swanson, Eric	WR	5-11	186	Tennessee
8.	Brown, Ray	G	6-5	257	Arkansas State
9.	Kafentzis, Kent	S	6-1	205	Hawaii
10.	Sikahema, Vai	RB	5-9	191	Brigham Young
10.	Smith, Wes	WR	5-11	194	East Texas State
11.	Dillard, Wayne	LB	6-2	232	Alcorn State
12.	Austin, Kent	QB	6-1	195	Mississippi

VETERAN ROSTER

No.	Name	Pos.	Ht.	Wt.	NFL Year	College
32	Anderson, Ottis	RB	6-2	225	8	Miami
60	Baker, Al	DE	6-6	270	9	Colorado State
52	Baker, Charlie	LB	6-2	234	7	New Mexico
74	Bergold, Scott	DT	6-7	263	2	Wisconsin
18	Birdsong, Carl	P	6-0	192	6	S.W. Oklahoma State
71	Bostic, Joe	G	6-3	265	8	Clemson
12	Brunner, Scott	QB	6-5	215	6	Delaware
64	Clark, Randy	C	6-4	270	7	Northern Illinois
66	Dawson, Doug	G	6-2	267	3	Texas
73	Duda, Mark	DT	6-3	279	4	Maryland
86	Duncan, Clyde	WR	6-2	211	3	Tennessee
31	Ferrell, Earl	RB	6-0	224	5	E. Tennessee State
65	Galloway, David	DT	6-3	279	5	Florida
87	Gray, Earnest	WR	6-3	191	8	Memphis State
81	Green, Roy	WR	6-0	195	8	Henderson State
75	Greer, Curtis	DE	6-4	258	7	Michigan
35	Griffin, Jeff	CB	6-0	185	6	Utah
78	Grooms, Elois	DT	6-4	250	12	Tennessee Tech
36	Harrington, Perry	RB	5-11	216	7	Jackson State
50	Harris, Bob	LB	6-2	205	4	Auburn
59	Howard, Thomas	LB	6-2	220	10	Texas Tech
42	Johnson, Bobby	S	6-0	187	4	Texas
54	Junior, E.J.	LB	6-3	235	6	Alabama
89	LaFleur, Greg	TE	6-4	236	6	Louisiana State
15	Lomax, Neil	QB	6-3	215	6	Portland State
40	Love, Randy	RB	6-1	224	8	Houston
47	Mack, Cedric	CB	6-0	194	4	Baylor
80	Marsh, Doug	TE	6-3	238	7	Michigan
76	Mays, Stafford	DE	6-2	255	7	Washington
14	McIvor, Rick	QB	6-4	210	3	Texas
30	Mitchell, Stump	RB	5-9	188	6	Citadel
51	Monaco, Rob	C	6-3	283	2	Vanderbilt
	Mumford, Tony	RB	6-0	215	2	Penn State
38	Nelson, Lee	S	5-10	185	11	Florida State
57	Noga, Niko	LB	6-1	235	3	Hawaii
28	Novacek, Jay	WR	6-4	217	2	Wyoming
53	Nunn, Freddie Joe	LB	6-4	228	2	Mississippi
23	Perrin, Benny	S	6-2	175	5	Alabama
72	Ralph, Dan	DT	6-4	260	2	Oregon
63	Robbins, Tootie	T	6-5	302	5	East Carolina
56	Scott, Carlos	C-T	6-4	285	4	Texas-El Paso
67	Sharpe, Luis	T	6-4	260	5	UCLA
84	Smith, J.T.	WR-PR	6-2	185	9	North Texas State
61	Smith, Lance	G	6-2	262	2	Louisiana State
45	Smith, Leonard	S	5-11	202	4	McNeese State
44	Smith, Wayne	CB	6-0	170	7	Purdue
55	Spradlin, Danny	LB	6-1	235	6	Tennessee
83	Tilley, Pat	WR	5-10	178	11	Louisiana Tech
33	Walker, Quentin	WR	6-1	200	2	Virginia
48	Washington, Lionel	CB	6-0	188	4	Tulane
42	Whitaker, Bill	S	6-0	182	5	Missouri
24	Wolfley, Ron	RB	6-0	222	2	West Virginia
43	Young, Lonnie	S	6-1	182	2	Michigan State

Wide receiver Roy 'Jetstream' Green could play a major role in bringing the Cardinals back into contention

WASHINGTON REDSKINS

Address Redskin Park, P.O. Box 17247, Dulles International Airport, Washington, D.C. 20041.

Stadium Robert F. Kennedy Stadium, Washington. *Capacity* 55,431 *Playing Surface* Grass (Prescription Athletic Turf).

Team Colours Burgundy and Gold.

Head Coach Joe Gibbs – sixth year.

Championships Division 1972, '83, '84;
Conference 1972, '82, '83;
NFL 1937, '42; Super Bowl 1982.

History NFL 1932-69, NFC 1970-
(Originally named the Boston Braves for the 1932 season only, they were renamed the Boston Redskins until, in 1937, they moved to Washington.)

Offense

Last year, the Redskins eased through a period of mini-transition. George Rogers became the senior running back ahead of John Riggins (he may be released); Gary Clark assumed the role of Art Monk's starting partner at wide receiver, and second-year quarterback Jay Schroeder did enough after Joe Theismann's Week Eleven injury to suggest that he could lead the club. It took a lot of nerve on the part of the Redskins ownership to trade with New Orleans for Rogers – players do not always perform up to scratch after a move, and there was some question of how he would share the playing time with Riggins in the Redskins' one-man backfield. Entering his fifth season, Rogers was expected to bring all the acceleration and speed that Riggins used to have and, at 229 pounds, he would not be short of power. He proved to be a good acquisition as, helped by a solid 677 yards from Riggins and the odd cameo performance from Keith Griffin (he rushed for 164 yards against Atlanta), he spearheaded the second-best rushing offense in the NFL. It was a team feat all the more remarkable for the absence of three of the Redskins' best offensive linemen. Right guard R.C. Thielemann (ex-Atlanta) missed most of the season, center Jeff Bostic missed six games, and left tackle Joe Jacoby was out for five. Between them, they have seven Pro Bowl selections and will line up together with Russ Grimm, a three-time Pro Bowler, at left guard, and Mark May at right tackle. Guard Ken Huff will probably rejoin the two good backups, tackle Dan McQuaid and guard Raleigh McKenzie. Tight ends Clint Didier and Don Warren are used predominantly as blockers, but Didier is a more-than-useful pass receiver. Last year, his fourth in the league, he doubled his number of career receptions with 41. At wide receiver, Malcolm Barnwell, who was obtained in a preseason trade with the Raiders, was not a success. And his former Raiders teammate, Calvin Muhammad, was out of touch before missing the last four games with injury. On the other hand, Clark was a sensation. A USFL defector and entering his first NFL season, he

rated only a few lines in the Redskins media handout but, by the end of the campaign, he and Monk, combined, had caught more passes than any other pair in the league. After establishing an NFL single-season record with 106 receptions in 1984, Monk followed up with 91 catches for his second 1,000-yards-receiving season in a row. With Theismann not certain to regain his former sparkle, quarterback Schroeder may have to shoulder the responsibility.

Defense

The feature of the 1985 defense was its amazing improvement, from 25th in 1984, to first in the entire league for defense against the pass – and this whilst fielding two rookies in place of injured veterans for much of the time. Raphel Cherry, who started in the final six games after injury to Tony Peters, should retain his place at strong safety. Defensive right tackle Dean Hamel, who had six sacks after coming in halfway through the season for the injured Darryl Grant, may have to step down. However, he will be an excellent reserve in company with second-round draftee Markus Koch. Elsewhere, several veterans turned in outstanding performances. Defensive ends Dexter Manley and Charles Mann had 15 and 14.5 sacks respectively, and defensive tackle Dave Butz had five sacks whilst taking the brunt of the run. Behind the four-man front, starting linebackers Mel Kaufman, Neal Olkewicz and Rich Milot, are very solid, with Monte Coleman available for spot duty. The secondary centres around free safety Curtis Jordan, who led the club with 178 tackles (Olkewicz had 174) and shared the lead with five pass interceptions. Of the starting cornerbacks, Vernon Dean confirmed his return to form with five interceptions, and Darrell Green added the extra dimension of great subtlety to his undoubted speed. Last year's rookie cornerback, Barry Wilburn, survived his baptism of fire and, together with Peters, gives the club sound reserves.

1986 SCHEDULE OF GAMES	September	
	7 PHILADELPHIA	1:00
	14 LOS ANGELES RAIDERS	1:00
	21 at San Diego	1:00
	28 SEATTLE	1:00
	October	
	5 at New Orleans	12:00
	12 at Dallas	12:00
	19 ST LOUIS	1:00
	27 at New York Giants (Mon.)	9:00
	November	
	2 MINNESOTA	4:00
	9 at Green Bay	12:00
	17 SAN FRANCISCO (Mon.)	9:00
	23 DALLAS	1:00
	30 at St Louis	12:00
	December	
	7 NEW YORK GIANTS	1:00
	13 at Denver (Sat.)	2:00
	21 at Philadelphia	1:00

Special Teams

Following the retirement of Minnesota's Jan Stenerud, placekicker Mark Moseley has become the NFL's leading active scorer (he has 1,321 points). Steady, as distinct from being a long-range field goal threat, he is returning for a 15th year. Punter Steve Cox took over from the injured Jeff Hayes and might well keep the position since he doubles as a reserve placekicker. Returning kickoffs, Ken Jenkins logged a 95-yarder in averaging a respectable 24.8. Also, Jenkins drives for that extra yardage on punt returns (he averaged a good 10.5 yards). However, the big return is always likely to come from cornerback Green, who averaged 13.4 yards on 16 attempts and was unfortunate to see two touchdowns nullified by infringements.

1986 DRAFT

Round	Name	Pos.	Ht.	Wt.	College
2.	Koch, Markus	DT	6-5	260	Boise State
2.	Murray, Walter	WR	6-3	200	Hawaii
3.	Walton, Alvin	S	5-11	191	Kansas
5.	Caldwell, Ravin	LB	6-3	224	Arkansas
6.	Rypien, Mark	QB	6-4	234	Washington State
6.	Huddleston, Jim	G	6-4	245	Virginia
7.	Badanjek, Rick	RB	5-8	217	Maryland
8.	Gouveia, Kurt	LB	6-1	213	Brigham Young
9.	Asberry, Wayne	DB	5-9	187	Texas A&M
11.	Fells, Kenny	RB	6-0	190	Henderson, Arkansas
12.	Yarber, Eric	WR	5-9	155	Idaho

VETERAN ROSTER

No.	Name	Pos.	Ht.	Wt.	NFL Year	College
58	Anderson, Stuart	LB	6-1	225	5	Virginia
67	Beasley, Tom	DE	6-5	248	9	Virginia Tech
53	Bostic, Jeff	C	6-2	260	7	Clemson
30	Branch, Reggie	RB	5-11	227	2	East Carolina
65	Butz, Dave	DT	6-7	295	14	Purdue
37	Cherry, Raphel	S	6-0	194	2	Hawaii
84	Clark, Gary	WR	5-9	173	2	James Madison
48	Coffey, Ken	S	6-0	190	3	Southwest Texas State
51	Coleman, Monte	LB	6-2	230	8	Central Arkansas
12	Cox, Steve	P	6-4	195	6	Arkansas
	Dailey, Darnell	LB	6-3	250	1	Maryland
32	Dean, Vernon	CB	5-11	178	5	San Diego State
86	Didier, Clint	TE	6-5	240	5	Portland State
77	Grant, Darryl	DT	6-1	275	6	Rice
28	Green, Darrell	CB	5-8	170	4	Texas A&I
35	Griffin, Keith	RB	5-8	185	3	Miami
68	Grimm, Russ	G	6-3	275	6	Pittsburgh
78	Hamel, Dean	DT	6-3	275	2	Tulsa
64	Hamilton, Steve	DE	6-4	255	2	East Carolina
5	Hayes, Jeff	P	5-11	175	5	North Carolina
61	Huff, Ken	G	6-4	265	12	North Carolina
66	Jacoby, Joe	T	6-7	305	6	Louisville
	Jenkins, Ken	RB-KR	5-8	185	4	Bucknell
82	Jones, Anthony	TE	6-3	248	3	Wichita State
22	Jordan, Curtis	S	6-2	205	10	Texas Tech
55	Kaufman, Mel	LB	6-2	218	6	Cal Poly-SLO
63	Kimball, Bruce	G	6-2	260	3	Massachusetts
16	Laufenberg, Babe	QB	6-2	195	3	Indiana
	Lee, Danzell	TE	6-2	232	1	Lamar
72	Manley, Dexter	DE	6-3	250	6	Oklahoma State
71	Mann, Charles	DE	6-6	260	4	Nevada-Reno
73	May, Mark	T	6-6	295	6	Pittsburgh
	McClearn, Mike	T	6-4	273	1	Temple
83	McGrath, Mark	WR	5-11	175	5	Montana State
63	McKenzie, Raleigh	G	6-2	262	2	Tennessee
60	McQuaid, Dan	T	6-7	278	2	Nevada-Las Vegas
57	Milot, Rich	LB	6-4	237	8	Penn State
81	Monk, Art	WR	6-3	209	7	Syracuse
3	Moseley, Mark	K	6-0	204	15	Stephen F. Austin
89	Muhammad, Calvin	WR	6-0	190	5	Texas Southern
	Newton, Mike	RB	5-11	227	1	South Connecticut
52	Olkewicz, Neal	LB	6-0	233	8	Maryland
	Orr, Terry	TE	6-3	227	1	Texas
	Osswald, Chris	C-G	6-4	255	1	Wisconsin
23	Peters, Tony	S	6-1	190	11	Oklahoma
80	Phillips, Joe	WR	5-9	188	2	Kentucky
44	Riggins, John	RB	6-2	240	15	Kansas
38	Rogers, George	RB	6-2	229	6	South Carolina
	Rosborough, Willie	DE	6-4	243	1	Washington
10	Schroeder, Jay	QB	6-4	215	3	UCLA
75	Slater, Bob	DT	6-4	265	1	Oklahoma
7	Theismann, Joe	QB	6-0	198	13	Notre Dame
69	Thielemann, R.C.	G	6-4	262	10	Arkansas
	Vital, Lionel	RB	5-9	195	1	Nicholls State
88	Walker, Rick	TE	6-4	235	10	UCLA
85	Warren, Don	TE	6-4	242	8	San Diego State
45	Wilburn, Barry	CB	6-3	186	2	Mississippi
47	Williams, Greg	S	5-11	185	5	Mississippi State
34	Williams, Kevin	CB	5-9	169	2	Iowa State
39	Wonsley, Otis	RB	5-10	214	6	Alcorn State

Russ Grimm (#68), the Redskins' dominating left guard, has been selected to the last three Pro Bowls

CHICAGO BEARS

NFC CENTRAL DIVISION

Address 250 N. Washington, Lake Forest, Illinois 60045.
Stadium Soldier Field, Chicago.
   Capacity 65,790 *Playing Surface* AstroTurf.
Team Colours Navy Blue, Orange, and White.
Head Coach Mike Ditka – fifth year.
Championships Division 1984, '85; Conference 1985;
   NFL 1921, '32, '33, '40, '41, '43, '46, '63; Super Bowl 1985.
History NFL 1920-69, NFC 1970-
   (Before 1922, they were known as firstly the Decatur
   Staleys and then the Chicago Staleys.)

Offense

It is difficult to find the slightest weakness in a Chicago squad which is knee deep in talent. Of the starting offensive linemen which rode shotgun for the league's best rushing offense, right tackle Keith Van Horne is the elder statesman, and he's only twenty-eight years old! Of the others, both left tackle Jim Covert and center Jay Hilgenberg started in the Pro Bowl. Left guard Mark Bortz is a very solid player, and at right guard, a position which could have been a problem, rookie Tom Thayer was outstanding as a replacement for Kurt Becker. Becker may not regain his starting spot. The NFL's all-time career rushing leader, Walter Payton, goes on and on. It is both testimony to his greatness and a sobering thought, that, after his retirement, his records could last into the twenty-first century. Matt Suhey will probably remain as Payton's partner, with Dennis Gentry, Calvin Thomas, Thomas Sanders and first-round draftee Neal Anderson ready to take full advantage of any opportunities which arise. Quarterback Jim McMahon has little more to prove. He's quick to move around in the backfield, throws a good pass, and is audacious in the Bears' mould. If he does have a weakness, it may be his very confidence which, at times, borders on the foolhardy. He'll take off and bootleg into the jaws of hell and, once or twice, even in Super Bowl XX, he appeared to throw the ball up for grabs. Wide receiver Willie Gault is tailor-made for McMahon's ambitious style of play. He is excellent when making those late adjustments before turning on his world-class speed. It comes as a surprise, however, to note that he caught only one touchdown pass in the 1985 regular season. Gault's starting partner, Dennis McKinnon, may be out all year with injury, and the Bears were fortunate to find David Williams, a fine prospect, still available in round three of the draft. McKinnon was the clutch receiver, brave and with terrific hands. Of the existing veterans, Ken Margerum is his obvious replacement, unless Williams turns out to be really special. The Bears could well have found a real star in tight end Tim Wrightman. It was known that he was a fine receiver, but his ability to block with such certainty was an unexpected bonus. For the moment, he may have to wait behind Emery Moorehead but, without doubt, he's the man for the future.

Defense

Former defensive coordinator Buddy Ryan took a good defense and turned it into one of the greatest of all time. He brought the best out of his squad by using a daring system, the '46 Defense'. Ryan's replacement, Vince Tobin, is said to be thinking of adopting a 3-4 alignment. Even so, the Bears are unlikely to be more generous than last year when they ranked first in the league. No NFL team, except perhaps Philadelphia, has a pair of defensive ends to merit comparison with the combination of Richard Dent and Dan Hampton. Despite attracting multiple coverage, Dent led the league with 17 quarterback sacks. And whilst Hampton had only 5.5, he too had to fight his way through the ranks massed to stop him. Both players are extremely versatile. Dent occasionally can be seen dropping back into pass coverage, and Hampton is virtually unstoppable when he lines up opposite the center. Undoubtedly, the play of these two helped to amplify the effectiveness of William Perry in his rookie year; nonetheless, the big lad did well enough, both as a defensive tackle and elsewhere, to justify his high position in the 1985 draft. The linebackers are awesomely good. Given the freedom to dog the quarterback, outside linebackers Otis Wilson and Wilber Marshall had 11.5 and six sacks respectively. Middle linebacker Mike Singletary calls out the defensive signals, mostly 'red for stop', and is widely regarded as the NFL's best in his position. The defensive secondary is still considered a relative weakness and they will miss cornerback Leslie Frazier, who led the team with six interceptions but is injured and may not play in 1986. Of the remaining starters, free safety Gary Fencik led the club in tackles, as usual, and strong safety Dave Duerson went to the Pro Bowl. Draftee Vestee Jackson will compete with Reggie Phillips and Ken Taylor to pair up with Mike Richardson in the cornerback positions.

1986 SCHEDULE OF GAMES	September	
	7 CLEVELAND	12:00
	14 PHILADELPHIA	12:00
	22 at Green Bay (Mon.)	8:00
	28 at Cincinnati	1:00
	October	
	5 MINNESOTA	12:00
	12 at Houston	12:00
	19 at Minnesota	12:00
	26 DETROIT	12:00
	November	
	3 LOS ANGELES RAMS (Mon.)	8:00
	9 at Tampa Bay	1:00
	16 at Atlanta	1:00
	23 GREEN BAY	12:00
	30 PITTSBURGH	12:00
	December	
	7 TAMPA BAY	12:00
	15 at Detroit (Mon.)	9:00
	21 at Dallas	3:00

Special Teams

The Bears have an edge in most areas of special-teams play. Gault and Dennis Gentry averaged 26.2 and 25.9 yards respectively, returning kickoffs. Gault scored on a 99-yard return and Gentry did likewise with a 94-yarder. Rookie placekicker Kevin Butler repeatedly turned good field position into points, missing on only six of 37 field goal attempts. Similarly, punter Maury Buford maintained a sound 42.2-yard gross average. Two adequate punt returners, Ken Taylor and Keith Ortego, should retain the least glamorous job in football.

1986 DRAFT

Round	Name	Pos.	Ht.	Wt.	College
1.	Anderson, Neal	RB	6-0	207	Florida
2.	Jackson, Vestee	CB	6-0	186	Washington
3.	Williams, David	WR	6-3	187	Illinois
4.	Blair, Paul	T	6-4	290	Oklahoma State
5.	Barnes, Lew	WR	5-8	163	Oregon
6.	Powell, Jeff	RB	5-10	170	Tennessee
7.	Jones, Bruce	DB	6-1	195	North Alabama
8.	Douglass, Maurice	CB	5-11	200	Kentucky
9.	Teltschik, John	P	6-1	207	Texas
10.	Hundley, Barton	DB	5-11	187	Kansas State
11.	Kozlowski, Glen	WR	6-1	193	Brigham Young

VETERAN ROSTER

No.	Name	Pos.	Ht.	Wt.	NFL Year	College
86	Anderson, Brad	WR	6-2	198	3	Arizona
60	Andrews, Tom	C	6-4	267	3	Louisville
84	Baschnagel, Brian	WR	6-0	193	10	Ohio State
79	Becker, Kurt	G	6-5	267	5	Michigan
62	Bortz, Mark	G	6-6	269	4	Iowa
8	Buford, Maury	P	6-1	191	5	Texas Tech
6	Butler, Kevin	K	6-1	204	2	Georgia
54	Cabral, Brian	LB	6-1	226	8	Colorado
74	Covert, Jim	T	6-4	271	4	Pittsburgh
95	Dent, Richard	DE	6-5	263	4	Tennessee State
22	Duerson, Dave	S	6-1	203	4	Notre Dame
88	Dunsmore, Pat	TE	6-3	237	3	Drake
45	Fencik, Gary	S	6-1	196	11	Yale
21	Frazier, Leslie	CB	6-0	187	6	Alcorn State
71	Frederick, Andy	T	6-6	265	10	New Mexico
4	Fuller, Steve	QB	6-4	195	8	Clemson
83	Gault, Willie	WR	6-1	183	4	Tennessee
23	Gayle, Shaun	CB	5-11	193	3	Ohio State
29	Gentry, Dennis	RB	5-8	181	5	Baylor
99	Hampton, Dan	DE	6-5	267	8	Arkansas
73	Hartenstine, Mike	DE	6-3	254	12	Penn State
63	Hilgenberg, Jay	C	6-3	258	6	Iowa
75	Humphries, Stefan	G	6-3	263	3	Michigan
98	Keys, Tyrone	DE	6-7	267	4	Mississippi State
89	Krenk, Mitch	TE	6-2	233	2	Nebraska
81	Maness, James	WR	6-1	174	2	Texas Christian
82	Margerum, Ken	WR	6-0	180	5	Stanford
58	Marshall, Wilber	LB	6-1	225	3	Florida
85	McKinnon, Dennis	WR	6-1	185	4	Florida State
9	McMahon, Jim	QB	6-1	190	5	Brigham Young
76	McMichael, Steve	DT	6-2	260	7	Texas
87	Moorehead, Emery	TE	6-2	220	10	Colorado
51	Morrissey, Jim	LB	6-3	215	2	Michigan State
89	Ortego, Keith	WR-PR	6-0	180	2	McNeese State
34	Payton, Walter	RB	5-10	202	12	Jackson State
72	Perry, William	DT	6-2	308	2	Clemson
48	Phillips, Reggie	DB	5-10	170	2	Southern Methodist
53	Rains, Dan	LB	6-1	220	3	Cincinnati
27	Richardson, Mike	CB	6-0	188	4	Arizona State
59	Rivera, Ron	LB	6-3	239	3	California
20	Sanders, Thomas	RB	5-11	203	2	Texas A&M
50	Singletary, Mike	LB	6-0	228	6	Baylor
26	Suhey, Matt	RB	5-11	216	7	Penn State
31	Taylor, Ken	CB-PR	6-1	185	2	Oregon State
57	Thayer, Tom	G-C	6-4	261	2	Notre Dame
33	Thomas, Calvin	RB	5-11	245	5	Illinois
52	Thrift, Cliff	LB	6-1	230	8	East Central Oklahoma
18	Tomczak, Mike	QB	6-1	195	2	Ohio State
78	Van Horne, Keith	T	6-6	280	6	Southern California
70	Waechter, Henry	DT	6-5	275	5	Nebraska
55	Wilson, Otis	LB	6-2	232	7	Louisville
80	Wrightman, Tim	TE	6-3	237	2	UCLA

Strong safety Dave Duerson took over from Todd Bell and made his first trip to the Pro Bowl

DETROIT LIONS

Address Pontiac Silverdome, 1200 Featherstone Road –
Box 4200, Pontiac, Michigan 48057.

Stadium Pontiac Silverdome.
Capacity 80,638 *Playing Surface* AstroTurf.

Team Colours Honolulu Blue and Silver.

Head Coach Darryl Rogers – second year.

Championships Division 1983; NFL 1935, '52, '53, '57.

History NFL 1930-69, NFC 1970-
(Until 1934, they were known as the Portsmouth (Ohio)
Spartans.)

Offense

The Detroit Lions went 7-9 on the season, beating Dallas, San Francisco, Miami, and the New York Jets, despite a rash of injuries which reached epidemic proportions. It takes some believing, but a total of thirty players missed, on average, nine games each because of injuries. On the offensive line, starting guards Don Greco and Chris Dieterich played together for only one quarter, missing eight and seven games respectively. It says a great deal for starting tackles Keith Dorney and rookie first-round pick Lomas Brown, and center Steve Mott, that the Lions had any kind of offense. Draftee tackle Joe Milinichik should help out. Top running back Billy Sims missed the entire year, and the man brought in to replace him, former Philadelphia player Wilbert Montgomery, too, was injured for nine games. It left James Jones to shoulder the burden, and the weight of his task is apparent from his low average per carry. Nonetheless, for his rushing and pro-ductivity as a receiver, he was voted the offensive MVP by his teammates. Draftee Garry James will inject a little pace into the offensive backfield. Another draftee, quarterback Chuck Long, could make a serious bid to start ahead of the incumbent, Eric Hipple. Long was considered to be one of the best two quarterbacks available and is sufficiently adaptable to make a quick adjustment to the pro style of play. However, Hipple will not be displaced easily – he's not what one might call a player of attractive style, but he's a tough competitor and he has seen off more than one challenger in the past. Wide receiver Leonard Thompson began catching passes back in 1976 and yet, even at the age of thirty-four, he remains at the top of his game. Last year, he caught a career-best 51 passes, and he is still extremely fast. His starting partner will be one of Mark Nichols, Jeff Chadwick, Pete Mandley and Carl Bland. All except Nichols caught passes for over 100 yards in a game last season, and he fell just short with 97 against Minnesota on Week Eleven. Tight end David Lewis was a first-round pick in 1984 but has yet to live up to that status. Nonethe-less, he will remain as the starter, ahead of Rob Rubick. Mark Brammer (ex-Buffalo), who has been acquired off waivers, may secure a place on the roster.

Defense

On defense, it was a similar story of injuries. Starting nose tackle Doug English, a four-time Pro Bowler, missed six games, and his replacement, Eric Williams, didn't return after taking a knock on Thanksgiving Day. Williams had been playing well at defensive end, where he had taken over from the injured Curtis Green, before moving inside. Continuing the game of musical linemen, Green replaced Williams at nose tackle, flanked by defensive ends Keith Ferguson and William Gay, the latter who played in the 1984 Pro Bowl. Williams should return, and though English has retired the Lions are quite well off in talent for the trenches. The linebacking corps, too, was ravaged by injuries, particularly important being those to starters Mike Cofer (nine games) and Ken Fantetti (eight games), the latter who has been released. Kurt Allerman missed five games, James Harrell nine, and the two rookies, James Johnson and Kevin Hancock, went down in training camp. Left outside linebacker Jimmy Williams had an excellent year, leading the club with 7.5 sacks, ahead of Gay and Green, who each had seven, and Eric Williams with 6.5. Again, perhaps by way of warning, the Lions can put out a very strong foursome to complement the front three. The starting secondary did stay healthy and helped the Lions to a ranking of 5th in the league for defense against the pass. They are all young – Demetrious Johnson is a veteran of three years whilst each of Bobby Watkins, William Graham and Bruce McNorton has played four – and have formed a really fine combination. Free safety Graham led the club in tackles (113) by some way from strong safety Johnson (97). There is adequate reserve strength in the speedy Alvin Hall, William Frizzell, and last year's rookies, Arnold Brown, John Bostic and Duane Galloway.

1986 SCHEDULE OF GAMES	September	
	7 at Minnesota	12:00
	14 DALLAS	1:00
	21 TAMPA BAY	1:00
	28 at Cleveland	1:00
	October	
	5 HOUSTON	1:00
	12 at Green Bay	12:00
	19 at Los Angeles Rams	1:00
	26 at Chicago	12:00
	November	
	2 CINCINNATI	1:00
	9 MINNESOTA	1:00
	16 at Philadelphia	1:00
	23 at Tampa Bay	1:00
	27 GREEN BAY (Thanksgiving)	12:30
	December	
	7 at Pittsburgh	1:00
	15 CHICAGO (Mon.)	9:00
	21 ATLANTA	1:00

Special Teams

Punter Mike Black is not spectacular but he's reliable and continues to average over 41 yards. Placekicker Eddie Murray is a good one. In 1985, he was successful on twelve consecutive field goal attempts and on 18 of the last 20. Pete Mandley averaged an excellent 10.6 yards over 38 punt returns, one of which he took 63 yards for a touchdown. He has the speed and moves to share the kickoff return duties with Alvin Hall.

1986 DRAFT

Round	Name	Pos.	Ht.	Wt.	College
1.	Long, Chuck	QB	6-4	211	Iowa
2.	James, Garry	RB	5-10	204	Louisiana State
3.	Milinichik, Joe	T	6-5	300	North Carolina State
4.	Mitchell, Devon	CB	6-1	194	Iowa
5.	Smith, Oscar	RB	5-9	203	Nicholls State
8.	Griffin, Allyn	WR	6-2	189	Wyoming
9.	Pickens, Lyle	CB	5-10	165	Colorado
10.	Johnson, Tracy	LB	6-1	244	Morningside
11.	Melvin, Leland	WR	5-11	175	Richmond
12.	Durden, Allan	DB	5-11	167	Arizona

VETERAN ROSTER

No.	Name	Pos.	Ht.	Wt.	NFL Year	College
95	Allerman, Kurt	LB	6-2	232	10	Penn State
68	Baack, Steve	NT-DE	6-4	265	3	Oregon
	Beauford, Clayton	WR	5-10	173	1	Auburn
11	Black, Mike	P	6-2	197	4	Arizona State
80	Bland, Carl	WR	5-11	182	3	Virginia Union
42	Bostic, John	CB	5-10	178	2	Bethune-Cookman
	Brammer, Mark	TE	6-3	235	6	Michigan State
23	Brown, Arnold	CB	5-11	185	2	North Carolina Central
75	Brown, Lomas	T	6-4	282	2	Florida
89	Chadwick, Jeff	WR	6-3	190	4	Grand Valley State
55	Cofer, Mike	LB	6-5	245	4	Tennessee
	Collins, Dwight	WR	6-1	208	2	Pittsburgh
50	Curley, August	LB	6-3	226	4	Southern California
44	D'Addio, Dave	RB	6-1	229	2	Maryland
72	Dieterich, Chris	G-T	6-3	260	7	North Carolina State
93	Dodge, Kirk	LB	6-1	231	2	Nevada-Las Vegas
70	Dorney, Keith	T	6-5	270	8	Penn State
66	Evans, Leon	DE	6-5	282	2	Miami
12	Ferguson, Joe	QB	6-1	195	14	Arkansas
77	Ferguson, Keith	DE	6-5	260	6	Ohio State
26	Frizzell, William	S	6-3	195	3	North Carolina Central
40	Galloway, Duane	CB	5-8	181	1	Arizona State
79	Gay, William	DE	6-5	260	9	Southern California
53	Glover, Kevin	C-G	6-2	267	2	Maryland
33	Graham, William	S	5-11	191	5	Texas
67	Greco, Don	G	6-3	265	5	Western Illinois
62	Green, Curtis	DE	6-3	258	6	Alabama State
35	Hall, Alvin	S	5-10	184	6	Miami (Ohio)
	Hancock, Kevin	LB	6-2	224	1	Baylor
58	Harrell, James	LB	6-1	230	7	Florida
17	Hipple, Eric	QB	6-2	198	7	Utah State
96	James, June	LB	6-1	218	2	Texas
21	Johnson, Demetrious	S	5-11	190	4	Missouri
	Johnson, James	LB	6-2	236	1	San Diego State
34	Jones, A.J.	RB	6-1	215	5	Texas
51	Jones, David	C-G	6-3	260	3	Texas
30	Jones, James	RB	6-2	229	4	Florida
92	King, Angelo	LB	6-1	222	6	South Carolina State
87	Lewis, David	TE	6-3	235	3	California
82	Mandley, Pete	WR-KR	5-10	191	4	Northern Arizona
98	Maxwell, Vernon	LB	6-2	235	4	Arizona State
29	McNorton, Bruce	CB	5-11	175	5	Georgetown, Kentucky
36	Meade, Mike	RB	5-11	227	5	Penn State
28	Montgomery, Wilbert	RB	5-10	195	10	Abilene Christian
24	Moore, Alvin	RB	6-0	194	4	Arizona State
52	Mott, Steve	C	6-3	265	4	Alabama
3	Murray, Ed	K	5-10	175	7	Tulane
86	Nichols, Mark	WR	6-2	208	6	San Jose State
84	Rubick, Rob	TE	6-3	234	5	Grand Valley State
65	Stevenson, Mark	G-C	6-3	285	2	Western Illinois
71	Strenger, Rich	T	6-7	276	3	Michigan
39	Thompson, Leonard	WR	5-11	192	12	Oklahoma State
60	Turnure, Tom	C-G	6-4	253	6	Washington
27	Watkins, Bobby	CB	5-10	184	5	Southwest Texas State
76	Williams, Eric	DE-NT	6-4	270	3	Washington State
59	Williams, Jimmy	LB	6-3	230	5	Nebraska
18	Witkowski, John	QB	6-1	205	2	Columbia

Linebacker Jimmy Williams was voted the club's outstanding defensive player by his teammates

GREEN BAY PACKERS

Address 1265 Lombardi Avenue, Green Bay, Wisconsin 54307-0628.

Stadium Lambeau Field, Green Bay, and Milwaukee County Stadium, Milwaukee.
Capacity (Lambeau Field) 56,926, (Milwaukee County Stadium) 55,976 *Playing Surfaces* Grass, both stadia.

Team Colours Dark Green, Gold, and White.

Head Coach Forrest Gregg – third year.

Championships Division 1972;
NFL 1929,'30,'31,'36,'39,'44,'61,'62,'65,'66,'67;
Super Bowl 1966,'67.

History NFL 1921-69, NFC 1970-

Offense

There's nothing unusual when the Packers go 8-8 on the year – that's been their record in each of the last four full seasons. But the encouraging thing about last year was that they maintained par despite uncertainty, both on the offensive line and at quarterback. Injuries to veteran linemen Ron Hallstrom and Keith Uecker, and a late start by Greg Koch, disrupted the system at a time when they were blooding two rookies, left tackle Ken Ruettgers and left guard Rich Moran, and a second-year center, Mark Cannon. Later, tackle Karl Swanke, the Packers' best pass blocker, was injured. Head coach Gregg persisted with his young men, despite their inevitable early mistakes, and, towards the end of the season, they began to live up to their potential. Cannon was particularly impressive, having beaten off the competition from Blake Moore to occupy the position dominated for so long by the retired veteran, Larry McCarren. The quarterback position was unsettled, with all three of Lynn Dickey, Jim Zorn and Randy Wright seeing action. At one stage in the season, Dickey, who is seen as the superior player, appeared to have lost interest in the game. With the arrival of the enigmatic Vince Ferragamo to spice the pot, it may be late in the preseason before the picture clears. However, there's not much problem at wide receiver, where, last year, the mighty James Lofton caught 69 passes for 1,153 yards. Phil Epps had his finest campaign to date and, at tight end, the athletic Paul Coffman was at his reliable best. At running back, there's the solid punch provided by three consistently effective players, each of whom averaged 4.3 yards or better per carry. Using any two of Eddie Lee Ivery, Jessie Clark and Gerry Ellis, the Packers hammered to a rank of eleventh-best in the league. Top draftee Kenneth Davis brings that extra speed.

Defense

Careful drafting in recent years has brought about significant improvement in the Packers' defense. In 1983, they ranked 28th overall, 26th against the rush and 24th against the pass. In 1984, their numbers read 16th, 20th and 8th respectively, and last year, they were 12th, 16th and 13th. They still need help but, whereas they were having

trouble stopping the flood, the holes in the dyke are now plugged and they can afford to think of drafting by choice rather than out of necessity. The second-year players, defensive left end Alphonso Carreker and nose tackle Donnie Humphrey, have become established alongside the indestructible veteran defensive right end, Ezra Johnson. For some time, Johnson, who was a Pro Bowler in 1979, has fought a lone battle. In 1984, after undergoing back surgery, he was restricted to the role of pass rusher. However, a subsequent operation seems to have corrected his disc problem and he returned to full-time active duty, leading the club with 9.5 sacks. In Carreker, who had nine sacks, he has found a partner in demolition. Linebacking has always been a Green Bay strength, even through the lean years. However, two solid veterans, Mike Douglass and Rich Wingo, were released in May. Douglass had been a starter since the beginning of the 1979 season and Wingo was a good backup on the inside. John Anderson and Randy Scott take care of the left side and 1985 rookie Brian Noble, a 237-pound missile, has moved ahead of George Cumby to start at right inside linebacker. Noble shared the team lead in tackles. Draftee Tim Harris will compete with Guy Prather to take over from Douglass at right outside linebacker. The starting secondary of cornerbacks Mark Lee and Tim Lewis, and safeties Tom Flynn and Mark Murphy, is well respected. Opposing quarterbacks stayed clear of Flynn, who led the NFC with nine interceptions in 1984. Lewis, who had a team-leading four interceptions, is now showing the kind of form the Packers expected when they made him a first-round pick in 1983. Murphy, the strong safety, is coming off the second exceptional year in a row, having shared the club lead in tackles and registering four sacks. He will remain ahead of Mossy Cade, who was a 1984 first-round pick of San Diego and might have been expected to start elsewhere in the league.

1986 SCHEDULE OF GAMES	September	
	7 HOUSTON	12:00
	14 at New Orleans	12:00
	22 CHICAGO (Mon.)	8:00
	28 at Minnesota	12:00
	October	
	5 CINCINNATI at Milwaukee	12:00
	12 DETROIT	12:00
	19 at Cleveland	1:00
	26 SAN FRANCISCO at Milwaukee	12:00
	November	
	2 at Pittsburgh	1:00
	9 WASHINGTON	12:00
	16 TAMPA BAY at Milwaukee	12:00
	23 at Chicago	12:00
	27 at Detroit (Thanksgiving)	12:30
	December	
	7 MINNESOTA	12:00
	14 at Tampa Bay	1:00
	20 at New York Giants (Sat.)	12:30

Special Teams

The Packers could do with a little more sparkle in their special teams play. Al Del Greco is a respectable place-kicker but presents no threat from long range. Also, three of his field-goal attempts, including a 25-yarder, were blocked. Don Bracken took over as punter from Joe Prokop, during the second half of the season, but was not much more effective and could be challenged in training camp. Walter Stanley may be given more opportunities ahead of the senior returners, Epps and Ellis on kickoffs, and Epps on punts, after showing good form in his rookie year.

1986 DRAFT

Round	Name	Pos.	Ht.	Wt.	College
2.	Davis, Kenneth	RB	5-10	212	Texas Christian
3.	Bosco, Robbie	QB	6-2	188	Brigham Young
4.	Harris, Tim	LB	6-7	235	Memphis State
4.	Knight, Dan	T	6-5	283	San Diego State
5.	Koart, Matt	NT	6-6	245	Southern California
6.	Dent, Burnell	LB	6-1	223	Tulane
7.	Berry, Ed	DB	5-11	176	Utah State
8.	Cline, Michael	NT	6-3	240	Arkansas State
9.	Moore, Brent	NT	6-5	235	Southern California
10.	Spann, Gary	LB	6-1	215	Texas Christian

VETERAN ROSTER

No.	Name	Pos.	Ht.	Wt.	NFL Year	College
59	Anderson, John	LB	6-3	229	9	Michigan
17	Bracken, Don	P	6-0	205	2	Michigan
93	Brown, Robert	DE	6-2	250	5	Virginia Tech
39	Burgess, Ronnie	DB	5-11	175	2	Wake Forest
77	Butler, Mike	DE	6-5	269	8	Kansas
24	Cade, Mossy	DB	6-1	195	2	Texas
58	Cannon, Mark	C	6-3	258	3	Texas-Arlington
76	Carreker, Alphonso	DE	6-6	260	3	Florida State
23	Clanton, Chuck	DB	5-11	192	2	Auburn
33	Clark, Jessie	RB	6-0	233	4	Arkansas
82	Coffman, Paul	TE	6-3	225	9	Kansas State
	Collins, Glen	DE	6-6	265	5	Mississippi State

No.	Name	Pos.	Ht.	Wt.	NFL Year	College
52	Cumby, George	LB	6-0	224	7	Oklahoma
10	Del Greco, Al	K	5-10	195	3	Auburn
88	Dennard, Preston	WR	6-1	183	9	New Mexico
99	Dorsey, John	LB	6-2	235	3	Connecticut
42	Ellerson, Gary	RB	5-11	220	2	Wisconsin
31	Ellis, Gerry	RB	5-11	225	7	Missouri
85	Epps, Phillip	WR	5-10	165	5	Texas Christian
5	Ferragamo, Vince	QB	6-3	217	9	Nebraska
41	Flynn, Tom	S	6-0	195	3	Pittsburgh
65	Hallstrom, Ron	G	6-6	283	5	Iowa
27	Hayes, Gary	DB	5-10	180	3	Fresno State
25	Huckleby, Harlan	RB	6-1	201	7	Michigan
74	Huffman, Tim	G	6-5	282	6	Notre Dame
79	Humphrey, Donnie	NT	6-3	275	3	Auburn
40	Ivery, Eddie Lee	RB	6-0	214	7	Georgia Tech
90	Johnson, Ezra	DE	6-4	259	10	Morris Brown
43	Jones, Daryll	DB	6-0	190	3	Georgia
63	Jones, Terry	NT	6-2	253	8	Alabama
68	Koch, Greg	T	6-4	276	10	Arkansas
22	Lee, Mark	CB	5-11	188	7	Washington
89	Lewis, Mark	TE	6-2	218	2	Texas A&M
26	Lewis, Tim	CB	5-11	191	4	Pittsburgh
80	Lofton, James	WR	6-3	197	9	Stanford
94	Martin, Charles	DE	6-4	270	3	Livingston
28	McLeod, Mike	DB	6-0	180	3	Montana State
57	Moran, Rich	C-G	6-2	272	2	San Diego State
37	Murphy, Mark	S	6-2	201	6	W. Liberty State, W. Va.
91	Noble, Brian	LB	6-3	237	2	Arizona State
	Obrovac, Mike	G	6-6	275	4	Bowling Green
51	Prather, Guy	LB	6-2	229	6	Grambling State
35	Rodgers, Del	RB	5-10	202	3	Utah
75	Ruettgers, Ken	T	6-5	267	2	Southern California
55	Scott, Randy	LB	6-1	222	6	Alabama
87	Stanley, Walter	WR-KR	5-9	180	2	Mesa College
29	Stills, Ken	DB	5-10	185	2	Wisconsin
67	Swanke, Karl	T-C	6-6	262	7	Boston College
	Thomas, Bob	K	5-10	177	11	Notre Dame
70	Uecker, Keith	G-T	6-5	270	5	Auburn
86	West, Ed	TE	6-1	242	3	Auburn
61	Wingle, Blake	G	6-2	260	4	UCLA
16	Wright, Randy	QB	6-2	194	3	Wisconsin
18	Zorn, Jim	QB	6-2	200	11	Cal Poly-Pomona

Veteran defensive end Ezra Johnson (#90) returned to his best form and led the Packers in quarterback sacks

MINNESOTA VIKINGS

Address 9520 Viking Drive, Eden Prairie, Minnesota 55344.
Stadium Hubert H. Humphrey Metrodome, Minneapolis.
  Capacity 62,212 *Playing Surface* Super Turf.
Team Colours Purple, Gold, and White.
Head Coach Jerry Burns – first year.
Championships Division 1970, '71, '73, '74, '75, '76, '77, '78, '80;
  Conference 1973, '74, '76; NFL 1969.
History NFL 1961-69, NFC 1970-

Offense

It is a re-invigorated squad which enters the 1986 season under Bud Grant's long-time assistant, new head coach Jerry Burns. The Vikings have made a start towards improving the offensive line by acquiring Gary Zimmerman, a top-rated player who spent two seasons in the USFL after leaving college. He could start right away on the left side, ahead of either guard Brent Boyd or tackle David Huffman. The offensive line is not a dominating feature of the Vikings game but, on the right side, the regular starters, guard Terry Tausch and tackle Tim Irwin, should continue to give good service. The main purpose of the line is pass protection – Minnesota is not a club which tries to rush the daylights out of the opposition – and that means looking after quarterback Tommy Kramer. Despite having suffered severe injuries in the past, Kramer is still some way ahead of his backups, Wade Wilson and Steve Bono. With wide receiver Sammy White beginning to slow, Anthony Carter made a timely entry into the league, and he seems certain to add his name to a Vikings honour roll which includes White, Ahmad Rashad and John Gilliam. Carter equalled Gilliam's records for the most 100-yards-receiving games by a rookie, with five. Four of his big games came in the last six weeks. The quick-footed Mike Jones is a useful partner, indeed, he caught more passes than Carter though at an average of 13.9 yards compared with Carter's excellent 19.1. Starting tight end Steve Jordan has made dramatic improvement in each of the last three seasons and now is a fully paid-up partner in the company of receivers. Over his four-year career, he has caught passes for 42, 212, 414 and 795 yards respectively, the latter figure representing the best among NFC tight ends. If he could find a way of breaking into the end zone (he has only five career touchdowns, four by pass reception), he'd be a candidate for the Pro Bowl. Darrin Nelson was easily the most productive of the Vikings' four running backs and will continue to start, with Alfred Anderson as his partner, backed up by the versatile Ted Brown.

Defense

On defense, things haven't been all that rosy up in Minnesota for some time. And it would be rash to predict that they were going to dominate the league, and yet, they've improved steadily over the last three campaigns,

helped in no little part by last year's rookies, defensive end Keith Millard and nose tackle Tim Newton. Millard became established on the right side and led the team with 11 sacks. Newton is Minnesota's equivalent of Chicago's William Perry – he is known as the 'Icebox'. Unlike Perry, Newton didn't attract much media attention, but he did start in fourteen games, and that augurs well for the future. Defensive left end Doug Martin came back well after his inconsistent 1984 performance (in that year he was slowed by injuries) and, if he can return to anything like his best, the three-man front will soon be coining its own nickname. Another player who could be a factor is Neil Elshire, a former starter who went off the boil in 1984 but gave indications of returning to his best, seeing action as the specialist pass rusher. First-round draftee Gerald Robinson is the latest step in the Vikings' attempts to improve the front seven. He was a defensive end in college and, at 253 pounds, can handle himself. Indeed, he's the right size to compete for a spot at inside linebacker. The incumbents include outside linebacker Chris Doleman, a 1985 first-round pick, and the nine-year veteran, Scott Studwell, who plays on the inside and led the team with an astonishing 206 tackles (109 solos and 97 assists) last year. In the secondary, cornerback Rufus Bess will return from injury to challenge for a starting spot. On the same day that Bess established a Vikings club record by forcing three fumbles (Week One), strong safety Joey Browner equalled the NFL single-game record by recovering three fumbles. It was an early nudge for those who, later, would elect him to the Pro Bowl. John Turner, whose five interceptions led the club, holds down the free safety position, whilst Willie Teal is a fixture at right cornerback.

1986 SCHEDULE OF GAMES		
September		
7 DETROIT		12:00
14 at Tampa Bay		4:00
21 PITTSBURGH		12:00
28 GREEN BAY		12:00
October		
5 at Chicago		12:00
12 at San Francisco		1:00
19 CHICAGO		12:00
26 CLEVELAND		12:00
November		
2 at Washington		4:00
9 at Detroit		1:00
16 NEW YORK GIANTS		12:00
23 at Cincinnati		1:00
30 TAMPA BAY		12:00
December		
7 at Green Bay		12:00
14 at Houston		3:00
21 NEW ORLEANS		12:00

Special Teams

The Vikings are still searching for a placekicker to succeed the great Jan Stenerud, who has retired. But they're in good shape at punter, where Greg Coleman averaged 42.8 yards and ranked fourth in the NFC. Kickoff returner Buster Rhymes led the league, both in return yardage (1,345) and attempts (53), maintaining a really fine average of 25.4 yards. He gives the offense a valuable edge every time he lines up. Running back Nelson doubles as a steady punt returner with Anthony Carter available for occasional duty.

Buster Rhymes is always dangerous on kickoff returns

VETERAN ROSTER

No.	Name	Pos.	Ht.	Wt.	NFL Year	College
46	Anderson, Alfred	RB	6-1	213	3	Baylor
58	Ashley, Walker Lee	LB	6-0	231	3	Penn State
21	Bess, Rufus	CB	5-9	187	8	South Carolina State
59	Blair, Matt	LB	6-5	239	13	Iowa State
13	Bono, Steve	QB	6-3	211	2	UCLA
62	Boyd, Brent	G	6-3	275	6	UCLA
23	Brown, Ted	RB	5-10	206	8	North Carolina State
47	Browner, Joey	S	6-2	205	4	Southern California
84	Carroll, Jay	TE	6-4	230	3	Minnesota
81	Carter, Anthony	WR	5-11	162	2	Michigan
8	Coleman, Greg	P	6-0	180	10	Florida A&M
56	Doleman, Chris	LB	6-5	250	2	Pittsburgh
73	Elshire, Neil	DE	6-6	261	6	Oregon
64	Feasel, Grant	T-C	6-8	278	3	Abilene Christian
50	Fowlkes, Dennis	LB	6-2	236	4	West Virginia
80	Gustafson, Jim	WR	6-1	185	1	St Thomas
61	Hamilton, Wes	G	6-3	267	10	Tulsa
30	Holt, Issiac	CB	6-1	197	2	Alcorn State
51	Hough, Jim	C	6-2	268	9	Utah State
99	Howard, David	LB	6-2	225	2	Long Beach State
72	Huffman, David	G	6-6	255	7	Notre Dame
76	Irwin, Tim	T	6-7	288	6	Tennessee
89	Jones, Mike	WR	5-11	180	4	Tennessee State
83	Jordan, Steve	TE	6-3	231	5	Brown
9	Kramer, Tommy	QB	6-2	202	10	Rice
39	Lee, Carl	DB	5-11	185	4	Marshall
87	Lewis, Leo	WR	5-8	172	6	Missouri
63	Lowdermilk, Kirk	C	6-3	265	2	Ohio State
71	MacDonald, Mark	G	6-4	267	2	Boston College
57	Martin, Chris	LB	6-2	230	4	Auburn
79	Martin, Doug	DE	6-3	255	7	Washington
53	Meamber, Tim	LB	6-3	228	2	Washington
75	Millard, Keith	DE	6-6	260	2	Washington State
35	Morrell, Kyle	S	6-1	189	1	Brigham Young
86	Mularkey, Mike	TE	6-4	233	4	Florida
77	Mullaney, Mark	DE	6-6	242	12	Colorado State
20	Nelson, Darrin	RB	5-9	185	5	Stanford
96	Newton, Tim	NT	6-0	302	2	Florida
49	Nord, Keith	S	6-0	188	7	St Cloud State
88	Rhymes, Buster	WR	6-1	212	2	Oklahoma
36	Rice, Allen	RB	5-10	198	3	Baylor
28	Rosnagle, Ted	S	6-3	202	2	Portland State
68	Rouse, Curtis	G-T	6-3	318	5	Tenn.-Chattanooga
74	Smith, Robert	DE	6-5	245	2	Grambling State
55	Studwell, Scott	LB	6-2	231	10	Illinois
67	Swilley, Dennis	C	6-3	245	9	Texas A&M
66	Tausch, Terry	T	6-5	270	5	Texas
37	Teal, Willie	CB	5-10	192	7	Louisiana State
27	Turner, John	CB	6-0	199	9	Miami
85	White, Sammy	WR	5-11	200	11	Grambling State
11	Wilson, Wade	QB	6-3	210	6	East Texas State
	Zimmerman, Gary	T-G	6-5	271	R	Oregon

1986 DRAFT

Round	Name	Pos.	Ht.	Wt.	College
1.	Robinson, Gerald	DE	6-4	253	Auburn
4.	Phillips, Joe	NT	6-4	290	Southern Methodist
5.	Jones, Hassan	WR	6-0	198	Florida State
6.	Rooks, Thomas	RB	6-1	209	Illinois
7.	Hilton, Carl	TE	6-3	229	Houston
8.	Schippang, Gary	T	6-4	268	West Chester State
9.	Slaton, Mike	DB	6-2	191	South Dakota
10.	Cormier, Joe	TE	6-6	223	Southern California
11.	Armstrong, John	DB	5-9	190	Richmond
12.	Solomon, Jesse	LB	6-1	240	Florida State

TAMPA BAY BUCCANEERS

Address One Buccaneer Place, Tampa, Florida 33607.
Stadium Tampa Stadium, Tampa.
   Capacity 74,270 *Playing Surface* Grass.
Team Colours Florida Orange, White, and Red.
Head Coach Leeman Bennett – second year.
Championships Division 1979, '81.
History AFC 1976, NFC 1977-

Offense

Leading up to the collegiate draft, there was much speculation over whether or not the Buccaneers would use their prime option to select Bo Jackson. When came the day, they had no hesitation in picking a player who is said to be the greatest running back to emerge since O.J. Simpson – and that's praise indeed. It is not yet clear if Jackson will opt for playing pro football – he is also a first-class baseball player and could command an even higher salary were he to choose that career. If he does go to Tampa Bay, he will add breathtaking speed to an offensive backfield which, already, boasts the teak-toughness and outstanding versatility of James Wilder. If the offensive line is able to maintain anything like reasonable protection, the Buccaneers will become a force to be reckoned with. Head coach Leeman Bennett was sufficiently confident in his existing unit not to seek help with any of the Buccaneers' next four picks. The star of the offensive line would have to be Sean Farrell. Formally a right guard, he easily made the transition to left tackle when starter George Yarno was injured in mid-season. Marvin Powell (ex-Jets) will probably displace Yarno, enabling Farrell to move back to guard. Rick Mallory moved in at right guard and did enough to preserve his status as a good backup. Elsewhere, Randy Grimes took over from the Bucs' faithful veteran, Steve Wilson, as the starting center, whilst both left guard Steve Courson and right tackle Ron Heller confirmed their seniority. In the 1985 preseason, Steve DeBerg won his quarterback battle against Jack Thompson, who was subsequently released. However, he has given way to Steve Young, a good prospect who tried his hand in the USFL before coming to Tampa Bay. Let's reserve a few thoughts for DeBerg, a fine player, who lost out to Joe Montana at San Francisco and then John Elway at Denver. Young will be aiming his bombs in the direction of wide receiver Kevin House, a player with blazing speed who has averaged 17.2 yards per reception over his six NFL years. The other starting wide receiver, Gerald Carter, functions as an excellent foil for House and, in his own right, is a receiver of high class. Speaking of class, tight end Jimmie Giles is now back where he belongs, amongst the league's best.

Defense

The Buccaneers' All-Pro defensive end, Lee Roy Selmon, has lost his fight with injury and, after missing all last season, he has retired. However, last year's top rookie,

Ron Holmes, went some way towards making up for the absence of the great man, charging in from the defensive right end position. David Logan began his NFL career as a twelfth-round pick in 1979, but he has developed into one of the league's better nose tackles, not least for his ability to pressure the quarterback – he led the Bucs with 6.5 sacks in 1985. John Cannon is another honest competitor and holds down the defensive left end spot. The departure of outside linebacker Hugh Green, who was traded to Miami, was a severe blow. However, his replacement could have arrived via the draft, in which Jackie Walker and Kevin Murphy were taken in the second round. The Bucs like big linebackers and, at 241 pounds, Walker fits the bill. Murphy will be converted from defensive end, a position in which he starred at Oklahoma. It's a fearsome sight when the current starters, Ervin Randle, Jeff Davis, Scot Brantley and Chris Washington, settle into the 'ready' position. Reserve linebacker Keith Browner tackles with the force of a freight train. Of the four-man secondary, cornerbacks Jeremiah Castille and John Holt, and safety Ivory Sully started in every game. Strong safety David Greenwood had a mini-competition with Craig Curry but regained the starting spot he relinquished for six games halfway through the season. Draftee cornerback Rod Jones wasn't rated highly by the scouting combines but the Bucs liked him enough to make him their second pick in the first round.

Special Teams

Donald Igwebuike made a good start in the NFL and his field goal percentage was not helped by three failures, two from 62 yards and one from 55 yards out. He landed field goals of 53, 51 and 50 yards. Frank Garcia punted for a respectable 42.0-yard average. Leon Bright was burning up the ground, returning punts at an average of 10.3 yards, before being injured on Week Eight. His replacement, Mike Prior, was less effective. Rookie wide receiver Phil Freeman worked hard, returning kickoffs for 1,085 yards, and was unlucky not to go the distance with a 58-yarder.

1986 SCHEDULE OF GAMES	September	
	7 SAN FRANCISCO	1:00
	14 MINNESOTA	4:00
	21 at Detroit	1:00
	28 ATLANTA	4:00
	October	
	5 at Los Angeles Rams	1:00
	12 ST LOUIS	1:00
	19 at New Orleans	12:00
	26 at Kansas City	12:00
	November	
	2 BUFFALO	1:00
	9 CHICAGO	1:00
	16 vs. Green Bay at Milwaukee	12:00
	23 DETROIT	1:00
	30 at Minnesota	12:00
	December	
	7 at Chicago	12:00
	14 GREEN BAY	1:00
	21 at St Louis	12:00

1986 DRAFT

Round	Name	Pos.	Ht.	Wt.	College
1.	Jackson, Bo	RB	6-2	225	Auburn
1.	Jones, Roderick	CB	5-11	175	Southern Methodist
2.	Walker, Jackie	LB	6-5	245	Jackson State
2.	Murphy, Kevin	LB	6-2	230	Oklahoma
4.	Swoope, Craig	S	6-1	195	Illinois
5.	Maarleveld, J.D.	T	6-6	300	Maryland
6.	Walker, Kevin	CB	5-11	180	East Carolina
9.	Barnhardt, Tommy	P	6-2	205	North Carolina
10.	Reed, Ben	DE	6-5	270	Mississippi
11.	Drenth, Mark	G	6-5	280	Purdue
12.	Miller, Clay	G	6-4	280	Michigan
12.	Crawford, Mike	RB	5-10	200	Arizona State

VETERAN ROSTER

No.	Name	Pos.	Ht.	Wt.	NFL Year	College
	Aldredge, Corwyn	TE	6-5	225	1	Mississippi State
82	Bell, Jerry	TE	6-5	230	5	Arizona State
83	Bell, Theo	WR	6-0	190	10	Arizona
	Bendross, Jesse	WR	6-0	200	3	Alabama
52	Brantley, Scot	LB	6-1	230	7	Florida
29	Bright, Leon	RB-PR	5-9	200	6	Florida State
57	Browner, Keith	LB	6-5	240	3	Southern California
78	Cannon, John	DE	6-5	265	5	William & Mary
87	Carter, Gerald	WR	6-1	190	7	Texas A&M
23	Castille, Jeremiah	CB	5-10	175	4	Alabama
72	Courson, Steve	G	6-1	275	9	South Carolina
31	Curry, Craig	S	6-0	190	3	Texas
58	Davis, Jeff	LB	6-0	230	5	Clemson
17	DeBerg, Steve	QB	6-3	210	10	San Jose State
80	Dunn, K.D.	TE	6-3	235	2	Clemson
26	Easmon, Ricky	CB	5-10	160	2	Florida
62	Farrell, Sean	G	6-3	260	5	Penn State
65	Fielder, Don	DE	6-3	260	2	Kentucky
81	Freeman, Phil	WR	5-11	185	2	Arizona
5	Garcia, Frank	P	6-0	210	4	Arizona
88	Giles, Jimmie	TE	6-3	240	10	Alcorn State
30	Greenwood, David	S	6-3	210	2	Wisconsin
60	Grimes, Randy	C	6-4	270	4	Baylor
73	Heller, Ron	T	6-6	280	3	Penn State
90	Holmes, Ron	DE	6-4	255	2	Washington
21	Holt, John	CB	5-11	180	6	West Texas State
89	House, Kevin	WR	6-1	185	7	Southern Illinois
1	Igwebuike, Donald	K	5-9	185	2	Clemson
56	Johnson, Cecil	LB	6-2	235	10	Pittsburgh
55	Johnson, Dennis	LB	6-3	235	7	Southern California
79	Kaplan, Ken	T	6-4	275	3	New Hampshire
59	Kubin, Larry	LB	6-2	234	5	Penn State
75	Lindstrom, Chris	DE	6-7	260	3	Boston University
76	Logan, David	NT	6-2	250	8	Pittsburgh
86	Magee, Calvin	TE	6-3	240	2	Southern
68	Mallory, Rick	G	6-2	260	2	Washington
67	Morgan, Karl	NT	6-1	255	3	UCLA
38	Peoples, George	RB	6-0	215	4	Auburn
	Powell, Marvin	T	6-5	270	10	Southern California
24	Prior, Mike	DB	6-0	200	2	Illinois State
54	Randle, Ervin	LB	6-1	250	2	Baylor
7	Risher, Alan	QB	6-2	190	2	Louisiana State
74	Sanders, Gene	T	6-3	285	7	Texas A&M
64	Shearin, Joe	G	6-4	250	4	Texas
20	Springs, Ron	RB	6-2	225	8	Ohio State
71	Studaway, Mark	DE	6-4	275	3	Tennessee
44	Sully, Ivory	S	6-0	200	8	Delaware
84	Verser, David	WR	6-1	200	6	Kansas
51	Washington, Chris	LB	6-4	230	3	Iowa State
32	Wilder, James	RB	6-3	225	6	Missouri
85	Witte, Mark	TE	6-3	240	4	North Texas State
66	Yarno, George	T	6-2	265	7	Washington State
8	Young, Steve	QB	6-2	200	2	Brigham Young

Dual-purpose running back James Wilder is as tough as they come

ATLANTA FALCONS

Address Suwanee Road at I-85, Suwanee, Georgia 30174.
Stadium Atlanta-Fulton County Stadium.
   Capacity 60,748 *Playing Surface* Grass.
Team Colours Red, Black, White, and Silver.
Head Coach Dan Henning – fourth year.
Championships Division 1980.
History NFL 1966-69, NFC 1970-

Offense

The strength of the Falcons' offense lies in its rushing game, led by Gerald Riggs. It's no longer appropriate to regard Riggs as a stand-in for the injured William Andrews. Last year, when for much of the time he was a one-man offense, he led the NFC with 1,719 yards rushing, and trailed the NFL leader, Marcus Allen, by only 40 yards. Astonishingly, Riggs has now handled the ball 483 straight times (rushing and catching passes) without fumbling. The return of Andrews would be welcomed, but he could hardly improve on the existing ground game, and he might even disrupt a system which, currently, uses only one running back. Andrews' value would now be his ability to double as a pass receiver coming out of the backfield. There's an opening created by the release of Joe Washington, who was acquired from the Redskins to play that role. With the arrival of quarterback Turk Schonert, the former Cincinnati player who came to Atlanta in April, in exchange for the Falcons' 1986 third-round draft option, the passing game could be set for a change in style. Schonert has never been given an extended run, and he could turn out to have been a bargain acquisition. Still, he will have to establish his superiority over David Archer in training camp. As his prime targets, the starter will have wide receivers 'Downtown' Charlie Brown, Stacey Bailey and Billy 'White Shoes' Johnson. One of the original Washington 'Smurfs', Brown saw only limited action last year but, in the final two games, after shaking off his injuries, he looked sharp. Bailey needs to rediscover his form of the 1984 season, when he caught 67 passes for 1,138 yards and six touchdowns. Johnson is the kind of pro who could wear any number. (If he played cricket, he'd be the one who just picked up a bat at random and then went out and scored a century.) He has a fine pair of hands, good speed and he's cheeky with it. The Falcons use their tight ends mostly as blockers but, despite that responsibility, Arthur Cox has improved steadily as a receiver. The offensive line performed adequately, clearing the way for the rushers, but, for the second year in a row, they ranked dead last in the NFL for sacks yielded. The trio of center Jeff Van Note, left tackle Mike Kenn (he is a five-time Pro Bowler), and the outstanding 1985 rookie, Bill Fralic (he can play at either guard or tackle), gives the line a first-class nucleus. But there's an obvious need for another dominant player.

Defense

The statistics tell the story; the Falcons had trouble on defense for much of last year, when they gave up the highest number of points in the league. But wait a minute. Draftee Tony Casillas could be the superman they've been looking for, and he should make an immediate impact in the defensive line, where both left end Rick Bryan and left tackle Mike Pitts are former first-round picks. Each with 7.5 sacks, they shared the club lead. And it's always an indication of work-rate when two linemen come high in the list for solo tackles – they ranked second and third respectively. Defensive right end Mike Gann, a 1985 second-round pick, came through to start and had five sacks. If Casillas might turn out to be Superman, draftee Tim Green could be Captain Marvel at linebacker, which is another area in need of help. In trades with Philadelphia, the Falcons acquired Reggie Wilkes, a 1985 starter, and Joel Williams, who led the NFC with 16 sacks when playing for Atlanta in 1980. One of them will step in for Al Richardson, who has been released. On the inside, Green might start in partnership with Buddy Curry, who has led the team in tackles in all six of his years as a pro. Cornerback Bobby Butler, who led the team with five interceptions, is the pick of a secondary which, otherwise, is modest.

Special Teams

There are several bright spots in this area. Placekicker Mick Luckhurst now ranks among the league's best (his sequence of successful field goals came to an end at 17, the fourth-highest total in league history). Punter Rick Donnelly led the NFC with a gross average of 43.6 yards and should be back from injury to displace Ralph Giacomarro. The kickoff coverage team was excellent, giving up only 18.3 yards per return and ranking second in the NFL behind Cleveland. However, when it comes to returning both punts and kickoffs, they could do with more speed, and there is a place open for one of those reckless rookies who wants to make a name for himself.

1986 SCHEDULE OF GAMES	September	
	7 at New Orleans	12:00
	14 ST LOUIS	1:00
	21 at Dallas	12:00
	28 at Tampa Bay	4:00
	October	
	5 PHILADELPHIA	1:00
	12 LOS ANGELES RAMS	1:00
	19 SAN FRANCISCO	1:00
	26 at Los Angeles Rams	1:00
	November	
	2 at New England	1:00
	9 NEW YORK JETS	1:00
	16 CHICAGO	1:00
	23 at San Francisco	1:00
	30 at Miami	1:00
	December	
	7 INDIANAPOLIS	1:00
	14 NEW ORLEANS	1:00
	21 at Detroit	1:00

VETERAN ROSTER

No.	Name	Pos.	Ht.	Wt.	NFL Year	College
85	Allen, Anthony	WR	5-11	182	2	Washington
31	Andrews, William	RB	6-0	213	6	Auburn
16	Archer, Dave	QB	6-2	203	3	Iowa State
39	Austin, Cliff	RB	6-0	207	4	Clemson
38	Ayres, John	CB	5-11	187	1	Illinois
82	Bailey, Stacey	WR	6-0	157	5	San Jose State
69	Benish, Dan	DT	6-5	280	4	Clemson
87	Benson, Cliff	TE	6-4	238	3	Purdue
53	Benson, Thomas	LB	6-2	235	3	Oklahoma
26	Britt, James	CB	6-0	185	3	Louisiana State
89	Brown, Charlie	WR	5-10	184	5	South Carolina State
77	Bryan, Rick	DE	6-4	270	3	Oklahoma
23	Butler, Bobby	CB	5-11	170	6	Florida State
25	Case, Scott	S	6-0	178	3	Oklahoma
20	Cason, Wendell	CB	5-11	183	2	Oregon
	Clark, Bret	S	6-2	195	R	Nebraska
88	Cox, Arthur	TE	6-2	255	4	Texas Southern
30	Croudip, David	DB	5-8	180	3	San Diego State
50	Curry, Buddy	LB	6-4	222	7	North Carolina
3	Donnelly, Rick	P	6-0	184	2	Wyoming
79	Fralic, Bill	T-G	6-5	280	2	Pittsburgh
58	Frye, David	LB	6-2	218	4	Purdue
76	Gann, Mike	DE	6-5	265	2	Notre Dame
70	Goff, Willard	DT	6-3	265	2	West Texas State
33	Greene, Tiger	CB	5-10	184	2	Western Carolina
71	Howe, Glen	T	6-6	292	2	Southern Mississippi
51	Jackson, Jeff	LB	6-1	228	2	Auburn
81	Johnson, Billy	WR	5-9	170	11	Widener
37	Johnson, Kenny	S	5-11	167	7	Mississippi State
78	Kenn, Mike	T	6-7	277	9	Michigan
63	Kiewel, Jeff	G	6-4	265	2	Arizona
80	Landrum, Mike	TE	6-2	231	2	Southern Mississippi
18	Luckhurst, Mick	K	6-2	183	6	California
52	Malancon, Rydell	LB	6-1	227	2	Louisiana State
93	Martin, Brent	C	6-3	255	1	Stanford
49	Matthews, Allama	TE	6-2	230	4	Vanderbilt
62	Miller, Brett	T	6-7	290	4	Iowa
64	Pellegrini, Joe	G-C	6-4	264	5	Harvard
74	Pitts, Mike	DT	6-5	277	4	Alabama
27	Pridemore, Tom	S	5-11	186	9	West Virginia
72	Provence, Andrew	DE	6-3	267	4	South Carolina
59	Rade, John	LB	6-1	220	4	Boise State
55	Radloff, Wayne	C-G	6-5	263	2	Georgia
42	Riggs, Gerald	RB	6-1	232	5	Arizona State
67	Sanders, Eric	T	6-7	280	6	Nevada-Reno
14	Schonert, Turk	QB	6-1	196	7	Stanford
61	Scully, John	G	6-6	265	6	Notre Dame
29	Stamps, Sylvester	RB	5-7	166	2	Jackson State
96	Taylor, Johnny	LB	6-4	235	3	Hawaii
66	Thomas, Chuck	C-G	6-3	277	2	Oklahoma
22	Thomas, Sean	DB	5-11	190	2	Texas Christian
32	Tyrrell, Tim	RB	6-1	201	3	Northern Illinois
57	Van Note, Jeff	C	6-2	264	18	Kentucky
36	Wagoner, Dan	DB	5-10	180	4	Kansas
92	Washington, Ronnie	LB	6-1	236	2	N.E. Louisiana State
45	Whisenhunt, Ken	TE	6-2	233	2	Georgia Tech
	Wilkes, Reggie	LB	6-4	235	9	Georgia Tech
	Williams, Joel	LB	6-1	225	8	Wisconsin-La Crosse

1986 DRAFT

Round	Name	Pos.	Ht.	Wt.	College
1.	Casillas, Tony	NT	6-3	280	Oklahoma
1.	Green, Tim	LB	6-2	249	Syracuse
6.	Dixon, Floyd	WR	5-9	170	Stephen F. Austin
6.	Williams, Keith	RB	5-9	180	Southwest Missouri State
8.	Hudgens, Kevin	DE	6-3	275	Idaho State
9.	Starks, Kevin	TE	6-4	219	Minnesota
10.	Baker, Tony	RB	5-10	175	East Carolina
11.	Hegg, Chris	QB	6-4	212	Northeast Missouri State
12.	Griffin, Steve	WR	5-11	178	Purdue

*Billy 'White Shoes' Johnson was the Falcons' leading
receiver in his tenth NFL season*

LOS ANGELES RAMS

Address 2327 West Lincoln Avenue, Anaheim, California 92801.

Stadium Anaheim Stadium, Anaheim.
Capacity 69,007 *Playing Surface* Grass.

Team Colours Royal Blue, Gold, and White.

Head Coach John Robinson – fourth year.

Championships Division 1973,'74,'75,'76,'77,'78,'79,'85; Conference 1979; NFL 1945,'51.

History NFL 1937-69, NFC 1970-
(Until 1946, they were known as the Cleveland Rams.)

Offense

It is not very often that a team with the third-worst offense in the league contests a conference championship game. But that was true of the Rams, who, even with their considerable array of talent, only rarely slipped into top gear. Imagine a club with the best pure running back in football, blistering speed at wide receiver, a choice of tight ends to suit the occasion and, on paper, the best offensive line in the conference. The one thing they lacked was a big-play quarterback. Dieter Brock, who is said to be able to throw the ball sixty yards from a sitting position, came into the NFL after eleven seasons in the Canadian Football League. However, though he finished the season with the eighth-best rating in the league, he never dominated in the manner expected of him. Only five times did he pass for more than 200 yards in a game and many of his 344 yards, on Week Eight, came when the 49ers were in prevent defense, protecting a 28-point lead. Without doubt, he will have learned a few tricks but, by way of insurance, the Rams have signed Steve Bartkowski, who is not unfamiliar with their type of one-back offense, having spent ten full seasons with Atlanta. The Rams' one-back is, of course, Eric Dickerson, who has recently signed a four-year agreement with the club. Not even Dickerson could give the likes of Marcus Allen and Gerald Riggs a two-game start, and he ended the season as the eighth-leading rusher. One has the feeling that he will be wishing to make a point in 1986. Barry Redden is a more-than-useful backup, and it was heart-warming to see Charles White remind the Californian fans of his days at USC. Discarded by the Browns, White was given a chance by John Robinson, his former coach at USC, and he filled in admirably in the first two games, for which Dickerson was unavailable. Of the wide receivers, all three of Henry Ellard, Bobby Duckworth and Ron Brown can go like the wind – hurricane variety. As a receiver, the cultivated tight end, Tony Hunter, ranked second in the club for both catches and yards. He really was a bargain acquisition from Buffalo. The other tight end, David Hill, is a stout blocker and he, too, merits the most careful watching when he slips into enemy territory. The Rams' offensive line reads like a pro football Who's Who. Left tackle Irv

Pankey is the odd man out, being the only one of the five starters never to play in the Pro Bowl. The others, left guard Kent Hill, center Doug Smith, right guard Dennis Harrah and right tackle Jackie Slater, have thirteen Pro Bowl elections between them. When anyone is injured, they just bring on the next man in line – and that means one of Tony Slaton, Russ Bolinger and on, and on, and on. Top draftees Mike Schad and Tom Newberry may have to bide their time.

Defense

It was the defense which kept the Rams in contention for much of the season. What had been expected to be a modest pass rush turned out to be an avalanche of bodies intent on creating mayhem. Where there used to be gaps open for the opposing rushers, there appeared blockhouses dressed in blue. And in the secondary, there was the flashing of gold as cornerbacks Gary Green and LeRoy Irvin each pounced for six pass interceptions, earning trips to the Pro Bowl. Second-year defensive end Doug Reed eased smoothly into position alongside nose tackle Charles DeJurnett and right end Reggie Doss. The pass-rushing defensive end, Gary Jeter, did his job well, logging 11 sacks. Before last season, outside linebacker Mike Wilcher had shown good form, and now he confirmed it with a club-leading 12.5 sacks. Charging from the left outside linebacker position, Mel Owens had nine sacks. Inside linebackers Jim Collins and Carl Ekern, the blockhouses, led the team with 140 and 118 tackles respectively. For the secondary, read 'thoroughbred'. Playing inside Green and Irvin, Nolan Cromwell and Johnnie Johnson form an excellent pair of safeties. Last year's first-round pick, cornerback Jerry Gray, had little chance of breaking into the lineup. But he's ready and so is Vince Newsome, a hard-tackling free safety.

1986 SCHEDULE OF GAMES		
September		
7	at St Louis	12:00
14	SAN FRANCISCO	1:00
21	at Indianapolis	12:00
28	at Philadelphia	1:00
October		
5	TAMPA BAY	1:00
12	at Atlanta	1:00
19	DETROIT	1:00
26	ATLANTA	1:00
November		
3	at Chicago (Mon.)	8:00
9	at New Orleans	12:00
16	NEW ENGLAND	1:00
23	NEW ORLEANS	1:00
30	at New York Jets	1:00
December		
7	DALLAS	6:00
14	MIAMI	1:00
19	at San Francisco (Fri.)	5:00

Special Teams

When it comes to returning kickoffs and punts, the Rams are the best. Ron Brown scored touchdowns on kickoff returns of 98, 86 and 86 yards, and he was stopped short of the goal line after running 89 yards with another. Punt returner Henry Ellard scored on an 80-yard romp and led the NFC with an average of 13.5 yards over 37 returns. Rookie Dale Hatcher maintained his booming average of 43.2 yards over 87 punts and, rightly, went to the Pro Bowl in preference to another good young player, Atlanta's Rick Donnelly. Mike Lansford usually sends his kickoffs deep and is secure on field goal attempts from sensible range.

1986 DRAFT

Round	Name	Pos.	Ht.	Wt.	College
1.	Schad, Mike	T	6-5	290	Queen's University, Ontario
2.	Newberry, Tom	G	6-1	279	Wisconsin-La Crosse
3.	Millen, Hugh	QB	6-5	215	Washington
6.	Cox, Robert	T	6-5	260	UCLA
6.	Williams, Lynn	RB	6-2	215	Kansas
8.	Jarecki, Steve	LB	6-2	217	UCLA
8.	Goebel, Hank	T	6-7	270	Cal State-Fullerton
9.	Watts, Elbert	DB	6-2	205	Southern California
10.	Breeland, Garrett	LB	6-1	230	Southern California
11.	Schwanke, Chul	RB	5-11	213	South Dakota
12.	Dupree, Marcus	RB	6-3	230	Oklahoma

VETERAN ROSTER

No.	Name	Pos.	Ht.	Wt.	NFL Year	College
52	Andrews, George	LB	6-3	225	7	Nebraska
	Bartkowski, Steve	QB	6-4	218	12	California
73	Bolinger, Russ	G	6-5	255	10	Long Beach State
34	Bradley, Danny	RB	5-9	178	1	Oklahoma
90	Brady, Ed	LB	6-2	235	3	Illinois
5	Brock, Dieter	QB	6-0	195	2	Jacksonville State
89	Brown, Ron	WR	5-11	181	3	Arizona State
50	Collins, Jim	LB	6-2	235	6	Syracuse
21	Cromwell, Nolan	S	6-1	200	10	Kansas
70	DeJurnett, Charles	NT	6-4	260	10	San Jose State
29	Dickerson, Eric	RB	6-3	218	4	Southern Methodist
8	Dils, Steve	QB	6-1	191	7	Stanford
71	Doss, Reggie	DE	6-4	263	9	Hampton Institute
82	Duckworth, Bobby	WR	6-3	196	5	Arkansas
55	Ekern, Carl	LB	6-3	230	10	San Jose State
80	Ellard, Henry	WR	5-11	170	4	Fresno State
48	Fox, Tim	S	5-11	186	11	Ohio State
25	Gray, Jerry	CB	6-0	185	2	Texas
27	Green, Gary	CB	5-11	191	10	Baylor
91	Greene, Kevin ·	LB	6-3	238	2	Auburn
44	Guman, Mike	RB	6-2	218	7	Penn State
60	Harrah, Dennis	G	6-5	265	12	Miami
26	Harris, Eric	CB	6-3	202	7	Memphis State
68	Harrison, Dennis	DE	6-8	280	9	Vanderbilt
3	Hatcher, Dale	P	6-2	200	2	Clemson
81	Hill, David	TE	6-2	240	11	Texas A&I
72	Hill, Kent	G	6-5	260	8	Georgia Tech
87	Hunter, Tony	TE	6-4	237	4	Notre Dame
47	Irvin, LeRoy	CB	5-11	184	7	Kansas
59	Jerue, Mark	LB	6-3	232	4	Washington
77	Jeter, Gary	DE	6-4	260	10	Southern California
	Johnson, Damone	TE	6-4	230	1	Cal Poly-SLO
20	Johnson, Johnnie	S	6-1	183	7	Texas
1	Lansford, Mike	K	6-0	183	5	Washington
57	Laughlin, Jim	LB	6-1	222	7	Ohio State
79	Love, Duval	G	6-3	263	1	UCLA
83	McDonald, James	TE	6-5	230	4	Southern California
69	Meisner, Greg	NT	6-3	253	6	Pittsburgh
94	Meyer, John	DE	6-6	255	1	Arizona State
98	Miller, Shawn	NT	6-4	255	1	Utah State
22	Newsome, Vince	S	6-1	179	4	Washington
58	Owens, Mel	LB	6-2	224	6	Michigan
75	Pankey, Irv	T	6-4	267	6	Penn State
43	Pleasant, Mike	CB	6-1	195	2	Oklahoma
30	Redden, Barry	RB	5-10	205	5	Richmond
93	Reed, Doug	DE	6-3	262	3	San Diego State
	Scott, Chuck	WR	6-2	202	1	Vanderbilt
65	Shiner, Mike	T	6-8	285	1	Notre Dame
78	Slater, Jackie	T	6-4	271	11	Jackson State
61	Slaton, Tony	C	6-4	265	3	Southern California
56	Smith, Doug	C	6-3	253	9	Bowling Green
51	Vann, Norwood	LB	6-1	225	3	East Carolina
33	White, Charles	RB	5-10	190	6	Southern California
54	Wilcher, Mike	LB	6-3	240	4	North Carolina
88	Young, Michael	WR	6-1	185	2	UCLA

LeRoy Irvin continued to make great progress in 1985 and is now one of the NFL's finest cornerbacks

NEW ORLEANS SAINTS

NFC WESTERN DIVISION

Address 1500 Poydras Street, New Orleans, Louisiana 70112.
Stadium Louisiana Superdome, New Orleans. *Capacity* 71,647 *Playing Surface* AstroTurf.
Team Colours Old Gold, Black, and White.
Head Coach Jim Mora – first year.
Championships None.
History NFL 1967-69, NFC 1970-

Offense

After nineteen years in the NFL, the Saints have yet to end the season better than par. They almost made it in both 1979 and 1983, when, on each occasion, they went 8-8. Only rarely, even at a time during the regular season, have they had more wins than losses. That was the case after five games last year, at which stage they were 3-2, having won three straight games for just the fifth time in their history. Always they have slipped back. Tradition, then, is one factor to be considered in assessing their chances for the coming season. Another, more sensible point, is the fact that their domestic competition includes San Francisco and the Rams – and that's a prospect which would be daunting for any club. To the outsider, your writer, it would appear that unsettlement in key areas has been a constant problem. Dave Wilson was to have been the quarterback for the 1980s, but he was placed in competition by the acquisition of Richard Todd from the Jets. More recently, Bobby Hebert has been thrown into the pot. Similarly, at running back, they seemed to be in excellent shape, with George Rogers backed up by Wayne Wilson and Hokie Gajan. But the then head coach, 'Bum' Phillips, chose to replace Rogers with Earl Campbell, who had been nothing less than a truly great runner and yet, must have left a good deal of that very greatness with Houston, the club of his origins. Nonetheless, Campbell can still scatter the opposition, as he demonstrated when rushing for 160 yards against Minnesota last season. And he will be helped by the drafting of Jim Dombrowski, a dominant tackle. Campbell is just the man to play in combination with a speedy rookie; and in Dalton Hilliard and Rueben Mayes, the Saints have made two excellent draft choices. Draftee Barry Word, one imagines, is the future fullback. Hebert did tolerably well last year and is projected to be the starter. His targets include Eugene Goodlow, a wide receiver who can really shift and is coming off a big-play campaign (he averaged 18.8 yards per reception). Last year's rookie wide receiver, Eric Martin, showed style and pace. Tight end Hoby Brenner was the most prolific receiver, catching a career-best 42 passes at the highly-impressive average of 15.5 yards, and he could be ready to emerge. The offensive line must surely improve with the acquisition of Dombrowski. There's certainly plenty of pedigree talent in right tackle Steve Brock, a former first-round pick, center Steve Korte and left guard Brad

Edelman, the latter who each were second-round picks. Kelvin Clark, a former starter who can play at both tackle and guard, will be back after injury.

Defense

The defense is far better than its 1985 rank of 24th in the league would suggest, and there are good players throughout the unit. Defensive end Bruce Clark, a former first-round pick of Green Bay, has started in every one of his games as a New Orleans player (55). He's a first-class performer and came second in the club with 8.5 sacks. Lying in wait just behind the defensive line, there is a mix of pure class and sheer brawling power. Outside line-backer Rickey Jackson, who led the team with 11 sacks, is simply formidable and has just appeared in his third consecutive Pro Bowl. Inside linebacker Glen Redd was the team-leading tackler with 112, 87 of them solo. Redd's inside partner, last year's rookie, Jack Del Rio, is surely destined for greatness. Certainly, he's a fine player already, and he's the type who always seems to be there when it matters. Five times he was on hand to recover fumbles (he equalled the Saints' single-season record), two of which resulted in touchdowns. He returned one himself, the other coming after he had lateralled to Frank Warren. The secondary is possibly the Saints' most secure area. Standing in for Russell Gary, strong safety Terry Hoage did well alongside the three experienced veterans, cornerbacks Dave Waymer and Johnnie Poe, and free safety Frank Wattelet.

Special Teams

If there's a placekicker in the league who is capable of beating the record for longest field goal (it stands at 63 yards), it is Morten Andersen, who went to his first Pro Bowl and carries a sequence of fourteen consecutive field goal successes into 1986. Second-year punter Brian Hansen, who went to the Pro Bowl in his rookie year, continued as one of the league's best. Returning the majority of punts, Willie Tullis had a disappointing year. And he achieved

1986 SCHEDULE OF GAMES	September	
	7 ATLANTA	12:00
	14 GREEN BAY	1:00
	21 at San Francisco	1:00
	28 at New York Giants	1:00
	October	
	5 WASHINGTON	12:00
	12 at Indianapolis	12:00
	19 TAMPA BAY	12:00
	26 at New York Jets	1:00
	November	
	2 SAN FRANCISCO	12:00
	9 LOS ANGELES RAMS	12:00
	16 at St Louis	12:00
	23 at Los Angeles Rams	1:00
	30 NEW ENGLAND	12:00
	December	
	7 MIAMI	12:00
	14 at Atlanta	1:00
	21 at Minnesota	12:00

only modest success returning kickoffs, a duty which Tyrone Anthony shared with similar effect. Tullis's big day came in his very first professional game with Houston, back in 1981, when he returned a kickoff 95 yards for a touchdown in the final minute to beat the Rams, 27-20.

1986 DRAFT

Round	Name	Pos.	Ht.	Wt.	College
1.	Dombrowski, Jim	T	6-5	289	Virginia
2.	Hilliard, Dalton	RB	5-8	196	Louisiana State
3.	Mayes, Rueben	RB	5-11	201	Washington State
3.	Swilling, Pat	LB	6-3	243	Georgia Tech
3.	Word, Barry	RB	6-2	220	Virginia
4.	Edwards, Kelvin	WR	6-2	192	Liberty Baptist
5.	Sutton, Reggie	DB	5-10	175	Miami
6.	Thompson, Robert	WR	5-9	174	Youngstown State
7.	Fenerty, Gill	RB	6-0	193	Holy Cross
8.	Mokofisi, Filipo	LB	6-1	232	Utah
9.	Jones, Merlon	LB	6-2	222	Florida A&M
10.	Dumbauld, Jon	DE	6-4	259	Kentucky
11.	Swoopes, Patrick	NT	6-3	262	Mississippi State
12.	Brown, Sebastian	WR	6-0	181	Bethune-Cookman

VETERAN ROSTER

No.	Name	Pos.	Ht.	Wt.	NFL Year	College
7	Andersen, Morten	K	6-2	205	5	Michigan State
37	Bennett, Rob	TE	6-5	250	1	West Virginia
85	Brenner, Hoby	TE	6-4	245	6	Southern California
67	Brock, Stan	T	6-6	288	7	Colorado
35	Campbell, Earl	RB	5-11	233	9	Texas
75	Clark, Bruce	DE	6-3	281	5	Penn State
68	Clark, Kelvin	G	6-3	273	8	Nebraska
50	Del Rio, Jack	LB	6-4	235	2	Southern California
63	Edelman, Brad	G	6-6	262	5	Missouri
99	Elliott, Tony	NT	6-2	300	5	North Texas State
43	Fowler, Bobby	RB	6-2	230	2	Louisiana Tech
46	Gajan, Hokie	RB	5-11	226	5	Louisiana State
20	Gary, Russell	S	5-11	196	6	Nebraska
97	Geathers, James	DE	6-7	267	3	Wichita State
77	Gilbert, Daren	T	6-6	285	2	Cal State-Fullerton
88	Goodlow, Eugene	WR	6-2	181	4	Kansas State
86	Groth, Jeff	WR	5-10	181	8	Bowling Green
10	Hansen, Brian	P	6-3	218	3	Sioux Falls, S.D.
87	Hardy, Larry	TE	6-3	246	9	Jackson State
92	Haynes, James	LB	6-2	227	3	Mississippi Valley State
3	Hebert, Bobby	QB	6-4	215	2	Northwestern Louisiana
61	Hilgenberg, Joel	C-G	6-3	253	3	Iowa
24	Hoage, Terry	S	6-3	199	3	Georgia
57	Jackson, Rickey	LB	6-2	239	6	Pittsburgh
21	Johnson, Earl	CB	6-0	190	2	South Carolina
55	Kohlbrand, Joe	LB	6-4	242	3	Miami
60	Korte, Steve	C	6-2	271	4	Arkansas
64	Lafary, Dave	T	6-7	285	9	Purdue
84	Martin, Eric	WR	6-1	195	2	Louisiana State
39	Maxie, Brett	DB	6-2	190	2	Texas Southern
19	Merkens, Guido	QB-WR	6-1	197	9	Sam Houston State
80	Miller, Mike	WR	6-0	183	3	Tennessee
74	Moore, Derland	NT	6-4	273	14	Oklahoma
51	Paul, Whitney	LB	6-3	218	11	Colorado
53	Pelluer, Scott	LB	6-2	227	6	Washington State
71	Perot, Petey	G	6-2	261	7	Northwestern Louisiana
25	Poe, Johnnie	CB	6-1	194	6	Missouri
47	Rackley, David	CB	5-9	170	2	Texas Southern
58	Redd, Glen	LB	6-1	231	5	Brigham Young
	Richardson, Al	LB	6-3	222	7	Georgia Tech
70	Rourke, Jim	T	6-5	263	7	Boston College
65	Schreiber, Adam	G	6-4	270	3	Texas
82	Tice, John	TE	6-5	243	4	Maryland
14	Todd, Richard	QB	6-2	212	11	Alabama
54	Toles, Alvin	LB	6-1	211	2	Tennessee
26	Tullis, Willie	CB	6-0	190	6	Troy State
73	Warren, Frank	DE	6-4	278	6	Auburn
49	Wattelet, Frank	S	6-0	185	6	Kansas
44	Waymer, Dave	CB	6-1	188	7	Notre Dame
94	Wilks, Jim	DE	6-5	265	6	San Diego State
79	Williams, Ralph	T	6-3	270	3	Southern
18	Wilson, Dave	QB	6-3	211	5	Illinois
30	Wilson, Wayne	RB	6-3	220	8	Shepherd, W.Va.
89	Young, Tyrone	WR	6-6	192	3	Florida

Quarterback Bobby Hebert is ready to lead the Saints to their first winning campaign

SAN FRANCISCO 49ers

Address 711 Nevada Street, Redwood City, California 94061.
Stadium Candlestick Park, San Francisco.
Capacity 61,413 *Playing Surface* Grass.
Team Colours Forty Niners Gold and Scarlet.
Head Coach Bill Walsh – eighth year.
Championships Division 1970,'71,'72,'81,'83,'84;
Conference 1981,'84; Super Bowl 1981,'84.
History AAFC 1946-49, NFL 1950-69, NFC 1970-

Offense

A few injuries, some lapses, and a bit of bad luck, made the 49ers' task of retaining their NFL Championship all the more difficult and, in the end, the combination was just too much. But it is inconceivable that this club could possibly slip from the NFL's upper echelons and, at the very least, they enter the 1986 season with the probability of reaching the playoffs. Despite a sequence of injuries, quarterback Joe Montana hung in and led the NFC with a passer rating of 91.3. Certainly, his rating reflects the 49ers' philosophy of high percentage, medium-range passing but, five times, almost six, he passed for more than 300 yards in a game. And he burned the luckless Falcons with 429 yards and five touchdowns, to establish career-best marks in each category. Quarterback Jeff Kemp has been acquired from the Rams as a possible replacement for Matt Cavanaugh, who has been traded to Philadelphia. Wide receiver Freddie Solomon has retired – he will be missed – but the expressive Jerry Rice had eased ahead of the old pro and, already, he has the scalps of Raiders' cornerbacks Mike Haynes and Lester Hayes in his trophy room. Operating down the opposite sideline, Dwight Clark caught ten touchdown passes and, increasingly, his name is becoming synonymous with reliable quality. These days, tight end Russ Francis doesn't hit the headlines, but he shows no signs of slowing. Indeed, last year, he established a personal best with 44 pass receptions in the regular season – and the value of his presence is in no way measured by numbers alone. Speaking of value, how about Roger Craig? Just for his rushing, he could start with any NFL club, but, in 1985, he became the first man in league history to go over 1,000 yards, in both rushing and pass receiving. His partner, Wendell Tyler, didn't rush for 1,000 yards – and that's newsworthy. In his own right, Tyler is a blue-chip running back who has averaged 4.8 yards on 1,313 carries over a nine-year career and there appears no reason why he could not maintain that level of performance in 1986. Montana, Craig and Tyler will be operating behind one of the better offensive lines in the league. Both center Fred Quillan and right tackle Keith Fahnhorst have played in the Pro Bowl, and another of that status, guard Randy Cross, will return after recovering from injury. 'Bubba' Paris is one of the few tackles who has controlled Chicago's Richard Dent, whilst, without fuss,

left guard John Ayers just goes out and destroys his opponent, week after week.

Defense

The 49ers' defense was less impressive than in their championship year but, still, they ranked second in the NFC for fewest points conceded – they bend but don't break. After only two years as a pro, starting nose tackle Michael Carter is considered to be one of the league's best. Another young player, defensive end John Harty, has overcome the problems with his left foot and came through to start in a three-man line anchored on the right side by the powerful Dwaine Board. It's on obvious passing downs that we're reminded of Super Bowl XIX. Defensive coordinator George Seifert selects from a treasure chest of pass rushers which includes Jim Stuckey, Jeff Stover and Gary 'Big Hands' Johnson. Specialist pass rusher Fred Dean is likely to retire. In terms of quarterback collars, Board led with 11.5, followed by Stover (10) and Carter (7). Outside linebackers Todd Shell and Keena Turner can go after the passer, secure in the knowledge that inside linebackers Riki Ellison and Mike Walter can jam up the middle. The steady veteran, Fulton Kuykendall, returns from injury. When safeties Ronnie Lott and Carlton Williamson launch into their tackles, the shudders can be felt in the back row of the bleachers. Lott, who intercepted a club-leading six passes, has turned out to be particularly versatile – he can play at either cornerback or safety with equal facility. Following the release of former starting left cornerback Dwight Hicks, last year's rookie, Tory Nixon, may take over. At right cornerback, Eric Wright is outstanding.

Special Teams

Placekicker Ray Wersching is steady enough but there are a few young boomers who might challenge Max Runager, whose gross punting average dropped to the level of his early days as a pro. Helped by Derrick Harmon, Carl Monroe handled most of the kickoffs,

1986 SCHEDULE OF GAMES	September	
	7 at Tampa Bay	1:00
	14 at Los Angeles Rams	1:00
	21 NEW ORLEANS	1:00
	28 at Miami	1:00
	October	
	5 INDIANAPOLIS	1:00
	12 MINNESOTA	1:00
	19 at Atlanta	1:00
	26 vs. Green Bay at Milwaukee	12:00
	November	
	2 at New Orleans	12:00
	9 ST LOUIS	1:00
	17 at Washington (Mon.)	9:00
	23 ATLANTA	1:00
	December	
	1 NEW YORK GIANTS (Mon.)	6:00
	7 NEW YORK JETS	1:00
	14 at New England	1:00
	19 LOS ANGELES RAMS (Fri.)	5:00

returning one 95 yards for a touchdown, and ranked fourth in the league. Monroe is the tough little runner who scored the first touchdown in Super Bowl XIX. Punt returner Dana McLemore had a poor year, averaging only 6.8 yards compared with his career-average of 12.1 coming into the season.

1986 DRAFT

Round	Name	Pos.	Ht.	Wt.	College
2.	Roberts, Larry	DE	6-3	260	Alabama
3.	Rathman, Tom	RB	6-0	223	Nebraska
3.	McKyer, Tim	CB	6-0	174	Texas-Arlington
3.	Taylor, John	WR	6-0	180	Delaware State
4.	Haley, Charles	LB	6-4	230	James Madison
4.	Wallace, Steve	T	6-5	267	Auburn
4.	Fagan, Kevin	NT	6-4	251	Miami
5.	Miller, Patrick	LB	6-1	211	Florida
6.	Griffin, Don	DB	6-1	170	Middle Tennessee State
8.	Popp, Jim	TE	6-5	240	Vanderbilt
9.	Cherry, Tony	RB	5-8	184	Oregon
10.	Stinson, Elliston	WR	5-9	160	Rice
10.	Hallman, Harold	LB	5-11	234	Auburn

VETERAN ROSTER

No.	Name	Pos.	Ht.	Wt.	NFL Year	College
68	Ayers, John	G	6-5	265	10	West Texas State
76	Board, Dwaine	DE	6-5	248	7	North Carolina A&T
95	Carter, Michael	NT	6-2	285	3	Southern Methodist
87	Clark, Dwight	WR	6-4	215	8	Clemson
69	Collie, Bruce	T	6-6	275	2	Texas-Arlington
33	Craig, Roger	RB	6-0	224	4	Nebraska
51	Cross, Randy	G	6-3	265	11	UCLA
50	Ellison, Riki	LB	6-2	225	4	Southern California
55	Fahnhorst, Jim	LB	6-4	230	3	Minnesota
71	Fahnhorst, Keith	T	6-6	273	13	Minnesota
54	Ferrari, Ron	LB	6-0	215	5	Illinois
81	Francis, Russ	TE	6-6	242	11	Oregon
86	Frank, John	TE	6-3	225	3	Ohio State
49	Fuller, Jeff	S	6-2	216	3	Texas A&M
24	Harmon, Derrick	RB-KR	5-10	202	3	Cornell
75	Harty, John	DE	6-4	260	5	Iowa
52	Hill, John	C	6-2	260	15	Lehigh
28	Holmoe, Tom	S	6-2	180	3	Brigham Young
	Huff, Charles	DB	5-11	195	1	Presbyterian State
97	Johnson, Gary	NT	6-2	261	12	Grambling State
	Kemp, Jeff	QB	6-1	201	6	Dartmouth
66	Kennedy, Allan	T	6-7	275	4	Washington State
57	Kovach, Jim	LB	6-2	239	8	Kentucky
	Kuykendall, Fulton	LB	6-4	228	11	UCLA
42	Lott, Ronnie	CB-S	6-0	200	6	Southern California
53	McColl, Milt	LB	6-6	230	6	Stanford
62	McIntyre, Guy	G	6-3	264	3	Georgia
43	McLemore, Dana	CB-KR	5-10	183	5	Hawaii
32	Monroe, Carl	RB-KR	5-8	180	4	Utah
16	Montana, Joe	QB	6-2	195	8	Notre Dame
20	Nixon, Tory	CB	5-11	186	2	San Diego State
77	Paris, Bubba	T	6-6	299	4	Michigan
56	Quillan, Fred	C	6-5	266	9	Oregon
80	Rice, Jerry	WR	6-2	200	2	Mississippi Valley State
30	Ring, Bill	RB	5-10	205	6	Brigham Young
4	Runager, Max	P	6-1	189	8	South Carolina
61	Sapolu, Jesse	G-C	6-4	260	2	Hawaii
90	Shell, Todd	LB	6-4	225	3	Brigham Young
	Steevens, John	G-C	6-3	265	1	Fresno State
72	Stover, Jeff	DE	6-5	275	5	Oregon
60	Stroth, Vince	T	6-3	256	2	Brigham Young
79	Stuckey, Jim	DE	6-4	253	7	Clemson
78	Tuiasosopo, Manu	NT	6-3	262	8	UCLA
58	Turner, Keena	LB	6-2	222	7	Purdue
26	Tyler, Wendell	RB	5-10	207	9	UCLA
99	Walter, Mike	LB	6-3	238	4	Oregon
14	Wersching, Ray	K	5-11	215	14	California
27	Williamson, Carlton	S	6-0	204	6	Pittsburgh
85	Wilson, Mike	WR	6-3	215	6	Washington State
21	Wright, Eric	CB	6-1	185	6	Missouri

Michael Carter (#95) has become a first-class nose tackle

1986 NATIONAL FOOTBALL LEAGUE SCHEDULE

(All times local)

FIRST WEEK

Sunday, September 7 — **Kickoff**

Atlanta at New Orleans	12:00
Cincinnati at Kansas City	3:00
Cleveland at Chicago	12:00
·Detroit at Minnesota	12:00
Houston at Green Bay	12:00
Indianapolis at New England	4:00
Los Angeles Raiders at Denver	2:00
Los Angeles Rams at St Louis	12:00
Miami at San Diego	1:00
New York Jets at Buffalo	4:00
Philadelphia at Washington	1:00
Pittsburgh at Seattle	1:00
San Francisco at Tampa Bay	1:00

Monday, September 8

New York Giants at Dallas	8:00

SECOND WEEK

Thursday, September 11

New England at New York Jets	8:00

Sunday, September 14

Buffalo at Cincinnati	1:00
Cleveland at Houston	12:00
Dallas at Detroit	1:00
Green Bay at New Orleans	12:00
Indianapolis at Miami	4:00
Kansas City at Seattle	1:00
Los Angeles Raiders at Washington	1:00
Minnesota at Tampa Bay	4:00
Philadelphia at Chicago	12:00
St Louis at Atlanta	1:00
San Diego at New York Giants	1:00
San Francisco at Los Angeles Rams	1:00

Monday, September 15

Denver at Pittsburgh	9:00

THIRD WEEK

Thursday, September 18

Cincinnati at Cleveland	8:00

Sunday, September 21

Atlanta at Dallas	12:00
Denver at Philadelphia	1:00
Houston at Kansas City	3:00
Los Angeles Rams at Indianapolis	12:00
Miami at New York Jets	1:00
New Orleans at San Francisco	1:00
New York Giants at Los Angeles Raiders	1:00
Pittsburgh at Minnesota	12:00
St Louis at Buffalo	1:00
Seattle at New England	1:00
Tampa Bay at Detroit	1:00
Washington at San Diego	1:00

Monday, September 22

Chicago at Green Bay	8:00

FOURTH WEEK

Sunday, September 28

Atlanta at Tampa Bay	4:00
Chicago at Cincinnati	1:00
Detroit at Cleveland	1:00
Green Bay at Minnesota	12:00
Kansas City at Buffalo	1:00
Los Angeles Rams at Philadelphia	1:00
New England at Denver	2:00
New Orleans at New York Giants	1:00
New York Jets at Indianapolis	3:00
Pittsburgh at Houston	12:00
San Diego at Los Angeles Raiders	1:00
San Francisco at Miami	1:00
Seattle at Washington	1:00

Monday, September 29

Dallas at St Louis	8:00

FIFTH WEEK

Sunday, October 5

Buffalo at New York Jets	4:00
Cincinnati vs Green Bay at Milwaukee	12:00
Cleveland at Pittsburgh	1:00
Dallas at Denver	2:00
Houston at Detroit	1:00

Indianapolis at San Francisco	1:00
Los Angeles Raiders at Kansas City	12:00
Miami at New England	1:00
Minnesota at Chicago	12:00
New York Giants at St Louis	12:00
Philadelphia at Atlanta	1:00
Tampa Bay at Los Angeles Rams	1:00
Washington at New Orleans	12:00

Monday, October 6

San Diego at Seattle	6:00

SIXTH WEEK
Sunday, October 12

Buffalo at Miami	1:00
Chicago at Houston	12:00
Denver at San Diego	1:00
Detroit at Green Bay	12:00
Kansas City at Cleveland	1:00
Los Angeles Rams at Atlanta	1:00
Minnesota at San Francisco	1:00
New Orleans at Indianapolis	12:00
New York Jets at New England	1:00
Philadelphia at New York Giants	4:00
St Louis at Tampa Bay	1:00
Seattle at Los Angeles Raiders	1:00
Washington at Dallas	12:00

Monday, October 13

Pittsburgh at Cincinnati	9:00

SEVENTH WEEK
Sunday, October 19

Chicago at Minnesota	12:00
Dallas at Philadelphia	1:00
Detroit at Los Angeles Rams	1:00
Green Bay at Cleveland	1:00
Houston at Cincinnati	1:00
Indianapolis at Buffalo	1:00
Los Angeles Raiders at Miami	1:00
New England at Pittsburgh	1:00
New York Giants at Seattle	1:00
St Louis at Washington	1:00
San Diego at Kansas City	3:00
San Francisco at Atlanta	1:00
Tampa Bay at New Orleans	12:00

Monday, October 20

Denver at New York Jets	9:00

EIGHTH WEEK
Sunday, October 26

Atlanta at Los Angeles Rams	1:00
Cincinnati at Pittsburgh	1:00
Cleveland at Minnesota	12:00
Detroit at Chicago	12:00
Los Angeles Raiders at Houston	12:00
Miami at Indianapolis	1:00
New England at Buffalo	1:00
New Orleans at New York Jets	1:00
St Louis at Dallas	3:00

San Diego at Philadelphia	1:00
San Francisco vs Green Bay at Milwaukee	12:00
Seattle at Denver	2:00
Tampa Bay at Kansas City	12:00

Monday, October 27

Washington at New York Giants	9:00

NINTH WEEK
Sunday, November 2

Atlanta at New England	1:00
Buffalo at Tampa Bay	1:00
Cincinnati at Detroit	1:00
Cleveland at Indianapolis	1:00
Dallas at New York Giants	1:00
Denver at Los Angeles Raiders	1:00
Green Bay at Pittsburgh	1:00
Houston at Miami	1:00
Kansas City at San Diego	1:00
Minnesota at Washington	4:00
New York Jets at Seattle	1:00
Philadelphia at St Louis	12:00
San Francisco at New Orleans	12:00

Monday, November 3

Los Angeles Rams at Chicago	8:00

TENTH WEEK
Sunday, November 9

Chicago at Tampa Bay	1:00
Cincinnati at Houston	12:00
Los Angeles Raiders at Dallas	3:00
Los Angeles Rams at New Orleans	12:00
Minnesota at Detroit	1:00
New England at Indianapolis	1:00
New York Giants at Philadelphia	4:00
New York Jets at Atlanta	1:00
Pittsburgh at Buffalo	1:00
St Louis at San Francisco	1:00
San Diego at Denver	2:00
Seattle at Kansas City	12:00
Washington at Green Bay	12:00

Monday, November 10

Miami at Cleveland	9:00

ELEVENTH WEEK
Sunday, November 16

Chicago at Atlanta	1:00
Cleveland at Los Angeles Raiders	1:00
Dallas at San Diego	1:00
Detroit at Philadelphia	1:00
Houston at Pittsburgh	1:00
Indianapolis at New York Jets	4:00
Kansas City at Denver	2:00
New England at Los Angeles Rams	1:00
Miami at Buffalo	1:00
New York Giants at Minnesota	12:00
New Orleans at St Louis	12:00
Seattle at Cincinnati	1:00
Tampa Bay vs Green Bay at Milwaukee	12:00

Monday, November 17

San Francisco at Washington	9:00

TWELFTH WEEK
Thursday, November 20

Los Angeles Raiders at San Diego	5:00

Sunday, November 23

Atlanta at San Francisco	1:00
Buffalo at New England	1:00
Dallas at Washington	1:00
Denver at New York Giants	1:00
Detroit at Tampa Bay	1:00
Green Bay at Chicago	12:00
Indianapolis at Houston	12:00
Kansas City at St Louis	3:00
Minnesota at Cincinnati	1:00
New Orleans at Los Angeles Rams	1:00
Philadelphia at Seattle	1:00
Pittsburgh at Cleveland	1:00

Monday, November 24

New York Jets at Miami	9:00

THIRTEENTH WEEK
Thursday, November 27 (Thanksgiving Day)

Green Bay at Detroit	12:30
Seattle at Dallas	3:00

Sunday, November 30

Atlanta at Miami	1:00
Buffalo at Kansas City	12:00
Cincinnati at Denver	2:00
Houston at Cleveland	1:00
Los Angeles Rams at New York Jets	1:00
New England at New Orleans	12:00
Philadelphia at Los Angeles Raiders	1:00
Pittsburgh at Chicago	12:00
San Diego at Indianapolis	1:00
Tampa Bay at Minnesota	12:00
Washington at St Louis	12:00

Monday, December 1

New York Giants at San Francisco	6:00

FOURTEENTH WEEK
Sunday, December 7

Cincinnati at New England	1:00
Cleveland at Buffalo	1:00
Dallas at Los Angeles Rams	6:00
Denver at Kansas City	12:00
Detroit at Pittsburgh	1:00
Houston at San Diego	1:00
Indianapolis at Atlanta	1:00
Miami at New Orleans	12:00
Minnesota at Green Bay	12:00
New York Giants at Washington	1:00
New York Jets at San Francisco	1:00

St Louis at Philadelphia	1:00
Tampa Bay at Chicago	12:00

Monday, December 8

Los Angeles Raiders at Seattle	6:00

FIFTEENTH WEEK
Saturday, December 13

Pittsburgh at New York Jets	12:30
Washington at Denver	2:00

Sunday, December 14

Buffalo at Indianapolis	1:00
Cleveland at Cincinnati	1:00
Green Bay at Tampa Bay	1:00
Kansas City at Los Angeles Raiders	1:00
Miami at Los Angeles Rams	1:00
Minnesota at Houston	3:00
New Orleans at Atlanta	1:00
Philadelphia at Dallas	12:00
St Louis at New York Giants	1:00
San Francisco at New England	1:00
Seattle at San Diego	1:00

Monday, December 15

Chicago at Detroit	9:00

SIXTEENTH WEEK
Friday, December 19

Los Angeles Rams at San Francisco	5:00

Saturday, December 20

Denver at Seattle	1:00
Green Bay at New York Giants	12:30

Sunday, December 21

Atlanta at Detroit	1:00
Buffalo at Houston	12:00
Chicago at Dallas	3:00
Indianapolis at Los Angeles Raiders	1:00
Kansas City at Pittsburgh	1:00
New Orleans at Minnesota	12:00
New York Jets at Cincinnati	1:00
San Diego at Cleveland	1:00
Tampa Bay at St Louis	12:00
Washington at Philadelphia	1:00

Monday, December 22

New England at Miami	9:00

Postseason

Sunday, Dec. 28	AFC and NFC First Round Playoffs
Saturday, Jan. 3	AFC and NFC Divisional Playoffs
Sunday, Jan. 4	AFC and NFC Divisional Playoffs
Sunday, Jan. 11	AFC and NFC Championship Games
Sunday, Jan. 25	Super Bowl XXI at Rose Bowl, Pasadena, California
Sunday, Feb. 1	AFC-NFC Pro Bowl, Honolulu, Hawaii

ALL-TIME HEAD-TO-HEAD RESULTS

	Buffalo	Indianapolis	Miami	New England	N.Y. Jets	Cincinnati	Cleveland	Houston	Pittsburgh	Denver	Kansas City	L.A. Raiders	San Diego	Seattle
Buffalo	—	15-15-1	7-32-1	23-28-1	26-25-0	5-8-0	2-5-0	9-17-0	3-6-0	13-9-1	14-11-1	11-12-0	9-17-2	0-2-0
Indianapolis	15-15-1	—	9-24-0	15-16-0	16-16-0	5-4-0	5-10-0	5-3-0	4-9-0	1-6-0	3-6-0	2-4-0	2-4-0	2-0-0
Miami	32-7-1	24-9-0	—	25-15-0	22-18-1	7-3-0	3-3-0	9-10-0	7-3-0	5-2-1	6-7-0	3-14-1	5-8-0	3-1-0
New England	28-23-1	16-15-0	15-25-0	—	22-29-1	6-3-0	2-6-0	14-13-1	2-5-0	12-11-0	7-11-3	12-12-1	13-12-2	5-1-0
N.Y. Jets	25-26-0	16-16-0	18-22-1	29-22-1	—	7-3-0	3-7-0	10-15-1	0-8-0	10-10-1	11-13-0	11-12-2	7-14-1	1-7-0
Cincinnati	8-5-0	4-5-0	3-7-0	3-6-0	3-7-0	—	16-15-0	20-13-1	14-17-0	6-8-0	7-8-0	4-12-0	7-10-0	3-2-0
Cleveland	5-2-0	10-5-0	3-3-0	6-2-0	7-3-0	15-16-0	—	20-11-0	41-31-0	3-8-0	4-5-1	1-9-0	4-5-1	2-7-0
Houston	17-9-0	3-5-0	10-9-0	13-14-1	15-10-1	13-20-1	11-20-0	—	9-24-0	18-10-1	12-20-0	10-21-0	12-16-1	3-2-0
Pittsburgh	6-3-0	9-4-0	3-7-0	5-2-0	8-0-0	17-14-0	31-41-0	24-9-0	—	5-7-1	9-4-0	6-9-0	8-4-0	3-2-0
Denver	9-13-1	6-1-0	2-5-1	11-12-0	10-10-1	8-6-0	8-3-0	10-18-1	7-5-1	—	18-33-0	14-36-2	24-27-1	11-7-0
Kansas City	11-14-1	6-3-0	7-6-0	11-7-3	13-11-0	8-7-0	5-4-1	20-12-0	4-9-0	33-18-0	—	21-30-2	24-26-1	8-7-0
L.A. Raiders	12-11-0	4-2-0	14-3-1	12-12-1	12-11-2	12-4-0	9-1-0	21-10-0	9-6-0	36-14-2	30-21-2	—	33-18-2	9-9-0
San Diego	17-9-2	4-2-0	8-5-0	12-13-2	14-7-1	10-7-0	5-4-1	16-12-1	4-8-0	27-24-1	26-24-1	18-33-2	—	9-6-0
Seattle	2-0-0	0-2-0	1-3-0	1-5-0	7-1-0	2-3-0	7-2-0	2-3-0	2-3-0	7-11-0	7-8-0	9-9-0	6-9-0	—
Dallas	3-1-0	6-3-0	2-3-0	5-0-0	3-0-0	2-1-0	9-15-0	4-1-0	11-12-0	3-1-0	2-1-0	1-2-0	2-1-0	3-0-0
N.Y. Giants	2-1-0	3-7-0	0-1-0	1-1-0	2-2-0	0-3-0	16-26-2	3-0-0	41-26-3	1-2-0	4-1-0	0-3-0	2-2-0	3-1-0
Philadelphia	3-1-0	5-5-0	2-3-0	3-2-0	3-0-0	0-4-0	11-29-1	3-0-0	42-25-3	3-1-0	1-0-0	1-3-0	1-2-0	2-0-0
St. Louis	3-1-0	5-4-0	0-5-0	4-1-0	2-1-0	1-2-0	10-30-3	3-1-0	20-29-3	0-1-1	0-3-1	1-1-0	1-2-0	2-0-0
Washington	2-2-0	6-15-0	2-4-0	3-1-0	3-0-0	3-1-0	8-31-1	2-2-0	40-27-3	2-1-0	1-2-0	1-4-0	3-0-0	2-1-0
Chicago	2-1-0	14-21-0	0-4-0	3-2-0	2-1-0	0-2-0	2-6-0	1-2-0	13-4-1	4-3-0	2-1-0	2-3-0	1-4-0	1-3-0
Detroit	1-1-1	16-17-2	1-2-0	2-2-0	2-2-0	2-1-0	12-3-0	1-2-0	13-8-1	2-3-0	2-2-0	2-3-0	3-2-0	1-2-0
Green Bay	1-2-0	18-17-1	0-4-0	1-2-0	1-4-0	2-3-0	7-5-0	2-2-0	16-10-0	1-3-0	1-1-1	1-4-0	3-1-0	3-1-0
Minnesota	4-1-0	5-12-1	1-4-0	1-2-0	1-3-0	2-2-0	7-1-0	2-1-0	5-4-0	2-2-0	2-2-0	1-5-0	3-3-0	1-2-0
Tampa Bay	2-1-0	1-2-0	1-2-0	0-2-0	1-3-0	1-2-0	0-3-0	1-2-0	0-3-0	0-2-0	2-3-0	0-2-0	0-2-0	0-2-0
Atlanta	2-2-0	0-8-0	0-4-0	2-2-0	2-1-0	1-4-0	1-6-0	4-1-0	1-6-0	3-3-0	0-2-0	1-4-0	2-0-0	0-3-0
L.A. Rams	3-1-0	14-20-2	1-3-0	1-2-0	2-2-0	2-3-0	7-8-0	3-1-0	12-4-2	3-2-0	3-0-0	1-4-0	2-1-0	3-0-0
New Orleans	1-2-0	0-3-0	1-3-0	0-4-0	1-3-0	2-3-0	1-8-0	2-2-1	4-4-0	0-4-0	2-2-0	0-3-1	0-3-0	1-2-0
San Francisco	1-2-0	14-21-0	1-4-0	3-1-0	3-1-0	4-1-0	4-8-0	3-2-0	6-6-0	2-3-0	3-1-0	2-3-0	1-3-0	2-1-0